RESEARCH HANDBOOK ON THE ECONOMICS OF ANTITRUST LAW

RESEARCH HANDBOOKS IN LAW AND ECONOMICS

Series Editors: Richard A. Posner, *Judge, United States Court of Appeals for the Seventh Circuit and Senior Lecturer, University of Chicago Law School, USA* and Francesco Parisi, *Oppenheimer Wolff and Donnelly Professor of Law, University of Minnesota, USA and Professor of Economics, University of Bologna, Italy*

Edited by highly distinguished scholars, the landmark reference works in this series offer advanced treatments of specific topics that reflect the state-of-the-art of research in law and economics, while also expanding the law and economics debate. Each volume's accessible yet sophisticated contributions from top international researchers make it an indispensable resource for students and scholars alike.

Titles in this series include:

Research Handbook on Public Choice and Public Law
Edited by Daniel A. Farber and Anne Joseph O'Connell

Research Handbook on the Economics of Property Law
Edited by Kenneth Ayotte and Henry E. Smith

Research Handbook on the Economics of Family Law
Edited by Lloyd R. Cohen and Joshua D. Wright

Research Handbook on the Economics of Antitrust Law
Edited by Einer Elhauge

Research Handbook on the Economics of Antitrust Law

Edited by

Einer Elhauge

Harvard Law School, USA

RESEARCH HANDBOOKS IN LAW AND ECONOMICS

Edward Elgar

Cheltenham, UK • Northampton, MA, USA

Published by
Edward Elgar Publishing Limited
The Lypiatts
15 Lansdown Road
Cheltenham
Glos GL50 2JA
UK

Edward Elgar Publishing, Inc.
William Pratt House
9 Dewey Court
Northampton
Massachusetts 01060
USA

A catalogue record for this book
is available from the British Library

Library of Congress Control Number: 2011927284

MIX
Paper from
responsible sources
FSC® C018575
www.fsc.org

ISBN 978 1 84844 080 7 (cased)

Typeset by Servis Filmsetting Ltd, Stockport, Cheshire
Printed and bound by MPG Books Group, UK

Contents

Figures and tables

FIGURES

TABLES

Contributors

Jonathan B. Baker
Professor of Law, American University Washington College of Law

Roger D. Blair
Walter J. Matherly Professor, Department of Economics, University of Florida

Anu Bradford
Assistant Professor, University of Chicago Law School

Nicholas Economides
Professor of Economics, Stern School of Business, New York University; Executive Director, NET Institute

Aaron Edlin
Richard Jennings Professor of Law and Professor of Economics, UC Berkeley and National Bureau of Economic Research

Einer Elhauge
Petrie Professor of Law, Harvard Law School

David S. Evans
Chairman, Global Economics Group; Lecturer, University of Chicago Law School

Jessica S. Haynes
PhD Candidate, Department of Economics, University of Florida

Benjamin Klein
Professor Emeritus of Economics, UCLA

Alvin K. Klevorick
John Thomas Smith Professor of Law and Professor of Economics, Yale University

Issa B. Kohler-Hausmann
JD Yale Law School; Ph.D Candidate in Sociology, New York University

John Kwoka
Neal F. Finnegan Distinguished Professor of Economics, Northeastern University

David Reitman
Vice President, Charles River Associates

Daniel L. Rubinfeld
Robert L. Bridges Professor of Law and Professor of Economics, U. of California Berkeley and Emeritus Professor of Law, NYU Law School

Howard A. Shelanski
Professor of Law, Georgetown University

Christopher Jon Sprigman
Class of 1963 Research Professor in Honor of Graham C. Lilly and Peter W. Low, University of Virginia School of Law

Abraham L. Wickelgren
Bernard J. Ward Centennial Professor of Law, University of Texas at Austin School of Law

Abbreviations

AAC	average avoidable cost
AMC	Antitrust Modernization Commission (US)
AVC	average variable cost
DOJ	Department of Justice (US)
FTC	Federal Trade Commission (US)
ICN	International Competition Network
IMF	International Monetary Fund
IP	intellectual property
LCC	low cost carrier
MC	marginal cost
MNC	multinational corporation
MR	marginal revenue
NTB	nontariff barrier
OECD	Organisation for Economic Co-operation and Development
OEM	original equipment manufacturer
OFT	Office of Fair Trading (UK)
PD	prisoner's dilemma
SSNIP	small but significant nontransitory increase in price
UNCTAD	United Nations Conference on Trade and Development
UPP	upward pricing pressure
WTO	World Trade Organization

1 Introduction and overview to current issues in antitrust economics

Einer Elhauge

Although economic analysis of law is increasingly important in many legal fields, perhaps no field of law is as dominated by economics as antitrust law. This no doubt reflects a confluence of factors. First, serious economic analysis of law really began with antitrust law, so economic analysis into antitrust issues has had time to go deeper and wider than economic analysis of other legal fields. Second, so much of standard microeconomics is directly relevant, given that antitrust involves regulating market competition. Third, the courts and enforcement agencies have grounded antitrust legal doctrines explicitly in concepts of antitrust economics. Fourth, because of the last factor, antitrust law creates a series of issues on which expert testimony on antitrust economics is relevant, meaning that every antitrust case of significance has at least one (often more) testifying expert on antitrust economics on each side. Antitrust law is thus unusual not only in the extent to which it turns on economics, but also in the extent to which that economics is vigorously debated in each case.

One might mistakenly think that such a long tradition would mean that there would be little new to say about antitrust economics. Yet antitrust economics is surprisingly dynamic and changing. In part, this is because new decisions or legal developments, often in response to old economic developments, tend to raise new economic issues. In part, it is because the continued testing of economic logic in adversarial economic testimony leads to continued self-reflection.

Given the rich literature in antitrust economics, this handbook does not purport to provide an exhaustive overview of all it has to tell us. This handbook focuses on those areas of antitrust economics that are most in flux because of new developments in law or the economics literature.

PART I MERGERS AND MARKET DEFINITION

Perhaps one of the most important recent developments is the promulgation of the 2010 US Horizontal Merger Guidelines. The new guidelines are notable in their increased emphasis on unilateral effects theory, their de-emphasis of market definition, and their inclusion of mergers that eliminate potential competition (which were previously classified as non-horizontal). Part I of this handbook includes a chapter on each of these three developments, illuminating the relevant economic issues.

Chapter 2 – Unilateral Effects Under Modern Merger Analysis. A merger is said to have unilateral effects when it reduces the incentives of the merged firm to compete aggressively, holding constant the strategies of non-merging rivals. Jon Baker and David Reitman's chapter provides a timely assessment of how mergers can produce adverse unilateral effects and what the best models are for assessing the likelihood and magnitude of unilateral effects, focusing on mergers in differentiated product markets. In differentiated markets, mergers can create unilateral effects because they allow the merged firm to recapture the profits they would otherwise lose to each other by raising prices, thus increasing their profit-maximizing price. A complementary explanation is that mergers can create unilateral effects by removing the competitive response of an important rival that would otherwise increase firm-specific demand elasticity. Baker and Reitman note that market shares may bear no relationship to such unilateral effects.

Baker and Reitman explore various simple models that can provide a quick preliminary read on likely unilateral effects with relatively light data requirements. They first address the Upward Pricing Pressure model proposed by Carl Shapiro and Joe Farrell, the Chief Economists for the Department of Justice and Federal Trade Commission, which is now included in the 2010 US Merger Guidelines. This model uses the diversion ratio, which is the fraction of customers who would switch from firm 1 to firm 2 in response to a firm 1 price increase. The model calculates that the recaptured profit equals the diversion ratio times the pre-merger profit margin on firm 2's product, and then observes that this recaptured profit has the same impact on firm 1's pricing as an increase in its marginal cost. The reason is that, after the merger, each successful sale of the firm 1 product now has the additional cost of losing that diverted profit on firm 2's product. Thus, such a merger will create upward pricing pressure when the recaptured profit is greater than any cost reduction produced by merger efficiencies. They propose using a standard deduction of some percentage of pre-merger costs. A related model, Compensating Cost Reduction, is similar to Upward Pricing Pressure, but uses the actual expected cost reduction rather than a standard deduction.

Baker and Reitman then address two other simple models. Critical Loss Analysis asks whether, given the demand elasticity for the merged firm's product and its pre-merger profit margin, the merged firm could profitably impose a small but significant nontransitory increase in price (SSNIP). Simple Price Effect models instead project merger price effects using the marketwide elasticity and an assumption that the diversion ratio is proportional to the market share of each brand. As Baker and Reitman observe, this assumption underestimates price effects if the merged products are relatively close substitutes and overestimates them if the merged products are relatively distant.

These simple models can reach decisions with relatively light data requirements that are more accurate than those one would reach using market definition and market concentration presumptions. However, the simple models can reach conclusions that conflict with each other. If the existing profit margins are high, the Upward Pricing Pressure model is more likely to conclude a merger is anticompetitive and Critical Loss Analysis is less likely to do so.

Further, the simple models sometimes deviate from the predictions reached using more complicated merger simulation models, which estimate demand functions for the differentiated products and parameters on costs and oligopoly behavior and then solve the merged firm's price-maximization decision. Assuming the merging firms have the same diversion ratios and profit margins, have constant costs unaltered by the merger, and do not engage in oligopolistic coordination, a Shapiro model shows the percentage price increase equals the diversion ratio times the profit margin divided by (with linear demand) two times the nondiversion ratio or (with constant elasticity) the nondiversion ratio minus the profit margin. More complicated models can quantify the degree of uncertainty in price predictions and take into account any merger-specific efficiencies. Merger simulations can also take into account rival reactions and cases where the merging brands are not the closest substitutes for each other.

Baker and Reitman also discuss measurement issues, as well as the possibilities that one might extend these models to take into account various possibilities excluded in standard unilateral effects models. First, they consider the possibility that firms might reposition their products post-merger. Although the Guidelines suggest this would only reduce predicted prices, they note that repositioning by the merged firm could increase price effects. Second, they consider the possibility that firms might price more strategically, noting that while such strategies are difficult to model *a priori*, they can help address deviations between the simple models and available evidence. Third, they consider bidding markets, noting that the unilateral effects models can be extended to them by assuming firms pick the bid they think most optimal given the need to beat the second best bid, which is sometimes the one offered by the merger partner. Fourth, they consider increasing marginal costs or capacity limits. Although such factors are usually assumed to increase price effects because they reduce the price constraint imposed by nonmerging rivals, they observe these factors can sometimes also reduce the merging firm's incentives to cut output post-merger, making the effects more mixed. Fifth, they consider the extent to which any merger cost-savings are passed on to customers.

Finally, Baker and Reitman observe that the most reliable empirical study of five approved mergers that seemed likely to have presented a close call for US antitrust agencies found that four of the five mergers increased prices by 3–7%. This may suggest the US agencies are being a bit too lax, unless efficiencies take longer to kick in. The increasing access to electronic sales data heralds more such retrospective merger studies in the future, refining our understanding about how best to analyse unilateral effects mergers.

Chapter 3 – Do We Need Market Definition? David Evans' chapter considers the current controversy about the need for market definition. As he notes, under the 2010 US Guidelines, one does not need market definition and the chief economists of the two US antitrust agencies have proposed abandoning it in merger analysis in unilateral effects cases.

Evans provides many arguments for lightening up on the emphasis on market definition. He points out that market definition is one of the few areas not supported by economics. A major problem is that product heterogeneity is the norm, not the exception, so that markets have no sharp boundaries. It thus often makes little sense to talk about 'the' market. Further, he observes that market share is not a reliable indicator of market power because the same market share can indicate much or little market power depending on the market elasticity and rival elasticity of supply. Moreover, he notes that, if we have the elasticity information necessary to do the SSNIP test that is needed to properly define a market, then we have enough information to directly assess the unilateral effects of a merger on price.

Nonetheless, Evans also argues that we should lighten up on the issue generally. In particular, while market definition should be less determinative, he argues that courts should continue to define markets because doing so provides information on competitive constraints. However, courts should not draw hard boundaries or make strong inferences about market power. Instead, as he would use it, market definition would consist more of a narrative about the potential competitive constraints.

This promises to be a hot issue in years to come. Although some cases suggest a need for market definition, many other cases have held that market definition is unnecessary when there is direct evidence of market power or anticompetitive effects.[1] Moreover, an increasing body of economic literature has indicated that market definition is not only unnecessary, but actually unnecessarily complicates and obscures the analysis, and thus should affirmatively be abandoned. I myself have argued that market definition should generally be abandoned on these grounds, other than in: (a) monopolization or exclusionary conduct cases, where market share may bear on whether a firm is a unitary actor who can exploit buyer collective action problems; or (b) oligopolistic coordination cases, where market definition may indicate whether a firm has few enough rivals to make coordination feasible.[2] A recent influential article by Professors Farrell and Shapiro argues that market definition should be abandoned just for mergers in differentiated markets.[3] Finally, a just-published article by Professor Kaplow takes the even more sweeping position that market definition should be abandoned in all antitrust cases.[4]

Evans' theory that market definition might still provide a useful narrative about potential competitive restraints seems to provide the best defense for keeping market definition. The more critical literature effectively responds that elasticities or diversion ratios would give us better and more precise information on competitive constraints, at least in some categories of cases. Still, it can be difficult to carry a matrix of elasticities or diversion ratios around in one's head when thinking about cases, especially in cases that involve the interaction of multiple market levels. For some forms of analytical analysis, it may be useful to exclude firms who, given those elasticities or diversion ratios, impose a weak enough competitive constraint that they are unlikely to change the analysis. Or at least one might want to do so for working purposes, as long as one then tests the ultimate conclusion against the possibility that their more marginal competitive constraint might matter. I would expect this debate to play out in the upcoming years.

Chapter 4 – Modern Analysis of Mergers that Eliminate Potential Competition. The 2010 US Horizontal Merger Guidelines are the first revisions since 1982 to update analysis of mergers involving potential competitors. It is thus particularly timely to address the antitrust analysis of mergers that may raise potential competition issues, which is the topic of John Kwoka's chapter. Whereas older versions classified mergers involving potential competitors as non-horizontal, the 2010 Guidelines call them horizontal.

Kwoka reviews the predicted market results with two firms under various standard

---

[1]   FTC v. Indiana Federation of Dentists, 476 U.S. 447, 460 (1986) (direct proof of anticompetitive effects obviates the need to prove market definition or power); Re/Max International v. Realty One, 173 F.3d 995, 1018 (6th Cir. 1999) (collecting cases holding that direct proof of market power obviates need to define markets); P. AREEDA, H. HOVENKAMP, and J.L. SOLOW, IIB ANTITRUST LAW 108 (3rd ed. 2007) (same).

[2]   E. Elhauge and D. Geradin, *Global Antitrust Law and Economics* 293–5 (Foundation Press, 2007); E. Elhauge and D. Geradin, *Global Antitrust Law and Economics* 316–18 (2d ed., Foundation Press, 2011).

[3]   J. Farrell and C. Shapiro, *Antitrust Evaluation of Horizontal Mergers: An Economic Alternative to Market Definition*, 10 B.E.J. THEORETICAL ECON. Iss. 1 (Policies and Perspectives), Article 9 (2010) (in differentiated markets, proving price effects directly is simpler and more accurate than market definition).

[4]   L. Kaplow, *Why (Ever) Define Markets?*, 124 HARVARD L. REV. 437 (2010).

models, assuming a homogeneous product and two identical firms. He shows that the Stackelberg leadership model, coupled with an assumption about the fixed costs of entry, allows an incumbent to set the output that it knows will deter entry. He offers formulas for calculating whether such entry deterrence is profitable, and to measure the increase in inefficiency and consumer harm that results. He then compares these formulas to the monopoly results in order to analyse the effects of a merger with a potential competitor, assuming only one potential entrant exists.

Kwoka finds that in each case a merger that fully compensates the potential competitor for the profits it could have earned from entry is profitable to the incumbent. He also derives formulas for calculating the increase in incumbent profits, inefficiency, and consumer harm that results from merging with a potential competitor. The harm is bigger the more competitive the market would have been without the merger. In the case of Stackelberg leadership, the incumbent would (without the merger) be setting output to deter entry, so the merger eliminates perceived potential competition rather than actual potential competition. He shows that mergers that eliminate perceived potential competition create smaller increases in profits, inefficiency, and consumer harm, consistent with intuition and empirical findings.

Kwoka then notes that, if we relax the assumption that only one potential entrant exists, the other potential entrants may offer enough of a competitive constraint to eliminate any harm from the merger. Also, if we alter assumptions to assume the entrant has higher per-unit costs than the incumbent, eliminating the entrant by merger is less profitable. Finally, if we assume a differentiated market, then one should analyse the merger like a merger between actual competitors, but the analysis is difficult because there is no actual diversion ratio so a projected diversion ratio would have to be estimated.

Kwoka also reports an empirical study finding that an airline merger increased prices by 10% when it eliminated an existing competitor and by 6% when it eliminated a potential competitor. Other empirical studies focus on the market effects of each additional potential entrant, a measurement that Kwoka points out reflects the *average* effect of a potential entrant and thus is likely to underestimate the effect of a merger, which is likely to focus on the *most* constraining potential entrant. Nonetheless these empirical studies have found statistically significant effects. One study found that each additional competitor in an airline market lowers prices by 4% and each additional potential competitor reduces prices by 1.4%. Other studies have replicated this conclusion, finding each additional potential entrant reduces prices by 0.25–2%, which is one-third to one-eighth of the effect they find for each additional actual competitor. Some studies find a particularly strong effect if the potential entrant is Southwest, which decreases prices by 12–33% if it is a potential entrant and by 46% if it is an actual competitor. Other studies have found that potential entrants significantly constrain prices in markets for railroads and pharmaceuticals. In cable television markets, potential entrants interestingly do not affect prices but instead affect quality, leading incumbents to offer more channels.

Kwoka thus concludes that, although enforcement against potential competition mergers declined from an earlier period, the theoretical and empirical literature indicates that mergers that eliminate potential competitors can have significant anticompetitive effects, even though those effects are less than those of mergers that eliminate existing competitors. He thus applauds the fact that the 2010 US Merger Guidelines include potential competition mergers in their analysis, and recognize that they can have significant anticompetitive effects, which he concludes will help elevate the importance of these issues in the future.

PART II   AGREEMENTS AND UNILATERAL CONDUCT

This handbook next moves on to consider various hot topics in the antitrust assessment of agreements and unilateral conduct. Some of these issues are hot because they involve conflicts in law among cases within the United States or between the United States and the EU and other nations. Other issues are hot because they involve issues that have been newly raised by recent Supreme Court decisions and cases.

Chapter 5 – The Recent Economic Literature on Tying, Bundled Discounts, and Loyalty Discounts. Probably the area of antitrust law and economics that is currently most contested is tying, bundled discounts, and loyalty discounts. A slew of recent cases in the United States have adopted diverging standards from each other and from EU cases.[5] It is thus particularly timely to have Nicholas Economides' chapter unpacking the findings of the economic literature.

Economides begins by clarifying the oft-neglected distinctions between fixed ratio ties, requirements ties, and volume-based ties, the parallel ones between fixed ratio bundled discounts, bundled loyalty discounts, and bundled volume-based discounts, and the distinction between loyalty commitments and conditions. He further observes that any nominal bundled or loyalty 'discount' can really be a penalty if the noncompliant price is set above the but-for price that would prevail without the program.

Economides then rebuts the single monopoly theory for such tying and bundling because they can extract consumer surplus through intra-product price discrimination, intra-consumer price discrimination, or inter-product price discrimination. Further, they can foreclose a substantial share of the tied market in a way that increases tied or tying market power.

Moving on to single-product loyalty discounts, he finds that all-units discounts are more problematic than incremental unit discounts. In particular, he finds that loyalty discounts on all-units can be equivalent to bundling incontestable and contestable demands. He also finds that share-based or individualized discounts are much more problematic than fixed volume-based discounts because the former can extract all consumer surplus and be tailored to exclude rivals.

Economides also rebuts the profit-sacrifice test, finding that no profit sacrifice is necessary to utilize these strategies is an anticompetitive way. The main reason is that buyers have a prisoner's dilemma that makes them willing to accept anticompetitive ties, bundled discounts, or loyalty discounts, as long as they get some trivial individual discount from the noncompliant price, even if the result is that collectively all buyers are harmed. Because no profit sacrifice is required, Economides concludes that the Antitrust Modernization Commission was mistaken to recommend requiring proof that a profit sacrifice was recouped.

Economides also demonstrates various problems with using cost-based tests to assess

---

[5]   Elhauge and Geradin, *supra* note 2, at 625–90 (2d ed).

bundled or loyalty discounts. First, if these tests use the defendant's costs, they can immunize cases where the conduct successfully made the rival less efficient. Second, these tests allow the exclusion of any less efficient rival, which can harm market efficiency and consumer welfare because such rivals can constrain market power. Third, these tests don't work well in differentiated markets. Fourth, allowing all above-cost bundled or loyalty discounts reduces price transparency. Fifth, the prisoner's dilemma problem means that buyers might accept above-cost bundled or loyalty discounts to avoid penalty pricing.

Economides instead recommends using a structured rule of reason that focuses on whether tying or bundling reduces consumer surplus. Because extracting consumer surplus requires tying market power, but does not require tied market power, a substantial tied foreclosure share, or failure of a price–cost attribution test, he concludes that legal doctrine likewise should require tying market power but not the other factors. However, legal doctrine should consider offsetting efficiencies. He concludes that a similar structured rule of reason should apply to bundled or loyalty discounts if the unbundled or disloyalty price is higher than the but-for price.

Chapter 6 – A New Theory of Predatory Pricing. Although the law on predatory pricing has become relatively stable within the United States, the US law on predatory pricing remains in considerable conflict with the EU and among other nations.[6] In his chapter, Aaron Edlin raises a broad-based attack that undermines the economic premises that underlie current US law's skepticism about predatory pricing and its usage of cost-based and recoupment tests. He proposes a new test, the consumer-betterment standard, to deal with cases of reactive above-cost price cuts that deter or drive out entrants who would offer consumers a better deal than the every-day price the monopolist charges when it does not confront entry.

Edlin begins by showing that predatory pricing is more plausible than had been argued by the Chicago School critique of predatory pricing. Even if one assumes symmetric information and costs, he finds that predation and non-predation are both economic equilibrium, and that which equilibrium holds turns entirely on expectations. He further shows that predation becomes even more likely if instead we have *a*symmetric information or costs: that is, either if entrants have to infer incumbent costs from incumbent pricing (giving the incumbent incentives to send false signals about its costs with predatory pricing) or if incumbents actually have lower costs (and thus can drive out entrants by cutting prices to levels above incumbent costs but below entrant costs). Finally, he argues that any theoretical ambiguity is resolved by empirical studies showing that predatory pricing does occur often, contrary to the opposite empirical premise asserted by some and relied on by some courts.

Edlin argues that, if one uses a price–cost test, the proper cost standard to use depends on whether the underlying test is a profit-sacrifice test or an equally-efficient-rival test. Under a profit-sacrifice test, he finds that courts should use 'inclusive' measures of costs that include the lost revenue from lowering prices to inframarginal buyers. (The same can be accomplished by using marginal revenue rather than price.) Under an equally-efficient-rival test, he finds that courts should use exclusive measures that exclude such costs.

However, Edlin finds that neither test is well-connected to the antitrust goal of

---

[6]   *Id.* at 352–98.

protecting consumer welfare. Edlin proposes that predatory pricing should instead be governed by a consumer-betterment test, which asks whether a monopolist's 'challenged practice is likely in the circumstances to exclude from the defendant's market a competitor who would provide consumers a better deal than they get from the monopoly'. He argues that this test does not prohibit limit pricing because there the deal offered by the firm is the limit price, which is better than consumers could get from an entrant. Further, he argues that the consumer-betterment test does not prohibit any permanent price cut in reaction to entry because then the deal offered would be the permanent price rather than the pre-entry price. However, the consumer-betterment test would prohibit a firm from normally pricing high pre-entry, using a temporary price cut to drive out an entrant, and then restoring high prices post-entry, because there the deal offered to consumers by the monopolist before and after the predatory period is worse than the entrant would offer.

This consumer-betterment test is an important new contribution, but one whose precise meaning may need to be fleshed out in future work and which may raise insuperable administrative problems. In particular, the consumer-betterment test requires some methodology for figuring out how to define what counts as the 'deal' offered by the monopolist and entrant in cases where their prices vary over time or with the conduct. For example, Edlin's application of his test suggests by implication that the monopolist's 'deal' does not include pre-entry prices in the event of a permanent price reduction, but does include both the monopolist's pre-entry and post-entry prices in the event of a temporary price increase (but does not include their temporary price reduction). But the underlying methodology for reaching those conclusions about what constitutes the 'deal' is not defined, and it is less clear what the consumer-betterment test would mean in other cases.

To illustrate, suppose a monopolist cut prices to a level above its costs but below an entrant's, and permanently kept them low, and this drove out the entrant. Suppose further that, without the price cut, the entrant would in the long run have become more efficient and lowered prices to below the monopolist's permanently-cut prices. Then, whether the consumer-betterment test allows the conduct turns on whether we deem the entrant's 'deal' to be: (a) the entrant's short-run price, in which case the test allows the conduct; (b) the long-run price the entrant would have offered, in which case the test prohibits the conduct, or (c) the present value of the entrant's short- and long-run prices, in which case the test outcome turns on whether this present value calculation exceeds the monopolist's permanent price. To the extent that the consumer-betterment test condemns such conduct, it differs from the Baumol test, which would allow all permanent price reductions, which is an interesting contribution. But condemning such price cuts would mean that the consumer-betterment test requires a court to project what the entrant's long-run price would have been (which will be hard), or to estimate what the present value of the entrant's stream of projected prices would be (which is even harder), in order to compare them to the monopolist's permanent price cut.

Or consider the following sort of situation. A monopolist prices at 100, an entrant enters at its cost of 76, the monopolist lowers its price to 75 and drives out the entrant. But after the entrant's exit, there is an increase in market quality, costs, or demand, so that, had the entrant remained in the market, the entrant would have increased its price to 90. Does the consumer-betterment test allow the monopolist to now increase its price to 89 because it is offering a deal that is better than the entrant 'would' have offered at the same time? If so, then this is another difference from the Baumol test, which would prohibit price increases after rival exit. Moreover, this difference is even more helpful because it neatly avoids some of the main critiques of Baumol's test, which were that the Baumol test would create inefficient incentives for the monopolist to evade the price cap by worsening quality or would inefficiently freeze pricing despite changes in costs or demand.[7] However, this interpretation of the consumer-betterment test would also put a lot of administrative burden on courts because it would require courts to adjust any price rule based on counterfactual projections of what the entrant would have charged at each point in time.

All this remains to be fleshed out in future work. For now, Edlin's consumer-betterment test offers a new intriguing possibility that avoids some of the problems of prior approaches. Time may tell whether the administrative problems it raises are so great it is unworkable, or so similar to the administrative problems raised by simply asking whether the conduct worsened consumer welfare that we might as well make that final ultimate question our test.

Chapter 7 – Vertical Price-Fixing After Leegin. Now that the 2007 *Leegin* decision has overruled the old per se rule against vertical price-fixing, it has raised new issues about how to assess claimed justifications and anticompetitive theories regarding vertical price-fixing. Those new issues will need to be addressed to conduct a rule of reason review, and are tackled in Ben Klein's chapter.

Assessing Procompetitive Justifications for Vertical Price-Fixing. Klein argues that the conventional free-rider justification for vertical price-fixing is too narrow and under-described because retailers can always engage in non-price competition that competes away the price floor. Thus, he argues that, even in free-riding scenarios, manufacturers would have to specify the performance they want, and that all vertical price-fixing provides in such cases is a profit margin that makes termination an effective penalty for nonperformance.

Moreover, Klein argues empirically that free-rider problems are not present in many actual cases. Free-riding on services is often inapplicable either because no service is being offered or because the terminated retailers provide the same services as other retailers. Free-riding on quality certification does not apply in many cases either because the product has a well-established brand name, because discounting retailers are terminated even when they have good quality reputations, or because the quality problem could easily be solved by the manufacturer simply refusing to sell the product to low-quality retailers.

Klein argues that the true justification for vertical price-fixing is usually different. It arises from the fact that retailers have discretion about which goods to carry and promote because each retailer has a group of loyal customers who get consumer surplus from going to that store. Thus, he concludes that retailer display or promotion decisions generally have 'significant inter-brand demand effects but little or no inter-retailer demand effects'. In Klein's view, the real reason manufacturers usually use vertical price-fixing is

---

[7]　E. Elhauge, *Why Above-Cost Price Cuts to Drive Out Entrants are Not Predatory – and the Implications for Defining Costs and Market Power*, 112 YALE L.J. 681, 822–5 (2003).

to give retailers a greater return that induces those retailers to exercise their discretion to favor the price-fixing manufacturers in display or promotion.

Klein acknowledges that manufacturers could simply pay directly for promotion or shelf-space, but he points out that this alternative may sometimes be hard to specify and monitor. For example, if may be hard to specify increased salesperson efforts and enthusiasm for a particular brand. Moreover, vertical price-fixing usefully ties the amount of payment to actual success in selling the product, thus aligning incentives and reducing monitoring costs. On this view, vertical price-fixing really solves a problem of contract economics that would be raised by trying to directly contract about promotion or display.

Students of Phillip Areeda may recall that he called this same theory the 'brand pushing' rationale, but that he classified it as anticompetitive rather than procompetitive. He argued that giving retailers greater returns on some brands in order to get them to push sales of it over others would distort retailer's advice to consumers and thus harm consumer welfare.[8] It would give retailers incentives to recommend the higher-profit brands even though their prices were higher and quality worse than other brands, either directly through salesperson recommendations or implicitly through promotions or display location. Moreover, Areeda reasoned that allowing vertical price-fixing would give each manufacturer incentives to adopt vertical price-fixing to prevent other brands from being pushed over its brand, with the result being a prisoner's dilemma where every manufacturer would use vertical price-fixing to get brand-pushing, but in the end no manufacturer would gain any relative advantage and all would suffer from excessive retail margins and unresponsive retail prices.[9] He anticipated the Klein type of argument that using vertical price-fixing to buy brand pushing reflects desirable competition for promotional services, but argued that bidding for promotional services is not procompetitive when the promotional service consists of retailer efforts to mislead consumers.[10]

So one basic issue that arises in the wake of *Leegin* is how we should think of this brand-pushing rationale for vertical price-fixing. Should we view it, as Klein does, as inherently procompetitive competition for retail distribution? Or should we view it, as Areeda argued, as an anticompetitive and inefficient effort to distort retailer advice and harm consumer welfare? I would expect this issue to be hotly contested in years to come, but the early legal returns seem to favor the Areeda approach. In *Leegin* itself, the Supreme Court held that one of the 'the potential *anti*competitive consequences of vertical price restraints' was that '[a] manufacturer with market power . . . might use resale price maintenance to give retailers an *incentive* not to sell the products of smaller rivals or new entrants'.[11] Thus, the *Leegin* Court treated as anticompetitive precisely what Klein characterizes as the principal procompetitive justification for vertical price-fixing.

Another issue arises from the rationale's premise that inter-retailer demand effects are low because that premise also suggests that retailers should not care what prices other retailers are charging for the same brand. The premise thus leaves it unclear why retailers

---

[8]   See VIII P. AREEDA, ANTITRUST LAW para. 1601(6) at 15, para. 1614 at 194–8 (1989).
[9]   *Id.* at 15, 197–8.
[10]   *Id.* at 197. In subsequent volumes of the antitrust law treatise, Professor Hovenkamp also adheres to the Areeda conclusions summarized in this paragraph. See VIII AREEDA AND HOVENKAMP, ANTITRUST LAW para. 1601 at 16–17, para. 1614 at 178–81 (3rd ed. 2010).
[11]   Leegin Creative Leather Products v. PSKS, Inc., 551 U.S. 877, 894 (2007) (emphasis added).

need vertical price-fixing at all. Each retailer could itself just determine the retail price for each brand that gives the retailer enough of a margin to cover the promotion and display the retailer chose for that brand, because the lack of inter-retailer demand effects makes the prices at other retailers irrelevant.

Moreover, given the premise of low inter-retailer demand effects, it is not clear why a manufacturer that wanted to encourage pushing of its brand could not do so without vertical price-fixing by simply lowering its wholesale price.[12] Cutting its wholesale price would give retailers a higher profit margin on its brand than on other competing brands at any given retail market price for the product. Cutting wholesale prices thus seems a less restrictive alternative for advancing brand-pushing. To be sure, this alternative would also encourage a prisoner's dilemma where every manufacturer lowered its whole-sale price to get brand-pushing, and thus none got it in the end. But, as shown above, using vertical price-fixing to incentivize brand-pushing also raises a prisoner's dilemma. Moreover, here the prisoner's dilemma is the virtuous one that underlies all competitive pricing, resulting in competitive low wholesale and retail prices, as well as in retailers whose advice to consumers is undistorted and who can vary retail prices with retailer cost variations over time and between retailers.

Finally, it should be noted that the Klein justification for vertical price-fixing is only potentially applicable to multi-brand dealers. If he is right that free-riding truly does not explain much vertical price-fixing, then that may leave little justification for the use of vertical price-fixing with single-brand dealers.

Assessing Anticompetitive Theories for Vertical Price-Fixing. Klein then assesses possible anticompetitive theories for vertical price-fixing after *Leegin*. He begins by considering manufacturer-motivated theories. One possible theory is that vertical price-fixing might facilitate a manufacturer cartel. It can do so either by decreasing manufacturer incentives to cut wholesale prices or by making it easier to detect such cuts. Klein acknowledges this possibility, and argues that proving it should require proving widespread use by rival manufacturers and sufficient market concentration. He also argues that the facilitating effects may be weaker than commonly supposed because each manufacturer still has incentives to cut wholesale prices to get its brand pushed. But his last point also raises the issue, noted above, about whether cutting wholesale prices is a less restrictive alternative for accomplishing what he finds to be the main rationale for vertical price-fixing.

A second manufacturer-motivated anticompetitive theory is that vertical price-fixing might allow a manufacturer to maintain its market power by giving retailers incentives not to carry smaller rivals or entrants. Here Klein critiques the *Leegin* Court's conclusion that it is anticompetitive to give retailers incentives to favor the powerful manufacturer over rival brands, arguing that doing so just reflects desirable competition. This argument

---

[12]   If instead inter-retailer demand effects are high, then intra-brand retail competition will be high, and lowering the wholesale price will predictably lower retail prices at all retailers and bring retailer profit margins back to competitive levels, eliminating the incentive to push. See VIII AREEDA, ANTITRUST LAW para.1614 at 195 (1989); VIII AREEDA AND HOVENKAMP, ANTITRUST LAW para.1614 at 178–9 (3rd ed. 2010). The same would be true of manufacturer efforts to achieve the same sort of brand-pushing by simply paying dealers a bonus for increased sales, which is equivalent to lowering the wholesale price. Thus, if inter-retailer demand effects are high, then vertical price-fixing does seem necessary to encourage brand-pushing, raising the issue of whether such brand-pushing is desirable.

raises the basic question, noted above, about whether to classify this effect as procompetitive under the Klein theory or anticompetitive under the *Leegin*-Areeda theory. Because Klein rejects the latter, he would require proof not only of manufacturer market power, but also of some actual or de facto exclusivity requirement. However, if the latter existed, we would really have a case of exclusive dealing, which is addressed under another antitrust doctrine. Thus, Klein effectively is arguing that mere vertical price-fixing imposed by a powerful manufacturer should be per se legal, unless one can prove it facilitates a manufacturer cartel.

Klein moves on to consider retailer-motivated anticompetitive theories. On both of these theories, the *Leegin* Court suggested it was relevant whether retailers were the source or initiator of the vertical price-fixing. However, Klein argues that this factor may not have economic significance because both manufacturers and retailers can benefit from vertical price-fixing, and thus either might suggest it. Although Klein emphasizes that either might initiate for procompetitive reasons, it is also true that either might initiate for anticompetitive reasons at either level.[13]

The first retailer-motivated theory that Klein considers is that vertical price-fixing might facilitate a retailer cartel. He argues that this theory requires evidence of a large share of retailers jointly communicating with the manufacturer. He further argues that this theory is strengthened by proof that the manufacturer market is unconcentrated. This latter point indicates that proving manufacturer market power should thus not be a requirement for all vertical price-fixing cases.

The second retailer-motivated anticompetitive theory is that a powerful retailer might use vertical price-fixing to impede competition from retailer rivals who are more efficient or innovative. Klein argues that this theory should require proof that a retailer has market power and that vertical price-fixing covers a significant share of the product market.

Finally, based on his premise that vertical price-fixing is generally procompetitive, Klein argues that the plaintiff should have to show anticompetitive effects before a defendant has to show procompetitive justification. However, if Klein is right that vertical price-fixing is usually motivated by encouraging brand-pushing rather than by curbing free-riding, and one instead adopts the Areeda-*Leegin* position that brand-pushing is anticompetitive, this would suggest the opposite conclusion: that vertical price-fixing is usually anticompetitive and that the defendant should have to prove a procompetitive justification first.

Klein also argues that proving increased prices should not suffice to show an anticompetitive effect because such a price increase is consistent with his procompetitive theory. Once again, this conclusion depends on his categorization of the brand-pushing rationale. He also argues that under all four anticompetitive theories, a plaintiff should have to show that the vertical price-fixing led to decreased market output and that the retailer-

---

[13]   E. Elhauge, *Harvard, Not Chicago,* 3 COMPETITION POLICY INT'L 59, 60–68 (Autumn 2007) ('Even if a dealer initiated the restraint, dealers have incentives to offer terms that they think manufacturers will find efficient and profitable. Further, even if a manufacturer initiated the restraint, any individual manufacturer has incentives to get dealers to carry its products by offering terms it knows a powerful dealer or dealer cartel will find profitable, even if those profits come at the expense of consumer welfare. Moreover, the Court itself acknowledged that manufacturers could have their own anticompetitive incentives for imposing vertical minimum price-fixing').

motivated theories should require proof of a decrease in the individual manufacturer's sales.

Chapter 8. Proving Horizontal Agreements After Twombly. The 2007 Supreme Court decision in *Twombly* creates new – but somewhat obscure – standards for alleging and proving horizontal agreements. In their chapter, Alvin Klevorick and Issa Kohler-Hausmann offer a descriptive theory that uses the notation of Bayesian probability to helpfully formalize the relevant standards. They argue that the case law shows the relevant standards differ on a motion to dismiss and on summary judgment.

On a motion to dismiss, they argue that, if the plaintiff does not allege direct evidence of a conspiracy, the *Twombly* plausibility standard requires that the plaintiff allege parallel conduct and at least one 'plus factor'. They use Bayesian analysis to define a 'plus factor' as a fact that makes the probability of a conspiracy (given the parallel conduct and that fact) higher than the probability of a conspiracy would be with just the parallel conduct and without that fact.

On summary judgment, they argue that, if the plaintiff lacks direct evidence of a horizontal conspiracy, the 'tends to exclude' standard requires that the plaintiff instead satisfy the following Bayesian standard. The plaintiff must show that the probability of a conspiracy (given the parallel conduct and *all* the plus factor evidence in combination) is higher than the probability of independent action (given the same evidence).

Chapter 9. Modern Analysis of Monopsony Power. Roger Blair and Jessica Haynes's chapter focuses on the monopsony issues that have been increasingly raised by the Supreme Court's 2007 *Weyerhaeuser* decision and by recent allegations of buyer cartels among Major League Baseball owners, the NCAA, antique dealers, hospitals, and timber bidders. They model monopsony problems, and show how to adapt the Lerner Index and standard dominant firm and oligopoly models to the monopsony context.

They further prove that the reduction in input prices reduces the monopsonist's output and thus leads to increased downstream prices, contrary to the lay intuition that reducing input prices should reduce downstream prices. Finally, they apply their analysis to cases, including *Weyerhaeuser.*

PART III   ANTITRUST ENFORCEMENT

The handbook ends by considering current issues of antitrust enforcement. One important choice is between public and private enforcement. This is a live current topic, as other nations like the EU member states consider adding significant private enforcement to their public enforcement regimes, and as US decisions curb private enforcement in favor of public enforcement. Another issue is the timing of enforcement, an issue that is raised not only by the increasing emphasis on retrospective private enforcement in many nations, but also by US agency efforts to attack some mergers retrospectively rather than prospectively. An even more fundamental choice is between using consumer welfare and total welfare standards to guide enforcement. This issue has become increasingly disputed in the economic literature, with the most interesting development being the development of literature indicating that using a consumer welfare standard may actually advance total welfare objectives better than a total welfare standard would.

Another major current topic concerns problems raised by the recent increase in multi-nation antitrust enforcement for any given merger or conduct that has resulted from the fact that markets are increasingly international and more nations have begun to adopt and seriously enforce antitrust laws. Other issues are raised by recent court decisions on the intersections between antitrust and patent law, and between antitrust and other regulatory statutes. Finally, recent economic literature has led to interesting insights about how best to measure damages. This final part of the handbook considers all these topics.

Chapter 10. New Developments in the Economic Analysis of Optimal Antitrust Enforcement. In his chapter, Abraham Wickelgren summarizes recent scholarship on optimal antitrust enforcement on a host of issues.

Public v. Private Enforcement. As Wickelgren notes, the EU has recently been considering procedural changes to increase its private enforcement of antitrust laws, so it is particularly timely to consider the literature on the optimal mix of public versus private enforcement. Private enforcement may lead to underenforcement or overenforcement because the expected damages may be less than or greater than the negative externality from an antitrust violation. Private enforcement also will not consider the deterrent effect (leading to underenforcement) or the social loss from defendant litigation costs (leading to overenforcement).

Compared to public enforcement, private enforcement has the advantage of being more likely to detect violations but the disadvantage that it may be used anticompetitively to disadvantage rivals because of the prospect of erroneous decisions. Wickelgren notes that a recent economic model finds that adding private enforcement to public enforcement increases welfare as long as courts are sufficiently accurate, but that if courts are less accurate it is optimal to rely solely on public enforcement. Relying solely on public enforcement is thus more likely to be optimal in nations that have relatively inaccurate judicial systems. Further, as a nation's judicial system becomes more accurate in assessing antitrust cases, the nation is likely to find it more optimal to increase private enforcement.

In deciding which cases to publicly enforce, Wickelgren focuses on two branches of literature that suggest shortfalls in private enforcement that might make particularly good cases for public enforcement. One paper found that, although competitor suits encourage entry that lowers prices, competitor suits can also soften post-entry competition because they give the incumbent incentives to increase prices to reduce its lost profit damages. Another paper found that, if consumers mentally discount cartel prices by their anticipated antitrust damages when deciding how much to consume and know the firms' costs, then consumer suits will deter cartels only if the damage multiple times the detection odds exceed 1. However, even if this figure is less than 1, consumer suits can deter cartels if consumers do not know the firms' costs and thus cannot be sure whether high prices reflect cartel pricing or costs. Moreover, it is unclear that real consumers mentally discount prices by anticipated antitrust damages or know the detection odds necessary to do so.

Enforcement Timing. Wickelgren also analyses the choice of whether to engage in ex ante enforcement (such as prospectively blocking mergers) or ex post enforcement (retrospectively challenging anticompetitive mergers or conduct). He finds that ex ante enforcement is more optimal the lower the prospective uncertainty about the effects and the higher the costs of reversing those effects (such as when it requires undoing a merger). Ex post review also has other mixed effects in that it can: (1) undermine a regulator's ability to commit to optimal policy, (2) induce more beneficial post-merger conduct, or (3) induce inefficient efforts to make it costly to undo a merger.

Consumer Welfare v. Total Welfare. Wickelgren also addresses the much-debated issue of whether consumer welfare or total welfare should be the standard agencies and courts use. He first points to reasons why total welfare should be the ultimate objective, but then explains why using a total welfare standard may not actually be best to achieve that objective.

On the reasons for making total welfare the ultimate objective, Wickelgren points out that consumer welfare has an imperfect fit with distributional concerns because antitrust victims are not always poorer than violator shareholders. Further, if one tried to limit the consumer welfare standard to cases where antitrust victims were poorer than violator shareholders, that would add legal expense and uncertainty and lead to the same work disincentives as the tax system, which could achieve redistribution better. However, Wickelgren does not respond to the point that, despite the imperfect fit, if antitrust victims are usually poorer than violator shareholders, then a consumer welfare standard applied across the board could further redistribution without work disincentives.[14] This may be more optimal than using the tax system to achieve more precise redistribution with greater work disincentives.

More interestingly, even on his assumption that total welfare should be the ultimate objective, Wickelgren finds that the economic literature indicates that this objective may sometimes be advanced better by using a consumer welfare standard. The reasons turn out to be numerous.

The first reason is that a total welfare standard will cause firms to choose the most profitable action among the actions that increase total welfare, which can differ from the profitable action that increases total welfare the most. A consumer welfare standard can drive firms to instead choose the action that increases total welfare the most. Indeed, the literature finds that, for uniform distributions, if the number of possible actions is four, then a pure consumer welfare standard is the one that maximizes total welfare. If the number of possible actions is less than four, the maximizing standard is somewhere between total and consumer welfare. If the number of possible actions is more than four, the maximizing standard is actually stricter than consumer welfare.

The second reason is that, if firms have private information about their efficiencies, then there is an enforcement probability that leads to firms proposing mergers only when they increase total welfare, but using such an enforcement probability would make all proposed mergers increase total welfare. Thus, an agency that used a total welfare standard would approve all mergers, thus deviating from the optimal enforcement probability. This analysis indicates that deviations from total welfare toward consumer welfare are likely to be optimal, though it does not necessarily support a pure consumer welfare standard.

Third, if monopolists dissipate their monopoly profits in efforts to obtain market power, then those monopoly profits wash out ex ante, and thus a consumer welfare standard may better maximize ex ante total welfare. An ex post total welfare standard would approve actions that increase monopoly profits by more than they harm consumer welfare, but if the increased monopoly profits are totally dissipated ex ante, such actions

---

[14]   See E. Elhauge, *The Failed Resurrection of the Single Monopoly Profit Theory*, 6(1) COMPETITION POLICY INT'L 155, 168 (Spring 2010).

would harm ex ante total welfare.[15] The greater the share of monopoly profits that are dissipated ex ante, the more likely it is that a consumer welfare standard does a better job of advancing ex ante total welfare than an ex post total welfare standard would.

A fourth point, which Wickelgren does not address, is that generally firms should be able to restructure any action that increases total welfare in a way that does not harm consumer welfare, perhaps by using their efficiency gains to fund consumer welfare trusts.[16] Given this, a consumer welfare standard usually seems unlikely to block action that increases total welfare, but instead would only induce the restructuring necessary to make sure that consumers benefit as well. This point also seems related to the first point above, because if manufacturers have to structure their actions to preserve consumer welfare, they might as well choose the action choice that maximizes total welfare because that will generally also maximize their profits given the lack of harm to consumer welfare.

Finally, a fifth point, also not addressed by Wickelgren, is that a consumer welfare standard makes it easier to coordinate international enforcement.[17] The reason is that concurrent international antitrust enforcement effectively allocates decisive power to the most aggressive enforcer, which is likely to result in decisive power being exercised by the importing nations that have the most incentive to be aggresive. Such importing nations have incentives to apply a consumer welfare standard correctly, but would have incentives to underweigh producer benefits if they were applying a total welfare standard.

International Enforcement. Although he does not consider its connection to the welfare standard, Wickelgren does briefly discuss international enforcement. He observes that, given concurrent international enforcement, a decision by the United States or the EU matters only if the other has approved the merger. He finds that this can lead to problems similar to the winner's curse in auctions, unless each takes into account the signals created by the decisions of others. The next chapter addresses international enforcement at greater length.

Chapter 11. Dealing With the Contemporary Increase in Multi-Nation Antitrust Enforcement. Anu Bradford's chapter focuses on the increasing importance of antitrust enforcement by multiple nations, given the proliferation of antitrust laws in more nations and the increasingly international nature of markets and thus of mergers or antitrust claims. She notes that without any overarching international antitrust regime, this multi-nation enforcement regime leads to three problems.

First, multi-nation enforcement can increase transaction costs and uncertainty for firms. For example, recent surveys have found that the typical international merger requires filing in six agencies and takes seven months and US $5 million to complete, even if the merger filing results in no serious investigation, with each additional jurisdiction increasing the delay and cost. Although the cost is only 0.11% of the costs of the average merger deal, she argues this amounts to a tax on international mergers that is regressive because it disproportionately burdens small mergers. Further, decisions by multiple regulators can conflict with each other, increasing uncertainty.

---

[15]   See Elhauge, *supra* note 14, at 169–72; E. Elhauge, *Tying, Bundled Discounts, and the Death of the Single Monopoly Profit Theory*, 123 HARVARD L. REV. 397, 439–42 (2009).
[16]   See Elhauge, *supra* note 14, at 168–9; Elhauge, *supra* note 15, at 438.
[17]   Elhauge, *supra* note 15, at 438.

However, she notes this concern may be overblown because very few mergers have actually produced a conflict and firms can always conform their behavior to the more aggressive regime.

Second, she argues that multi-nation enforcement can lead to antitrust protectionism. One possibility is that states might be influenced by their trade flows, overenforcing antitrust law if they are net importers and underenforcing antitrust law if they are net exporters. Bradford observes that this theory must assume nations are in a prisoner's dilemma that causes them to choose suboptimal enforcement and cannot reach binding agreements to prevent it. Moreover, she notes that trade flows are a relatively small percentage of any nation's GDP and fluctuate over time. Finally, she observes that Elhauge and Geradin have pointed out that net-importing nations actually have optimal enforcement incentives if they adopt a consumer welfare standard and that underenforcement by net-exporting nations is irrelevant given the enforcement by net-importing nations.

Antitrust protectionism might also arise from the fact that most nations exempt export cartels, thus allowing anticompetitive conduct that harms consumers outside their borders. However, just as Elhauge and Geradin's point means that a general underenforcement by net-exporting nations does not matter given enforcement by net-importing nations, so too it means that a specific underenforcement by a nation that exports a particular product does not matter given enforcement by the nations that import that product. Bradford stresses that this logic assumes the importing nations have the resources and evidentiary access to enforce their antitrust laws, which may not always be true.

Antitrust enforcement might also arise if states underenforce antitrust laws against domestic firms, while overenforcing them against foreign firms. However, she notes that the actual evidence is that the EU is half as likely to block a merger involving a US firm. On the other hand, early concerns have been raised about whether China's enforcement of its brand new antitrust statute is favoring domestic firms. This is an issue that can be expected to become increasingly controversial in years to come.

Third, following another argument from Elhauge and Geradin, Bradford observes that multi-nation enforcement can lead to global overenforcement because the most aggressive enforcer always prevails given concurrent antitrust jurisdiction. Thus, even if nations are equally likely to overenforce as underenforce, the overenforcing result will prevail. Further, it means that nations that favor less stringent antitrust enforcement (such as the United States) effectively cede de facto international authority to nations that favor more stringent enforcement (such as the EU).

Because of concurrent jurisdiction, international antitrust enforcement will not have the 'race to the top' or 'race to the bottom' character that international regimes do with choice of law rules that put one jurisdiction in charge of each firm. However, Bradford observes that this tendency to overenforcement may helpfully compensate for underenforcement by antitrust jurisdictions that lack enforcement capacity or prefer to free ride on the enforcement efforts of others.

Despite the above three problems, no overarching international regime has arisen. Bradford argues that one important reason for this is a substantive disagreement about what the optimal antitrust rules are. Thus, Bradford argues that the underlying game-theoretic problem is not a prisoner's dilemma (where both nations would favor the same agreement) but a coordination game, where the nations differ on which international agreement is optimal, even though they may both be better off with some agreement than with nonagreement. This may be the case because different sorts of antitrust laws are favored by the United States and EU, by developed and developing nations, or by net-importing and net-exporting nations.

Another reason for the nonadoption of international antitrust law is the perception that the net benefits of an international agreement would be small relative to the costs. Those net benefits might seem low because the actual transaction costs are a small percentage of deal costs, actual international conflict is rare, underenforcement by exporting nations is adequately addressed by enforcement by importing nations, and the general tendency for errors to cause overenforcement in a multiple-enforcer regime is offset by the underenforcement tendency caused by free-riding or weak antitrust regimes. The costs of international agreement may be relatively high because they include not only the costs of deviating from a nation's optimal antitrust regime, but also the negotiation costs of reaching an international agreement and the agency costs of having international enforcers who are difficult for individual nations to monitor.

Chapter 12. Current Issues in the Intersection of Antitrust and Regulation. Howard Shelanski's chapter addresses the intersection between antitrust and regulation. He argues that the issue has changed with the 2004 and 2007 Supreme Court decisions in *Trinko* and *Credit Suisse,* which weakened the historical reluctance of courts to hold that federal regulation triggered antitrust immunity. Before those decisions, the case law presumed that antitrust law could operate in parallel with regulatory laws unless a 'plain repugnancy' between them could be established. *Trinko,* he notes, might be read to make it harder to bring any novel antitrust claims against firms subject to regulatory oversight even when the regulatory law has an antitrust saving clause. *Credit Suisse* seemed to extend the concept of 'repugnancy' to include cases where judicial error might lead to conflict, although a narrow reading of the case might limit *Credit Suisse* to core areas regulated by securities law.

Shelanski notes that this doctrine is premised on the questionable empirical premise that false positives leading to antitrust overenforcement are more costly than false negatives that lead to regulatory underenforcement. On underdeterrence, he observes that regulatory agencies may fail to actively exercise their authority or erroneously fail to condemn conduct. On overdeterrence, he observes that the Antitrust Modernization Commission found that, although overdeterrence was a valid theoretical concern, '[n]o actual cases or evidence of systematic overdeterrence were presented to the Commission'. Further, many other Supreme Court cases have narrowed antitrust in a way that reduces overdeterrence, and empirical studies show that the lion's share of essential facility claims have been held not to raise a triable issue of fact. Moreover, the concerns about overdeterrence from self-interested private litigation do not apply to public litigation by antitrust agencies, and yet the regulatory exemption doctrines preclude both.

Shelanski suggests various ways to mitigate these problems. First, courts could read *Trinko* and *Credit Suisse* narrowly. Second, Congress or the Supreme Court could adopt clearer standards for antitrust immunity, which the lower courts could apply in a case-by-case way. Third, either could exempt the antitrust agencies from the *Trinko* and *Credit Suisse* rulings. Fourth, Congress could give regulatory agencies authority to make case-by-case antitrust-like rulings even without rulemaking, to make up for the displacement of such ex post case-specific review by antitrust courts.

Chapter 13. Current Issues in the Patent–Antitrust Intersection. Chris Sprigman's chapter addresses the intersection of patent and antitrust law. He argues that while earlier antitrust law was hostile to patents and aggressive exercises of patent rights, more recent antitrust case law has moved away from this hostility. He argues that there is a fundamental conflict between antitrust and intellectual property law because, while both seek to foster innovation and consumer welfare, antitrust seeks to do so by fostering competition, whereas intellectual property law does so by preventing competition in certain areas. However, he also notes that the right to exclude provided by intellectual property law does not differ from the right to exclude provided under other forms of property law, so that there is no real reason to treat exercises of the different property rights differently under antitrust law.

In the Supreme Court's *Kodak* decision, Sprigman notes that foreclosing rival service organizations may have been used to extend market power in parts beyond the length of the patents. He argues that while the 2006 *Illinois Tool Works* decision was right that most patents do not confer market power, the court should nonetheless have inferred market power from the ability to impose a burdensome requirements tie involving complementary products, arguing that such a burden could have been inferred not only from licensee objections but also from the fact that the tied product cost 2.5–4 times as much as identical alternatives. He argues that such ties produce price discrimination that reliably reduces consumer welfare but yield no reliable increase in total welfare. Sprigman also reviews antitrust analysis of patent licenses, patent pools, patents obtained by fraud, and the recent hot topic of reverse payments in settlements of pharmaceutical patent infringement cases.

Chapter 14. Modern Methods for Measuring Antitrust Damages. In the final chapter, Professor Rubinfeld provides an analysis of how to calculate antitrust damages. This is again quite timely given the growth of private antitrust enforcement outside of the United States, and reflects developments in modern economic analysis of antitrust damages.

Rubinfeld begins by analysing the measurement of overcharge damages, which he says generally use either the yardstick or benchmark approach. Under the yardstick approach, prices or margins in the violation market are compared to prices or margins in related nonviolation markets. The latter could be the same product in different but similar geographic markets, or it could be different but similar products in the same geographic market. Under the benchmark approach, prices during the violation period are compared to prices in the same market before or after the violation period.

Under either approach, one can use regression analysis to control for any differences in costs, demand, or degree of competition either between the violation market and yardstick market or between the violation period and benchmark period. Under the benchmark approach, one can also use either (1) a forecasting method that uses only data from the nonviolation period to predict but-for prices during the violation period, or (2) a dummy variable approach, which uses data from all periods but uses a dummy variable to distinguish periods when the violation occurred. He observes that one should also take into account that the violation may itself affect the correlation between the covariates and prices, and shows how to account for this in the regression.

How does one choose between these approaches when they conflict? Rubinfeld notes that if quantity is not correlated with the omitted variables, then the two approaches generate consistent predictions. However, the forecasting estimates vary more than the dummy variable estimates. On the other hand, a forecasting approach is less likely to be corrupted by the anticompetitive behavior during the violation period. Particularly worrisome is that if one uses a sufficient number of irrelevant variables, one can always use an in-sample model that produces a damage estimate of zero. Yet the disadvantage of the forecasting approach is that it may work less well if the relationship between prices and covariates is changing rapidly over time.

Rubinfeld notes that overcharge damages are underdeterring because they do not take into account the deadweight loss; that is, the fact that higher prices induce buyers to make fewer purchases. He notes that this underdeterrence may be offset by trebling damages. On the other hand, others have calculated that this failure to account for deadweight loss, coupled with the inability to recover for umbrella effects or pre-judgment interest, reduces treble damages to single damages on average.[18] Given that one needs some damage multiple to offset the odds of nondetection, this suggests underdeterrence.

Rubinfeld then turns to measuring lost profits damages. One method is to use the yardstick or benchmark method to estimate but-for prices, and then add estimates of but-for costs and a demand model to estimate but-for quantities. Another method is the market-share approach, which compares the profits the plaintiff in the actual and but-for worlds. The difficulties are that it may be difficult to control for other factors that affect market share or to apply the approach to new entrants.

Rubinfeld turns next to indirect purchaser cases, which are prohibited under current federal antitrust law but allowed under most state antitrust laws. He notes that indirect purchaser damages raise many complications, but that one should calculate them by using a reduced-form method to measure the pass-through rate. Under this method, one uses a regression to estimate the extent to which an increase in an intermediate firm's upstream costs leads to increases in its downstream prices. He observes that if the federal damages rule is optimal (on which he notes the evidence is weak), then adding indirect damages produces overdeterrence.

The Antitrust Modernization Commission suggested solving this duplicative damages problem by allowing indirect purchaser suits under federal law, but also allowing a pass-through defense to reduce damages from the direct purchaser. Rubineld notes a recent article finds that, in complex supply chains, direct purchaser overcharges underestimate the total antitrust harm. Another interesting paper finds that, if the direct purchaser is a monopolist, its deadweight loss from an upstream cartel equals the amount of the overcharge that it would pass through. Thus, an overcharge measure provides a good measure of the harm suffered by such a direct purchaser, but allowing the direct purchaser to recover the overcharge and the indirect purchasers to recover the pass-through would better approximate the total antitrust harm in the direct market (though understate the total harm given downstream effects).

Finally, Rubinfeld addresses the practice of awarding discount coupons rather than damages. He notes that one problem with these remedies is that the actual redemption rate tends to be low. Another problem is that, to the extent they are redeemed, they will lead to overconsumption by artificially lowering the price, and that the deadweight loss

---

[18]   See Robert H. Lande, *Five Myths About Antitrust Damages,* 40 U.S.F.L. Rev. 651 (2006).

from this can be comparable to that created by the overcharge itself. However, giving plaintiffs a choice between coupons and cash damages that are lower than the coupon amount can lead to superior results because it induces plaintiffs who suffer more harm to select coupons and other plaintiffs to select cash.

PART I

MERGERS AND MARKET DEFINITION

2 Research topics in unilateral effects analysis
*Jonathan B. Baker and David Reitman**

I INTRODUCTION

If a merger harms competition by leading the merged firms to compete less aggressively, holding constant the strategies adopted by nonmerging rivals, those harms are said to reflect adverse unilateral effects.[1] Adverse unilateral effects are usually modeled as higher prices, but they may also involve harm to buyers on other dimensions of competition, such as reduced output, lower quality, or slowed new product introduction.

Unilateral effects have been important in merger analysis since the late 1980s, when newly developed empirical methodologies and newly-available computerized point-of-sale scanner data for recording individual retail transactions began to make it possible to identify and measure the loss of direct competition among sellers of differentiated products.[2] The analytical framework the enforcement agencies began to employ was codified in the 1992 Horizontal Merger Guidelines,[3] and remains widely used today.[4]

Our focus in this chapter is on a subset of the possible unilateral effects that may arise from horizontal merger. We emphasize competitive effects that arise when the merging firms sell differentiated products without binding capacity constraints, and interact by

---

* We would like to thank Gopal Das Varma, Luke Froeb, Serge Moresi, Aviv Nevo, and Greg Werden for their comments and suggestions.

[1] For a similar definition, see Gregory J. Werden and Luke M. Froeb, *Unilateral Competitive Effects of Horizontal Mergers*, in HANDBOOK OF ANTITRUST ECONOMICS 43 (Paolo Buccirossi ed., 2008); Gregory J. Werden, *Unilateral Competitive Effects of Horizontal Mergers I: Basic Concepts and Models*, in ABA Antitrust Section, ISSUES IN COMPETITION LAW AND POLICY 1319 (2008). By contrast, if a merger harms competition by making coordination possible, or by making preexisting coordination more effective, those harms to competition are said to arise from coordinated effects. Coordinated industry outcomes arise from a repeated interaction among oligopolists, in which firm strategies depend on history, as with oligopoly supergames that arise from infinitely repeated play or finitely repeated play with uncertain termination.

[2] The history of unilateral effects is described in Jonathan B. Baker, *Why Did the Antitrust Agencies Embrace Unilateral Effects?*, 12 GEO. MASON L. REV. 31 (2003). Werden's sketch of the theory emphasizes the development of game-theoretic models of oligopoly conduct. Werden, *Unilateral Competitive Effects of Horizontal Mergers, supra* note 1.

[3] US Dep't of Justice and FTC, Horizontal Merger Guidelines § 2.2 (1992), reprinted in 4 Trade Reg. Rep. (CCH) para. 13,104. This analytical framework was preserved in the 2010 Horizontal Merger Guidelines; US Dep't of Justice and FTC, Horizontal Merger Guidelines § 6 (2010), available at www.ftc.gov/os/2010/08/100819hmg.pdf.

[4] An internal FTC study concluded that more than half of the mergers analysed between 1993 and 2005 were reviewed under a unilateral effects theory. Malcolm B. Coate, *Unilateral Effects and the Guidelines: Models, Merits, and Merger Policy* (April 2009) available at http://ssrn.com/abstract=1263474.

setting prices in one-shot games with Bertrand–Nash oligopoly conduct.[5] We also discuss extensions of the analysis to other types of oligopoly interaction and dynamic settings, and we refer briefly to bidding models.[6]

II   BASIC INTUITIONS[7]

A merger creates adverse unilateral effects by relaxing a competitive constraint that one or both merging firms previously imposed on the other. In the most common setting for unilateral effects analysis, the loss of direct competition among sellers of differentiated products, that dynamic can be described in two complementary ways: the merger allows one or both firms to recapture previously lost profits from raising price, and the merger removes for one or both firms the competitive response of an important rival.

These conclusions are evident from examining the effect of merger in a simple model of a differentiated product industry, in which each firm sells only one product. In the pre-merger setting, firm 1 charges price P^1 and sells Q^1 units. Before the merger, firm 1 recognizes that if it raises its price by a small amount, ΔP^1, it will lose ΔQ^1 in sales (where ΔQ^1 is defined as a positive number). The gains from doing so equal $\Delta P^1(Q^1)$,[8] while the losses equal $(P^1 - C^1)\Delta Q^1$, where C^1 equals marginal cost and $P^1 - C^1$ represents the price–cost margin the firm would have earned on the lost sales. The firm raises price to the point where the gains from a further price increase just equal the losses, that is to where

$$\Delta P^1(Q^1) = (P^1 - C^1)\Delta Q^1$$

After dividing both sides by P^1 and rearranging terms, this equation can be rewritten as

$$\frac{P^1 - C^1}{P^1} = \frac{\Delta P^1 Q^1}{\Delta Q^1 P^1}$$

---

[5]   Unilateral effects also arise in other settings, including the following four. First, in bidding markets and auctions, the merging firms compete by bidding for the business of one or more customers, or participate in an auction to supply services to one or more customers. This includes the case of price discrimination markets, where the suppliers compete to serve one customer or a group of similarly situated customers. Second, in markets with relatively homogeneous goods, firms may compete by choosing quantities, either production levels or capacities. Third, in a market with a dominant firm and competitive fringe, a merger may reduce fringe competition (or, in the limit, create a monopolist). Fourth, unilateral effects may also arise when the merged firm changes its strategy in the first stage of a two-stage game, for example if firms choose capacity in the first period and set prices in the second.

[6]   For a broader survey, including a discussion of quantity setting models and an expanded treatment of auction models, see Werden and Froeb, *supra* note 1.

[7]   This section was adapted from Jonathan B. Baker, *Market Concentration in the Analysis of Horizontal Mergers*, in ANTITRUST LAW AND ECONOMICS (Keith Hylton ed., 2010).

[8]   The gains are technically $\Delta P^1(Q^1 - \Delta Q^1) = \Delta P^1(Q^1) - \Delta P^1 \Delta Q^1$, but the $\Delta P^1 \Delta Q^1$ term, the product of two small numbers, is second order in magnitude and can be ignored.

This latter equation can be written in the form $L^1 = 1/\eta^1$, where $L^1 = (P^1 - C^1)/P^1$ is the firm's Lerner Index of price–cost margin and $\eta^1 = (\Delta Q^1 P^1)/(\Delta P^1 Q^1)$ is (the absolute value of) the elasticity of the residual demand facing the firm.[9] This equation is the first order condition for profit maximization by firm 1.

When the first firm raises price in the pre-merger setting, it loses sales as some buyers switch to their second choice product (which could be no product at all, but instead a decision not to purchase from any seller). Some of those buyers may switch to the product sold by a particular second firm.

Now suppose the first firm and the second firm agree to merge. This changes the merged firm's profit-maximization calculus with respect to the first product (the product formerly sold by the first firm). After the merger the direct gains from raising the price of the first product continue to equal $\Delta P^1(Q^1)$. But the net losses from raising price are no longer equal to $(P^1 - C^1)\Delta Q^1$. The reason is that some of the ΔQ^1 lost sales from the first product lead to increased purchases of the second product, allowing the merged firm to recapture some of the lost profits from raising the price of the first product in the form of increased profits on sales of the second product.[10] The increased profits on the second product can be represented as[11]

$$(P^2 - C^2)\Delta Q^2, \text{ with } 0 < \Delta Q^2 \leq \Delta Q^1$$

Now the merged firm's profits from raising the price of the first product to a small amount above the pre-merger price are unambiguously positive, as[12]

$$\Delta P^1(Q^1) + (P^2 - C^2)\Delta Q^2 > (P^1 - C^1)\Delta Q^1$$

Before the merger, the first firm declined to raise price further because the gains from doing so were not more than the losses. After the merger, the new firm recognizes that

---

[9]   A firm's residual demand function describes how its quantity sold responds to changes in its price, after taking into account the competitive responses of rivals. It differs from the more familiar structural demand function, which describes how a firm's quantity sold responds to changes in its price holding constant the prices charged by rivals. For further discussion, see generally Jonathan B. Baker and Timothy F. Bresnahan, *Estimating the Residual Demand Curve Facing a Single Firm*, 6 INT'L J. INDUS. ORG. 283 (1988).

[10]   Note that firm 2's product does not have to be the best substitute for firm 1's product – perhaps more of the lost sales go to some third firm's product. What matters is that a significant group of firm 1's customers would respond to a higher price for firm 1's product by switching to firm 2's product. For those customers, firm 2's product is their second choice at pre-merger prices. Accordingly, a merger between sellers of differentiated products may harm competition even when most of the customers switching away from firm 1's product select the products of non-merging firms or do without the product entirely, and even when some third product is the second choice for more of firm 1's customers than is the product sold by firm 2.

[11]   That is, the increased profits equal the price–cost margin on the second product, which could be different from the price–cost margin on the first product, times the increase in second product sales (which will be a portion of the lost sales on the first product).

[12]   In this representation, sources of incremental profits from a small price rise are placed on the left hand side of the equation, while sources of incremental losses are placed on the right.

it can recapture some of those losses, so now finds it profitable to raise the price of the first product.[13]

This is not the end of the story for the merged firm, as it may also have an incentive to increase the price of the second product. The higher price for the second product may lead some of the ΔQ^1 customers who switched from the first product to the second to instead stick with the first product (increasing the profits from raising the price of the first product) or switch to a third alternative (reducing the profits from raising the price of the first product). The merged firm will choose a profit-maximizing price for both products simultaneously, taking a range of direct effects and feedbacks like these into account.[14] It will also consider price and 'repositioning' responses by third firms.[15] But one central idea underlying unilateral effects is captured in the example: a merger allows the firm to recapture some of the profits that would previously have been lost as a result of competition with its merger partner, removing a constraint on pricing and leading to higher prices.

A complementary way to understand unilateral competitive effects is to recognize that before the merger, competition from all firm 1's rivals, including competition from firm 2, contributed to determining η^1, the elasticity of the residual demand function facing firm 1. The more aggressive was firm 2's competitive response to firm 1 pre-merger – the less willing firm 2 was to match firm 1's price increase or the more that firm 2 would expand output when firm 1's output contracted – the greater firm 1's loss of sales to firm 2 would have been if firm 1 raised price pre-merger, so the more elastic was firm 1's pre-merger residual demand. By merging with firm 2, firm 1 removed the competitive response of product 2 to a price increase on product 1.[16] In consequence, the residual demand for product 1 will become less elastic, making it profitable for the merged firm to increase the first product's price.[17] This example captures an alternative

---

[13]   An alternative intuition arising from the same model arises from observing that after the merger, output expansion by the first firm leads it to cannibalize some of the sales that would otherwise have gone to its merger partner. From this perspective, the merger can be thought of as lowering the marginal revenue obtained from selling the first product or, equivalently, as raising that product's marginal cost (understood as incorporating an opportunity cost). Accordingly, the acquisition gives the merged firm an incentive to reduce output of the first product. The marginal cost perspective is emphasized in Joseph Farrell and Carl Shapiro, *Antitrust Evaluation of Horizontal Mergers: An Economic Alternative to Market Definition* (28 November 2008) available at http://faculty.haas.berkeley.edu/shapiro/alternative.pdf, as we discuss in the following section.

[14]   The mathematics of the profit-maximization calculus for the merged firm are treated in, for example, Werden and Froeb, *supra* note 1 at 45, including a discussion of various assumptions about the structure of buyer preferences and the interaction among sellers.

[15]   Firms may reposition products by altering their physical or non-physical attributes. As we discuss in more detail below, rival repositioning could counteract or deter the exercise of market power by the merged firm, so must be accounted for in a full analysis of the unilateral competitive effects of merger.

[16]   Following the merger, firm 1 likely has an incentive to raise the price of both products. The merged firm has an incentive to raise the price of the first product because it knows that the acquisition will allow it to recapture some of the lost profits through increased sales of the second product. It similarly has an incentive to raise the price of the second product, making the pricing response of the second product less aggressive than it would have been pre-merger.

[17]   This idea is implemented empirically in Jonathan B. Baker and Timothy F. Bresnahan,

way of understanding unilateral effects: the merger removes for one or both firms the competitive response of an important rival, removing a constraint on pricing and leading to higher prices.

Even when a merger among rivals threatens adverse unilateral effects, because it relaxes a competitive constraint that one or both merging firms previously imposed on the other, competition is not invariably harmed. Mergers among rivals also routinely benefit competition, by permitting the firms to reduce costs or to develop new or better products. If merger-related marginal cost reductions are sufficiently large, the net impact on the merged firm's pricing decisions may result in lower prices in the post-merger market equilibrium. Accordingly, merger analysis must also ask whether the anticompetitive pricing incentive outweighs the procompetitive synergy incentive for the merger.

III   SIMPLE MODELS USED TO IDENTIFY UNILATERAL EFFECTS

The Horizontal Merger Guidelines establish presumptions indicating when a horizontal merger entails a sufficient increase in concentration to raise competitive concerns.[18] These presumptions are related to changes in concentration given the merging firms' share of the market. Presumptions about which mergers are more likely to be of concern can improve the transparency, consistency, and efficiency of the merger review process. However, in the context of price-setting differentiated product markets, the Merger Guidelines presumptions are not directly linked to unilateral merger effects. Those presumptions are based on market shares, which may bear no relationship to the loss of direct competition between merging firms.[19]

In contrast, the models discussed in this section are built around the key drivers of unilateral effects in price-setting markets. We classify them as simple models because they do not attempt to incorporate all the interactions and strategic possibilities that can arise in a fully specified model of post-merger competition. The data requirements for these models are, in consequence, less demanding than for a fully specified model. That

---

The Gains from Merger or Collusion in Product Differentiated Industries, 33 J. INDUS. ECON. 427 (1985). This method offers a way of approximating the post-merger incentive to raise price based on the assumption that the merged firm reduces output of both products by the same percentage. However, it does not provide an exact solution to the merged firm's joint profit maximization problem. This approach does not require knowledge of the oligopoly solution concept or reliable estimates of the level of marginal cost. Information about oligopoly conduct is instead inferred empirically from the past reactions of the nonmerging firms.

[18]   Horizontal Merger Guidelines, *supra* note 3, § 5.3.

[19]   In differentiated product markets, a firm's market share reflects the fraction of potential customers who select its product as their first choice. But the constraint imposed by any particular rival depends instead on its customers' second choices – in particular, on the extent to which its merger partner's product is the second choice for those of its customers who would switch rather than stay loyal were the first firm to raise price. Thus, market shares are informative as to likely unilateral effects only to the extent that customer second choices are distributed similarly to customer first choices. Farrell and Shapiro, *supra* note 13, at 4 argue that the market definition exercise diverts attention from the analysis of the loss of competition between the merging firms.

simplicity makes these models candidates to be an alternative initial screen for whether a particular merger is likely to raise competitive concerns, or else as a basis for a safe harbor to deflect potential concerns.

In some cases these models may be precursors to a more thorough quantitative assessment of unilateral effects claims using the simulation methods discussed in the next section. But in other cases, where data on demand, transactions, or consumer preferences are limited or unavailable, these models may be the only quantitative evidence used in assessing the likelihood of an anticompetitive unilateral price increase. The different models in this section emphasize different elements of the drivers of unilateral price increases, which correspond to the different intuitive bases for unilateral effects discussed above.

A   Upward Pricing Pressure

The upward pricing pressure (UPP) measure of Farrell and Shapiro starts with the recaptured customer effect resulting from a horizontal merger.[20] Suppose firm 1 and firm 2 merge. When firm 1 raises the prices of its products, some customers who would have bought from firm 1 buy from firm 2. Of the customers who stop buying firm 1's product in response to a price increase by firm 1, the fraction that switch to buying firm 2's product is D^{12}, the diversion ratio from firm 1 to firm 2.[21] Let P^2 and C^2 be the price and marginal cost, respectively, of firm 2's product.[22] Then for each customer who leaves firm 1 in response to a price increase, the expected recaptured profit is $D^{12}(P^2 - C^2)$, which is the probability that the customer switches to firm 2 times the gross profit earned on firm 2 customers. A central insight of the UPP concept is that this expected recaptured profit has the same impact on firm 1's pricing post-merger as an increase in marginal cost: both will induce the firm to charge a higher price. In order for there to be no net incentive to raise prices post-merger, the marginal cost savings due to merger-induced synergies must be at least as large as the recaptured profit component. For the purposes of implementing a screen for upward pricing pressure, Farrell and Shapiro propose using a 'standard deduction' of some percentage, E, of pre-merger costs, rather than trying to measure actual synergies. Thus, a merger creates upward pricing pressure if $D^{12}(P^2 - C^2) > EC^1$. The UPP test captures the central role element of eliminating direct competition between the merged firms, while limiting the data requirements to

---

[20]   Farrell and Shapiro, *supra* note 13; see also Daniel O'Brien and Steven Salop, *Competitive Effects of Partial Ownership: Financial Interest and Corporate Control*, 67 ANTITRUST L.J. 559 (2000), which derives a similar measure of pricing pressure. This approach to measuring the value of diverted sales is described in the 2010 Merger Guidelines, *supra* note 3, § 6.1.

[21]   The diversion ratio can be written as a function of the own and cross-price elasticities of demand: if ε^{11} is the own price elasticity of demand for product 1 and ε^{21} is the cross-price elasticity of demand for product 2 with respect to the price of product 1, and if Q^1 and Q^2 are the outputs of products 1 and 2, respectively, then $D^{12} = -(\varepsilon^{21}Q^2)/(\varepsilon^{11}Q^1)$.

[22]   This discussion presents the simplest version of the UPP test; the authors discuss extensions of the test that incorporate multiproduct firms and that internalize the feedback from price increases on one product to other products. Farrell and Shapiro, *supra* note 13, at 13, 26.

an estimate of diversion ratios between the merging firms and prices and margins for those firms.[23]

B Critical Loss

Critical loss is fundamentally a tool for market definition. It starts with the hypothetical monopolist test for a proposed market definition, and asks what fraction of customers would the hypothetical monopolist have to lose in order to make a small but significant nontransitory increase in price (SSNIP) unprofitable.[24] That minimal level of lost sales is the critical loss.[25] Critical loss has also been used as a tool for unilateral effects analysis because of the similarity between a substantial unilateral post-merger price increase by a merged firm and a SSNIP for a hypothetical monopolist: if the merged firm would be able to raise prices substantially, that suggests that the products of the merged firm themselves constitute a relevant antitrust market.[26] Conversely, if the merged firm's products are not by themselves an antitrust market, then the merged firm will generally not be able to raise prices by more than a SSNIP post-merger, though it may still be able to raise prices enough to be of antitrust concern.[27] Critical loss (or critical elasticity) implements the intuition that a merger will reduce the elasticity of the residual demand function faced by the merged firm, which in turn induces the merged firm to raise prices somewhat (in the absence of cost reductions). The question is whether the elasticity of demand for the merged products is reduced enough to make a SSNIP profitable. For a given level of SSNIP, the critical loss depends only on the margins earned by the merged firms: the higher the margins, the lower the critical loss needed to make a SSNIP unprofitable.[28] It

---

[23] There can nevertheless be substantial issues in measuring both of those components, as discussed below.

[24] Critical loss was introduced in Barry Harris and Joseph Simons, *Focusing Market Definition: How Much Substitution is Necessary?*, 12 Res L. and Econ. 207 (1989). The hypothetical monopolist test is described in the Merger Guidelines, *supra* note 3, § 4.1.1.

[25] A variant of critical loss, critical elasticity, is defined similarly: what is the minimal market elasticity for the proposed market that would make a SSNIP unprofitable for the hypothetical monopolist.

[26] The similarity between market definition and unilateral effects analysis arises because the same economic force, buyer substitution, is central to each. They are not identical, however; in particular, they make different assumptions about whether nonmerging firms raise prices in response to a price increase by the merging firms.

[27] The connection between post-merger unilateral price increases and market definition played a prominent role in the court's decision in the Oracle–PeopleSoft merger (United States v. Oracle Corp., 331 F. Supp. 2d 1098 (N.D. Cal. 2004); see the roundtable discussion in *Unilateral Effects Analysis After Oracle*, Antitrust 8 (Spring 2005); see also Werden, *supra* note 1, at 1333.

[28] A criticism of critical loss analysis, as commonly applied, is that it does not require consistency between estimates of margins and estimates of demand elasticities. The critics point out that margins also inform the actual losses a firm would sustain from a SSNIP, with higher pre-merger margins indicating low demand elasticity and relatively little substitution away from the merged firm following a price increase. See Daniel O'Brien and Abraham Wickelgren, *A Critical Analysis of Critical Loss Analysis*, 71 Antitrust L. J. 161 (2003); Michael Katz and Carl Shapiro, *Critical Loss: Let's Tell the Whole Story*, Antitrust 49 (Spring 2003).

is thus among the simplest quantitative tests to implement for unilateral effects analysis, and has been used both to argue that a merger is unlikely to lead to unilateral effects because the firms compete in a broader market, in cases such as *SunGard*[29] and *Whole Foods*,[30] and to argue that a merger would be anticompetitive, as in *XM-Sirius*.[31]

C   Compensating Cost Reduction

In contrast to the proposed standard deduction for synergies used in UPP, Gregory J. Werden derives the precise marginal cost reductions necessary for a merger to have no impact on prices.[32] Werden observes that the compensating cost reduction can be determined without knowledge of the demand function beyond the elasticity at the pre-merger equilibrium, simply by solving the post-merger first order conditions for the level of costs at which the optimal prices remain at the pre-merger level.[33] As such, this test implements the intuition that unilateral effects reflect an imbalance between the anticompetitive incentive to exploit a reduction in competitive constraints with the pro-competitive benefits of synergies. Comparing actual (anticipated) cost reductions with the benchmark produced by the test shows whether the balance tilts toward a unilateral price increase or price reductions post-merger. As with UPP, an advantage of this test is that the conclusion does not depend on assumptions about the shape of the demand curve.[34]

D   PCAIDS and ALM

The PCAIDS (proportionality-calibrated almost ideal demand system) model of Epstein and Rubinfeld is designed to compute merger price effects using a simplified model with relatively light data requirements.[35] The earlier antitrust logit model (ALM) of Werden and Froeb similarly implements a merger simulation with minimal data requirements.[36] The key element of both models is that they infer buyer substitution patterns among brands in the market from market shares. Thus, the models could provide a basis for interpreting the market share based screens of the Merger Guidelines.

---

[29]   United States v. SunGard Data Systems, Inc., 172 F. Supp. 2d 172 (2001).

[30]   FTC v. Whole Foods Markets. Inc., 548 F.3d 1028 (D.C. Cir. 2008). For an analysis of the use of critical loss in that case, see Kevin Murphy and Robert Topel, *Critical Loss Analysis in the Whole Foods Case,* GLOBAL COMPETITION POLICY (17 March 2008).

[31]   See *Expert Declaration of J. Gregory Sidak Concerning the Competitive Consequences of the Proposed Merger of Sirius Satellite Radio, Inc. and XM Satellite Radio, Inc.* (16 March 2007) at 10, available at http://fjallfoss.fcc.gov/prod/ecfs/retrieve.cgi?native_or_pdf=pdf&id_document=6519008261.

[32]   Gregory J. Werden, *A Robust Test for Consumer Welfare Enhancing Mergers Among Sellers of Differentiated Products,* 44 J. INDUS. ECON. 409 (1996).

[33]   The resulting cost reduction is shown in the next section, *infra* at note 56.

[34]   An additional similarity is that both tests can predict an ambiguous overall merger effect, with price predicted to increase for one or more merging products and decrease for others.

[35]   Roy J. Epstein and Daniel L. Rubinfeld, *Merger Simulation: A Simplified Approach with New Applications,* 69 ANTITRUST L.J. 833 (2002).

[36]   Gregory J. Werden and Luke M. Froeb, *The Effects of Mergers in Differentiated Products Industries: Logit Demand and Merger Policy,* 10 J.L. ECON. AND ORG. 407 (1994).

The relationship between shares and substitution patterns is most clearly seen with the logit model of demand. In that model, customers rank alternatives based on a index for each product, which in a simple version is $v^i = \alpha^i + \beta P^i + \varepsilon^i$, where ε^i is a random term with an extreme value distribution.[37] This functional form coupled with the particular error term distribution implies that the probability that a customer will choose brand i is $e^{v^i}/\Sigma_j e^{v^j}$. This in turn means that, if s^i is the market share for firm i, the diversion ratio from product i to product j is $D^{ij} = s^j/(1 - s^i)$.[38] In other words, the diversion to another product is proportional to the share of that product,[39] as would be the case if buyer second choices are distributed similarly to buyer first choices.[40] Thus, the models can be calibrated using market shares and an overall measure of market elasticity and/or the propensity to choose the 'outside good'.[41] Unlike the other simple models discussed above, these models provide a measure of the unilateral price impact, rather than just whether there is likely to be a price increase resulting from the merger. But PCAIDS and ALM can be regarded as preliminary screens because they measure the extent of a unilateral price effect under the proportional diversion assumption, before asking whether the merged products are relatively close or distant substitutes, which would increase or decrease the predicted unilateral effect.

E   Discussion

The advantage of using these simple models to analyse unilateral effects is that they can provide a preliminary read on the likely impact of the merger quickly and with relatively light data requirements.[42] In part this is because the models rely upon parameters describing selected aspects of the market, whether diversion between the merging parties, aggregate elasticity, margins, synergies, or market shares, without requiring a full simulation model that incorporates all of these elements and more.

---

[37]   See Werden and Froeb, *supra* note 1, at 53 and Margaret E. Slade, *Merger Simulations of Unilateral Effects: What Can We Learn from the UK Brewing Industry?*, in CASES IN EUROPEAN ECONOMIC POLICY: THE ECONOMIC ANALYSIS 316 (Bruce Lyons ed., 2009) for more details on the logit model, including the derivation of own and cross-price elasticities implied by the model.

[38]   The PCAIDS model, similarly assumes that diversion is proportional to market revenue shares within an AIDS (almost ideal demand system) model.

[39]   More complex substitution patterns are possible when using a nested logit, which allows products that are presumed to be close substitutes to be grouped together in nests. The resulting substitution patterns between products depends on the choice of which products are in which nests as well as parameters governing choice between nests. Additional flexibility can be obtained using the distance-metric demand model. See Slade, *supra* note 37, at 317.

[40]   For example, if (hypothetically) 30% of soft drink buyers select Coke as their first choice at current prices and 10% pick 7Up, then this functional form presumes that $(30\% / (100\% - 10\%))$ = 33% of those buyers who select 7Up as their first choice would pick Coke as their second choice.

[41]   Slade shows that estimated elasticities are sensitive to the choice of the outside good, so that this choice plays a role similar to market definition when the analysis of competitive effects is based on market concentration. Slade, *supra* note 37, at 316, 339.

[42]   While to varying extents these models are envisioned as preliminary screens, they may frequently end up being the primary quantitative model used, either because data for a more detailed study are not available, or because the simplicity of these models makes them an appealing vehicle for presenting evidence about the likelihood of unilateral effects.

   That selectivity comes with at least two potential costs. One is that conclusions based on only some aspects of the market will at times differ from those drawn from analysis of the overall impact of the merger based on all available data.[43] The other is the possibility that having multiple preliminary models using different categories of information will resemble the proverbial blind men and the elephant, reaching different conclusions based on the components of the market being used in the analysis. In markets for products with high margins, the UPP model will tend to conclude that mergers will be anticompetitive, since the profit gained from recaptured sales is large and the standard deduction for efficiencies will have a relatively small impact on prices. In contrast, critical loss analysis would typically show that the critical loss for the merged firm is relatively low in such markets, suggesting that the market is broader and the merger is less likely to present a competitive issue. In addition, these models to varying degrees simplify aspects of competition that would be incorporated in a more complete simulation of competition in the market. Examples include allowing multiproduct firms to have different post-merger price increases for different products, and incorporating the competitive response of nonmerging firms. This suggests exploring how likely the models are to reach different conclusions, both from each other and from a fully-specified merger model. Particularly if these models are to be used as preliminary screens for potentially problematic mergers, it is important to gauge how reliable they are both as a predictor for the results of a more thorough study and for predicting actual anticompetitive effects.

IV   MERGER SIMULATION

Merger simulations combine a model of industry conduct with information or assumptions about the parameters to predict the effect of the merger on industry outcomes, usually prices. Simulation modeling usually begins by estimating demand functions for the differentiated products at issue, and incorporates parameters from those estimates into a model that also accounts for costs and oligopoly behavior. Then the structure of the model is modified to account for the merger by allowing the merged firm to optimally select all the decision variables previously chosen independently by the merger partners, and the model solved for the post-merger equilibrium conditions (using the parameters estimated on pre-merger data).[44]

   This approach is made clear in a benchmark calculation (essentially a simple simulation model) presented by Carl Shapiro.[45] For this calculation, Shapiro assumes (1) each

---

   [43]   After comparing predicted merger effects from a series of increasingly detailed models, Slade concludes that 'the predictions about markups and merger effects that can be obtained from simple models are often misleading'. Slade, *supra* note 37, at 338.
   [44]   This is not the only way that merger effects may be simulated, but it is the most common. For an example of a different approach to merger simulation, using a reduced form model that relates price to market structure, see Orley Ashenfelter, David Ashmore, Jonathan B. Baker, Suzanne Gleason, and Daniel S. Hosken, *Empirical Methods in Merger Analysis: Econometric Analysis of Pricing in* FTC v. Staples, 13 INT'L J. ECON. BUS. 265 (2006).
   [45]   Carl Shapiro, *Mergers with Differentiated Products*, 10 ANTITRUST 23, 26–7 (Spring 1996). Derivations are set forth in Carl Shapiro, *Unilateral Effects Calculations* (September 2007), available at http://faculty.haas.berkeley.edu/shapiro/unilateral.pdf.

merging firm has one product, (2) demand functions are linear, (3) the merging products are symmetric in demand prior to the merger, in the sense that the two diversion ratios (from each to the other) are identical (and denoted α), (4) marginal costs are constant, (5) the merging products have the identical price–cost margins $L = (P - C)/P$ prior to the merger, and (6) the interaction between firms is characterized by Bertrand–Nash behavior. Under the above assumptions, Shapiro finds that

$$\Delta P/P = \alpha L/[2(1 - \alpha)]$$

where $\Delta P/P$ represents the percentage price increase from merger for each product. If assumption (2) is altered so that demand functions are constant elasticity, then[46]

$$\Delta P/P = \alpha L/(1 - \alpha - L)$$

Shapiro's benchmark formulae can be used to illustrate some of the benefits of simulation modeling. First, simulation modeling can synthesize a great deal of empirical information (here information about diversion ratios and margins) in a logically consistent way. Second, and relatedly, simulation modeling provides a metric for understanding the strength of the incentive to raise price implied by key parameters, particularly those associated with demand (elasticities or diversion ratios).[47] In the Shapiro example, if $\Delta P/P$ is an economically significant amount, that result would suggest a concern about adverse unilateral effects of merger.[48] Third, simulation modeling can help identify the critical uncertainties in model specification or parameter estimates on which the strength of that incentive depends.[49] In the example, if $\Delta P/P$ is economically significant when demand is taken to follow a constant-elasticity form, but not economically significant if demand is assumed linear, that difference would suggest the importance of gathering information about the functional form for demand.[50]

---

[46] The formula assumes that $(1 - \alpha - L) > 0$; otherwise, under the assumptions of the model and with constant elasticity of demand, the merged firm would raise price without limit.

[47] Because the simulation procedure necessarily combines estimates and assumptions about which there may be significant uncertainty, the output of the procedure – a set of projected price changes – is better viewed as an indicator of the strength of incentives to raise price post-merger, rather than as a forecast.

[48] There is no consensus among antitrust economists about how large the price increase must be, or how long it must last, to be considered economically significant. In practice, a 3% price increase is often treated as economically significant, but, legally, any price increase from merger could be actionable. This issue is related to the choice of the standard deduction for efficiencies in Farrell and Shapiro's UPP framework.

[49] One aspect of identifying critical uncertainties involves testing for consistency in simulation models with overidentified model restrictions. For example, margins implied by demand elasticities and pre-merger profit maximizing conditions can be compared to actual margins derived from accounting data; see Steven Tenn, Luke Froeb, and Steven Tschantz, *Mergers When Firms Compete by Choosing Both Price and Promotion* (2009) at 2, available at http://papers.ssrn.com/sol3/papers.cfm?abstract_id=980941.

[50] The price increase in Shapiro's model is greater when demand elasticities are assumed constant because linear demand functions grow more elastic as price increases. This difference can be substantial; for example, with 40% margins and a 20% diversion ratio between the merging firms,

Simulation modeling has other potential benefits, not illustrated by the Shapiro formulae. It can in principle be used to quantify the degree of uncertainty in the price increase forecasts resulting from sampling error in the statistical estimation of model parameters (and the equivalent uncertainty when parameters are determined based on qualitative information).[51] It can also offer a way to net the unilateral incentive to raise price resulting from merger against the incentive to lower price that arises from merger-related synergies.

The mechanics of simulation will be described using a more general setup than Shapiro employed.[52] The first step is to specify a model and work out the pre-merger and post-merger equilibria. The model in this example assumes, as Shapiro did, that each merging firm has one product and that the interaction between firms is characterized by Bertrand-Nash behavior. But each product i's demand has a more general functional form $Q^i(P^i, P^j)$, where P^j is a vector of prices for the $n - 1$ products sold by rivals.[53] This general functional form allows for demand elasticities to differ across products, and permits asymmetric demand cross-elasticities (or diversion ratios). Marginal cost $C^i(Q^i(P^i, P^j))$ is also more general than in Shapiro's simple framework: it now varies with firm output and may differ across products. With Bertrand–Nash conduct, the pre-merger equilibrium is characterized by n first order conditions $L^i = -1/\varepsilon^{ii}$, where $L^1 = (P^1 - C^1)/P^1$ is the Lerner index for product i and ε^{ii} is the own elasticity of demand for product i.

If brands i and j merge, the post-merger first order condition for product i becomes

$$L^i = -1/\varepsilon^{ii} - L^j(\varepsilon^{ji}/\varepsilon^{ii})(Q^jP^j/Q^iP^i)$$

where ε^{ji} is the cross-elasticity of demand of product j with respect to the price of product i.[54] The post-merger first order condition for product j is analogous and the first order conditions for the other $n - 2$ products do not change.

To simulate a merger in this framework, it is necessary to estimate the parameters of the demand system (to recover own and cross-elasticities of demand, as functions of price) and to estimate the parameters of the cost functions for each merging firm (to infer the marginal cost functions).[55] Some of the parameters of these functions are chosen

---

the predicted price increase in the linear model is 5%, while under the constant elasticity model the predicted price increase is 20%.

[51]   For an example of a procedure for specifying confidence intervals for predicted price changes, see Oral Capps, Jeffrey Church, and H. Alan Love, *Specification Issues and Confidence Intervals in Unilateral Price Effects Analysis*, 113 J. ECONOMETRICS 3 (2003); see additional references in Oliver Budzinski and Isabel Ruhmer, *Merger Simulation in Competition Policy: A Survey*, 6 J. COMP. L. AND ECON. 305 (2009).

[52]   This model is taken from Werden and Froeb, *supra* note 1, at 51.

[53]   With no loss of generality, and with empirical estimation in mind, the demand function can also incorporate a vector of exogenous variables affecting demand.

[54]   Werden and Froeb specify the first order conditions in an equivalent form that uses diversion ratios rather than cross-elasticities. Werden and Froeb, *supra* note 1, at 51.

[55]   In this model, if marginal cost is assumed to be constant, its level can be inferred by solving the first order conditions for firm profit-maximization, allowing the merger to be simulated without data on marginal cost. For a discussion of estimating cost functions in the context of merger simulation, see Slade, *supra* note 37, at 320.

by calibrating to match pre-merger prices, outputs, and costs. Once the parameters are determined by estimation or calibration, they are used to specify the system of *n* pre-merger first order conditions (which may be nonlinear). These first order conditions are solved simultaneously to make inferences about other terms in the model; this is a form of calibration. The next step is to specify the first order conditions that pertain to the post-merger market after accounting for joint ownership of the merged firm. Then the system of *n* post-merger first order conditions is solved for the post-merger price and output vectors.[56] If the cost functions are expected to change as a result of merger-related efficiencies, those new functions can be employed in deriving the post-merger equilibrium.[57]

Full-fledged simulation modeling incorporates substantial technical complexity in specifying and solving the model and estimating its parameters. It is as yet unclear whether the payoff in more accurate enforcement determinations is worth the effort.[58] Absent such modeling, unilateral effects can be (and are) demonstrated with less technically demanding evidence that shows that the merging firms' products are close substitutes in demand.[59]

In addition to the benefits of simulation methods just discussed (synthesizing information, providing a metric for the degree of anticompetitive concern, and identifying critical parameters) merger simulations appear to have three primary advantages relative to informal methods of proving unilateral effects. First, they may be able to identify unilateral effects when the merging firms' products are substitutes but not the closest substitutes, so the magnitude of the post-merger incentive to raise price is not initially obvious. This advantage is potentially important in markets where sellers are densely distributed (either product markets with brand proliferation, such as breakfast cereals, or geographic markets, such as gas stations or hospitals). The advantage of simulation methods here comes from incorporating the full set of own and cross-price elasticities in a demand system. But a large demand system may be difficult to estimate with precision, and agencies and courts may be reluctant to base merger enforcement decisions on the implications of econometric estimates of the parameters of a large demand system unless those conclusions are confirmed by other, more qualitative evidence that the merging firms' products are substitutes in demand.

Second, simulation methods promise to account for supply-side limitations on unilateral price increases, and in particular rival reactions. However, existing methods

---

[56] The simultaneous solution of a system of nonlinear equations can raise computational issues not treated here.

[57] Alternatively, Werden shows that the post-merger first order conditions can be solved to find the cost reduction necessary to preserve pre-merger prices. In the case of symmetric merging products, the necessary post-merger marginal cost is $\hat{C} = C/1 - L(1 + 1/\varepsilon^{ii} + \varepsilon^{ji})$. Werden, *supra* note 32.

[58] For a discussion of the application and impact of merger simulations in six cases reviewed or challenged by competition authorities in the United States and Europe, see Budzinski and Ruhmer, *supra* note 51, at 20.

[59] The types of evidence used to demonstrate demand substitution may include buyer surveys, demand elasticity studies, information about buyer switching costs, inference from company documents and monitoring of competitors, and views of third party experts on the market. See Jonathan B. Baker, *Market Definition: An Analytical Overview*, 74 ANTITRUST L.J. 129, 139–41 (2007) (discussing types of evidence in the context of market definition).

commonly treat rival reactions as a matter of assumption (as by imposing Bertrand–Nash behavior) rather than viewing oligopoly conduct as something to estimate.[60] One might expect that the choice of solution concept would make a difference to the inferred equilibrium prices, because it alters the first order conditions defining the pre- and post-merger equilibria.[61]

Consistent with this expectation, Peters' merger retrospective involving the airline industry found that the predicted price changes from merger implied by several common simulation methods could be improved by incorporating more information about rival reactions.[62] On the other hand, the airline industry may be relatively undifferentiated, so supply-side factors may matter particularly in simulating unilateral effects in such markets. In any case, Peters found that all the simulation methods he studied properly identified the substantial price increases arising from loss of competition in the five markets studied.[63] Accordingly, Peters' study is not inconsistent with Baker and Bresnahan's judgment that in product differentiated industries, 'an enquiry that looks only at demand substitution to address market definition and identify market power, ignoring supply-side factors like costs and strategic conduct, is in general likely to be largely right'.[64]

Baker and Bresnahan also note that '[c]areful attention to the supply-side along with demand becomes important only when the question shifts from whether the firm

---

[60]   See Budzinski and Ruhmer, *supra* note 51, at 4 ('there is a widespread consensus that Bertrand competition is the first choice for heterogeneous oligopolies') and Slade, *supra* note 37, at 321 ('Bertrand competition is an obvious focal point for the estimation of unilateral effects in markets where products are differentiated'). Simulation methods relying on residual demand estimates are an exception because rival reactions are incorporated into residual demand functions. See Jonathan B. Baker and Timothy F. Bresnahan, *The Gains from Merger or Collusion in Product Differentiated Industries*, 33 J. INDUS. ECON. 427 (1985).

[61]   The pre-merger first order condition for each differentiated product seller of a single product can be written independent of solution concept as $L = -1/\eta$, where η is the elasticity of the firm's residual demand. (This is because a differentiated product seller can be thought of as a monopolist of its residual demand.) The residual demand elasticity equals the own elasticity of demand if the solution concept is Bertrand–Nash (as in the Werden and Froeb example in the text) but under other solution concepts it will also include terms reflecting cross-elasticities of demand and best response functions.

[62]   Craig Peters, *Evaluating the Performance of Merger Simulation: Evidence from the U.S. Airline Industry*, 49 J.L. AND ECON. 627 (2006). *Cf.* David Genesove and Wallace P. Mullin, *Testing Static Oligopoly Models: Conduct and Cost in the Sugar Industry, 1890–1914*, 29 RAND J. ECON. 355 (1998) (finding that empirical models using changes in demand elasticities and cost components in order to infer oligopoly market power and unobserved components of marginal cost provide the best fit to data directly measuring cost when conduct is estimated as a free parameter). For a review of additional tests comparing structural models and merger effects, see Tenn, Froeb, and Tschantz, *supra* note 49, at 2, and Budzinski and Ruhmer, *supra* note 51, at 36.

[63]   Peters, *supra* note 62, at 641, 644 (tables 3 and 4).

[64]   Jonathan B. Baker and Timothy F. Bresnahan, *Economic Evidence in Antitrust: Defining Markets and Measuring Market Power*, in HANDBOOK OF ANTITRUST ECONOMICS 27 (Paolo Buccirossi ed., 2008). Consistent with this view, Baker and Shapiro propose creating presumptions of anticompetitive effect in unilateral effects cases by focusing only on demand-side factors. Jonathan B. Baker and Carl Shapiro, *Reinvigorating Horizontal Merger Enforcement*, in WHERE THE CHICAGO SCHOOL OVERSHOT THE MARK: EFFECT OF CONSERVATIVE ECONOMIC ANALYSIS ON U.S. ANTITRUST 264–6 (Robert Pitofsky ed., 2008).

or firms exercise market power – the issue in market definition or unilateral effects of merger among sellers of differentiated products – to whether changes in supply, as from the efficiencies that may result from firm conduct or the increased competition that could result from firm remedies, would counteract the exercise of market power in such markets'.[65] This observation suggests the third primary advantage of simulation methods over informal methods of proving unilateral competitive effects: the promise that they can be used to trade off merger-related efficiencies against the anticompetitive incentive to raise price. Whether this promise can be fulfilled in practice, however, depends on the ability to measure the two incentives – to raise price and lower price – with sufficient precision to make a comparison reliable.[66] It is unclear whether the available methods and data allow for such comparisons outside of cases in which one incentive is powerful and the other weak – the setting where sophisticated simulation methods provide the least advantage over simpler methods of unilateral effects analysis.[67]

V EXTENSIONS

While the models discussed thus far differ with respect to such things as symmetry assumptions and demand specifications, they make many of the same simplifying assumptions in abstracting from real-world settings to tractable models. One assumption is that the products available post-merger are unchanged, both in terms of product characteristics and the number of brands or brand extensions offered for sale. Another assumption underlying these models is that firms choose prices according to a static Nash equilibrium, rather than engaging in more complex dynamic equilibrium behavior or taking into account longer term drivers of strategic choices. A third assumption is that prices are picked by sellers rather than being determined through bidding in an auction setting. Fourth, firms' abilities to expand output post-merger are not constrained by increasing marginal costs or capacity limitations. And finally, the models typically do not explicitly consider the extent to which cost savings will be passed on to customers. Rather, pass-through rates are determined by adoption of a specific demand model. This section discusses relaxing each of these assumptions.

---

[65]   Baker and Bresnahan, *supra* note 64, at n.92.

[66]   In this regard, we note that current practice does not generally attempt to quantify the uncertainty around the point estimate of simulation forecasts. That is a difficult task because it combines sampling uncertainty in the econometric measurement of demand with model specification uncertainty. The latter uncertainty can be addressed with sensitivity analyses but is hard to summarize succinctly. Models that attempt to estimate the confidence intervals around merger simulation predictions were discussed earlier at *supra* note 51.

[67]   We note two additional benefits of simulation modeling that may pertain in some applications. Simulation models can be adapted to account for atypical elements of a market setting such as partial cross-ownership, regulations, or capacity constraints that may be difficult to incorporate in an informal analysis. In addition, they can be useful in evaluating the extent to which alternative divestiture proposals mitigate concerns about a post-merger price increase.

A   Product Repositioning

Just as both merging and nonmerging firms in a price-setting, differentiated product market will generally have an incentive to revise their prices in the post-merger market, they will also generally have an incentive to change their product positioning.[68] Prior to the merger, the merging firms positioned their brands to compete against all other firms in the market, including each other. Post-merger, the two merging firms 'have each other's back' and no longer need to consider competing against each other. As a result, there is an incentive to reposition their products to compete more directly against other firms. This in turn will induce nonmerging firms to adjust their product positions until equilibrium conditions for both price and position are satisfied. In addition, as the head-to-head competition between merging firms is eliminated, there may be an incentive for nonmerging firms to fill that competitive vacuum by repositioning existing products or introducing new product varieties that replace some of the pre-merger competitive interactions.

The incentive facing nonmerging firms is discussed in the Merger Guidelines.[69] The description suggests that consideration of post-merger repositioning will make unilateral effects less of a concern than would be the case in a less flexible model with fixed product characteristics. This is not the only possibility: repositioning by the merged firm can also potentially lead to higher average prices across the market as a whole. The merged firm may reconfigure its products so that they serve a broader cross-section of the market rather than competing head-to-head for the same customers.[70] Thus, an extended unilateral effects model that incorporates product repositioning could lead to either higher or lower average price increases than a model in which all product offerings are fixed.

Introducing product repositioning into unilateral effects models raises several issues. One is simply the additional complexity of the model, particularly if product characteristics are treated as a multidimensional space that allows a full range of differentiation between products.[71] In addition, adding product location as a choice variable can make

---

[68]   This assumes that repositioning a product is not sufficiently costly that the incentives to change product position are outweighed by the adjustment cost. The same assumption is routinely made with respect to prices: in some cases there may be adjustment costs to reconfiguring prices, at least in the short term, which may mitigate the ability of firms to take advantage of the post-merger incentive to raise prices. Adjustment costs with respect to prices are rarely discussed in the context of unilateral effects analysis; adjustment costs with respect to product positioning are presumably more common, and may often be sunk, so there is a correspondingly greater need to incorporate them into unilateral effects models of product repositioning.

[69]   'A merger is unlikely to generate substantial unilateral price increases if non-merging parties offer very close substitutes for the products offered by the merging firms. In some cases, non-merging firms may be able to reposition their products to offer close substitutes for the products offered by the merging firms.' Horizontal Merger Guidelines, *supra* note 3, § 6.1. According to the Guidelines, repositioning is 'evaluated much like' entry. *Id.* § 6.1.

[70]   After the Princess–Carnival cruise line merger, the merging firm repositioned its brands to target niche customers (premium customers in the case of the Cunard Line and British customers in the case of P&O Cruises) that the merging firms had not served as effectively prior to the merger. Amit Gandhi, Luke M. Froeb, Steven Tschantz, and Gregory J. Werden, *Post-Merger Product Repositioning*, 56 J. IND. ECON. 49 (2008).

[71]   As an example of how limited dimensionality limits differentiation possibilities, suppose that location is modeled using a single dimension (products are ordered along a line). If products A and

the best response functions discontinuous, and thus substantially harder to solve for an equilibrium. A third issue is the prevalence of multiple equilibria in games where firms choose both locations and prices, since often various configurations of the different firms can be Nash equilibria given the locations chosen by other firms.[72]

One alternative approach to finding a tractable model may be to replace the assumption that firms choose their brand positions simultaneously with one in which the merged firm is a Stackelberg leader in choosing locations. The merged firm is naturally positioned as a leader since nonmerging firms have no incentive to change their location until the merged firm changes its location or prices. Anticipating how the merged firm might reposition is complicated if there are multiple equilibria that could emerge post-merger. That suggests that other firms may let the merged firm adjust brand locations first, and then react optimally. Such a structure could simplify finding the equilibrium, as the merged firm would solve for its optimal location given the best responses of nonmerging firms, though the solution may still be challenging to the extent that response functions are discontinuous. In addition, while costless repositioning is a natural modeling assumption to make when exploring how repositioning can affect unilateral effects outcomes, repositioning may not be costless in many markets, so repositioning models that neglect adjustment costs likely overstate repositioning incentives.[73] In some markets, costly repositioning may resolve the problem of multiple equilibria: if the cost of repositioning is increasing in the amount of change in product characteristics, reducing the cost of repositioning could play the role of a selection criterion in determining what equilibrium will result post-merger.

In addition to changing the attributes of brands, firms can change their competitive posture by introducing addition brands or line extensions into the market.[74] Post-merger price increases or repositioning by other firms can make more profitable a new product introduction that was unprofitable pre-merger given the cost of start-up. While the merged firm may have new profitable opportunities to introduce products post-merger, the more compelling possibility is that an existing nonmerging firm will introduce a new product to replace some of the competitive interactions that are lost if two of the merging firm brands are close substitutes. Not only could a product introduction introduce

---

B are equally differentiated from C, then either A and B are identical products, or they are twice as far apart as each is from C. With multiple dimensions, all intermediate degrees of differentiation between A and B are also possible. Demand models based on product characteristics, which are discussed in the next section, provide a promising avenue for incorporating strategic decisions over a more complex and realistic description of product locations.

[72]   Gandhi, Froeb, Tschantz, and Werden, *supra* note 70, explore the range of outcomes that come into play when costless product repositioning is allowed by limiting the product space to a single dimension (brands are arrayed along a line). They use a selection criterion to deal with multiple equilibria that picks out the equilibrium with the most separation between brands.

[73]   If those costs are sunk or repositioning takes time, moreover, additional strategic considerations reducing the likelihood of repositioning may come into play.

[74]   Such post-merger changes differ from the analysis of entry of non-committed market participants because they involve firms already competing in the market pre-merger, who expand their product offerings post-merger. Incumbent firms may have advantages over *de novo* entrants through shared costs and the incentive to internalize customer substitution between existing brands and brand extensions. This suggests that, at least in contexts where additional product varieties can be introduced relatively cheaply, there is value for incorporating brand extensions in unilateral effects models directly rather than treating it as entry.

additional competition into the post-merger market, but in some cases anticipation of such an introduction (particularly if offering a brand extension can be done relatively cheaply and quickly) could constrain a post-merger price increase by the merged firm as it attempts to limit competitive opportunities for rivals.[75]

B   Dynamic Models

The various unilateral effects models discussed thus far share one common element: they are all based on the Nash equilibrium of a static game, in which firms choose their optimal strategies as if there is a one-time interaction between the firms post-merger. In reality, of course, firms compete in ongoing interactions that make possible a much richer menu of strategic options than are possible in a one-shot game. These richer strategies fall into at least two categories. First, repeated interaction expands the range of price-quantity outcomes that emerge as equilibria of the market when firms engage in history- or state-dependent strategies. Rather than the single Nash equilibrium which generally characterizes the static equilibrium used in unilateral effects models, the set of sustainable equilibrium profits in the dynamic game (as characterized by the folk theorem) ranges from the static equilibrium outcome of the one-shot game to something close to full collusive profits.[76] In addition, firms may engage in a variety of complex intertemporal pricing strategies such as intertemporal price discrimination, durable goods pricing that takes into account competition against the installed base, or penetration pricing where current sales increase future demand through word-of-mouth advertising or network effects.[77]

If the modeling goal was solely to predict the equilibrium of a game in which firms can use dynamic pricing strategies rather than static strategies, then the multiplicity of possible equilibria in a dynamic model would often only expand the range of plausible outcomes. But in the context of unilateral effects analysis, particularly in a setting where there is abundant data available, a dynamic model can help to resolve evidence that may otherwise be incompatible.[78] Suppose, for example, that sufficient data is available to estimate individual firm demand functions, and that the cross-elasticity matrix is used to calibrate the pre-merger equilibrium, which results in marginal cost estimates for each product. However, these imputed marginal costs diverge substantially from the margins

---

[75]   Draganska, Mazzeo, and Seim offer one such model, in which the locations of possible brand offerings for each firm are fixed, but firms choose which of the menu of available products they will put on the market pre- and post- merger. Michaela Draganska, Michael Mazzeo, and Katja Seim, *Beyond Plain Vanilla: Modeling Joint Product Assortment and Pricing Decisions*, 7 QUANT. MARKETING AND ECON. 105 (2009).

[76]   See JEAN TIROLE, THE THEORY OF INDUSTRIAL ORGANIZATION 245 (1988).

[77]   For the analysis of the price effect of mergers in durable goods markets, see Ari Gerstle and Michael Waldman, *Mergers in Durable-Good Industries: A Re-Examination of Market Power and Welfare Effects* (2004), available at http://law.bepress.com/cgi/viewcontent. cgi?article=1038&context=alea; and David Reitman, *Mergers in Durable Goods Markets with Rational Customers* (Economic Analysis Group Discussion Paper No. EAG 01, 8 September 2001), available at http://ssrn.com/abstract=288342.

[78]   An inconsistency between demand and marginal cost estimates could also be due to mismeasurement of demand or costs, as discussed in the next section.

inferred using cost data. Rather than assuming that one or the other estimate is unreliable, an alternative explanation is that the pre-merger outcomes reflect an equilibrium in which firms are using dynamic pricing strategies. If calibrated margins are larger than actual margins, firms might be using penetration pricing, deliberately setting lower prices than what would maximize prices in the short run in order to expand the market in future periods.[79] If calibrated margins are smaller than actual margins, it may be because firms are able to sustain higher prices than in the static equilibrium by using dynamic pricing strategies. In both cases, a unilateral effects model that incorporates the dynamic strategies implied by the pre-merger data may more accurately predict the post-merger outcome than a model based on a static equilibrium that does not incorporate all the information in the pre-merger data.

Adapting the unilateral effects model to incorporate equilibria other than that of the one-shot game does not necessarily require a full dynamic model. If conjectural variations parameters are constants, the pre-merger equilibrium can be calibrated using them in the first order condition for profit maximization. For example, suppose firm i expects that when it raises its price by one dollar, in equilibrium other firms will raise their price by μ_i (that is, the firm conjectures, correctly, that $\partial P^j/\partial P^i = \mu_i, \forall j \neq i$.) Then, in the simple one product per firm case, the first order conditions in the pre-merger equilibrium are given by

$$Q^i + (P^i - C^i)\left[\frac{\partial Q^i}{\partial P^i} + \mu_i \sum_{j \neq i} \frac{\partial Q^i}{\partial P^j}\right] = 0, \ \forall i$$

Given estimated demand parameters and margins, the first order conditions can be solved for the conjectural variation parameters that characterize the pre-merger equilibrium.[80]

Once the conjectural variation parameters or other parameters of the pre-merger equilibrium are calibrated, the natural assumption is to assume that those same parameters carry over to the post-merger equilibrium. That assumption is subject to criticism: it may be that a different equilibrium of the post-merger merger dynamic game as reflected by the conjectural variation parameters will be selected, or that the incentives to engage in time dependent pricing strategies with respect to consumers will change

---

[79]   In the XM–Sirius merger, the parties argued that they deliberately set low prices to increase current demand, since word-of-mouth advertising means that additional customers now produce more customers in the future. Short-run profits would increase by raising prices now, but long-run profits would suffer. Not only would dynamic pricing reconcile the observed margins and elasticities, but it provides a procompetitive benefit of the merger: the merged firm would internalize the demand expanding effect of word-of-mouth advertising on the rival firm, resulting in a greater incentive to engage in penetration pricing post-merger. See Steven C. Salop, Steven R. Brenner, Lorenzo Coppi, and Serge X. Moresi, *Economic Analysis of the Competitive Effects of the Sirius-XM Merger*, paper filed at the Federal Communications Commission, In the Matter of XM Satellite Radio Holdings Inc., Transferor, and Sirius Satellite Radio Inc., Transferee, Consolidated Application for Authority to Transfer Control of XM Radio Inc. and Sirius Satellite Radio Inc., MB Docket No. 07-57 (24 July 2007).

[80]   This discussion assumes that demand and cost (hence margins) are observable but oligopoly conduct is not.

with fewer firms in the market.[81] However, the same assumption about unchanging pre- and post-merger parameters is implicit in static models, with the parameters stuck at the default value inherent in the static model. Incorporating such parameters explicitly at least provides an opportunity to consider how ad hoc assumptions about post-merger changes in those parameters would affect the unilateral effects results. It remains to be seen how closely a unilateral effects model using conjectural variations parameters to capture long-run steady state equilibria resembles the results of an explicitly dynamic model.

C   Auction Models

In some markets, price determination more closely resembles an auction than either the posted price mechanism in differentiated Bertrand models or the quantity choice and market clearing prices in Cournot models. In order to better capture predicted price effects in such markets, unilateral effects analysis can be undertaken using an auction model rather than the price and quantity setting models we have discussed thus far.[82] The underlying intuition for unilateral effects is analogous in an auction setting. When suppliers offer bids at which they are willing to sell their product, they take into account the expected bids of other suppliers. The optimal bid is chosen to beat the second best offer made to a customer. In the pre-merger market, that second best bid is sometimes offered by the merger partner. However, after the merger, when bidding for customers for whom the merger partner would have been the second best alternative, the optimal bid need only beat the third best alternative. Thus firms bid less aggressively post-merger, by an amount that depends on the frequency of sales opportunities in which the merging firms' products would have been the customer's first and second choices. Unilateral effects arise because the merger removes the competitive constraint imposed by the merger partner when the latter firm is the second best alternative for some customers.

Merger simulation using auctions follows much the same algorithm as with price-setting models.[83] A particular auction model is picked, with an eye toward capturing important facts of the market in question. The parameters of the model are chosen so that the equilibrium of the model is calibrated to prices and shares in the pre-merger market. Then the auction is simulated in the post-merger market, allowing for coordinated bidding of the merged firm's products. The resulting prices are then compared to the pre-merger prices to compute the predicted unilateral effects from the merger. Such a model was used by the plaintiff's expert in the *Oracle*[84] case to simulate the

---

[81]   Note that the first of these criticisms blurs the line between unilateral and coordinated merger effects, and may be handled better through an explicit coordinated effects model.

[82]   See Werden and Froeb, *supra* note 1, at 57, and generally Paul Klemperer, *Competition Policy in Auctions and Bidding Markets*, in HANDBOOK OF ANTITRUST ECONOMICS 583 (Paolo Buccirossi ed., 2008). Another auction model, emphasizing the possibility that firms selling indivisible goods, and unable to expand output because of capacity constraints, may be able to induce price increases by making 'all-or-nothing' offers, is sketched in Jonathan B. Baker, *Unilateral Competitive Effects Theories in Merger Analysis*, 11 ANTITRUST 21 (Spring 1997).

[83]   See, e.g., Keith Waehrer and Martin K. Perry, *The Effects of Mergers in Open-Auction Markets*, 34 RAND J. ECON. 287 (2003).

[84]   United States v. Oracle Corp., 331 F. Supp. 2d 1098 (N.D. Cal. 2004).

increase in prices for enterprise software that would result from a merger of Oracle and PeopleSoft.[85]

The court did not directly evaluate the simulation but found the results to be unreliable because the market shares used to calibrate the model had already been determined to be unreliable. Nevertheless, that simulation highlights a way in which many auction models used to evaluate unilateral effects ignore relevant information that could be used to improve their predictions. The model does not directly capture whether two products are close or distant substitutes, but instead infers the frequency with which the products are the first and second choices for customers from market shares. When additional empirical information about demand is available, such as information (for example, from win-loss reports) on which products are most often first and second choices, it can be employed to calibrate patterns of head to head competition more accurately before predicting unilateral effects. An additional question is the extent to which differentiated product models like UPP can be adapted to an auction context to provide an initial screen for identifying which mergers are likely to lead to unilateral effects without requiring a full auction simulation.

D   Other Extensions

We briefly discuss two other possible extensions of unilateral effects models. One concerns whether pass-through can be modeled explicitly in a unilateral effects simulation. Pass-through describes the relationship between cost changes experienced by firms and price changes received by customers. It can be a contentious issue in merger cases, as in *Staples*.[86] Typically pass-through is determined by assumption, as a byproduct of the functional forms used in a merger simulation model (a linear demand model produces a pass-through rate of 50%, for example). But in some cases it may make sense to model pass-through directly, setting parameters by using the available evidence as to oligopoly conduct and the curvature of demand.[87] For example, in a merger of products sold in supermarkets, the pass-through rate would be determined not only by wholesale competition and the consumer demand function but also by the retail pricing equilibrium among supermarkets. Rather than developing a full two-stage model of competition (only one stage of which is directly affected by the merger) it may be sufficient to capture the effect of the retail stage using a pass-through parameter.

One final area for extending unilateral effects models is the impact of nonlinear cost functions or capacity constraints. Intuitively, if nonmerging firms are less willing to

---

[85]   Werden and Froeb, *supra* note 1, at 70 describe the *Oracle* case as 'the only U.S. merger case in which a merger simulation was introduced at trial'.

[86]   FTC v. Staples, Inc., 970 F. Supp. 1066 (D.D.C. 1997). For a discussion of econometric issues in that case, including the measurement of pass-through rates, see Jonathan B. Baker, *Econometric Analysis in FTC v. Staples,* 18 J. PUBLIC POLICY AND MARKETING 11 (1999). See also Luke Froeb, Steven Tschantz, and Gregory J. Werden, *Pass Through Rates and the Price Effects of Mergers,* 23 INT'L J. INDUS. ORG. 703 (2005) (claiming that the estimated merger effect in *Staples* was inconsistent with the estimated pass-through rate, conditional on restrictive assumptions about the functional form of demand).

[87]   The importance of curvature of demand (the elasticity of the elasticity) to pass-through is emphasized in Jeremy I. Bulow and Paul Pfleiderer, *A Note on the Effect of Cost Changes on Prices,* 91 J. POL. ECON. 182 (1983).

expand output following a merger because costs rise as output expands or because they run into capacity constraints, those firms will provide less of a constraint on post-merger pricing, which would tend to increase adverse unilateral effects. On the other hand, if the merging firms' output was constrained by rising marginal costs or capacity constraints pre-merger, they will have less incentive to cut output post-merger, which will tend to reduce unilateral effects. In one set of simulations that allowed simultaneously for both possibilities, the second effect tended to dominate.[88]

VI   MEASUREMENT ISSUES

A number of measurement issues arise in analysing unilateral effects, regardless of whether informal methods or merger simulation are employed to measure incentives to raise price post-merger. This section considers several such topics.

A   Demand

Most simulation modeling begins by estimating a demand system for the products at issue.[89] Doing so raises familiar econometric issues, including the choice of functional form, simultaneity and identification, and the possibility of omitted variable bias.[90] Our brief discussion highlights a number of issues that frequently arise when demand system parameters are employed for merger simulation. The same issues necessarily arise when informal methods are used to infer demand elasticities, but they are generally not exposed (and may not be recognized when present) in such settings.

First, in differentiated product settings, there is commonly no reason to expect symmetry in demand elasticities or diversion ratios across products.[91] Such asymmetries can

---

[88]   Luke Froeb, Steven Tschantz, and Philip Crooke, *Bertrand Competition with Capacity Constraints: Mergers Among Parking Lots*, 113 J. ECONOMETRICS 49 (2003).

[89]   For a technical survey of recently developed empirical techniques for analysing demand, see Daniel Ackerberg, C. Lanier Benkard, Steven Berry, and Ariel Pakes, *Econometric Tools for Analyzing Market Outcomes*, in 6A HANDBOOK OF ECONOMETRICS 4171 (James J. Heckman and Edward E. Leamer eds., 2006), available at www.stanford.edu/~lanierb/research/tools8l-6-8.pdf.

[90]   For a discussion of some of these in an antitrust context, see Jonathan B. Baker and Daniel L. Rubinfeld, *Empirical Methods in Antitrust Litigation: Review and Critique*, 1 AM. L. AND ECON. REV. 386, 406–14 (1999). Identification issues in estimating logit models of demand for differentiated products are discussed as an application in Aviv Nevo and Adam Rosen, *Identification with Imperfect Instruments* (NBER Working Paper No. W14434, October 2008) available at SSRN: http://ssrn.com/abstract=1289668. It is worth noting that demand for many retail products peaks at certain holidays (roses on Valentine's Day, etc.) or in certain seasons. The empirical literature generally finds that firms charge lower prices in thick markets, because they are able to exploit scale economies. These exogenous shifts in demand could exacerbate the problem of identifying the parameters of demand functions.

[91]   Even if (hypothetically) most Dr Pepper drinkers view Coca-Cola as their second choice soft drink at current prices, Coke drinkers might nevertheless largely see Pepsi as their second choice, for example. See generally Jonathan B. Baker, *Contemporary Empirical Merger Analysis*, 5 GEO. MASON L. REV. 347, 357 (1997) ('there is no basis, theoretical or empirical, for presuming absent evidence from the market at issue that the cross elasticities are symmetric').

have a large effect on the outcome of a merger simulation, so demand estimation should allow for that possibility. Second, some limits will invariably be placed on the scope of products included in the demand study. The decision whether to include or exclude a relatively distant substitute for the products of the merging firms generally has little practical effect on the simulated price increases, however.

Third, if the merger simulation model accounts for the possibility that cost savings will be passed through to price, it must incorporate parameters related to the curvature of demand.[92] To infer such parameters statistically, it will be necessary to estimate demand using flexible functional forms that allow demand elasticities to vary freely with price.

The latter issue points to a more general tradeoff in merger simulation between tractability (which pushes toward reducing the number of parameters that must be estimated or inferred) and flexibility (which pushes toward increasing the number of parameters). Limiting the number of parameters can be particularly important for tractability when estimating demand in differentiated-product industries where each firm sells a wide range of product variants.[93]

On one extreme, some merger simulation methods, such as the PCAIDS and ALM models discussed earlier, rely on a limited number of demand parameters. These parameters are sometimes assessed informally using qualitative evidence, without quantitative estimation of a demand system, or inferred from market shares. Other methods, with more complex computational requirements, infer demand parameters from market shares and product characteristics.[94] Still another way of restricting the number of demand parameters in estimation characterizes demand as resulting from multistage budgeting, and assumes separability of demand between the products in various sub-aggregates.[95]

A fourth issue in estimating demand arises in settings where dynamic behavior is important.[96] In many retail markets, the combination of short-term seller promotions and household inventorying create short-run buyer responses to price changes that

---

[92]   We discuss pass-through of cost savings above.

[93]   Relatedly, Budzinski and Ruhmer emphasize the expense and time required for sophisticated merger simulation. Budzinski and Ruhmer, *supra* note 51, at 34; see also Slade, *supra* note 37, at 338 (discussing the tradeoffs between simplicity and accuracy in differentiated product merger simulation models).

[94]   Steven Berry, James Levinsohn, and Ariel Pakes, *Automobile Prices in Market Equilibrium*, 63 ECONOMETRICA 841 (1995); Timothy F. Bresnahan, Scott Stern, and Manuel Trajtenberg, *Market Segmentation and the Sources of Rents from Innovation: Personal Computers in the Late 1980s*, 28 RAND J. ECON. S17 (1997); Aviv Nevo, *Mergers with Differentiated Products: The Case of the Ready-to-Eat Cereal Industry*, 31 RAND J. ECON. 395 (2000); Aviv Nevo, *A Practitioner's Guide to Estimation of Random-Coefficients Logit Models of Demand*, 9 J. ECON. AND MANAGEMENT STRATEGY 513 (2000); Aviv Nevo, *Measuring Market Power in the Ready-to-Eat Cereal Industry*, 69 ECONOMETRICA 307 (2001); Michelle Sovinsky Goree, *Limited Information and Advertising in the U.S. Personal Computer Industry*, 76 ECONOMETRICA 1017 (2008).

[95]   Jerry Hausman, Gregory Leonard, and Douglas J. Zona, *Competitive Analysis with Differentiated Products*, 34 ANNALES D'ECONOMIE ET DE STATISTIQUE 159 (1994).

[96]   We are grateful to Aviv Nevo for discussion of these issues.

differ from how buyers behave over a longer run more relevant to antitrust analysis.[97] Demand estimates that use high frequency (daily or weekly) data and do not explicitly model these dynamics may estimate inconsistent coefficients[98] and, even if they do not, may measure short-run effects that differ from the elasticities of interest for simulating unilateral effects.[99]

A final issue relates to out-of-sample predictions. If price variation is limited in the data used to identify demand, it may be possible to identify empirically local demand elasticities with precision without precisely identifying the curvature of demand. Yet mergers can substantially alter market structure, leading to discrete, not localized, movements in prices and output. The curvature of demand can be very influential in determining the price changes that result from loss of direct competition in this context, and it is central to determining the rate at which the merged firm would pass through marginal cost savings to price. If price variation is limited in the data, it may still be possible to exploit other types of informal experiments, particularly the entry and exit of products or locations, to gauge the curvature of demand.[100]

---

[97]   See generally Baker, *supra* note 91, at 352–5.

[98]   See Igal Hendel and Aviv Nevo, *A Simple Model of Demand Anticipation* (11 September 2009) and Tenn, Froeb, and Tschantz, *supra* note 49. Another common problem arises when demand systems are estimated on weekly store data: cross-price effects not infrequently have the 'wrong' sign (likely substitutes appearing to be complements). This may reflect a failure to account properly for promotional activity and household inventory. In a personal communication with one of us, Aviv Nevo suggested instead that this may arise from a lack of independent exogenous variation in prices (that is, variation in the part of price explained by the instrumental variables). The problem is less common in estimating logit models of demand, mainly by assumption. The discrete choice framework tends to require that products be substitutes by virtue of the assumption that if buyers do not purchase one product they select another.

[99]   See generally Igal Hendel and Aviv Nevo, *Measuring the Implications of Sales and Consumer Inventory Behavior*, 74 ECONOMETRICA 1637 (2006). Hendel and Nevo find in their data that static demand estimates, which neglect dynamics, overestimate own-price elasticities and underestimate cross-price elasticities – likely leading simulation modeling to underpredict the effects of mergers. Another example of biases from inattention to dynamics is the problem of estimating demand in markets in which sellers facing capacity constraints periodically sell out their stock, making their product temporarily unavailable. Christopher T. Conlon and Julie Holland Mortimer, *Demand Estimation Under Incomplete Product Availability* (Harvard Institute of Economic Research Discussion Paper No. 2174, 16 March 2009), available at http://ssrn.com/abstract=1394476. *Cf.* Steven Tenn and John M. Yun, *Biases in Demand Analysis Due to Variation in Retail Distribution* (FTC Working Paper No. 287, February 2007) (discussing estimation of logit models when product assortments vary across stores).

[100]   For example, if a supermarket or other multilocation retailer opens at a new location, it in effect lowers the price for its products at that location from what was the delivered price (the price at the nearest neighboring location plus transportation costs). Entry and exit events may also allow identification of the relationship between price and market structure, which can be used to simulate the effects of merger. Orley Ashenfelter, David Ashmore, Jonathan B. Baker, Suzanne Gleason, and Daniel S. Hosken, *Empirical Methods in Merger Analysis: Econometric Analysis of Pricing in FTC v. Staples*, 13 INT'L J. ECON. BUS. 265 (2006).

B   Marginal Cost

Another set of measurement issues involves marginal cost. The profit recapture perspective on unilateral effects emphasizes that any effort to calibrate demand elasticities or diversion ratios – to determine whether those demand parameters imply a large or small incentive to raise price – values the lost sales from a unilateral price rise (an amount determined by the shape of demand) by weighting them by the contribution margin on those sales. The contribution margin in turn depends on measurement of marginal cost – most importantly its level, and secondarily how it varies with output.[101] Putting aside the analysis of efficiencies, the unilateral effects model in differentiated products industries thus uses marginal cost mainly to determine the lost contribution to profit from a reduction in output by the merging firms.

It is typically possible even for industry outsiders to observe changes in prices of some key inputs into production or distribution of differentiated products.[102] But detailed accounting information about the components and level of average variable cost, a common proxy for marginal cost, is generally only available to industry insiders, who can make it available for antitrust analysis.[103] Some simulation methods treat marginal cost as unobservable, and infer cost and price–cost margins from demand using the first order conditions for firm profit-maximization. This approach allows mergers to be simulated without data on marginal cost. The resulting inferences as to marginal cost and the effect of the merger on price and output can be sensitive, however, to various assumptions, particularly as to the functional form of demand[104] and to the oligopoly solution concept (for example, that it is Bertrand–Nash).[105]

Other difficulties with measuring marginal cost derive from the possibility that the merging firm's marginal decision relevant to merger analysis is not the same as the decision implicit in the accounting data from which its average variable cost is computed.[106] For example, if the merged firm reduces output of the products sold by either (or both) merger partners in order to raise price, it might on the one hand lose out on volume discounts previously available or the ability to access low-cost channels of

---

[101]   Understatement of marginal cost (markup overestimate) limited to one firm may lead to an overstatement of the unilateral incentive to raise price arising from merger. Marginal cost underestimation across the board (for all firms) will likely lead to a misstatement of the unilateral incentive to raise price, but the bias could go either way. Baker, *supra* note 91, at 358 n.43.

[102]   This type of information can often be used to identify demand econometrically.

[103]   It is often necessary to interview executives to understand the technology of production and distribution and clarify the interpretation of accounting data from the merging firms. For an example of the kind of analysis required to develop a convincing measure of average variable cost even when *detailed accounting* data is available, see Genesove and Mullin, *supra* note 62, at 359–61.

[104]   See Slade, *supra* note 37, at 334.

[105]   See generally Genesove and Mullin, *supra* note 62. Even if firms experience their conduct as setting price rather than output, their behavior is not necessarily consistent with Bertrand–Nash competition, a common assumption in that context. See, e.g., David M. Kreps and José A. Scheinkman, *Quantity Precommitment and Bertrand Competition Yield Cournot Outcomes*, 14 Bell J. Econ. 326 (1983).

[106]   That is, the accounting data may implicitly assume that the merged firm reduces output (loses sales) over a different time period or different scale than contemplated by the unilateral effects model.

distribution, raising per unit costs above what is recorded in the accounting data. On the other hand, the merged firm might free itself from paying the higher costs associated with approaching a capacity constraint, or from rising marginal costs in marketing a differentiated product,[107] thus lowering per unit costs below what is recorded in the accounting data.

Similarly, an accounting measure of average variable cost that excludes all expenditures on advertising and promotion may underestimate marginal cost. The marginal cost relevant to pricing includes those advertising and promotional expenditures that would change were the firm to adopt a different pricing strategy over a full promotion and inventory cycle – a time period more relevant to merger analysis than the short-run period over which average variable cost is often computed.[108]

Other problems in measuring marginal cost may arise when firms sell multiple products; we highlight issues arising when either or both merging firms sell demand complements for the products of concern.[109] Suppose, for example, the unilateral effects concern from a proposed (and entirely hypothetical) merger involves the merging firms' sale of shampoo, and that one or both firms also sell conditioner under the same brand name (where adverse competitive effects are not threatened). No firm in this hypothetical example sells shampoo combined with conditioner, many but not all consumers of shampoo also use conditioner, and consumers of a particular shampoo brand tend to use the same brand of conditioner. Under such circumstances, if a merging firm reduces the output of shampoo (to profit from anticompetitive unilateral effects), it will lose sales and profits in conditioner as well. Accordingly, the lost contribution to profit in conditioner resulting from a marginal increase in the shampoo price should be included in assessing the marginal cost of shampoo. An analysis of unilateral effects that does not account for this dynamic will understate the cost of raising the price of shampoo to the merging firm, and, in consequence, likely overstate the unilateral incentive to raise price.[110] Moreover,

---

[107]   The marginal cost of distributing a differentiated product will slope upward if the firm sells first to buyers who can be informed or persuaded least expensively. That is, firms selling differentiated products may experience decreasing returns to scale in promotion and distribution even if they experience constant returns to scale in production.

[108]   This idea might justify using average operating cost or average total cost rather than average variable cost as a proxy for marginal cost in some cases. If the merged firm reduces output in order to raise price, marginal cost might also be reduced to the extent the output reduction leads the firm to cut back on planned investments such as capacity expansion. The marginal cost reduction could go beyond the direct savings to include any 'real option' benefit arising when investment decisions are deferred.

[109]   There are three other cases. First, if a merging firm also sells products that are complements in supply (joint products, like beef and hides), an anticompetitive reduction in output by the merged firm will reduce the contribution to profit from the supply complement. This lost profit should be seen as part of the marginal cost of producing the product of concern. Second, if a merging firm sells products that are substitutes in demand, its profit-maximizing output decision with respect to that good is presumably accounted for directly in the analysis of unilateral effects. Third, if it sells products that are substitutes in supply, any contribution to profit obtained from shifting the marginal unit of production or distribution capacity to that supply substitute would reduce the marginal cost of the product of concern for the purpose of unilateral effects analysis.

[110]   Note, however, that if all firms in the market sell complementary products, and if as a result

if current sales of a product make future sales more likely, as would arise, for example, if buyers learn about product attributes from trial or from network effects, then future sales can be viewed as a demand complement for current sales and a similar analysis would apply.[111]

C   Nonprice Dimensions of Competition

Much competition takes place on nonprice dimensions, including improvements in product quality, modification of product features or geographic locations, and new product introductions. Unilateral effects analyses that focus on output and price likely incorporate some of these dimensions by measuring price and output in quality-adjusted units. But it is an open question whether that analysis fully proxies for unilateral reductions in these other dimensions of competition, which might take the form of slowed innovation.[112]

VII   TESTING OF UNILATERAL EFFECTS ANALYSES

Merger retrospectives are difficult to conduct and rare, but a recent study by Orley Ashenfelter and Daniel Hosken offers the most reliable test of unilateral effects analyses to date.[113] Their study examines the price effects of merger following five recent branded consumer products acquisitions using scanner data. The mergers were selected for analysis based on data availability and on indications that the merger, though not challenged, might have presented a close call for the US antitrust enforcement agencies.[114] The mergers were in industries where the likely competitive effects theory was the loss of direct competition among sellers of differentiated products – historically the primary concern of unilateral effects analysis.

The study employs a difference-in-difference empirical strategy to control for factors that might affect prices other than the merger. It compares the change in prices for the merged firm's products from before the merger to after the merger (using various definitions of price and various definitions of before and after) to the change in prices of products in two control groups: private label products in the same industry and branded consumer products sold by rivals. In four of the five cases, the study finds that the merger led to price increases (typically between 3% and 7%) relative to prices in the control groups, while leading to no price increase in the fifth case.

These results suggest that the marginal unilateral effects merger – one that would be a

---

the cost of raising price is understated for all firms, then the bias in the unilateral effects analysis could go either way; see Baker, *supra* note 91, at 358 n.43.

[111]   See Salop, Brenner, Coppi, and Moresi, *supra* note 79, at 61.

[112]   For a recent effort to make product characteristics endogenous, see Draganska, Mazzeo, and Seim, *supra* note 75.

[113]   Orley C. Ashenfelter and Daniel S. Hosken, *The Effect of Mergers on Consumer Prices: Evidence from Five Mergers on the Enforcement Margin*, 53 J.L. AND ECON. 417 (2010).

[114]   Those indications include apparent high market concentration and, in some cases, evidence of an active enforcement agency review before the merger was allowed to proceed.

close call to antitrust enforcers – raised price, at least in the short run, before all efficiencies kicked in. This conclusion implies that the antitrust agencies, in employing unilateral effects analysis, are successfully targeting transactions that would have an anticompetitive effect on prices.

In future retrospective analyses of unilateral cases, it would be useful to extend this result, in analysing these or other transactions. Many other questions could be studied. Did rival repositioning undermine or counteract the harm in these or other mergers? Did efficiencies from merger make these transactions procompetitive in the long run? Do the agencies do as well when the unilateral effects theory involves a bidding model?

3 Lightening up on market definition
David S. Evans*

I INTRODUCTION

'Market definition' refers to the process of determining the set of products, and locations from which those products are sold, that are relevant for analysing the antitrust issue at hand. That set of products and locations defines '*the* market'. Courts have long treated market definition as the first step in analysing an antitrust matter.[1] Among other things they rely on the relevant antitrust market to calculate market shares from which they infer the existence of market power. At least since *Alcoa*,[2] the courts have drawn hard market boundaries. A product is either in or out of the market. The placement of this fence often determines the final outcome of the matter.[3] As a result, market definition sets up a battle between the 'we-win because it is a narrow market' plaintiffs and the 'you-lose because it is a broad market' defendants.[4] Both sides naturally invest significant resources in trying to persuade the courts where to build the fence.

Many economists have argued that there is seldom a solid market boundary in practice.[5] Products from different vendors are often heterogeneous and compete along a continuum. Economists have also observed that there is no particular need to define a rigid boundary. Ultimately antitrust is about ascertaining effects on prices, output, and other factors that influence consumer welfare. It is possible to address those effects directly without taking a firm position on a market boundary. In recent years, the US Department of Justice (DOJ) and the Federal Trade Commission (FTC) have, in the merger context, agreed with this view.[6] They have tried to block several transactions in which they focused

---

* I would like to thank Howard Chang, Dale Collins, Douglas Ginsburg, Michael Salinger, and Richard Schmalensee for helpful comments and Dhiren Patki for excellent research support.

[1] See PHILLIP E. AREEDA, JOHN L. SOLOW, AND HERBERT HOVENKAMP, IIA ANTITRUST LAW 187–8 (2d ed., Aspen Law & Business, 2002).

[2] United States v. Aluminum Co. of America, 148 F.2d 416 (2d Cir. 1945).

[3] Robert Pitofsky, *New Definitions of Relevant Market and the Assault on Antitrust*, 90 COLUMBIA L. REV. 1805, 1807 (1990) ('Knowledgeable antitrust practitioners have long known that the most important single issue in most enforcement actions – because so much depends on it – is market definition').

[4] See, e.g., the discussion of *FTC v. Staples*, *infra* note 72. The federal district court and the DC Circuit Court of Appeals both concluded that the outcome hinged entirely on market definition.

[5] For an excellent summary see Gregory J. Werden, *The History of Antitrust Market Delineation*, 76 MARQ. L. REV. 123 (1992). For older and newer statements of the complaint by economists see FRANKLIN M. FISHER, JOHN J. MCGOWAN, and JOEN E. GREENWOOD, FOLDED, SPINDLED, AND MUTILATED: ECONOMIC ANALYSIS AND U.S. v. IBM (MIT Press, 1983) and Joseph Farrell and Carl Shapiro, *Antitrust Evaluation of Horizontal Mergers: An Economic Alternative to Market Definition* (2008), available at http://ssrn.com/abstract=1313782.

[6] See US Dep't of Justice and Fed. Trade Comm'n, Commentary on the Horizontal Merger Guidelines (2006) available at www.ftc.gov/os/2006/03/CommentaryontheHorizontal

mainly on demonstrating the effect of the combination. The courts have insisted on defining *the* market in reviewing motions to enjoin these mergers.[7]

This chapter proposes a workable truce to the market definition war that has raged with varying intensity for almost seven decades. Market definition should remain the first step in the analysis of mergers and anticompetitive practices. The exercise should focus on understanding the economic relationships that would have a bearing on the practice at issue before the court or agency. For many modern firms this exercise entails learning about the complex ecosystem in which the firm operates.[8] A key part of this broader inquiry concerns how other products are substitutes or complements for the products at issue in the inquiry. It will often prove informative to calculate shares based on tentative but credible delineations of the relevant players. The courts should not, however, draw a firm boundary around a particular set of products and make all subsequent steps in their analysis depend on where that boundary is drawn or on calculations of precise market shares. Plaintiffs and defendants, and their economic experts, would of course assist the court, as they do now, in understanding market relationships.

Quite simply the truce merely involves taking the '*the*' out of 'the market'. That definite article has led to wooden analysis. It is time to lighten up.

This truce would make the court's approach toward market definition consistent with modern economic thinking. The US courts have embraced economic reasoning in almost every aspect of their approach to antitrust.[9] Market definition, and the related subject of market power, is one of the few remaining areas in which the courts rely on an approach that is not supported by economic science.[10] To align themselves with the modern economic approach to antitrust the courts would have to make but a modest change from their long-standing jurisprudence. They would merely need to abandon their insistence on drawing hard boundaries and making all subsequent analytical steps depend on where those lines are drawn. They would continue to have market definition as the first step in the analysis and build their subsequent narratives off of it. They would only have to avoid economically unsupported conclusions drawn from artificial market boundaries. Nothing in the antitrust statutes prevents this result. Section 7 of the Clayton Act refers

---

MergerGuidelinesMarch2006.pdf. Also see US Dep't of Justice & Fed. Trade Comm'n, Horizontal Merger Guidelines for Public Comment (2010) available at www.ftc.gov/os/2010/04/100420hmg. pdf ('[The market definition exercise] is useful to the extent it illuminates the merger's likely competitive effects'), at 7.

[7] See United States v. Oracle Corp., 331 F. Supp. 2d 1098 (N.D. Cal. 2004) and FTC v. Whole Foods Mkt., Inc., 533 F.3d 869 (D.C. Cir. 2008).

[8] See David S. Evans, *Two Sided Market Definition*, forthcoming in MARKET DEFINITION IN ANTITRUST: THEORY AND CASE STUDIES (ABA Section of Antitrust Law ed.), available at http://papers.ssrn.com/sol3/papers.cfm?abstract_id=1396751.

[9] See, e.g., Leegin Creative Leather Prods. v. PSKS, Inc., 551 U.S. 877 (2007).

[10] As some of the earlier references indicate this is hardly a new point. For a particularly insightful analysis see Richard Schmalensee, *On the Use of Economic Models in Antitrust*, 127 U. PA. L. REV. 994, 1004 (1978) ('the standard market share approach to the measurement of monopoly power is inherently incapable of providing definite answers to the relevant economic questions in the ReaLemon case, even though both sides apparently assumed that it could do so').

to 'lines of commerce' but it is hard to imagine Congress intended that to require drawing hard boundaries.[11] The Sherman Act is silent on the subject of markets, referring only generally to 'trade or commerce'.[12] Competition authorities have demonstrated the ability to draft coherent decisions on mergers without drawing hard market boundaries.[13] There is no reason the courts cannot do so as well.

To arrive at this truce this chapter proceeds as follows.

Section II describes the current practice of market definition. It shows that drawing hard market boundaries generally does not make economic sense because most businesses differentiate their products from rivals so the products are imperfect substitutes that compete along a continuum. This section is brief because the point is oft-told and widely recognized. Section III then shows that the main role of market definition in antitrust analysis is to help identify competitive constraints and assess the extent of market power. The crux of most antitrust matters is the extent to which competitive forces limit market power and more generally the ability to inflict consumer harm. Drawing hard market boundaries provides an awkward approach for assessing the subset of these competitive constraints resulting from demand-side substitution. Section IV reviews current approaches for market definition. The courts have mainly relied on informal analyses of demand and supply substitution. The US antitrust authorities introduced the seemingly more rigorous hypothetical monopoly test for market definition. Economists have developed sophisticated technical methods for implementing this definition. The analyses have tried to nail down something that seldom exists: a hard market boundary. Section V argues that from the standpoint of reaching the right conclusion, and minimizing error costs, there are few benefits and significant costs to drawing precise market boundaries. Section VI develops the truce in detail and explains why it is ultimately in the interest of the consumers that the antitrust laws seek to protect. Section VII makes some concluding observations.[14]

II THE NATURE OF COMPETITION AND HARD BOUNDARIES

The traditional approach to market definition involves making informed but ultimately subjective judgments concerning, on the demand side, the extent to which products are interchangeable or have high cross-price elasticities of demand and, on the supply side, the extent to which firms can easily switch production to offer substitutable products. The courts do not require perfect interchangeability or perfect supply-side substitution.[15] This approach can provide an accurate assessment of competitive constraints resulting from

---

[11]   Clayton Act, 15 U.S.C. § 18 (1914).

[12]   Sherman Act, 15 U.S.C. § 2 (1890).

[13]   See, e.g., UK Office of Fair Trading, Anticipated acquisition of the online DVD rental subscription business of Amazon Inc. by LOVEFiLM International Limited ME/3534/08, 8 May 2008.

[14]   The chapter focuses only on the United States. However, the same criticisms apply to the use of market definition to assess dominance under Article 102 of the EU Treaty and merger control in the EU.

[15]   See generally ANTITRUST LAW, *supra* note 1, at 293–310.

demand-side and supply-side substitutes when firms produce very similar products and compete mainly on price. In this case, it is straightforward to determine which products are reasonably interchangeable with each other. These similar products should also have positive and significant cross-elasticities with each other and not with any other products.

Few markets, however, involve competition over homogeneous products. Consider the market for wheat, which is often cited as the textbook example of a homogeneous product industry.[16] According to www.wheatflourbook.org:[17]

> One of the major strengths of the U.S. grain production and marketing system is the variety of grades, classes, and prices that it can offer customers around the world. Dramatic differences in topography, soils, and climate from one region to another make this variety possible. By building on these natural advantages, seed breeders, researchers, farmers, grain handlers, and merchandisers are continually seeking to expand both the type and quality of wheat the United States can make available to its customers.

In evaluating whether products are differentiated it is important to recognize that almost all products are multidimensional in that they involve a product that has several attributes, including quality, and comes bundled with various kinds of services and other complementary products. Aspirin, for example, is a homogeneous product from a chemical standpoint yet there are significant price differences between different brands.

Product heterogeneity is the norm, not the exception. It is seldom the case that consumers are selecting among equivalent products mainly on the basis of price. Sometimes firms produce different products because they lack the knowhow or resources to produce the same product as a competitor. A wheat farmer may have land whose topography only supports a particular kind and grade of wheat. More generally firms do not want to compete intensely with each other. They often try to figure out ways to differentiate their products from other firms through physical differentiation, service, quality, advertising, branding, location, and many other factors. Firms are aided in their efforts to distinguish themselves in part because consumers, whether people or other businesses, are heterogeneous as well. Consumers have varying tastes for the many possible dimensions of a product. Firms try to devise sets of product attributes that are desired by groups of consumers. Consumers also may differ in their ability to pay for higher quality products. As incomes increase people switch from inferior to superior products.

To see why drawing hard market boundaries is problematic in real-world markets it is useful to consider the simple case shown in Figure 3.1. The product under consideration, say product 6, has two attributes (such as horsepower and mileage; sweetness and crunchiness; battery life and screen resolution) which are measured on the horizontal and vertical axes as well as a price which is measured by the size of the bubble. Other products have higher or lower prices but provide different combinations of the other two attributes. Consumers, in this example, do not have uniform views on the value of the attributes so at the same price products with high and low values of attributes can find enough customers

---

[16]   See Dennis W. Carlton and Jeffrey M. Perloff, Modern Industrial Organization 203 (Addison Wesley, 2005).
[17]   See www.wheatflourbook.org/Main.aspx?p=52.

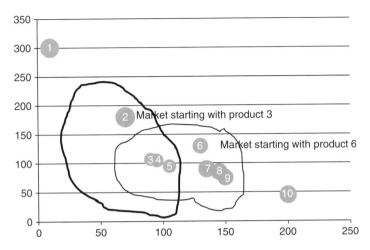

Note: Each product has two attributes with values as shown by the horizontal and vertical axes. The size of the bubble reflects the price, which ranges from 30 for product 10 to 14 for product 2.

Figure 3.1 Market definition for a group of differentiated products

to sustain provision of the product. Some products seem more similar to the product in question: product 5 seems closer to product 6 than product 9. But an increase in the price of 6 could lead a significant portion of consumers of product 6 to switch to product 1. For example, product 6 could be a Nokia smart phone and with an increase in price people switch to an iPhone. There is no obvious basis for drawing a fence at any particular distance from the original product.[18] We will see later that the hypothetical monopolist test was a valiant but problematic effort to draw that boundary.

The example in Figure 3.1 also helps show that there is no such thing as '*the* market'. No method for drawing a fence around some group of heterogeneous products can lead to a unique 'market' for those products. Suppose product 6 is at the center of an antitrust inquiry and that one of the standard approaches to market definition (such as the hypothetical monopoly test) determines that the market encompasses the products shown. Now suppose that product 3 which was included in the market for product 6 is at the center of an inquiry. The same approach to market definition will almost certainly find that the market for product 3 includes products that were not in the market for product 6 and that the market for product 6 does not include products (including possibly product 3) that were included.

This point is well recognized by the courts and antitrust professionals. Careful writers use the phrase '*the* "relevant antitrust" market' to reflect the fact that what is 'relevant' varies from case to case and that the word 'market' refers to a concept that is different

---

[18]   As we will see later, the extent to which some of the products may provide competitive constraints to the product at issue in the matter depends in part on how easily the makers of these products could alter their attributes (reposition them in the parlance of marketing professionals) in response to a price increase for the product at issue.

than how this word is understood in common as well as business parlance. The courts[19] and authorities[20] observe that the relevant antitrust market can be different than how businesses that compete with each other use the term market.

'*The* market' varies depending upon the reference point from which it is considered. It is therefore unlike assessing objective (nonsituational) concepts such as price or whether there is a tie. In fact, the purpose of market definition is to identify substitutes that are relevant for evaluating the competitive constraints on the party at issue. The collection of these demand- (and possibly supply-)side substitutes is called *the* market for the case at hand. For other cases those competitive constraints may differ and therefore it is not surprising that *the* market for a matter involving a somewhat similar product could be different.

Although the language of market definition seems to suggest that it is attempting to identify an invariant fact – *the* market – it is really a process for identifying certain competitive constraints that are relevant to the matter at hand and for assessing market power. Unfortunately, locating hard market boundaries and calculating shares based on those boundaries are not reliable methods for assessing the extent of competitive constraints or the degree of market power. In fact, as we will argue later, it is better to reposition market definition so that it involves analysing a broad range of competitive constraints whose presence or absence can determine the significance of the matter at issue on welfare.

III   COMPETITIVE CONSTRAINTS AND MARKET POWER

Antitrust jurisprudence recognizes that whether a particular suspect practice harms consumers, benefits them, or has no material effect on them depends on the facts and circumstances of the case. Economics shows that the answer hinges on the strength of the 'competitive constraints' on the ability and incentives of the firm(s) at issue to increase its profits by engaging in the practice at hand.[21] Sometimes the practice involves removing a competitive constraint. In that case the antitrust question revolves around the significance of the competitive constraint that has been, or will be, eliminated and the strength of the competitive constraints that will remain. The courts, and economists that specialize in antitrust, sometimes use the notion of 'market power'[22] to summarize the net effect of these constraints.[23] A firm is said to have significant market power if it faces relatively weak competitive constraints and is therefore able to raise prices above the level that would prevail under competition.[24] The main goal of market definition is to

---

[19]   See, e.g., FTC v. Staples, 970 F. Supp. 1066, 1075 (D.D.C. 1997) where the court noted that '[t]he mere fact that a firm may be termed a competitor in the overall marketplace does not necessarily require that it be included in the relevant product market for antitrust purposes'.

[20]   See Horizontal Merger Guidelines (2010), *supra* note 6, at 11.

[21]   See MASSIMO MOTTA, COMPETITION POLICY THEORY AND PRACTICE 45–8 (Cambridge University Press, 2004).

[22]   Depending on the context this may be referred to as monopoly power or significant market power.

[23]   As we will discuss below, however, market power is not a well-defined analytical concept.

[24]   Alternatively, market power is sometimes defined as the ability to control price since in a truly competitive market firms must take price as given and therefore do not have any control over

help understand these competitive constraints and thus the degree of market power. This section provides the background for assessing the extent to which locating hard market boundaries and calculating market shares helps achieve this goal. It also provides background for introducing the techniques of market definition in the next section.

Subsection A describes the main practices in antitrust and explains how competitive constraints are helpful in sorting out whether these practices are harmful to consumers. Subsection B then provides a summary of the sources of competitive constraints. Subsection C relates these constraints to the notion of market power.

A   Business Practices and Competitive Constraints

Consider two products x and y which are produced by separate firms A and B. Some consumers would substitute x for y if the price of y went up and the price of x did not (and vice versa). There is therefore a positive cross-price elasticity of demand between x and y.[25] When firm A decides on the price of product x it would need to consider the extent to which customers would switch to product y provided by firm B. Firm A would tend to charge a lower price the more sales it loses to firm B. Firm B's product y similarly imposes a competitive constraint on firm A's product x. Both firm A and firm B may face competition from other sources and they may face other competitive constraints that limit their ability to make decisions that adversely affect consumers, as we discuss in more detail below. Call these other competitive constraints z from a collection of sources we denote by C.[26] The competitive constraints z are not necessarily substitutes for x or y. For example, as we discuss below, firm A may produce a complement to x in which case the loss of profits from the sales of this complement constrains the willingness of A to increase the price of x.

The competitive constraints between A, B, and C are generally relevant for assessing whether suspect actions taken by A, B, or both are harmful to consumers. Consider a proposed merger between A and B. To evaluate the effect of this, economists would want to know the extent to which A and B constrain each other's decisions towards products x and y. If they impose a significant constraint on each other, the merger, in effect, removes that constraint and could allow them to raise prices.[27] To put this in the language of merger analysis, before the merger, a further price increase by A for x is unprofitable because it leads to a loss of sales and profits to B; after the merger, a further price increase by AB for x could be profitable because the combined firm captures the increase in profits resulting from the increased sales of y. If these products do not impose significant constraints on each other, and if the combination generates enough efficiencies[28] to offset

---

it. See US Dep't of Justice, *Competition and Monopoly: Single-Firm Conduct Under Section 2 of the Sherman Act* (2008) available at www.justice.gov/atr/public/reports/236681.pdf.

   [25]   See equation (2) below and the discussion preceding it for a technical definition of cross-price elasticity of demand.

   [26] C in this formulation also includes factors that would reduce competitive constraints such as entry barriers.

   [27]   Michael L. Katz and Carl Shapiro, *Critical Loss: Let's Tell the Whole Story*, ANTITRUST MAGAZINE (Spring 2003) at 43.

   [28]   These could be cost efficiencies which provide an incentive to decrease price and thereby

whatever minimal price increase that might occur, we would conclude that the merger would not likely harm consumers. We would also want to know the extent to which C constrains A and B. Many factors could limit the combined firm from adversely affecting the terms of trade with consumers even if x and y constrained A and B's practices before the merger. Consumers could switch to other products, new firms could enter, existing firms could expand supply, existing firms could reposition themselves, or the likelihood of a drastic innovation that would displace x and y could increase.

In many respects the same considerations come into play in other antitrust matters. Consider exclusionary practices cases in which price or nonprice methods are used to soften the competitive constraints on A coming from B or C. In a predatory pricing case the issue involves the elimination of B's production of y by A. This could harm consumers only if y imposes a significant constraint on x and if z does not discourage A from adversely affecting consumers. More generally, for the discussion of antitrust, we can think of firm B and product y as standing in for all the firms and products that firm A is excluding, in whole or in part, from competing against it for sales of x. The core issue involves the extent to which the competitive constraints coming from y are significant, the extent to which the practice softens those competitive constraints, and the extent to which z provides enough competitive constraints to prevent consumer harm.

The key point is that antitrust inquiries are ultimately about competitive constraints. They involve looking into whether the competitive constraint that is eliminated is important and whether the remaining competitive constraints are sufficient to prevent the firm(s) engaged in the business practice from harming consumers. Market definition is useful to the extent it helps understand these competitive constraints. As we will see, while the process of market definition provides useful insights into these constraints, the requirement that this process end with the erection of a wall that precludes consideration of anything beyond this boundary can lead to a distorted view of competitive constraints. Moreover, for the purposes of merger assessment, the antitrust authorities limit market definition to a particular set of competitive constraints arising from demand-side substitutability.

B   Competitive Constraints

We have used the phrase 'competitive constraint' loosely but it is helpful to have a formal definition. A competitive constraint is any factor that tends to reduce the expected profit that a firm can earn from taking some action that would harm consumers. If firm A increased the price[29] for x it might realize lower profits as a result of losing sales of x, losing sales of complementary products, foregoing indirect network or scale effects, spurring entry, and many other reasons. The following is a nonexhaustive survey of the possible sources of competitive constraints.

---

offset the demand-side incentives to increase price or they could be quality improvements so that the consumer's willingness to pay increases by more than the price increase.

[29]   We will generally use an increase in price as a stand-in for any action that reduces the consumer surplus that the consumer receives where surplus is defined as the difference between the value the consumer receives for the good (which is the consumer's maximum willingness to pay) and the cost of that good (which includes the price the consumer pays for the good plus any other costs).

1 Role of substitutes in demand

If a firm tried to turn the terms of trade against consumers it would first and foremost need to worry that consumers would reduce spending on its product. That could happen through some combination of consumers purchasing less, switching to alternative products that meet their needs, or switching to some other product altogether. It is helpful for us to focus on this source of constraint because it enables us to introduce several of the standard economic tools that are used in the analysis of market definition and market power.

If the price of Chimay Ale[30] goes up, for example, you might consume fewer bottles, switch to another beer, change to wine, or stop drinking alcohol altogether. All of these factors are summarized as a matter of theory in the demand schedule that a firm faces. Each point on that schedule summarizes how much consumers would purchase at various prices. As price goes up or down the demand schedule reflects the extent to which consumers would increase or decrease spending for all possible reasons. The own-price elasticity of demand at the price that the firm is charging before considering raising its price summarizes the effect of a small price change. The own-price elasticity of demand e_x for product x is defined as the percent change in the quantity sold that would result from a 1% increase in price:

$$(1) \quad e_x = \frac{dq_x/q_x}{dp_x/p_x}$$

where roughly speaking 'd' is the calculus symbol for 'small change in',[31] q_x is the quantity of product x, and p_x is the price of product x. A larger own-price elasticity means that consumers reduce purchases to a greater degree for the various reasons mentioned above.[32]

We can say more about what determines the elasticity of demand by introducing another measure known as the cross-price elasticity of demand. It equals the percent change in the quantity of a good that results from a 1% change in the price of a given good. A 1% increase in the price of y would lead to an increase in the demand for x given by the cross-elasticity of demand between x and y:

$$(2) \quad e_{xy} = \frac{dq_x/q_x}{dp_y/p_y}$$

When the cross-price elasticity is positive the goods are substitutes in the sense that an increase in the price of one results in consumers moving spending to the other. When the cross-elasticity is negative the goods are complements in the sense that an increase in the price of one results in consumers spending less on the other.

As a matter of simple accounting the elasticity of demand is a linear function of the

---

[30] At least in the United States, Chimay Ale is a high quality expensive ale. At Beacon Hill Liquors on Charles Street in Boston, bottles of Chimay cost US$5.20 for slightly less than a 12 ounce bottle vs US$6.25 for a six-pack of Miller 12 ounce cans.

[31] Technically the ds are all referring to partial derivatives.

[32] The convention is to use the absolute value of the price elasticity of demand which in effect puts a minus sign in front of the expression in (1). A price elasticity of 2 implies that a 1% increase in price leads to a 2% reduction in the quantity demand.

cross-elasticities of demand for all other goods. Your demand for Chimay Ale could be more elastic (that is, you could be more sensitive to price) if you thought you had a very good substitute for Chimay Ale or if there were several other products that you could collectively divert spending to. The same considerations apply when we consider the overall demand facing a firm. In the face of a price increase consumers could switch to a few close substitutes, or spread their spending across many, and anything in between.

2   Role of suppliers of substitutes

When firm A increases the price for x, firms that produce substitutes may change their current actions. What they do affects competitive constraints. There are at least three considerations.

First, do competitors increase their output in response to the higher price? If they can expand their output they may respond to the higher price charged by firm A by trying to take over some demand from A by, for example, poaching A's customers. A key consideration is the extent to which these competitors can and will increase their output. If they face capacity constraints they might have limited ability to expand; if they have a great deal of excess capacity they might be able to expand easily and quickly. Economists often point to the dominant firm with a competitive fringe model to illustrate this. The elasticity of demand facing firm A would depend on the industry demand elasticity, the share held by the dominant firm, and the elasticity of supply of the competitive fringe firms (i.e. the percent change in output that would follow from a 1% increase in market price):[33]

$$(3) \qquad e_x = \frac{e_M + (1 - S_x)e_f}{S_x}$$

where e_M is the market demand schedule, S_x is the share of the firm under consideration, and e_f is the elasticity of supply of the competitive fringe. Firm A's elasticity of demand for x – again, the measure of the extent to which it would lose sales if prices go up – is larger when the fringe firms have a larger share and those fringe firms have more elastic supply.

Second, do competitors increase their prices in response to the price increase by firm A? In a highly competitive market we would expect that firms would not increase their prices at all if another small player tried to increase its price. Many standard economic models of oligopoly, however, predict that the competitors will tend to increase their prices in response to a unilateral increase in price by another firm.[34] But this does not have to be the case. Firms may decide to use the price increase as an opportunity to steal their rival's customers and increase their own market share.

Third, would competitors reposition their product as a result of the price increase? In many industries firms offer products that are differentiated from one another, often to appeal to particular groups of customers.[35] Consumers sort themselves out across the various alternatives based on the price and product attributes being offered. If one firm raises

---

[33]   See William M. Landes and Richard A. Posner, *Market Power in Antitrust Cases*, 94 HARVARD L. REV. 937 (1981).

[34]   See Gregory J. Werden and Luke M. Froeb, *Unilateral Competitive Effects of Horizontal Mergers*, in HANDBOOK OF ANTITRUST ECONOMICS (Paolo Buccirossi ed., 2008).

[35]   See CARLTON AND PERLOFF, *supra* note 16, at 203–5.

price it presents an opportunity for other firms to go after that product niche. For example, if a magazine targeted towards well-off fashion-conscious women raised its price a competing magazine that targeted a more down-market crowd could consider altering its content.

These factors all affect competitive constraints. The firm may anticipate these responses and temper its decision to alter the terms of trade with consumers. Alternatively, the competitive response of other firms may mitigate the harm to consumers.

3   Role of entry

Increasing prices may alter the incentives for other firms to start producing substitute products. Existing firms may diversify into the product at issue (what the courts consider supply-side substitution) or new firms may form. In considering raising its price, firm *A* would therefore want to consider the possibility that the price increase will attract entry. That entry would reduce firm *A*'s expected future profits and offset any gains from its price increase. It would therefore temper firm *A*'s enthusiasm for a price increase.

Whether a price increase would likely attract entry depends, according to economic theory, on a complex set of factors. A price increase would attract entry if competitors could come in quickly to capture demand and exit easily if the incumbents lower the price. That depends in part on whether there are sunk (that is, unrecoverable) costs of entry. With imperfect information among firms on demand and costs an increase in price provides a signal to entrepreneurs that there may be profit opportunities. That can encourage entry.

As a related matter, prices can also affect the incentives to engage in incremental or disruptive innovation. Firms face competition when entrepreneurs introduce better products or come up with an entirely new way to satisfy consumer needs. Current prices provide signals to innovators on where they should place efforts. A firm may find that it is better to keep prices low, especially if it faces the risk of innovation that could effectively displace it. On the other hand, it may have intellectual property or scale advantages that make this unlikely.

4   Role of complements, indirect network effects, and two-sided markets

Many firms produce multiple products and have numerous sources of revenue. When firm *A* increases the price of product *x* it may lose revenue from the sale of complementary products.[36] Consider a company that produces a music player and also has an online music store. An increase in the prices for the online music store would tend to reduce the sales of its music player.

In addition, the number of users of one product may increase the value of the other product; that is, there may be indirect network effects, or positive feedback effects, between the two products.[37] Video game console makers, for example, sell video game consoles to consumers and license game makers. An increase in the game royalties would tend to reduce the supply of games, and increase their prices, and thereby reduce the demand for the consoles.

---

[36]   In the simple framework we used these would be included in *z*, the group of other products that are the sources of competitive constraints.

[37]   See Michael L. Katz and Carl Shapiro, *Systems Competition and Network Effects*, 8 J. Econ. Perspectives 93 (1994).

Many firms operate multisided platforms (what are sometimes called 'two-sided markets') which depend on getting multiple groups of interdependent customers together in some way.[38] An increase in the price to one group of customers will typically reduce the value to the other group of customers. That was the case with video consoles. It is also the case with advertising-supported media. An increase in the effective price to readers (which adjusts for the value of the content they are receiving) would reduce the revenue that the media business would obtain from advertisers.

In common for all these cases is that an increase in the price of one product results directly or indirectly in the reduction of revenue. Those possible reductions therefore impose a competitive constraint in the sense that they reduce the incentive to increase price.

5   Other competitive constraints

There are many reasons why firms may face greater or lesser constraints on their pricing ability. The ones listed above are not meant to be exhaustive. To take one example, the government may factor into the firm's calculations. A firm may be able to rely on government regulations that make it more difficult for firms to challenge it. That was historically the case in the telecommunications industry in the United States and many other countries. Such restrictions would factor into the analysis of entry. Alternatively, increases in price may spur the government to impose regulations that could limit a firm's profitability. An increase in price might result in demands for legislation. But in any event it is these competitive constraints that are relevant for assessing the matter at hand.

C   Market Power

Antitrust analysis often uses the concept of market power to summarize the degree of competitive constraints that are faced by a firm.[39] According to Kaplow and Shapiro:[40]

> The concept of market power is fundamental to antitrust economics and to the law. Except for conduct subject to per se treatment, antitrust violations typically require the government or a private plaintiff to show that the defendant created, enhanced, or extended in time its market power. . . . the inquiry into market power is usually a threshold question; if sufficient market power is established, it is then asked whether the conduct in question – say, a horizontal merger

---

[38]   See Evans, *supra* note 8; David S. Evans and Richard Schmalensee, *Markets with Two-Sided Platforms*, in 1 Issues in Competition Law and Policy 667 (ABA Section of Antitrust Law ed., 2008), available at http://papers.ssrn.com/sol3/papers.cfm?abstract_id=1094820.

[39]   The US courts and antitrust authorities use market power in various ways. For the purposes of merger analysis the US Department of Justice and the Federal Trade Commission Horizontal Merger Guidelines define market power as 'the ability to maintain prices above competitive levels for a significant period of time'. Horizontal Merger Guidelines (2010), *supra* note 6, at 1. Under section 1 of the Sherman Act market power is defined as concerted refusal to deal. See NW Wholesale Stationers v. Pac. Stationery, 472 U.S. 284, (1985). Under section 2 of the Sherman Act monopoly power is defined as the 'power to control prices or exclude competition'. See United States v. du Pont (Cellophane), 351 United States 377, 391 (1956). Monopoly power requires substantial market power. See Motta, *supra* note 21, at 39.

[40]   See Louis Kaplow and Carl Shapiro, *Antitrust* 2 (Harvard Law and Economics Discussion Paper No. 575, 2007) available at http://papers.ssrn.com/sol3/papers.cfm?abstract_id=961264&download=yes.

or an alleged act of monopolization – constitutes an antitrust violation. If sufficient market power is not demonstrated, the inquiry terminates with a victory for the defendant.

Unfortunately, market power is a poorly defined concept in antitrust law and economics.[41] Its use can obscure the role of competitive constraints that are relevant for the analysis. These problems are accentuated by the delineation of hard market boundaries and the calculation of market shares.

Market power is generally defined by economists as the ability of a firm to charge a price that exceeds the competitive level. In practice, the competitive level is usually defined as the price that equals marginal cost. For example, in the textbook model of perfect competition, firms are price takers and produce at the point where the market price just equals their marginal cost of production. It is widely recognized that virtually all firms charge prices in excess of marginal cost even though they operate in industries that seem quite competitive. Therefore most discussions of market power refer to 'significant market power'.

The Lerner Index is a commonly used measure of market power especially in the analysis of mergers. Profit-maximizing firms set price and output so that marginal revenue equals marginal cost. Under certain assumptions that apply in simple markets[42] that profit-maximizing condition results in the standard Lerner Index:

$$(4) \qquad m_x = \frac{p_x - c_x}{p_x} = \frac{1}{e_x}$$

where c_x is marginal cost. The left-hand side is a measure of profitability: the profit margin as a percent of price. This measure of profitability is inversely related to the firm's elasticity of demand which reflects all factors including competitive responses that would result in a loss of sales.[43] A firm realizes a smaller margin when it has a larger elasticity of demand. This formula captures the notion of demand-side substitutes discussed above. When consumers can readily switch to one or more alternatives as price increases (as shown in equation (3)) the firm faces greater limitations on increasing its price.

The fundamental problem with the economic treatments of market power is that these treatments attempt to replace the analysis of competitive constraints with metrics that are sometimes subject to serious measurement or conceptual problems. Consider the Lerner Index. The analyst needs to measure marginal cost, which can be difficult to do as we discuss in some detail below. Furthermore, once the analyst has calculated the Lerner

---

[41]   See EINER ELHAUGE AND DAMIEN GERADIN, GLOBAL COMPETITION LAW AND ECONOMICS 257–68 (Hart Publishing, 2007) for discussion.

[42]   The result that the price–cost margin is inversely proportional to the own-price elasticity of demand assumes, among other things, that there are no complementary products and indirect network efforts and that there are no strategic considerations such as entry concerns that would lead a firm to reduce the margin. Therefore one must be cautious about inferring the own-price elasticity of demand from the observed price–cost margin or from estimating the price–cost margin from estimates of the own-price elasticity of demand. As we will discuss below, there are empirical issues concerning how costs are measured.

[43]   This is generally called the 'residual demand elasticity'. See Jonathan B. Baker and David Reitman, Chapter 2.

Index it is not possible to infer that the observed margin reflects a significant departure from competition without a further inquiry into the margins that are necessary for the firm to recover its fixed costs.[44] Alternatively, consider determining whether the firm's prices exceed the level that would enable the firm to recover its risky investments and cover its fixed costs. In practice, these calculations are subject to a number of difficulties. For example, the level of risk that entrepreneurs and investors faced in making investments in an industry are generally unknown. In principle one could infer that risk from examining the failure rate of entrants and their investments but such data are seldom available.[45]

There are also conceptual problems. The measures of market power that are based on deviations from a hypothetical competitive level may not be useful for the purpose for which they are intended. On the one hand, a firm may have the ability and incentive to exclude a more efficient rival even though it is earning a competitive rate of return after adjusting for fixed costs or after adjusting for risky investments as well as fixed costs. By excluding the rival it prevents a decline in its profits; it is immaterial that its profits are currently at the competitive level. On the other hand, a firm may lack the ability and incentive to exclude a more efficient rival even though it is charging a price that is considerably higher than marginal cost. If the rival also has to charge a high price to recover its fixed costs, its entry may not reduce the market price much; or it may be so easy to enter the industry that it is implausible that the firm could prevent competitive entry.

This brings us back to competitive constraints. Most antitrust matters ultimately hinge on the nature and degree of the competitive constraints that the firm faces. Market power can be used as shorthand to summarize these competitive constraints. Investigating market power therefore requires examining all of the constraints mentioned above and assessing their significance for the matter at hand. Metrics such as price–cost margins and measures of risk-adjusted rates of return can provide further information on the importance of these constraints but must be used carefully.

Antitrust runs the greatest risk of error when it places too much weight on a single indicator of competitive constraints. We have already seen that with respect to the various measures of market power used by economists and the courts. They may provide relatively limited information on whether firms have the ability or incentive to engage in practices that cause consumer harm. Analysts can also make mistakes by focusing

---

[44]   For example, in an industry in which firms incur fixed costs to operate, and average variable costs are not increasing, it is not possible for firms to maintain long-run viability if they charge a price equal to marginal cost. Kaplow and Shapiro show in the simple case of linear demand and constant average variable costs that the firm's price–cost margin would have to equal the ratio of the firm's fixed cost to its revenue for the firm to break even. Thus, if fixed costs were 20% of annual revenue the firm would have to earn a margin of 20%. See Kaplow and Shapiro, *supra* note 40. The importance of fixed costs depends on the time horizon considered. In the very long run all costs are variable. The price–cost margin is a more reliable indicator of market power when long-run marginal costs are considered and these costs include a return on risk-taking.

[45]   One can also estimate market power by examining the extent to which a firm's rate of return exceeds the risk-adjusted competitive rate of return. There are various measurement issues for rates of return as well. See Franklin M. Fisher and John J. McGowan, *On the Misuse of Accounting Rates of Return to Infer Monopoly Profits*, 73 Am. Econ. Rev. 82 (1983) for the classic treatment of this.

narrowly on one factor such as demand substitutability. The 'cellophane fallacy' is the classic example of this.[46] Starting from the competitive level a firm with market power will raise its price until so many consumers would switch to other products that a further price increase would be unprofitable.[47] Thus, a firm with significant market power would continue raising its price until at the margin some consumers would find other products substitutable. The fact that consumers have substitutes to which to turn – parchment paper instead of cellophane – does not necessarily mean that the firm lacks market power.

D Market Power, Market Definition, and Market Shares

Antitrust analysts can guard against these mistakes by focusing on the broad range of competitive constraints that are relevant to analysing the matter at hand. The courts have, however, tended to infer the existence of market power primarily from market shares. To do this they first define a market, as we discuss in the next section. They infer the magnitude of market power from the share of this market possessed by the firm. They then decide whether these shares are large enough, and presumably indicate large enough market power, to trigger further analysis. Judge Learned Hand famously observed that for determining whether a firm had monopoly power 33% was not enough, 60% was doubtful, and 90% was sufficient.[48] For tying cases the Supreme Court decided that a 30% share was not enough for a per se tying prohibition.[49]

The economic literature provides no support for any of these bright-line tests, either as a matter of theory or of empirical fact. Nor, more generally, does the literature find that market shares are reliable predictors of the magnitude of competitive constraints.[50] As noted earlier, most firms try to make their products different from rivals. In this case economic models generally find no systematic relationship between market shares and measures of market power.[51] In addition, dynamic models of competition find that high market shares can result from more efficient and innovative firms gaining more

---

[46] See Morris A. Adelman, *Economic Aspects of the Bethlehem Option*, 45 VA. L. REV. 684 (1959); Gregory J. Werden, *The 1982 Merger Guidelines and the Ascent of the Hypothetical Monopolist Paradigm*, 71 ANTITRUST L.J. 253 (2003); ANTITRUST LAW, *supra* note 1, at 241–6.

[47] Technically, with positive marginal costs a firm that faces a downward sloping demand schedule and therefore has pricing discretion will always set price at a point on that demand schedule at which the absolute value of own-price elasticity of demand is greater than 1.0 (i.e. demand is 'elastic' so that a 1% increase in price leads to a more than 1% decrease in the quantity demanded).

[48] *United States v. Aluminum Co. of America*, *supra* note 2, at 424. (The percentage we have already mentioned – 90% – results only if we both include all 'Alcoa's' production and exclude 'secondary'. That percentage is enough to constitute a monopoly; it is doubtful whether 60 or 64% would be enough; and certainly 33% is not. Hence it is necessary to settle what he will treat as competing in the ingot market.)

[49] Jefferson Parish Hosp. Dist. v. Hyde, 466 U.S. 2, 7 (1984).

[50] See KEITH N. HYLTON, ANTITRUST LAW: ECONOMIC THEORY AND COMMON LAW EVOLUTION 243 (Cambridge University Press, 2003) ('market share by itself says very little about the degree of market power possessed by a firm') and Richard Schmalensee, *Studies of Structure and Performance*, in 2 HANDBOOK OF INDUSTRIAL ORGANIZATION 984–5 (Richard Schmalensee and Robert Willig eds, 1989).

[51] See Werden and Froeb, *supra* note 34, and Baker and Reitman, *supra* note 43.

customers.[52] Most importantly, there is no basis in economics for inferring anything about the degree of competitive constraints from precise share figures, as some courts have done. Nor is there any basis for concluding that a single critical market share figure could be applied to all market situations.[53] Market share cannot be used like a thermometer based on universal laws on when water freezes or boils.

The current practice of market definition provides a limited and distorted view of competitive constraints. It largely focuses primarily on demand-side substitutes which, while important, are only one source of competitive constraints.[54] It draws a hard boundary between products for consideration as substitutes even when there is no economic basis for concluding that a particular product should be classified as in or out. It then uses this boundary to calculate market shares which may provide a limited basis for assessing competitive effects. Although courts and authorities consider other sources of competitive constraints, *the* market and its associated shares tend to weigh most heavily in the analysis.

IV   MARKET DEFINITION

When the courts first started looking at antitrust cases they naturally began using the term 'market'. In 1898, Justice Peckham concluded that there was a broad market for selling cattle and rejected a much narrower definition by the plaintiffs.[55] The focus on market shares seems to have begun with Learned Hand's opinion in *Alcoa* in 1945. He concluded that a firm had to have a high enough share of the market to be a monopolist. To determine if it reached that threshold it was therefore necessary to determine which products were in the market.[56] Over time that approach evolved into the practice of making the definition of hard market boundaries and the calculation of market shares the first step in antitrust analysis.

---

[52] See, e.g., F. MICHAEL SCHERER, INDUSTRIAL MARKET STRUCTURE AND ECONOMIC PERFORMANCE 288–92 (Houghton Mifflin Company, 1980); Richard Blundell, Rachel Griffith and John Van Reenen, *Market Share, Market Value and Innovation in a Panel of British Manufacturing Firms*, 66 REV. ECON. STUDIES 529 (1999); Zoltan J. Acs and David B. Audretsch, *Innovation, Market Structure, and Firm Size*, 69 REV. ECON. AND STAT. 567 (1987).

[53] There is an extensive empirical literature in economics, largely conducted from the early 1950s to the early 1980s, that attempted to examine whether there was a systematic relationship between measures of firm profitability and the degree of industry concentration. That literature finds that manufacturing industries with higher concentration tended to be more profitable. However, there are many possible reasons for that and the literature did not reach robust conclusions on the extent to which those industries were more profitable because the leading firms in those industries were more efficient, as opposed to being more profitable because they faced fewer competitive constraints. Moreover, this literature does not provide a basis for making any precise predictions about the relationship between market shares and market power. See CARLTON AND PERLOFF, *supra* note 16, at 259–67; SCHERER, *supra* note 52, at 288–92 and Schmalensee, *supra* note 50, at 984–5.

[54] The US Merger Guidelines only consider demand-side substitutability in defining the market. See US Dep't of Justice and Fed. Trade Comm'n, Horizontal Merger Guidelines (1997) available at www.justice.gov/atr/public/guidelines/horiz_book/hmg1.html.

[55] A search of the keywords 'market' and 'Sherman' finds that the first reference to 'market' in a Sherman Act case was in 1898.

[56] See *United States v. Aluminum Co. of America, supra* note 2.

Market shares are a handy way of summarizing data about an industry. They tell us something about the relative importance of different firms and something about the structure of competition. Looking at market shares is a perfectly sensible thing to do as part of the overall analysis of competitive constraints facing a firm. The consideration of market shares has led, however, to two unfortunate developments. One of these has been the tendency to use market shares as stand-alone metrics for assessing the degree of market power and establishing flash points to identify significant market power or monopoly power. As noted above, there is no basis in economic theory or empirical evidence that could support this 'market share as thermometer' approach as a general matter.[57]

The other, which results from the desire to use market shares to infer market power, is the focus on identifying the denominator for calculating market shares. That has led to market definition becoming a central focus in antitrust cases and one that can determine the outcome. As Jonathan Baker has observed:

> throughout the history of U.S. antitrust litigation, the outcome of more cases has surely turned on market definition than any other substantive issue. Market definition is often the most critical step in evaluating market power and determining whether business conduct has or likely will have anticompetitive effects.[58]

This section surveys the state of the current approaches to market definition.[59]

A   Market Definition in the Courts

The courts have tried to define markets primarily by focusing on demand and to a lesser extent supply substitutability.[60] On the demand side, one line of attack examines whether products are interchangeable in the sense that they are functionally equivalent from the standpoint of the consumer. Another approach involves looking at the cross-price elasticities of demand among various products. These are ways of assessing whether consumers have other alternatives to which they could switch. On the supply side, the courts consider whether firms that are producing dissimilar products would switch production to compete if prices increased above the competitive level.[61]

---

[57]   In an industry with homogeneous products a small market share indicates the lack of market power.

[58]   See Jonathan B. Baker, *Market Definition: An Analytical Overview*, 74 ANTITRUST L.J. 129. Robert Pitofsky observes, 'Knowledgeable antitrust practitioners have long known that the most important single issue in most enforcement actions – because so much depends on it – is market definition'. See Pitofsky, *supra* note 3.

[59]   For comprehensive discussions of market definition see Baker, *supra* note 58; Jonathan B. Baker and Timothy F. Bresnahan, *Economic Evidence in Antitrust: Defining Markets and Measuring Market Power* (Stanford Law and Economics Olin Working Paper No. 328, 2006), available at http://ssrn.com/abstract=931225.

[60]   See ANTITRUST LAW, *supra* note 1, at 184.

[61]   Starting with the *Brown Shoe* decision, *infra* note 79, the courts have considered the possibility of a broad market that has submarkets that should be treated as distinct markets for antitrust purposes. These would be situations in which a particular group of customers would have difficulty switching to an alternative or where a firm could engage in price discrimination with respect to that group of customers. A number of Antitrust Law and economics scholars have argued against this

The degree of interchangeability, the cross-price elasticities of demand, and the elasticities of supply are all continuous variables. The courts, however, make binary decisions on whether particular products, alternative suppliers, or geographic locations should be considered as either 'in' the market or 'out of' the market. The capacity that is 'in' the market is then used as the denominator for calculating market shares.

The analysis of market power is built off of this edifice. First, the court calculates market shares, which provide a reading on the market share thermometer for assessing whether the firm has significant market power or monopoly power under the relevant case law. Second, the market delineation largely determines the set of competitive constraints that the court will consider in examining the possibility that the practice at issue will harm consumers. Demand and supply substitutes that are excluded at the market definition stage are not considered in further analyses. The courts do, however, consider whether the prospect of entry into the market will temper the market power that might otherwise be inferred from the shares.

B   Hypothetical Monopolist Test

The US Department of Justice introduced a different approach for establishing market boundaries in its 1982 Merger Guidelines.[62] After some slight changes in language the Guidelines say:[63]

> A market is defined as a product or group of products and a geographic area in which it is produced or sold such that a hypothetical profit-maximizing firm, not subject to price regulation, that was the only present and future producer or seller of those products in that area likely would impose at least a 'small but significant and nontransitory' increase in price, assuming the terms of sale of all other products are held constant.

This has become known as the 'hypothetical monopolist test' or the SSNIP test. Small but significant is generally taken to mean at least 5%.[64]

---

approach which has lost favor in the courts. See ANTITRUST LAW, *supra* note 1, at 185; ELHAUGE AND GERADIN, *supra* note 41. Judge Brown's opinion for the DC Circuit in *Whole Foods* resurrected the concept in overturning a lower court decision to deny the FTC's motion for a preliminary injunction to enjoin the Whole Foods acquisition of organic supermarket competitor Wild Oats. *FTC v. Whole Foods Mkt., supra* note 7.

[62]   US Dep't of Justice, Merger Guidelines (1982) available at www.justice.gov/atr/hmerger/11248.pdf.

[63]   US Dep't of Justice and Fed. Trade Comm'n, Horizontal Merger Guidelines 4 (1992) available at www.justice.gov/atr/public/guidelines/hmg.pdf.

[64]   The market obtained from the hypothetical monopolist test depends on the benchmark for assessing the price increase. For merger analysis the increase in price is ordinarily taken relative to prevailing prices at the time of a merger. The argument for doing so is that the purpose of market definition is to help determine whether the merger would result in an increase in price. Therefore even if a product would not constrain a competitive firm from increasing its price it may constrain firms that have already increased price and therefore pushed customers to consider more distant substitutes. See Gregory J. Werden, *Market Delineation and the Justice Department's Merger Guidelines*, DUKE L.J. 514 (1983). For monopolization cases, there is an argument for using the competitive price as the benchmark. Otherwise one would commit the cellophane fallacy of concluding that a monopolist faces competition because it has raised price so high that consumers

The test provides some rigor to the decision on where to draw the market boundary. The idea is that if the hypothetical profit-maximizing firm in the definition could not raise price much then there must be demand substitutes that constrain it. If it attempted to raise price by a small but significant amount its profits would fall because too many customers would desert it. As the hypothetical firm takes over more demand substitutes it eventually reaches the point at which it can impose a small but significant price increase because there are no longer enough demand substitutes, not under its control, to which consumers could turn. The SSNIP test draws a hard market boundary at this level. The products beyond the boundary are individually and collectively weak substitutes in the sense that their presence would not constrain the hypothetical firm from increasing prices.

The introduction of the SSNIP test has led to a technical literature by economists on how to implement it, along with a vibrant literature by antitrust law and economics scholars on the reliability of various approaches.[65] Critical loss analysis is the most popular technique for implementing the SSNIP test.[66] For the conjectured hypothetical monopolist the analyst calculates the loss of sales that would result in a 5% price increase having no net effect on profits. This *critical loss* can be calculated based on information of the profit margin for the hypothetical firm.

$$(5) \qquad L_x = \frac{g}{g + m_x}$$

where g is the small but significant price increase considered (for example, g=.05 or 5%) and m_x is the price–cost margin from equation (4).

If the *actual loss* of sales that would result based on a consideration of demand-side substitution would exceed this then that price increase would be unprofitable. The actual loss can be calculated based on information concerning the residual demand elasticity, cross-price elasticities of demand, or proxies for this based on estimates of the diversion of sales to alternative producers. For example, suppose it was possible to observe the portion of sales D_{xy} that would be diverted to the target of the acquisition. Then Katz and Shapiro show that the actual loss would be:[67]

$$(6) \qquad A_x = (1 - D_{xy}) \times \frac{g}{m_x}$$

where D_{xy} is the fraction of sales lost by firm A for product x to firm B's product y.

If the actual loss exceeds the critical loss then the market would be expanded because there must be demand substitutes not under the control of the hypothetical firm. If the actual loss is less than the critical loss then that price increase would be profitable. The analyst would conclude that the market must be at least as narrow as what has been considered for the

would consider highly inferior substitutes at the margin. See CARLTON AND PERLOFF, *supra* note 16, at 646–7.

[65] For a summary see Kaplow and Shapiro, *supra* note 40.

[66] See Barry C. Harris and Joseph J. Simons, *Focusing Market Definition: How Much Substitution is Necessary*, 12 RES. L. AND ECON. 207 (1989); Katz and Shapiro, *supra* note 27.

[67] Katz and Shapiro, *supra* note 27, at 56.

hypothetical monopolist. In theory the analyst begins with the products at issue and then expands the market out until actual loss just falls short of critical loss. Under the Merger Guidelines the market is defined entirely by reference to demand substitutability.[68] Firms that would supply output to this market in response to a 5% price increase are then included.

While the hypothetical monopoly test was viewed as a significant methodological advance when it was introduced in 1982, the antitrust profession has become less enamored with it over time.[69] To implement the hypothetical monopoly test it is necessary to construct a firm consisting of multiple products and measure the profit margin of that firm as well as substitution from all of the products for that firm to all of the other products that have not been consolidated into the hypothetical firm. In practice it is difficult enough to obtain accurate measures of these parameters for a single firm. Obtaining them for many firms and simulating the behavior of the hypothetical firm is a challenge. The outcome of the hypothetical monopolist test – that is, the location of the market boundary – depends on the order in which additional products are added to the hypothetical firm.

The other reason economists and competition authorities have become less enchanted with the hypothetical monopolist test for mergers is that, if there is enough information to determine the market under the SSNIP test, there is almost surely enough information to determine directly whether the merger will, within the framework of the simple economic model behind the test, result in a unilateral increase in the prices charged by the firm that has been created through the merger. We turn to this next.

C   Going Right to Effects

Courts and antitrust authorities use market definition as a screen for focusing resources on cases in which it is plausible that the practices in question could harm consumers. They define a market, calculate shares, and infer the degree of market power from these shares. If a firm lacks market power in a monopolization case or if merged firms would lack market power then there is no need to invest further resources in evaluating the effects of the practice on consumers. But suppose the courts and antitrust authorities had readily at their disposal all of the information necessary for evaluating effects. In that case it would not, one could argue, make any sense to expend effort on market delineation and assessing market power. In principle it would be possible to spend fewer resources (by eliminating the market definition inquiry and just looking at effects) and to make fewer mistakes (since the screen will necessarily result in some false negatives that would lead to stopping the inquiry into effects too soon).[70]

At least in the merger context it became apparent to the antitrust authorities that this was precisely the situation they were in. Once they have collected the information necessary for conducting the SSNIP they have enough information for assessing the unilateral effects of the merger on price. For example, suppose the authority has collected information on the price–cost margins for the merging parties and evidence on the diversion of sales

---

[68]   See Horizontal Merger Guidelines (1992), *supra* note 63.
[69]   For a recent discussion by two authors who have contributed some of the key technical papers see Farrell and Shapiro, *supra* note 5.
[70]   For an earlier discussion of this point see FISHER, MCGOWAN AND GREENWOOD, *supra* note 5.

between the acquiring firm and the target; this is all data it would need for a SSNIP test of market definition. In the case of linear demand the predicted effect on price would be:[71]

$$(7) \qquad \frac{dp_x}{p_x} = \frac{m_x D_{xy}}{2(1 - D_{xy})}$$

There may be other situations in which the authorities have direct evidence on the likely effects of a merger. In *Staples*, the Federal Trade Commission was able to compare local areas in which Staples and Office Depot both operated with ones in which only one operated.[72] They found that areas in which only one store operated had higher prices than where two stores operated. From this they inferred that the merger would reduce prices significantly.

As a result, the US Department of Justice and the Federal Trade Commission have de-emphasized market definition.[73] In their joint Commentary on the Guidelines they argued that 'market definition is not isolated from the other analytic components in the Guidelines. The Agencies do not settle on a relevant market definition before proceeding to address other issues'. In effect they allow for the possibility that they will analyse the competitive effects of the merger first and then construct a market in which those competitive effects would occur.

The chief economists of the US DOJ and the FTC have gone further in a paper they wrote shortly before assuming their current positions.[74] Farrell and Shapiro argue against relying on binary market definition and the use of concentration measures for evaluating mergers. As an alternative screening device they propose a measure (based largely on the same economic considerations that underlie the critical loss test and diversion ratios) of whether the contemplated merger would place an upward pressure on price. In the case where the merging firms are symmetric one version of the formula is:

$$(8) \qquad D_{xy} m_x - E_x (1 - m_x) > 0$$

where E_x is the fraction by which marginal cost would decline as a result of the merger. Symmetry means that the margins, diversion ratios, and efficiencies are the same for both merging firms. The left-hand side is a measure of the 'upward pricing pressure' from the merger. Under their approach the agency would adopt a default assumption concerning the likely efficiencies resulting from mergers; as an example, they use 10% in their paper. As a practical device this approach results in screening mergers based on diversion ratios and margins. The agency invests resources in investigating the merger further only if these

---

[71]   See Kaplow and Shapiro, *supra* note 40, at 10.

[72]   FTC v. Staples, 970 F. Supp. 1066 (D.D.C. 1997).

[73]   See William Baer and Deborah Feinstein, *Changing Emphasis: How Whole Foods Advances the FTC's Efforts to Transform Merger Litigation*, GLOBAL COMPETITION POL'Y (1 September 2008) at 9.

[74]   See Joseph Farrell and Carl Shapiro, *Antitrust Evaluation of Horizontal Mergers: An Economic Alternative to Market Definition* (UC Berkeley, Competition Policy Center, Institute of Business and Economic Research, 2008) available at http://escholarship.org/uc/item/8z51b1q8; Farrell and Shapiro, *supra* note 5.

are 'high enough' based on whatever default efficiency level is assumed by the agency. For example, with a diversion ratio of .4, a margin of .5, and efficiency of .1 the left-hand side is .15 and therefore the agency would consider the merger further; if on the other hand the diversion ratio was .2 and the margin was .3, the left-hand side would be −.01 and the merger would not be considered further.

D   Standoff with the Courts

The US DOJ and the FTC have made several attempts to downplay market definition and focus mainly on competitive effects.[75] The *Whole Foods* case provides a good indication of where economists, the authorities, and the courts stand on market definition in the case of mergers. Whole Foods wanted to buy Wild Oats. They are both premium natural organic supermarkets. They sell the similar array of products as traditional supermarkets but, in some cases, sell a natural organic variant in place of usual products. The FTC concluded that the merger would result in raising prices largely because the two stores were closer competitors to each other than they were to other supermarkets. The FTC submitted evidence that Whole Foods lost more to Wild Oats than did supermarkets when a Wild Oats entered, and econometric evidence that Whole Foods earned higher margins in markets in which it did not face competition from Wild Oats. It became apparent on appeal that the FTC believed that market definition was at best a distraction from its findings on competitive effects.

The FTC sought a preliminary injunction. At the lower court level market definition was the determinative issue. As the District Court judge observed:[76]

> [If] the relevant product market is, as the FTC alleges, a product market of 'premium natural and organic supermarkets' consisting only of the two defendants and two other non-national firms, there can be little doubt that the acquisition of the second largest firm in the market by the largest firm in the market will tend to harm competition in that market. If, on the other hand, the defendants are merely differentiated firms operating within the larger relevant product market of 'supermarkets', the proposed merger will not tend to harm competition.

The judge found the consumers could readily turn to other supermarkets in the face of a price increase by the premium natural organic supermarkets. As a result he defined a market that consisted of all supermarkets and denied the preliminary injunction.

The FTC appealed. One of its grounds was that the lower court had erred in making market definition a threshold question. In a split 2–1 decision, the DC Circuit first took the FTC to task for advancing this claim.[77] According to Judge Brown:[78]

> Inexplicably, the FTC now asserts a market definition is not necessary in a § 7 case, Appellant's Br. 37–38, in contravention of the statute itself, see 15 U.S.C. § 18 (barring an acquisition 'where in any line of commerce . . . the effect of such acquisition may be substantially to lessen com-

---

[75]   See Horizontal Merger Guidelines (2010), *supra* note 6, at 12–14.

[76]   FTC v. Whole Foods Mkt., Inc., 502 F. Supp. 2d 1, 8 (D.D.C. 2007).

[77]   The opinion of the court was delivered by Judge Brown. Judge Tatel delivered an opinion that concurred that the district court erred and Judge Kavanaugh a dissenting one.

[78]   *FTC v. Whole Foods Mkt.*, *supra* note 7, at 875.

petition') . . . The FTC suggests 'market definition . . . is a means to an end – to enable some measurement of market power – not an end in itself'. Appellant's Br. 38 n.26. But measuring market power is not the only purpose of a market definition; only 'examination of the particular market – its structure, history[,] and probable future – can provide the appropriate setting for judging the probable anticompetitive effect of the merger'. *Brown Shoe*, 370 U.S. at 322 n.38.

The DC Circuit then examined the lower court's analysis of market definition. The two judges in the majority argued that the lower court had not adequately considered the possibility of a submarket of consumers who did not see regular supermarkets as possible substitutes for premium natural organic supermarkets. According to Judge Brown:

> In sum, the district court believed the antitrust laws are addressed only to marginal consumers. This was an error of law, because in some situations core consumers, demanding exclusively a particular product or package of products, distinguish a submarket. The FTC described the core PNOS customers, explained how PNOS cater to these customers, and showed these customers provided the bulk of PNOS' business. The FTC put forward economic evidence – which the district court ignored – showing directly how PNOS discriminate on price between their core and marginal customers, thus treating the former as a distinct market.

Both he and Judge Tatel endorsed the submarket approach from *Brown Shoe*.[79]

Despite the FTC's desire to focus on competitive effects, market definition became the central focus of the *Whole Foods* case as it wound its way through the courts. The district court said as much, as did Judge Tatel, who concurred in the decision of the DC Circuit.[80] The courts felt they had to choose between two extremes: either the regular supermarkets competed so much with the premium natural organic supermarkets that they were essentially interchangeable and therefore in the same market; or the premium natural organic supermarkets were not interchangeable for some set of customers and therefore in different markets than the regular supermarkets. The courts could not consider the possibility the regular supermarkets and the premium natural organic supermarkets were imperfect substitutes and examine whether the regular supermarkets would, or would not, provide a sufficient competitive constraint. More importantly, the analysis of market definition was ill-suited to helping assess the competitive effects of the proposed merger. As Farrell and Shapiro note:[81]

> Whether or not the merger between Whole Foods and Wild Oats was anticompetitive, the market definition inquiry addressed that question at best indirectly. Only clumsily could it ask how strongly Whole Foods and Wild Oats were differentiated from traditional supermarkets. To this key question, it was open to only two answers: either they are so strongly differentiated that they are (almost) their own separate market, making it a merger (almost) to monopoly, or they are so weakly differentiated that one should treat them as two rather small players among all supermarkets. Neither answer seems a good way of expressing substantial-but-not-overwhelming product differentiation.

---

[79]   Brown Shoe Co., Inc. v. United States, 370 U.S. 294 (1962).

[80]   'I agree with the district court that this "case hinges"– almost entirely – "on the proper definition of the relevant product market"', for if a separate natural and organic market exists, 'there can be little doubt that the acquisition of the second largest firm in the market by the largest firm in the market will tend to harm competition in that market.' *FTC v. Whole Foods Mkt.*, *supra* note 7, at 883.

[81]   Farrell and Shapiro, *supra* note 74.

V   MARKET DEFINITION, ERROR COSTS, AND THE CURSE OF FALSE PRECISION

Market definition would not be so important if it were not so important. Any analysis of business practices has to start with an understanding of the competitive landscape. That is largely what market definition is all about. The battle over the contours of the landscape, however, often determines who wins the war. The reason is simple. Courts use market definition to calculate market-share 'tests'. Defendants who convince the courts to load more substitutes into the market sail smoothly into a safe harbor by making their shares small. Plaintiffs who convince the courts to exclude more things get the wind behind their sails for the race to the finish line: they establish market power and remove from consideration potential competitive constraints that could affect the analysis of competitive effects. As we saw above, Whole Foods can consummate its merger if the courts are convinced to look at a landscape that includes all supermarkets while the FTC can block the merger if the courts look only at Whole Foods and Wild Oats.

This section looks at the accuracy of market definition and the costs that ensue when the courts get the boundaries wrong. The Supreme Court has recognized the importance of error costs in several landmark antitrust decisions and has modified judicial rules as a result of finding that they were likely to result in costly mistakes.[82] In subsection A we introduce the error-cost framework and apply it to market definition. Then, in subsection B, we consider the error risks for the traditional approach taken by the courts to market definition and market power, which focuses heavily on the interchangeability of products and the use of market shares. We turn in subsection C to the prospects of errors for the hypothetical monopoly test and its various empirical implementations. Our conclusion is that using market definition analyses to draw hard boundaries and to infer market power from shares based on those boundaries results in significant and unnecessary error in antitrust analysis.

A   Error Costs

The error-cost framework has become the backbone of American antitrust analysis. It recognizes that when imperfect human beings base decisions on imperfect information they make mistakes and that those mistakes have costs. There is no way to avoid errors. But we can devise rules that help us make the decisions that maximize our wellbeing net of the costs of making mistakes. In developing these rules we need to take the likelihood and cost of errors into account. False positives result when a rule, or test, finds that the subject has the condition when in fact they do not. False negatives result when a test finds that the subject does not have the condition when in fact they do. Both errors lead to costs. Judge Richard Posner first applied error-cost analysis, which is based on decision theory,

---

[82]   See Matsushita Electric Industrial Co, Ltd v Zenith Radio Corp, 475 U.S. 574 (1986); Brooke Group Ltd. v. Brown & Williamson Tobacco Corp., 509 U.S. 209 (1993); Verizon Communications Inc. v. Law Offices of Curtis V. Trinko, LLP, 540 U.S. 398, 407 (2004); and Pac. Bell Tel. Co. v. LinkLine Commun's., Inc., 129 S. Ct. 1109 (U.S. 2009).

to the law in 1973.[83] Judge Easterbrook pioneered its application to antitrust rule-making in his classic article on predatory pricing.[84]

The Supreme Court hinted at the error-cost framework in dismissing the predatory pricing claims against 21 Japanese companies. It noted 'mistaken inferences in cases such as this one are especially costly, because they chill the very conduct the antitrust laws are designed to protect'.[85] In *Brooke Group* the Court placed it conclusions in *Matsushita* more explicitly in the error-cost framework:[86]

> As we have said in the Sherman Act context, 'predatory pricing schemes are rarely tried, and even more rarely successful', *Matsushita, supra*, at 589, and the costs of an erroneous finding of liability are high. '[T]he mechanism by which a firm engages in predatory pricing – lowering prices – is the same mechanism by which a firm stimulates competition; because "cutting prices in order to increase business often is the very essence of competition . . . [;] mistaken inferences . . . are especially costly, because they chill the very conduct the antitrust laws are designed to protect"'. *Cargill, supra*, at 122, n. 17 (quoting *Matsushita, supra*, at 594). It would be ironic indeed if the standards for predatory pricing liability were so low that antitrust suits themselves became a tool for keeping prices high.

In *Brooke Group* the Court required that plaintiffs establish the likelihood that the defendant would recoup allegedly predatory losses. This rule change made it less likely that courts would wrongly condemn procompetitive low pricing. Other decisions have followed this approach.[87]

The Supreme Court has invoked the error-cost framework mainly to limit 'false positives' in which defendants lose even though their actions are procompetitive. The framework itself does not require that result.[88] When anticompetitive actions are frequent, false positives uncommon and cheap, and false negatives are infrequent or expensive, the error-cost framework implies that businesses should face very high hurdles for defending those actions.[89] Hard-core horizontal price-fixing is per se unlawful because the courts believe the benefits are seldom large and the cost of allowing price-fixing is significant.[90] If the courts developed more accurate tests of anticompetitive behavior, perhaps because of advances in economics, or if businesses developed more egregious or hard-to-detect

---

[83]   See Richard A. Posner, *An Economic Approach to Legal Procedure and Judicial Administration*, 2 J. Legal Studies 399 (1973).

[84]   See Frank H. Easterbrook, *The Limits of Antitrust*, 63 Tex. L. Rev. 1 (1984); Frank H. Easterbrook, *Predatory Strategies and Counterstrategies*, 48 U. Chi. L. Rev. 263 (1981).

[85]   *Matsushita Electric Industrial Co., Ltd v. Zenith Radio Corp.*, *supra* note 82, at 594.

[86]   See *Brooke Group Ltd. v. Brown & Williamson*, *supra* note 82, at 226.

[87]   See *Verizon Communications Inc v. Law Offices of Curtis V. Trinkoi*, *supra* note 82; *Pac. Bell Tel. Co. v. LinkLine Commun's.*, *supra* note 82; and Weyerhaeuser Co. v. Ross-Simmons Hardwood Lumber Co., 549 U.S. 312 (2007).

[88]   See David S. Evans, *Why Different Jurisdictions Do Not (and Should Not) Adopt the Same Antitrust Rules*, 10 Chi. J. Int'l L. 161 (2009) available at http://papers.ssrn.com/sol3/papers.cfm?abstract_id=1342797.

[89]   See David S. Evans, *Economics and the Design of Competition Law* in Issues in Competition Law and Policy (W. Dale Collins ed., 2008) available at http://papers.ssrn.com/sol3/papers.cfm?abstract_id=827465.

[90]   See Hylton, *supra* note 50, at 116.

methods for anticompetitive exclusion, the error-cost framework would imply that the courts should focus more on limiting false negatives. Academics whose views span the spectrum on the desirable vigor of antitrust enforcement advocate the application of the error-cost framework to analysing antitrust rules.[91] Jonathan Baker, for example, has argued for a stricter approach to monopolies because the failure to detect anticompetitive behavior by a monopolist can lead to reduced innovation and therefore significant welfare losses.[92]

Market definition can result in mistakes in the outcome of antitrust matters largely because it affects the information that is considered in subsequent steps of the analysis. The seriousness of the errors depends on the interaction between analyses of market definition, market power, and competitive effects. At the market definition stage the court decides whether a demand- or supply-side substitute is either in or out of the market. That could result in including a product that does not provide a significant competitive constraint, or excluding a product that does provide a significant competitive constraint.

The courts typically rely on market shares as one way, and sometimes the main way, to assess market power. Consider the finding that the market consists of products x, y, z_1 but not z_2. The market power of x is effectively measured by:

$$(9) \qquad S_x = \frac{q_x}{q_x + q_y + q_{z_1}}$$

The quantities could be measured by units sold or revenue earned.[93] Product z_2 has been excluded and therefore effectively receives a weight of 0 in the share calculation. The magnitude of the competitive constraint resulting from a product included in the market is measured through its inclusion in the denominator of the share for S_x. The inclusion of a product that is not a significant constraint inflates the denominator of the share measure for the product under consideration and thereby understates market power. The exclusion of a product that is a competitive constraint overstates market power by making the denominator too small.

There is a further potential source of error at this point. The share calculations are based on the assumption that quantity or revenue is a proxy for the competitive constraint that results from a substitute. That may not be the case. For example, product z_1 may have a larger share than product y but its customers may be less likely to switch to product x than would the customers of product y.[94] Although the courts may consider factors other than market share in considering market power, they do not consider demand substitutes that have been excluded at the market definition stage and they generally ignore demand

[91]   See, e.g., C. Frederick Beckner, III and Steven C. Salop, *Decision Theory and Antitrust Rules*, 67 ANTITRUST L.J. 41 (1999); David S. Evans and Jorge A. Padilla, *Designing Antitrust Rules for Assessing Unilateral Practices: A Neo-Chicago Approach*, 72 U. CHI. L. REV. 73 (2005) available at http://papers.ssrn.com/sol3/papers.cfm?abstract_id=580882.

[92]   Jonathan B. Baker, *Beyond Schumpeter vs. Arrow: How Antitrust Fosters Innovation*, 74 ANTITRUST L.J. 575 (2007) available at http://ssrn.com/abstract=962261.

[93]   Revenue is usually the preferable measure and has the merit that it implicitly takes some quality differences into account and in a very crude way adjusts for product differentiation.

[94]   The variation in within-market substitution is ordinarily ignored in traditional market definition analysis.

substitutes that have been included at the market definition stage. Thus, market definition can result in false positives (finding significant market power for a firm that lacks it) or false negatives (not finding significant market power for a firm that has it) at this stage. Both errors have material impacts on the results of the case. A false negative result leads to a win for the defendant and in some cases a false positive result almost guarantees a win for the plaintiff.

Mistakes in market definition also affect the analysis of competitive effects. When a substitute is excluded from the market the court usually does not consider it further in assessing the ability and incentive of the party under consideration to engage in a practice that is anticompetitive. Alternatively, by wrongly including a substitute the court may overstate the constraints that would limit a defendant, for example, from profitably excluding a rival. The next two parts of this section consider the extent to which major methods of market definition are likely to make mistakes.

B   Hard Boundaries and Market Shares in the Courts

The traditional approach to market definition lacks defining principles when it must deal with differentiated products. Products differ in their degrees of interchangeability and the magnitudes of the cross-elasticities of demand. Suppose the defendant proposes that product z_2 is a substitute for product x that is the main focus of the case. The jurisprudence has not developed any meaningful guidance for telling a judge, or a jury, the degree of interchangeability or cross-elasticity of demand that would warrant the inclusion of that candidate product in the market. That absence of guidance is reflected in the common decision by the parties to advocate wildly divergent positions.

We would therefore expect that the traditional approach would be quite prone to error. The battle may take place over extreme positions. Depending on which party is more persuasive, the court or the jury may include products that pose no competitive constraints in the market or exclude products that pose significant competitive constraints from the market. There is no apparent reason to expect that false positives or false negatives are more likely.

C   Hypothetical Monopolist Test

The hypothetical monopolist test was designed to provide guiding principles based on economics for market definition. It adopts an operational definition for deciding whether products provide strong enough competitive constraints to be included in the market. If product z_2 would prevent a hypothetical monopolist over x, y, and z_1 from raising its price by 5% or more that product must be a strong substitute; it should therefore be included in the market. If product z_2 would not prevent a monopolist over x, y, and z_1 from raising its price by 5% or more, then that product is not a serious competitive constraint; it should therefore be excluded. This algorithm can in principle lead the antitrust analyst to a market that includes all of the demand-side substitutes that are important.

This test was seen as a major methodological advance when it was introduced. Over time it has become apparent that it is hard to implement reliably and it tends to lead to markets that seem implausibly narrow, as we discuss below.

1   Empirical implementations of the hypothetical monopolist test

Critical loss analysis is the major method used in practice to implement the SSNIP test. To determine the critical loss it is only necessary to know the profit margin for the products in question. For the economic theory under which the critical loss test has been derived, that profit margin should reflect the incremental profit realized from the change in output over the time period contemplated by the test. The SSNIP test envisions a small increase in price, such as 5%. With a demand elasticity of 2.0 (which would imply a 50% profit margin based on the Lerner Index) a 5% change in price would result in a 10% change in output. The SSNIP test also envisions that the change in price would take place over a time period of about a year. As a result the estimated incremental profit margin for the purpose of the test should pertain to a small but significant (probably 10% or more) change in output over about a year.

Analysts often use the operating margin for a company's product to estimate the price–cost margin for the critical loss analysis. That operating margin generally equals the average difference between revenue and variable costs for the product. It therefore does not necessarily estimate the *incremental* margin except in the case where there are constant returns to scale.[95] It also does not necessarily estimate the *incremental* margin for a relatively large increase in output over a year. For a 10% change in output over a year, for example, we would expect that fixed costs such as marketing and advertising would change as well. It is possible to estimate the correct metric but in practice that may be difficult.

Conceptually, the critical loss analysis requires an estimate of the incremental price–cost margin for every product that is considered for the hypothetical monopolist test. Two problems arise. It is often difficult to obtain these data. The parties to a merger would not be able to obtain them in most cases. The authorities could but would have to identify and collect these data for all products to be considered and then estimate the correct incremental price–cost margin for each. It may be appropriate in some cases to assume that all firms have similar margins but in many cases, especially when the products are differentiated, there may be sound reasons to expect that the margins will differ across firms.

A significant problem in practice involves estimating actual loss. This calculation is often straightforward in the case of two firms. It is possible to estimate the actual loss from a small but significant price increase from diversion ratios for two products produced by the two firms. Company records on wins or losses for their sales teams, bid results, or market studies sometimes provide estimates of diversion. Under some simplifying assumptions this information can be used to determine whether a hypothetical monopolist consisting of these two firms would raise price by 5% or more (all else equal). This calculation is equivalent, on a first approximation, to assessing whether a merger of these two firms would have unilateral effects. Things become more complicated and conjectural as the market is expanded out beyond two firms. Then it is necessary to estimate the extent to which the sales of a hypothetical merger of multiple firms would be diverted to other firms in the event of a price increase. Unlike the two-firm cases, this

---

[95]   If there are diseconomies of scale, marginal cost is higher than average variable cost, which is lower than average total cost.

diversion estimate cannot be read directly from historical data. One needs to estimate the extent to which sales would be diverted from each hypothetical monopolist considered to the next product considered for inclusion. The hypothetical monopolist consists of several firms under one roof; the analyst needs to assess how the sales would be allocated among these firms and the prices set since that will determine the diversion to the next firm considered for inclusion.

Implementing actual and critical loss analysis generally requires making an assumption about the shape of the demand schedules around the price and quantity levels being considered. Over the years it has become apparent that the results of the analysis are highly dependent on what is assumed about this shape, which among other things determines the extent to which cost changes are passed through to consumers.[96] A common assumption is that the demand schedule can be approximated by a straight line at the equilibrium. For small changes, that is mathematically quite sensible. Unfortunately, a 5% change in price (and a larger change in quantity ordinarily) is not a small change. The result of the hypothetical monopolist test depends on the curvature of the demand schedule. For a unilateral effects analysis involving MCI and Sprint, Froeb *et al.* found that the estimated price effect was seven times greater using a constant-elasticity demand schedule (where the log of quantity is a function of the log of price) than using a linear demand schedule (where quantity is a linear function of price).[97] The curvature of the demand schedule is often difficult to determine for a single firm and more so as we consider hypothetical combinations of firms.[98]

2 Plausibility of SSNIP-based markets

The SSNIP test as it is implemented under the Merger Guidelines asks a quite narrow question. To see this it helps to focus on a hypothetical monopolist consisting of two firms that seek to merge. In this case the market definition question and the unilateral effects questions are similar. The SSNIP test asks whether a single owner of these two firms would have the ability and incentive to increase price. Assuming that the products of these two firms are substitutes, and setting efficiencies aside, the answer to this question is always that the merger would result in an increase in price. Before the merger, an increase in price would result in sales and profits being lost to the competing product, while after the merger, an increase in price would result in these sales profits being captured by the combined firm. If each firm is maximizing profit before the merger the fact that they internalize these losses after the merger means that they have an incentive to raise price.

The theoretical prediction that mergers inevitably raise price does not seem to accord with reality. Mergers take place all the time in the economy and there is no evidence that they lead to inexorable price increases. Mergers result in efficiencies, such as scale economies, that could offset these predicted price increases. Other changes in the market, such as competitive responses including product repositioning by other firms, discourage merged

---

[96] This issue is related to the degree to which a firm will 'pass-through' a cost increase to consumers. See E. Glen Weyl and Michal Fabinger, *Pass-Through as an Economic Tool* (2009) available at http://papers.ssrn.com/sol3/papers.cfm?abstract_id=1324426.

[97] Luke Froeb, Stephen Tschantz, and Gregory Werden, *Pass-Through Rates and the Price Effects of Mergers*, 23 INT'L J. INDUS. ORG. 703 (2005).

[98] See generally Weyl and Fabinger, *supra* note 96.

firms from raising prices or defeat price increases that are tried. Competition authorities do not in fact take this theoretical prediction seriously and rarely block mergers.[99]

In implementing the hypothetical test it is possible to 'adjust' for these ignored factors by increasing the size of the price increase required for finding that a price increase is significant. By choosing 5% the authorities have already afforded a margin of error. However, there is no economic basis for selecting 5% as the 'fudge factor' nor is there any reason to believe that the fudge factor should be the same across market circumstances.

When firms have relatively high price–cost margins the SSNIP test will often find markets that 'seem' quite narrow. As mentioned earlier, the price–cost margins that can support competitive firms depend on the level of fixed costs incurred when average variable costs are not increasing. Firms that have relatively high fixed costs must have relatively high margins to fund those costs. There is no necessary relationship between the price–cost margin and whether the firm can earn a supracompetitive profit.[100] Farrell and Shapiro explain the issue nicely in the context of their analysis in which, for the quote below, A reflects aggregate diversion for the hypothetical monopolist and $s = .05$ reflects the price increase:[101]

> Proposition 1 implies that a seemingly narrow group of products will often form a market according to the Guidelines. With the standard SSNIP of $s = .05$ and with a moderate margin of $m = .45$, a group of products forms a market if $A \geq 0.1$. In many intuitively defined 'industries', the Aggregate Diversion Ratio would be far higher, so narrower markets may well exist within the industry. For instance, if the price of one model, or brand, of cars were to rise by a SSNIP, quite a few customers would no doubt substitute away – but we would expect that most of them would substitute away to some other car. Thus, if gross margins are about 45%, there would be a product market considerably narrower than 'cars'. For example, if 20% of BMW customers would substitute to Mercedes or Audi following a SSNIP by BMW, and conversely, then the hypothetical monopolist test suggests that 'German luxury cars' would be a market.

It is also possible, of course, that the Mercedes 500 series and the BMW 740 Series (their respective large luxury models) could form a market as well.[102]

The issue is not with that math. Within the narrow construct of the question being asked it could well be that the correct answer is that a hypothetical monopolist over a seemingly narrow set of products would have the incentive to raise price. The problem is that the SSNIP test provides a very narrow view of the competitive landscape. It assumes away at the market definition stage many relevant competitive constraints with a promise, under the Guidelines, that they could be considered in the analysis of competitive effects.

---

[99]   Between 1999 and 2008 almost 23,000 merger actions were filed with the FTC/DOJ; of these, 309 saw some sort of enforcement action thus representing an enforcement rate of about 1.3%. See FTC Competition Enforcement Database, www.ftc.gov/bc/caselist/merger/index.shtml; US Dep't of Justice, Antitrust Division, Workload Statistics, www.justice.gov/atr/public/workstats. pdf and FTC, Bureau of Competition: Annual Competition Enforcement Reports, www.ftc.gov/bc/anncompreports.shtm.

[100]   See ANTITRUST LAW, *supra* note 1, at 115–16 and Schmalensee, *supra* note 50, at 973.

[101]   See Farrell and Shapiro, *supra* note 74, at 5.

[102]   I would speculate that the antitrust authorities often do not advance the narrowest market that they could under the hypothetical monopolist test because such market would seem so grossly implausible. That is no defense of the test and in fact suggests that it can be invoked to justify any narrow market that one would like to advance.

At least at the market definition stage of the inquiry, the hypothetical monopolist test has the potential of excluding demand-side substitutes that could constrain market power. Unlike the court's test it is biased towards false positives. Not surprisingly the courts have been reluctant to rely on markets based on this test. As Farrell and Shapiro observe:[103]

> When gross margins are substantial, [the SSNIP] algorithm often leads to relatively narrow markets. But the merging parties (who typically argue for broader markets, in which their shares are smaller) can point to some competition between their products and products outside a Guidelines market or other relatively narrow proposed market. Courts have been inclined to define markets relatively broadly, including all 'reasonable substitutes' to the products offered by the merging firms. Thus the agencies have not always succeeded when they have gone to court advancing relevant markets based on the algorithm from the Guidelines.

D   Hard Boundaries and Errors

It is not possible to design a method for drawing hard market boundaries that produces few false positives or false negatives for the simple reason that hard market boundaries seldom exist in the real world of business. It is therefore hardly surprising that no one has developed a satisfactory method of market definition or that the two leading approaches can result in significant errors. Those who search for rigorous market definition are often chasing a chimera. It is time to abandon hard market boundaries and market share divinations.

VI   A PROPOSED TRUCE BETWEEN COURTS, AUTHORITIES, AND ECONOMISTS

The current process of market definition provides many great ingredients for cooking an antitrust decision. Locating demand and supply-side substitutes is important for understanding the competitive constraints that determine market power and provide information for analysing competitive effects. No serious economic analyst would want to skip this inquiry into substitutes. It is true that one could analyse the competitive effects of the merger by examining only the diversion of sales between the two firms, along with a few other economic facts about these two companies. But that would involve doing economic analysis with blinders on. Diversion ratios and other parameters used in the analysis of competitive effects are invariably measured with error because neither data nor the techniques for making inferences from data are precise. It is therefore important to consider other information that could be used to check an economic analysis of competitive effects. In addition, a myriad of factors outside the purview of the two firms in the merger could affect the likelihood that a price increase would occur. The same considerations apply in monopolization and other antitrust cases. One cannot conduct a reliable assessment whether a firm has market power, or whether a practice has anti-competitive effects, without a full appreciation of competitive constraints, including

---

[103]   *Supra* note 74.

the demand- and supply-side substitutes that are often considered as part of the market definition inquiry.

A   First Pillar of the Truce: Market Definition Comes First

The market definition examination should therefore remain the first step in merger and antitrust inquiries. This inquiry should, however, be opened up and expanded so that it provides a fuller context for understanding the panoply of competitive constraints – or lack thereof – that might affect the ability and incentive of the subjects of the inquiry to harm consumers. Judge Vaughan Walker, for example, has argued that it would be useful for lawyers for the parties to provide more history and background:[104]

> All companies and industries have a history and background. Companies and industries don't just happen; they originate, grow, and develop. The shape and habits of companies and industries are, at least in part, owed to their pasts. In most instances, these histories are rich in narratives. All companies of any size and certainly any industry of any scope will admit a past that is replete with sagas of accomplishment, success, and failure.

Many businesses operate in complex ecosystems. Their success depends on providers of complementary products as well as providers of substitutes and on a variety of vertical relationships. Reducing competitive constraints these businesses face to a list of demand- and supply-side substitutes can eliminate many important nuances about the environment in which these businesses operate. A number of industries, including many businesses that involve software or the Web, are centered on multisided platforms (also known as 'two-sided markets') that serve as intermediaries between several groups of customers and providers of complementary products. These relationships are often better described through the narrative form suggested by Judge Walker than through quantitative measures such as shares or other mechanical devices.[105]

Market definition in this form would provide the historical and current background for understanding the panoply of competitive constraints that are relevant for analysing the practices at hand. This exercise would ordinarily involve calculations for revealing the relative significance of businesses in various competitive dimensions. In some cases the most convenient way to express these calculations would involve shares. In *Whole Foods*, for example, a trier-of-fact or other decision-maker might want to know the share of Whole Foods and Wild Oats among supermarkets that specialize in premium natural organic foods, among large supermarket chains more broadly, and perhaps even among a broader category of grocery sellers. The other aspects of competitive constraints would also be considered. This market inquiry should, for example, look at the ability of firms to reposition their products and therefore change the patterns of substitution. Of course, the parties to the dispute would provide evidence and testimony on these issues so the court could assess the weight to accord to various competitive constraints. We would not exclude the possibility that the parties

---

[104]   See Vaughn Walker, *Merger Trials: Looking for the Third Dimension*, 5(1) COMPETITION POLICY INTERNATIONAL 43 (Spring 2009).
[105]   See Evans, *supra* note 8, at 35.

could advance, and the court could pick, a hard market boundary. But it should not be insisted upon.

This approach to market definition is much broader, and more tied to assessing competitive constraints, than is the current approach. The US DOJ/FTC Horizontal Merger Guidelines, for example, only consider demand-side substitution in the analysis of market definition. Other factors, such as product repositioning and entry, are considered mainly in assessing competitive effects. This approach, to the extent it is followed, has the effect of setting up a presumption that the chosen market defines the arena of competition and the main sources of competitive constraints. It can, in practice, shift the burden to the merging parties to demonstrate that constraints beyond demand-side substitutability are important. Similarly, in Sherman section 2 cases, the focus on demand- and supply-side substitutability can result in a market that excludes many other sources of competitive constraints. While in principle these other factors could be raised at other points in the analysis, the hard market boundaries chosen have the effect of setting up presumptions for the remainder of the case.

B   Second Pillar of the Truce: Market Boundaries are Soft

The courts should not, however, insist on establishing hard market boundaries when the facts of the industry do not support this. Most of the problems with market definition have come from an effort to identify something that seldom exists in real-world markets. For building their narratives of a case, the courts could still talk about markets. In some cases the courts might find that a group of products are quite substitutable and that other products are relatively weak substitutes. They could therefore comfortably talk about a market for those products and note the existence of imperfect substitutes outside of that market. In other cases the courts may find that it is more difficult to draw a line. Even here they could make a preliminary determination that a group of products forms a market so long as they note that other products closely substitute. By dropping the use of hard market boundaries the courts avoid having to make a firm decision on whether to consider certain products near the boundary either in or out of the market. They also reduce the incentives of the parties to argue so vigorously about the precise placement of the boundary.

The courts should also not place significant reliance on market shares. As noted earlier, there is no basis in economics for using market shares, as a general matter, by themselves to draw inferences about the presence or significance of market power. Tentative market shares could be used to establish the relative importance of competitors, to help describe the competitive landscape, and as one of several sources of information for assessing competitive constraints.

It is true that many antitrust cases since *Alcoa* have insisted on the determination of hard market boundaries and relied on shares. But as mentioned earlier, the statutes do not require this exercise. The courts have moved away from antitrust precedent when they have had good reason to doubt the intellectual rigor of their previous cases.[106]

---

[106]   For recent cases, see *Leegin Creative Leather Prods. v. PSKS, Inc.*, *supra* note 9; *Verizon Communications Inc. v. Law Offices of Curtis V. Trinko*, *supra* note 82; and State Oil Co. v. Khan, 522 U.S. 3 (1997).

There seems to be far more consensus among economists on the unreliability of drawing hard boundaries and using market shares in product differentiated markets than the circumstances under which vertical restraints such as resale price maintenance should be lawful.

The UK Office of Fair Trading (OFT) decision in the proposed merger between Amazon and LOVEFiLM's online DVD rental subscription businesses provides an example of drafting a decision that does not take a hard position on market boundaries. Amazon and LOVEFiLM were the only providers of online DVD rentals in the United Kingdom. There were many other channels by which consumers could obtain film and television video content. Consumers could rent DVDs at bricks and mortar stores such as Blockbuster, buy DVDs at places such as WHSmith, watch on pay-per-view channels or specialty film channels provided with their cable packages, download movies over the Internet, or watch movies and television shows on free television stations.

None of these alternatives is a perfect substitute for online DVD rentals. A traditional market definition approach would largely determine the case. If the market were defined as online DVD rentals then the parties would have a 92% share (effectively a merger to monopoly), while if the market were defined to include all the alternatives listed above the merged firm would have only a 9% share. Rather than making a decision on a firm market boundary, the OFT reported this information, which was obviously helpful in understanding the marketplace, but did not take a position on the market boundary. They noted that a critical loss analysis was consistent with a narrow market but that the data showed that this conclusion was a close call and that the presence of competition from other channels made the conclusion that there was a narrow market open to debate.

In this particular matter, the OFT took an approach that more or less followed that suggested by Farrell and Shapiro.[107] They used a diversion ratio analysis submitted by the parties to assess whether there was evidence that the merger could raise prices. They found that '[t]aken at face value the illustrative price increases' calculated from the diversion ratios and margins (following equation (7) above) showed that there was a presumption that the merger could increase the prices based on this evidence.[108] However, they then considered extensive evidence from the files of the companies that demonstrated that Amazon's online DVD rental business was a relatively weak constraint on LOVEFiLM and that the merging parties acted as if they faced considerable competition from the other channels, including the bricks and mortar stores. The OFT therefore presented a narrative that demonstrated that, in effect, there were enough constraints coming from the other providers of video and television shows that the merged firm would not be able to raise price significantly.

It would seem that US courts should also be able to write decisions that, as the OFT has done in *LOVEFiLM*, provide a coherent analysis of whether there is a competitive problem without deciding on hard market boundaries.[109] US courts write many deci-

---

107   *Supra* note 13.
108   *Supra* note 13, para. 41.
109   It is likewise very difficult to see how the market definition approach taken by the US courts, as applied to *LOVEFiLM*, could have resulted in a sound decision. A US court, following the approach taken by the courts in *Whole Foods*, would most likely have decided the issue based

sions that are not based on establishing bright-line tests. One should be optimistic that the courts could write antitrust decisions without pinning down hard market boundaries and relying on market shares.

C Third Pillar of the Truce: Economists Exhibit Care in Identifying and Validating Assumptions

Economics has revolutionized modern antitrust. Supreme Court as well as lower court decisions frequently cite either the economics literature or law review articles that rely on that literature. Many of the modifications in older approaches have resulted from the courts learning from and adopting economic reasoning. Almost all antitrust cases involve economic experts. Nevertheless, the courts are sometimes skeptical of economic analysis.[110]

The history of the hypothetical monopoly test helps explain why. When first proposed the test sounded like a significant methodological advance. Over the years, economists developed models for implementing the test. Some of these models, such as critical loss, were quite attractive because they seemed to enable economists to reach conclusions on market definition with a relative minimum of data that were often available. However, as with all economic models, these were based on assumptions. In our enthusiasm for putting the models to work it took some time to expose these assumptions and to assess their importance. It took a surprisingly long time for economists to focus on such important and obvious assumptions as the actual shape of the demand curve. Twenty years after critical loss analysis was proposed[111] the chief economists of the two US antitrust authorities have proposed, as academic economists, abandoning the hypothetical monopolist test altogether.[112]

Economists need to come to grips with the tradeoffs between false precision and imprecision. Analysis that examines qualitative evidence can seldom yield precise answers. The traditional approach to market definition, with its emphasis on the interchangeability of products, can at best result in a subjective and impressionistic understanding of demand- and supply-side substitutes. It is necessarily imprecise. Analysis that is based on mathematical models and estimated with hard data can yield precise answers, such as where to draw a market boundary or the percent by which price will rise (down to many digits after the decimal point) as a result of an action. In practice, this precision can be a mirage because it is based on assumptions that may not hold and data that are measured with error. This is false precision. Model- and data-based methods that yield precise numerical answers could be more or less reliable, on average, than qualitative methods that do not yield precise numerical answers. Unfortunately, economists, and those who rely on

---

on a debate over whether there was an online DVD subscription market (the position that would have likely been advanced by a plaintiff) or a broader market for videos and television shows (the position that would likely have been advanced by a defendant) even though neither really captures the relevant market dynamics.

[110]   See Vaughn Walker, *supra* note 104.

[111]   See Harris and Simons, *supra* note 66.

[112]   Farrell and Shapiro, *supra* note 5.

economists, have not invested much in ascertaining the reliability of the techniques. The limited work on estimates of price effects for mergers has not been encouraging.[113]

That does not mean that economists should soften up and forgo the use of math and data. The economics profession has made tremendous progress in understanding product differentiated markets, estimating demand, understanding the nuances of competitive effects through rigorous modeling and data analysis. However, the problem of false precision does have three implications for market definition. First, economists should be more explicit about the assumptions behind their theoretical models and statistical techniques; do more to validate those assumptions as part of their analysis; and evaluate the reliability of data they are using. Second, economists need to do more work on assessing the reliability of tools that they are developing for policy-making. Third, economists should more carefully consider the tradeoff between imprecision and false precision and adopt more qualitative approaches when these are likely to be more informative than highly quantitative approaches.

D   Fourth Pillar of the Truce: Antitrust Authorities Should Not Go Directly to Competitive Effects

The antitrust authorities should not focus on competitive effects and relegate market definition to an ancillary role as they have done in recent cases and as they seem to have proposed in the Draft Merger Guidelines that were released in April 2010. Doing so runs the risk of having tunnel vision in analysing the possible effects of business practices.

That is particularly likely as the authorities and their economists focus on estimates of unilateral effects based on diversion ratios and margins. While these techniques and data provide a useful source of evidence, they are based on numerous assumptions and run the risk of giving the lawyers and economists a false sense of precision. By going directly to effects, the authorities could focus on data analyses without ever looking in detail at the industry, or business ecosystem, in question. They would never see information that would allow them to question the plausibility of the data analyses or assess whether there are countervailing factors.

One could argue that this concern is a straw man because the authorities would ordinarily study the industry in detail as part of any inquiry. In some cases that may well be correct. The OFT in *LOVEFiLM* focused on competitive effects rather than market definition. But they supplemented a data-driven unilateral effects pricing analysis with documentary evidence on the competitive dynamics faced by the merging parties. In other cases, however, one can imagine that the authorities would latch onto evidence of

---

[113]   See Orley Ashenfelter *et al.*, *Empirical Methods in Merger Analysis: Econometric Analysis of Pricing in FTC vs. Staples*, 13 INT'L J. ECON. BUS. 265 (2006); Matthew Weinberg, *The Price Effects of Horizontal Mergers*, 4 J. COMPETITION L. AND ECON. 433 (2007); MATTHEW WEINBERG AND DANIEL HOSKEN, USING MERGERS TO TEST A MODEL OF OLIGOPOLY (FTC, 2008) available at www.ftc.gov/be/workshops/microeconomics/2008/docs/weinberg.pdf; Orley Ashenfelter, Daniel Hosken, and Matthew Weinberg, *Generating Evidence to Guide Merger Enforcement*, 5 COMPETITION POL'Y INT'L 57 (2009) and Dennis Carlton, *The Need to Measure the Effect of Merger Policy and How to Do It* (US Dep't of Justice, Antitrust Division, Economic Analysis Group Discussion Paper 07-15, 2007) available at http://papers.ssrn.com/sol3/papers.cfm?abstract_id=1075707.

competitive effects based on narrow pricing studies and use that to insist that there are no significant competitive constraints.

The advantage of beginning with market definition is that, done properly and without focusing on hard boundaries, it provides an understanding of the business ecosystem and its competitive dynamics and therefore a basis for evaluating the plausibility of evidence on competitive effects.

VII   CONCLUSION

Market definition – in the sense of understanding the environment in which a firm operates – is an important element of antitrust analysis. The courts should not drop it nor should the competition authorities. It provides critical background for understanding competitive constraints that ultimately determine whether the practice at issue will cause the kind of consumer harm that antitrust is designed to prevent. The difficulty with market definition results from two specific problems that can be solved without abandoning what the courts have considered the primary step in antitrust.

The first problem involves drawing hard market boundaries that do not exist in many situations. Product differentiation is the norm of business and as a result products usually substitute along a continuum.

The second problem involves calculating market shares and relying on those shares for triggering safe harbor provisions. There is no basis in economics, as a general matter at least, for drawing hard boundaries or putting so much analytical weight on market shares.

The solution proposed here is to keep market definition but to eliminate the two problems that have made it controversial and subject to derision. Doing so would have no material impact on the ability of courts to collect market definition information and to build this into the narratives of their decisions.

4 Mergers that eliminate potential competition
John Kwoka

I INTRODUCTION

Modern merger analysis began with the promulgation of the 1982 Merger Guidelines by the Antitrust Division of the Department of Justice and the Federal Trade Commission. Those Guidelines focused on harm to competition from various types of mergers, primarily those between direct horizontal competitors but also including vertical mergers and those that 'eliminate[d] specific potential entrants'.[1] As part of the latter concern, section 4.11 of the Guidelines endorsed the 'theory of potential competition' – the proposition that a merger between an incumbent firm and another at the 'edge of the market' could adversely affect competition – and outlined an analytical framework for policy toward such mergers.

From that point the doctrine of potential competition has had an unusual history, both in subsequent revisions of the Merger Guidelines and in enforcement practice. The revisions issued in 1984, 1992, and 1997 extended and clarified the Guidelines with respect to particular issues (entry, efficiencies, and competitive effects) but they notably omitted any explicit reference to potential competition. While the agencies provided an accompanying statement asserting there was 'no change in their policy toward non-horizontal mergers'[2] (a category that included potential competition), it seemed clear that potential competition concerns had been downgraded. The reasons for this change in policy appeared to be a combination of a more stringent legal standard of proof for potential competition mergers and a progressive decline in overall merger challenges as the antitrust agencies and courts came to view mergers in a more favorable light.[3]

Interestingly, therefore, an explicit statement of concern with mergers eliminating potential competition reappeared in the 2010 Horizontal Merger Guidelines.[4] Indeed, the very first sentence of those Guidelines states that they 'outline the principal analytical techniques, practices, and enforcement policy of the Department of Justice and the Federal Trade Commission . . . with respect to mergers and acquisitions involving actual *or potential* competition'.[5] This renewed attention to such mergers was likely due to two factors: (a) the growing body of economic evidence demonstrating that mergers eliminating potential competitors may well relax the competitive constraint on incumbent firm

---

[1] US Department of Justice and Federal Trade Commission, Horizontal Merger Guidelines (1982).

[2] The 1992 Horizontal Merger Guidelines: Commentary and Text 21 (1992).

[3] Jonathan Baker and Carl Shapiro, *Reinvigorating Horizontal Merger Enforcement*, in How Chicago Overshot the Mark (Robert Pitofsky ed., 2008).

[4] US Department of Justice and the Federal Trade Commission, Horizontal Merger Guidelines (19 August 2011).

[5] *Id.* at 1. Emphasis added.

pricing, and (b) the fact that mergers raising such concerns were not infrequent, perhaps even of growing frequency.

This chapter will examine the analytical underpinnings of concern with mergers eliminating potential competition, as well as the policy standards and actual practice toward such mergers. It begins with an outline of the legal foundations of antitrust policy toward mergers between an incumbent and a potential entrant. This is followed by a formalization of the theory of such mergers that demonstrates both the incentive of firms to merge and the competitive harm that they produce. We then note a key judicial ruling that reflected doubts about the basis for the doctrine of potential competition and heightened the evidentiary standard for challenging potential competition mergers. The subsequent section provides evidence dispelling such doubts, evidence both old and new that demonstrates the constraining effect of potential competition and the deconstraining effect of merging the potential competitor out of existence. This is followed by an examination of a number of cases raising potential competition concerns, with attention to methods used by the antitrust agencies to preserve and employ this doctrine in the face of heightened standards of proof and a skeptical judiciary. The final substantive section discusses the restoration of explicit mention of potential competition in the 2010 Merger Guidelines.

II   EARLY POLICY DECISIONS

Recognition of the importance of potential competition dates back at least to the Temporary National Economic Committee (TNEC) in 1941. In conjunction with the TNEC's investigation into economic concentration and market power, a congressional staff report concluded:[6]

> Potential competition . . . as a substitute for . . . [actual competition] may restrain producers from overcharging those to whom they sell or underpaying those from whom they buy . . . Potential competition . . . may compensate in part for the imperfection characteristics of actual competition in the great majority of competitive markets.

The legal doctrine of potential competition was the collective product of several decisions of the Supreme Court dating from the mid-1960s through the early 1970s. This section reviews those decisions, focusing on important details of the doctrine and the criteria that they established

The four leading cases are commonly considered to be *El Paso Natural Gas*, *Procter & Gamble*, *Falstaff Brewing*, and *Penn-Olin*. The named party in *United States v. El Paso Natural Gas*[7] was a large Texas-based supplier of natural gas to California, by itself accounting for one-half of that state's total supply. El Paso had a contract for so-called interruptible supply with a major California utility, Southern California Edison. Pacific Northwest Pipeline Corporation was another out-of-state gas supplier that had previously bid on contracts for So Cal Edison's business, offering both cheaper service

---

6   UNITED STATES STAFF OF SENATE TNEC, INVESTIGATION OF CONCENTRATION OF ECONOMIC POWER: COMPETITION AND MONOPOLY IN AMERICAN HISTORY 7–8 (1941), quoted in United States v. Penn-Olin, 378 U.S. 158, 174 (1964).

7   United States v. El Paso Natural Gas Co., 376 U.S. 659, 661 (1964).

and 'firm' or non-interruptible supply. The difficulty with Pacific Northwest's offer was that the company had no existing pipeline directly serving California, although Pacific Northwest and So Cal Edison had in fact entered into an agreement providing for the construction of the necessary pipeline. One immediate result of that agreement was that El Paso reduced its price to So Cal Edison by 25% and offered its supply on a firm basis. The other result was that El Paso proposed to acquire Pacific Northwest.

The Justice Department sued to block the acquisition and the Supreme Court upheld the challenge. The Court reviewed evidence of the effect of Pacific Northwest's bidding on El Paso's offer prices and concluded that 'the mere efforts of Pacific Northwest to get into the California market, though unsuccessful, had a powerful influence on El Paso's business attitudes within the state'.[8] The fact that Pacific Northwest was not currently supplying natural gas was irrelevant. The Court asserted that 'unsuccessful bidders are not less competitors than the successful one. The presence of two or more suppliers gives buyers a choice'.[9]

While the *El Paso* opinion provided a strong endorsement of the application of potential competition in that case, it offered limited policy guidance regarding the standard for challenging mergers eliminating potential competitors. It stated only that 'the effect on competition in a particular market through acquisition of another company is determined by the nature or extent of that market and by the nearness of the absorbed company to it, that company's eagerness to enter that market, its resourcefulness, and so on'.[10] The Court soon had opportunities to clarify and advance its thinking.

United States v. Penn-Olin[11] expanded the reach of the potential competition doctrine to cover joint ventures between two potential entrants into the same market, that is, between two firms neither of which produced in the market in question. Pennsalt Chemicals produced sodium chlorate but not in the southeastern United States, a region where Olin Mathieson had a distribution system for sodium chlorate (indeed, for Pennsalt) but no production. Growing demand in the southeast had prompted both companies to consider starting production there, but ultimately they decided to form a single joint venture production facility.

The Justice Department challenged the joint venture. In the district court's view, the relevant question was whether 'as a matter of reasonable probability both Pennsalt and Olin would have built plants in the southeast if Penn-Olin [the joint venture] had not been created'.[12] Concluding that was unlikely, the court observed that the outcome of the joint venture was the creation of one new competitor – the most that otherwise would have occurred – and therefore held for the parties. The Supreme Court reversed, asserting that the lower court had failed to consider the possibility that, even if only one of the companies actually entered, 'Penn-Olin eliminated the potential competition of the corporation that might have remained at the edge of the market, continually threatening to enter'.[13]

---

[8]   *Id.*
[9]   *Id.*
[10]   United States v. Penn-Olin, 378 U.S. 158, 660 (1964).
[11]   *Id.* at 378.
[12]   United States v. Penn-Olin Chem. Co., 217 F. Supp. 110, 131 (D. Del. 1963), *vacated.*
[13]   378 U.S. 158, 173 (1964).

The Court found evidence that both companies had a basis for independent entry. It acknowledged the fact that since neither company had competed in the market in question, 'it is impossible to demonstrate the precise competitive effects of elimination of either Pennsalt or Olin as a potential competitor'. It nonetheless noted that 'the existence of an aggressive, well equipped and well financed corporation in the same or related lines of commerce waiting anxiously to enter an oligopolistic market would be a substantial incentive to competition which cannot be underestimated'.[14] On this basis, it remanded the case for rehearing.[15]

Two later cases sharpened and extended the doctrine of potential competition. In *Procter & Gamble*,[16] the Court was confronted with that company's acquisition of Clorox, which was the largest seller of household liquid bleach. Procter & Gamble (P&G) was a large manufacturer of various household products, but contended that it never intended to enter the bleach market itself. There was evidence that P&G had considered but apparently rejected that alternative, and as a result the lower court approved the acquisition. The Supreme Court reversed, noting a number of factors indicating that P&G had both the ability and incentive to enter the market *de novo* or through a smaller toehold acquisition. As for intent, the Court concluded that P&G's internal decision not to enter was actually motivated by the fact that 'the acquisition of Clorox would enable Procter to capture a more commanding share of the market'.[17] In summary, the court stated that 'the market behavior of the liquid bleach market was influenced by each firm's predictions of the market behavior of its competitors, actual and potential'.[18] Thus, it seemed, elimination of a firm perceived to be a potential entrant could violate the antitrust statutes much as a merger between actual competitors.

The fourth significant case of this era involved the acquisition of Narragansett, a large New England brewer, by Falstaff Brewing. Falstaff was at the time the fourth largest national brewer but without a presence in the region. It had considered but, according to its executives, rejected other alternatives for entering the New England market, including building a new brewery, acquiring a smaller local brewer, or shipping its beer from its existing breweries. Based on this evidence, the lower court approved the acquisition but the Supreme Court again reversed, this time on somewhat different grounds.

The Court did not directly dispute the conclusion that Falstaff would not otherwise in fact have entered. Rather, it argued that independent of that, consideration had to be given to the possibility that 'Falstaff was a potential competitor in the sense that it was so positioned on the edge of the market that it exerted beneficial influence on competitive conditions in the market'.[19] The Court directed attention to underlying market conditions and observed that 'if it would appear to rational beer merchants in New England that Falstaff might well build a new brewery to supply the northeastern market then its entry

---

[14]   *Id.* at 176.
[15]   On rehearing, the district court found that neither of the two firms would have entered independently, thus permitting the joint venture to go forward.
[16]   FTC v. Procter & Gamble Co., 386 U.S. 568 (1967).
[17]   *Id.* at 578.
[18]   *Id.*
[19]   410 U.S. 526, 532 (1973).

by merger becomes suspect'.[20] Thus, the Court endorsed the proposition that a company that is perceived as a potential competitor may be prohibited from merging with an incumbent, regardless of whether it was in fact intending separate entry.

The opinions in the *El Paso*, *Penn-Olin*, *P&G*, and *Falstaff* cases – three of which were reversals of narrower interpretations by lower courts – expanded the reach of the antitrust laws. The Supreme Court made clear that merger enforcement should encompass not only mergers of actual competitors but also mergers between incumbents and potential competitors. Moreover, the latter category included potential competitors in the sense of firms actually contemplating entry and those perceived to be possible entrants. The former represented constraining influences on incumbent behavior ('perceived potential competitors' or 'constraining competitors') while the latter, absent the merger, would enter and thereby help to reduce industry concentration ('actual potential competitors' or 'deconcentrating competitors').[21] In what follows, we focus primarily on the case of a constraining competitor, or what is sometimes termed 'pure' potential competition.

III   ECONOMIC FOUNDATIONS OF THE POTENTIAL COMPETITION DOCTRINE

The economic framework for evaluating the competitive consequences of a merger eliminating a potential competitor is similar to that for a merger between two incumbent firms in a market. The key question in both cases is whether or not the merger relaxes the competitive constraint on pricing by the remaining firms. To be sure, there are differences between the cases that require differences in the analyses. For example, since the potential entrant is not committed to the industry to the same degree as an incumbent with sunk costs and dedicated operations, the behavior of the potential entrant in response to certain price or profit signals may differ. In addition, unlike an actual competitor, the potential entrant does not currently produce in the relevant market, requiring a different method for assessing its importance and the effect of its elimination.

Despite these differences, there is much in common in the analyses of a merger between actual competitors and one involving a potential competitor. This section illustrates several fundamental points by use of a simple analytical model. We begin by contrasting the competitive and monopoly outcomes in a specific market setting, and then consider how that market equilibrium changes in the presence of a second actual or potential competitor. Since a merger between a single incumbent and that second competitor will preserve or restore the monopoly result, the difference in profits to the incumbent is a measure of its incentive to merge. Corresponding changes in allocative efficiency and in consumer harm measure the adverse effects of the merger on market equilibrium.

---

[20]   *Id.* at 533.

[21]   The terminology of 'perceived' and 'actual' potential competitors is standard but somewhat opaque. The alternative of 'constraining' and 'deconcentrating' competitors has therefore been suggested. John Kwoka, *Non-Incumbent Competition: Mergers Involving Constraining and Prospective Competitors*, 52 CASE W. RES. L. REV. 173 (2001).

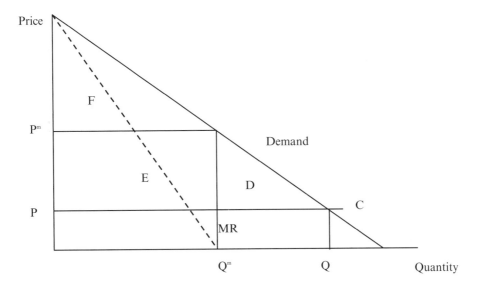

Figure 4.1   Benchmark cases: perfect competition and monopoly

A   Effect of Actual and Potential Competition

From among the limitless possible specifications of market demand, firm costs, and behavior, we employ a simple, but familiar and tractable, example. Though specific in its details, this example serves as a guide for intuition about the effects of various types of competition between incumbent firms and with a potential entrant, and ultimately a guide to the effects of merger that eliminates the latter. Throughout we assume a linear inverse market demand curve $P = A - bQ$, where P and Q are market price and quantity, respectively. All firms are initially assumed to have constant and identical unit costs – that is, no scale economies and no differences among firms, actual or potential. This assumption implies a cost function $C = cq$, where c is marginal cost and q is any single firm's output. A later cost function will add fixed costs F to C. This market demand curve and cost curve are shown in Figure 4.1 (the other entries will be explained momentarily). Firm profit may be written simply as $\pi = Pq - cq$.

We begin with two benchmark cases: perfect competition and then unconstrained monopoly. In the perfectly competitive case, the market equilibrium is determined by setting price equal to marginal cost. Thus, $P = c$, which implies that market quantity $Q = (A - c)/b$. These results are shown in Table 4.1, column (a), and illustrated in Figure 4.1. Given the fragmented nature of a perfectly competitive industry, each individual firm's output is negligible and its profits (as well as those of the entire industry) are zero. Consumer surplus – the difference between consumers' valuation of the product and the price they must pay – is graphically the total of areas D, E, and F in Figure 4.1. Under competition, area DEF constitutes the maximum total of consumer surplus possible in this market, so that 'consumer harm' at the competitive point of operation is zero. These, too, are shown in Table 4.1.

We next turn to the case of a simple monopoly unconstrained by the threat of entry.

Table 4.1 Market and firm outcomes under various competitive scenarios

	(a) Perfect competition	(b) Monopoly	(c) 2-firm Cournot	(d) Stackelberg leadership	(e) Stackelberg entry deterrence
market quantity	$\dfrac{A-c}{b}$	$\dfrac{A-c}{2b}$	$\dfrac{2(A-c)}{3b}$	$\dfrac{3(A-c)}{4b}$	$\dfrac{A-c-2\sqrt{bF}}{b}$
market price	c	$\dfrac{A+c}{2}$	$\dfrac{A+2c}{3}$	$\dfrac{A+3c}{4}$	$c+2\sqrt{bF}$
incumbent quantity	–	$\dfrac{A-c}{2b}$	$\dfrac{A-c}{3b}$	$\dfrac{A-c}{2b}$	$\dfrac{A-c-2\sqrt{bF}}{b}$
incumbent profit	–	$\dfrac{(A-c)^2}{4b}$	$\dfrac{(A-c)^2}{9b}$	$\dfrac{(A-c)^2}{8b}$	$\dfrac{2(A-c)\sqrt{bF}}{b}-5F$
entrant quantity	–	–	$\dfrac{A-c}{3b}$	$\dfrac{A-c}{4b}$	–
entrant profit	–	–	$\dfrac{(A-c)^2}{9b}$	$\dfrac{(A-c)^2}{16b}$	–
allocative inefficiency	0	$\dfrac{(A-c)^2}{8b}$	$\dfrac{(A-c)^2}{18b}$	$\dfrac{(A-c)^2}{32b}$	2F
consumer harm	0	$\dfrac{3(A-c)^2}{8b}$	$\dfrac{5(A-c)^2}{18b}$	$\dfrac{7(A-c)^2}{32b}$	$\dfrac{2(A-c)\sqrt{bF}}{b}-3F$

Such a firm maximizes profit $\pi = (Pq - cq)$ by setting its marginal cost c equal to marginal revenue in the market. For the demand curve in Figure 4.1, marginal revenue is also a straight line but with twice the slope of demand. Again for this example, the intersection of c with marginal revenue MR is at $Q^m = (A - c)/2b$, or one-half the competitive output. Market price P^m is readily determined to be $(A + c)/2$, which in turn implies profits (shown as area E) in the amount

$$(1) \qquad \Pi^m = (A - c)^2/4b$$

This profit represents a transfer from consumers to producers and is one portion of consumer harm from monopoly. The other portion is the loss of surplus on output that the monopolist does not produce, i.e. between Q^m and Q. This added harm, sometimes called deadweight loss, is shown as D in Figure 4.1 and in the present case equals one-half of the amount of profit, or $(A - c)^2/8b$. Together with profit, total consumer harm consists of D plus E, specifically, $3(A - c)^2/8b$. All of these results are summarized in Table 4.1.

If the competitive case serves as a benchmark against which to compare other outcomes, monopoly represents the extreme alternative that maximizes profit extraction from the market. In addition, the monopoly outcome is also the objective that firms in more constrained market conditions seek to realize by merger. We next specify a range of such other market conditions and then measure the gains that firms in each case realize from merger.

The 'shared monopoly' case involves joint profit maximization by the incumbent firm and the second firm (the potential entrant) when the latter indeed does enter the market. If those two firms jointly maximize profit, there would be no difference in overall market outcomes. Rather, under present assumptions, they would share the market equally, so that the incumbent firm's profit would decline from the full monopoly level to one-half that amount. The remaining half would simply become the entrant's profit.

More likely than such perfect cooperation would be a post-entry equilibrium that involves some shortfall of total profit from the monopoly case. That equilibrium might range from nearly perfect cooperation down to intense competition with zero profit to both the incumbent firm and the entrant. Here, we focus on a standard intermediate case, namely, the Cournot model, which can be taken as illustrative of equilibria between those extremes.[22]

In the familiar Cournot model, each firm acts independently, choosing its output in the belief that its rival will not change its own output from the observed level. From this behavioral assumption, firm and market equilibria can be derived. In the present case entry results in two identical firms each with profit-maximizing output given by the usual formula:

$$(2) \qquad q_1^c = q_2^c = (A - c)/3b$$

---

[22]   Discussion of the Bertrand, Cournot, and other modes of competition discussed in this section can be found in standard industrial organization texts. See, e.g., JEFFREY CHURCH AND ROGER WARE, INDUSTRIAL ORGANIZATION: A STRATEGIC APPROACH (2000).

so that total $Q^c = 2(A - c)/3b$. That in turn implies market price $P^c = (A + 2c)/3$, from which it follows that each firm's profit

$$(3) \qquad \pi_1^c = \pi_2^c = (A - c)^2/9b$$

Total output in the market has now increased relative to the monopoly result, since

$$(4) \qquad 2(A - c)/3b > (A - c)/2$$

Deadweight loss has been reduced to $(A - c)^2/18b$ and total consumer harm reduced to $5(A - c)^2/18b$. These results appear in Table 4.1 as column (c). As is apparent, Cournot outcomes lie between the competitive result and full monopoly.

B   The Deterrence Option

The joint profit maximization and Cournot models presume some accommodation of the potential entrant by the incumbent. Alternatively, the incumbent can seek to deter the potential entrant altogether by setting a price (or equivalently, output) that results in non-positive profits to that firm upon entry. Under present assumptions about costs, that crucial price (the 'limit price') would be equal to the entrant's unit cost c. Any higher price would permit profitable sales by the entrant in the market. In setting that price, however, the incumbent also guarantees zero profit to itself, making entry deterrence supremely costly. Unless the incumbent finds some other advantage in entry deterrence, this case seems unlikely to arise.

A more interesting strategy is the leader–follower model originally developed by Stackelberg. In this model the incumbent firm exploits its advantage of already being in the market to move prior to the entrant. As a result, when the entrant or follower calculates its optimum output, it is confronted with the incumbent's existing output and must maximize its profit given that output. But that in turn permits the incumbent or leading firm to factor into its own profit calculation the later output decision of the follower, thereby allowing the leader to increase its share of sales and profit.[23]

Formally, the follower's residual demand is given by

$$(5) \qquad P_2(q_1, q_2) = A - bq_1 - bq_2$$

and so its profits can be written

$$(6) \qquad \pi_2(q_1, q_2) = (A - bq_1 - bq_2) q_1 - cq_2$$

Equating marginal revenue to marginal cost gives the follower's best response function

---

[23]   As is well known, this requires the leader's output choice to be irreversible. A common interpretation is therefore that q denotes capacity, rather than output. See, e.g., CHURCH AND WARE, *supra* note 22.

$$(7) \qquad q_2 = R_2(q_1) = \frac{A - bq_1 - c}{2b}$$

The leader's profit function can be written as follows:

$$(8a) \qquad \pi_1(q_1, q_2) = P(Q) q_1 - cq_1$$

$$(8b) \qquad = (A - bq_1 - bq_2) q_1 - cq_1$$

Now substituting for q_2 what is known to be the follower's output response yields the leader's profit as

$$(9) \qquad \pi_1(q_1, R_2(q_1)) = (A - bq_1 - bR_2(q_1)) - cq_1$$

Maximizing with respect to its own q_1 implies the leader's profit-maximizing output as $q_1^s = (A - c)/2b$. Substituting this into equation (7) gives the follower's output as $q_2^s = (A - c)/4b$, so that total market quantity $Q^s = 3(A - c)/4b$ and price $P^s = (A - 3c)/4$. Profit earned by the leading firm is readily calculated to be $\pi_1^s = (A - c)^2/8b$, while the follower earns only half that amount, or $\pi_2^s = (A - c)^2/16b$.

Note that total output under Stackelberg exceeds that under Cournot, so that total industry profits decline. The profits of the leading firm rise, however, reflecting its first-mover advantage, while the second firm/follower's profits fall substantially. The increase in total output ensures that both deadweight loss and consumer harm decline. The former is now $(A - c)^2/32b$ and the latter $7(A - c)^2/32b$, both less than under Cournot and much less than under monopoly.

Our final example modifies the Stackelberg model in a manner that best illustrates entry deterrence rather than accommodation in any form. It also illustrates a crucial motivation for merger eliminating a potential competitor. The key modification to the previous model is the inclusion of a fixed and irreversible ('sunk') cost F, so that $C = cq + F$. The incumbent firm again moves first, but now solves for the state of residual demand that is just insufficient for an entrant with fixed costs F to be able to cover its full cost of operation in the market. The necessary residual demand is determined by the incumbent's choice of output, so the incumbent can maximize its profitability conditional on entry deterrence. Its profitability will be less than the unconstrained level, of course, but will generally exceed that from simple Stackelberg leadership, which after all accommodated some level of output by the entrant.

Formally, the entrant's profit function in the presence of fixed cost F will be given by

$$(10) \qquad \pi_2(q_1, q_2) = (A - bq_1 - bq_2) q_1 - cq_2 - F$$

Substituting the entrant's best response function from equation (5), we can solve for the entrant's profit:

$$(11) \qquad \pi_2(q_1) = \frac{(A - bq_1 - c)^2}{4b} - F$$

Table 4.2   *Change in profit and inefficiency for merger that eliminates actual or potential competition*

	(a) 2- firm Cournot	(b) Stackelberg leadership	(c) Stackelberg entry deterrence
leader's gain in profit	$\dfrac{(A-c)^2}{36b}$	$\dfrac{(A-c)^2}{16b}$	$\dfrac{(A-c)^2}{4b} - \dfrac{2(A-c)\sqrt{bF}}{b} + 4F$
increase in allocative inefficiency	$\dfrac{5(A-c)^2}{72b}$	$\dfrac{3(A-c)^2}{32b}$	$\dfrac{(A-c)^2}{8b} - 2F$
increase in consumer harm	$\dfrac{7(A-c)^2}{72b}$	$\dfrac{5(A-c)^2}{32b}$	$\dfrac{3(A-c)^2}{8b} - \dfrac{2(A-c)\sqrt{bF}}{b} + 2F$

The incumbent's entry-deterring ('limit') output is found by setting this equal to zero and obtaining an explicit expression for q_1^d. In this model, that is given by

$$(12) \quad q_1^d = \frac{A-c}{b} - 2\sqrt{\frac{F}{b}}$$

All of these are shown in column (e) of Table 4.1. Not surprisingly, the limit output depends upon the magnitude of fixed cost F. A larger F implies that the entrant needs larger output to break even, so that the incumbent is free to restrict its output to a greater degree (i.e. more closely approximating the monopoly level) without inducing entry.

It should be noted that entry deterrence may not in all cases result in greater profit relative to accommodation. Whether that holds can be determined by comparing the incumbent's profit from Stackelberg leadership and from entry deterrence. As shown in Table 4.2, that difference will depend on the value of F. Assuming, however, that the incumbent's profits are greater from entry deterrence, total market quantity is reduced even though the incumbent itself produces more than it did under simple leadership. The actual values again depend on the magnitude of fixed cost F. Market price $P^d = c + 2\sqrt{bF}$ and deadweight loss is simply given by 2F. Total consumer harm is again the sum of deadweight loss and profit and depends in a complicated way on the magnitude of fixed cost.

This analysis has demonstrated a variety of possible outcomes when an incumbent firm is faced with either the threat of entry or its realization. The outcome depends on such factors as the nature of post-entry competition, a possible first-mover advantage, and the existence and size of fixed costs. Common to all scenarios is the fact that the incumbent's profits are reduced relative to unconstrained monopoly. We shall now explore another alternative strategy, namely, merger to eliminate that second firm.

C   The Merger Option

Faced with a constraining potential entrant, the incumbent may pursue an entirely different strategy, namely, merging with that firm and thereby eliminating the constraint. Here we examine three key effects of the merger option: the increase in the incumbent's profit, the increase in allocative inefficiency from the merger, and the increase in total consumer harm. The first measures the incumbent's incentive to merge the constraining competitor out of existence, while the latter two capture different aspects of the adverse consequences of such a merger.

Central to this analysis is the fact that, under present assumptions, elimination of the potential entrant results in the incumbent achieving (or restoring) the unconstrained monopoly outcome.[24] Table 4.2 reports the differences in incumbent profits, in allocative inefficiency, and in consumer harm for the three alternatives to monopoly that have been examined. Each of these differences is net of the cost to the leading firm of acquiring the potential competitor. For example, in the case of Cournot competition, entry would result in each firm earning $(A - c)^2/9b$ in profit. In order to eliminate the potential rival by merger, the leading firm would have to compensate the rival for its foregone profit, presumably through the purchase price. The incumbent can afford to pay that amount to eliminate the rival since the resulting unconstrained monopoly yields more than sufficient incremental profit.

This can be illustrated with an example from Table 4.1. As shown there, profits from an unconstrained monopoly total $(A - c)^2/4b$ whereas each firm in the two-firm Cournot case earns profits of $(A - c)^2/9b$. Assuming that the incumbent fully compensates the potential entrant in the process of acquisition, the target firm therefore collects $(A - c)^2/9b$ from the acquirer. After payment of that amount, the remaining firm still earns positive net profit relative to the Cournot outcome, since monopoly profit exceeds the sum of its original profit plus the cost of eliminating its rival

$$(13)\quad ((¼ - 2/9\,)(A - c)^2/b) = (A - c)^2/36b > 0^{[25]}$$

It is this *net* profit gain that is recorded in column (a) of Table 4.2.[26]

Since the monopoly outcome produces the maximum profit to the incumbent, all

---

[24]   To this point we have assumed that the potential entrant is unique. The next subsection examines the effect of modifying this assumption.

[25]   Knowing this, the rival might demand more than $(A - c)^2/4b$, but we leave complications of bargaining strategies aside here. It is also possible that the potential entrant is producing profitably in another market, in which case its foregone profits from being eliminated from production of this product are reduced.

[26]   These entries represent per-period profits, whereas the rival would presumably be paid a lump-sum equal to the present value of its profit stream. The results are equivalent. It should also be noted that, despite the Cournot environment, this merger does not run afoul of the paradoxical result that mergers in a Cournot industry are generally not profitable. That result arises for mergers among incumbents, not, as here, between an incumbent and a potential entrant. See S. Salant, S. Switzer, and R. Reynolds, *Losses from Merger: The Effects of an Exogenous Change in Industry Structure on Cournot-Nash Equilibrium*, QUARTERLY J. ECONOMICS 185 (May 1983).

merger scenarios in fact result in net profit increases, implying that the incumbent generally has an incentive to merge the constraining potential entrant out of existence. Columns (b) and (c) of Table 4.2 report the net profits to the leading firm from eliminating its rival in the case of Stackelberg leadership and of entry deterrence, respectively. While the algebraic expressions become increasingly complex, suffice it to say that positive net profits result in each case. Comparison reveals that the gain is greater in the case of Stackelberg leadership, while the case of entry deterrence depends on the magnitude of fixed cost F (more on this below).

The other rows in Table 4.2 report the increase in deadweight loss from a merger that creates a monopoly from a market previously characterized by Cournot behavior, Stackelberg leadership, and entry deterrence. Deadweight loss, for example, rises by $5(a - c)^2/72b$ when Cournot competition is eliminated, and consumer harm rises by $7(A - c)^2/72b$. When the pre-merger market involves Stackelberg leadership, these increases are larger than in the Cournot case since the elimination cost of the rival is smaller in the case of Stackelberg leadership. For the case of entry deterrence, once again the magnitude of fixed cost affects the conclusion.

These results confirm two important propositions. First, merging with a constraining competitor – actual or potential – generally is a profitable course of action to the leading or incumbent firm. Second, such a merger can produce competitive harm, and that harm will be larger when the competition that would have existed absent the merger is stronger.

The case in which the incumbent firm initially behaved so as to deter entry is closest to our concern with mergers that eliminate a constraining firm. In this case merging with that constraining outside firm increases the incumbent's profit as well as allocative inefficiency and consumer harm by amounts that depend in complicated ways on the magnitude of fixed cost. The profit gain is more modest than in other scenarios,[27] in part because with fixed costs preventing entry, the incumbent is already earning substantial profit. This result corroborates the proposition (and empirical finding) that eliminating a constraining potential competitor is likely to have a smaller effect than the elimination of an actual competitor.

Since the complexity of some of the formulas in Table 4.2 may obscure their significance, we offer a numerical example. Suppose simply that A = 9, b = 1, c = 1, and F = 2. Thus, demand can be written as P = 9 − Q and total cost as either C = q or C = q + 2. Table 4.3 reports the increases in profit, inefficiency, and consumer harm from merger eliminating a second firm, either an actual or potential competitor, much as in Table 4.2 but now for this numerical example. As is again evident from the Table 4.3 entries, all of these changes are positive, indicating that there is private gain (profit) from such mergers, but also social losses (allocative inefficiency and consumer harm). Most significantly for present purposes, if a potential entrant that has been deterred by a Stackelberg incumbent is eliminated by that incumbent, the incumbent's net profit rises by 1.4, whereas allocative

---

[27]   In order to calculate correctly the change in profit when the incumbent eliminates a constraining potential entrant, the cost functions of the monopoly and Cournot incumbents must include the same fixed cost term F as the entry-deterring Stackelberg leader. This departs from the earlier models of monopoly and Cournot firms, whose cost functions have no fixed cost term. Alternatively, 'profits' could be interpreted throughout as variable profits, i.e. apart from any fixed costs.

Table 4.3 *Change in profit and inefficiency for merger that eliminates actual or potential competition: numerical example*

	(a) 2-firm Cournot	(b) Stackelberg leadership	(c) Stackelberg entry deterrence
leader's incentive to merge	1.8	4.0	1.4
increase in allocative inefficiency	4.4	6.0	4.0
increase in consumer harm	6.2	10.0	5.4

Note: Calculations based on model $P = 9 - Q$, $c = 1$, $F = 2$.

inefficiency rises by 4.0 and consumer harm by 5.4. Relative to industry revenues of 21.2, this represents a 6.6% gain in profit, an 18.9% increase in allocative inefficiency, and a 25.4% rise in consumer harm – all nontrivial effects.

D Some Generalizations

The above model has been based on a number of specific assumptions, including a single potential entrant, identical incumbent and entrant, and a homogeneous product. Here we re-examine these assumptions to determine to what extent they may alter the constraint and any results.

We first consider the possibility that there exist two (or more) potential entrants. If both are identical and also identical to the incumbent, then in the Cournot model the incumbent faces the prospect of entry by both outside firms and profits at the Cournot triopoly level. A merger with one potential entrant would increase the incumbent's profits only to the duopoly level while costing one full triopoly level of profit, making such a transaction uneconomic. Merging with both potential entrants would cost two triopoly profits but yield the larger full monopoly profit. Such a merger would therefore be profitable to the incumbent. In the Stackelberg case, it is again generally true that merger with one of two or more potential entrants is likely uneconomic since the remaining potential entrant(s) serves to limit the profit gain from the merger. Merging with both (or all) potential entrants would naturally increase the leader's gain but it is also possible that the follower could not be adequately compensated for being merged, since its operation on the fringe may well have been quite profitable. In this case, regardless of the efficiency effects, the merger may simply not be endogenous.

Next we return to the case of a single potential entrant but allow the possibility that the entrant's unit costs c_1 exceed those of the incumbent, that is, $c_1 > c$. The constraint imposed by that potential entrant is now of lesser magnitude, since even without merger the incumbent can raise price to $P_1 = c_1$ and earn unit profit $(P_1 - c) = (c_1 - c) > 0$ without inducing entry. It also follows that the elimination of such a potential entrant is less beneficial to the incumbent under any scenario, since the incumbent's but-for profits are larger.

These two generalizations might arise simultaneously insofar as there are multiple potential entrants with different costs. For concreteness, suppose that there are two potential entrants, one with costs identical to those of the incumbent ($c_1 = c$) while the second has higher unit costs c_2. As before, a merger between the incumbent and the most efficient potential entrant relaxes the constraint on price, but in this case the magnitude of the effect is limited to the difference between the unit cost of the most efficient potential entrant and that of the next most efficient entrant, that is, $c_2 - c_1$. This difference could be a very small increment if the potential entrants are nearly identical, or larger as their costs differ by more.

All of the above has assumed that the incumbent and the potential entrant(s) produce the same product and that they differ, if at all, in their unit costs. These assumptions make the analysis straightforward, but in many real-world settings, firms' products in fact differ in substantive ways ('quality') or in intangibles ('reputation'). As a result the potential entrant's unit costs do not fully determine its constraining effect, since a lower cost entrant may offer a lower quality product that is dispreferred by many customers. A determination of the constraining effect of any potential entrant and hence the value of its elimination through merger requires a different framework.

That framework is provided by the differentiated-products Bertrand model. For competition among multiple incumbents, that model assumes a set of products with varying characteristics that have some appeal to all customers, but each appealing more strongly to some. As is well-known, a merger between two incumbents in such a market setting may have anticompetitive effects that depend on the degrees of substitutability between the two products and also with other products in the relevant set.[28] When one of the merging parties is a potential entrant whose product, upon entry, would be differentiated, the same considerations apply. The entrant's degree of product differentiation would determine the extent of constraint imposed prior to entry as well as the extent to which the constraint is relaxed by merger. Calculation of effects is not straightforward,[29] but the basic methodology would follow that used to evaluate mergers between incumbents with differentiated products.

IV   SECOND THOUGHTS AND HEIGHTENED STANDARDS

The cases reviewed in Section II constituted the foundation of an antitrust policy toward mergers that eliminated a potential competitor that was consistent both with policy toward mergers between actual competitors and with the underlying economics. Despite this, the Supreme Court soon appeared to have misgivings about this position. These misgivings manifested themselves in changes in evidentiary standards articulated by the Court in the next such case before it. Those new standards had the effect of circumscribing that policy. This section examines that case, with particular attention to the standard of proof.

---

[28]   Church and Ware, *supra* note 22.
[29]   For example, there are no diversion ratios to estimate post-merger shares, since the potential entrant by definition has no pre-merger sales.

The case in question involved Marine Bancorporation,[30] the parent of a large Seattle bank that sought to acquire Washington Trust, a midsize bank headquartered in Spokane. Under state banking laws, *de novo* entry into the Spokane area would have been virtually impossible, but the government contended that Marine Bancorp could have entered in some other less anticompetitive manner. The district court concurred and prohibited the merger, but the Supreme Court reversed. It held that actual potential competition required that the firm have some other feasible means to enter that 'offer[ed] a substantial likelihood of ultimately producing deconcentration of that market or other significant procompetitive effects'.[31] Based on its view that Washington state banking laws rendered infeasible any method of entry other than acquisition, it concluded that the government's theory of the case was flawed.

The Court took the opportunity presented by *Marine Bancorporation* to expound on its modified views of the potential competition doctrine in general and the standards of proof in particular. It addressed actual potential competition and perceived potential competition separately. With respect to the former, it opined that '[u]nequivocal proof that an acquiring firm actually would have entered *de novo* but for a merger is rarely available'.[32] This passage at once suggests that the Court would henceforth seek 'unequivocal proof' and that it did not expect to find it.

The Court then declared that potential competition issues primarily involved perceived potential competition: '[t]he principle focus of the doctrine is on the likely effects of the premerger position of the acquiring firm on the fringe of the target market'. And with respect to such potential competition, it offered this guidance:[33]

> In developing and applying the doctrine, the Court has recognized that a market extension merger may be unlawful if the target market is substantially concentrated, if the acquiring firm has the characteristics, capability, and economic incentive to render it a perceived potential *de novo* entrant, and if the acquiring firm's premerger presence on the fringe of the target market in fact tempered oligopolistic behavior on the part of existing participants in that market.

This statement sets out three criteria for applying the doctrine of potential competition. The first – that the market be concentrated – is straightforward and consistent with previously developed economic theory. From an economic and business perspective, the same may be said about the second criterion, that requiring the potential entrant to have relevant 'characteristics, capability, and economic incentive'. The third element, on the other hand, is quite different. It requires evidence that the potential entrant 'in fact' restrained non-competitive behavior by incumbent firms, that is, a demonstration of a market effect from the pre-merger interaction of the potential entrant and one or more incumbent firms. While such evidence is obviously important when available, this standard is considerably more stringent than that which has conventionally governed challenges to mergers between two incumbents. For the most part, the latter has derived from economic understanding of the effect of concentration and mergers on price,

---

[30]   United States v. Marine Bancorporation, 418 U.S. 602 (1974).
[31]   *Id.* at 633.
[32]   *Id.* at 636.
[33]   *Id.*

supplemented, to be sure, with whatever evidence of likely actual effects there might be.[34] For mergers that eliminate potential competition, by contrast, the Court seemed to signal that evidence of actual constraining interactions would be required.

The evidentiary standard set out by the Supreme Court in the *Marine Bancorporation* case has been adopted and in some cases extended by the antitrust agencies.[35] It has made antitrust challenges to mergers eliminating a potential competitor considerably more difficult. No doubt this was the intent, reflecting the Court's unease with proceeding against such mergers based on its understanding of the economic evidence. As we shall now see, however, evidence of the effects of eliminating potential competition was (and is) quite substantial, as substantial as that for mergers reducing actual competition.

V   ECONOMIC EVIDENCE ON THE EFFECT OF POTENTIAL COMPETITION

Economic evidence of the effect of potential competition and the effect of its elimination falls into two broad categories. One type of evidence consists of studies of markets with different or changing numbers of potential entrants. With appropriate controls and modeling, empirical analysis can then determine how equilibrium price in the market varies with the number of potential competitors. The second type of evidence is the direct study of mergers that eliminate a potential, as opposed to an actual, competitor. Again with appropriate controls for other possible influences, a merger-specific study directly measures the change in price in markets where an incumbent firm in fact merges with a potential entrant.

Although merger-specific studies lack the generality of cross-sectional evidence, they have two distinct advantages over those examining numbers of potential competitors. The first advantage is simply that merger-specific studies directly address the key question, whereas studies of the presence of potential competitors rely on inference with respect to mergers. Indeed, merger-specific studies can be viewed as tests of the theory developed in section III that sets out the gain in incumbent profit from removing a constraining potential entrant.

A second advantage of a merger-specific study is that it avoids a bias that likely affects the evidence from studies of different or changing numbers of potential competitors. A merger is a purposeful pairing of particular firms, for example, a firm acquiring a particularly constraining competitor. By contrast, studies that compare market equilibria with differing numbers of potential entrants cannot capture the unique effect of eliminating

---

[34]   This approach has itself undergone transformation, albeit much more recently. See Warren Grimes and John Kwoka, *A Study in Merger Enforcement Transparency: The FTC's Cruise Merger Decision and the Presumption Governing High Concentration Mergers*, The Antitrust Source 1 (May 2003), available at www.abanet.org/antitrust/at-source/03/05/metstudy.pdf.

[35]   The Federal Trade Commission, for example, seemed intent on further circumscribing such challenges by adding crucial adjectives to *Marine Bancorp* principles. In re B.A.T. Industries, 104 F.T.C. 852 (1984) it held that determination of potential entry requires '*clear* proof of *concrete* internal plans for independent entry that have been at least tacitly *approved* at the *governing levels* of corporate management' (emphasis added).

a particular potential entrant. Rather, they measure something like the average effect across all potential entrants. Hence, the effect of its elimination via merger is likely to be greater than the effect from a simple reduction by one in the total number of potential competitors in some market.

We now turn to summaries of both types of empirical evidence.

A   Merger Eliminating Potential Competition

Empirical study of mergers eliminating potential competition is in principle no different than the study of mergers between incumbent firms. In practice, however, potential competition mergers pose distinctive challenges, most especially because of the difficulty of reliably identifying firms that are potential entrants. Firms that by virtue of their 'characteristics, capability, and economic incentive' can enter quickly and cheaply are not always obvious. For this reason, until recently there appears to have been no empirical studies examining the effects of an actual merger eliminating potential competition. One such study now exists.

That study, by Kwoka and Shumilkina,[36] examines a merger in the airline industry, where mergers have been numerous, where the requisite data on prices and competitors are readily available,[37] and where it is considerably more straightforward to identify potential entrants than in other markets. Airline markets are conventionally defined as city-pairs, and potential entrants are taken as those carriers that serve either or both endpoints but not the route itself. Endpoint-serving carriers are viewed as uniquely and advantageously positioned to enter service on the route quickly, cheaply, and easily, for at least three reasons. First, such carriers have in place some of the ground infrastructure required to serve the route. Second, they have market-specific information useful in developing and providing service for local needs. And third, they have the feed or connecting traffic that makes entry more likely profitable relative to a stand-alone new route.

Studies of airline pricing share a common methodology that is relevant to the investigation of potential competition and mergers that eliminate potential competitors. Figure 4.2 illustrates the standard market setting, with letters X, Y, and Z denoting incumbent firms on the route from A to B, while M and N are endpoint-serving firms, i.e. potential entrants. Note that M serves one endpoint while N serves both, but in neither case does the carrier serve the route itself. Whereas standard studies of airline pricing examine the effect of concentration among incumbents X, Y, and Z, or the effect of changes in concentration caused by a merger between two incumbents (e.g., X and Y), our focus is a merger between one incumbent and one endpoint-serving potential entrant (e.g., X and M). In this latter case, concentration on the route itself does not change, since the incumbent carriers do not change in number, identity, or share. The key question is whether

---

[36]   John Kwoka and Evgenia Shumilkina, *The Price Effect of Eliminating Potential Competition: Evidence from an Airline Merger*, J. INDUSTRIAL ECONOMICS 767 (December 2010).

[37]   As a vestige of their regulated days, airlines are required to report to the Department of Transportation considerable information from a 10% sample of all tickets written each quarter. That database is publicly available, permitting research into a variety of pricing, concentration, and other aspects of airlines' presence in markets throughout the country.

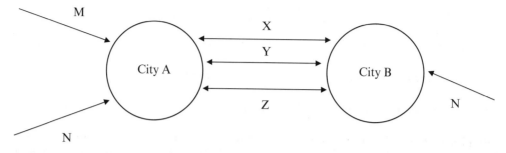

Note: X, Y, and Z are actual competitors; M and N are potential competitors

Figure 4.2   Airline route competition: actual and potential competitors

route pricing nonetheless changes as a result of the elimination of a particular potential competitor by merger.

The Kwoka–Shumilkina study examines the 1987 merger between US Air (now US Airways) and Piedmont Airlines.[38] The data employed in this study consist of 132,000 observations on pricing by carrier, by route, and by time (four quarters before the merger and four quarters after, with a break at the time of merger to minimize transition effects). Routes are separated into several categories, most importantly, (a) those where US Air was an incumbent and Piedmont a potential entrant, or the reverse; (b) those where both US Air and Piedmont were incumbents (permitting measurement of the usual merger effect); (c) those where either US Air or Piedmont was an incumbent and the other neither an incumbent nor a potential entrant; and (d) those where neither carrier was an incumbent or a potential entrant. The latter two categories serve as benchmarks since they represent markets not affected by the merger. In addition, the regression models (technically, a difference-in-difference approach) include a number of other standard control variables.

The results of this study are as follows. Where US Air and Piedmont were both incumbents, the merger resulted in a statistically significant price increase of 10.2% relative to routes unaffected by the merger. This result is consistent with other studies of the price effect of competitively-problematic airline mergers, including two previous studies of this US Air–Piedmont merger by Peters[39] and by Morrison.[40] Most importantly for present purposes, where one of the two carriers was an incumbent and the other a potential entrant, the merger caused a 6% price increase on the route. This result is the most direct test of the effect on pricing from a merger eliminating a constraining potential competitor. In this case that effect was a statistically significant price increase more than half as large

---

[38]   At the time of the study US Air–Piedmont was the most recent merger of major carriers not involving a bankrupt or financially distressed airline. The merger of Delta and Northwest occurred subsequently.

[39]   Craig Peters, *Evaluating the Performance of Merger Stimulation: Evidence from the U.S. Airline Industry*, 49 J. LAW AND ECONOMICS 627 (2006).

[40]   Steven Morrison, *Airline Mergers: A Longer View*, 30 J. TRANSPORT ECONOMICS AND POLICY 237 (1996).

Table 4.4   *Estimated price increases (%) from US Air–Piedmont merger*

Elimination of actual competition	10.2
Elimination of potential competition	
(a) Overall	6.0
(b) When potential competition is:	
large	6.2
small	5.4
(c) When HHI is:	
high	3.9
medium high	7.9
medium low	7.6
low	3.5
(d) When potential competition is at:	
two endpoints	5.9
one endpoint	6.1
(e) When incumbent is:	
US Air	6.8
Piedmont	5.1

Source: John Kwoka and Evgenia Shumilkina, *The Price Effect of Eliminating Potential Competition: Evidence from an Airline Merger*, J. INDUSTRIAL ECONOMICS 767 (December 2010).

as that from eliminating an actual competitor, and occurred even though concentration on the route itself did not change.[41]

This study analysed some variations on this result. These included the following (all results summarized in Table 4.4).

(1)   The price-constraining effect of either US Air or Piedmont as a potential competitor was statistically the same whether that potential competitor was large or small, as measured by the size of their endpoint operations. It appears that the threat itself, more than size, constrains the incumbent.

(2)   The effect of the loss of a potential competitor varies with the degree of concentration among incumbents in the market. The effect is greatest for mid-ranges of Herfindahl concentration, lower both when concentration is high (presumably reflecting already successful market coordination) and when concentration is low (presumably because coordination is more difficult, with or without the potential entrant).

(3)   The price effect from the loss of either US Air or Piedmont as a potential competitor on routes where the other carrier is an incumbent is statistically the same regardless of whether that potential competitor serves just one endpoint or both endpoints.

(4)   The effect is greater when US Air is the incumbent facing Piedmont as the potential

---

[41]   It is also noteworthy that the total value of consumer harm from this merger was 40% as large as that from reduced competition on routes involving the reduction of actual competition, although this effect is the result of these carriers' route configurations.

entrant, than when their roles are reversed. This scenario is consistent with the fact that US Air initiated the merger, presumably because of the considerable constraint that Piedmont imposed on its pricing.

This study appears to be unique in the literature in that it provides direct evidence on the question of the effect of eliminating a constraining potential competitor.

B   Presence of Potential Competitors

Insight into the effect of eliminating potential competition by merger can also be gleaned from estimates of price differences in markets with and without potential competitors, or more generally with varying numbers of potential competitors. The previously expressed caveat to this approach is that the full effect of a merger between a particular incumbent and a particular potential competitor is likely to be underestimated by comparison of two markets that simply differ in their numbers of potential competitors. The latter is the mean effect of reducing the number of potential competitors by one, whereas a merger – or at least one that raises competitive concerns – should have a distinctly greater effect since it eliminates a potential competitor that is particularly constraining.

The Kwoka–Shumilkina study has already demonstrated this difference. Table 4.4 reported the estimated price effect from the merger on routes where one of the carriers was an incumbent and the other a potential entrant to be 6%. In the full regression model not reported here, the estimated effect of another variable that counts the number of potential entrants (other than US Air or Piedmont) implies that one fewer such firm increases price by 1.9%. Thus, reducing the number of 'anonymous' potential entrants has less than one-third the price effect compared to the case where the merger eliminated the merger partner as a potential entrant. The difference between these two effects is statistically significant, confirming the tendency of studies of the presence of potential competitors to substantially underestimate the price effect from merger eliminating a particular potential competitor.

With that caveat in mind, we nonetheless review studies of varying numbers of potential competitors, since properly interpreted, they do cast some further light on merger effects. The relevant studies derive from four industries: airlines (again), railroads, pharmaceuticals, and cable TV. This subsection summarizes those studies.

1   Airlines

By far the largest group of studies is in the airline industry. The reasons for the attention to airlines have already been mentioned, and we also have described their standard empirical approach: across many different city-pair markets, data are compiled on incumbent concentration, the number of potential competitors, and various control variables. Concentration is usually measured by HHI or sometimes by its inverse, 'numbers-equivalent',[42] and potential competitors are the count of carriers serving either endpoint

---

[42]   The HHI, or Herfindahl-Hirschman Index of concentration, is defined as the sum of the squares of each firm's market share. If firms are equal in size, HHI equals 10,000 divided by the number of firms, e.g., five identical firms would result in an HHI equal to 2,000. Although

but not the route itself, as shown in Figure 4.2. These data are then used in a regression model on price on the route (generally, yield per mile), controlling for other possible influences.

A good example of such a study is that by Morrison and Winston,[43] who investigated 769 airline markets in 1983. After controlling for various other factors and adjusting for service quality, they found that each additional actual carrier on a route causes price to fall by 4%, and that one more potential competitor brings price down by 1.4%. Both effects are statistically significant, and the difference between them is also significant. The Morrison and Winston results establish two important, and intuitive, propositions: in equilibrium, the number of potential competitors does matter, and each potential competitor matters less than an actual incumbent.

This methodology, with many variations, has been employed in a substantial number of studies of the airline industry. Most are reviewed elsewhere,[44] permitting a briefer summary of those studies together with somewhat closer attention to a few additional contributions. Twelve previous studies of the airline industry have included potential competition as a causal factor in explaining prices, one of those studies being that by Morrison and Winston described in detail above. Most studies use a count of endpoint-serving airlines as their measure of potential competition, with some variation in details. All 12 studies find that potential competition results in lower prices by incumbent carriers, in 10 cases by statistically significant amounts. Except as noted below, the amounts range from one-quarter of 1% to about 2%, and in all cases are less than the amount of the price decline from one additional *actual* competitor, specifically, from one-eighth to one-third as large. These results corroborate the proposition that potential competitors indeed do constrain incumbents' pricing behavior and hence alter market equilibrium toward a more competitive outcome.

Two of those studies, together with one published subsequent to that review, find a larger effect from potential competition in airline markets when the potential entrant is Southwest Airlines. Southwest's historically low costs, its distinctive service, and until recently its unique business strategy have made it a particularly potent constraint on its rivals. Richards[45] found a substantial and significant 'Southwest effect' when that carrier served one endpoint of a route, and indeed the effect was essentially the same effect as when it served the route itself. Morrison[46] reports a 33% reduction in price when Southwest serves both endpoints and a 12–13% effect when it serves one endpoint of a route. These magnitudes should be compared to a 46% reduction when it serves the

---

real markets do not consist of equal-size firms, any actual value of HHI can be interpreted as deriving from some number of equal-size firms, calculated as 10,000/HHI. Thus, any market with an HHI of 2,000 could be interpreted as having a 'numbers-equivalent' of five equal-size firms.

[43]   Steven Morrison and Clifford Winston, *Empirical Implications and Tests of the Contestability Hypothesis*, 30 J. LAW AND ECONOMICS 53 (1987).

[44]   Kwoka, *supra* note 21.

[45]   Krista Richards, *The Effects of Southwest Airlines on U.S. Airlines Markets*, 32 J. LAW AND ECONOMICS 179 (1996).

[46]   Steven Morrison, *Actual, Adjacent and Potential Competition: Estimating the Full Effect of Southwest Airlines*, 35 J. TRANSPORT ECONOMICS AND POLICY 240 (2001).

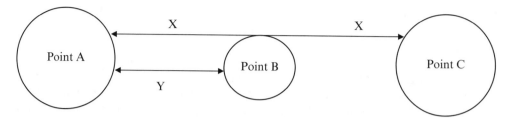

Figure 4.3   Railroad route competition: actual and potential competitors

route itself.[47] Goolsbee and Syverson[48] estimate a structural model of entry and find that incumbents lower their prices as soon as Southwest is perceived to be positioning itself for entry. Price reductions prior to entry range up to about 19% and are followed by further declines up to 13% upon actual entry. All of these results demonstrate the constraining effect of potential competition in these markets, and in particular the enormous impact of Southwest Airlines, which has an effect much like a maverick firm even when it is only a potential competitor.

2   Railroads

Much as in the case of airlines, identifying potential competitors in geographic space is somewhat easier than with respect to product market competition. Accordingly, two studies have examined pricing in the railroad industry in ways that cast light on the effect of potential competition. The setting is described in Figure 4.3, where one railroad X serves the entirety of the origin-to-destination route A–C, whereas a second carrier Y operates only on segment A–B and can therefore offer its customers only inferior 'interline' service, i.e. involving a transfer between carriers at point B. By virtue of its proximity to B–C, however, carrier Y can likely enter into operation on that segment B–C, and hence offer full through service more quickly and cheaply than other carriers.

Two studies of railroad pricing surveyed elsewhere[49] have examined the effects on incumbent pricing of service on A–C from the existence of another carrier serving A–B in Figure 4.3. Despite the obvious greater expense and time required for entry into rail markets, these studies nonetheless find substantial and significant price reductions on routes where such competitors were poised to enter.

3   Cable TV

In markets where product rather than geography determines potential competition, studies must confront the task of identifying such firms in some other way. The remaining industry studies reviewed here employ a variety of strategies for doing so. Savage

---

[47]   All of these results are statistically significant. Morrison notes that Southwest's pervasive and enormous presence meant that it accounted for more than half of the total gains from airline deregulation.

[48]   Austan Goolsbee and Chad Syverson, *How Do Incumbents Respond to the Threat of Entry? Evidence from the Major Airlines* (NBER Working Paper 11072, 2005).

[49]   Kwoka, *supra* note 21.

and Wirth[50] examine cable TV markets where technologies such as wireless cable, local telephone companies, second cable operators, and other sources provide threatened or actual competition. The Savage–Wirth study first estimates the probability of entry into a particular market by such alternative providers, depending on various cost, demographic, and local industry characteristics. Those estimated probabilities are used to explain prices charged by the incumbent cable TV monopoly.

Interpreting the estimated entry probabilities as a measure of the constraining effect of potential competition, the Savage–Wirth results imply that potential competition has a substantial effect on incumbents' behavior. Interestingly, however, the effect is not to force prices down, but rather to increase 'quality' by adding channels. As the probability of entry rises from 3 to 42%, the incumbent monopoly cable operator responds by offering six additional channels, a substantial increase over the mean of 32 channels. This evidence corroborates the competitive effect of potential entry, although the precise reasons that the response takes the form of a quality increase rather than a price reduction requires further study.

4   Pharmaceuticals

The pharmaceutical industry has been the focus of several studies of the effects of potential competition. Each study has a somewhat different method for identifying potential entrants. The first, illustrated in Cool *et al.*,[51] involves estimating a 'presence vector' of overlapping segments in the operations of existing pharmaceutical firms. Overlap between firms is taken as an indication of their similar interests and comparable resources and hence their potential to enter each other's segment. The profitability of 22 leading pharmaceutical firms in the United States between 1963 and 1982 is then related to actual rivalry and potential rivalry, as measured by overlap, after controlling for other factors. Cool *et al.* find that both greater actual competition and greater potential competition are effective in reducing return on sales. The effects are roughly comparable up through the late 1970s, after which actual competition has had a larger effect than does potential competition. Both effects, however, remain statistically significant.

The other approach for isolating the role of potential competition in specific drug markets exploits the important patent feature of the industry.[52] During the period of a drug's patent protection, of course, there can be no competition. But the pricing strategy of the incumbent firm during this period of time reflects the prospect of future entry and

---

[50]   Scott Savage and Michael Wirth, *Price Programming and Potential Competition in US Cable Television Markets*, 27 J. REGULATORY ECONOMICS 25 (2005).

[51]   Karel Cool, Lars-Hendrik Roller and Benoit Leleux, *The Relative Impact of Actual and Potential Rivalry on Firm Profitability in the Pharmaceutical Industry*, 20 STRATEGIC MANAGEMENT J. 1 (1999).

[52]   Another practice involving pharmaceutical patents may also illustrate the effect of potential competition (though not its merger-related elimination). So-called 'reverse payments' involve an agreement between an incumbent drug company with a patented product that enters into an agreement with a generic entrant to postpone entry in trade for a direct payment. One interpretation is that the incumbent is seeking to buy off the constraining competitor, although the practice has other interpretations. For discussion of non-merger related issues raised by potential competition, see John Bigelow and Robert Willig, *'Reverse Payments' in Settlements of Patent Litigation*, in THE ANTITRUST REVOLUTION (John Kwoka and Lawrence White eds, 2009).

competition. Moreover, after patent expiration the incumbent is faced with actual generic entry or at least the bona fide threat of such entry at any time. Two studies make use of these facts to measure the effect of potential competition.

Ellison and Ellison[53] examine marketing, product proliferation, and pricing strategies of an incumbent pharmaceutical company in the period leading up to patent expiration. Conditioned by the prospect of generic entry (but without any fear of hastening it), the incumbent's typical response is found to be to increase its price on the branded version of the drug in the period immediately before patent expiration. The reason is that the incumbent seeks to preserve the high-margin branded segment of the market, while ceding to lower-cost generic rivals the more price-sensitive segments of the market. As a result, somewhat paradoxically, prospective competition increases pre-entry price in a market subject to such segmentation, although post-entry prices generally decline at least moderately.

Work by Bergman and Rudholm[54] examines drug pricing in Sweden, specifically, the behavior of post-patent-expiration price in markets where entry has actually occurred, and separately in markets without actual but with potential entry. This study finds that prices fall by essentially the same amount in both cases, about 4 to 8% – a result that they interpret as evidence of the substantial importance of the constraining effect of potential competition. Notably, the reason for the smaller price reductions in this study compared to the Ellison and Ellison finding is that in Sweden the incumbent firm commits to what is effectively a maximum price for a drug during the lifespan of its patent. This creates a powerful incentive for a lower base price throughout the patent period, and hence a smaller price reduction after patent expiration, compared to the US experience.

5   Summary of evidence

As the above makes clear, there is a substantial body of evidence regarding the effect of the presence of potential competitors on equilibrium in a wide variety of markets. In conjunction with the one study of an actual merger eliminating a potential competitor, this evidence provides considerable support for the proposition that such mergers can have significant anticompetitive effects, support analogous to that underlying policy toward mergers between incumbent firms.

VI   CURRENT APPROACHES TO POTENTIAL COMPETITION MERGERS

Despite these theoretical and empirical bases for concern with the elimination of potential competition, the evidentiary hurdles set for challenges to such mergers have chilled enforcement efforts. At the same time potential competition matters continue to arise, perhaps most especially in industries where deregulation has blurred traditional distinctions between services, and in high technology industries, where the possibility of product

---

[53]   GLENN ELLISON AND SARA FISHER ELLISON, STRATEGIC ENTRY DETERRANCE AND THE BEHAVIOR OF PHARMACEUTICAL INCUMBENTS PRIOR TO PATENT EXPIRATION (MIT, 2000).

[54]   Mats Bergman and Niklas Rudholm, *The Relative Importance of Actual and Potential Competition: Empirical Evidence from the Pharmaceutical Market*, 51 J. INDUSTRIAL ECONOMICS 455 (2003).

changes creates more abundant opportunities for entry. Despite the importance of such matters, the antitrust agencies have limited their challenges to potential competition mergers, and when they have pursued them, have modified the manner in which they proceed.

These cases and matters largely fall into three categories.[55] First, a few merger cases involving potential competition have gone to trial. Where this has occurred, however, potential competition has been raised as a secondary matter, with the primary allegation being the loss of actual competition. Notable among such cases is the Staples–Office Depot matter, where in addition to evidence of price differences between them due to varying amounts of actual competition, the documents made clear that pricing decisions were altered as a result of the threat of possible entry by the other merging party.[56] Both actual and potential competition concerns were in the complaint.

A second and larger category of cases involving the elimination of a potential competitor are those that have settled rather than going to trial. Settlements are particularly useful tools for resolution of issues where the agencies prefer to avoid judicial review of legal or economic theories. A number of such cases have arisen in the pharmaceutical, airline, technology, and other industries, including the Primestar–News Corporation merger,[57] the proposed US Air–United merger,[58] Google–DoubleClick,[59] the Hospira–Mayne merger,[60] and Ticketmaster–LiveNation.[61] Many of these cases have involved considerable concessions by the parties in the face of agency concerns over the loss of potential competition that would result from the merger, but notably, none has undergone full judicial review.

Thirdly, many examples of mergers arguably eliminating potential competition have arisen in regulated or partially deregulated industries. In many instances primary jurisdiction over competition matters lies with the regulatory agency rather than the antitrust agencies. Regulatory agencies' 'public interest' standard permits a broader approach to mergers eliminating potential competition than strictly antitrust standards, although agencies have dismissed concerns over such mergers at least as often as they have used their authority creatively. Examples include the various mergers between the Bell Operating

---

[55]   Summaries can be found in Kwoka, *supra* note 21; in Darren Bush and Salvatore Massa, *Rethinking the Potential Competition Doctrine*, WISCONSIN L.R. 1035 (2004); and in Darren Tucker, *Thoughts on Revising the Horizontal Merger Guidelines*, THE ANTITRUST SOURCE 1 (October 2009). Also of interest are two recent potential competition mergers that have been the subject of extensive reports by the UK Competition Commission. See *A Report on the Proposed Acquisition by SvitzerWijsmuller A/S of AdSteam Marine Ltd* (UK Competition Commission, 2007); also, *Ticketmaster and Live Nation Merger Inquiry: Provisional Findings Report* (UK Competition Commission, 2009).

[56]   FTC v. Staples, Inc., 970 F. Supp. 1066 (D.D.C. 1997).

[57]   United States v. Primestar, No. 1:98CV01193 (D.D.C. 12 May 1998).

[58]   US Department of Justice, *Department of Justice and Several States Will Sue to Stop United Airlines from Acquiring U.S. Airways*, Washington, DC, 27 July 2001.

[59]   Statement of the Federal Trade Commission Concerning Google DoubleClick, FTC File No. 071-0170, 2007.

[60]   Complaint, In the Matter of Hospira, Inc., and Mayne Pharma Ltd, FTC Docket No. C-4182.

[61]   Competitive Impact Statement, United States v. Ticketmaster and LiveNation, 25 January 2010.

Companies in the telecommunications sector (reviewed by the Federal Communications Commission),[62] railroad mergers such as that between the Union Pacific and Southern Pacific (reviewed by the Surface Transportation Board),[63] and natural gas pipelines and electric power companies (reviewed by the Federal Energy Regulatory Commission).[64]

These cases and others illustrate several propositions. First, mergers involving potential competitors continue unabated, and indeed may even be on the increase. Second, these cases involve major industries and companies, suggesting broad importance to the issues. And third, the agencies have sought to avoid direct challenges to such mergers, undoubtedly due to concern about their likelihood of prevailing.

VII   REVISED GUIDELINES AND RENEWED ATTENTION

The promulgation of the 2010 Horizontal Merger Guidelines represents a significant advance in many aspects of antitrust policy toward mergers, certainly including the case of mergers that eliminate potential competition. As previously noted, the very first sentence of those Guidelines explicitly states their focus to be on 'mergers and acquisitions involving actual *or potential* competitors'.[65] This policy position not only restores the doctrine of potential competition to the Guidelines, but in fact elevates it to a more prominent status than that in the original 1982 Guidelines.

Moreover, the new Guidelines make clear that potential competition mergers raise issues analogous to those involving actual competitors, and they provide some guidance as to how such mergers will be evaluated. A subsequent section states, 'The lessening of competition from such a merger [involving a potential competitor] is more likely to be substantial, the larger is the market share of the incumbent, the greater is the competitive significance of the potential entrant, and the greater is the competitive threat posed by this potential entrant relative to others'.[66] These criteria reflect economic theory and evidence,[67] and their articulation represents a major step forward in bringing stated merger policy into conformance with contemporary economics.

As always, actual practice may diverge from stated policy. Consequently, it will be important to observe how this policy statement and criteria will be applied in actual merger investigations and case bringing. It is nonetheless a major step for the agencies

---

[62]   Steven Brenner, *Potential Competition in Local Telephone Service: Bell Atlantic-Nynex*, in The Antitrust Revolution (John Kwoka and Lawrence White eds, 1999).

[63]   John Kwoka and Lawrence White, *Manifest Destiny? The Union Pacific and Southern Pacific Railroad Merger*, in The Antitrust Revolution, *supra* note 62.

[64]   Diana Moss, *Natural Gas Pipelines: Can Merger Enforcement Preserve the Gains from Restructuring?*, in Competition Policy and Merger Analysis In Deregulated and Newly Competitive Industries (Peter Carstensen, George Young-Bascom, and Susan Beth Farmer eds, 2008). Also, FERC, Order Authorizing Merger, Duke Energy Corporation and Cinergy Corp. Docket No. EC05-103-000, 2005.

[65]   Horizontal Merger Guidelines 2010, at 1 (emphasis added).

[66]   *Id.* at 18.

[67]   These arguments were made to the FTC-DOJ Merger Guidelines Review Project by this author, both in the Project Workshop held in Washington, DC, January 2010, and in subsequent Comments Submitted to the Horizontal Merger Guidelines Review Project, 26 January 2010.

to announce that they will monitor and review mergers that eliminate potential competition and look for indications of likely anticompetitive effects that in principle are little different from those that may arise in mergers between direct competitors.

VIII CONCLUSIONS

This chapter has examined the economic and policy issues raised by mergers that eliminate potential competitors. For some time, policy and practice did not reflect the importance of such mergers, largely due to the standards set by judicial precedent and the resulting marginalization of concerns with potential competition in the FTC-DOJ Merger Guidelines of 1984, 1992, and 1997. As reviewed herein, however, both economic theory and empirical evidence are clear that mergers that eliminate potential competitors can relax the competitive constraint on incumbent firm pricing, with substantial adverse effects on consumers. These concerns have now been elevated to substantial importance in the new 2010 Horizontal Merger Guidelines.

While existing evidence is substantial, further research into the effects of potential competition and the effects of eliminating particular potential competitors would provide additional corroboration of and details about those effects. Most important would be direct studies of actual mergers eliminating potential competitors that constrain incumbent firm behavior. Mergers that have been allowed to proceed in the belief that there would be no adverse effects would provide particularly useful insights into possible effects. Such research efforts would aid in making the criteria in the 2010 Merger Guidelines for policy toward mergers eliminating potential competition yet more sophisticated and rigorous.

PART II

AGREEMENTS AND UNILATERAL CONDUCT

5 Tying, bundling, and loyalty/requirement rebates

*Nicholas Economides**

I TYING AND BUNDLING: DEFINITIONS

Tying of two products (or services) occurs when a seller sells one good on the condition that the buyer buys the other good from that seller:

> A tying arrangement is 'an agreement by a party to sell one product but only on the condition that the buyer also purchase a different (or tied) product, or at least agrees that he will not purchase that product from any other supplier.'[1]

Of particular interest are cases when the seller has market power in the tying product (call it product A) which is the one required to be sold with the other (tied) product. The tied product (call it product B) is the one that the buyer has to take to get the tying product.

There are many different ways in which the sale of a product can be conditioned on the sale of another. The tie that comes first to mind is the sale of two goods together in a 1:1 ratio or, more generally, in a fixed ratio. But there are also other more sophisticated ways to condition tying. A tying condition may require a certain number of units of the tied good to be bought from the same seller. An even more restrictive condition resulting in a 'requirements tie' is an agreement to sell the tying product only if the buyer buys all or most of its requirements of the tied product from that seller. The 'requirements tie' conditions pricing on the number of units that a buyer buys from a rival. As we will see, the requirements tie has quite different effects from the fixed ratio tie, as well as from the ties that are based on the number of units bought from the same seller.

Bundling is a general term describing selling collections of goods (A, B, C, . . .) as a package. Such collections may vary in their composition and in the conditions that apply to the availability of special pricing for the collections.

Bundling discounts can be based on a variety of conditions. There can be fixed ratio bundles, such as buying a desktop computer and a video monitor at a lower price than à la carte. There can be bundled discounts based on a requirement to buy a certain number of units from the same seller. And there are more sophisticated bundling programs, such as a bundled loyalty agreement where a buyer agrees to buy from a seller all or most of the buyer's needs of two products, generally for terms preferable to those given to buyers who don't buy most or all of their needs of two products from the seller. As we

---

* I thank Douglas Broder, Einer Elhauge, William Hebert, and Ioannis Lianos for comments on an earlier draft.
[1]   Kodak, 504 U.S. 461 (quoting Northern Pacific R. Co. v. United States, 356 U.S. 1, 5–6 (1958)). See, e.g., Yentsch v. Texaco, Inc., 630 F.2d 46, 56–7 (2d Cir. 1980).

will see,[2] bundles with fixed ratios have effects similar to ties with fixed ratios, bundles with a requirement to buy a certain number of units from the same seller are similar to ties under the same condition, and bundled loyalty agreements have effects similar to requirements ties.[3]

In some cases in a requirement tie, the available prices outside the bundle (the à la carte prices) are so high that there are no à la carte sales, so that bundling under a requirement tie is de facto tying. Then we can think of tying as a special case of bundling.[4]

II   CHICAGO SCHOOL THEORY OF A SINGLE MONOPOLY SURPLUS AND WHY IT TYPICALLY FAILS

In a series of early decisions, the Supreme Court ruled that tying was per se illegal, so specific analysis of economic harm was unnecessary to find liability.[5] In the late 1970s prominent antitrust scholars (Posner, Easterbrook, Bork) proposed instead that tying should be per se legal, and only in exceptional circumstances can there be antitrust liability.[6] Their reasoning was based on early work by Director and Levy (1956) which

---

[2]   Also see Nicholas Economides, *Loyalty/Requirement Rebates and the Antitrust Modernization Commission: What is the Appropriate Liability Standard?*, 54 ANTITR. BULL. 259 (2009), available at www.stern.nyu.edu/networks/Economides_Loyalty_Discounts_AntitrustBulletin.pdf; Nicholas Economides and Ioannis Lianos, *The Elusive Antitrust Standard on Bundling in Europe and in the United States at the Aftermath of the Microsoft Cases*, 76 ANTITR. L.J. 483, 510–34 (2009), available at www.stern.nyu.edu/networks/Economides_Lianos_Bundling.pdf; Einer Elhauge, *Tying, Bundled Discounts, and the Death of the Single Monopoly Profit Theory*, 123 HARV. L. REV. 397, 451–3, 457–8 (2009).

[3]   It is also useful to distinguish bundled loyalty conditions (which simply make receipt of favorable terms conditioned on actually meeting loyalty conditions) from bundled loyalty commitments (where the buyer commits in advance to meet the loyalty conditions in order to get the favorable terms), because they have slightly different effects. For a summary of differences see Elhauge, *supra* note 2, at 460–61, 470–72. Also see Einer Elhauge, *How Loyalty Discounts Can Perversely Discourage Discounting*, 5 J. COMPETITION L. AND ECON. 189 (2009).

[4]   See Dennis W. Carlton, Patrick Greenlee, and Michael Waldman, *Assessing the Anticompetitive Effects of Multiproduct Pricing,* 53 ANTITR. BULL. 587, 597 (2008); Economides, *supra* note 2.

[5]   See Jefferson Parish Hospital District No. 2 v. Edwin G. Hyde, 466 U.S. 2, 12 nn. 12–14 (1984). See also Motion Picture Patents Co. v. Universal Film Co., 243 U.S. 502 (1917); United States Steel Corp. v. Fortner Enterprises, 429 U.S. 610, 619–21 (1977); Fortner Enterprises v. United States Steel Corp., 394 U.S. 495, 498–9 (1969); White Motor Co. v. United States, 372 U.S. 253, 262 (1963); Brown Shoe Co. v. United States, 370 U.S. 294, 330 (1962); United States v. Loew's Inc., 371 U.S. 38 (1962); Northern Pacific R. Co. v. United States, 356 U.S. 1, 5 (1958); Black v. Magnolia Liquor Co., 355 U.S. 24, 25 (1957); Times-Picayune Publishing Co. v. United States, 345 U.S. 594, 608–9 (1953); Standard Oil Co. of California v. United States, 337 U.S. 293, 305–6 (1949); International Salt Co. v. United States, 332 U.S. 392, 396 (1947). For an historical perspective on this case law, see V.H. Kramer, *The Supreme Court and Tying Arrangements: Antitrust as History*, 69 MINNESOTA L. REV. 1013 (1985).

[6]   See ROBERT BORK, THE ANTITRUST PARADOX 375 (1978); RICHARD A. POSNER, ANTITRUST LAW: AN ECONOMIC PERSPECTIVE (2001); RICHARD POSNER AND FRANK EASTERBROOK, ANTITRUST CASES, ECONOMIC NOTES, AND OTHER MATERIALS 802–10 (2d ed., St. Paul, Minn., West Publishing (Co., 1981).

has become known as the Chicago School 'one surplus theory'.[7] This theory essentially stated that a monopolist in good A has no reason to tie product B except when there are cost savings or other efficiencies in the joint production or distribution of A and B. In the Chicago School line of reasoning, tying only occurs when it is efficient (because of cost savings), and therefore tying should be allowed in principle, and only occasionally and in special circumstances might be found illegal.

At the heart of the Chicago School analysis, the first question is 'why does the monopolist want a second monopoly?'[8] Clearly, the Chicago School is correct to state that cost savings in production and distribution are a possible reason for any firm, even a monopolist, to want a second monopoly, not for the second monopoly's revenue and profits, but for the cost savings created in selling the combination of the two goods. However, the Chicago School's proposition that cost savings in joint production and distribution are the *only* reason for tying and bundling is incorrect, as we see below.[9]

The question 'why does a monopolist want a second monopoly?' is insufficient to

---

[7]   See Aaron Director and Edward H. Levi, *Law and the Future: Trade Regulation*, 51 Nw. U. L. Rev. 281, 290 (1956).

[8]   See Posner and Easterbrook, *supra* note 6, at 802.

[9]   See Economides, *supra* note 2, at 262–4; Economides and Lianos, *supra* note 2; Nicholas Economides and Ioannis Lianos, *A Critical Appraisal of Remedies in the EU Microsoft Cases*, Columbia Bus. L. Rev. 346 (2010), available at www.stern.nyu.edu/networks/Economides_Lianos_Critical_Appraisal_Microsoft_Remedies.pdf; Elhauge, *supra* note 2. Also see Michael D. Whinston, *Tying, Foreclosure, and Exclusion*, 80 Am. Econ. Rev. 838 (1990); Barry Nalebuff, *Bundling as an Entry Barrier*, 119 Q. J. Econ. 159 (2004); Bruce H. Kobayashi, *Does Economics Provide a Reliable Guide to Regulating Commodity Bundling by Firms? A Survey of the Economic Literature*, 1 J. Competition L. and Econ. 707 (2005); Bruce H. Kobayashi, *The Economics of Loyalty Rebates and Antitrust Law in the United States*, Competition Pol'y Int'l 115 (Autumn 2005); Thomas A. Lambert, *Evaluating Bundled Discounts*, 89 Minn. L. Rev. 1688 (2005); Daniel L. Rubinfeld, *3M's Bundled Rebates: An Economic Perspective*, 72 U. Chi. L. Rev. 243 (2005); David Spector, *Loyalty Rebates: An Assessment of Competition Concerns and a Proposed Structured Rule of Reason*, Competition Pol'y Int'l 89 (Autumn 2005); Daniel A. Crane, *Multiproduct Discounting: A Myth of Nonprice Predation*, 72 U. Chi. L. Rev. 27 (2005); Kai-Uwe Kuhn *et al.*, *Economic Theories of Bundling and Their Policy Implications in Abuse Cases: An Assessment in Light of the* Microsoft *Case*, 1 Eur. Competition J. 85 (2005); Christian Ahlborn and David Bailey, *Discounts, Rebates and Selective Pricing by Dominant Firms: A Trans-Atlantic Comparison*, in Handbook of Research In Transatlantic Antitrust 195 (Philip Marsden ed., 2006); Herbert Hovenkamp, *Discounts and Exclusion*, Utah L. Rev. 841 (2006); Robert H. Lande, *Should Predatory Pricing Rules Immunize Exclusionary Discounts?*, Utah L. Rev. 863 (2006); Frank P. Maier-Rigaud, *Article 82 Rebates: Four Common Fallacies*, 2 Eur. Competition J. 85 (2006); Martin Beckenkamp and Frank P. Maier-Rigaud, *An Experimental Investigation of Article 82 Rebate Schemes*, 2 Competition L. Rev. 1 (Supp. 2006); John Simpson and Abraham L. Wickelgren, *Bundled Discounts, Leverage Theory, and Downstream Competition*, 9 Am. L. and Econ. Rev. 370 (2007); Gregory K. Leonard, *The Competitive Effects of Bundled Discounts*, in Economics of Antitrust: Complex Issues in a Dynamic Economy 3 (Laurence Wu ed., 2007); Timothy J. Brennan, *Bundled Rebates as Exclusion Rather than Predation*, 4 J. Competition L. and Econ. 335 (2008); Damien Geradin, *A Proposed Test for Separating Pro-Competitive Conditional Rebates from Anti-Competitive Ones*, 32 World Competition 41 (No. 1, 2009); Patrick Greenlee *et al.*, *An Antitrust Analysis of Bundled Loyalty Discounts* (Econ. Analysis Group, Discussion Paper No. 04-13, 2004), available at http://papers.ssrn.com/sol3/papers.cfm?abstract_id=600799; Janusz A. Ordover and Greg Shaffer, *Exclusionary Discounts* (Centre for Competition Policy, Working Paper No. 07-13, 2007), available at http://papers.ssrn.com/sol3/papers.cfm?abstract_id=995426).

describe the incentives of a monopolist to impose tying and bundling. The key to understanding the motives behind the decision to tie or bundle is that a monopolist can extract surplus in varying degrees from buyers. Thus, the word 'monopoly' does not describe sufficiently the extent of extraction of consumer surplus[10] by the seller. In some markets, monopolists are able to extract all consumer surplus by selling each unit to every buyer at his/her willingness to pay, a practice called perfect price discrimination. In most markets, this very complex pricing is unfeasible. Perfect price discrimination may be unfeasible for at least three reasons: (i) the seller does not know the willingness to pay for each unit that every buyer may be willing to buy; (ii) the pricing schedule to be implemented is very complex; and (iii) resale among the users (arbitrage) makes price discrimination unfeasible.

The incentive of a monopolist to impose tying or bundling practices depends on the extent to which he is able to extract surplus from each buyer and on the extent to which each buyer is left with some consumer surplus before tying or bundling is imposed. In particular, if a monopolist is able to extract *all* consumer surplus from every buyer without imposing tying or bundling, there is no incentive for tying or bundling that does not create a substantial foreclosure share in the tied product except in the presence of cost savings from joint production and distribution.[11] So, in this very special setting where the monopolist is able to extract *all* consumer surplus from every buyer and the tie does not foreclose a substantial share of the tied product market, the Chicago School theory is correct.[12] But extracting *all* consumer surplus from every buyer is very unlikely to occur in practice, and thus, the Chicago School's theory fails most of the time.

The Chicago School theory is developed under the assumption of a homogeneous monopolized good and a homogeneous tied good. If there is consumer demand for variety or quality product differentiation, the Chicago School theory can easily fail because entry of even an inefficient rival in a new variety or quality can add to consumer surplus.

Besides extracting additional consumer surplus from its current degree of tying market power, a monopolist might be able to gain if it forecloses a substantial share of the tied product and that (1) gives the firm tied market power it can use against tied product buyers who were not subject to the tie, or (2) increases the degree of tying market power.[13]

---

[10]   Consumer surplus is the difference between what consumers are cumulatively willing to pay and what they cumulatively actually pay in a market. It represents the net benefit to consumers from the existence of the market. As long as a consumer or different consumers have varying valuations for different units of a good, and the good is sold at a single price, consumer surplus is positive.

[11]   Full consumer surplus can be extracted when each buyer buys only one unit and the seller is able to sell to each buyer at the price that buyer is willing to pay, thereby leaving no consumer surplus for any buyer. Or, more generally, a seller sells many units to each buyer, but is able to offer very sophisticated, individually tailored pricing that extracts all consumer surplus from all units bought by each buyer.

[12]   Even with full consumer surplus extraction by the seller and tying not creating substantial foreclosure in the tied product, the Chicago School theory can fail if a buyer has made complementary investments that require the use of a certain amount of the relevant goods. By manipulating the prices and ratios of tied goods in the tying contract, the monopolist can effectively threaten not to sell the amounts that the buyer counted on buying when making the complementary investments, and thereby the buyer can extract even more surplus. In this case, the buyer would be willing to give up more surplus so as not to lose the value of the complementary investments.

[13]   See section IIIC and Elhauge, *supra* note 2, at 413–19.

The specific inabilities of a monopolist to extract the full consumer surplus from all buyers define a roadmap of how tying and/or bundling without a substantial foreclosure share can profitably be used by a monopolist to extract additional surplus in the absence of joint production and distribution cost savings. If buyers buy one unit each but vary in willingness to pay, a single-price monopolist will fail to extract all consumer surplus. The monopolist can then use tying and/or bundling mechanisms to extract more surplus from buyers. If a buyer buys more than one unit and values each unit differently, again a single-price monopolist will fail to extract all consumer surplus, and can use tying and bundling practices to extract more surplus from buyers. Typically each buyer buys more than one unit of varying valuations *and* buyers differ in their valuations, so even sophisticated nonlinear pricing by the monopolist will have a very hard time extracting *all* surplus from *all* buyers. Then the availability of tying and bundling strategies increases the ability of a monopolist to extract consumer surplus.

III   STRATEGIC REASONS FOR TYING AND BUNDLING

I now analyse a number of reasons/settings that provide an incentive to a monopolist to impose tying restrictions that go beyond cost savings, as described above. I assume no cost savings from joint distribution and production and no substantial foreclosure share and look for other reasons that may drive a monopolist in good A to tie product B or to create a bundling contract that involves A and B.[14] If cost savings from joint distribution and production exist, they can be taken into consideration as efficiencies to counterbalance consumer losses, but cost savings are not a necessary cause for a dominant firm to profitably introduce tying and/or bundling, including a loyalty/requirement discount program.

A   Use of Tying and Bundling to Extract Consumer's Surplus Through Intra-Product Price Discrimination

The first strategic reason for tying is when tying helps extract more consumer surplus of product A than the monopolist is able to extract through single-price monopoly of good A. In this practice, the main objective is not appropriating additional surplus from product B. Instead, the main objective of tying that I identify in this section is to appropriate more consumer surplus from product A.[15] The key assumption here is that, absent tying, the monopolist in A is unable to implement perfect price discrimination, and therefore unable to extract all the consumer surplus of product A as its profits. Tying A with B and requiring that only the monopolist's product B is used with A (rather than a rival's B) can be used as a metering device for the use of A, and can implicitly reveal the willingness to pay of a buyer of A if the willingness to pay for A is highly

---

[14]   The arguments can be easily extended to ties and bundles that involve more than two goods.

[15]   This does not imply there may not be other incentives for tying, such as increasing tying power in A and increasing market power in B. Also monopolization of the B market raises concerns about the loss of consumer surplus of buyers of B who do not buy A, as well as common concerns of monopolization such as elimination of competitive pressure for cost reduction and innovation.

positively correlated with use of B. Once B is tied and sold at a supracompetitive price, the monopolist can extract more surplus than without tying. Of course, if a consumer uses A and B in fixed proportions, increasing the price of B will have the same effect as increasing the price of A, and tying B would be unnecessary to implement intra-product price discrimination. Therefore, for the tying of B to be profitable and useful to the seller of A in intra-product price discrimination, it is necessary that A and B are not sold/demanded in fixed proportions.[16]

The arguments for the strategic reason for tying outlined above work both when each buyer buys a single unit of A or many units of A, as long as the pricing conditions in the absence of tying leave some consumer surplus to the buyer or buyers.

A good example of intra-product discrimination may be found in *IBM v. United States.*[17] There, IBM required lessees of tabulating machines to buy paper cards used by these machines only from itself. The extent of use of paper cards can measure the use of the machine and may be closely correlated with the willingness to pay for the lease. Clearly, the same setup applies more generally to tying a durable good with a complementary consumable, such as a printer with replacement ink. Sometimes companies use patents in an attempt to implement the tie as well as go around the antitrust issues that arise in tying.[18]

Tying in this context typically reduces consumers' surplus in A and forecloses rival firms in good B.[19] Firms may not be able to enter the market for B unless they also enter the market for A.[20] Posner and Easterbrook (1981) claim that, since this tying is based on price discrimination, whether such behavior is anticompetitive is debatable, depending on whether price discrimination in the particular case can be proved to reduce consumers' surplus and therefore be deemed illegal.[21] However, the law disallows the exclusion effects

---

[16]   As we will see in section IIID, tying with a fixed ratio between the products can also accomplish inter-product price discrimination. Also see Elhauge, *supra* note 2, at 405–7, 455–6.

[17]   See International Business Machines Corp. v. United States, 298 U.S. 131, 56 S.Ct. 701, 80 L.Ed. 1085 (1936).

[18]   See, e.g., Microsoft Corp., 253 F.3d 34, 63 (D.C. Cir. 2001); C.R. Bard, Inc. v. M3 Sys., Inc., 157 F.3d 1340 (Fed. Cir. 1998); Image Technical Servs., Inc. v. Eastman Kodak Co., 125 F.3d 1195 (9th Cir. 1997). For a recent example, see Xerox v. Media Sciences, Civil Action No. 06-CV-4872 (RJH), US DC SDNY. Media Sciences is the only rival to Xerox in the market for replacement ink used in Xerox printers. Xerox patented the design of the entry chute for the replacement ink so as to exclude Media Sciences from the replacement ink market. See also Nicholas Economides and William Hebert, *Patents and Antitrust: Application to Adjacent Markets*, 6 J. TELECOMM. AND HIGH TECH. L. 455, 463–81 (2008), available at www.stern.nyu.edu/networks/Economides_Hebert_Patents_and_Antitrust.pdf.

[19]   Also see Barry Nalebuff, *Price Discrimination and Welfare*, 5 COMPETITION POL'Y INT'L 221, 231–2 (2009); Einer Elhauge, *The Failed Resurrection of the Single Monopoly Profit Theory*, 6 COMPETITION POL'Y INT'L 155, 186–92 (2009).

[20]   Such tying forecloses rivals in B from selling to buyers subject to the tie, but may not foreclose rivals from market B in general since rivals may be able to sell product B to buyers who are not subject to the tie.

[21]   Note that the Posner and Easterbrook argument about case-by-case analysis is inconsistent with the claim that ties should be per se legal, but is consistent with the quasi per se rule which actually is based on a case-by-case analysis (despite its name). See Elhauge, *supra* note 2, at 425–6. Some claim that tying should be legal when it results in intra-product price discrimination. See POSNER, *supra* note 6, at 203–4; 9 PHILLIP E. AREEDA and HERBERT HOVENKAMP, 9 *Antitrust Law* paras. 1705, 1710c4, at 99–100, 1711b, at 102–7, 1711e, at 110–12. However, implementing price

of tying and has no exception for tying when the objective of tying is to implement price discrimination. Additionally, often it is very difficult, if not impossible, to implement perfect price discrimination, so one cannot argue that the same outcome would have been achieved absent tying.

Bundling with a requirement condition can work very much like tying in extracting consumer surplus through intra-product price discrimination. In this setup, the monopolist in A can demand that a very large percentage of the needs in product B of a buyer be bought from it instead of requiring that all product B be bought from it. Additionally, the monopolist in A can increase the à la carte price of A as it institutes this bundling program, even to an above-monopoly level, to induce consumers to accept the bundle. These issues are discussed in detail in section IV

B Use of Tying and Bundling to Extract Consumer's Surplus Through Intra-Consumer Price Discrimination

As long as some consumer surplus is left to a buyer of a good even when this good is sold by a monopolist, the monopolist can use tying and/or bundling to extract the remaining surplus from the buyer. This setup requires that a buyer buy more than one unit, and that he values some unit(s) more than another (or other units). In other words, the buyer values one or more infra-marginal units more than the marginal unit. Some surplus left to a buyer means that the seller, absent tying and bundling, is unable to implement intra-consumer perfect price discrimination.

Under these conditions, the monopolist in market A leverages the remaining surplus with a buyer in market A to induce him to buy the monopolist's product in market B. That is, the seller's tying essentially threatens the buyer with loss of all his ex ante remaining consumer surplus to induce him to buy B from this seller. This requires that, without the use of tying and/or bundling strategies, some consumer surplus is left to affected buyers in market A, for example, because they purchase multiple units of the tying product. The threat of appropriation of this surplus by the monopolist is used in the tying or bundling scheme to induce the affected buyers to buy the monopolist's product in market B. Again, some consumer surplus is needed to be left with affected buyers under monopoly before tying and bundling is implemented. Therefore the necessary assumption (no consumer surplus left ex ante) for the Chicago School theory to work is violated and it fails.[22]

I now go into the details of how this tying and/or bundling program works. Suppose that a buyer buys goods A and B and, in the absence of bundling and tying, is left

---

discrimination without tying requires no resale (to avoid arbitrage) and knowledge of the willingness to pay of specific buyers and specific units for each buyer. Tying a second product that is highly correlated with usage of the first product allows the discovery of the value of each unit of the first good. Tying also eliminates the need for the no resale requirement. Finally, tying may be a much easier pricing scheme than the very complex pricing required for perfect price discrimination. For additional reasons why the analogy to price discrimination does not justify changing tying doctrine, see Elhauge, *supra* note 2, at 427–34.

22 See M.L. Burstein, *The Economics of Tie-In Sales*, 42 REV. ECON. AND STAT. 68 (1960); M.L. Burstein, *A Theory of Full-Line Forcing*, 55 NORTHWESTERN L. REV. 62 (1960).

with some consumer surplus $CS_{monop.A}$ in the monopolized market A at monopoly pricing and with consumer surplus $CS_{comp.B}$ in market B. For simplicity assume that the market in product B is originally competitive, although this is not necessary. Then the introduction of tying between A and B can force the buyer to give more surplus to the seller.

This works as follows. Before tying, a buyer has total consumer surplus from the two goods $CS_{monop.A} + CS_{comp.B}$. The monopolist seller in A refuses to offer A by itself but offers it only with B which he now sells at a monopoly price (and may offer A à la carte at a prohibitively high price in a bundling setting, as discussed later in the chapter). The buyer's consumer surplus from B in the tied arrangement is $CS_{monop.B}$ which is lower than without tying, $CS_{monop.B} < CS_{comp.B}$. The consumer surplus from both products under tying is $CS_{monop.A} + CS_{monop.B}$, which is lower than in the but-for world, $CS_{monop.A} + CS_{monop.B} < CS_{monop.A} + CS_{comp.B}$. Therefore (i) the buyer is worse off under tying compared to the but-for world (which was the original monopoly in A only); and (ii) the seller extracts additional surplus (and has higher profits) by tying.[23]

The buyer has the option of not buying the tied goods A and B from the monopolist, which means foregoing A altogether and buying B from a rival. If the buyer does not buy the tied products A and B from the monopolist, he loses his pre-tying consumer surplus from good A, $CS_{monop.A}$, and is left with only his consumer surplus from B at a competitive price, $CS_{comp.B}$. Because of this, the buyer may prefer to buy under tying, specifically when the alternative, that is, buying only B at competitive prices, is not as desirable. Therefore, in the world when tying is offered, the buyer prefers to buy under tying when $CS_{monop.A} + CS_{monop.B} > CS_{comp.B}$ even though he is worse off compared to the but-for, pre-tying, world.[24] Greenlee *et al.* (2008) also show that even when a buyer prefers not to buy under tying, the introduction of tying reduces consumer surplus.[25]

Notice that the price discrimination implemented through tying here is intra-consumer price discrimination, and requires that a buyer buys more than one unit and values units differently, and that the seller is unable to implement perfect price discrimination on each buyer, so a buyer is left with some consumer surplus absent tying and bundling. Since the price discrimination implemented through tying is among the units bought by the same consumer and is done separately for each consumer, it does not depend on differences across consumers. The tying scheme can be applied even if all buyers are identical in their valuations of the two products. Additionally, there is no requirement that market power and market share in the tied market B are significant before tying starts. However, once the tying scheme is in effect, the acceptance by many buyers to buy the tied products A

---

[23]   See Patrick Greenlee, David S. Reitman, and David S. Sibley, *An Antitrust Analysis of Bundled Loyalty Discounts*, 26 INT'L J. INDUS. ORG. 113 (2008); Barry Nalebuff, *Bundling as a Way to Leverage Monopoly* (Yale Working Paper, October 2004); Frank Mathewson and Ralph Winter, *Tying as a Response to Demand Uncertainty*, 28 RAND J. ECON. 566 (1997); and Elhauge, *supra* note 2, at 407–13.

[24]   If both A and B have linear demand curves and constant marginal costs, the condition of accepting to buy under tying, $CS_{monop.A} + CS_{monop.B} > CS_{comp.B}$, is equivalent to $CS_{monop.A} > 3CS_{monop.B}$ or equivalently $CS_{comp.A} > 3CS_{comp.B}$. See Greenlee *et al.*, *supra* note 23, at 1137; Elhauge, *supra* note 2, at 410.

[25]   See Greenlee *et al.*, *supra* note 23, at 1137; Elhauge, *supra* note 2, at 410–11.

and B (rather than forego A altogether) increases the seller's market power in the tying market.

Bundling with a requirement condition can work very much as tying in extracting consumer surplus through intra-consumer price discrimination. I discuss this in section IV under loyalty/requirement programs.

C   Tying Can Implement Inter-Product Price Discrimination to the Detriment of Consumers

Tying and bundling as described in the previous two subsections are mainly instruments to implement price discrimination and extract more consumer surplus from a single monopolized market with the caveats stated in the previous subsections. In those settings, the monopolization of the second market through tying and bundling is typically not the monopolist's main goal. However, there are settings where the objective of tying and bundling is the extraction of surplus in the second (tied good) market.

In the presence of substantial market power in the tying market,[26] when consumers buy two goods and their demands do not have very strong positive correlation, introduction of tying or bundled pricing can increase profits and reduce consumer surplus.[27] This applies for both fixed and variable ratio tying and bundling. The starting point for this analysis is the Supreme Court's decision in *United States v. Loew's Inc.*,[28] which banned fixed ratio bundles of movies, and Stigler's subsequent analysis of this case.[29] For illustration, suppose that consumers are distributed uniformly according to type x in [0, 100] so that consumer x has willingness to pay $p(x)$ for good A and willingness to pay US\$100 − $p(x)$ for good B. Additionally, let the willingness to pay for consumer of type x be inversely related to his type, $p(x) = 100 - x$. Then, if the goods are sold separately, a single-price monopolist will charge US\$50 for each of goods A and B, and, in each of these markets, consumer surplus will be US\$1,250.[30] However, if A and B are tied in a 1:1 ratio, the willingness to pay for AB is US\$100 for every consumer. The monopolist charges US\$100 for the bundle, all consumers buy the good, and consumers are left with zero consumer surplus. Although this example is constructed with negative correlation between the willingness to pay for the two goods, similar results can be established when the correlation between the willingness to pay for the two goods is not too positive.[31]

---

[26]   Substantial market power in the tied good or foreclosure effect is not required.

[27]   See also Elhauge, *supra* note 2, at 405–7, 415; Economides and Hebert, *supra* note 18, at 465.

[28]   371 U.S. 38 (1962).

[29]   See George J. Stigler, *United States v. Loew's Inc.: A Note on Block-Booking*, SUP. CT. REV. 152 (1963).

[30]   For a linear demand consumer surplus is the triangle below the demand curve from zero units to the market equilibrium quantity, here of area US\$(50) x (50)/2 = US\$1,250.

[31]   See Richard Schmalensee, *Gaussian Demand and Commodity Bundling*, 57 J. BUS. S211 (1984); Richard Schmalensee, *Commodity Bundling by Single-Product Monopolies*, 25 J.L. and ECON. 67 (1982); William James Adams and Janet L. Yellen, *Commodity Bundling and the Burden of Monopoly*, 90 Q.J. ECON. 475 (1976); R. Preston McAfee *et al.*, *Multiproduct Monopoly, Commodity Bundling, and Correlation of Values*, 104 Q.J. ECON. 371 (1989).

D   Use of Tying and Bundling to Disadvantage Rivals in the Tied Market and Foreclose Entry in the Tied Market

Tying and bundling, including under a loyalty/requirement program, can be used by a monopolist in A to foreclose rivals, reduce their scale of operations, and thereby increase their unit costs and reduce their competitiveness.[32] This can be profitable even when products A and B are tied in fixed proportions or the tied product has no other use. Tying and bundling can also be used by a monopolist to foreclose rivals in the tied market or reduce their scale of operations and increase their costs.[33] This requires that a substantial share of the tied market be foreclosed.[34]

Facing a smaller market, rivals with entry costs may not enter the tied market, resulting in less competition and lower consumer surplus. Based on the same argument, a company that only produces one of the tied products may exit the market as a result of tying.

A dominant firm with market power in two markets where a typical buyer buys both products can protect itself from entry in either of the markets by tying (or by offering a requirement/loyalty program). Thus, tying (and requirement/loyalty programs) may be used as entry-deterring devices by making it economically unprofitable for an entrant to enter one market without simultaneously entering the second market.[35]

IV   BUNDLING AND LOYALTY/REQUIREMENT PROGRAMS

A   A Loyalty 'Discount' is Equivalent to a 'Disloyalty Penalty'

In a typical loyalty/requirement bundling contract, a dominant firm in market *A* also sells in market *B* à la carte. Based on a requirement that a particular buyer buys a large percentage or 100% of his needs in both products from the dominant firm, the dominant firm also offers discounts on all units of either *A*, or *B*, or both,[36] or provides a lump sum discount.[37] The requirement/loyalty programs can be sufficiently tailored to the scale of

---

[32]   See Economides *supra* note 2, at 268; Economides and Lianos, *supra* note 2, at 511–16; Elhauge, *supra* note 2, at 413–19.

[33]   See Barry Nalebuff, *Bundling as an Entry Barrier*, 119 Q.J. Econ. 159 (2004); Economides and Hebert, *supra* note 18, at 466. Also see Phillip Aghion and Patrick Bolton, *Contracts as a Barrier to Entry*, 77 Amer. Econ. Rev. 388 (1987). The paper shows that a monopolist can extract a new entrant's technology advantage using contracts which require 100% of a customer's total purchases.

[34]   See Elhauge, *supra* note 2, at 413–19. Creating tied market power with ties cannot be profitable if the tie or bundle is in fixed proportions and the tied product has no use other than with the tying product. See Elhauge, *supra* note 2, at 416.

[35]   See, e.g., Barry Nalebuff, *Bundling as an Entry Barrier*, 119 Q.J. Econ. 159 (2004); Daniel L. Rubinfeld, *3M's Bundled Rebates: An Economic Perspective*, 72 U. Chi. L. Rev. 243, 257 (2005); Aaron S. Edlin and Daniel L. Rubinfeld, *Exclusion or Efficient Pricing? The 'Big Deal' Bundling of Academic Journals*, 72 Antitrust L.J. 119 (2004).

[36]   This setup can easily be extended to collections of more than two goods.

[37]   Need for monitoring implies that such discounts are typically not offered to final consumers but to companies.

each buyer (based on a percentage of his purchases of similar products) so that additional surplus is extracted by the monopolist.[38]

Bundling at a first glance seems procompetitive since, in terms of actual prices offered, the bundle price is lower than the à la carte price. However, this is highly misleading because the comparison of the actual price under the bundle/condition with the à la carte price is done in the presence of the bundle and the requirement condition. The correct comparison is comparing the actual prices (à la carte and bundled) with prices in the but-for world (without bundling). Note that the difference between the price under the bundling condition and the à la carte price can also be thought of as a penalty for not accepting the bundle, a 'disloyalty penalty'.[39]

B   A Loyalty 'Discount' Can be Illusory; No Profit Sacrifice is Needed in Loyalty/ Requirement Pricing

When bundled pricing is introduced, a dominant firm can simultaneously increase the à la carte prices above the but-for levels. And this can also result in the price of the bundle being higher than the but-for prices, so that the discount is in fact illusory and also results in higher market share for the dominant firm.[40]

Suppose that, in the but-for world, unit cost is US$150, but the dominant firm sells at US$250.[41] As the loyalty discount is introduced, the seller can increase the à la carte (or no commitment) price to US$300 (or more) while offering a price of US$250 under the commitment (by offering a US$50 discount per unit). As more buyers accept the commitment, the market power and the market share of the dominant firm increase, and simultaneously the collective market share of the rivals decreases. This allows the monopolist to increase price or at least maintain it at the old monopoly level. So the loyalty discount program enables the monopolist to increase market share without decreasing price. In implementing a loyalty/requirement program, the monopolist does not need to suffer any profit sacrifice. See also the detailed discussion in section IIIB.

---

[38]   One may also distinguish bundled loyalty/requirement conditions (which simply make receipt of favorable terms conditioned on actually meeting loyalty conditions) from bundled loyalty/requirement *commitments* (where the buyer commits in advance to meet the loyalty conditions in order to get the favorable terms). For a summary of their slightly different effects see Elhauge, *supra* note 2, at 460–61, 470–72; Einer Elhauge, *How Loyalty Discounts Can Perversely Discourage Discounting*, 5 J. Competition L. and Econ. 189 (2009).

[39]   See Economides, *supra* note 2, at 260; Economides and Lianos, *supra* note 2, at 513: Elhauge, *supra* note 2, at 402–3, 450; Einer Elhauge, United States Antitrust Law and Economics 406, 408 (2008).

[40]   See Economides and Lianos, *supra* note 2, at 513; Elhauge, *supra* note 39, at 406, 408; Greenlee *et al.*, *supra* note 23; Daniel L. Rubinfeld, *3M's Bundled Rebates: An Economic Perspective*, 72 U. Chi. L. Rev. 243, 252 (2005); Elhauge, *supra* note 2, at 402–3, 450.

[41]   In the example, the dominant firm is able to sell at a higher price than unit cost in the but-for world because of its market power.

C   Buyers Find Themselves in a 'Prisoners' Dilemma'

Given a choice between buying a bundle at a discount under a loyalty/requirement program and buying à la carte, many buyers will buy under the loyalty/requirement program, for the reasons explained in section IIIB. Even though buyers may each prefer to buy under the bundle when it is offered, this does not imply that buyers are better off than in the but-for world (where the loyalty/requirement program is not offered) for the reasons as explained in section IIIB.[42]

Additionally, if many buyers accept to buy under the bundle, the seller's market power will increase thereby making the buyers worse off. The situation is similar to the well-known game of the 'prisoner's dilemma'. In this game, two prisoners are offered a lower sentence if they accept a 'deal' with the prosecutor. The prisoner who accepts the deal is better off if the other prisoner does not accept the deal. But once they both have accepted the deal, they are both worse off than when neither accepted the deal. Similarly, here each buyer is better off by buying under the bundle assuming the bundling and à la carte prices are not affected by his decision and the decision of other buyers. But once many buyers buy under the requirement, the market power of the monopolist increases and he is able to increase both the à la carte and bundled prices. Therefore buying under the requirement does not make buyers better off than in the but-for world.[43]

D   Differences Among Types of Discounts

It is important to distinguish between different types of discounts. First, there can be standardized quantity discounts that are triggered once a buyer passes a certain quantity threshold. Among these there can be (i) discounts for the incremental units above a threshold; or (ii) discounts for all units once a threshold has been achieved, sometimes called 'first unit discounts' and sometimes 'retroactive discounts'. Second, there can be individualized discounts that are conditioned on the share of the requirements/needs of a buyer that are bought from the monopolist, or are conditioned on individualized quantities for each buyer. Again these discounts may be (i) for the incremental units above a threshold; or (ii) for all units (first unit or retroactive discounts). It should be clear that a discount on the share of the requirements of a buyer is an individualized discount because buyers generally have different requirements and it will apply at a different quantity for each buyer. Also note that a lump sum discount is a special case of an all-units discount.

We should be much more concerned about individualized loyalty/requirement discounts than about standardized discounts.[44] Individualized discounts can be tailored

---

[42]   See Economides, *supra* note 2, at 271–2; Economides and Lianos, *supra* note 2, at 513; Elhauge, *supra* note 2, at 451–5; Einer Elhauge, *The Failed Resurrection of the Single Monopoly Profit Theory*, 6 COMPETITION POL'Y INT'L 155, 177–83 (2009).

[43]   See Economides, *supra* note 2, at 260; Economides and Lianos, *supra* note 2, at 513–14; Elhauge, *supra* note 2, at 456.

[44]   The European Commission distinguishes between individualized-threshold and standardized-threshold discounts. Individualized-threshold discounts are based on a percentage of the total

to exclude rivals. If the same discount is available to all buyers who buy the same quantity (or combinations of quantities of A and B), a quantity-based price discount will leave some consumer surplus with buyers when buyers vary in their demand for the product(s). But an individualized loyalty/requirement pricing scheme with a condition based on the percentage sales by the monopolist of the needs of a buyer can be tailored to extract more surplus for the monopolist. A loyalty/requirement program can be written so that the discount will apply to different buyers according to the percentage of their purchases from the dominant firm, and therefore it can affect different units for each buyer. For example, a discount based on a 90% requirement/loyalty program affects different units when applied to a buyer of 100 units than when applied to a buyer of 1,000 units. Of course, pricing that depends on an individual buyer's demand and gives the same discount to one buyer for, say, unit number 100 as to another buyer for unit 1,000 is very hard to justify on efficiency considerations.[45] Finally, a volume discount will tend to be less restrictive since it will not require that fewer purchases be made from the rival(s) and leaves open the possibility for the buyer to buy from the rival(s) at competitive prices.[46]

We should also be much more concerned about conditional discounts that apply to all units than about discounts that apply only to incremental units. Table 5.1 summarizes this discussion.

E   Loyalty/Requirement Pricing Switches Competition from the Last Unit to Competition for Large Chunks of the Demand

Consider a buyer who buys 100 units in total from the dominant firm and the rival. If the dominant firm's lump sum rebate kicks in at the 90th unit, it is very unlikely that the buyer will buy 89 units, just short of achieving the quota necessary for the rebate. A buyer that might have bought 80 units in the but-for world in the absence of the rebate will consider buying 90 units to receive the rebate. Thus, competition is no longer for the last unit (the

---

requirements of a buyer or an individualized target volume, while the standardized-threshold discounts are the same for all customers. Article 82 of the EU Treaty applies to both types of discounts, although standardized discounts are treated more leniently. See Communication from the Commission, Guidance on the Commission's enforcement priorities in applying Article 82 of the EC Treaty to abusive exclusionary conduct by dominant undertakings [2009] OJ C 45/7, para. 45 (hereinafter 'EU Guidance'), also available at http://eur-lex.europa.eu/LexUriServ/LexUriServ. do?uri=OJ:C:2009:045:0007:0020:EN:PDF: 'It is normally important to consider whether the rebate system is applied with an individualized or a standardized threshold. An individualized threshold – one based on a percentage of the total requirements of the customer or an individualized volume target – allows the dominant supplier to set the threshold at such a level as to make it difficult for customers to switch suppliers, thereby creating a maximum loyalty enhancing effect. By contrast, a standardized volume threshold – where the threshold is the same for all or a group of customers – may be too high for some smaller customers and/or too low for larger customers to have a loyalty enhancing effect. If, however, it can be established that a standardized volume threshold approximates the requirements of an appreciable proportion of customers, the Commission is likely to consider that such a standardized system of rebates may produce anticompetitive fore-closure effects'.

[45]   Also see Elhauge, *supra* note 39, at 415.
[46]   See Elhauge, *supra* note 2, at 412 n.27.

Table 5.1   Types of loyalty/requirement discounts

Qualifier/requirement	To which units the discount applies	
	Discount on incremental units	Discount on all units
Standardized quantity discounts	Not a concern if after-discount price is above unit cost Concern about the effects on rivals if after-discount price is below unit cost	Concern if after-discount prices are below unit cost for some users
Individualized buyer-specific share or buyer-specific quantity discounts	May be a concern if tailored to exclude rivals	Major concern since this type of discount is typically aimed at excluding rivals

81st unit to be sold by the dominant firm) as in the but-for world, but for whole chunks of the demand, here units 81 to 90. This favors the monopolist and can lead to foreclosure of the rival who has to fight not only for the 81st unit of the dominant firm (his 19th unit) as in the but-for world, but-for units 81–90 (his units 10–19). This can create significant foreclosure, as underlined by the European Commission:

> Retroactive rebates may foreclose the market significantly, as they may make it less attractive for customers to switch small amounts of demand to an alternative supplier, if this would lead to loss of the retroactive rebates.[47]

Furthermore, many companies, once they buy a large percentage of their needs from one seller, may not want to buy a small percentage of their needs from another. This may be to avoid training personnel in a new product, compatibility issues, necessity of investments in complementary goods, and other reasons. Thus, often once a buyer commits to buying a very large share of his needs from one seller, he may end up buying *all* his needs from the same seller. Therefore the impact of the loyalty/requirement program may be larger than the share thresholds on which it is based.

F   Use of Loyalty/Requirement Programs to Disadvantage Rivals and Foreclose Entry

The commitment to buy under a loyalty/requirement program reduces the scale of rival(s) and, in the presence of fixed costs, increases the costs of rivals. The monopolist can also deter a new entrant by locking customers into a requirement/loyalty program. All other things equal, the customer will decide to break the contract with the monopolist only if it is compensated by the new entrant's lower price; that is, the monopolist has lowered the incentives for entry and thus created barriers for potential new entrants to compete as an efficient competitor.

---

[47]   See EU Guidance, *supra* note 44, para. 40.

G   Foreclosure

Loyalty/requirement programs can lead to substantial foreclosure, even if the loyalty commitment requirement is less than 100%. Foreclosure should be calculated marketwide. For example, if the loyalty/requirement program foreclosed 95% of sales of 80% of buyers, then the foreclosure percentage in market B is 76%.[48] Bundling, like tying, can impair the competitiveness of a rival through market foreclosure. A rival that is forced to a small market share will have higher unit costs when there are fixed costs (costs that do not vary with output), and will thus be marginalized or forced to exit the market.

V   LOYALTY/REQUIREMENT PRICING CAN BE EQUIVALENT TO BUNDLING 'INCONTESTABLE' AND 'CONTESTABLE' UNITS OF A SINGLE GOOD

A very similar setting to multiproduct loyalty/requirement contracts arises in a single-product market.[49] Suppose that a dominant firm in a market sells at a constant per unit price. Provided the particular buyer commits to buying a large percentage or all of his 'needs' from the dominant firm, the seller also offers a 'retroactive'[50] 'discount' on all units

---

[48]   The foreclosure percentage of the market is larger than a 100% foreclosure of 75% of the buyers. See also Elhauge, *supra* note 2, at 457.

[49]   Some prominent single-product loyalty discounts cases are the ones involving Intel. In the United States: Advanced Micro Devices, Inc. v. Intel Corp., No. 05-441 (D. Del. filed 27 June 2005, settled on 12 November 2009; New York v. Intel Corp., 1:2009cv00827 (D. Del. filed 4 November 2009) available at www.oag.state.ny.us/media_center/2009/nov/NYAG_v_Intel_COMPLAINT_ FINAL.pdf; Complaint, Intel Corp., FTC Docket No. 9341 (16 December 2009), available at http://www.ftc.gov/os/adjpro/d9341/091216intelcmpt.pdf. In the European Union, see Commission Decision, COMP/C-3/37.900—Intel Corp., 13 May 2009, available at http://ec.europa.eu/competition/sectors/ICT/intel.html. *Intel* involved both a single-product loyalty requirement program and a loyalty requirement program on bundles involving chip sets. The FTC case was settled with Intel on 29 October 2010. See the proposed 'Decision and Order' at www.ftc.gov/os/adjpro/ d9341/101102inteldo.pdf and the 'Analysis of Proposed Consent Order' at www.ftc.gov/os/adjpro/ d9341/100804intelanal.pdf. The FTC/Intel settlement has three prongs. First, it prohibits certain pricing practices in single products and in bundles. Second, it prohibits 'predatory design' of products that would disadvantage rivals without improving efficiency. Third, it prohibits deception relating to benchmarking of performance. We discuss here only the prohibition of pricing practices which are detailed in Section IV (at 9 onwards) of the Decision and Order. Section A1 prohibits sole sourcing, that is, buying all the relevant products from Intel. Section A2 prohibits giving benefits to a buyer on the condition that he does not buy from Intel's rivals. Sections A3–4 prohibit Intel giving benefits to a buyer on the condition that he does not buy complementary goods from Intel's rivals. A5 prohibits giving benefits to a buyer on the condition that he limits his share of rival purchases of the basic or complementary products. Section A6 prohibits bundling and other discounts that if attributed to any product of the bundle would lead to a price below total cost. A7 prohibits lump sum discounts based on a threshold amount in units or in share except for such discounts applied only to purchases beyond a threshold (incremental discounts). All the restrictions proposed are in line with the arguments of this chapter except A6 which is weak because (i) it is based on total and not incremental cost; and (ii) attribution is on all units and not on the contestable ones.

[50]   The term 'retroactive' is used because the 'discount' (or difference between prices adhering to and not adhering to the requirement) applies to all units sold in a time period or a subset

or a subset of units below a certain threshold, such as 90% of the buyer's purchases in market *A* during a defined time period. The retroactive discount can be a lower price on all units below the threshold or a subset of these, or it can be a lump sum discount. The requirement may be 'sole-sourcing', that is, a requirement that a particular buyer buys 100% of his purchases from the dominant firm, or the discount may be available only if a large percentage of the buyer's purchases in market *A*, say 90%, are from the dominant firm.[51] The requirement, the base prices, the extent of the discounts, and even the time period on which it applies can vary across buyers.

It makes sense to apply the same antitrust standard for discounts on loyalty/requirement practices irrespective of whether we are in a single-product or multiproduct case. In the former case, the demand is divided between an incontestable part that is always purchased from the dominant firm and a contestable part of the demand where the customer may buy from any firm.[52] In both the multiproduct and single-product cases, the dominant firm leverages its monopoly or dominant position to obtain higher sales in the remaining market. The only difference is that in the multiproduct case, sales in market *A* are leveraged to obtain higher sales in market *B*, while in the single-product case, the uncontested sales in market *A* are leveraged to obtain the contested sales also in market *A*.

If the seller commits to charge loyal buyers a discount from any future price it charges to disloyal buyers, this can result in higher prices. This is akin to a 'most favored nation' clause. It makes it more costly to the seller to cut prices to non-committed buyers because then prices will have to be cut to committed buyers. Therefore it leads to higher prices at equilibrium.[53]

VI   DEFECTS OF THE DISCOUNT ATTRIBUTION TEST AS A LIABILITY STANDARD FOR LOYALTY/REQUIREMENT PROGRAMS

A   Background

The Antitrust Modernization Commission (AMC) proposed using a discount 'attribution test'. Separately, the European Union (EU) proposed a different discount attribu-

---

thereof, while it may be announced in the last part of this time period. This discount is distinguished from an 'incremental' discount which is applied only to the last unit or units sold. For similar definitions, see Commission of the European Communities, EU Guidance, *supra* note 44, para. 42.

[51]   For the arguments I make here it is not necessary to have the discount apply to all units.

[52]   This conforms with the definitions used by the European Commission. See EU Guidance, *supra* note 44.

[53]   *See* Steven Salop, *Practices that (Credibly) Facilitate Oligopoly Coordination*, in NEW DEVELOPMENTS IN THE ANALYSIS OF MARKET STRUCTURE (Joseph E. Stiglitz and G. Frank Mathewson eds, MIT Press, 1986). Also see Elhauge, *supra* note 2, at 449–61; Einer Elhauge, *How Loyalty Discounts Can Perversely Discourage Discounting*, 5 J. COMPETITION L. AND ECON. 189 (2009); and E. Elhauge and A.L. Wickelgren, *Robust Exclusion Through Loyalty Discounts* (Harvard Law School Discussion Paper No. 662, January 2010).

tion test.[54] The AMC test takes all discounts on a bundle and attributes them to the more competitive of the two products, that is, subtracts the discounts from the total revenue of the competitive product, and divides by a sales quantity of the competitive product. Then it tests whether the resulting hypothetical 'effective' price established through the attribution is above a measure of avoidable cost (average variable cost).[55] It finds an antitrust violation if (i) the effective price is below the average variable cost of product B of the monopolist in product A; (ii) the dominant firm is likely to recoup its losses; and (iii) the requirement contract is likely to have anticompetitive conse-quences.[56] As I show below, this test is inappropriate for finding liability of loyalty/requirement programs.[57]

The AMC proposed (and the US Department of Justice (DOJ) under President George W. Bush agreed) that a safe harbor should be established if the hypothetical effective price established through the attribution process is above avoidable cost of the monopolist for product B.[58] The present DOJ under President Obama withdrew this recommendation.[59] The idea of the discount attribution test was to eliminate plaintiff claims from ineffi-cient competitors. The first prong of the AMC test was adopted by the Ninth Circuit in *PeaceHealth*.[60] In contrast, the same Circuit upheld a jury verdict finding liability in the loyalty/requirement case *Masimo Corporation v. Tyco Health Care Group*,[61] based on the argument that Masimo 'could not price its sensors low enough' to meet the effective price

---

54   For an analysis, see Economides and Lianos, *supra* note 2, at 501–10. For a criticism of the Commission's approach, see Ioannis Lianos, *The Price/Non Price Exclusionary Abuses Dichotomy: A Critical Appraisal*, 2 CONCURRENCES REV. (2009), available at SSRN: http://ssrn.com/abstract=1398943.

55   The AMC uses the words 'incremental cost' in its cost criterion. Often average variable cost (AVC) is used instead. The EU uses the terminology average avoidable costs (AAC) to denote costs that can be avoided if the units in question are not produced. However, it should be understood that AAC and AVC include the cost of additional plants (or plant expansion) and fixed investment required to produce the additional units. Also see Einer Elhauge, *Why Above-Cost Price Cuts to Drive out Entrants Do Not Signal Predation or Even Market Power – and the Implications for Defining Costs,* 112 YALE L.J. 681, 707–26 (2003).

56   Antitrust Modernization Commission, *Report and Recommendations* 99 (April 2007): ('Courts should adopt a three-part test to determine whether bundled discounts or rebates violate section 2 of the Sherman Act. To prove a violation of section 2, a plaintiff should be required to show each one of the following elements (as well as other elements of a section 2 claim): (1) after allocating all discounts and rebates attributable to the entire bundle of products to the competitive product, the defendant sold the competitive product below its incremental cost for the competitive product; (2) the defendant is likely to recoup these short-term losses; and (3) the bundled discount or rebate program has had or is likely to have an adverse effect on competition').

57   Also see Economides and Lianos, *supra* note 2, at 506–10; Lianos, *supra* note 54. See also Elhauge, *supra* note 2, at 463–4.

58   See US Dep't of Justice, *Competition and Monopoly: Single-Firm Conduct Under Section 2 of the Sherman Act* 101 (September 2008).

59   See *Justice Department Withdraws Report on Antitrust Monopoly Law*, at www.usdoj.gov/atr/public/press_releases/2009/245710.htm.

60   See Cascade Health Solutions v. PeaceHealth, 515 F.3d 883, 906–10 (9th Cir. 2008).

61   No. CV-02-4770 (MRP), 2006 WL 1236666 (C.D. Cal. 22 March 2006), *aff'd*, 30 Fed. App'x 95 (9th Cir. 2009).

of Tyco based on the volume for which it could compete – an implicit acceptance that Masimo could compete only for a contestable quantity.[62]

B   Which Quantity of the Competitive Product Should be Used in the Attribution Test?

In calculating the hypothetical attribution price, AMC used the total sales quantity of the 'competitive' product. In contrast, the EU differentiated between 'contestable' and 'incontestable' parts of the demand.[63] In many markets, a significant portion of the sales of the dominant firm is uncontested by competitors because of reputation, fear of punishment of executives if something goes wrong when they do not buy from the dominant firm, complementary investments by buyers of the dominant product, limitations in the production capacity of the competitor, availability of a full range of varieties, and other reasons. The contestable part of the market is defined in the EU Guidance Paper for Article 82 as 'how much of a customer's purchase requirements can realistically be switched to a rival'.[64]

A dominant firm does not offer a loyalty discount to attract buyers to the incontestable part of the demand since it already is able to sell these units at full price. The requirement/loyalty 'discount' is offered to attract customers in the contestable part of the demand. Therefore its effects have to be analysed on that part of the demand.

The EU correctly noted that the loyalty/requirement program aims to win for the monopolist the contestable part of the demand. The monopolist does not offer a loyalty discount to attract buyers to the uncontested part of the demand since it already is able to sell these units at full price. Therefore, the EU correctly reasoned, the appropriate number of units to which the attribution is applied should be only the contestable ones.

Clearly, which units a discount should be attributed to is crucial if this test is being used as a basis for liability. For example, suppose a firm has a monopoly in A and sells 80 units out of a total demand of 100 units in product B for a specific buyer. Suppose the monopolist offers to this buyer a lump sum discount of US$1,000 if this buyer commits

---

[62]   See Jonathan Jacobson, *A Note on Loyalty Discounts*, ANTITR. SOURCE 3–4 (June 2010).

[63]   See EU Guidance, *supra* note 44, para. 39. Also note that the EU Guidance may find a violation if the resulting effective price is above average avoidable cost of the monopolist, based on more detailed examination. In particular, the Commission notes: 'Where the effective price is between [average avoidable cost, AAC] and [long run average incremental cost, LRAIC], the Commission will investigate whether other factors point to the conclusion that entry or expansion even by efficient competitors is likely to be affected. In this context, the Commission will investigate whether and to what extent rivals have realistic and effective counterstrategies at their disposal, for instance their capacity to also use a 'non contestable' portion of their buyer's demand as leverage to decrease the price for the relevant range. Where competitors do not have such counterstrategies at their disposal, the Commission will consider that the rebate scheme is capable of foreclosing equally efficient competitors'. See EU Guidance, para. 44.

[64]   In applying this standard in its *Intel* decision, the European Commission notes that the contestable part of the market can be small. EU Press Release, 'Antitrust: Commission imposes fine of €1.06 bn on Intel for abuse of dominant position; orders Intel to cease illegal practices', (13 May 2009), available at http://europa.eu/rapid/pressReleasesAction.do?reference=IP / 09 /745&fonnat=HTML: 'Because computer manufacturers are dependent on Intel for a majority of their x86 CPU supplies, only a limited part of a computer manufacturer's x86 CPU requirements is open to competition at any given time'.

to buy 90 units of his demand of B from him.[65] The AMC test may attribute the discount to all units of B presently sold by the monopolist in A, and then the discount will be US$12.50 (US$1,000/80) per unit. The EU will apply the discount to the contested units. One may argue that the contestable units are the difference between the existing sales of the monopolist in B (80 units) and the requirement amount (90 units), but of course this is a fact issue that the court can determine. Then the discount for these 10 contested units is US$100 per unit – a huge difference from the US$12.50 attributed discount of the AMC test. Typically the liability test will be more likely to find liability if the discount is applied to the contestable units rather than all sales of the monopolist in A. If, for example, the unit cost of good B is US$20 and the market price is US$40, the AMC application of the attribution test results in an effective price of US$28.50 (US$40 − US$12.50), which is above unit cost, and therefore in the safe harbor. In contrast, the correct application of the attribution test to contestable units as posited by the EU results in a below-zero effective price of −US$60 (US$40 − US$100) which is obviously below unit cost and implies liability.[66]

C   Which Company's Costs Should be Used in the Attribution Test?

Both the AMC and the EU use the monopolist's costs to calculate avoidable cost. This is incorrect. In the presence of economies of scale, the monopolist's average costs at its high level of market share are lower than those of a rival who is equally efficient, that is, a rival which has the same average cost *function* (average cost as a function of quantity) as the monopolist. A rival should not be deemed less efficient because its scale of production forces its costs to be higher even though it would have the same average cost as the monopolist if the two had the same scale of operation (or market share). In fact, it would be ironic to use the large scale of the monopolist which may be an effect of its anticompetitive actions to weaken the test and make it more likely that the monopolist is found to have no liability.[67]

---

[65]   Similar examples can be created for a percentage discount on the contestable units rather than a lump sum discount. See Jonathan Jacobson, *A Note on Loyalty Discounts*, ANTITRUST SOURCE 7 (June 2010).

[66]   In its *Intel* decision (Case COMP/C-3/37.990—Intel, Comm'n Decision (13 May 2009), available at http://ec.europa.eu/competition/antitrust/cases/decisions/37990/provisional_decision_en.pdf), the European Commission provides an example of a rival (AMD) to the monopolist (Intel) that was unable to 'sell' its product at zero price because of Intel's loyalty/requirement practice. A buyer (computer manufacturer) refused to accept to 'buy' AMD's CPUs at zero price because, if it did, it would forego Intel's loyalty discount which was based on the requirement that this buyer buys a very large share of its CPU needs from Intel. 'Moreover, in order to be able to compete with the Intel rebates, for the part of the computer manufacturers' supplies that was up for grabs, a competitor that was just as efficient as Intel would have had to offer a price for its CPUs lower than its costs of producing those CPUs, even if the average price of its CPUs was lower than that of Intel. For example, rival chip manufacturer AMD offered one million free CPUs to one particular computer manufacturer. If the computer manufacturer had accepted all of these, it would have lost Intel's rebate on its many millions of remaining CPU purchases, and would have been worse off overall simply for having accepted this highly competitive offer. In the end, the computer manufacturer took only 160,000 CPUs for free.'

[67]   See Economides and Lianos, *supra* note 2, at 20–24; Elhauge, *supra* note 2, at 412, 463–4. If the qualities of the products of the dominant firm and the rival differ, the costs can be appropriately adjusted for quality differences.

D　Survival of Higher Cost Rival Can Benefit Consumers

Even a higher cost competitor can constrain price and increase consumer surplus, therefore inefficient rivals should not be automatically excluded. In the presence of monopoly pricing, the entry of an inefficient (higher cost) rival can result in a lower market price and higher consumer surplus.[68] It is a very significant flaw of the attribution test that it aims to exclude all inefficient competitors irrespective of their influence on price and consumer surplus. The fact that such entrants are excluded creates a lack of correspondence between consumer surplus comparisons and liability established under this test. Since change in consumer surplus is the right criterion for liability, the AMC attribution test clearly fails since it points to no liability even when the monopolist's bundling action reduces consumer surplus.

E　AMC Attribution Test Fails When Products are Differentiated

In the presence of product differentiation (either in variety or in quality) the AMC attribution test makes little sense. Since a rival to the dominant firm does not offer the same products, why should we be using the dominant firm's costs to evaluate the survival of the rival's products that differ in quality and variety from the dominant firm's ones? Additionally, when the products are differentiated, consumers may gain in surplus from the presence of additional varieties and qualities offered by the rival even if the rival prices above the dominant firm.[69]

F　A Loyalty/Requirement Program Reduces Price Transparency

Introduction of a loyalty/requirement makes the calculation of the price paid by a buyer for the monopolist's product B opaque to a rival because this price typically depends on the sales of A by the monopolist to this buyer, which a rival does not know. Thus, it will be difficult for a rival to accurately calculate the effective price offered by the dominant firm to particular buyers, and therefore attempt to match it. This uncertainty may tend to reduce price competition. This is ignored by the AMC attribution test.

G　Even When a Buyer Accepts the Bundle, He may be Worse Off Than in the But-For World; Buyers Find Themselves in a Prisoner's Dilemma

As discussed earlier, a buyer accepting to buy under the loyalty/requirement program does not necessarily imply higher consumers' surplus compared to the but-for world, since the monopolist has the opportunity to increase prices as he implements the loyalty/requirement program. Still, it may be optimal individually for each buyer to buy under the requirement bundle so that he is not penalized by the higher prices outside the

---

[68]　See Economides, *supra* note 2; see Economides and Lianos, *supra* note 2, at 508–9; Elhauge, *supra* note 2, at 462–3; Elhauge, *supra* note 8, at 413.
[69]　See Nicholas Economides, *Quality Variations in the Circular Model of Variety-Differentiated Products*, 23 REGIONAL SCI. AND URB. ECON. 235 (1993).

requirement. However, individual buyer's acceptance to buy under the requirement does not imply that collectively buyers are better off compared to the but-for world.[70]

Even if each buyer is better off individually when he buys under the requirement bundle, collectively buyers may be worse off because they find themselves in a prisoner's dilemma setting. Collectively all buyers lose because of the increase in market power of the monopolist as more buyers accept the requirement.

H   Recoupment is Unnecessary

The recoupment prong of the AMC test is irrelevant because it is not clear that the monopolist actually loses money under the requirement contract compared to the but-for world. The difference between prices under the requirement contract and without it does not necessarily imply losses for the monopolist because the monopolist can increase both the uncontested and contested prices on the introduction of the loyalty/requirement program.

The fact that a dominant firm's profit sacrifice is not necessary in a requirement/loyalty rebate is shared by the European Commission:[71]

> Conditional rebates can have such [actual and potential foreclosure] effects without necessarily entailing a sacrifice for the dominant undertaking.

The text is accompanied by this footnote:

> In that regard, the assessment of conditional rebates differs from that of predation, which always entails a sacrifice.[72]

Additionally, as explained earlier, acceptance of the requirement contract gives the monopolist more market power. As discussed earlier, when the dominant firm's price outside the requirement/loyalty contract is higher than in the but-for world, this is an indication that the action is anticompetitive.[73] Additionally, bundling can also be used to create threats of higher à la carte prices, even if all consumers buy under the bundle and therefore the threat of buying at higher à la carte prices is not enforced at equilibrium.[74]

VII   STRUCTURED RULE OF REASON[75]

I propose the 'structured rule of reason' standard as the correct approach to establish liability. The court should look at a number of variables to ascertain whether tying,

---

[70]   See also Einer Elhauge and Abraham L. Wickelgren, *Robust Exclusion Through Loyalty Discounts* (Harvard Law School, Discussion Paper No. 62, January 2010).

[71]   EU Guidance, *supra* note 44, para. 37.

[72]   *Id.* at 13, n.3.

[73]   See Greenlee *et al.*, *supra* note 23; Economides and Lianos, *supra* note 2; Elhauge, *supra* note 2.

[74]   See Barry Nalebuff, *Tried and True Exclusion*, 1 COMPETITION POL'Y INT'L 41 (2005).

[75]   See also Elhauge's 'quasi per se' rule. See Elhauge, *supra* note 38, at 358–9; Elhauge, *supra* note 2, at 442–3.

Table 5.2   Summary of requirements and effects of tying in implementing different types of price discrimination

Type of price discrimination that tying implements	Significant market power in the tying market	Market power in the tied market and foreclosure in the tied market	Tying gives additional profits to monopolist even when A and B are demanded in fixed proportion	Consumer surplus (CS) can decrease because of tying
Inter-product price discrimination	Necessary for tying resulting in CS reduction	Unnecessary for tying resulting in CS reduction	Yes	Yes
Intra-product price discrimination	Necessary for tying resulting in CS reduction	Unnecessary for tying resulting in CS reduction	No	Yes
Intra-consumer price discrimination	Necessary for tying resulting in CS reduction	Unnecessary for tying resulting in CS reduction	No	Yes

bundling, and a loyalty/requirement rebates program violate antitrust law, with the central question being whether the introduction of tying and bundling, including a loyalty/requirement rebates program, reduces consumer surplus.

This chapter explains how tying can result in consumer harm in a variety of different settings. The common feature of these settings is substantial market power in the tying good, which is necessary for tying implementing intra-product price discrimination (section IIIA), intra-consumer price discrimination (section IIIB), inter-product price discrimination (section IIIC), and tying used to disadvantage rivals in the tied market and foreclose entry in the tied market (section IIID). In the cases of sections IIIA to IIIC, where tying is used to implement intra-product, intra-consumer, and inter-product price discrimination, market power in the tied market is not required to establish liability. In contrast, disadvantaging rivals in the tied market and preventing entry in this market require substantial foreclosure in the tied market.

When A and B are demanded in fixed proportions, a monopolist does not have an incentive to use tying to implement intra-product or intra-consumer price discrimination.[76] However, even when A and B are demanded in fixed proportions, a monopolist in A using inter-product price discrimination can increase its profits and decrease consumer surplus. Finally, the court should consider whether there are sufficient offsetting efficiencies to balance the anticompetitive effects in each of these cases.

Table 5.2 summarizes the requirements and effects of the various types of price discrimination that tying implements.

Therefore the crucial requirement to establish tying liability is market power in the tying good, and insubstantial offsetting efficiencies. Substantial foreclosure in the tied

---

[76]   Also see Elhauge, *supra* note 2, at 407–13 and Mathewson and Winter, *supra* note 23.

market is not required, although, in its presence, the monopolist can disadvantage rivals in the tied market and can prevent rivals from entering.

For bundling and loyalty/requirement programs, I should first note that a safe harbor cannot be established based on a price/cost attribution test. This is because changes in consumer surplus as a result of entry or expanded operation of a rival non-dominant firm do not, in general, correspond directly to any price/cost attribution test comparisons, as I have shown above. Under the structured rule of reason standard, a violation can be established even when none is found by the attribution tests, and, in particular, even when the calculated effective price in the attribution test is above the average variable cost of the dominant firm.[77]

For bundling and loyalty/requirement programs, liability can be established when the dominant firm's price outside the requirement/loyalty contract (that is, the à la carte price) is higher than in the but-for world.[78] This is very close to tying to implement intra-consumer price discrimination (see section IIIB) and does not require market power in the tied good. Otherwise liability can be established when there is substantial foreclosure of the tied market.

---

[77] In LePage's v. 3M Co. 324 F.3d 141 (3d Cir. 2003), the court did not require a price/cost test to establish liability.

[78] See Economides, *supra* note 2, at 277–8; Greenlee *et al.*, *supra* note 23; Elhauge, *supra* note 2, at 402–3, 450–55, 468–9.

6 Predatory pricing
*Aaron Edlin**

I INTRODUCTION

Antitrust aims to make markets more competitive, with the ultimate aim of low consumer prices, or more generally of high consumer welfare.[1] On these terms, predatory pricing may appear a paradox, because a predatory pricing claim asserts that a low price is anticompetitive.[2] Some put a point on the matter, saying that a predatory pricing claim asserts that a price is *too* low.

The so-called paradox is not a deep one, however, and is misleading, because while a rival complains of the low price, antitrust courts would ignore the complaint absent some convincing story that links the low price to a higher price; this higher price is the real policy concern guiding the law. Thus, the traditional story of predatory pricing has an incumbent or would-be monopolist driving an entrant or existing rival out of the market so that the incumbent can later raise prices. The threat is not the low price but the high price. Edlin[3] emphasizes instead the danger of an unnecessarily high pre-predatory, pre-entry price. He points out that banning the price cut can encourage the incumbent to charge low prices in the first place. Again, the threat is not the low price (entailed by the price cut), but the absence of an everyday low price 'requiring' the cut.

Whatever the timing, the competition problem is a high price during a period without competition or with less intense competition. Predatory pricing claims are less a paradox than they are a challenge. The challenge for law and competition policy is to distinguish low prices or price cuts that raise average or 'regular' prices from those that lower them. When this challenge proves frustrating, the temptation is to abandon the venture and declare predatory pricing beyond the scope of competition law and policy.

---

*   I owe a deep debt to my co-author Joseph Farrell whose work with me laid the foundation for the consumer betterment proposal. (See *Freedom to Trade and the Competitive Process*, by Aaron Edlin and Joseph Farrell, NBER Working Paper No. 16818, http://www.nber.org/papers/w16818.) I am also grateful for discussions with Jon Baker, Michal Gal, David Gilo, Justin McCrary, Ralph Moore, Daniel Rubinfeld, Christopher Sagers, Steve Salop, Carl Shapiro, Eric Talley, Abe Wickelgren, audiences at NYU School of Law, UC Berkeley, and the 2010 Meeting of the Law and Economics Association, and especially Louis Kaplow. I am also grateful for the research assistance of Omari French.
[1]   Reiter v. Sonotone Corp., 442 U.S. 330, 342 (1979); see also Statement of Commissioners Harbour, Leibowitz and Rosch on the Issuance of the Section 2 Report by the Department of Justice, Federal Trade Commission, September 2008, and R.H. Lande, *Wealth Transfers as the Original and Primary Concern of Antitrust: The Efficiency Interpretation Challenged*, 32 Hastings L.J. 67 (1982).
[2]   See, e.g., Robert Bork, Antitrust Paradox (1978).
[3]   Edlin, *infra* note 6.

Below, I begin by summarizing and critiquing prominent thinking about predatory pricing. Section II argues that Judge Breyer's bird in hand is a fallacy. I explain in section III that the strongest Chicago School skepticism of the existence of predatory pricing has weak theoretical foundations even in its wheelhouse (the case of symmetric costs and information). When information is asymmetric and/or when the monopoly has cost advantages, these foundations liquify as section IV explains. Following this theoretical discussion, section V examines the state of empirical knowledge.

Sections VIA and B distinguish two strands of thought that courts and commentators have tangled into a thick knot: one is the sacrifice justification of price–cost tests; and the other is the equally efficient competitor justification. The two strands lead to distinct conceptions of the 'appropriate' measure of cost. The sacrifice notion requires implementing an 'inclusive' measure of cost or price; in contrast, the more common 'exclusive' notion is appropriate (under certain assumptions, anyway) to prevent the exclusion of equally efficient competitors. I introduce and define inclusive and exclusive notions of cost and price in section VIA.

Oddly, neither protecting equally efficient competitors nor preventing sacrifice are closely connected to the predominant welfare goal of antitrust, which is the protection of consumer welfare. Section VIC therefore introduces a new consumer betterment standard for identifying exclusion in monopolization cases;[4] the standard proposes asking whether a monopoly's actions are likely to exclude from its market a competitor who would provide consumers a better deal than they get from the monopoly.[5] As I will explain, the consumer betterment standard is not the same as maximizing consumer welfare. Applying the consumer betterment standard to the *American Airlines* case might have allowed the Department of Justice to win on the evidence they presented and would have provided a different avenue of proof more directly geared to consumer welfare, as section VII explains. Although recoupment is not itself an element under the consumer betterment standard, raising prices after a predatory episode is an important part of a case.

Section VIII discusses the relationship of consumer betterment to the price freezes of Baumol and Edlin.[6] All have in common that they can condemn pricing patterns that never dip below cost, and all are designed to increase the gains that consumers get from entry. In the case of reactive price cuts, as in *American Airlines*, the Baumol price freeze and the consumer betterment standard are both less aggressive than an Edlin price freeze; on the facts of *American Airlines* both standards would likely have allowed the Department of Justice to win. In some reactive pricing cases, however,

---

4   As far as I know, the standard is new but I fully expect that various historians of antitrust will soon inform me of its antecedents and I look forward to learning of them. Little in truth is new under the sun.

5   The consumer betterment standard for distinguishing anticompetitive from procompetitive exclusion is inspired by my work with Joseph Farrell. See Aaron Edlin and Joseph Farrell, *Freedom to Trade and the Competitive Process* (NBER Working Paper No. 16818), available at www.nber.org/papers/w16818.

6   Aaron Edlin, *Stopping Above-Cost Predatory Pricing*, 111(4) YALE L.J. 941 (2002). W.J. Baumol, *Quasi-Permanence of Price Reductions: A Policy for Prevention of Predatory Pricing*, 89(1) YALE L.J. 21 (1979).

the consumer betterment standard yields different and perhaps more appealing results than the Baumol price freeze. Consumer betterment also has general application in monopolization cases not just in predation; the Baumol price freeze is a specialized rule for predatory pricing.

II   BREYER'S BIRD-IN-HAND FALLACY

One of the main reasons that noninterventionists argue that plaintiffs should jump a high hurdle to prove a predation case is the view that alleged predation generally involves unarguably competitive behavior (a good) whereas any consequent bads involve arguable and uncertain claims. Judge Stephen Breyer (now Justice Breyer) put a colorful point on the matter in *Barry Wright*.[7] He said there that to declare illegal an above-cost price cut would be to sacrifice a bird in hand (the price cut) for a speculative bird in the bush (preventing exit and a future price rise).[8] Breyer's 'bird in hand' view has enormous gravitational pull[9] and suggests that we must beware of interventionist policies.

The bird-in-hand view, however, is simply a fallacy. The important effects of court decisions and legal rules are prospective, which is to say the important effects are future effects on markets and potential cases.

The price cut only happens if and when there is entry and entry is not a bird in hand. In theory, entry may never occur, and in practice a very permissive rule that allows aggressive price cuts post-entry may make entry rare or delayed. If the entrant anticipates being outcompeted or predated post-entry, why would it enter? Breyer's bird-in-hand view presumes entry, and thus is just as speculative a proposition as the fear of high prices post-exit.

The predatory pricing rule can affect the price before entry, the probability of entry during any given time period, and pricing post-entry if there is entry. In reality all effects are more like birds in the bush than birds in hand.

Some will be tempted to doubt this position and wonder how I can deny the fact of the real benefits that have actually occurred in the case under consideration from the price war that precipitated the instant court battle. How can these consumer benefits not be a bird in hand? True, at the time of trial those gains are in fact real, but the trial's results will not take them from consumers in any event. The relevant birds are all in prospective cases, not in the present case.

---

[7]   Barry Wright Corp. v. ITT Grinnell Corp., 724 F.2d 227, 234 (1st Cir. 1983).

[8]   Specifically, Breyer wrote '[T]he antitrust laws very rarely reject such beneficial "birds in hand" for the sake of more speculative (future low-price) "birds in the bush"'.

[9]   See Einer Elhauge, *Why Above-Cost Price Cuts to Drive Out Entrants are Not Predatory – and the Implications for Defining Costs and Market Power*, 112(4) YALE L.J. 681 (2003), at sections I.B, IV.E, collecting sources stating that the tradeoff of banning above cost pricing entails a 'certain short-term loss for an uncertain long-term gain'.

III   IS PREDATORY PRICING COMMON? IF BUSINESS FOLK THINK SO, IT IS

Robert Bork concluded that predatory pricing is 'a phenomenon that probably does not exist'.[10] Professor Frank Easterbrook concurred in 1981, writing that predatory pricing is like 'dragons' – everywhere in literature and nowhere in the world.[11] When I presented my 2002 paper at the University of Chicago,[12] it appeared to me that Judge Easterbrook had come to think that predatory pricing might be even more rare than that.[13]

Why so? Why did (and does) the Chicago School of Antitrust see predatory pricing as generally implausible, a claim that ultimately convinced the US Supreme Court to write that 'predatory pricing schemes are rarely tried, and even more rarely successful'.[14]

Bork reasons thus:

> A firm contemplating predatory price warfare will perceive a series of obstacles that make the prospect of such a campaign exceedingly unattractive. The losses during the war will be proportionally higher for the predator than for the victim; merger law will make it all but impossible for the predator to purchase the victim, so the campaign will have to last until the victim's organization and assets are dissolved; ease of entry will be symmetrical with ease of exit; and anticipated monopoly revenues, being deferred, must be discounted at the current interest rate.

The beginning of the Chicago logic is the idea that the predator's losses during the predatory period will typically be large and larger than the prey. To understand this claim, consider the way the matter is taught to undergraduates in the leading industrial organization textbook written by Professors Dennis Carlton and Jeffrey Perloff.[15] See Figure 6.1 (which is their Figure 11.1). Imagine a market that is big enough for two identical firms to produce at efficient scale as depicted in Figure 6.1. Can one firm oust the other through predatory pricing? Label the predator-incumbent 'i' and the prey-entrant 'e'. The predation, of course, need not follow entry – it can simply be an effort to end an unsatisfactory sharing of the market.

The entrant will presumably not consider exit so long as price exceeds the minimum of its average cost. In fact, it should only consider exit if price is below the minimum of its average avoidable cost (AAC), where 'avoidable costs' are those that would be avoided by the exit. (As the time to exit expands, presumably more and more costs become avoidable by exit and AAC becomes closer to average total costs.) But in order to drive price to some level p* below AAC, the entrant must expand output enough to keep the price at that level. After all at a price of p* less than the minimum of AC, if the entrant stays in

10   Bork, *supra* note 2, at 154.

11   F. Easterbrook, *Predatory Strategies and Counterstrategies*, 48(2) U. Chicago L. Rev. 263 (1981). Jonathan Baker says that Chicago adherents see predation as like either a white tiger (if it exists at all) or a unicorn (if it does not). J. Baker, *Predatory Pricing after Brooke Group: An Economic Perspective*, 62 Antitrust L.J. 585 (1984).

12   Edlin, *supra* note 6.

13   Kenneth Elzinga and David Mills take a slightly more open view comparing successful price predation to an individual scoring over 65 points in a basketball game. K. Elzinga and D. Mills, *Predatory Pricing and Strategic Theory*, 89(8) Georgetown L. J. 2475, 2479 (2001).

14   Matsushita Elec. Indus. Co. v. Zenith Radio Corp., 475 U.S. 574, 589 (1986).

15   Dennis Carlton and Jeffrey Perloff, Modern Industrial Organization (2005).

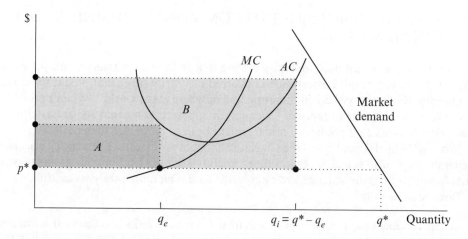

Figure 6.1   Predation

the market, the entrant will reduce its output to some q_e such that $MC(q_e) = p^*$. In order to keep price at p^*, the incumbent will need to increase its production to $q_i = q^* - q_e$.

As shown in the figure, the losses for the entrant, the dark shaded area A, are considerably smaller than those for the incumbent, the shaded area B. In fact, even if rectangle A were taller than rectangle B, it must have smaller area because the area of rectangle B equals that of rectangle A plus the extra losses that the incumbent suffers on all units between q_e and q_i (i.e. the area under MC and above p^* between q_e and q_i). [16] So during the predatory period, in this example anyway, the predator loses more per month than the prey.

In general, successful predation requires:

(1) *low prices:* price must be sufficiently low to tempt rivals to exit (generally below AAC) or otherwise to chasten them;
(2) *credibility:* the threat must be credible that the predator will keep prices low until rivals exit; and
(3) *no re-entry:* re-entry or new competition must be sufficiently delayed that the predator can recoup its losses from predation.

Let's begin by focusing on requirements (1) and (2) and assuming for the time being that re-entry will not occur after an exit has been forced.

In order to satisfy condition (1), the market price must be driven below the prey's AAC. If the two firms have symmetric costs as in the example, and the predator's average costs rise with additional output as depicted in Figure 6.1, then the predator will lose more than the prey. As Bork, Carlton, and Perloff and many others see the matter, this makes

---

[16] $B = A + \displaystyle\int_{q_e}^{q_i} [MC(q) - p^*]dq.$

it implausible that the predator will continue such behavior.[17] And if it is not plausible that the predator will continue, then the prey will not exit, and if the prey will not exit, the predator will never start, or at least rationally should never start.

Their presumption seems sensible enough: if the predator is losing money by the boat-load, shouldn't the prey expect that the predator will give up its foolishness before long? Particularly if the prey makes it clear that it will stick it out, by sticking it out! The logic has its appeal, but then consider that the prey is also losing money, albeit less. And, the predator too may make its own obstinance clear by sticking around.

In fact, in a game theoretic sense, there are (at least) two equilibria. In the no-predation equilibrium, the prey will persevere (perhaps rationalizing this decision on a comparison of relative losses), no matter how far the game continues, because he always expects that the predator will quit the next moment; the predator's corresponding strategy in this equilibrium is always to quit predation at the next moment no matter how long he has been in the market. If we restrict attention to any particular subgame, these two strategies restricted to the subgame constitute a Nash equilibrium. Hence, these two strategies are a subgame perfect equilibrium of the overall predation game.

But successful predation is also a subgame perfect equilibrium.[18] In that equilibrium, the predator expects the prey to drop out next period if predation continues and so at all points the predator wants to continue predation; correspondingly, the prey expects that the predator will continue indefinitely and so drops out quickly or immediately. These two strategies are just as consistent and sensible as the no-predation equilibrium.

Condition (3) is thought by many to be the real rub. After all, if the predator raises price, won't this simply invite re-entry? Maybe. But this 'no re-entry' condition may not be so tough to satisfy. Condition (3) has a certain self-fulfilling character. If predation is known to be generally unsuccessful and implausible, then if by some stroke of luck, although rarely tried, predation is tried, and if although it rarely succeeds, by luck again it does succeed in inducing exit, the predatory strategy may still be unsuccessful taken as a whole. After all, for full success the predator must not just induce exit, but must also satisfy condition (3). And if, despite this success, entrants are not worried about further predation, the monopoly will be short-lived because the monopoly will invite entry just as a vacuum invites gas.

But, suppose on the other hand that predation is a generally successful strategy. Then, entry (post-predation) would seem foolish, as it will only be met with more predation. In this case, the period of monopoly rents will be long. And, if the recoupment period is long, this return will tend of course to justify a long and large investment in the preda-tory period; and if a large investment is justified, then a large investment won't even be necessary because the prey will likely get out early, realizing that it won't be fruitful to wait the predator out. Now observe that if the prey gets out early, then the long post-entry

---

[17]   Carlton and Perloff, *supra* note 15, conclude: 'The reason that predatory pricing is unlikely to succeed where firms have identical costs is that the predatory firm suffers greater losses than its intended victim'.

[18]   This is demonstrated formally in Appendix A of P. Milgrom and J. Roberts, *Predation, Reputation, and Entry Deterrence*, 27(2) J. ECONOMIC THEORY 280 (1982). The predation equilib-rium can be eliminated if there is a known finite end to the game as in R. Selten, *The Chain Store Paradox*, 9(2) THEORY AND DECISION 127, but this possibility is extremely unusual.

period will not only be long, but contrary to Bork's suggestion, also not be delayed, so the discounting that Bork emphasizes becomes relatively inconsequential.

There are two basic points to understand here. The first is that requirements (2) and (3) are not so very different and do not really compound the difficulties of successful predation, contrary to what many suppose.[19] Staying in a market is easier and cheaper than entering a market. Hence, if a firm in the market will and does exit in response to predation, no firm with a similar cost structure will enter.

The second point is that the plausibility of predation is much more self-fulfilling than often realized. Starting at the end and reasoning backward, if predation is a plausible strategy, then re-entry will be rare. The recoupment period will be long. It is then credible that the predator will continue its predation long enough to drive the prey out and hence the prey sees no advantage to staying in the market after it begins losing money with respect to its AAC. If the prey will leave quickly and the recoupment period is long, then the predator will rationally persist. And if predation leads to quick exit and long recoupment without re-entry, then when firms consider re-entry this will be unattractive (because they will face predation). Hence, all the assumptions of plausibility are self-fulfilling.

There is a fair bit of stability to the equilibrium of a deep short price cut, followed by quick exit, and a long period without re-entry. Who but a madman, or a firm with extremely low costs, would enter such a market? And with the expectation of a quick exit and long recoupment period, a rational predator is willing to stick to its price cut despite large losses for a long time; after all, the predator in this equilibrium rationally believes that the prey is always hanging on by a thread and likely to leave shortly and without return. The unlikely event that the prey persists in the market for a long period may of course mean the predatory strategy turns out to be unprofitable ex post. But it does not mean that the predatory strategy is unprofitable ex ante. After all, this event is unlikely; in the extreme case, it is out of equilibrium and a zero probability event. And it does not mean that continuing the predatory strategy is unprofitable in conditional expectation from any point in time; quite the contrary, the prey is expected by the predator to exit at any moment and the long period of recoupment is always expected to be very close. In the unlikely or out-of-equilibrium event that the prey persists for a long time in the market, it is only the 20-20 hindsight of the Supreme Court in *Matsushita* that makes it appear that the predator's strategy was irrational because recoupment was so delayed.[20]

This logic suggests that if predator and prey have consistent expectations, the Bork–Easterbrook view could be right, but it could also be completely wrong. What creates the expectations? Economics offers no solid theory to answer that question. In economic theory, expectations are 'read' off the equilibrium; if there are multiple equilibria with different expectations, economics does not have a definite prediction of which will obtain.

Possibly, financial constraints might play a role in defining expectations, as suggested

---

[19]   At the 70,000 foot level this is an instance of Stiglitz and Dasgupta's principle that 'the more competitive ex post competition (competition is after entry) the less effective is the market discipline provided by potential competition'. J.E. Stiglitz and P. Dasgupta, *Potential Competition, Actual Competition, and Economic Welfare*, EUROPEAN ECONOMIC REV. 566 (1988).

[20]   Matsushita v. Zenith Radio Corp., 475 U.S. 574 (1986).

long ago by Telser and more recently by Bolton and Scharfstein or by Bolton, Brodley and Riordan.[21] If the prey has capital constraints, one might think that it cannot persist for long. Perhaps the predatory equilibrium is more likely then. It is tempting, then, to imagine that a predatory equilibrium will be more plausible when a large firm preys on a small firm (though this effect may be offset if the predator's losses exceed the prey's).

We have seen that the home-run point about the relative losses of predator and prey is not such a home run despite its intuitive appeal. Whether predation is a successful strategy depends very much on whether predator and prey believe it is a successful strategy. Only if the Bork–Easterbrook skepticism is as contagious among business people as it has been among courts and in academe will predation be like dragons. If business people read Supreme Court opinions, perhaps the skepticism of *Matsushita* and *Brooke Group* would produce a world in which that skepticism were fully justified. Few, however, do.[22]

IV ASYMMETRIC INFORMATION AND ASYMMETRIC FUNDAMENTALS

Thus far, I have argued that predation is plausible even in the world of symmetric costs and symmetric information in which the Chicago attacks seem strongest. The main stream of literature on predation, however, took a different tack. The progress of Chicago School skepticism led to a wave of critiques in the 1980s by many of the greatest names in economics such as Drew Fudenberg, David Kreps, Paul Milgrom, John Roberts, Steven Salop, Jean Tirole, and Robert Wilson.[23] They pointed out that if firms have asymmetric fundamentals (e.g., costs of production or finance or discounting) and asymmetric information about these costs, then predation makes perfect sense in that a firm with high costs may cut price in an effort to convince entrants that it has low costs and that they should therefore exit.[24] It turns out that even without asymmetric information, asymmetric fundamentals by themselves, at least if they entail incumbent advantages, can make it more likely that incumbent price cuts are socially undesirable.

---

[21] L. Telser, *Cutthroat Competition and the Long Purse*, 9 J. LAW AND ECONOMICS 259 (1966); P. Bolton, J. Brodley and M. Riordan, *Predatory Pricing: Strategic Theory and Legal Policy*, 88(8) GEORGETOWN L.J. 2239 (2000); P. Bolton and D. Scharfstein, *A Theory of Predation Based on Agency Problems in Financial Contracting*, 80(1) AMERICAN ECONOMIC REVIEW 93 (1990).

[22] See generally Matsushita Elec. Indus. Co. v. Zenith Radio Corp., 475 U.S. 574, 589 (1986); see also Brooke Group Ltd. v. Brown & Williamson Tobacco Corp., 509 U.S. 209 (1993).

[23] S.C. Salop, *Strategic Entry Deterrence*, 69 AMERICAN ECONOMIC REV. 335 (1979); Milgrom and Roberts, *supra* note 18; J. Roberts, *A Signaling Model of Predatory Pricing*, 75 (Oxford Economic Papers, New Series, 38 (supp.), 1986); D. Fudenberg and J. Tirole, *A Signal-Jamming Theory of Predation*, 17 (3) RAND J. ECONOMICS 366; D. Kreps and R. Wilson, *Reputation and Imperfect Information*, 27(2) J. ECONOMIC THEORY 253 (1982).

[24] Ordover and Saloner [1989] provide an excellent review of these asymmetric information models. See J.A. Ordover and G. Saloner, *Predation, Monopolization, and Antitrust*, in THE HANDBOOK OF INDUSTRIAL ORGANIZATION, Richard Schmalensee and Robert D. Willig (eds) (2007), Amsterdam: North Holland, pp. 537–96.

A   Asymmetric Information Models of Predation

Suppose that incumbents come in two types – low cost and high cost – and entrants or rivals cannot directly observe which is which. For the low-cost firms fighting entry is short-term optimal and for the high-cost firms accommodation is short-term optimal. Rivals lose money if they face a firm that fights, but otherwise make money. For the high-cost incumbents fighting is only optimal if it induces exit or deters further entry. Will the high-cost incumbents predate, thereby sacrificing short-run returns to induce exit or to discourage others from entry?

If information were symmetric and the game ended tomorrow, then incumbents would not predate today because regardless of what they do today, rivals know that tomorrow they will accommodate (Selten showed that a similar backward reasoning applies to games of arbitrary length as long as the parties know when they will end).[25] However, if rivals must infer the incumbents' costs from their behavior, then some of the high-cost firms will surely fight in any equilibrium. How do we know? Simple. If none did, so that all fighters have low cost, then by fighting even a high cost firm can make others believe it to be low cost, which by assumption will induce exit or deter entry. Thus, the equilibrium involves some high-cost firms fighting even though they lose money in the short run by doing so. If the game is long, then the proportion fighting can grow toward one. Fast reactions are, of course, equivalent to a long game with low discount rates, so when reactions can be fast, predation becomes very likely.

B   Asymmetric Fundamentals Models of Predation

Edlin[26] has argued that even if information is symmetric, asymmetric fundamentals, like cost or product quality, allow an incumbent with advantages to predate on disadvantaged entrants and drive them from the market. Unlike the arguments in section II, and like the arguments above, Edlin's arguments apply in both finite and infinite horizons.

Consider, as Edlin suggests, a monopoly incumbent charging a high price H. The monopoly is known to have low costs L. Will a potential rival with costs M between L and H enter the market? Not if the monopoly will respond with the price just under M (or equivalently beat whatever price the entrant charges). The capacity to cut price from H to M after entry allows the monopoly to charge H forever without fear of entry. Or, if the rival firm is already in the market, the monopoly can drive it from the market and raise price to H without fear of re-entry.

This straightforward competition problem is likely to be endemic. After all, it is common that an incumbent monopoly has cost or other advantages over rivals considering entry. If not for some advantage how else did the firm come to be or to retain a monopoly? (Well, predation is one possible answer, but surely advantages are another and indeed a complementary one.) A monopoly may have lower costs due to fortuity, ingeniousness, or increasing returns. Its products could enjoy a quality advantage due

---

25   Selten, *supra* note 18.
26   Edlin, *supra* note 6.

to network externalities[27] or simply superior production; such quality advantages can roughly be thought of as cost advantages. At the very least, there is frequently a 'switching cost' that buyers incur if they switch suppliers; such a cost will give the monopoly an advantage at keeping customers – at a minimum, if the entrant charges the same price as the monopoly it should expect very little if any business (even though in the 'standard' model, it would get half the market).

In general, then, the canonical model of a monopoly and entrant should probably not have identical costs but assume at least that (most) potential entrants have higher costs or some other disadvantage. As a result, the incumbent may be able to force entrants to exit the market without incurring losses at all. Such 'above-cost predation' may even be profit maximizing in the short run; it will be profit maximizing in the short run if the firms have constant marginal costs and sell identical products.

Once one thinks of predation as including price matching or price beating by a monopoly that succeeds in significantly limiting entry, it becomes evident that such pricing patterns are roughly as common as entry in monopoly and nothing like dragons. Perhaps the Bork–Easterbrook vision of below-cost predation is like dragons (though the discussion in section I may lead one to doubt it); but above-cost predation of the Edlin ilk is not.

There is a question in the minds of many (and of the courts) about whether above-cost pricing can be termed predatory at all, but if not, choose another word and call it 'anti-competitive' above-cost pricing. As Professor Einer Elhauge points out, to *define* predation as entailing below-cost pricing rather than *arguing* that only below-cost pricing is worthy of concern is a cheap rhetorical ploy with no fundamental import.[28] To sum up, even if one believes the expectational assumptions that make predation rare in the case of symmetric costs, symmetric information, decreasing returns to scale, and no switching costs, once one deviates from these assumptions, one moves from thinking that price cuts can sometimes be anticompetitive to thinking that they frequently can be.

V   THE EMPIRICAL EVIDENCE ON PREDATORY PRICING

What is the empirical evidence on predatory pricing? It depends a great deal of course on how we define predatory pricing. Thus, Elzinga[29] did not find predatory pricing in the gunpowder trust, defining predatory pricing as below marginal-cost pricing. Yet, Zerbe and Mumford found it in 5 of 11 cases by including above marginal-cost pricing intended to drive a rival from business or to induce a rival to join a cartel.[30]

---

[27]   Joseph Farrell and Michael Katz, *Competition or Predation? Consumer Coordination, Strategic Pricing and Price Floors in Network Markets*, 53 J. INDUSTRIAL ECONOMICS, 203 (1986).

[28]   Elhauge, *supra* note 9, at 698–9 (writing that '[o]ne unfortunate tendency has been to declare victory by definition – asserting that a "predatory" price must be below cost or that low above-cost prices involve "competition on the merits"').

[29]   K. Elzinga, *Predatory Pricing: The Case of the Gunpowder Trust*, 13(1) JOURNAL OF LAW AND ECONOMICS 223–40 (1970).

[30]   R. Zerbe Jr. and M. Mumford, *Does Predatory Pricing Exist? Economic Theory and the Courts after* Brooke Group [Ltd. v. Brown & Williamson Tobacco Corp., 509 US 209 (1993)], 41 ANTITRUST BULLETIN 949–85 (1996).

Elzinga and Mills see no evidence of successful predation by General Foods in the 1970s to protect its Maxwell House coffee in the eastern United States from the incursion of Procter & Gamble's Folgers coffee, which was the most popular brand in the West.[31] They emphasize in particular that the price cuts of General Foods did not in the end stop Folgers from moving east and becoming a national brand. Patrick Bolton, Joseph Brodley, and Michael Riordan, on the other hand, argue that it is plausible that General Foods successfully engaged in test-market predation: success was measured by Folgers delaying its entry for seven to eight years; they suggest that this delay of competition in the east is an important harm to be considered.[32]

Most empirical studies are case studies that attempt to tease out of observed data what firms were trying to do and what they in fact did do. David Bunch and Robert Smiley take a different approach.[33] They survey managers and ask how frequently those in their industry engage in a variety of practices to deter entry. One striking finding is that limit pricing is the most rare of the surveyed strategies. Interestingly these authors do not survey firms about deterring future entry by predatory pricing in response to current entry (they do survey about 'giving the impression through media' that entrants will be greeted with 'especially rigorous' competition). Capacity expansion tends to be used more when incumbents are larger and when the cost disadvantage to being small is greater, according to Bunch and Smiley.[34]

Burns[35] found that American Tobacco was able to purchase rivals at lower prices after predation as would be expected in a reputation model and contrary to McGee's[36] early arguments that merger was a substitute (and superior) strategy to predation. Scott Morton[37] found that when newer or smaller entrants faced off with the British shipping conference they were more likely than larger firms to confront a price war and be driven from the market. This is consistent with Telser's long purse theory. Genesove and Mullin[38] have provided evidence of successful below-cost predation in the sugar industry in the early twentieth century. An excellent and extensive literature survey has been written by Bruce Kobayashi; a pithier one is found in Kaplow and Shapiro.[39] Chris Sagers has surveyed all available information on airline price predation and concludes

---

[31]   See In re General Foods, 103 F.T.C. 204 (1984); see Elzinga and Mills, *supra* note 13.

[32]   Bolton, Brodley and Riordan, *supra* note 21.

[33]   David Bunch and Robert Smiley, "*What Deters Entry? Evidence on the Use of Strategic Entry Deterrents,*" Rev. Economics and Statistics 509 (1992).

[34]   *Id.* at 517.

[35]   Malcolm Burns, *Predatory Pricing and the Acquisition Costs of Competitors*, 94 J. Political Economy 266–96 (1986); Malcolm Burns, *New Evidence of Price Cutting*, 10 Managerial & Decision Economics 327–30 (1989).

[36]   J.S. McGee, *Ocean Freight Conferences and American Merchant Marine*, 27 Univ. Chicago Law Rev. 191–314 (1960).

[37]   Fiona Scott Morton, *Entry and Predation: British Shipping Cartels 1879–1929*, 6(4) J. Economics & Management Strategy 679–724 (1997).

[38]   David Genesove and Wallace Mullin, *Predation and Its Rate of Return: The Sugar Industry, 1887–1914*, 37(2) Rand J. Economics 47–69 (1997).

[39]   Bruce Kobayashi, *The Law and Economics of Predatory Pricing*, in Antitrust Law and Economics, Keith N. Hylton (ed.) (2010) Edward Elgar, pp. 116–56. Louis Kaplow and Carl Shapiro, *Antitrust*, 2 Handbook of Law and Economics (A. Mitchell Polinsky and Steven Shavell eds, 2007).

'that predation not only occurs in airline markets, but has been a key tool to preserve market power held by the surviving legacy carriers'.[40]

What is learned from this empirical evidence? Even if one takes a narrow view of predatory pricing and considers only below-cost pricing as candidates for predation, the view that predation is as rare as dragons is not born of the empirical evidence. If you hold that view strongly as a prior,[41] then it is possible that papers such as Genesove and Mullin's won't sway you much. On the other hand, you shouldn't expect to cite Koller (1971), McGee (1960, 1980) and Easterbrook (1981) as the Supreme Court did in its *Matsushita* ruling and convince someone that predation never occurs if that someone is predisposed to think predation possible.[42]

If one expands one's view of predation to include cases where a monopoly drives out entrants and deters future entry to the detriment of consumers, then the frequency of predation surely goes up, but the empirical literature does not tell us how much.

VI TESTS, STANDARDS, AND RATIONALES

I have argued that the Chicago School's skepticism about the existence of predatory pricing was unfounded,[43] particularly if one considers above-cost predation. Left unanswered is what if anything should be done? In particular, what should be the legal standard of illegal pricing?

The Supreme Court in the United States (at least in oligopoly markets) endorses a test of predatory pricing requiring proof that the predator prices below its cost and that it has either a reasonable prospect or probability of recouping the losses from so doing.[44] In contrast, the European Union has found abuse of dominance when above-cost price cuts

---

[40] Christopher Sagers, *Rarely Tried, and . . . Rarely Successful: Theoretically Impossible Price Predation Among the Airlines*, 74 J. AIR L. AND COM. 919 (2009).

[41] By a 'prior', I mean a belief held prior to reviewing the empirical evidence. Bayesian statisticians speak of this prior belief and the posterior belief resulting from updating the prior in light of the evidence.

[42] See Matsushita, *supra* note 14, 475 U.S. at 589. See also Ronald H. Koller, *The Myth of Predatory Pricing: An Empirical Study*, 4 (Summer) ANTITRUST LAW AND ECONOMICS REV. 105–23 (1971); J.S. McGee, *Ocean Freight Conferences and American Merchant Marine*, 27 UNIV. CHICAGO LAW REVIEW 191–314 (1960); J.S. McGee, *Predatory Pricing Revisited*, 23(2) J. LAW AND ECONOMICS 289–330 (1980).

[43] Of course this skepticism itself has two strands: one is a theoretical contention that low prices harmful to competition are rare or nonexistent, and the other is that little can be done about it without doing more harm than good. So far, I have tackled only the theoretical claim.

[44] Most commentators assume that Brooke Group Ltd. v. Brown & Williamson Tobacco Corp., 509 U.S. 209 (1993) applies equally to oligopolies and monopolies. On the other hand, Edlin, *supra* note 6, and later the court in LePage's, Inc. v. 3M, 324 F.3d 141 (3rd Cir. 2003) found that the *Brooke Group* precedent may not be applicable to monopolies: '[n]othing in the decision suggests that its discussion of the issue is applicable to a monopolist with its unconstrained market power'. *Lepage's*, 324 F.3d at 151. Unfortunately, Weyerhauser v. Ross-Simmons Hardwood Lumber, 127 S. Ct. 1069 (2007) probably puts an end to such arguments as it extended the *Brooke Group* rule to the case of monopsony.

were intended to drive rivals from the market.[45] The US Supreme Court pays at least lip service to the idea that above-cost price cuts can be undesirable but says they are 'beyond the practical ability of a judicial tribunal to control without courting intolerable risks of chilling legitimate price-cutting'.[46]

The connection between restricting attention to below-cost price cuts and the goal of protecting consumer welfare is indirect and somewhat loose. One idea (Breyer's bird in hand) is that price cuts benefit consumers and so we should be loath to condemn them. Another would be that in the long run, low costs drive low prices and so we should be alert (only) to firms who may drive lower cost rivals from the market.

The cost-based tests used in the United States present many implementation issues. Costs are notoriously difficult to measure, and once one begins measuring them, one immediately discovers that they come in many varieties: short-run marginal cost, long-run marginal cost, average variable cost, average avoidable cost, average incremental cost, and more. If the test for predation involves pricing below cost, what measure of cost is the right one to use? The US Supreme Court has said that price should be compared with the *appropriate* level of cost, but declined to decide what measure was appropriate.[47]

One can't really consider what the appropriate level of cost is without explaining first why one is comparing price with cost to ferret out predation. Here I distinguish two cost-based rationales, and take each in turn: sacrifice rationales and excluding equally efficient competitor rationales. Oddly, American courts say at various times that they are about either or both and rarely seem to discern that they are different.

After I discuss the two traditional rationales and the test each implies, I introduce a consumer betterment standard. This standard is more closely related to protecting consumer welfare than the two traditional standards, which either protect equally efficient competitors or prevent profit sacrifice.

A   Sacrifice Standard

Sacrifice theories observe that if a price is below cost, this reflects a sacrifice, and sacrifice raises the question – 'what for?' One possible answer is that the sacrifice was suffered 'to exclude competition', and if this is the answer, then an antitrust problem emerges. Under

---

[45]   Key cases in this line include AKZO, Compagnie Maritime (known as Cewal), and Irish Sugar. Case C-62/86, AKZO Chemie BV v. Commission, [1991] E.C.R. I-3359 paras 70–73 EC (holding that above variable cost but below total cost pricing is illegal if intended to eliminate a competitor). See also Joined Cases T-24/93, T-25/93, T-26/93, and T-28/93, Compagnie Maritime Belge Transps. SA v. Commission, [1996] E.C.R. II-1201 paras 138–53 (Ct. First Instance); aff'd by Joined Cases C-395/96 P and C-396/96 P, Compagnie Maritime Belge Transps. SA v. Commission, [2000] E.C.R. I-1365 paras 117–20, ECJ. (European Court of Justice affirming that selective above-cost price cuts to meet an entrant were illegal when a firm with over 90% market share has purpose of eliminating entrant). Case T-228/97, Irish Sugar PLC v. Commission, [1999] E.C.R. II-2969 173–93, Ct. First Instance, aff'd on other grounds, C-497/99 P, [2001] E.C.R. I-5333, ECJ.

[46]   *Brooke Group, supra* note 44, 509 U.S. at 223.

[47]   *Brooke Group*, 509 U.S. at 211 n.1 ('we again decline to resolve the conflict among the lower courts over the appropriate measure of cost').

sacrifice theories of predation, the cost (and price) definition should be geared to identify sacrifice.

Areeda and Turner[48] is the usual point of departure for sacrifice tests. Their theory is premised on the observation that in perfectly competitive markets, price equals short-run marginal cost, and so if, and only if, prices are below that level, does the question 'what for?' emerge. Thus, the *AMR* (*American Airlines*) court wrote, following *Advo*, that 'the ideal measure of cost would be marginal cost because "[a]s long as a firm's prices exceeded its marginal cost, each additional sale decreases losses or increases profits"'.[49]

Others such as Ordover and Willig[50] followed at least this much of the Areeda–Turner logic: if a firm undertakes actions that it would not undertake absent the effects of its action on reducing future competition, then the action is anticompetitive (but otherwise not). The Ordover–Willig definition urges that proving predation entails demonstrating first, a short-run profit sacrifice and second, that recouping the sacrifice is only possible due to reductions in competition.[51] With some modification of rationale, this logic developed into the two-pronged Brooke Group test (prong (1), P<C; prong (2), recoupment).[52]

What measures of cost and of price does a sacrifice theory suggest? Areeda and Turner, Ordover and Willig, and the courts in *AMR* and *Advo* advocate comparing price with marginal cost (MC) at least when possible. And indeed, output expansions when p<MC do involve a sacrifice.

But does P>MC imply lack of sacrifice? If MC were the dividing line between sacrifice and lack of sacrifice, then the test would be unbiased. However, contrary to the assumption of the *AMR* court and the *Advo* court, P>MC is quite consistent with sacrifice, as these terms are used in basic microeconomics texts. A price above marginal cost does not mean that an additional sale 'decreases losses or increases profits'.[53]

Additional sales generally require lowering prices on all goods sold not just on the additional sales. As a result, marginal revenue (defined as the revenue from an additional sale) is almost always below price for firms that charge uniform prices. Only in idealized perfectly competitive markets can a firm increase output without lowering price, and such markets are pretty irrelevant to the contexts of antitrust (monopoly and market power).

---

[48]   P. Areeda and D. Turner, *Predatory Pricing and Related Practices under Section 2 of the Sherman Act*, 88(4) HARVARD L. R. 697 (1975).

[49]   United States v. AMR, 335 F.3d 1109 1116 (10th Cir. 2003) quoting Advo, Inc. v. Phila. Newspapers, Inc., 51 F.3d 1191, 1198 (3d Cir. 1995).

[50]   J.A. Ordover and R.D. Willig, *An Economic Definition of Predation: Pricing and Product Innovation*, 91 YALE L.J. 8–53 (1981).

[51]   For a critique of the idea that profit sacrifice is necessary for an antitrust violation, see Steven Salop, *Exclusionary Conduct, Effect on Consumers, and the Flawed Profit-Sacrifice Standard*, 73 ANTITRUST L.J. 311 (2006). Jonathan Baker also discusses critiques of profit sacrifice in *Preserving a Political Bargain: The Political Economy of the Non-Interventionist Challenge to Monopolization Enforcement*, 76(3) ANTITRUST L.J. 605–54 (2010).

[52]   *Brooke Group*, 509 U.S. at 226 citing Kenneth Elzinga and David Mills, *Testing for Predation: Is Recoupment Feasible?*, 34 ANTITRUST BULLETIN 869 (Winter 1989); C.S. Hemphill, *The Role of Recoupment in Predatory Pricing Analyses*, 53(6) STANFORD L. REV. 1581 (2001) (providing a particularly insightful analysis of recoupment).

[53]   See *AMR*, 335 F. 3d at 1116; see also *Advo,* 51 F.3d at 1198, *supra* note 49.

The more market power a firm has, all else equal, the greater will be the excess of price over marginal revenue.

Here are two simple ways to frame a price–cost comparison as a necessary and sufficient test of sacrifice, which appears (sometimes) to be what the *AMR* court sought. Suppose that Dell sells one million computers each year for US$1,000 each, and pays US$900 to produce each computer. To sell 1,000,001 computers it must lower price by one cent to US$999.99. One cost of selling the extra computer is lowering price on one million computers by one cent each, which cost amounts to US$10,000 in lost revenue. As a result, even though the last computer sells for US$999.99 and this 'price' exceeds the production cost of US$900, the sale involves an enormous sacrifice. Profits fall because

$$US\$999.99 < US\$10,900$$

The real full cost of selling the extra computer is actually US$10,900. The *Advo* assertion holds true only if marginal cost includes the cost of losing US$10,000 of revenue on the first million computers.[54] Unlike the 'production' measure of marginal cost, this 'inclusive' definition of marginal cost can be compared to price to yield an unbiased measure of sacrifice. (I here introduce and utilize the terminology 'inclusive' and 'exclusive' which is inspired by the tax literature where prices are referred to as being tax-inclusive or tax-exclusive).

There is another way to think about the matter, which is to reconceptualize price and not see price as US$999.99. Economists speak of marginal revenue (MR), which is the increment to revenue from the last sale. In this case, marginal revenue is negative. It is:

$$MR = US\$999.99 - US\$10,000 = -US\$9,000.01$$

Extra output involves sacrifice if and only if MR<MC. Marginal revenue can be seen as an inclusive notion of price. It includes revenue effects. The alternative way to measure sacrifice is to talk about an inclusive notion of revenue that includes the lost revenue on inframarginal units; an inclusive notion of price can be compared to the exclusive production cost of US$900. In this example, as −US$9,000.01<US$900.00, MR<MC, and the output increase is unprofitable.

The Department of Justice (DOJ) *implicitly* put forward these inclusive definitions of price (or maybe cost) in the *AMR* case.[55] AMR had added a number of planes to a route. The DOJ compared incremental revenue to incremental cost, where the 'increment' was the additional flights. In a sense the price at which AMR was selling the extra flights was the amount by which its revenues increased (i.e. incremental revenue) rather than, say, the sum of ticket prices of passengers who traveled on the extra flights. There are at least two problems with simply counting the ticket prices on the extra flights: first, that would count

---

[54]   This example is a variant of one in PHILLIP AREEDA, LOUIS KAPLOW AND AARON EDLIN, ANTITRUST ANALYSIS: PROBLEMS, TEXT AND CASES 478–9 (6th ed. 2004).

[55]   Oddly, the Department of Justice briefs in *AMR* were not straightforward in explaining the difference between inclusive and exclusive notions of price and cost. The briefs embrace Areeda–Turner who probably had in mind comparing exclusive measures of price and cost, but then proceeded to implement tests that used inclusive measures of one or the other.

revenue even if the only thing that happened was that passengers switched from existing American Airlines flights to the new ones, and second, it would not account for the full impact (on existing flights) of any overall price decreases that American Airlines made to fill its expanded schedule of flights. With this inclusive definition of price as incremental revenue the DOJ proved a sacrifice. There is a strong sense in which the price at which American Airlines sold these extra flights equals the incremental revenue of adding them and not the narrow and exclusive measure of the revenues from tickets on the flights.

The district and appellate courts, however, did not accept these inclusive notions in *AMR*. The appellate court objected, using an example drawn from Elhauge, that the DOJ test 'effectively treats foregone or "sacrificed" profits as costs, and condemns activity that may have been profitable as predatory'.[56] The Elhauge example involves an airline that adds a flight with direct costs of US$500,000. Passengers on that flight purchase US$1,000,000 of tickets, but the revenue of the rest of the route falls by US$600,000 so that the net incremental revenue is US$400,000.[57] Adding the flight lowers profits by US$100,000 and involves a profit sacrifice. How then does the court come to view the added flight as profitable? It does so by comparing the US$1,000,000 exclusive price on the incremental capacity to its US$500,000 exclusive cost. Elhauge objects to the inclusive notions of cost or price saying 'it is vital for analytical clarity to avoid using cost measures that effectively include forgone profits . . . otherwise, one cannot keep predatory theories based on a failure to maximize short-term profits analytically distinct from theories based on pricing below costs'.[58]

Why, though, should one want to keep predatory theories based on profit sacrifice[59] analytically distinct from theories based on pricing below cost? One of the central rationales for price–cost tests is that pricing below cost indicates short-run profit sacrifice and that sacrifice may indicate anticompetitive exclusionary activity. In defense of Elhauge here, his statement makes perfect sense if one views price–cost tests as the exclusive domain of equally efficient competitor standards rather than sacrifice standards. His point becomes one of truth in advertising, which is that price–cost tests do not measure profit–sacrifice so one should distinguish profit sacrifice tests from price–cost tests. My objection to that truth-in-advertising point is that, for better or worse, price–cost tests have been adopted by courts at least in part to identify profit sacrifice and if price or cost is measured inclusively then the tests can do so admirably. What I think is clearly false advertising is to use exclusive measures of price and cost in an effort to measure sacrifice.

Additional output involves a sacrifice if and only if marginal revenue is less than

---

56   *AMR*, 335 F.3d at 1118 n. 13.
57   Elhauge, *supra* note 9, at 694; *AMR*, 335 F.3d at 1118 n. 13.
58   Elhauge, *supra* note 9, at 694.
59   Here I have substituted the words 'profit sacrifice' for Elhauge's 'failure to maximize short-run profits' because the latter may be a more inclusive term and because (to the extent that profit sacrifice and failure to maximize profits differ) profit sacrifice is the concept central to predation analysis. The Department of Justice distinguished between sacrifice theories and failure to maximize short-term profits theories by pointing out that its efforts to identify (large) profit sacrifices from adding incremental capacity in response to entry are different than obligating a firm to always maximize profits. The Department of Justice would not, for example, have argued that a firm that priced low in the first place before entry was unlawfully excluding competition because it failed to maximize short-run or long-run profits.

marginal cost. Comparing exclusive notions of price to exclusive notions of marginal cost gives a free pass to sacrifices that are not too great. Counterproductively, bigger free passes are handed out to firms with greater market power because for them the wedge between marginal revenue and price is greater. In fact, the free pass can be huge: in the example above, the goods were sold when the loss from so doing was 10 times the price.

To the extent that one is trying to measure the intent to limit the competition from rivals – and to the extent that short-term sacrifice is seen as a useful signal of such intent – comparing marginal revenue with marginal cost is a more accurate test of sacrifice than comparing exclusive notions of price with exclusive notions of marginal cost or price with average variable cost.

Saying that marginal (or incremental) cost should when possible be compared to marginal (or incremental) revenue to identify sacrifice does not transparently answer all questions, of course. The following application is more subtle. Consider two-sided markets in which types A and types B are simultaneously served by a 'market-maker' and the service consists of intermediation between As and Bs. Examples abound: a nightclub serves and matches men and women; credit card networks simultaneously serve customers and merchants; and an academic journal serves readers and authors. In fact any distributor of goods or reseller can be thought to provide its distribution services both to suppliers and customers – ultimately it matches them together.

Suppose the immediate cost of serving A is X and the market maker sells to A at p<X. Is the price below the 'appropriate' measure of cost? Not necessarily. It sells below the exclusive cost, but not necessarily the inclusive cost. The inclusive cost is less than X because by serving A the market maker gets a higher price from B, or sells to more Bs. Such an adjustment seems necessary. (Some readers should be careful before following me down this garden path, however, as I don't see how they could consistently admit these adjustments and not admit the inclusive adjustments in *AMR* that Elhauge and the *AMR* courts eschew.)

If the inclusive adjustment isn't allowed, on what grounds? In what fundamental sense can we say that X is the cost of serving A? The servicing of A can be viewed as an input to the service of B; perhaps A should be being paid and not paying. Is the processing of my credit card payments a service to me or to the merchant network of Visa who wants my business?

There are, of course, innumerable subtle issues involved in determining profit sacrifice. The main point here is that to measure profit sacrifice in an unbiased way using a price–cost test requires using either an inclusive notion of marginal or incremental cost or an inclusive notion of price that amounts to marginal or incremental revenue.

B   Equally Efficient Competitor Standard

A second strand of thinking asserts that we should only be concerned about price predation when such pricing excludes equally or more efficient competitors. To achieve this end with a price–cost test, 'price' and 'cost' should be defined with an eye to ensuring as much as possible that prices above cost are too high to exclude equally efficient competitors, but that prices below cost threaten to do so.

Hence, Baumol and Posner come to favor an average variable cost test not as an approximation for marginal cost like the Areeda–Turner school, but rather as the *right* test. They recast it as an average avoidable cost test, where 'avoidable costs' are those that would be avoided if the firm did not make the challenged increment of output – some would call this the average incremental cost test. (NB: If one challenges the last unit of output, this test converges to the Areeda–Turner marginal-cost test but with an exclusive measure of cost and price.)

If a firm prices below average avoidable cost, then the firm may exclude a rival who could more efficiently produce the allegedly predatory increment of output. Prices above AAC can, they would argue, only exclude less efficient entrants because, if an entrant were equally or more efficient in the sense of having lower avoidable cost on the output increment, presumably that entrant could win the business when competing against a price above its cost.[60]

Thus, the standard of Baumol and Posner is 'the equally efficient competitor standard'.[61] Prices that exclude an equally or more efficient competitor are predatory. Prices that don't are not. Elhauge argues for the equally efficient competitor standard for predatory pricing (but importantly not for other monopolization[62]) based on welfare effects, not as an axiom. Indeed, Elhauge concludes that '"costs" should be defined in whatever way satisfies the condition that an above-cost price could not deter or drive out an equally efficient firm'.[63] Thus, if in some instance average avoidable cost did not do the trick and allowed an above-cost price to drive out an equally efficient firm, Elhauge would define 'cost' as whatever higher cost measure precluded this result.

The US Supreme Court has at times embraced this focus on the relative efficiency of excluded firms, at least in dicta. For example, in *Brooke Group*, the Court made a statement that could be interpreted as implicitly defining competition on the merits as excluding those who are less efficient and only those who are less efficient.[64] This is certainly one view of 'the merits'. It describes productive merits.

The average avoidable cost test raises many issues in application. Consider that American Airlines moves an aircraft from a profitable route in New York to add to its allegedly predatory campaign on the Dallas to Wichita route. Using the aircraft on the

---

[60] This proposition has an undeniable strength, though it is not as self-evident in practice as it is in theory. In the typical theoretical model, an equally good product at a lower price captures the whole market. In practice, an entrant whose products are unknown may find itself selling little without (and sometimes even with) extraordinary marketing and sales expenses. There is a sense in which this entrant is less efficient in that its products won't sell without these marketing and sales expenditures; or, one might say that its products are not truly equally good because one aspect of a product is being known.

[61] R. POSNER, ECONOMIC ANALYSIS OF LAW, 194–5 (6th ed., Aspen Publishers, 2002); W. Baumol, *Predation and the Logic of the Average Variable Cost Test*, 39(1) J. LAW AND ECONOMICS (1996).

[62] For example, Elhauge rejects the standard in the case of loyalty discounts: see *Tying, Bundled Discounts, and the Death of the Single Monopoly Profit Theory* at 67, 16 October 2009, available at www.law.harvard.edu/faculty/elhauge/pdf/Elhauge_629_Revised2.pdf.

[63] *Id.* at 689.

[64] The Court wrote that 'As a general rule, the exclusionary effect of prices above a relevant measure of cost either reflects the lower cost structure of the alleged predator, and so represents competition on the merits, or is beyond the practical ability of a judicial tribunal to control without courting intolerable risks of chilling legitimate price-cutting'. *Brooke Group*, 113 S.Ct. 2578 at 2588. A recent OECD report suggests, on the other hand, that there is no consensus on the meaning of competition on the merits, see www.oecd.org/dataoecd/10/27/37082099.pdf.

Wichita route is avoidable, but what is its cost? Is the lost net income on the New York route a cost? It is certainly what economists call an opportunity cost. In fact, if consumers on the New York route lost consumer surplus one might argue that too should be counted in a true equally efficient competitor test (it is a social opportunity cost). Remarkably, the court in *AMR* was unreceptive to seeing aircraft costs as includable in any fashion.[65] In contrast, even the defendant's expert in *Spirit v. Northwest* wanted to include the lost profits on other routes as the cost of an extra aircraft on the predatory route.[66]

Fixed costs present a vexing issue in predation cases. Costs that are truly fixed in that they don't vary with the increment in question are not avoidable. That said, it is all too easy for a court or an economic expert to assume that a great many costs like rent (or aircraft ownership costs) are fixed, particularly when a company's accountants label them as such. However, as businesses grow the amount of money that they spend on what accountants label as fixed costs grow as well, suggesting that these costs are not actually fixed in the long run.

Are these costs fixed in the short run? They may be, at least in a sense. Thus, it is understandable that the district and appellate courts in *AMR* objected to including costs such as 'dispatch, city ticket offices, certain station expenses, certain maintenance expenses, American's flight academy, flight simulator maintenance, general sales and advertising'.[67] The court's exclusion of these costs as unavoidable is plausible but not as compelling as the court thought. There are many hidden costs in the use of facilities, whether a city ticket office or a flight simulator. Use of facilities can create crowding and waiting costs. If employees work harder than usual until new employees are hired, there may be a morale cost. One might argue that the reason new employees are hired or larger facilities are purchased is because those decisions are cheaper than the alternatives of continuing to bear crowding, morale, or other like costs.[68] Once one delves into the details, cost measurement becomes ever murkier, unfortunately.

C   Consumer Betterment Standard

An alternative view of competition on the merits which derives from my ongoing joint work with Joseph Farrell would focus not on the productive merits of a firm but on

---

[65]   See *AMR*, 335 F.3d at 1119 n. 12 approving of the district court's conclusion that 'VAUDNC-AC overstates short-run cost because it includes fixed, unavoidable aircraft-ownership costs'.

[66]   Spirit Airlines, Inc. v. Northwest Airlines, Inc., 431 F.3d 917, 925 (6th Cir. 2005). To include only lost profits (and not lost consumer surplus) on the other route actually misses the point if one is asking about the total economic avoidable cost of shifting the extra aircraft to the predatory route. If, on the other hand, one is trying to implement a sacrifice test, then these forgone profits are the relevant measure. Indeed, for similar reasons, if one is trying to identify sacrifice, then the forgone profits on the existing (pre-expansionary) flights on the predatory route would also be relevant as discussed in section VA. Oddly, many would take the position, as the defendant's expert in *Spirit* did, that the relevant cost measure would include one forgone profit and yet not the other.

[67]   *AMR*, 335 F.3d at 1117 (2003).

[68]   I am grateful to my co-author Joseph Farrell for teaching me this. We discuss it in *The American Airlines Case: A Chance to Clarify Predation Policy*, in THE ANTITRUST REVOLUTION (John Kwoka and Lawrence White eds, 3rd ed, Oxford University Press, 2003).

the merits of the offer it makes to customers.[69] Thus, while Posner and Baumol see monopolization where a

> challenged practice is likely in the circumstances to exclude from the defendant's market an equally or more efficient competitor (equally efficient competitor standard)[70]

I propose seeing monopolization where a

> challenged practice is likely in the circumstances to exclude from the defendant's market a competitor who would provide consumers a better deal than they get from the monopoly (consumer betterment standard).[71]

The Posner–Baumol standard focuses on production efficiency, asking: is a cheaper producer excluded from the market? The consumer betterment standard focuses on increases in consumer surplus, asking: is a better deal for consumers excluded from the market? The better deal might be a lower price or higher quality. This approach flows fairly directly from the view espoused by the US Supreme Court that antitrust is intended to protect consumer welfare.[72] As such, focusing directly on consumer betterment for monopolization generally or predatory pricing specifically flows naturally in the river of antitrust. In fact, it seems odd that the main stream of monopolization thinking interprets competition on the merits as equivalent to the triumph of the firm with the greater productive merits, regardless of whether those merits will be passed on to consumers.

What are the differences at a theoretical level between these two definitions of monopolization? Observe that, if a firm promised to sell forever at a price below its average avoidable cost and maintained its monopoly in this way, it would violate the equally efficient competitor standard as more efficient competitors are likely to be excluded. The same firm would not, however, violate the consumer betterment standard, because no better offers are likely to be excluded. As the firm's offer is a boon to consumers, in this case, the consumer betterment standard furthers antitrust's dominant welfare goal. However, we should not make much of this advantage because this scenario is implausible. Perhaps the equally efficient competitor standard is justified because the only entrants who will plausibly increase

---

[69]   Edlin and Farrell, *supra* note 5.

[70]   Quote is from Posner, *supra* note 61; Baumol, *supra* note 61.

[71]   I call this a consumer betterment standard (as opposed to consumer welfare) because it is a process standard that indicates anticompetitive exclusion and need not require a final welfare analysis.

[72]   Reiter v. Sonotone Corp., 442 U.S. 330, 342 (1979); see also Statement of Commissioners Harbour, Leibowitz and Rosch on the Issuance of the Section 2 Report by the Department of Justice, Federal Trade Commission, September 2008; R.H. Lande, *Proving the Obvious: The Antitrust Laws were Passed to Protect Consumers (not Just to Increase Efficiency)*, 50 HASTINGS L.R. 959, 963–6 (1999) (citing over twenty scholars who agree with the wealth transfer thesis); R.H. Lande, *Wealth Transfers (Not Just Efficiency) Should Guide Antitrust*, 58 ANTITRUST L.J. 631, n. 27 (1989); and Lande, *supra* note 1. See also the Court's rationale for the recoupment requirement in *Brook Group* that although below-cost pricing is inefficient, it is a 'boon to consumers' if prices don't rise later (recoupment). ('Without [recoupment], predatory pricing produces lower aggregate prices in the market, and consumer welfare is enhanced. Although unsuccessful predatory pricing may encourage some inefficient substitution toward the product being sold at less than its cost, unsuccessful predation is in general a boon to consumers'. *Brook Group*, *supra* note 22, 509 U.S. 209, 224.)

consumer welfare by entry are those with lower costs and the only (or main?) threat to consumer wellbeing is a monopoly's exclusion of such more efficient rivals? Not so, I argue.

Inefficient rivals often provide important competition, or at least could provide important competition if competition law limited their exclusion, as emphasized by Edlin and Baker.[73] To understand the bite of the consumer betterment standard in a plausible scenario, consider an efficient incumbent that sells at high prices but forestalls entry (from less efficient firms) because it 'advertises' a credible threat (or makes a contractual promise) to cut prices post-entry to levels below the average costs of entrants but above its own avoidable costs. If entrants would otherwise provide consumers with better deals, then this incumbent monopolizes according to the consumer betterment standard. The incumbent does not monopolize according to the equally efficient competitor standard because the excluded entrants are inefficient.

Entrants in this example stand willing to provide consumers with a better deal than the incumbent actually gives consumers, but entrants don't do so because the efficient incumbent would drive them from the market. Those worried solely about productive efficiency are not concerned about productively inefficient entrants, of course, but why should antitrust focus on the exclusion of productively efficient firms if consumer welfare is its ultimate consequentialist goal?

A refuge for those who favor the equally efficient competitor standard is to say that the forestalled entry problem is theoretically possible but can't be reliably identified. How would you know in the example above that entrants stood ready to provide better offers? No doubt this will often be difficult. Yet, in cases such as *AMR* or *Spirit Airlines*, the problem can be identified, often because an entrant actually does offer a better deal for a time before the incumbent responds. Where proof that a monopoly is excluding those likely to offer better deals is unavailable the defendant should win.

A last important question is whether the consumer betterment standard is the same as an overall consumer welfare standard that approves tactics that improve consumer welfare and condemns those that reduce them. The two are related but distinct. The consumer betterment standard is largely a process-based rule, protecting the competitive process, rather than a standard demanding an ultimate consumer welfare calculus. The distinctions will become clearer with an example.

VII   AN APPLICATION OF THE THREE STANDARDS: *AMERICAN AIRLINES*

A concrete example may help to illustrate the three predatory pricing standards I have discussed and show that defining predation according to consumer betterment might be practical and appealing. Consider the *American Airlines* case brought by the Department of Justice, a case discussed extensively by Edlin, Edlin and Farrell, and Elhauge.[74]

---

[73]   J. Baker, *Preserving a Political Bargain: The Political Economy of the Non-Interventionist Challenge to Monopolization Enforcement*, 76(3) ANTITRUST L.J. 605–54 (2010).

[74]   *AMR*, *supra* note 49, 335 F.3d at 1109. See Edlin, *supra* note 6; Edlin and Farrell, *supra* note 68; Elhauge, *supra* note 9.

American Airlines reacted to entrants who offered low fares by overriding 'its own capacity-planning models for each route' and increasing the number of flights on the route, despite the fact that American Airlines' models suggested such increases would be unprofitable, by matching the entrant's prices, and 'making more seats available at the new, lower prices'.[75] The court found the pattern well illustrated by the DFW–Wichita route, where average prices were roughly US$100 pre-'predation', dropped to US$60 during 'predation', rose to US$95 for the year after 'predation', and were over US$100 thereafter.[76]

The question in the case was whether the quotation marks around 'predation' should be removed. The appeals court wrote that:

> In each instance, American's response produced the same result: the competing LCC failed to establish a presence, moved its operations or ceased its separate existence entirely. Once the [entrant] ceased or moved its operations, American generally resumed its prior marketing strategy, reducing flights and raising prices to levels roughly comparable to those prior to the period of low-fare competition.[77]

The appeals court opinion seemed ambivalent about whether it was applying the equally efficient competitor standard or the sacrifice standard. At times one has the feeling that the court thought they were the same, while at other times the court made a sharp point to critique profit-maximization requirements.[78] In particular, it quoted *Advo* to the effect that '[a]s long as a firm's prices exceed its marginal cost, each additional sale decreases losses or increases profits'[79] – an assertion that we have seen is false unless inclusive notions of price or marginal cost are used, and the court did not allow the Department of Justice's inclusive notions; that is, if the additional sale lowers profit margins on earlier sales, then a sale at a price above production cost can easily lower profits.

If the *AMR* case had been decided squarely using profit sacrifice, the DOJ should have won the case or at least gotten to the recoupment stage of proof. After all, the court found that American Airlines overrode its own capacity planning model. In addition, the DOJ showed that the addition of extra flights (and the extra sales that were part of this strategy) caused overall profits to fall. The appeals court tried to say that the extra flights were still 'profitable', but this was really a statement that the ticket revenues of passengers on these flights exceeded the production cost of those flights, not an inclusive cost measure that included forgone revenues as passengers switched from the existing American Airlines flights to the new ones, or that included losses as fares fell on existing flights, or that included the opportunity cost of moving aircraft to the route. The court

---

[75]   *AMR*, 335 F.3d at 1113.
[76]   *Id.* at 1112.
[77]   *Id.* at 1113.
[78]   The Department of Justice tried to distinguish profit sacrifice tests from requiring profit maximization as follows. Under a profit sacrifice test for predatory pricing, it is predatory to make a large output expansion in response to entry when that expansion lowers profits beyond what the entry itself does. However, a failure to maximize profits in general, by for example charging prices that are lower than profit maximizing prior to entry or by charging prices above profit-maximizing levels, is not predatory pricing.
[79]   *AMR*, 335 F.3d at 1115.

explicitly jettisoned inclusive cost measures distinguishing 'actual costs' from opportunity costs or 'forgone or "sacrificed" profits'.[80] In so doing, the *AMR* court ultimately applied the equally efficient competitor test, despite the confusing justifications of AVC tests as a proxy for MC and the court's erroneous explanation that sales at prices above MC increase profits.

Under the equally efficient competitor test, the *AMR* opinion may be correctly decided. The DOJ was unable to show that a noninclusive measure of incremental revenues was less than a noninclusive measure of avoidable incremental cost. Although low-cost carriers (LCCs) have lower costs of operating flights, American Airlines has the advantage of operating a hub and spoke system so that it can fill much of its plane with through-passengers, which can justify the flight with very low prices for the direct-customers with whom it competes with LCC entrants.

How then might *AMR* be analysed under the consumer betterment standard? The key question is whether American Airlines' behavior is likely to exclude entrants who would otherwise provide consumers with substantially better deals than American Airlines offers. We must therefore decide the relevant benchmark by which to measure the deals that American Airlines offers. Is it the US$100 pre-predation price, the US$60 predatory price, or the final US$110 post-predation price? And what exclusion concerns us?

There are three exclusions of potential concern in considering the Dallas–Wichita route. The first is the actual exclusion of Vanguard, the airline that entered, charged low prices and ended up exiting. The second is the probabalistic exclusion of all the potential rivals in the future who may not enter after observing American Airlines' behavior. Obviously the second presents evidentiary challenges. Finally, one might well be concerned about exclusion of likely competitors on all of American Airlines' other routes.

Suppose the facts had been different. Assume that American Airlines had excluded Vanguard with the US$60 price but then kept its price at US$60 forever. We may surmise that Vanguard was unwilling to offer consumers better deals than the US$60 price that American Airlines did and was excluded for that reason. That observation suggests that American Airlines has not violated the consumer betterment standard in this hypothetical case because it did not exclude a rival who would have offered better than American Airlines did (US$60).

Under the actual facts, however, American Airlines raised its price after Vanguard exited. American Airlines' typical price was therefore US$100. Let's assume that American Airlines' average price over a five-year period was roughly US$100 or more except for the short period when Vanguard entered and it charged US$60. I would argue then that the relevant benchmark comparison is US$100, American Airlines' price before and after the predatory period. Then the consumer betterment test asks whether American Airlines' behavior is likely to exclude rivals who would willingly offer better deals, better than American Airlines' usual price of US$100. The answer here is 'yes'. In fact, just such a rival was excluded.

---

[80]   In particular, the appellate court complained that 'Test One effectively treats forgone or "sacrificed" profits as costs, and condemns activity that may have been profitable as predatory'. *AMR*, 335 F.3d at 1119. The appellate court further wrote, quoting the district court, that 'It is clear, therefore, that, in proffering Test One, the government has not "attempted to identify the actual costs associated with the capacity additions". *AMR Corp.*., 140 F. Supp.2d at 1202'.

Perhaps the evidence presented in *AMR* doesn't conclusively clinch the case (perhaps that particular rival exited for some reason other than American Airlines' actions). Then, the case might hinge upon the likelihood of the exclusion of future would-be entrants. Suppose that in addition, the DOJ proved that there were five entrants who would definitely enter the market and charge prices of US\$75 or below on the Dallas–Wichita route but these firms are unwilling to do so because they witnessed American Airlines' prior response and expect a similar response. In that case, the DOJ would have proved its case under a consumer betterment standard.

Defining predation according to consumer betterment has two advantages. The more straightforward is that it allows consumers to enjoy the fruits of more entry holding constant pre-entry pricing, and to enjoy those fruits for longer. The subtler effect is that defining predation according to consumer betterment provides monopolies like American Airlines the incentive to price low in the first instance to make their deal better and thereby make entry and predation cases harder. American Airlines might likewise price lower post-predation to make predation cases harder to bring because it will be harder to find plausible would-be entrants. For these reasons, a consumer betterment standard for adjudicating predatory pricing has the prospect of making consumers better off when facing a monopoly.

Consumer betterment focuses on the competitive process and the exclusion of competitors who would offer a better deal. Although it is inspired by consumer welfare it is not the same as a consumer welfare standard, which condemns behavior that ultimately hurts competitors and allows behavior that ultimately benefits consumers.[81] Under consumer betterment, I have argued that American Airlines could escape liability by leaving its price low. Potentially, consumers are worse off under such a rule than an Edlin price freeze rule that didn't allow American Airlines to lower its price at all in reaction to entry; potentially, an Edlin rule would induce American Airlines to price lower in the first place or induce more entry than consumer betterment. Likewise, it is conceivable that consumer betterment would invite entrants who will innovate less and ultimately lead to lower consumer welfare in the long run than existing predatory pricing law. I don't see any reason to believe that, but the point is that consumer betterment does not, however, demand a final consumer welfare analysis; it asks instead an immediate question about whether rivals who would offer better deals now are excluded.

VIII   THE RELATIONSHIP OF THE CONSUMER BETTERMENT STANDARD TO BAUMOL'S AND EDLIN'S PRICE FREEZES

The preceding discussion of *American Airlines* and the application of the consumer betterment standard to that case may remind some readers of the price freeze proposals

---

[81]   See Steven C. Salop, *Question: What is the Real and Proper Antitrust Welfare Standard? Answer: The* True *Consumer Welfare Standard*, 22(3) LOYOLA CONSUMER L. REV. 336–53 (2010); Steven C. Salop, *Exclusionary Conduct, Effect on Consumers and the Flawed Profit-Sacrifice Standard*, 73 ANTITRUST L.J. 312, 314 (2006).

made by Edlin[82] in 2002 and by Baumol[83] in 1979 (a very different Baumol than the Baumol who in 1996 proposed the equally efficient competitor standard). After all, the Baumol and Edlin price freezes and consumer betterment are all geared to maximize the value that consumers derive from entry. Additionally, all three proposals assert that firms can predate without pricing below cost, a controversial idea. It is therefore worth considering, at a finer level of detail, what they have in common and how they differ.

In the simplest case, where all competition is price competition, the Edlin price freeze proposes that if an entrant substantially undercuts a monopoly (perhaps by 20% or more), then the monopoly cannot respond for a sufficient period to encourage such entry (perhaps 18–24 months). More generally, Edlin proposes protecting entrants who offer substantial consumer value vis-à-vis the incumbent offer. The idea is to encourage monopolies to price low or otherwise offer value in the first place (pre-entry) as they would in a contestable market, and if they don't do so to encourage entry by those willing to offer better value.

Baumol proposes that if the monopoly chooses to cut its price after entry, the monopoly cannot raise its price after the entrant exits or is chastened. Liability in Baumol attaches on the price rise, whereas in the Edlin price freeze it attaches to the price cut.

Like the consumer betterment standard, the price freezes of Edlin and Buamol are each geared to increase the value that consumers get from entry. The Edlin rule focuses more on lowering pre-entry pricing and on increasing the chance of entry. The Baumol rule focuses more on getting the most from entry that occurs so that if the monopoly cuts its price those benefits can be enjoyed forever (or at least for a long time).[84]

How do the Edlin and Baumol price freeze rules relate to the consumer betterment standard in the *American Airlines* application? In the *American Airlines* application, the Edlin rule would have found American Airlines guilty of monopolization even if it had left the price at US$60, because American Airlines' reactive price cut triggers liablity. But in such a case, could we fairly say that a competitor has been excluded who would provide consumers with a better deal than they get from the monopoly? Probably not. The monopoly ended up offering consumers fares of US$60 and Vanguard was not providing better value than that. Only a very aggressive interpretation of the consumer betterment standard would go so far as to condemn such a monopoly.

The Baumol rule would have found American Airlines liable when it raised its price after Vanguard exited (but not before). Hence, if American Airlines had left its price at US$60 after Vanguard exited, then it could not be found to have monopolized. That result is broadly consistent with what the consumer betterment standard suggests, so in this case Baumol and consumer betterment converge, and are both less aggressive rules than Edlin's price freeze.

The consumer betterment standard is not always identical to a Baumol price freeze, however. To see why, suppose that a monopoly prices at 100 until another firm enters and

---

[82]   Edlin, *supra* note 6.

[83]   Baumol, *supra* note 6.

[84]   The Edlin proposal does have one policy lever geared to increasing the value derived from entry given entry, which is the threshold of increased value that the entrant must bring to consumers to earn protection. As that threshold increases (to a point) consumers will get more value from a given entrant.

prices at 70. To drive the entrant from the market, the incumbent monopoly prices at 50. Once the entrant exits, the monopoly raises price to 70, which it charges thereafter. What result? Under the Baumol price freeze, the monopoly has committed predation. Under consumer betterment, however, there is no evidence here that the monopoly which offers either 50 or 70 has excluded better deals. It excluded a deal of 70. Thus, plaintiff has no case under consumer betterment.

Consumer betterment is a general interpretation of competition on the merits and, unlike a Baumol price freeze, is a general standard for monopolization cases, not just predatory pricing cases. If pervasive long-term exclusive dealing contracts prevented a better product from getting to market, for example, they might run afoul of consumer betterment. A Baumol price freeze is inapplicable to exclusive dealing arrangements, so the generality of consumer betterment distinguishes it from the Baumol price freeze.

Within the predatory pricing context, a consumer betterment standard may be either a less or more aggressive antitrust standard than a Baumol price freeze. I gave above an example where consumer betterment is more permissive for an incumbent monopoly. Here is an example where it is less so. Consider, for example, the case of the preemptive threat discussed earlier. A monopoly charges a high price, and potential competitors would willingly offer lower prices, but don't enter because the monopoly credibly threatens in a press conference that it will crush any low-priced entrants. Under the consumer betterment standard, if an entrant proves that it would otherwise have entered and offered consumers a better deal, but was excluded by the credible threat, the entrant has a case. Under the Edlin price freeze rule, the entrant must actually enter and offer a very low price; monopolization only occurs when the monopoly comes through on its threat and matches or beats the entrant's price. Under Baumol, liability does not attach unless the monopoly subsequently raises price (after the entrant exits or is disciplined).

Is a consumer betterment standard too aggressive in finding liability for a preemptive threat? I don't think so. The preemptive threat provides no social benefit and comes at what is a substantial consumer welfare cost if it is actually shown that the threat prevented entry. Another angle is this. By condemning preemptive threats, the consumer betterment standard also promotes competition, if competition is understood as the process by which firms offer better and better deals to buyers. Both competition and consumer welfare are goals of antitrust, and consumer betterment can serve each master.

Elhauge and Above-Cost Predation

One potential objection to the consumer betterment standard is that it can condemn pricing patterns that never dip below cost. Professor Elhauge has recently argued that no predatory pricing rule should condemn above-cost pricing.[85] His main arguments, though, seem to apply more to Edlin's price freeze than to Baumol's price freeze or to consumer betterment.[86]

Elhauge's main objection to Edlin's price freeze was that it could protect high-cost

---

[85]   Elhauge, *supra* note 9.
[86]   Elhauge, *supra* note 9, at 822–6, however, made supplementary critiques of Baumol's price freeze, some (but not all) of which would apply to consumer betterment.

entrants and Elhauge believes that such entrants have very little to offer in the end to consumers.[87] Elhauge's idea is that even if such entrants offer consumers substantial short-run surplus, if one adopts a rule that an incumbent cannot (for a time) match or beat the price of an entrant who offers a better deal, little is gained in the long run because once the bar on incumbent price reductions is lifted, the incumbent can drive the entrant from the market. Even if Elhauge is correct about the effects of Edlin's price freeze, the same cannot be said of Baumol's or of consumer betterment. Under either Baumol or consumer betterment, consumers will derive lasting benefits from competition because if they do not, then the monopoly's reactive low pricing will be viewed as predatory rather than competitive.

Elhauge's second objection also seems to apply more to Edlin's price freeze than to Baumol's or to consumer betterment. He worries that limiting aggressive incumbent responses to entry could hurt consumers post-entry because it limits post-entry competition in cases where entry would occur regardless of antitrust protections[88] (i.e. in cases where the Edlin competition problem doesn't exist). This response applies more to the Edlin price freeze than to Baumol or consumer betterment, because both Baumol and consumer betterment allow post-entry competition. Baumol and consumer betterment simply insist that if the monopoly decides to compete against a low-priced entrant by improving its offer, consumers get lasting benefits from the improved offer and it not be too ephemeral and transitory.

In the end then, whatever the force of Elhauge's criticisms of Edlin's price freeze, the criticisms do not seem to apply to consumer betterment or to the Baumol price freeze.[89]

IX   OLIGOPOLY VS MONOPOLY PREDATION

Most of our discussion has concerned cases of monopoly predation. Of course, plaintiffs will sometimes complain of predatory pricing in oligopoly industries. The economics in such industries are, of course, quite different. In fact, the skepticism of the Supreme Court in *Brooke Group* and *Matsushita* seems in many ways more warranted in light of the fact that both cases involved oligopolies.[90]

A canonical story of predatory pricing in an oligopoly is where a maverick firm (Liggett in the case of Brooke Group) decides to increase its market share by undercutting the

---

[87]   See *id.* at 687.

[88]   *Id.* at 687.

[89]   Another of Elhauge's objections is that it is difficult to identify the moment of entry (see *id.* at 688, 809–12) or of exit (823). These critiques are specific to Edlin's and Baumol's price freezes. I have ignored here Elhauge's fourth argument about price discrimination (e.g., 686–7) because it is far afield from the current discussion. Elhauge has critiques that definitely do apply to the consumer betterment standard, such as the difficulty of identifying exit or exclusion and the potential manipulability of those by entrant or incumbent; it is worth noting though that administrative difficulties in identifying illegal conduct are pervasive in antitrust, however illegal has been defined. Whether consumer betterment is administrable will vary with the case. In the *American Airlines* case, it would seem to be administrable.

[90]   See *Brooke Group, supra* note 22, 509 U.S. at 212; *Matsushita, supra* note 22, 475 U.S. at 589.

oligopoly pricing equilibrium.[91] Either all firms together or a few alone respond by engaging in a price war until this firm relents and raises its price.

In oligopoly industries, raising prices after the predatory episode does not just require discouraging entry, but also requires discouraging competition from many competitors. In principle that is possible, but of course it may require a degree of coordination that is impossible without explicit agreements.

Is an oligopoly price war following a maverick's price cut predatory? Does that depend upon whether its motivation is to encourage higher prices? One approach would be to say that this is essentially a cartel problem and the question is whether the firms have a price-fixing agreement, whether tacit or explicit. Under section 1 of the Sherman Act, when the maverick agrees with its rivals to raise price (if indeed it does agree) and end the predatory episode, they have created an agreement in restraint of trade. The whole endeavor of predation may also be an aspect of an agreement to charge and maintain supercompetitive prices, and if this can be proven, then one has a price-fixing agreement.

Absent evidence of agreement, many would believe that the story is not a plausible one (rumor has it that the plaintiff in *Brooke Group* did not want to play the cartel card because it itself might wind up in trouble). Absent evidence of a cartel agreement or some other mechanism to coordinate a price increase, the price rise, like that in *Brooke Group*, is more likely explained by an increase in demand or a decrease in market demand elasticity.

In *Brooke Group*, the Supreme Court argued that Brown and Williamson only had one-ninth of the market and so most of the returns from its predation would accrue to other firms.[92] This made the plaintiff's whole theory suspect to the Court. This much made sense.[93] On the other hand, this cartel-dependent observation undermines the Court's rationale for the recoupment requirement. The rationale offered in *Brooke Group* was that without recoupment, 'predatory pricing produces lower aggregate prices in the market, and consumer welfare is enhanced'. Even if that equivalence between recoupment and consumer injury held for a monopoly (and it holds only roughly at best) it is evidently far from holding if only one in nine high-priced purchases accrues to Brown and Williamson but consumers suffer with each one.

---

[91]   This description is contested, as Elzinga and Mills view Liggett as the incumbent in the discount segment it pioneered and Brown and Williamson (the larger firm in the main market) as the entrant to the discount segment. See Kenneth G. Elzinga and David E. Mills, *Trumping the Areeda-Turner Test: The Recoupment Standard in Brooke Group* (*Symposium: Predatory Pricing after Brooke Group*), ANTITRUST L.J. 559–84 (1994).

[92]   Specifically, the court wrote: 'In this case, for example, Brown & Williamson, with its 11–12% share of the cigarette market, would have had to generate around $9 in supracompetitive profits for each $1 invested in predation; the remaining $8 would belong to its competitors who had taken no risk'.

[93]   It makes sense anyway, if one discounts as the Supreme Court did Brown and Williamson's internal assessments of what was at stake. See Walter Adams, James Brock, and Norman Orbst, *Is Predation Rational? Is it profitable?*, 11 REV. INDUSTRIAL ORGANIZATION 753 (1996) (arguing that Brown and Williamson would have profited in expected value even if the predation had been fairly unlikely to succeed and that it in fact did succeed). But see Kenneth Elzinga and David Mills *supra* note 91(disagreeing vehemently, and arguing that the documents relied on by Adams, Brock, and Orbst were taken out of context and were unreliable). See finally, Walter Adams, James W. Brock, and Norman P. Obst, *Is Predation Rational? Is it Profitable? – A Reply*, 11 Rev. INDUSTRIAL ORGANIZATION 767 (1996).

Given the economic differences between cartel situations and monopoly ones, it is odd that many courts in monopoly cases of predatory pricing in the United States feel bound by rules of predation that were codified in oligopoly cases like *Matsushita* and *Brooke Group*. This observation motivates the arguments of Edlin and later the court in *LePage's* that oligopoly precedents should not apply in monopoly cases where anticompetitive pricing practices seem much more plausible and problematic.[94] This point is consistent with the emphasis of Joskow and Klevorick on industrial structure as the first step of analysis in predatory pricing cases.[95]

X   RECOUPMENT

Brooke Group makes clear that an essential element of a predation case is proving that losses can be recouped (at the least for oligopoly cases). Left unclear is what this means and why this element is required.

The Court wrote that a reasonable jury might have concluded that Brown and Williamson priced below its cost[96] but that it could not reasonably have hoped to recoup the ensuing losses in an oligopoly industry where it sold only 12% of the output.[97]

Kenneth Elzinga and David Mills, who were economic experts in the case and whose academic writings the Court cited regarding the importance of recoupment, describe predation as follows:

> the predator prices at nonremunerative levels to drive rivals or an entrant from the market, or to coerce rivals to cede price leadership to the predator. In the second stage, the predator flexes its monopolistic muscles by charging supracompetitive prices and recouping the losses sustained during the initial stage.

It is straightforward to leap from this description to the two-prong test of *Brooke Group*.

But does the leap make sense? Some would argue that firms don't ordinarily price at 'nonremunerative' levels absent prospects of recoupment so that recoupment should be presumed. Why should a predator choose to suffer short-term losses if it does not expect to recoup them? Will a court's expectations be more reasonable or accurate than the alleged predator's? The *Brooke Group* Court did not address these questions, so one is left to wonder.[98]

Whether we take the sacrifice view or the equally efficient competitor view of predatory

---

[94]   See *LePage's*, *supra* note 44, 324 F.3d at 151 (the *LePage's* court made two distinctions: it argued that *Brooke Group* does not apply to monopolies and second that the plaintiff in *LePage's* did not allege predatory pricing).

[95]   Paul L. Joskow and Alvin K. Klevorick, *A Framework for Analyzing Predatory Pricing Policy*, 89 YALE L.J. 213, 219–20 (1979).

[96]   *Brooke Group*, *supra* note 22, 509 U.S. at 233.

[97]   *Id.*

[98]   The Supreme Court *tries* to address this issue in *Brook Group* at 226 ('Evidence of below-cost pricing is not alone sufficient to permit an inference of probable recoupment and injury to competition') but actually explains why consumers will not be hurt if recoupment is impossible rather than explaining why it is unreasonable to infer recoupment.

pricing, the recoupment element as a distinct element may seem superfluous. On the other hand, if we adopt the consumer betterment standard for predation, then it is more straightforward that something close to recoupment becomes important. The question under this standard is whether consumers typically pay higher prices than they might absent the predatory behavior. If the predator never raises prices in a reactive entry situation, then this case will be hard to prove. If the predator quickly raises price after the predatory episode, we have a high-priced benchmark to refer to when asking: 'Are rivals who would provide better deals than the incumbent likely to be excluded from the market?' The consumer betterment standard does not beg us to explicitly consider the predator's rationality or the profitability of a predatory strategy, but like in a search for recoupment, high prices post-predation will be relevant.

XI CONCLUSIONS

What can we conclude? US predatory pricing law is built on two foundations. One is a shaky premise, which is that economic reasoning predicts and experience confirms that predatory pricing is rare if existent at all. Neither the theoretical nor the empirical literature provides strong support for this premise. The other foundation is a healthy question: what can be done about predatory pricing without overly discouraging desirable price competition? However, that question is often not put in sharp focus. Presumably, it is true, for example, that most price cuts are procompetitive, as Kaplow and Shapiro point out.[99] However, no antitrust proposals attack all price cuts, so that sample is irrelevant. Can we say that drastic price cuts by monopolies (who apparently could have priced much lower in the first place) are mostly procompetitive, even when these price cuts destroy an entrant who has provided large surplus to consumers? Much less clear.

Here, I introduce a consumer betterment standard to test for monopoly exclusion as an alternative to the equally efficient competitor test. When applied to the *American Airlines* case, we see that the result might have been different and more pro-consumer. This test has the benefit (unlike Edlin's proposal) that it is a standard that can be applied to any type of monopolization case.

If courts continue to apply sacrifice and equally efficient competitor tests, then I urge them to sharply distinguish the two, and if sacrifice is to be identified, that courts should use inclusive notions of cost or revenue as I have described.

---

[99] Specifically, Kaplow and Shapiro write that 'beneficial price cuts will vastly outnumber predatory ones, so heavy attention to false positives is nevertheless sensible'. Kaplow and Shapiro, *supra* note 39.

7 Assessing resale price maintenance after *Leegin*
*Benjamin Klein**

Antitrust evaluation of resale price maintenance under the rule of reason standard adopted in *Leegin*[1] requires economic analysis of the likely anticompetitive effects and procompetitive benefits that may be associated with a resale price maintenance arrangement. Unfortunately, the economic focus on the prevention of retailer free-riding as the primary, if not the sole, procompetitive efficiency motivation for resale price maintenance distorts this antitrust analysis. Concentrating on free-riding not only narrows the potential procompetitive rationale for the use of resale price maintenance, but also overstates the anticompetitive significance of a manufacturer's adoption of resale price maintenance in response to retailer complaints about price discounting.

This chapter broadens the standard economic view of resale price maintenance by explaining how manufacturers often are procompetitively motivated to use resale price maintenance as a way to achieve effective distribution of their products even when there is not a retailer free-riding problem. Since retailers usually have significant discretion regarding what products they will stock and actively promote, manufacturers must create distribution arrangements where retailers expect to earn a sufficient return on their retailing assets (their shelf space and sales efforts) if they decide to distribute the manufacturer's products. Section I demonstrates how resale price maintenance is competitively used in many circumstances because it is an economically efficient way for manufacturers to obtain desirable retail distribution by assuring retailers a sufficient expected return. Section II then applies this broader view of the economics of resale price maintenance to the factors one should consider when conducting antitrust analysis of specific resale price maintenance arrangements.

I   PROCOMPETITIVE USE OF RESALE PRICE MAINTENANCE

Manufacturers generally wish to have their products distributed by retailers at the lowest retail margin. Everything else equal, a lower retail margin, that is, a lower retail price for any given wholesale price, will increase the sales of the manufacturer's products. However, in addition to minimizing retailing costs, profit-maximizing manufacturers also desire effective retail distribution of their products by what they consider to be the optimal number and type of retailers.

The idea that manufacturers actively determine the optimal retail distribution of their

---

*   This chapter is based, in part, on Benjamin Klein, *Competitive Resale Price Maintenance in the Absence of Free-Riding*, 76 ANTITRUST L.J. 431 (2009) and my testimony at the Federal Trade Commission Hearings on Resale Price Maintenance, Washington, DC, 17 February 2009.

[1]   Leegin Creative Leather Prods., Inc. v. PSKS, Inc., dba Kay's Kloset, 551 U.S. 877 (2007).

products is an obvious business reality. However, the economic basis of this phenomenon is not obvious within the standard economic framework. Because retailing is generally highly competitive, it superficially may appear that manufacturers could leave the retailing of their products 'up to the market' without controlling retailer competition in any way. This is what has led to the economic assumption that the existence of inter-retailer externalities or some other 'market imperfection' is required to explain why manufacturers generally do not find it profitable to leave the distribution of their products entirely up to uncontrolled retailer competition.

One such 'market imperfection' that is used as a rationale for manufacturer intervention into the competitive retailing process, including the possibility of manufacturer-imposed resale price maintenance, is inter-retailer 'free-riding' on pre-purchase retailing services. Manufacturers intervene in the competitive retailing process because individual retailers would otherwise take advantage of the retailing services supplied by other retailers, leading to the supply of less than the optimal overall quantity of retailing services. The theoretical foundation and empirical relevance of this commonly recognized economic factor is discussed in section IA.

However, even when there is no inter-retailer free-riding, manufacturers are likely to find it economically efficient to intervene in the competitive retailing market to determine who will distribute their products and on what terms such distribution occurs. The fundamental economic reason for this is that, although retailing is highly competitive, retailers have significant discretion in determining what products to stock and to actively promote. Because such retailer decisions generally do not have large inter-retailer demand effects, manufacturers must compete with one another to obtain desired retail distribution. In this environment, discussed in section IB, a manufacturer may find it economic to use resale price maintenance to assure retailers a sufficient expected return so that they distribute and adequately promote the manufacturer's products.

A   How Resale Price Maintenance Prevents Retailer Free-Riding

It is widely recognized by economists and has been accepted in the law since *Sylvania* that 'discounting retailers can free-ride on retailers who furnish services and then capture some of the increased demand those services generate'.[2] The classic form of such free-riding involves consumers who first visit a full-service retailer to obtain valuable services, such as product information and demonstration, but then purchase the product at a lower price from a discount retailer that does not supply the costly pre-sale services.

For example, consider the commonly discussed case of high-end audio and video equipment. The demand facing manufacturers of such products is said to depend upon retailer supply at the point-of-sale of product information and demonstrations. When retailers supply such services, the demand for the manufacturer's products increases. It is assumed that manufacturer-supplied promotion, such as national advertising, is not an efficient, complete substitute for these point-of-sale retailer promotional efforts, which explains the manufacturer's desire for retailers to supply such point-of-sale services.

---

[2]   Continental T.V., Inc. v. GTE Sylvania, Inc., 433 U.S. 36, 55 (1977).

Since retailer-supplied point-of-sale services such as product demonstrations are valuable to many consumers, retailers that supply such services will experience a significant increase in their demand. Therefore, retailers could be expected to compete with one another by providing these services to consumers; and consumers in principle will choose a high-price, full-service retailer or a low-price, low-service retailer depending on whether they demand such services. However, a valid economic concern of manufacturers is that retailers will have an incentive to free-ride on the point-of-sale services supplied by other retailers. Specifically, non-service supplying discount retailers may encourage consumers to first visit a full-service retailer to determine what particular product and features they desire before purchasing that product from the non-service retailer at a lower price. In this way, discount retailers are free-riding on the investments made by full-service retailers by capturing some of the increased demand generated by the services provided by full-service retailers.

The discount, non-service providing retailer can sell the product at a lower price because it has lower costs by not supplying pre-sale product information and demonstration services. However, economic analysis of free-riding emphasizes that this is not the likely final market equilibrium. Since retailers do not have an economic incentive to supply services unless they are compensated by increased sales, full-service retailers will reduce their provision of services in response to free-riding by discount retailers. The standard analysis concludes that the reduction in retailer-supplied services in response to free-riding, therefore, will ultimately lead to both consumers and the manufacturer being worse off – consumers are worse off because they do not receive desired pre-sale retailer services and the manufacturer is worse off because the demand for its products is reduced.

Exactly how resale price maintenance is used by manufacturers to prevent retailers from free-riding and, instead, to incentivize retailers to supply pre-sale product demonstration and other services is not adequately described in the common formulation of the free-riding theory of resale price maintenance. The usual economic analysis of resale price maintenance is that the elimination of retailer price discounting prevents retailer free-riding because it removes the incentive of consumers to patronize free-riding retailers and forces retailers to compete on non-price dimensions.[3] Most statements of the theory reach this conclusion by assuming that the only way retailers can compete, once they cannot reduce price, is by supplying the retail services desired by the manufacturer.[4] However, free-riding retailers often will be able to compete more effectively in other ways.

For example, audio equipment retailers that sell the product at the resale-maintained price could provide other non-price services that have larger inter-retailer demand effects, such as free installation or liberal return privileges or possibly even more general services such as convenient free parking, fast check-out, or other services that lower the effective

---

[3]   The economics of this efficiency justification for resale price maintenance is presented in Lester Telser, *Why Should Manufacturers Want Fair Trade?*, 3 J.L. AND ECON. 86 (1960). Similar economic reasoning can be found much earlier in T.H. Silcock, *Some Problems of Price Maintenance*, 48 ECON. J. 42 (1938), and F.W. Taussig, *Price Maintenance*, 6 AM. ECON. REV., SUPPLEMENT, PAPERS AND PROCEEDINGS 170 (1916).

[4]   All models that include only two variables, price and desired retailer services, implicitly make this assumption.

price or make the shopping and purchase experience more pleasant. Competing retailers cannot free-ride on these services since their customers cannot consume the services at another retailer and then use the services when purchasing the product at their store. Therefore, audio equipment retailers will have an incentive to compete through the supply of these services while free-riding on retailers that provide product demonstrations and other free-rideable services.

Consequently, even within the standard free-riding theory, manufacturers must do more than merely fix minimum retail prices to assure provision of the retail services desired by the manufacturer. Manufacturers also must monitor and enforce retailer performance with regard to the provision of desired retail services. A manufacturer accomplishes this by informing retailers regarding what it desires and expects in terms of retailer performance, and then compensating those retailers that perform as desired while terminating those retailers that do not perform as desired. In this way the manufacturer 'self-enforces' its distribution arrangement with retailers.[5]

The primary economic role served by resale price maintenance in this self-enforcement framework is that it efficiently compensates retailers for supplying the increased point-of-sale services desired by the manufacturer. Resale price maintenance accomplishes this by providing retailers with a profit margin that is somewhat more than sufficient to cover the retailer's increased costs of supplying desired services. In this way the arrangement is self-enforcing because retailers then have something valuable to lose (an expected future profit stream) if they are terminated for non-performance.[6]

The *Leegin* court recognized this economic motivation for resale price maintenance: 'Offering the retailer a guaranteed margin and threatening termination if it does not live up to expectations may be the most efficient way to expand the manufacturer's market share by inducing the retailer's performance.'[7] This increased retailer incentive to perform was also relied upon in Justice Scalia's opinion in *Sharp*, which stated that vertical restraints work by ensuring a dealer profit margin that 'permits provision of the desired

---

[5] Benjamin Klein and Kevin M. Murphy, *Vertical Restraints as Contract Enforcement Mechanisms*, 31 J.L. AND ECON. 265 (1988). Manufacturer self-enforcement of retail distribution arrangements as described in this chapter does not imply the existence of an agreement in the sense required for antitrust analysis of resale price maintenance under the *Colgate* doctrine (United States v. Colgate & Co., 250 U.S. 300 (1919)) as it has legally evolved (Monsanto Co. v. Spray-Rite Serv. Corp., 465 U.S. 752 (1984); Business Elecs. Corp. v. Sharp Elecs. Corp., 485 U.S. 717 (1988)). The fact that transactors often unilaterally self-enforce, rather than legally court-enforce, their business relationships is the fundamental empirical insight of Stewart Macaulay, *Non-Contractual Relations in Business: A Preliminary Study*, 28 AM. SOC. REV. 55 (1963).

[6] Klein and Murphy, *supra* note 5. For a distribution arrangement to be self-enforcing the present discounted value of retailer profit when performing as desired by the manufacturer must be greater than the additional short-run profit the retailer can earn by not performing as desired. The fundamental economic reason a profit stream above retailer costs is required for self-enforcement is because manufacturer detection and termination of non-performing retailers is not perfect or immediate. Therefore, without any profit premium the retailer will always be better off not performing as desired and instead collect the increased manufacturer compensation in the short run before termination occurs. See Benjamin Klein and Keith B. Leffler, *The Role of Market Forces in Assuring Contractual Performance*, 89 J. POL. ECON. 615 (1981).

[7] *Leegin, supra* note 1, 551 U.S. at 892.

services'.[8] Similarly, Judge Frank Easterbrook writes that 'the manufacturer can't get the dealer to do more without increasing the dealer's margin'.[9]

These three judicial statements focus on an economic motivation for resale price maintenance that is somewhat distinct from the standard prevention of free-riding explanation. Resale price maintenance does not merely eliminate the option for consumers to purchase a product at lower-priced retailers after receiving pre-sale services from full-service retailers; resale price maintenance is recognized to be an efficient way for manufacturers to 'pay' retailers for supplying increased services, 'free-rideable' or not. However, Judge Easterbrook, Justice Scalia, and the *Leegin* court do not explain why competitive retailers in the absence of free-riding may not have a sufficient independent incentive to provide the type or quantity of services desired by the manufacturer. Hence, they do not explain why the manufacturer must create a distribution arrangement where its retailers are compensated for supplying more retailing services than they would otherwise be forced by competition to provide in the absence of free-riding.

B   Resale Price Maintenance in the Absence of Free-Riding

Many cases of resale price maintenance, even when adopted by extremely small firms such as Leegin, do not fit the procompetitive prevention of free-riding paradigm. Robert Pitofsky has asked us to 'think for a moment about the product areas in which resale price maintenance has appeared – boxed candy, pet foods, jeans, vitamins, hair shampoo, knit shirts, men's underwear. What are the services we are talking about in these cases?'[10] The type of retailer services that fit the classic definition of free-riding, such as product demonstrations by audio and video retailers, do not appear to be applicable in these cases. Therefore, Pitofsky and other prominent antitrust commentators conclude that free-riding is not a widespread phenomenon that can justify most cases of resale price maintenance, including the recent cases where resale price maintenance was used for women's shoes,[11] athletic shoes,[12] and the leather products that were the subject of *Leegin*.[13]

In these and many other resale price maintenance cases a free-riding rationale does not appear applicable because manufacturers prevent discounting even when both discount and non-discount retailers provide similar point-of-sale services. Discount retailers are terminated not for failing to supply sufficient point-of-sale services, but solely

---

[8]   Business Elecs. Corp. v. Sharp Elecs. Corp., 485 U.S. 717, 728 (1988).

[9]   Frank Easterbrook, *Vertical Agreements and the Rule of Reason*, 53 ANTITRUST L.J. 135, 156 (1984).

[10]   Robert Pitofsky, *Why 'Dr. Miles' Was Right*, 8 REGULATION 27, 29 (1984). A similar list of products was repeated in Robert Pitofsky, *Are Retailers Who Offer Discounts Really 'Knaves'?: The Coming Challenge to the Dr. Miles Rule*, ANTITRUST 61, 63 (Spring 2007).

[11]   Order Granting in Part Petition to Reopen and Modify Order Issued April 11, 2000, Nine West Group Inc., FTC Docket No. C-3937 (May 6, 2008), available at www.ftc.gov/os/caselist/9810386/080506order.pdf.

[12]   Keds Corp., 117 F.T.C. 389 (April 1, 1994); Reebok Int'l Ltd., 120 F.T.C. 20 (July 18, 1995); New Balance Athletic Shoe, Inc., 122 F.T.C. 137 (September 10, 1996).

[13]   The absence of a free-riding problem is one of the principal bases of Justice Breyer's dissent in *Leegin*. *Leegin, supra* note 1, 551 U.S. at 915 (Breyer, J. dissenting).

because they sell below suggested prices. This specifically appears to describe the facts of *Leegin*, where product shipments were suspended to the plaintiff retailer, Kay's Kloset, solely because it was selling Leegin's Brighton brand of leather products below required minimum prices.

1 Retailers have discretion regarding what products to promote

The way to understand the use of resale price maintenance in these and other cases where there is not a free-riding problem is to recognize, first of all, that retailers often have considerable discretion regarding the particular products they can decide to stock and promote. Although retailing is highly competitive, the result of retailer competition is that retailers often will have a group of loyal customers who receive some consumer surplus from shopping with them. Consumers choose to shop at a retailer where they expect to receive the greatest consumer surplus, taking account of the retailer's reputation for low average prices, good product selection, service quality, convenient location, and other possible demand factors. Consumer demand faced by an individual retailer is assumed to be highly elastic with regard to this overall product package, but not perfectly elastic. Therefore, while a significant degree of inter-retailer competition exists, individual consumers receive different amounts of consumer surplus relative to their next best alternative retailer based on their particular product preferences, the location of the retailer in relation to their residence, and other factors.[14]

Because each retailer has a group of loyal customers earning some consumer surplus on the overall price, product variety, and service package the retailer is supplying, retailers will have some discretion in choosing the particular products they stock and actively promote when such retailer decisions have little or no inter-retailer demand effects. As we shall see, in these circumstances retailers must be compensated by manufacturers to devote their retailing assets to the sale of a manufacturer's products.

To illustrate the economic forces at work, consider retailer supply of point-of-sale promotional services such as prominent display of a manufacturer's products. Since consumers are likely to be indifferent to which of the products stocked by the retailer are prominently displayed, the retailer has total discretion with regard to this decision. However, this retailer promotional decision will significantly affect demand for the particular manufacturer's products that are promoted, so that manufacturers clearly are not indifferent. If a manufacturer's products are prominently displayed at a store, a fraction of the customers that come into the store will see and buy the manufacturer's products who would not otherwise have done so. The retailer's prominent shelf space therefore is valuable for the manufacturer.

---

[14] The fact that each individual retailer faces a somewhat negatively sloped demand with respect to the package of price, product variety, service, and other characteristics it supplies in competition with other retailers does not mean that individual retailers possess any antitrust market power in the sense of the ability to affect overall market prices. This distinction between a firm's own elasticity of demand and antitrust market power is described in Benjamin Klein, *Market Power in Antitrust: Economic Analysis After* Kodak, 3 S. Ct. Econ. Rev. 43 (1993), which shows that defining antitrust market power in terms of the ability to affect market prices, not in terms of the firm's own elasticity of demand, is consistent with the definition of market power in antitrust law.

For example, if a leather products retailer such as Kay's Kloset (the plaintiff in *Leegin*) decides to prominently display a particular manufacturer's handbag, rather than another brand of handbag it stocks, Kay's Kloset's sales of the displayed handbag will increase. The consumers who choose to purchase the displayed handbag when they observe it can be labeled 'marginal consumers', rather than the 'inframarginal consumers' who know they wish to buy the handbag and will do so without the retailer's promotional display services. However, while some marginal consumers choose to purchase the displayed brand rather than another brand, few if any consumers are likely to shift the store at which they shop based on which particular handbag the retailer decides to display. The retailer's decision to prominently display or otherwise promote at the point-of-sale one manufacturer's products and not another manufacturer's products has significant inter-brand demand effects but little or no inter-retailer demand effects.

Another type of manufacturer-desired retailer promotional service with large inter-brand demand effects and little inter-retailer demand effects that induces incremental manufacturer sales is additional salesperson attention devoted to the sale of a particular manufacturer's products. Although such retailer promotional efforts are the type of retailer service described in the standard free-riding analysis, such manufacturer-specific promotional efforts often do not involve a significant free-riding problem. For example, many consumers who are convinced by a salesperson in a department store to purchase a particular article of clothing may not be likely to then go to another store that does not provide point-of-sale assistance in the hope of buying that product at a lower price. And, once again, because the retailer's consumers may be largely indifferent to which of the retailer's products are actively promoted, the absence of inter-retailer demand effects means that the retailer will have significant discretion regarding which manufacturer's products to actively promote.

2 Manufacturers must compensate retailers for the supply of promotional services

The absence of significant inter-retailer demand effects from retailer decisions regarding manufacturer-specific promotional services is the fundamental economic reason manufacturers find it necessary to design distribution arrangements where they compensate retailers for the provision of point-of-sale promotional services for their products. Without such manufacturer compensation, the absence of inter-retailer demand effects implies that retailers will not have the independent incentive to provide point-of-sale promotional services for the manufacturer's products. The profits earned by a manufacturer on the incremental sales produced by a retailer's decision to provide point-of-sale promotional services for the manufacturer's products, which often are substantial, will be substantially greater than the additional profits earned by the retailer from such manufacturer-specific promotion, which may be close to zero. Although the retailer earns some profit on the incremental sales of whatever products it decides to promote, the retailer experiences reduced sales and profits on other products that it now does not prominently display or devote increased salesperson efforts to. The absence of significant inter-retailer demand effects means that the retailer does not also earn profits on additional overall sales, as it does when it provides non-manufacturer-specific retail services, such as free convenient parking or a pleasant selling environment, services which are valued by consumers more generally (not solely consumers who are marginal with respect to demanding a particular manufacturer's products) and which influence consumer decisions regarding where to shop.[15]

It is the profit differential between a manufacturer and its retailers that creates an incentive incompatibility with regard to retailer supply of manufacturer-specific point-of-sale promotional efforts that prevents manufacturers from relying entirely on retailer competition and the absence of free-riding to assure retailer supply of desired promotional services for their products.[16]

Instead, manufacturers must compete with other manufacturers for desired retailer promotional efforts, and not passively leave retailing of their products up to whatever results from retailer competition for consumers. This manufacturer competition for desired retailing requires manufacturers to assure retailers that they can expect to earn a competitive return on the retailing assets they devote to the sale of a manufacturer's products.

To appreciate why non-free-riding retailers have an insufficient incentive to supply the point-of-sale promotional services desired by the manufacturer, consider Russell Stover's use of resale price maintenance in the sale of boxed candy. This arrangement, challenged by the Federal Trade Commission,[17] is particularly difficult to place in the standard prevention of free-riding framework. Russell Stover distributed its boxed candies primarily through drug, card, gift and department stores, and these retailers did not provide any significant pre-sale product demonstrations or other services that other retailers could free-ride upon.

The primary point-of-sale services Russell Stover wanted its retailers to provide were the services of displaying its products. Specifically, display of Russell Stover's products could be expected to significantly increase its sales since a large number of consumers purchase candy only after they notice it when they are shopping for something else. This has been labeled in the marketing literature as 'impulse purchases', where consumers

---

[15]   The supply of these services, which have significant inter-retailer demand effects and generally little or no inter-brand demand effects, generally can be left up to uncontrolled retailer competition. Benjamin Klein, *Competitive Resale Price Maintenance in the Absence of Free-Riding*, 76 ANTITRUST L.J. 431 (2009).

[16]   This incentive incompatibility was originally described in Klein and Murphy, *supra* note 5, at 295, where the manufacturer-specific point-of-sale promotion was considered equivalent to a targeted price discount to marginal consumers. The economic analysis described here is related to Ralph Winter, *Vertical Control and Price Versus Nonprice Competition*, 108 Q.J. ECON 61 (1993), where a manufacturer–retailer incentive incompatibility is similarly based on the assumption of a lack of significant inter-retailer demand effects from retailer supply of non-price services. Winter justifies the assumption of a lack of significant inter-retailer demand effects by making the additional assumption that consumers who value a retailer's non-price services are likely to be the retailer's inframarginal consumers and hence largely unresponsive in terms of inter-retailer demand effects with regard to retailer-supplied non-price services. This, however, misleading aggregates all types of retailer-supplied non-price services. Consumers may prefer a particular retailer's location, services, and other amenities but be indifferent between brands and therefore highly sensitive to brand-specific point-of-sale retailer promotion. The Winter framework also has a fundamentally different view of the role of resale price maintenance in alleviating the manufacturer–retailer incentive incompatibility, claiming that resale price maintenance by itself eliminates the incentive incompatibility. In contrast, the economic role of resale price maintenance presented here is a way for the manufacture to compensate retailers for desired brand-specific promotion and thereby facilitate self-enforcement of retailer performance. See Klein and Murphy, *supra* note 5.

[17]   Russell Stover Candies, Inc., 100 F.T.C. 1 (July 1, 1982).

who have no prior intent to purchase a product do so after observing the product on display.[18] Moreover, even when consumers have a prior intent to purchase a particular type of product such as candy, they may not be committed to purchase a particular brand of the product, so that they may be influenced to purchase the particular brand on display. It is unlikely that such retail display services that induce incremental manufacturer sales will involve a significant free-riding problem. Consumers will not, for example, observe Russell Stover boxed candy on display, decide at that moment that they want to purchase the product, but then visit another retailer where the candy is not displayed to make their purchase.

The Russell Stover case illustrates that the retailing services of concern to a manufacturer are likely to include retailer stocking of the manufacturer's products. While a retailer's failure to stock a well-known, highly demanded product will influence some consumers' decisions regarding where to shop, retailers generally will have considerable discretion regarding which of many products in a product category they decide to stock. Retailer product stocking decisions often will have relatively small inter-retailer demand effects because consumers that lose their preferred brand will be offset to some extent by consumers whose preferred brand is now stocked. Moreover, when the retailer is a supermarket or department store that sells many types of products, it is less likely that a consumer will switch retailers because of the loss of one preferred product. The consumer surplus and loyalty to the retailer depends on the retailer's overall selection of many products, not merely the particular brand chosen in the one particular product class.[19]

3 Resale price maintenance is an efficient way for manufacturers to compensate retailers for their promotional efforts

Manufacturer compensation of retailers for the increased point-of-sale promotional services they provide in connection with the sale of a manufacturer's products, such as stocking or more prominently displaying the manufacturer's product or devoting greater salesperson efforts to selling the manufacturer's product, must entail a sufficient manufacturer payment to cover the retailer's opportunity cost of devoting its retailing assets (primarily its shelf space and sales staff) to the promotion of the manufacturer's products. That is, the manufacturer's payment must equal or exceed the return the retailer alternatively could earn by promoting another manufacturer's products. The expected payment received by the retailer more generally will consist of a combination of expected retailer sales of the manufacturer's products and an expected retailer profit margin on those sales.

Manufacturers therefore will frequently use some form of restricted distribution that increases either retailer sales or the retailer margin, or both, so that retailers earn a sufficient expected return to induce desired promotional efforts. For example, a manufacturer may lower the wholesale price and institute minimum resale price maintenance

---

[18] Charles Areni, Dale Duhan, and Pamela Kiecker, *Point-of-Purchase Displays, Product Organization, and Brand Purchase Likelihoods*, 27 J. ACAD. MKTG. SCI. 428 (1999). It has been estimated that 60% of all consumer purchases are unplanned. PACO UNDERHILL, WHY WE BUY: THE SCIENCE OF SHOPPING 57 (2009).

[19] Furthermore, any loss of consumer surplus may be offset by higher stocking payments made by the manufacturer of the substitute product, which may be passed on in somewhat lower average prices on other products sold in the store.

to generate a higher retailer margin or provide retailers with exclusive territories and use some form of maximum resale price maintenance to generate higher retailer sales. Rather than solely preventing free-riding, both resale price maintenance and exclusive territories should be more generally thought of as efficient compensation mechanisms for increased retailer promotional efforts.[20]

Alternatively, manufacturers may compensate retailers directly for their promotional services. For example, a manufacturer may compensate retailers for their costs of providing local advertising of the manufacturer's products. Retailer compensation on a per unit time basis may also sometimes be a reasonable form of compensation. The retailer costs of providing preferential or increased product display are largely per unit time shelf space costs and the retailer costs of providing increased point-of-sale salesperson services also largely may be per unit time (wage rate) costs. However, although manufacturer compensation of retailers for shelf space services may occur with per unit time payments similar to supermarket shelf space slotting arrangements,[21] the services provided by retailers of the products subject to resale price maintenance often are substantially more complex and therefore more difficult to specify and monitor than supermarket shelf space.

Consider, for example, the point-of-sale promotional services that take the form of increased salesperson efforts. What is the measureable unit of service the manufacturer is purchasing that could be the basis of a per service retailer compensation formula? Because of the difficulties of specifying detailed retailer performance, it is more common for manufacturers to enter more general understandings with their retailers regarding the promotional efforts they expect retailers to devote to the sale of their products and to leave it up to the retailer to determine the details of how this should be accomplished.[22]

Furthermore, there is likely to be a significant economic advantage in these circumstances to compensate retailers for dedicated retailing services in relation to the volume of the manufacturer's products the retailer sells because this creates an increased incentive for retailers to promote the manufacturer's products. This is what is accomplished with resale price maintenance since the increased retailer profit margin on the manufacturer's products increases the retailer's profitability on incremental sales, which increases the retailer's incentive to supply additional promotional services in connection with the

---

[20]   An exclusive territory in some circumstances may have an advantage over resale price maintenance as a way of compensating retailers because it more effectively reduces inter-retailer free-riding problems and provides retailers with increased pricing flexibility compared to resale price maintenance. The major economic advantage of resale price maintenance, on the other hand, is that it permits the manufacturer to have a larger number of retailers within an area selling its products. When the number of retailers in an area that sell a manufacturer's products has a significant positive effect on total demand for the manufacturer's products, an exclusive territory arrangement is a relatively inefficient way to generate retailer compensation for a promotional effort; in that case, resale price maintenance is the preferred restricted distribution arrangement.

[21]   See Benjamin Klein and Joshua D. Wright, *The Economics of Slotting Contracts*, 50 J.L. AND ECON. 421 (2007).

[22]   This is what the Supreme Court in *Leegin* is referring to when it states that 'it may be difficult and inefficient for a manufacturer to make and enforce a contract with a retailer specifying the different services the retailer must perform'. As a consequence, the Court notes that it is often efficient for the manufacturer to let the retailer 'use its own initiative and experience in providing valuable services' that most effectively encourage increased sales of the manufacturer's products. *Leegin*, *supra* note 1, 551 U.S. at 892.

manufacturer's products. The retailer's independent economic incentive to perform therefore becomes more closely aligned with the retailer performance desired and paid for by the manufacturer. And the manufacturer's costs of monitoring and enforcing retailer performance, a consideration that is economically more important when retailer promotional efforts are more complex, are reduced.

Although the increased retail profit margin created by resale price maintenance provides the retailer with an increased independent incentive to supply promotional services, it is important to recognize that on the margin the retailer does not have the incentive to supply all the promotional services the manufacturer has purchased and expects to receive. This is because resale price maintenance compensates retailers for increased promotional efforts in the form of a payment based on all of a retailer's sales, not solely a retailer's incremental sales. Therefore, when a retailer reduces its promotional efforts and its sales of the manufacturer's products decrease, the retailer still receives additional compensation on its remaining sales of the manufacturer's products. Hence, the retailer has an economic incentive not to supply all the promotional services paid for by the manufacturer.[23]

That is why, in addition to monitoring minimum retail prices and preventing free-riding, the manufacturer also must monitor retailer performance and terminate those retailers who are not supplying all the manufacturer-specific promotional efforts they have been compensated to provide. The increased independent retailer incentive to provide manufacturer-specific selling services that is created by a resale price maintenance form of retailer compensation, however, means that the manufacturer need not devote as much resources to monitoring retailers and that the manufacturer need not provide retailers with as large a profit stream in order to assure retailer performance.

4   Retailer price discounting disrupts the manufacturer's retail distribution network

An implication of this analysis is that discount retailers that reduce their prices of a manufacturer's products may disturb the manufacturer's desired retail distribution network. This is because price discounting retailers reduce the sales of other retailers that are promoting the manufacturer's products and therefore reduce the compensation received by the other retailers. Since retailers require a minimum expected return to stock, display, and otherwise promote a product, the reduction in compensation will lead the other retailers to reduce the promotional efforts they devote to sale of the manufacturer's products, and in some cases will result in other retailers dropping distribution of the manufacturer's products entirely. This disruption in distribution occurs even if the discount retailers continue to provide desired retailing services and are not free-riding on the services supplied by other retailers.[24]

---

[23]   The attempt to base compensation solely on retailer incremental sales, for example, by paying a bonus solely on sales increases over some benchmark level, has obvious measurement difficulties and increases the incentive of retailers to expand sales by violating resale price maintenance.

[24]   The discounting retailer in this context can be said to be 'free-riding' on the manufacturer's compensation arrangement for the increased supply of point-of-sale retailer promotional services. The discounting retailer is increasing its sales to price-sensitive inframarginal consumers who already know that they want to purchase the product and switch their purchases to the price-discounting retailer. Because resale price maintenance involves retailer compensation on the

These inter-retailer effects caused by retailer price discounting may sound superficially like the effects of normal price competition among retailers, which manufacturers should be in favor of since manufacturers wish to have their products sold most efficiently at the lowest retail margin. But manufacturers also wish to have their products adequately promoted and effectively distributed by retailers. If discounting by a retailer competes away the compensation a manufacturer has provided its retailers for increased point-of-sale promotion of the manufacturer's products, and this leads some retailers to reduce their promotional efforts and possibly drop distribution of the manufacturer's products, the manufacturer's sales and profit may decline in spite of the fact that its products are now sold at a lower retailer margin. This injures the manufacturer, as well as the consumers who now no longer purchase the manufacturer's products. A manufacturer's fear of reduced sales from the loss of effective retail distribution therefore is a reasonable and common competitive business motivation for the use of resale price maintenance.

This highlights that effective retailer distribution for a manufacturer may consist, in addition to each retailer supplying adequate retail promotion of its products, in an appropriate number and type of retail outlets. A sufficient number of outlets is particularly important for products where significant sales are made to consumers when they observe a product display while shopping, such as in the Russell Stover boxed candy case. Wide retail distribution provides increased product display and hence the potential for increased impulse sales; it also provides increased opportunities for manufacturers to reach a greater number of consumers with other types of point-of-sale retailer promotional efforts that induce incremental sales. Consumers shopping for products do not search every retailer, and sometimes do not even search more than one retailer. Therefore, a manufacturer has access to a larger number of potential customers when a greater number of retail outlets stock and display its products. Resale price maintenance, by creating and protecting an increased retailer margin, is one way in which a manufacturer may guarantee that its retail distribution network is preserved with an increased number of retailers in equilibrium that carry its products.[25]

This analysis provides an economic basis for the 'outlets hypothesis' explanation for resale price maintenance originally presented by Gould and Preston,[26] where the demand for a manufacturer's products is assumed to be positively related to the number of retail outlets that sell the manufacturer's products. However, Gould and Preston do not explain why competitive retailers operating in an unrestricted retail environment will result in less than the profit-maximizing number of outlets. The economic forces described in this chapter imply that manufacturers often may desire a greater number of retail

---

basis of all of a retailer's sales, this shift in sales implies that the compensation received by the discount retailer from the manufacturer increases, while the non-discounting retailers that lose sales receive less compensation from the manufacturer. The shift in sales therefore means that the price-discounting retailer is overcompensated and the other retailers are undercompensated for the supply of desired promotional services.

[25]   The preservation of the manufacturer's retail distribution network was a primary economic rationale offered by Dr. Miles for its use of resale price maintenance. Dr. Miles claimed that as a consequence of retail price competition, a majority of retail druggists had dropped the Dr. Miles products as unprofitable. Dr. Miles Med. Co. v. John D. Park & Sons Co., 220 U.S. 373, 375 (1911).

[26]   J.R. Gould and L.E. Preston, *Resale Price Maintenance and Retail Outlets*, 32 ECONOMICA 302 (1965).

outlets selling their products than would be generated by retailer competition because an additional outlet that sells the manufacturer's products increases point-of-sale retail promotional services (such as product displays), which induces profitable incremental manufacturer sales.[27]

A manufacturer's use of resale price maintenance to obtain a larger number of retail outlets may explain Leegin's use of resale price maintenance. Rather than investing in national advertising or focusing on sales through major department stores, Leegin used resale price maintenance to increase the retail margin in order to support the sale of its leather products through a wide distribution network of more than 5,000 relatively small US specialty retail outlets.[28] Allowing retailers such as Kay's Kloset to discount prices would have left other Leegin retail outlets with reduced sales and profit and, if permitted to continue, would have resulted in some of these other outlets reducing their promotion of Leegin products or dropping distribution of Leegin products entirely. Other retail outlets would have insufficient sales to cover the retailers' opportunity costs associated with the shelf space and promotional efforts dedicated to Leegin products. Leegin has to prevent retailer price discounting in order to insure that a sufficient number of retailers will continue to distribute and adequately promote its products. [29]

In addition to using resale price maintenance to assure that they have an adequate number of retailers that distribute their products, manufacturers also will use resale price maintenance to assure that they have the desired types of retailers in their retail distribution network. In particular, there are likely to be some retailers that the manufacturer considers to be 'high-quality', in the sense that the retailers have a loyal customer base which includes a significant number of likely incremental customers for the manufactur-

---

[27]   Raymond Deneckere, Howard P. Marvel, and James Peck, *Demand Uncertainty, Inventories, and Resale Price Maintenance*, 111 Q.J. ECON. 885 (1996), use the fact that manufacturers often justify resale price maintenance as a way to support an increased number of retail outlets as supporting evidence for their theory that resale price maintenance is commonly motivated by a desire to induce retailers to hold greater inventories. However, a manufacturer's desire for a greater number of retail outlets is economically distinct from a manufacturer's desire for greater retailer inventories. One reason a manufacturer may want retailers to hold increased inventories (separate from the inter-retailer free-riding externality the Deneckere *et al.* model assumes with regard to individual retailer inventory decisions) may be because retailer and manufacturer incentives do not coincide with regard to the level of inventories, since a retailer that runs out of a manufacturer's products may be able to switch consumers to another brand. In cases where the manufacturer's desire for increased retail inventories is economically important, the manufacturer is likely to accomplish this with more direct financial incentives, such as subsidizing the financing of inventories, the use of liberal return policies, or providing wholesale price refunds, rather than with resale price maintenance.
[28]   *Leegin, supra* note 1, 551 U.S. at 882.
[29]   Pitofsky, *supra* note 10, at 63, mistakenly claims that the economic importance of resale price maintenance as a way to support an increased number of retail outlets is only relevant for new entrants that have to establish a distribution network. Because Leegin already had a large distribution network, Pitofsky concludes that this economic rationale cannot justify Leegin's use of resale price maintenance. However, established manufacturers also receive significant economic benefits from a distribution network that includes many retailers, including increased point-of-sale display and other retail promotional services that induce incremental manufacturer sales.

er's products.[30] In order for these 'high-quality' retailers to decide to stock and promote the manufacturer's products, the manufacturer must assure the retailer that they likely will earn a sufficient return on the sale of the manufacturer's products so that it is worthwhile for the retailers to devote their valuable shelf space and promotional efforts to the manufacturer's products.

One way for a manufacturer to assure high quality retailers a sufficient return may be by reducing the number of authorized retailers that carry its products, bearing the costs associated with reduced overall product display from a reduced number of outlets. But to assure 'high-quality' retailers a sufficient return on their retailing assets in most circumstances this will have to be accompanied by resale price maintenance.

For example, if Rolex watches were sold at a significant price discount at discount retailers, this would significantly reduce the sales of Rolex at full-price 'high-quality' retailers, leading some of those retailers to stop carrying the product. Although total Rolex sales may increase in the short run as a result of the price discounting, Rolex sales eventually will decrease when 'high-quality' retailers adjust by no longer carrying or promoting Rolex products because of the insufficient return they are earning on their retailing assets.[31]

This long-run reduction in demand as a result of price discounting is separate from any effect of retailers free-riding on the 'quality certification' services supplied by high-quality retailers.[32] According to the 'quality certification' theory, consumers 'decide to buy the product because they see it in a retail establishment that has a reputation for selling high-quality merchandise'.[33] For example, a reputable department store that stocks and displays a product is claimed to be certifying quality and thereby increasing overall demand for the manufacturer's products in the marketplace, which other discount retailers then free-ride upon.

Many cases of resale price maintenance involve products that already have well-established brand names, so that in these cases 'quality certification' by a reputable retailer is unlikely to be an especially important determinant of demand at discount retailers.[34] Moreover, most firms that insist on resale price maintenance will terminate

---

[30]   It is important to emphasize, once again, that the fact that some retailers may have loyal customers has nothing to do with the presence of retailer market power. Retailers, who may be relatively small, will create a loyal customer base that may be valuable to specific manufacturers because they provide consumers with the particular retailing services they desire (e.g., desired product selection, convenient locations, knowledgeable service, etc.) in the competitive retailing market.

[31]   A theoretical alternative to resale price maintenance as a way for the manufacturer to preserve desirable retail distribution may involve the manufacturer selling the product to higher-quality established retailers at a lower wholesale price than to discount retailers. However, this involves potential Robinson-Patman problems and does not prevent established retailers trans-shipping products purchased at a low price to discount retailers, a generally much more difficult problem for the manufacturer to monitor and control than setting minimum retail prices.

[32]   Howard P. Marvel and Stephen McCafferty, *Resale Price Maintenance and Quality Certification*, 15 RAND J. ECON. 346 (1984).

[33]   *Leegin*, 551 U.S. at 891.

[34]   For example, Sharon Oster claims that free-riding on retailer quality certification services was the economic motivation for Levi's use of resale price maintenance. FTC v. Levi Strauss & Co., 92 F.T.C. 171 (1978). However, Levi had established an independent reputation for its products at the time of the litigation. Rather than attempting to reconcile this apparent inconsistency, Oster

discounting retailers even when the discounters are reputable sellers of high-quality merchandise. This fact also undercuts the inter-retailer 'quality-image' demand externality argument, where it is claimed that the overall demand for a manufacturer's product decreases when the product is seen by consumers in discount stores associated with the sale of lower quality products.[35]

A manufacturer wishes to have 'high-quality' retailers sell its products to enhance and protect the 'quality image' of its products not because of the positive demand externality it creates, or because of the negative demand externality that is avoided when the manufacturer's products are sold at a store that generally sells lower quality products, but because the manufacturer wishes to have 'high-quality' retailers promote its products to their loyal customers. Rolex wishes to have high-quality retailers display and promote its products in order to obtain access to the consumers that shop at such high-quality retailers. That is why 'effective' distribution of Rolex products includes distribution by 'high-quality' image retailers and why Rolex may use resale price maintenance to assure that such high-quality retailers receive an adequate expected return on the promotion and sale of Rolex products.

These economic forces also explain why manufacturers will be more concerned about price discounting if retailers are permitted to publicly advertise their discount prices. Widely disseminated advertising of discount prices will result in a greater shift of consumer purchases to the discounting retailer, exacerbating the deleterious effects on the manufacturer's retail network. On the other hand, in-store promotion of price reductions may have primarily within-store inter-brand effects without producing significant inter-retailer intra-brand demand effects. Therefore, a manufacturer may sometimes permit within-store retailer price discounting but prevent significant adverse effects on its retail network by adopting a minimum advertised price policy.

These considerations also explain why a manufacturer may find it necessary to adopt distribution policies to control Internet retailing. Uncontrolled Internet retailing and price discounting is likely to lead to both a decrease in the number and a shift in the type of retailers that sell the manufacturer's products, which may result in a long-run reduction in the manufacturer's sales. The primary problem may not be that discounting Internet retailers free-ride on the services provided by brick-and-mortar retailers, as consumers first obtain relevant product information at a brick-and-mortar store before purchasing the product at a lower price online.[36] Even without such Internet retailer free-riding on brick-and-mortar

---

concludes that the FTC did Levi Strauss a favor by stopping its economically unnecessary use of resale price maintenance. Sharon Oster, *The FTC v. Levi Strauss: An Analysis of the Economic Issues,* in IMPACT EVALUATIONS OF FEDERAL TRADE COMMISSION VERTICAL RESTRAINT CASES 47 (R.N. Lafferty, R.H. Lande, and J.B. Kirkwood eds, FTC Bureau of Competition and Bureau of Economics, 1984).

[35]   See, e.g., Jacob Jacoby and David Mazursky, *Linking Brand and Retailer Images: Do the Potential Risks Outweigh the Potential Benefits?*, 60 J. RETAILING 105 (1984). If the sale of a product in low reputation stores reduces the demand for the product in high reputation stores, it generally can be prevented by manufacturer control of distribution, namely, by refusing to sell to low reputation stores and preventing inter-retailer transshipping; it often may not be necessary for the manufacturer to control the retail price.

[36]   A number of commentators have noted that there may be more free-riding in the opposite direction, with consumers first finding out what they wish to purchase by searching online and then purchasing the product at a brick-and-mortar store. A survey of these marketing studies in

retailers, the equilibrium that results from uncontrolled Internet price discounting, with the resulting significant increase in Internet sales and corresponding loss of sales by brick-and-mortar retailers, is not likely to maximize the manufacturer's sales and profitability.

Manufacturers must decide how best to distribute their products through various distribution channels, including optimally encouraging incremental sales by high-quality brick-and-mortar retailers who may intensively promote the manufacturer's products at the point-of-sale as well as making their products conveniently available on the Internet. The desired number and various types of retailers chosen by manufacturers to distribute their products have shifted over time in response to changes that have occurred in the technology of retailing and in consumer preferences. At any point in time, manufacturers will take these underlying shifts in supply and demand for retailing services into account in analysing the tradeoffs involved when deciding what is the optimal number and type of retailers that should sell their products. However, it is unlikely that the competitive retailing process will result in the desired distribution of a manufacturer's products without any manufacturer intervention whatsoever.

II ANTITRUST ANALYSIS OF RESALE PRICE MAINTENANCE

Christine Varney, Assistant Attorney General of the Antitrust Division of the Department of Justice, outlines in an important recent article a structured rule of reason framework for the analysis of resale price maintenance.[37] Varney's rule of reason framework requires, first of all, that the plaintiff establish a *prima facie* showing of a likely anticompetitive effect within the context of the four potential anticompetitive theories outlined by the Supreme Court in *Leegin*. These anticompetitive theories are described in section IIA, and the conditions for the likely existence of each anticompetitive theory within the context of the broader procompetitive economic analysis of resale price maintenance emphasized above are discussed in section IIB.[38] The antitrust policy standard for resale price maintenance is discussed in section IIC.

Gregory T. Gundlach, Joseph P. Cannon, and Kenneth C. Manning, *Free Riding and Resale Price Maintenance: Insights from Marketing Research and Practice*, 55 ANTITRUST BULL. 381 (2010) shows that this type of free-riding by brick-and-mortar retailers on the services provided by Internet retailers occurs more frequently than free-riding by Internet retailers on brick-and-mortar retailers. However, these forms of free-riding are separate 'distortions' that cannot be just netted out against one another; the manufacturer wants to mitigate both of them. Specifically, the manufacturer wants to assure a sufficient supply of product information on the Internet, which it may do in part by supplying product information itself; and the manufacturer also wants to assure a sufficient supply of brick-and-mortar retailer face-to-face retailing services, which it may do in part with the use of resale price maintenance. It is not clear that resale price maintenance, the solution to the problem of an insufficient number of brick-and-mortar stores promoting the manufacturer's products, has a significant marginal effect in terms of exacerbating the other problem of reducing the supply of Internet product information available to consumers.

[37] Christine A. Varney, *A Post-*Leegin *Approach to Resale Price Maintenance Using a Structured Rule of Reason*, ANTITRUST 22 (Fall 2009).

[38] Once the plaintiff has established the existence of a likely anticompetitive effect, Varney's framework then shifts the burden 'to the defendant to demonstrate either that its RPM agreements

A   Anticompetitive Theories of Resale Price Maintenance

The Court in *Leegin* made it clear that, although resale price maintenance may increase a product's retail price, the appropriate antitrust standard should not focus solely on the short-term, or even long-term, effect of a vertical restraint on a product's price.[39] Instead, the Court focused on four potential anticompetitive theories of resale price maintenance, two manufacturer-motivated anticompetitive theories and two retailer-motivated anticompetitive theories. Specifically, the Court described the use of resale price maintenance (i) by a group of manufacturers to facilitate a manufacturer cartel; (ii) by a dominant manufacturer to maintain its market power; (iii) by a group of retailers to facilitate a retailer cartel; and (iv) by a dominant retailer to maintain its retail market power.[40] As Varney outlines, antitrust analysis of resale price maintenance should involve, as a first step, an economic evaluation of the risks associated with each of these potential anticompetitive theories.

1   Anticompetitive manufacturer-motivated resale price maintenance

A manufacturer would not appear to have an anticompetitive economic interest in increasing retail margins. Manufacturers are in effect purchasing retailing services at an implicit price equal to the retail margin defined by the gap between the retail price paid by consumers and the wholesale price received by manufacturers. Hence, the lower the retail margin, or the manufacturer's implicit purchase price of retailing services, the lower is the retail price for any given level of wholesale price, and therefore the greater are the manufacturer's sales and profits at any given wholesale price. Consequently, it would not appear to make economic sense for a manufacturer to institute resale price maintenance if the increased retailer margin and the associated increased implicit manufacturer cost of retailing services produced by resale price maintenance did not compensate retailers for supplying services that created consumer value and procompetitively increased the demand for the manufacturer's products.

The *Leegin* Court described two anticompetitive exceptions to this general proposition that manufacturer-motivated resale price maintenance must be procompetitive. The first anticompetitive manufacturer motivation involves the use of resale price maintenance by a group of manufacturers to facilitate a manufacturer cartel.[41] Resale price maintenance may facilitate a horizontal price-fixing agreement among manufacturers in two ways: (a) by decreasing the incentive of individual manufacturers to cheat on the cartel by reducing their wholesale prices below collusively set wholesale prices; and (b) by increasing the ability of cartel members to detect manufacturers that do cheat on the cartel by reducing their wholesale prices.

With regard to the first mechanism by which resale price maintenance may facilitate a collusive agreement, the economic forces described in this chapter imply that resale price

---

are actually – not merely theoretically – procompetitive or that the plaintiff's characterizations of the marketplace [when describing the anticompetitive effect] were erroneous'. *Id.* at 22.

[39]   Leegin Creative Leather Prods., Inc. v. PSKS, Inc., dba Kay's Kloset, 551 U.S. 877, 895–7 (2007).

[40]   *Id.* at 892–4.

[41]   *Id.* at 892.

maintenance will not entirely eliminate the incentive of individual manufacturer cartel members to cheat on the cartel. A manufacturer that reduces its wholesale price while continuing to maintain retail prices with resale price maintenance creates an increased incentive for retailers to promote its products at the expense of rival products. And in some circumstances, this manufacturer incentive to encourage preferential retailer promotional activity may substantially destabilize a cartel in spite of resale price maintenance. However, because resale price maintenance restrains the ability of retailers to reduce prices, resale price maintenance will decrease the incentive of manufacturers to cut wholesale prices and will be a factor that stabilizes a cartel.

The other mechanism by which resale price maintenance may facilitate a collusive agreement, by making it easier to detect manufacturers who cheat on a cartel by reducing wholesale price, is likely to have a much weaker cartel-stabilizing effect. Even if there were not resale price maintenance, observing a retailer's lower prices would be an indication that a cheating manufacturer may have violated the conspiracy by lowering its wholesale prices; and even with resale price maintenance, lower retail prices do not necessarily mean that the manufacturer has lowered its wholesale prices.

The second manufacturer-motivated anticompetitive theory of resale price maintenance described by the Court in *Leegin* involves the use of resale price maintenance by a dominant manufacturer to maintain its market power, either by driving smaller manufacturing rivals out of the market or by preventing new competitive manufacturing rivals from entering the market.[42] It is not clear exactly how this anticompetitive theory operates. One way may involve the dominant manufacturer combining resale price maintenance with the threat to terminate retailers that carry the products of competing rivals or new entrants. This anticompetitive theory therefore amounts to the use of resale price maintenance by a dominant firm as a way to pay retailers for de facto exclusive dealing.

Evaluating the potential anticompetitive effects of resale price maintenance used by a dominant manufacturer under this interpretation of the anticompetitive theory requires us to focus on the question of whether there are likely to be anticompetitive effects from exclusive dealing. This generally involves a determination of whether, given economies of scale in manufacturing or economies of scope in distribution for the manufacturer, the dominant manufacturer is able to place rival manufacturers at a significant competitive disadvantage by foreclosing rivals' access to a sufficiently large share of retailing. Under this exclusivity scenario, an anticompetitive effect is certainly possible; but resale price maintenance itself has no anticompetitive significance. In this anticompetitive framework resale price maintenance is merely the way in which a dominant manufacturer may pay for exclusivity.

The Court in *Leegin* does not describe the potential anticompetitive effects of a dominant firm's use of resale price maintenance in this way, namely as a method of compensating retailers for a de facto exclusive agreement. Instead, the Court describes the potential anticompetitive effects of a dominant firm's use of resale price maintenance as a way for the dominant firm to maintain its market power because it 'give[s] retailers an incentive not to sell the products of smaller rivals or new entrants'.[43] In particular, it is claimed that

---

[42]   *Id.* at 894.
[43]   *Id.*

retailers have a reduced incentive to carry a rival brand because retailers operating under resale price maintenance are earning a protected, higher than normal margin on sales of the dominant manufacturer's brand. However, absent the dominant manufacturer's threat to terminate retailers that carry rival products, that is, absent a de facto exclusivity agreement, there is no reason why retailers would not also carry competing products.

All that is necessary for retailers to carry rival products is that they expect to earn a sufficient return on the rival products. When a retailer's return on the dominant manufacturer's established brand is protected with resale price maintenance, this is likely to increase what competing manufacturers of rival products must offer retailers to obtain distribution. But rival product manufacturers could also assure retailers that they will earn a sufficient return by compensating them with resale price maintenance. In these circumstances, resale price maintenance is not exclusionary; it is just an element of the normal competitive process by which manufacturers compete for retail distribution. Small new manufacturers, as well as large established manufacturers, may use resale price maintenance within this competitive framework as an effective way to compensate retailers for stocking and promoting their products.

2   Anticompetitive retailer-motivated resale price maintenance

The Court in *Leegin* describes two forms of anticompetitive retailer-motivated resale price maintenance. One involves a group of colluding retailers that force the manufacturer to institute resale price maintenance in order to limit inter-retailer competition and thereby collusively increase retailer margins. This is the most obvious anticompetitive theory of resale price maintenance.

The other anticompetitive retailer-motivated resale price maintenance theory described by the Court in *Leegin* involves a dominant retailer that anticompetitively uses resale price maintenance in an attempt to maintain its market power by preventing the entry of new, lower-cost retailers. The theory is that if lower-cost retailers entered and were able to discount prices, the dominant retailer would lose market share. Therefore, the dominant retailer 'might request resale price maintenance to forestall innovation in distribution that decreases costs'.[44] And the manufacturer may acquiesce to the dominant retailer's demands because 'it has little choice but to accommodate the retailer's demands for vertical price restraints if the manufacturer believes it needs access to the retailer's distribution network'.[45]

This statement of the dominant retailer-initiated anticompetitive theory of resale price maintenance is similar to the retailer cartel theory in the sense that it would appear not to be in the interests of the manufacturer to prevent the entry of a new, lower-cost retailer. Since the manufacturer wishes to purchase retailing services at the lowest implicit cost, entry of a new innovative retailer that has lower retailing costs would increase the manufacturer's profits. The theory assumes the manufacturer is forced against its economic

---

[44]   *Id.* at 893.

[45]   *Id.* at 893–4 (citing Thomas R. Overstreet, *Resale Price Maintenance: Economic Theories and Empirical Evidence* 31 (Federal Trade Comm'n Bureau of Economics staff report, November 1983); Phillip E. Areeda and Herbert Hovenkamp, 8 Antitrust Law: An Analysis of Antitrust Principles and Their Application 47 (2d ed. 2004); and Toys 'R' Us, Inc. v. FTC, 221 F.3d, 928, 937–8 (7th Cir. 2000)).

interests by the dominant retailer to use resale price maintenance to prevent the new, lower-cost retailer from reducing its retail prices. In this way, it is claimed that the established retailer protects its dominant position because consumers will not have the incentive to shift their purchases to the new, lower-cost retailer that is charging the same price, thereby deterring, or at least delaying, the entry of the lower-cost retailer.

B   Economic Conditions to Establish a Likely Anticompetitive Effect

The four anticompetitive theories of resale price maintenance described by the *Leegin* Court each imply a set of necessary economic conditions that must be present before a plaintiff can meet the first *prima facie* anticompetitive effects requirement of the antitrust analysis of resale price maintenance arrangements. Since the necessary economic conditions, described below, vary substantially depending on the particular anticompetitive theory of resale price maintenance, plaintiffs at the outset should be required to specify which theory is claimed to be the anticompetitive motivation for the resale price maintenance arrangement they are challenging.

1   Anticompetitive manufacturer-motivated resale price maintenance

The conditions for finding a likely anticompetitive effect are fairly restrictive under the two manufacturer-motivated anticompetitive theories of resale price maintenance. The claim that resale price maintenance may be used by a group of manufacturers to stabilize a manufacturer cartel requires, first of all, that resale price maintenance is used by a large fraction of firms in the industry and, secondly, that the industry is sufficiently concentrated that manufacturer collusion is likely.[46]

It is important to emphasize that the role of resale price maintenance under the manufacturer cartel anticompetitive theory of resale price maintenance is only a potential cartel-facilitating practice and is not anticompetitive in itself. Therefore, to establish the likely existence of this anticompetitive use of resale price maintenance one must meet the other common conditions for the presence of a collusive horizontal conspiracy among manufacturers to fix wholesale prices. Specifically, one must demonstrate that individual manufacturers are acting contrary to their independent economic self-interests absent a conspiracy. Without such evidence, the widespread use of resale price maintenance in an industry, by itself, should not be considered anticompetitive. Without evidence of a conspiracy, the widespread use of resale price maintenance in an industry more likely suggests the existence of an important efficiency reason for independent manufacturer adoption of resale price maintenance in the industry.[47]

---

[46]   Overstreet, *supra* note 45, at 71–82 concludes that most resale price maintenance arrangements are generally unlikely to be cartel-stabilizing devices because the concentration ratio is too low in the industries where resale price maintenance has been widely used to credibly suggest the presence of a manufacturer conspiracy.

[47]   This is consistent with the relevance assigned by the Federal Trade Commission to the widespread use of resale price maintenance in an industry in the FTC's modification of the *Nine West* consent order. Although the FTC rejected Nine West's contention that prohibiting its use of resale price maintenance when many other women's shoe manufacturers were using resale price maintenance placed Nine West at a competitive disadvantage, the FTC also failed to infer any

A likely anticompetitive effect under the alternative dominant manufacturer-motivated anticompetitive theory of resale price maintenance requires, first of all, that the manufacturer employing resale price maintenance have a large share of the relevant market. Resale price maintenance established by a relatively small manufacturer, such as Leegin, therefore should fall into a safe harbor of per se legality under this anticompetitive theory.[48] If this safe harbor screen is exceeded, plaintiffs then should be required to demonstrate the likely applicability of the dominant firm anticompetitive theory of resale price maintenance, recognizing that in most cases the anticompetitive use of resale price maintenance to effectively exclude rivals is highly unlikely without some form of actual or de facto exclusivity agreement with retailers. And such exclusivity agreements should be evaluated separately from resale price maintenance for anticompetitive effects.

2   Anticompetitive retailer-motivated resale price maintenance

The two retailer-motivated anticompetitive theories described by the Court in *Leegin* implicitly assume that the manufacturer is being forced by retailers to act against its economic interests in adopting resale price maintenance. The Court refers to situations where retailers are 'the source' or 'the impetus' for resale price maintenance as something that indicates 'a greater likelihood that the restraint facilitates a retailer cartel or supports a dominant inefficient retailer'.[49] The economic rationale for such reasoning is that the 'potential procompetitive uses of RPM identified in *Leegin* involve tangible benefits to manufacturers, so manufacturers need not be coerced to adopt RPM when it serves any of these purposes'.[50]

However, it is unclear exactly what the Court means by retailers being the 'source' or 'impetus' for a resale price maintenance arrangement. It certainly does not mean that the retailer is the only one benefiting from the arrangement and therefore a retailer cartel or a dominant retailer is coercing the manufacturer to adopt resale price maintenance against its interests. The economic analysis of resale price maintenance presented in this chapter describes how resale price maintenance is often part of a transaction between a manufacturer (who is buying retailing services) and its retailers (who are selling retailing services) and therefore both the manufacturer and the retailers are benefiting from the

---

anticompetitive significance from the fact that resale price maintenance was widely used in the industry. FTC, Nine West Order, *supra* note 11, at 16.

[48]   This also is consistent with the antitrust liability standard adopted by the Federal Trade Commission when modifying the Nine West consent order. The FTC concluded that resale price maintenance established by a manufacturer that does not possess market power is a sufficient condition to infer the absence of any anticompetitive effects, and is therefore legal under *Leegin*. *Id.* at 17.

[49]   *Leegin*, *supra* note 1, at 897–8.

[50]   Varney, *supra* note 37, at 24. William Comanor and Frederic Scherer state in their *Leegin* Amicus Brief, that '[t]o the knowledge of the amici, there are no arguments in economic analysis supporting restraints arising from distributor actions or pressures'. Brief for William S. Comanor and Frederic M. Scherer as Amicus Curiae Supporting Neither Party, Leegin Creative Leather Products, Inc. v. PSKS, Inc., 127 S. Ct. 2705 (2007), 2007 WL 173679, at 8. Comanor and Scherer therefore advocate a presumptively per se illegal antitrust standard for resale price maintenance when it is initiated by retailers. *Id.* at 9.

transaction. In these circumstances the identity of 'the source' or 'the initiator' of the resale price maintenance arrangement may not have much economic significance.

For example, think about a case where a manufacturer asks a retailer to stock (or more intensively promote) its products, and the retailer in response then asks the manufacturer how it intends to organize distribution of its products – a clearly relevant business consideration for the retailer. The retailer may ask the manufacturer who else is (or will be) carrying the manufacturer's products in the retailer's area and what will be the manufacturer's other terms of retail distribution. As part of these business communications that are part of the normal competitive process, there is no economic significance related to whether (a) it is the manufacturer that says it plans to institute resale price maintenance and expects the retailer to intensively promote its products, or (b) it is the retailer that offers to carry and more intensively promote the products but says it expects the manufacturer to maintain retail margins. The manufacturer may have already decided to adopt some minimum pricing arrangement or may realize during its conversations with retailers that such an arrangement would be the best way to maximize its sales and effectively compete with other manufacturers.

Since the fundamental economics involves the manufacturer purchase of retailing services and the retailer sale of retailing services, both the manufacturer and retailer expect to be better off as a result of the transaction. It certainly would be incorrect to infer that 'the initiator' of the arrangement is the only one benefiting from it and is coercing the other party to adopt the arrangement against its interests.

The economic conditions for establishing a likely anticompetitive effect under retailer-motivated anticompetitive theories of resale price maintenance therefore must involve evidence of retailer coercion, and not merely retailer initiation or encouragement of manufacturers to adopt resale price maintenance.

The necessary conditions for the presence of retailer coercion are perhaps easiest to recognize under the retailer cartel anticompetitive theory of resale price maintenance. Resale price maintenance established by a retailer cartel against the wishes of a manufacturer requires that resale price maintenance be used by a large share of the relevant retailers who are jointly communicating with the manufacturer. Joint retailer ability to coerce is also facilitated by unconcentrated manufacturing, since a large manufacturer can more easily thwart a retailer conspiracy.

The evidence indicates that a very small minority of resale price maintenance arrangements are instituted as a result of organized retailer group pressure of manufacturers consistent with the existence of an anticompetitive retailer cartel.[51] The fact that multiple retailers may make simultaneous demands upon a manufacturer to stop retailer price discounting and adopt resale price maintenance should not be interpreted as an antitrust problem analogous to a retailer cartel. The economic theory of resale price maintenance presented in this chapter implies that the existence of extensive retail price discounting may mean that retailers are not earning a competitive return on their retailing assets, such as their shelf space and sales staff, and therefore that it may be in each retailer's independent economic interest to complain to the manufacturer about the retailer price discounting and to communicate their plans to drop distribution or reduce promotion of

---

[51] Overstreet, *supra* note 45, at 13–19, 80, 140–44, 161–3.

the manufacturer's products if the manufacturer does not prevent such price discounting. In contrast, when retailer demands are jointly made through a retailer trade association or otherwise involve joint retailer action, it may legally be considered concerted action.[52]

Establishing the anticompetitive use of resale price maintenance by a dominant retailer is analytically similar to a retailer cartel in that it requires evidence that the manufacturers adopting resale price maintenance are being forced to act contrary to their economic interests by the exercise of the dominant retailer's market power. Therefore, this anticompetitive theory requires that the dominant retailer has a significant market share and the market power to coerce manufacturers to act contrary to their economic interests.

In addition, anticompetitive market effects require that the resale price maintenance agreements cover a significant share of sales in the relevant product market. If competing retailers have access to enough alternative uncovered products, they will be able to sell at a discount in competition with the dominant retailer and therefore defeat the dominant retailer's anticompetitive scheme. Furthermore, if the resale price maintenance arrangement covers a significant share of product market sales solely with a contract with a single large manufacturer that has a large share of the relevant market (or with a small group of large manufacturers), it is less likely that the dominant retailer obtained the contract by coercing the large manufacturer or manufacturers to act contrary to their interests.

Whether the dominant retailer has, in fact, exercised its market power by coercing manufacturers to act contrary to their economic interests requires, once again, more than evidence that the dominant retailer informed a manufacturer that it will drop distribution (or stop active promotion) of the manufacturer's products if retailer price discounting is not eliminated. If other, non-dominant retailers are similarly complaining to manufacturers about the adverse effects of retailer discounting on their business and stating the future actions they expect to take, this is an indication that the dominant retailer's communications, by themselves, are not an exercise of its market power. In these circumstances all retailers are just informing the manufacturer about market conditions. Moreover, if the manufacturers' internal business documents indicate concern about the adverse effects of retailer price discounting on their retail distribution networks, independent of dominant retailer complaints, that also is an indication that dominant retailer communications with manufacturers regarding the adoption of resale price maintenance do not involve the exercise of retailer market power to force manufacturers to act contrary to their interests.

As opposed to communications between horizontal competitors, continuous communications between manufacturers and their retailers about market conditions are expected as part of the normal competitive process. Inferring the existence of an agreement on the basis of communications between firms that are vertically related to one another is different from inferring a collusive agreement on the basis of communications between horizontal competitors. In contrast to communications between horizontal rivals, there is a clear competitive economic rationale for vertically related firms to communicate with one another in order to form expectations regarding one another's performance. It is certainly reasonable to expect retailers to communicate with the suppliers of the products they sell,

---

[52]   See, e.g., United States v. General Motors Corp., 384 U.S. 127 (1966).

including communicating about market conditions that they believe may make it difficult for them to profitably sell a supplier's products.

As noted by the Supreme Court in *Mansanto v. Spray-Rite*, 'the fact that a manufacturer and its distributors are in constant communication about prices and marketing strategy does not alone show that the distributors are not making independent pricing decisions'. To support an inference of an agreement, the Court continues, 'something more than evidence of complaints is needed . . . there must be evidence that tends to exclude the possibility of independent action by the manufacturer and distributor'.[53] Retailer communication about a manufacturer's price or distribution policy certainly is not evidence that 'tends to exclude the possibility of independent action'.

If a manufacturer takes account of retailer complaints and other communications in formulating and enforcing its pricing policies, for example, by terminating price discounting retailers, this is not economically equivalent to the manufacturer being coerced by a dominant retailer to act contrary to its economic interests. If the manufacturer knows that retailer price discounting is occurring, and expects that it would ultimately lead retailers, including the dominant retailer, to unilaterally conclude that it no longer pays to devote their selling space or other promotional efforts to the manufacturer's independent products, it would be in the manufacturer's economic interest to terminate the price discounting retailers. The manufacturer would terminate price discounting retailers in these circumstances even if the manufacturer had not received any retailer warnings.

A manufacturer may receive some short-term increased sales benefits as a result of retailer price discounting, and therefore bear a short-term cost of reduced sales when it terminates discounting retailers. However, the manufacturer also recognizes that not terminating price discounting retailers would reduce the overall long-run demand for its products because it would be unable to obtain or maintain adequate retail distribution of its products. If there is evidence that each manufacturer's decision is driven by what it believes would promote its own independent long-run economic interests in maintaining an effective distribution network of retailers, then this is evidence that the dominant retailer is not coercing the manufacturers to act contrary to their interests.

Evidence that would permit one to infer the presence of a possible coercive agreement would be a decrease in the individual manufacturer's long-run sales and profits after the adoption of resale price maintenance. It is important, once again, not to focus on short-term effects on the manufacturer's sales of a change in the manufacturer's price policies. As described above, a manufacturer may lose sales in the short run when it terminates a price discounting retailer, but this change may have been necessary to preserve the manufacturer's overall efficient retailer distribution network over the long term.

Finally, an additional factor that may be consistent with the possible presence of a coercive agreement is evidence that the manufacturer adopted resale price maintenance only reluctantly and has continually attempted to evade enforcement of its pricing policies. Such behavior may be analytically similar to the usual evidence of cartel 'cheating' by manufacturers that is used to demonstrate that the manufacturers have entered into a horizontal collusive arrangement which forces them to act contrary to their independent self-interests.

---

[53]   Monsanto Co. v. Spray-Rite Serv. Corp., 465 U.S. 752, 762, 764, 768 (1984).

C   Antitrust Policy Standard

The reasoning underlying *Leegin* is that because resale price maintenance often is the result of procompetitive market forces, plaintiffs should be legally required to demonstrate the existence of a likely anticompetitive market effect in order to successfully challenge a resale price maintenance arrangement. Under this interpretation, the four anticompetitive motivations for resale price maintenance noted by the Court in *Leegin* should serve as legal screening devices, with defendants not needing to prove the existence of procompetitive efficiencies to avoid antitrust liability unless plaintiffs first demonstrate a *prima facie* anticompetitive effect under one of these theories.[54]

However, because resale price maintenance often does not appear to be motivated by the procompetitive prevention of free-riding, as a practical matter, some have interpreted the plaintiff's initial legal burden of demonstrating a potential anticompetitive effect to be more easily met. Specifically, the fact that resale price maintenance increases a product's price, at least in the short run, and there is an absence of free-riding, may be mistakenly considered by some to be sufficient to fulfill the initial likely anticompetitive effect requirement.[55] Once we recognize the common procompetitive role of resale price maintenance in the absence of free-riding, this shortcut in the economic analysis required to establish a likely anticompetitive effect is clearly mistaken.

In addition to the conditions outlined in section IIB, a necessary condition for demonstrating an anticompetitive effect of resale price maintenance is a decrease in market output. If resale price arrangements established by manufacturers to assure effective retail distribution of their products instead lead to an increase in market output, this should be a sufficient condition for categorizing the arrangement as procompetitive. And all we need to reject the retailer-motivated anticompetitive theories of resale price maintenance is that the individual manufacturer's sales increase, clearly indicating the absence of dominant retailer or retailer cartel coercion of the manufacturer to act contrary to its independent economic interests.

William Comanor and Frederic Scherer claim that an increase in a manufacturer's sales as a result of resale price maintenance does not necessarily imply an increase in total consumer welfare.[56] They argue that the point-of-sale retailing services which manufacturers desire as a way to profitably increase the demand for their products, and which are, in

---

[54]   This interpretation of *Leegin* is consistent with the Federal Trade Commission's recent modification of the *Nine West* consent decree, *supra* note 11. Although the FTC did not accept the procompetitive justifications for resale price maintenance offered by Nine West, the FTC modified the consent decree because it found Nine West's use of resale price maintenance unlikely to have had an anticompetitive effect.

[55]   The absence of obvious procompetitive rationales for most resale price maintenance arrangements has led some antitrust commentators to argue that resale price maintenance should be subject to a stricter truncated or 'quick look' rule of reason legal standard that requires establishment of a procompetitive rationale. See, e.g., Robert L. Hubbard, *Protecting Consumers Post-Leegin*, ANTITRUST 41 (Fall 2007).

[56]   Comanor and Scherer, *Leegin* Amicus Brief, *supra* note 50. This is a long-standing position of both Comanor and Scherer. See, e.g., William B. Comanor, *Vertical Price-Fixing, Vertical Market Restrictions, and the New Antitrust Policy*, 98 HARV. L. REV. 983 (1985); and Frederic M. Scherer, *The Economics of Vertical Restraints*, 52 ANTITRUST L.J. 687 (1983).

effect, purchased from retailers with increased retail margins created by resale price maintenance, are not retail services demanded by all consumers. Consequently, some consumers are better off, but other consumers worse off, as a result of the manufacturer's actions.

Specifically, Comanor and Scherer note that while marginal consumers who respond to retailing services such as product display and promotion by increasing their purchases of the manufacturer's products value and hence benefit from the increased retailing services that result from resale price maintenance, inframarginal consumers who would have purchased the manufacturer's products in any event without, for example, the preferable display space or extra time devoted by sales staff to a manufacturer's products, are worse off since they are now paying higher prices without receiving any benefit from the retailer's increased supply of manufacturer-specific retailing services. Comanor and Scherer therefore conclude that the net welfare effect of the increased manufacturer-specific retailer services induced by resale price maintenance depends on the relative number of inframarginal and marginal consumers that purchase the manufacturer's products.

However, Comanor and Scherer incorrectly assume that inframarginal consumers would necessarily pay lower prices in the absence of resale price maintenance. Manufacturers create the retail margin required to compensate retailers for supplying desired promotional services by reducing wholesale prices in combination with resale price maintenance. In the absence of resale price maintenance, manufacturers will substitute less efficient ways to purchase the promotional services they desire, such as increased manufacturer advertising in combination with higher wholesale prices, or possibly the direct supply by manufacturers of desired point-of-sale retailing services by vertically integrating into retail distribution. These and other alternative arrangements may very well result in higher retail prices than under resale price maintenance. Furthermore, even if retail prices fall in the absence of resale price maintenance, inframarginal consumers may be worse off if this leads some retailers to drop distribution of the consumers' preferred products, so that some inframarginal consumers would have to shop for their preferred products at a less desirable store or purchase a less desirable product.

More fundamentally, it is important to recognize that the procompetitive role of resale price maintenance described in this chapter is part of a larger competitive process by which manufacturers compete with one another for retail distribution. This competition between manufacturers for retail distribution has the immediate effect of benefiting retailers because retailers earn profit on the sale of their retailing assets and manufacturer access to their loyal customer base. However, the highly competitive nature of retailing implies that any retailer return from the provision of manufacturer-specific retailer promotion and distribution services that is greater than retailer costs of supplying these retail distribution services will lead to retailer entry or be largely passed on to consumers as part of the competitive retailing process. Since manufacturer payments to retailers for retail services with resale price maintenance are related to a retailer's sales, retailers will compete with one another to develop a loyal customer base that increases both their sales and the compensation they will receive from manufacturers for their retail distribution and sales efforts. Consequently, retailers face long-run competitive pressures to use any manufacturer payments they receive in excess of costs to either lower their overall average prices (when the retailer is a multiproduct retailer) or to supply consumer services that have large inter-retailer demand effects. Such price and non-price inter-retailer competition results in the manufacturer payments for retail distribution and promotion ultimately benefiting consumers.

While there are likely to be differing effects across consumers when a manufacturer uses resale price maintenance to compensate retailers for distribution and promotional efforts, this is a normal consequence of competition. Some consumers are likely to gain and other consumers likely to lose from most marketing practices adopted by competitive firms. For example, many competitive retailers provide services, such as free delivery, that are not consumed by all customers.

The provision of free sales assistance is another obvious example. One customer may try on 20 different pairs of shoes over an hour-long period before making a purchase while another customer purchases a similar pair of shoes in five minutes without trying on any shoes. The fact that retailer provision of free sales assistance may increase retail prices without any offsetting benefit to inframarginal consumers who do not demand the assistance does not mean that we should prohibit retailers from supplying such services, or prohibit manufacturers from compensating retailers for supplying such services. Although inframarginal consumers could be made better off as a result of such a prohibition on free sales assistance, this does not make such a prohibition procompetitive. The provision of free services that are valuable to only a subset of consumers is a pervasive part of the normal competitive process undertaken by firms without any market power.

Antitrust policy leaves it up to firms competing in the marketplace to determine which services will be supplied by retailers, often with financial assistance provided by manufacturers to retailers for the supply of services devoted to the sale of the manufacturer's products. The role of antitrust is not to microregulate this competitive process by calculating whether a particular marketing practice in a particular circumstance produces a net consumer welfare gain or not. Although the ultimate purpose of the antitrust laws is to maximize consumer welfare, that does not mean that antitrust law should consist of the measurement of consumer welfare changes. It is highly unlikely that a court could empirically estimate the differential effects between marginal and inframarginal consumers and accurately determine when total consumer welfare was or was not reduced in every particular situation. Moreover, independent of these difficult empirical considerations, when a small competitive firm, such as Leegin, independently decides to adopt a particular retailing arrangement as a way to increase point-of-sale retailing services and therefore the demand for its products, this should be considered an element of the normal competitive process independent of any potential distribution effects across consumers that may occur as a result. The antitrust laws do not require the courts post-*Leegin* to second-guess this competitive process.

8 The plausibility of *Twombly*: proving horizontal agreements after *Twombly*

*Alvin K. Klevorick and Issa B. Kohler-Hausmann**

I INTRODUCTION

One of the most settled, and indeed commonly applauded, elements of US antitrust law is the prohibition of horizontal agreements among competing firms with regard to their price and quantity decisions. The seemingly simple language of section 1 of the Sherman Act states, 'Every contract, combination in the form of trust or otherwise, or conspiracy, in restraint of trade or commerce ... is declared to be illegal'.[1] Yet, since the statute's early days, courts and commentators have struggled to specify exactly what sort of evidence ought to suffice to show the existence of an unlawful agreement. This has been especially troublesome in the context of oligopolistic markets in which it is notoriously difficult to discern whether the appearance of parallel behavior is the product of coordinated conspiracy or simultaneous strategic, yet independent firm decisions.[2]

Section 1's broad but vague prohibition of agreements in restraint of trade has spawned a long common law battle over justiciable standards. In particular, is anything more required than interdependent behavior that achieves supracompetitive returns, and if so, what more is needed and how is it to be established? There is even dispute about what constitutes interdependent behavior as opposed to independent behavior.

Two important and yet conflicting policy imperatives fuel the debate over standards of proof in section 1 cases. On one hand, courts recognize the difficulty (or, in some cases, the impossibility) of obtaining direct evidence of an explicit unlawful antitrust conspiracy. Accordingly, they seek to fashion sufficiently permissive evidentiary requirements so that savvy conspirators who successfully conceal traces of explicit unlawful agreements do not go unpunished. That is, the courts are concerned about the likelihood and social cost of false negative errors, of not punishing illegal behavior. On the other hand, courts are concerned that excessively permissive evidentiary standards risk punishing or chilling legitimate business activity that is merely interdependent. Here, they worry about the probability and social cost of making false positive errors.

Even when the Supreme Court has directly addressed the requirements for showing an agreement under section 1 at various stages of litigation, its general language has often led to a proliferation of semantic reformulations by lower courts and antitrust scholars. Few commentators in the law and economics literature have attempted to formalize the

* The authors thank Bruce Ackerman, Daniel Crane, William Eskridge, and Louis Kaplow for helpful comments and Mishele N. Kieffer, Yale Law School Class of 2010, and Catherine S. Simonsen, Yale Law School Class of 2011, for their excellent research assistance.

1 15 U.S.C. § 1 (2006).
2 See *infra* notes 16–18 and accompanying text.

reigning tests in federal courts for establishing a horizontal agreement. Significant debate continues as to exactly what the doctrine requires at specific points in litigation of antitrust plaintiffs who claim section 1 violations. The Supreme Court's 2007 decision in *Bell Atlantic v. Twombly* is the Court's most recent pronouncement on the question of what exactly an antitrust plaintiff claiming a violation of section 1 must show, in this case at the pleading stage, and as with some past decisions, it has engendered more questions than answers about this long-running doctrinal question.[3]

Our major goal here is to offer what we believe is the most compelling interpretation and formalization of the Supreme Court's statements on evidentiary and procedural standards for showing a section 1 violation, while recognizing that, as some have claimed, the Court has addressed the required proof of pleading without a well-articulated definition of agreement or, more narrowly, conspiracy.[4] Our contribution attempts to formalize what we believe is the most reasonable interpretation of the Court's reigning rules, which now include the one in *Twombly*. For now we do not offer a normative prescription for those rules based on foundational policy principles, such as promotion of efficiency or minimization of social costs, which include the costs of errors in the decision process. This is not to say that those policy concerns do not motivate the doctrine we are addressing, but rather that here we set ourselves to the more limited task of presenting the most plausible and reasonable interpretation of the doctrine and of formalizing it in a way that aids understanding.

Whether in celebration or lamentation, many legal academics have labeled *Twombly* a paradigm-shifting case. Some have hailed it as ushering in a new era of more stringent and efficient pleading standards for antitrust plaintiffs by moving the standard for ruling on motions to dismiss closer to the one for deciding summary judgment motions. The decision, they say, allows courts to weed out nonmeritorious claims at the pleading stage by eschewing the traditional fact–law distinction of the strict notice pleading regime and thereby promotes economic and judicial efficiency.[5] Other commentators have interpreted *Twombly* as striking a serious blow to the notice- pleading norms established by the 1938 Federal Rules of Civil Procedure by announcing a new anti-plaintiff posture in civil procedure law generally.[6]

---

[3]　Bell Atl. Corp. v. Twombly, 550 U.S. 544 (2007).

[4]　In his recent insightful piece, *On the Meaning of Horizontal Agreements in Competition Law*, Louis Kaplow argues that the problem with section 1 jurisprudence runs deeper than the pleading and evidentiary requirements. It strikes, he argues, at the core of the canonical violation because section 1 antitrust law lacks a coherent definition of agreement. Louis Kaplow, *On the Meaning of Horizontal Agreements in Competition Law*, Harvard John M. Olin Discussion Paper No. 691, available at www.law.harvard.edu/programs/olin_center/.

[5]　For example, see Richard Epstein, Bell Atlantic v. Twombly, *How Motions to Dismiss Become (Disguised) Summary Judgments*, 25 WASH. U. J.L. AND POL'Y 61 (2007), where Epstein argues: 'The fact/law distinction that organizes civil procedure does not work as well in the context of modern litigation as it does in the simpler cases that originally animated the Federal Rules'. *Id.* at 65. Epstein further argues that, 'as the costs of discovery mount, the case for terminating litigation earlier in the cycle gets ever stronger, and should be realized, especially in those cases where the plaintiff relies on public information, easily assembled and widely available, that can be effectively rebutted by other public evidence'. *Id.* at 66–7. He interprets the *Twombly* decision as setting forth a 'mini-summary judgment' standard authorizing judges to evaluate the persuasiveness of the facts pled by a plaintiff and to dismiss the claims if the facts fail to make out a reasonable conspiracy case. *Id.* at 81.

[6]　One commentator stated that *Twombly*'s plausibility standard represents a significant departure from the 'liberal ethos' of notice pleading, which traditionally required only minimal

In the Supreme Court's May 2009 decision in *Ashcroft v. Iqbal*,[7] the Court confirmed that the pleading standard it announced in *Twombly* is applicable to 'all civil actions and proceedings in the United States district courts'.[8] The Court's decision in *Iqbal* dispelled any possibility that *Twombly*'s 'plausibility' requirement would be applied only to antitrust cases or to another well-defined set of civil causes of action alleging some form of conspiracy or potentially engendering massive discovery costs. Irrespective of their assessments of *Twombly*'s merits, most commentators agree that the case represents a landmark civil procedure decision.[9] With respect to antitrust law, many commentators have predicted that *Twombly* will have a chilling effect on plaintiff prosecution of conspiracy claims because its holding imposes a heightened, perhaps even unfairly elevated, standard specifically for antitrust conspiracy plaintiffs.[10]

By far the most pronounced and consistent reaction to *Twombly*'s holding is that it is confusing. Across the spectrum of reactions, courts and commentators have described the standard to evaluate a Rule 12(b)(6) motion announced by Justice Souter's majority opinion as somewhat unclear, calling it 'inartfully drafted',[11] 'fuzzy',[12] 'ambiguous',[13]

---

factual specificity and tolerated conclusory legal terms. The 'liberal ethos' of notice pleading was committed to 'the facilitation of litigant access in the interest of reaching merits-based resolutions of cases'. Benjamin Spencer, *Plausibility Pleading*, 49 B.C. L. REV. 431, 479 (2008). Spencer asserts that *Twombly* represents 'the latest and perhaps final chapter in a long saga that has moved the federal civil system from a liberal to a restrictive ethos'. *Id.* See also Saritha Komatireddy Tice, *Recent Developments: A 'Plausible' Explanation of Pleading Standards:* Bell Atlantic Corp. v. Twombly, 31 HARV. J.L. AND PUB. POL'Y 827, 830 (2008) ('The Court's decision in *Twombly* is an important change. It reflects a significant shift away from the litigation-promoting mindset embodied in *Conley* and instead solidifies what has been a growing hostility toward litigation. The decision, however, gives lower courts and plaintiffs little guidance on the future of pleading standards, leaving lower courts to define precisely the meaning of the "plausibility" standard and requiring plaintiffs simply to divine what is expected of them . . . The implications of *Twombly* extend far beyond the field of antitrust. The decision reaches toward the foundations of what it means for a civil complaint to be sufficient').

[7]   Ashcroft v. Iqbal, 129 S. Ct. 1937 (2009).

[8]   *Id.* at 1953 (quoting FED. R. CIV. P. 1).

[9]   See, e.g., Scott Dodson, *Pleading Standards After* Bell Atlantic Corp. v. Twombly, 93 VA. L. REV. BRIEF 135, 137–8 (2007) ('*Bell Atlantic* is a significant statement from the Court from a proceduralist perspective (even if perhaps unremarkable from an antitrust perspective)'); Ettie Ward, *The After-Shocks of* Twombly: *Will We 'Notice' Pleading Changes?*, 82 ST. JOHN'S L. REV. 893, 910–19 (2008).

[10]   '*Twombly* will shrink substantially the ability of antitrust plaintiffs to file a complaint and find conspiracies through discovery.' Randal C. Picker, Twombly, Leegin *and the Reshaping of Antitrust*, SUP. CT. REV. 161, 164 (2008); Ward, *supra* note 9, at 910–11.

[11]   Martin H. Redish and Lee Epstein, Bell Atlantic v. Twombly *and the Future of Pleading in the Federal Courts: A Normative and Empirical Analysis* 24 (Research Symposium on Empirical Studies of Civil Liability, 10 October 2008). Redish and Epstein state that the 'confusion in the district courts over the meaning of *Twombly* is staggering'. *Id.*

[12]   Epstein, *supra* note 5, at 77.

[13]   'Because *Twombly*'s holding is somewhat ambiguous, however, lower courts and plaintiffs' lawyers have significant leeway to tease out the meaning of "plausibility" in different contexts.' Tice, *supra* note 6, at 827. 'The Court's decision creates uncertainty among lower courts and practitioners.' *Id.* at 838.

'sending mixed messages',[14] and introducing '[c]onsiderable uncertainty concerning the standard for assessing the adequacy of pleadings'.[15] We believe that as a matter of antitrust jurisprudence, *Twombly* deserves a more favorable reception. To support our argument, we review the history of a number of key antitrust decisions that addressed the requirements of section 1 at different procedural stages. We also offer a conceptual scheme for understanding the development of this line of cases that addresses what is required of a plaintiff to show a horizontal agreement. Drawing on simple applications of probability, we present a formalization of the rules announced in those decisions. We endeavor to show that *Twombly*'s holding in many ways helps to formalize and make more definite the rules enunciated in prior Supreme Court cases addressing the question of what is required at different procedural stages to establish a section 1 violation.

The conceptual task of *defining* an unlawful agreement under section 1 and the evidentiary or procedural one of delineating what is required to *show* (or *plead*, as the case may be) the existence of such an agreement as a matter of substantive antitrust law and civil procedure are closely tied. Indeed, attending to the former would seem to be a prerequisite to addressing the latter: namely, how does the existence of an agreement differ from independent or interdependent firm behavior? Many use the term 'independent' firm behavior to characterize firm decisions that do not rely on the anticipated actions of other firms as a *ground* or *basis* for the firm's decision, even if the firm is aware of or can anticipate the reactions of other firms. For example, if the price of an important input were to increase, the price of each firm in a perfectly competitive market would increase. But the fact that other firms' prices are expected to rise is not the basis of the firm's decision, although it anticipates that reaction to the input price increase. Independent behavior is often contrasted with 'interdependent' behavior where, in making its price and quantity decisions, a firm expressly considers the content of other firms' price and quantity decisions in reaction to its own, and the expected course of action of other firms affects the content of the firm's decision.[16]

As many have pointed out, whether a firm's decision about its price, quantity, or other strategy is interdependent in such a way that it runs afoul of section 1 requires specification of the sort of understanding underlying the interdependent behavior that constitutes an *illegal agreement*.[17] A firm can choose to price above the competitive level in the expectation that other firms will also do so pursuant to an explicit unlawful arrangement it has with them, or a firm can choose such a price above the competitive level with the strategic expectation that other firms will also do so. Both types of behavior are independently executed but

---

[14]   'Justice Souter's opinion, joined by all but two dissenters, sent mixed messages on pleadings to the bench and bar.' Ward, *supra* note 9, at 904.

[15]   *Iqbal v. Hasty*, 490 F.3d 143, 155 (2d Cir. 2007), rev'd and remanded, 129 S. Ct. 1937 (2009).

[16]   See Kaplow, *supra* note 4, at 11–13; Richard A. Posner, *Oligopoly and the Antitrust Laws: A Suggested Approach*, 21 STAN. L. REV. 1562, 1564 (1969).

[17]   See, e.g., Kaplow, *supra* note 4, at 10–17; Posner, *supra* note 16, at 1576 (stating that '[t]here is no distortion of accepted meanings, however, in viewing what I have termed tacit collusion as a form of concerted rather than unilateral activity'); Donald F. Turner, *The Definition of Agreement Under the Sherman Act: Conscious Parallelism and Refusals to Deal*, 75 HARV. L. REV. 655, 666 (1962) (stating that 'there is fair ground for argument that oligopoly price behavior can be described as individual behavior – rational individual decision in the light of relevant economic facts – as well as it can be described as "agreement"').

interdependently calculated, and whether the latter is an unlawful form of 'tacit collusion' proscribed by section 1 is a question that has long divided courts and commentators alike.[18]

Here we use the term 'independent' to characterize that class of behavior that could be interdependent but *not* pursuant to an illegal agreement. Of course, this begs the question of definition of an illegal agreement, but for now we bracket that question. At a later point in the chapter, we shall discuss how this question of definition merges with our question at hand, which is the evidentiary or procedural question of what is required to plead or to show an illegal agreement. In section VIII we discuss how the open definitional question of whether or not 'tacit collusion' constitutes an illegal agreement under section 1 interfaces with our task of formalizing the evidentiary rules we explore.

The primary target of our interpretive task is the Supreme Court's 2007 decision in *Twombly*, which is the most recent installment in a line of cases that has addressed the requirements for establishing the existence of an agreement as a matter of substantive antitrust law and civil procedure. We begin, in section II, by locating *Twombly* in the context of Sherman Act section 1 jurisprudence that courts have adopted to try to minimize overall expected error costs in deciding conspiracy cases. In section III, we describe a leading – perhaps the leading – approach that courts have followed in delineating the types of facts a plaintiff relying on circumstantial evidence must adduce to prove her section 1 conspiracy claim, the doctrine commonly know as 'plus factors'. This discussion is complemented in section IV by an account of how *Monsanto Co. v. Spray-Rite Corp.*[19] and *Matsushita Electric Industrial Co. v. Zenith Radio Corp.*[20] together set the standard for how much of that type of evidence such a plaintiff needs to offer to withstand a motion for summary judgment. In these sections we introduce a conceptual distinction between the *type* and *quantum* of proof and argue that it is key to understanding and formalizing the rules announced in the line of cases addressing evidentiary sufficiency of section 1 claims. Consequently, this duality will help us distinguish the issues in *Monsanto* and *Matsushita* from the motion to dismiss question addressed in *Twombly*.

We bring these two elements of types of evidence and quantum of evidence together in section V, where we describe how the circuit courts integrated the consideration of plus factors and the holding in *Matsushita* into a test the plaintiff must pass at the summary judgment stage. In this section we introduce the notation of Bayesian probability to formalize the tests that have emerged across the circuit courts for section 1 plaintiffs to withstand summary judgment. This formalization is helpful for the final sections, where we seek to distinguish the reigning tests for summary judgment from the standard announced in *Twombly* for a motion to dismiss on the pleadings.

The case of principal concern, *Twombly*, takes center stage in section VI, where we describe the difference between the district court's and the Second Circuit's analyses of the case, and in section VII, which takes up the argument between the parties at the Supreme Court. Finally, in section VIII, we offer our reading of the Supreme Court's

---

[18]   This was the subject of the famous Posner–Turner debate. See Posner, *supra* note 16; Turner, *supra* note 17. See also Posner's brief discussion in *JTC Petroleum Co. v. Piasa Motor Fuels, Inc.*, 190 F.3d 775, 780 (7th Cir. 1999); and Alan Devlin, Note, *A Proposed Solution to the Problem of Parallel Pricing in Oligopolistic Markets*, 59 STAN. L. REV. 1111 (2007).

[19]   Monsanto Co. v. Spray-Rite Corp., 465 U.S. 752 (1984).

[20]   Matsushita Elec. Indus. Co. v. Zenith Radio Corp., 475 U.S. 574 (1986).

Twombly decision and propose a formalization of our interpretation again using the notation of Bayesian probability. The latter helps to distinguish our proposed reading of the case's holding from the settled doctrine around summary judgment. We briefly conclude in section IX with remarks on the future of *Twombly*'s 'plausibility' standard and the task of proving horizontal agreements in the future.

Some brief background on the *Twombly* case is helpful. The plaintiffs comprised a class of telephone and Internet service users. The class filed a complaint alleging that five incumbent local exchange carriers (ILECs), or incumbent local telecommunication companies, violated section 1 of the Sherman Act by conspiring in two respects to monopolize and restrain trade in their respective geographic markets inherited from the breakup of AT&T. The plaintiffs alleged that the ILECs conspired to resist the mandates of the Telecommunications Act of 1996[21] by erecting unlawful barriers against the entrance of competitive local exchange carriers (CLECs) into the incumbent telecommunication companies' respective territories and by mutually agreeing not to compete in the territories of another ILEC.[22] In 2003 the District Court for the Southern District of New York dismissed the class plaintiffs' complaint for failure to state a claim; it held that the complaint alleged only parallel conduct and failed to specify 'plus factors' that would 'tend[ ] to exclude independent self-interested conduct as an explanation for defendants' parallel behavior'.[23] The Second Circuit reversed the district court's dismissal as it held that 'plus factors are not required to be pleaded to permit an antitrust claim based on parallel conduct to survive dismissal'.[24]

The Supreme Court reversed the Second Circuit's decision and remanded the case for further proceedings consistent with the Supreme Court's opinion. Justice Souter's opinion rehearsed the general pleading standards that had been developed to evaluate a complaint attacked by a motion to dismiss for failure to state a claim and then applied 'these general standards to a § 1 claim', holding that 'stating such a claim requires a complaint with enough factual matter (taken as true) to suggest that an agreement was made'.[25] Although the Court claimed merely to apply the traditional general Rule 12(b)(6) standard, it made a point of 'retiring'[26] the famous language from *Conley v. Gibson* that had guided federal courts for decades, which stated the standard as follows: 'the accepted rule [is] that a complaint should not be dismissed for failure to state a claim unless it appears beyond doubt that the plaintiff can prove no set of facts in support of his claim which would entitle him to relief'.[27] After rejecting the *Conley* 'no set of facts' standard, the Court articulated a novel 'plausibility' standard to evaluate a complaint that is subject to a motion to dismiss for failure to state a claim. It held that a plaintiff must plead 'facts that are suggestive enough to render a § 1 conspiracy plausible'.[28]

---

[21]   Pub. L. No. 104-104, 110 Stat. 56 (1996).

[22]   Amended Complaint at para. 47, Twombly v. Bell Atl. Corp., 313 F. Supp. 2d 174 (S.D.N.Y. 2003) (No. 02 CIV. 10220 (GEL)) (quoted in Bell Atl. Corp. v. Twombly, 550 U.S. 544, 549–53 (2007)).

[23]   *Twombly*, 313 F. Supp. 2d at 179.

[24]   Twombly v. Bell Atl. Corp., 425 F.3d 99, 114 (2d Cir. 2005).

[25]   *Twombly*, 550 U.S. at 555–6.

[26]   '[A]fter puzzling the profession for 50 years, this famous observation has earned its retirement.' *Id.* at 563.

[27]   Conley v. Gibson, 355 U.S. 41, 45–6 (1957).

[28]   *Twombly*, 550 U.S. at 556. The Supreme Court opinion will be discussed at length, see section VII. A few other quotations give a sense of the Court's explanation of the standard: 'allegations

Some of the *Twombly* commentary seems to assume that because the Supreme Court reversed the Second Circuit in favor of the defendants, it implicitly endorsed the district court's or petitioner-defendants' position and rejected all of the Second Circuit's reasoning. Such an interpretation would indeed mark the *Twombly* standard as significantly heightened over the test historically employed for a motion to dismiss. Under such an interpretation, applying the *Twombly* standard most likely would be equivalent to applying the summary judgment standard to the allegations in the complaint.[29] Many commentators' discussions of the decision suggest that they understand it in precisely such terms. For example, arguing that the *Twombly* decision merely underscored the importance of 'substantive sufficiency' in the pleading, Allan Ides states that the Supreme Court held that a claim alleging 'parallel conduct unsupported by plus-factor evidence . . . as the sole basis for establishing the existence of an anti-competitive agreement' is insufficient to survive a Rule 12(b)(6) motion.[30] Ides argues that 'inferences allowed at the pleading stage must be the same as the inferences available at the "proof" stage', lest we 'permit a complaint that was materially deficient as a matter of law – no allegations or inferences of an agreement – to survive a Rule 12(b)(6) motion to dismiss'.[31] Richard Epstein also endorses a reading of *Twombly* that equates the summary judgment and motion to dismiss standards where the plaintiffs are relying on 'public' factual information to state the claim.[32] He argues, moreover, that this is the correct outcome on the merits.[33]

Various other commentators, while not necessarily endorsing such a standard, have also read *Twombly* as bringing the motion to dismiss standard close to the summary judgment standard, if not equating the two. Randal Picker characterizes the case as follows: 'In *Twombly*, in a 7–2 decision authored by Justice Souter, the Court transplanted its prior decision in *Matsushita* regarding summary judgment standards to a motion to dismiss for failure to state a claim (Rule 12(b)(6))'.[34] A major antitrust treatise also interprets the Supreme Court's plausibility standard as equivalent to the district court's plus factor pleading requirement: 'the Supreme Court recently indicated that the plus factor must be alleged within the complaint itself in order to survive a motion to dismiss'.[35] Finally, Ettie Ward observes that equating the two standards is a fair reading of the Court's 'sleight-of-hand'.[36]

---

of parallel conduct . . . placed in a context that raises a suggestion of a preceding agreement', *id.* at 557; 'allegations plausibly suggesting (not merely consistent with) agreement', *id*; 'enough facts to state a claim to relief that is plausible on its face', *id.* at 570.

[29] See, e.g., Ward, *supra* note 9, at 916–17, asking if *Twombly*'s holding was in fact 'conflating the standards for motions to dismiss and motions for summary judgment and directed verdicts' by 'sleight-of-hand'.

[30] Allan Ides, Bell Atlantic *and the Principle of Substantive Sufficiency Under Federal Rule of Civil Procedure 8(a)(2): Toward a Structured Approach to Pleading Practice*, 243 F.R.D. 604, 627 (2006).

[31] *Id.* at 628.

[32] Epstein, *supra* note 5, at 79–81.

[33] *Id.* at 62.

[34] Picker, *supra* note 10, at 162 (footnotes omitted).

[35] 2 ANTITRUST LAWS AND TRADE REGULATION: DESK EDITION (MB) § 11.02[2].

[36] 'This directed verdict and summary judgment standard based on "evidence" somehow morphs into an appropriate pleading standard.' Ward, *supra* note 9, at 917.

We share the concerns of those commentators alarmed at the possible chilling effect of a stringent pleading standard on the private enforcement of antitrust laws. We believe, however, that there is a reading of *Twombly* – indeed the most compelling reading of it – that does not necessitate such an outcome in the area of antitrust. Our interpretation comes from within the context of the common law development of section 1 of the Sherman Act. We argue that one can make sense of *Twombly*'s holding only by viewing the case in light of the progression of those decisions that have sought to articulate justiciable standards for antitrust plaintiffs alleging conspiracy while balancing the risk of chilling legitimate business activity against the risk of discouraging legitimate prosecution of the antitrust laws. Viewed in this light, we shall argue that *Twombly*'s 'plausibility' standard should not be interpreted as a heightened, ratcheted-up test for section 1 plaintiffs. If *Twombly* does not introduce new stringent requirements in the antitrust context in which it was decided, then perhaps it ought not to be interpreted as imposing new stringent requirements on pleading in other civil causes of action.

Although the *Twombly* Court reversed the Second Circuit's decision and remanded the case to the district court for further proceedings consistent with the Court's opinion, we shall argue that the Supreme Court's decision should not be read as a vindication of the defendants' litigation position or necessarily an endorsement of the district court's opinion that was overturned by the Second Circuit. The lower court decisions, as well as the briefs and arguments submitted to the Supreme Court, reveal a debate over the appropriateness of applying terms and standards from the summary judgment context to the motion to dismiss phase. But these terms and standards are conspicuously absent from the Supreme Court's final decision. Instead, the Court forged a noticeably novel standard for the motion to dismiss. It held that a complaint that alleges nothing more than parallel conduct is not sufficient to withstand a motion to dismiss.[37] The Court went on to hold that a plaintiff must identify in the complaint 'facts that are suggestive enough to render a § 1 conspiracy plausible',[38] and it determined that in *Twombly* itself 'the plaintiffs rest their § 1 claim on descriptions of parallel conduct and not on any independent allegation of actual agreement'.[39]

To be sure, the Supreme Court sought to make clear, as it had in a line of other cases concerning other stages of section 1 conspiracy litigation, that at the pleading stage as well *something* more than allegations of mere parallel conduct is necessary. The *Twombly* decision did *not*, however, as the petitioners and their amici urged in briefs and arguments to the Court, equate the standard for evaluating the motion to dismiss with the standard for ruling on a defendant's motion for summary judgment in the context of antitrust law. It also did not vindicate the 'plus factor pleading rule' promoted in the district court's opinion, one that would at minimum import much of the doctrinal baggage from the summary judgment standard, if not set the substantive standard precisely at the same level. We shall argue that the 'plausibility' standard articulated by Justice Souter was not 'fuzzy'[40] for lack of analytical clarity on the part of the opinion's author, but rather

---

[37]   Bell Atl. Corp. v. Twombly, 550 U.S. 544, 556–7 (2007).
[38]   *Id.* at 556.
[39]   *Id.* at 564.
[40]   Epstein, *supra* note 5, at 77.

intentionally indeterminate consistent with antitrust's common law tradition of allowing lower courts to articulate and elaborate workable and economically intelligent standards through the process of applying the standard to a range of factual contexts.

Moreover, in recognition of the principles inherent in the Federal Rules of Civil Procedure's notice pleading regime, this novel language establishes a standard distinct from the summary judgment standard. The summary judgment standard is used to assess the *evidentiary sufficiency* of the plaintiff's case after the conclusion of discovery to determine if she has amassed sufficient proof to submit a question of fact to the jury. But the motion to dismiss standard governs assessment of the *legal sufficiency* of the plaintiff's complaint to determine if the plaintiff has sufficient grounds for her claim in the law and in the facts she has pled to proceed to discovery. Our interpretation of *Twombly* is compelling because it respects this distinction.

In this chapter we offer an alternative reading of *Twombly* as we interpret its language in the context of the lower court decisions the Supreme Court reviewed and the arguments of the parties before it, and we place the decision in the historical context of the common law development of section 1 of the Sherman Act. Using these interpretive guideposts to examine *Twombly*'s holding, we find that although *Twombly* does indeed make clear that antitrust plaintiffs must satisfy a specific substantive standard (which we describe below), the standard is not nearly so rigid and elevated as some have feared. In announcing the novel 'plausibility' standard, the Supreme Court self-consciously rejected articulations of the motion to dismiss standard advanced by the defendants and in the district court opinion that would have fashioned it in the image of the summary judgment standard. We shall endeavor to show that Justice Souter's majority opinion rejected that equivalence in favor of a flexible standard compatible with the notice pleading paradigm.

Indeed, we find the articulated 'plausibility' standard to be quite in line with the flexible, pragmatically evolving common law rules that have developed to make the Sherman Act's broad and vague proscriptions at once justiciable and adaptable. Although we share the concerns Justice Stevens articulated in his dissent regarding the importance of protecting the notice pleading regime,[41] we believe our reading of *Twombly* could neutralize many of the decision's most troubling implications, at least in the area of antitrust law. If we are right that *Twombly*'s holding in the context of antitrust does not imply a major tightening of the standard under which antitrust complaints are evaluated for legal sufficiency, then perhaps the decision and its application in *Iqbal* do not spell the end of the notice pleading regime after all.

II   *TWOMBLY'S* COMMON LAW CONTEXT: THE DILEMMA OF SECTION 1

The most compelling interpretation of *Twombly* considers the case in the context of the historical common law development of antitrust law of which it is a part. A major issue in that development has been the forging of justiciable standards for section 1 cases that allow plaintiffs legitimately pleading conspiracy to proceed on the basis of circumstantial

---

[41]   *Twombly*, 550 U.S. at 570 (Stevens, J., dissenting).

evidence without punishing or, through the threat of punishment, chilling lawful business activity. Allowing plaintiffs to proceed with circumstantial evidence for a section 1 claim represents a concession to the actual circumstances in which conspiracy claims arise: sophisticated defendants avoid making direct records of their unlawful agreements, and directly probative evidence is most often under the defendants' control. At various points in the history of section 1 jurisprudence, the Supreme Court has given lower courts standards to apply at various procedural points regarding the type and quantum of evidence required of a plaintiff who relies on circumstantial evidence of conspiracy.

Twombly should be viewed as the newest episode in this long-running doctrinal drama produced by the tensions inherent in section 1 of the Sherman Act. The prohibitions are fairly straightforward: 'Every contract, combination in the form of trust or otherwise, or conspiracy, in restraint of trade or commerce . . . is declared to be illegal'.[42] But courts have faced a central dilemma in determining justiciable standards of proof necessary to demonstrate a 'contract, combination, . . . or conspiracy' in restraint of trade. On the one hand, courts are concerned with Type I errors or false positives that result when a decision punishes parallel, even consciously parallel, business behavior that is not undertaken pursuant to an explicit agreement among rivals.[43] Parallel business choices, whether with regard to price, output, distribution policy, responses to new entrants, or any other strategic variable, may often have benign justifications. For example, competing businesses in a concentrated industry face the same market signals, and all the firms may independently make similar choices based on independent calculations of their own self-interest. In tight oligopolistic markets, interdependent firms may be able to calculate the optimal price and production levels by correctly anticipating their rivals' reactions, with the result that conduct that may appear to be coordinated is actually the result of independently chosen acts.

On the other hand, courts are also concerned with Type II errors or false negatives that result from the failure to punish conspirators who do undertake parallel conduct pursuant to an agreement to restrain trade but go unpunished because no direct proof of the agreement can be had. Sophisticated business agents attempting to restrain trade in violation of the law are cognizant of the criminal and civil penalties prescribed by the Sherman Act, and they therefore avoid creating any record of unlawful activities and take steps to conceal any unlawful coordination undertaken in furtherance of a conspiracy.[44] Therefore, plaintiffs seeking to establish the existence of an agreement often cannot identify any direct proof of conspiracy.

Doctrinal constructions of section 1 have navigated between these two concerns in an

---

[42]   15 U.S.C. § 1 (2006).

[43]   Richard Epstein argues that we should not weigh false positives and false negatives equally in the determination of antitrust principles because market forces tend to inhibit the formation and stability of conspiracies, and because chilling lawful business activity is more costly than not punishing the occasional conspiracy. Epstein, *supra* note 5, at 68. This claim entails complex questions of both fact and value, and its validity is, at a minimum, contestable.

[44]   The Department of Justice, Antitrust Division has sought to overcome this informational disadvantage by instituting what it calls the 'leniency program', offering both corporations and individuals the possibility of avoiding criminal conviction and sanctions if they are the first members of a conspiracy to confess, were not the cartel leaders, and fully cooperate with the investigation. See Leniency Program: Antitrust Division, available at www.usdoj.gov/atr/public/criminal/leniency.htm.

attempt to attain the appropriate balance between overdeterrence and underdeterrence. In the course of Sherman Act litigation, the Supreme Court has issued a number of decisions, applicable to various procedural postures, that attempt to fashion justiciable standards that steer between the risks of punishing parallel but lawful behavior and the risks of disregarding unlawful conspiracies because legitimate plaintiffs cannot produce direct proof.

Given these dual concerns, questions naturally arose as to the kind and quantum of evidence sufficient to prove conspiracy under section 1. Must plaintiffs put forward direct evidence of an express or implied agreement, or may they put forward circumstantial evidence from which the existence of an agreement can be inferred? Beginning in the late 1930s, the Supreme Court recognized what has come to be known as the doctrine of 'conscious parallelism' that allows, under some circumstances, a plaintiff to make out a case of conspiracy from evidence that several competitors acted in a similar fashion with knowledge that each would take the same course of action. In *Interstate Circuit, Inc., v. United States*, the Supreme Court upheld a finding of section 1 conspiracy on purely circumstantial evidence.[45] Here, eight film distributors undertook the same actions after receiving from two related theater chains a letter demanding minimum prices on second-run showings (and a restriction on double features), and listing the addresses of all competitors receiving a copy of the letter.[46] The Court explained:

> It is elementary that an unlawful conspiracy may be and often is formed without simultaneous action or agreement on the part of the conspirators. Acceptance by competitors, without previous agreement, of an invitation to participate in a plan, the necessary consequence of which, if carried out, is restraint of interstate commerce, is sufficient to establish an unlawful conspiracy under the Sherman Act.[47]

In 1946, the Court in *American Tobacco Co. v. United States*[48] addressed the evidentiary requirement for showing a conspiracy based on circumstantial evidence, although largely in dicta because certiorari was granted to decide if actual exclusion of competitors was a necessary element of section 2 conspiracy to monopolize. The Court held that antitrust plaintiffs need not adduce direct evidence of a formal explicit agreement. It said:

> No formal agreement is necessary to constitute an unlawful conspiracy. Often crimes are a matter of inference deduced from the acts of the person accused and done in pursuance of a

---

45   Interstate Circuit, Inc. v. United States, 306 U.S. 208 (1939).

46   *Id.* at 226–7. The Court held: 'While the District Court's finding of an agreement of the distributors among themselves is supported by the evidence, we think that in the circumstances of this case such agreement for the imposition of the restrictions upon subsequent-run exhibitors was not a prerequisite to an unlawful conspiracy. It was enough that, knowing that concerted action was contemplated and invited, the distributors gave their adherence to the scheme and participated in it. Each distributor was advised that the others were asked to participate; each knew that cooperation was essential to successful operation of the plan. They knew that the plan, if carried out, would result in a restraint of commerce, which, we will presently point out, was unreasonable within the meaning of the Sherman Act, and knowing it, all participated in the plan. The evidence is persuasive that each distributor early became aware that the others had joined'. *Id.*

47   *Id.* at 227 (citations omitted).

48   Am. Tobacco Co. v. United States, 328 U.S. 781 (1946).

criminal purpose. Where the conspiracy is proved, as here, from the evidence of the action taken in concert by the parties to it, it is all the more convincing proof of an intent to exercise the power of exclusion acquired through that conspiracy. The essential combination or conspiracy in violation of the Sherman Act may be found in a course of dealing or other circumstances as well as in an exchange of words. Where the circumstances are such as to warrant a jury in finding that the conspirators had a unity of purpose or a common design and understanding, or a meeting of minds in an unlawful arrangement, the conclusion that a conspiracy is established is justified.[49]

This doctrine of conscious parallelism thus developed to address the Court's concern with false negatives – allowing conspiracies in restraint of trade to go unpunished because plaintiffs were not able to locate and put forward direct evidence of an agreement.

The Court, however, has also been concerned with Type I errors (false positives) – punishing behavior that is parallel but *not* the result of an illegal agreement or conspiracy in restraint of trade. The Court has been careful to maintain a clear requirement that a plaintiff, whether she relies on direct or circumstantial evidence, must demonstrate the existence of an *agreement* as opposed to merely demonstrating parallel behavior, which by itself is not in violation of the Sherman Act. One of the most cited statements for this proposition comes from *Theatre Enterprises, Inc. v. Paramount Film Distributing Corp.*:

> this Court has never held that proof of parallel business behavior conclusively establishes agreement or, phrased differently, that such behavior itself constitutes a Sherman Act offense. Circumstantial evidence of consciously parallel behavior may have made heavy inroads into the traditional judicial attitude toward conspiracy; but 'conscious parallelism' has not yet read conspiracy out of the Sherman Act entirely.[50]

Together, *Theatre Enterprises, Interstate Circuit,* and *American Tobacco* instructed lower courts that something more than mere parallel conduct must be demonstrated to make out a section 1 violation based on circumstantial evidence. This left lower courts with two tasks. First, they had to identify the *types* of evidence that should qualify as the 'something more' necessary to augment evidence of parallel conduct to make out a section 1 case. Second, lower courts needed to determine the *level* of probative sufficiency to which such evidence must rise to justify a finding of conspiracy by the trier of fact. Although these questions are closely related, it is conceptually useful to separate them. The first question relates to the *types* of facts a plaintiff must put forward to make out a violation of section 1 on circumstantial evidence; the latter concerns the *level* of evidentiary sufficiency that the plaintiff's entire set of evidence must attain to establish his claim.

III   THE SOLUTION OF PLUS FACTORS: TYPE OF PROOF

Lower courts pioneered a solution to the problem of developing evidentiary standards for section 1 that would accurately distinguish between conspiracy and merely parallel

---

[49]   *Id.* at 809–10. The Court went on to say, 'Neither proof of exertion of the power to exclude nor proof of actual exclusion of existing or potential competitors is essential to sustain a charge of monopolization under the Sherman Act'. *Id* at 810.

[50]   Theatre Enterprises, Inc. v. Paramount Film Distrib. Corp., 346 U.S. 537, 540 (1954). In *Theatre Enterprises,* the Court postulated that the defendants' behavior was not interdependent.

behavior – namely, the doctrine of 'plus factors'.[51] Courts sought to identify a type of evidence that, when presented in conjunction with evidence of parallel behavior, could give rise to a legitimate inference of conspiracy and thus allow a reasonable jury to find for the plaintiff.

The first reference to the term 'plus factor' in a federal case dates to 1952 in the Ninth Circuit case *C-O-Two Fire Equipment Co. v. United States*.[52] This was an appeal from a bench trial decision finding that the defendants had violated section 1 of the Sherman Act by conspiring to fix prices as well as the terms and conditions of sale of portable fire extinguishers in Southern California. The defendants challenged the legal sufficiency of the evidence by arguing that the proof offered at trial consisted solely of circumstantial evidence showing parallel behavior without any direct proof of conspiracy. The appeals court noted that antitrust violations could be made out on circumstantial evidence alone where, as in the case at issue, the court has evidence:

> in addition to price uniformity, [of] the other so-called plus factors hereinbefore treated . . . [which] include a background of illegal licensing agreements containing minimum price maintenance provisions, an artificial standardization of product, a raising of prices at a time when a surplus existed in the industry, and a policing of dealers to effectuate the maintenance of minimum price provisions in accordance with price lists published and distributed by the corporate defendants.[53]

The court concluded that these 'so-called plus factors' considered in concert with the parallel pricing behavior constituted 'facts . . . not only consistent with the guilt of appellants, but also inconsistent with any other reasonable hypothesis'.[54]

The next federal court case to employ the term was *Delaware Valley Marine Supply Co. v. American Tobacco Co.* in 1961.[55] The Third Circuit upheld a directed verdict for the defendants, a number of tobacco companies that had individually declined to sell cigarettes to an upstart company looking to market to ships in port in Philadelphia.[56] The Circuit Court affirmed the dismissal because it found that the plaintiffs had adduced evidence of only conscious (or in some instances unconscious) parallel conduct. In a footnote the court noted:

> In other cases utilizing the theory of conscious parallelism to find conspiracy, at least two of the following three circumstances are present: 'plus' factors such as those emphasized in the simple refusal to deal cases; parallelism of a much more elaborate and complex nature; a web of circumstantial evidence pointing very convincingly to the ultimate fact of agreement.[57]

---

[51]   See generally PHILLIP E. AREEDA AND HERBERT HOVENKAMP, 6 ANTITRUST LAW: AN ANALYSIS OF ANTITRUST PRINCIPLES AND THEIR APPLICATION para. 1434 (2d ed. 2003); 2 ANTITRUST LAWS AND TRADE REGULATION: DESK EDITION § 11.02[2][b][i].

[52]   C-O-Two Fire Equip. Co. v. United States, 197 F.2d 489, 493 (9th Cir. 1952).

[53]   *Id.* at 497.

[54]   *Id.*

[55]   Delaware Valley Marine Supply Co. v. Am. Tobacco Co., 297 F.2d 199 (3d Cir. 1961).

[56]   *Id.* at 201. The plaintiff company approached several major tobacco companies requesting a 'direct listing' that would enable it to purchase cigarettes tax-free. Each company denied the request citing prior business relationships or sufficient direct suppliers in the port area selling the defendant's products.

[57]   *Id.* at 205 n.19 (citations omitted).

Various textbooks soon began citing the term 'plus factors' to refer to that class of evidence courts had recognized as necessary for a plaintiff without direct evidence of conspiracy to present in conjunction with parallel conduct to establish a section 1 case. For example, Phillip Areeda's 1967 textbook *Antitrust Analysis* refers to both *Delaware Valley* and *C-O-Two Fire Equipment,* and cites the term 'plus factor' in a section discussing the necessary elements to prove horizontal conspiracy.[58] But the book contains no definition or discussion of the term. Areeda's 1974 edition notes the Ninth Circuit's use of the term 'plus factor' in the *C-O-Two Fire Equipment* case but does not explicate the term in the text or define it as an established doctrinal tool in identifying conspiracy in the face of circumstantial evidence.[59] In the 1981 edition of the textbook, Areeda explicitly uses the term 'plus factor' to describe the additional evidence courts have required to demonstrate a contract, combination, or conspiracy that has been suggested by parallel behavior.[60] He states that courts usually have held that 'parallelism accompanied by some other fact supports a jury verdict or that parallelism is insufficient even to get to the jury unless some other fact is established'.[61] Areeda then goes on to state, 'These other facts that serve to transform parallelism into conspiracy (or that allow a jury to do so) are often characterized as "plus factors"'.[62]

Lawrence Sullivan's 1977 *Handbook of the Law of Antitrust* identifies plus factors as a doctrinal tool used to distinguish unlawful conspiracy from lawful parallel conduct emerging from a line of cases beginning with *Interstate Circuit*.[63] Sullivan states that in each case in which a court has recognized conscious parallelism as the evidentiary basis for inferring conspiracy, 'there was something additional, a "plus factor" as the Ninth Circuit has called it'.[64] He goes on to warn us that '[t]alk about "plus factors" should not lead to a mechanistic response; the question is whether all of the evidence warrants an inference of common, rather than individual, conduct'.[65]

The term plus factor appears in several district court and Circuit Court opinions from the late 1960s through the 1970s, where it usually refers to the evidentiary element a plaintiff must provide in addition to parallel conduct in the context of summary judgment or a directed verdict.[66] These courts generally employed the term consistently with

---

[58]   PHILLIP AREEDA, ANTITRUST ANALYSIS: PROBLEMS, TEXT, CASES 222–3 nn.22–3 and accompanying text (1st ed. 1967).
[59]   PHILLIP AREEDA, ANTITRUST ANALYSIS: PROBLEMS, TEXT, CASES 304 n.44 (2d ed. 1974).
[60]   PHILLIP AREEDA, ANTITRUST ANALYSIS: PROBLEMS, TEXT, CASES 372–4 (3d ed. 1981).
[61]   *Id.* at 372.
[62]   *Id.* at 372–3.
[63]   LAWRENCE A. SULLIVAN, HANDBOOK OF THE LAW OF ANTITRUST 317 (1977).
[64]   *Id.* (referencing the 1952 *C-O-Two* case for the 'plus factor' terminology).
[65]   *Id.*
[66]   See, e.g., Edward J. Sweeney & Sons, Inc. v. Texaco, Inc., 637 F.2d 105, 129 (3d Cir. 1980) (Sloviter, J., dissenting) ('The search for "something more" stems from the line of cases where the plaintiffs have sought to have the trier of fact infer the requisite combination or conspiracy from mere parallel action, usually refusals to deal, when there is no direct evidence of combined action . . . This "plus factor", as it is sometimes called, has been used in the parallel action cases even in the absence of evidence of communication between the alleged conspirators to permit the inference of a combination from external factors. Of course, in this case, there was direct evidence of communication, and therefore the requirement of a "plus factor" for that purpose

Areeda's circular definition – to identify those items of proof that had been recognized in various federal courts as sufficiently probative of a conspiracy that, when presented in conjunction with consciously parallel action, were adequate to raise the proof to the level necessary to survive either a summary judgment motion or a directed verdict motion.

The set of plus factors adduced in section 1 cases covers a wide range of evidence. Borrowing Judge Posner's terms in *In re High Fructose Corn Syrup Antitrust Litigation*, plus factor evidence can be of the 'economic' or 'noneconomic' variety.[67] 'Economic' plus factors relate to the structure of the market, the character of the goods sold by the firms in question and other structural traits that, according to most economic theory, would make it more probable that a conspiracy could be formed, monitored, and sustained. 'Noneconomic' evidence would relate to the opportunity for conspiracy or actual instances of collusion among the defendants in question.

Thus, the doctrine of plus factors developed as an answer to the first question regarding the *types* of facts that a plaintiff relying on circumstantial evidence must put forward to make out a violation of section 1. During this period the term did not entail a specific answer to the second question regarding exactly *how* probative these facts needed to be *in toto* to establish a section 1 violation. At least, the Supreme Court doctrine did not explicitly specify just how probative a lower court judge must find this plus factor evidence to enable the plaintiff to withstand a motion for summary judgment and to allow a trier of fact, whether in a bench or jury trial, to decide the case.

---

is superfluous') (footnotes and internal citations omitted); Gainesville Utilities Dep't v. Florida Power & Light Co., 573 F.2d 292, 301 (5th Cir. 1978) (reviewing the district court's denial of plaintiff's motion for a judgment notwithstanding the verdict and finding that at least one piece of evidence, extensive correspondence between top executives of different companies, constituted a 'so-called plus factor, which, in addition to parallel activity, points so strongly to the existence of a conspiracy that "reasonable men could not arrive at a contrary verdict"') (internal citations omitted); Harlem River Consumers Coop., Inc. v. Associated Grocers of Harlem, Inc., 408 F. Supp. 1251, 1278 (S.D.N.Y. 1976) (granting directed verdict and dismissal with respect to some plaintiffs because 'consciously parallel business behavior does not of itself constitute a violation of the antitrust laws. Some "plus" factors must be present, such as a showing that the actions of the defendants were inconsistent with normal independent business methods') (citations omitted); Seago v. North Carolina Theatres, Inc., 42 F.R.D. 627, 640 (E.D.N.C. 1967) (granting summary judgment because 'Plaintiff has alleged many things which when taken with some other factors, which are lacking here, could be considered evidence of a conspiracy . . . Plaintiff's evidence does not show the required plus factor and, therefore, he has not raised a genuine issue of material fact').

[67] In re High Fructose Corn Syrup Antitrust Litig., 295 F.3d 651, 655 (7th Cir. 2002) ('The evidence upon which a plaintiff will rely will usually be and in this case is of two types – economic evidence suggesting that the defendants were not in fact competing, and non-economic evidence suggesting that they were not competing because they had agreed not to compete. The economic evidence will in turn generally be of two types, and is in this case: evidence that the structure of the market was such as to make secret price fixing feasible (almost any market can be cartelized if the law permits sellers to establish formal, overt mechanisms for colluding, such as exclusive sales agencies); and evidence that the market behaved in a noncompetitive manner').

IV   THE SOLUTION OF *MONSANTO* AND *MATSUSHITA*: QUANTUM OF PROOF

Thirty years after lower federal courts pioneered the doctrine of plus factors to address the question of the *types* of proof necessary to establish a circumstantial section 1 case, the Supreme Court decided two cases that gave lower courts substantive guidance on answering the question of the *level* of proof required. In two important antitrust cases from the 1980s, *Monsanto Co. v. Spray-Rite Service Corp.*[68] and *Matsushita Electric Industrial Co. v. Zenith Radio Corp.*,[69] the Court gave lower courts a specific answer to the second question regarding the requisite probative level to which a plaintiff's circumstantial evidence must rise in two different procedural contexts.

Monsanto presented 'a question as to the standard of proof required to find a vertical price-fixing conspiracy in violation of § 1 of the Sherman Act', and came to the Court in the posture of an appeal from the denial of a motion for a directed verdict for the defendant.[70] The plaintiff, a discount distributor of agricultural chemical products, Spray-Rite, claimed that the termination of its distributorship was executed pursuant to an unlawful agreement between Monsanto, a producer of agricultural herbicides, and various retail distributors conspiring to fix prices and to curtail Spray-Rite's discount operation. Therefore, the case involved both vertical and horizontal conspiracy allegations. The alleged vertical conspiracy consisted of an agreement between Monsanto and its other distributors to set prices above the level at which Spray-Rite was selling Monsanto's products. The alleged horizontal conspiracy consisted of an agreement (tacit or explicit) among distributors to set prices and to refuse to sell directly to Spray-Rite on favorable terms after Monsanto terminated its distributorship.

A jury found the defendants guilty of section 1 violations as it determined that Spray-Rite's dealership was terminated pursuant to a conspiracy between Monsanto and several of the other retailers.[71] On appeal, the Seventh Circuit upheld the jury verdict.[72] The court held that the plaintiff's evidence that its distributorship had been terminated in response to complaints from other distributors regarding its pricing practices was sufficient to survive a motion for a directed verdict.[73] The appeals court determined that proof of termination pursuant to, or merely following, competitor complaints about pricing practices constituted sufficient indirect evidence of concerted action to warrant a jury finding of conspiracy.

The Supreme Court found this standard too permissive. The Court re-articulated its concern that lawful, economically rational, independent conduct not be deterred or punished by allowing an inference of conspiracy to be drawn from ambiguous evidence.[74] It also restated the central tension in section 1 cases, namely, the practical need to rely on circumstantial evidence, which necessarily involves the risk of false positives.[75] Previous

---

[68]   Monsanto Co. v. Spray-Rite Serv. Corp., 465 U.S. 752 (1984).
[69]   Matsushita Elec. Indus. Co. v. Zenith Radio Corp., 475 U.S. 574 (1986).
[70]   *Monsanto*, 465 U.S. at 755.
[71]   *Id*. at 757–8.
[72]   Spray-Rite Serv. Corp. v. Monsanto Co., 684 F.2d 1226, 1232 (7th Cir. 1982).
[73]   *Id*. at 1238.
[74]   *Monsanto*, 465 U.S. at 762–3.
[75]   *Id*. at 760–64.

distributor termination cases, the Court stated, had established two key principles, namely, 'the doctrines enunciated in *Sylvania* and *Colgate*'.[76] In *Colgate*, the Court held that a manufacturer has a 'right to deal, or refuse to deal, with whomever it likes, as long as it does so independently'.[77] In *Sylvania*, the Court determined that nonprice restrictions are 'judged under the rule of reason, which requires a weighing of the relevant circumstances of a case to decide whether a restrictive practice constitutes an unreasonable restraint on competition'.[78] The Court warned, 'If an inference of such an agreement may be drawn from highly ambiguous evidence, there is a considerable danger that the doctrines enunciated in *Sylvania* and *Colgate* will be seriously eroded'.[79]

The Court reiterated that there is a 'basic distinction between concerted and independent action . . . Section 1 of the Sherman Act requires that there be a "contract, combination . . . or conspiracy" between the manufacturer and other distributors in order to establish a violation. Independent action is not proscribed'.[80] Addressing the Seventh Circuit's holding, the Court found that '[t]he flaw in the evidentiary standard adopted by the Court of Appeals in this case is that it disregards this danger [of making false positive errors]'.[81]

The Supreme Court therefore set out to formulate a more rigorous evidentiary standard calibrated to minimize false positives. The Court held that 'something more' than evidence of conduct consistent with individually rational parallel behavior is needed to submit a case to the jury; '[t]here must be evidence that *tends to exclude* the possibility that the manufacturer and nonterminated distributors were acting independently'.[82] Thus, the *Monsanto* Court sought to provide guidance to lower courts that had been operating under a fuzzy standard that allowed merely feasible stories of conspiracy to proceed to a jury. The standard of 'tends to exclude' independent action prescribes a more stringent level of evidentiary sufficiency that a plaintiff must meet to survive a directed verdict motion.

The *Monsanto* standard itself, however, is not crystal clear. The Court does not define or characterize the essential features of 'independent action'. As Judge Posner has emphasized, this important remaining ambiguity has created problems in the lower courts as '[m]ost courts mistakenly regard tacitly collusive behavior as independent and therefore infer from the dictum in *Monsanto* that the plaintiff must negate the possibility that supracompetitive pricing was achieved without explicit agreement'.[83] The Supreme Court has yet to state explicitly whether tacit collusion is prohibited by section 1, and the Circuit Courts and commentators are divided on the question.[84]

---

[76]   *Id.* at 763.
[77]   *Id.* at 761 (referring to United States v. Colgate & Co., 250 U.S. 300, 307 (1919)).
[78]   *Monsanto,* 465 U.S. at 761 (citing Continental T.V., Inc. v. GTE Sylvania Inc., 433 U.S. 36 (1977)).
[79]   *Monsanto,* 465 U.S. at 763.
[80]   *Id.* at 760 (citations omitted).
[81]   *Id.* at 763.
[82]   *Id.* at 764 (emphasis added).
[83]   Richard A. Posner, Antitrust Law 100 (2d ed. 2001). He observes as well how peculiar it is to require a plaintiff 'to prove a sweeping negative'. *Id.*
[84]   See In re High Fructose Corn Syrup Antitrust Litigation, 295 F.3d 651, 654 (7th Cir. 2002), for various cases addressing the issue; and Devlin, *supra* note 18.

Matsushita further specified the *Monsanto* standard in the context of summary judgment. The *Matsushita* plaintiffs, US consumer electronic products manufacturers, alleged that a group of Japanese competitors had conspired to monopolize the American market through predatory pricing in violation of sections 1 and 2 of the Sherman Act. The district court granted the defendants' summary judgment motion, the Third Circuit reversed, and the defendants appealed to the Supreme Court. The Court first noted the general standard for evaluating a summary judgment motion: the moving party must show that there is no 'genuine issue for trial', or, stated otherwise, that the case is one '[w]here the record taken as a whole could not lead a rational trier of fact to find for the nonmoving party'.[85] Applying this general Rule 56 standard to the context of section 1 cases, the Court held: 'To survive petitioners' motion for summary judgment, respondents must establish that there is a genuine issue of material fact *as to whether petitioners entered into an illegal conspiracy* that caused respondents to suffer a cognizable injury'.[86] Here, the 'genuine issue of material fact' does not refer to any potential contestation of the plaintiff's circumstantial evidence, but rather to the fact of conspiracy itself – 'whether petitioners entered into an illegal conspiracy'.[87] The Court went on to say, 'It follows from these settled principles that if the factual context renders respondents' claim implausible – if the claim is one that simply makes no economic sense – respondents must come forward with more persuasive evidence to support their claim than would otherwise be necessary'.[88]

Matsushita did not leave lower courts free to determine varying levels of proof sufficient to present a genuine issue of material fact on the question of conspiracy. Rather, the Court established a substantive level of evidence of conspiracy necessary to pose an issue of material fact and therefore to survive a defendant's motion for summary judgment. The Court arrived at its substantive standard as follows. First, it repeated the oft-stated requirement that on summary judgment all inferences must be drawn in the light most favorable to the nonmoving party.[89] But the Court went on to say that 'antitrust law limits the range of permissible inferences from ambiguous evidence in a § 1 case'.[90] Furthermore, 'in [*Monsanto*], we held that conduct *as consistent with permissible compe-*

---

[85]   Matsushita Elec. Indus. Co. v. Zenith Radio Corp., 475 U.S. 574, 587 (1986) (citations omitted). Note that the Court's reference to viewing the 'record as a whole' in this context reinforced to lower courts that they ought to look at the totality of plaintiff's circumstantial evidence to determine if it substantiates the claim of a conspiracy.

[86]   *Id.* at 585–6 (citing FED. R. CIV. P 56(e)) (emphasis added).

[87]   *Matsushita*, 475 U.S. at 586.

[88]   *Id.* at 587. Note that the *Matsushita* decision employs the language of 'plausibility' at several points. For example, 'In *Monsanto*, we emphasized that courts should not permit factfinders to infer conspiracies when such inferences are implausible, because the effect of such practices is often to deter procompetitive conduct'. *Id.* at 593. '[T]he absence of any plausible motive to engage in the conduct charged is highly relevant to whether a 'genuine issue for trial' exists within the meaning of Rule 56(e). Lack of motive bears on the range of permissible conclusions that might be drawn from ambiguous evidence: if petitioners had no rational economic motive to conspire, and if their conduct is consistent with other, equally plausible explanations, the conduct does not give rise to an inference of conspiracy.' *Id.* at 596–7.

[89]   *Id.* at 587 (quoting United States v. Diebold, Inc., 369 U.S. 654, 655 (1962)).

[90]   *Matsushita*, 475 U.S. at 588.

tition as with illegal conspiracy does not, standing alone, support an inference of antitrust conspiracy'.[91] Therefore, the Court concluded:

> To survive a motion for summary judgment or for a directed verdict, a plaintiff seeking damages for a violation of § 1 must present evidence 'that tends to exclude the possibility' that the alleged conspirators acted independently. Respondents in this case, in other words, must show that the inference of conspiracy is reasonable in light of the competing inferences of independent action or collusive action that could not have harmed respondents.[92]

Matsushita established two principles for lower courts to employ in evaluating a plaintiff's evidence when presented with a motion for summary judgment. First, the evidence must be evaluated as a whole, and the court must consider all possible reasonable inferences that could be drawn from such evidence. The court must comparatively weigh the competing inferences proposed by the plaintiff indicating conspiracy and the reasonable inferences offered by defendants indicating lawful, independent conduct, and the court must determine which is the more likely account.

Second, the Court established a substantive level of evidentiary sufficiency that the totality of this evidence must surpass to create a genuine issue of material fact regarding the question of conspiracy. The *Matsushita* Court stated that to defeat a motion for summary judgment the 'opponent must do more than simply show that there is some metaphysical doubt as to the material facts . . . Where the record taken as a whole could not lead a rational trier of fact to find for the nonmoving party, there is no "genuine issue for trial"'.[93] Because the Court stated that 'conduct as consistent with permissible competition as with illegal conspiracy does not, standing alone, support an inference of antitrust conspiracy', this standard requires that when competing inferences of lawful and unlawful conduct stand as equally plausible, the case must be decided in favor of the defendants.[94] This, in turn, implies the standard a party must meet to withstand a motion for summary judgment: namely, it must be possible that a rational trier of fact could find for the nonmoving party. But the general civil standard requires the trier of fact to find for a party if and only if there is a preponderance of evidence in that party's favor. Hence, *Matsushita* requires that to defeat a motion for summary judgment in an antitrust conspiracy case the plaintiff must establish that there is a positive probability that the evidence adduced yields a probability of nonindependent action that exceeds one-half.

Matsushita's substantive standard thus requires judges to evaluate the totality of the plaintiff's proof at the summary judgment phase to determine if the circumstantial evidence warrants an inference in favor of conspiracy that is stronger than the one in favor of independent action. According to this standard, only if the judge finds that the evidence presented by the plaintiff in opposition to summary judgment warrants a stronger inference of conspiracy may she submit the case to the jury.

The *Matsushita* dissent, written by Justice White and joined by Justices Brennan, Blackmun, and Stevens, expressed concerns that the substantive, evaluative summary

---

[91]   *Id.* (emphasis added).
[92]   *Id.* (quoting Monsanto Co. v. Spray-Rite Service Corp., 465 U.S. 752, 764 (1984)) (citations omitted).
[93]   *Matsushita*, 475 U.S. at 586–7.
[94]   *Id.* at 588.

judgment standard articulated by the majority would encourage a judge to 'invade the factfinder's province'.[95] The dissenting Justices worried that '[s]uch language suggests that a judge hearing a defendant's motion for summary judgment in an antitrust case should go beyond the traditional summary judgment inquiry and decide for himself whether the weight of the evidence favors the plaintiff'.[96] They further argued that *Monsanto* did not require such a conclusion. The dissent understood *Monsanto* to have held that one particular fact proffered alone – namely, post-complaint termination of a dealer by its supplier – was not sufficient to warrant an inference of conspiracy. Contrary to the majority's interpretation, '*Monsanto* does not hold that if a terminated dealer produces some further evidence of conspiracy beyond the bare fact of postcomplaint termination, the judge hearing a motion for summary judgment should balance all the evidence pointing toward conspiracy against all the evidence pointing toward independent action'.[97]

Therefore, there was concern on the sharply divided *Matsushita* Court that the standard articulated by the majority's 'tends to exclude' language was problematic even at the summary judgment phase because it invited the trial judge to engage in a weighing and evaluation of evidence that was inappropriate for that stage of litigation. Whether or not this test is appropriate for the summary judgment inquiry, which takes place *after* the conclusion of at least limited discovery, we shall argue in section VIII that such a test is decidedly not suitable at the motion to dismiss phase. At that much earlier point in the proceedings, the relevant issue is the complaint's legal sufficiency to proceed to discovery, and the plaintiff has not had the benefit of any discovery to establish the factual predicate of the complaint.

This brief overview of central aspects of Sherman Act conspiracy jurisprudence provides essential context for interpreting *Twombly* because its holding can be appropriately understood only against the backdrop of section 1's common law tradition. Section 1's vague yet broad prohibitions presented a set of dilemmas to courts concerned with minimizing the cost of false positive errors while allowing legitimate allegations of conspiracy based on circumstantial evidence to go forward. First, courts had to identify the *types* of evidence that a plaintiff seeking to establish a section 1 conspiracy claim must present in addition to evidence of parallel conduct. Second, courts had to determine just *how* probative such evidence must be to justify a jury finding of conspiracy.

Prior to *Monsanto* and *Matsushita*, lower courts developed the plus factor doctrine in response to the first question. They identified as plus factors those elements of evidence or circumstances that, developed through the common law tradition, they found 'serve to

---

[95]   *Id.* at 601 (White, J., dissenting). Justice Stevens revived similar concerns about the appropriateness of evidentiary assessment in pre-trial litigation phases in his *Twombly* dissent. For example, he criticized the majority's reworking (to retire) the *Conley* standard for a motion to dismiss, saying that the *Conley* Court 'would have understood the majority's remodeling of its language to express an evidentiary standard, which the *Conley* Court had neither need nor want to explicate'. Bell Atl. Corp. v. Twombly, 550 U.S. 544, 580 (2007) (Stevens, J., dissenting). He also stated that recent cases had affirmed that pleadings are not an appropriate stage to judge the merits of a plaintiff's proof. Citing Swierkiewicz v. Sorema N.A., 534 U.S. 506, 511 (2002), Justice Stevens noted, 'We . . . observed that Rule 8(a)(2) does not contemplate a court's passing on the merits of a litigant's claim at the pleading stage'. *Twombly*, 550 U.S. at 585 (Stevens, J., dissenting).

[96]   *Matsushita*, 475 U.S. at 600 (White, J., dissenting).

[97]   *Id.* at 600 n.1.

transform parallelism into conspiracy (or that allow a jury to do so)'.[98] Taking *Monsanto* and *Matsushita* together, the Supreme Court answered the second question by establishing the requisite level of probativeness to which an antitrust plaintiff's circumstantial evidence must rise in a conspiracy case to survive a motion for summary judgment or a motion for a directed verdict as a matter of federal law. The Court held that the plaintiff must present evidence of conspiracy that 'tends to exclude' the possibility of independent conduct.

One plausible interpretation of that phrase would require only that the plaintiff's evidence increases the probability of concerted over independent action. Under this interpretation, the criterion that the evidence 'tends to exclude the possibility of independent action' requires that in light of the evidence (E) the posterior probability of independent action (I) is lower than the prior probability of I based on only the existence of parallel conduct (PC). This could be formalized as follows:

$$P(I \mid PC \text{ \& } E) < P(I \mid PC) \text{ or } P(C \mid PC \text{ \& } E) > P(C \mid PC)$$

where C is conspiracy. We characterize this as the *weak* reading of the *Matsushita* standard because it would require only that plaintiffs adduce some evidence, in addition to parallel conduct, that would make a rational fact-finder revise upwards the inferential probability of conspiracy from a baseline probability of conspiracy given by mere evidence of parallel behavior. It does not specify a *threshold* probability that this revised estimate must surpass, just a *relational* requirement that with the new evidence the behavior is more consistent with conspiracy than it was without the new evidence.

But the Court's other language in *Matsushita* indicates that it intended to require plaintiffs to show more than that to meet its 'tends to exclude' standard. Namely, the Court implies that the plaintiff needs to show that the probability of conspiracy is greater than one-half, that is, $P(C \mid PC \text{ \& } E) > 0.5$.[99] The Court requires that based on the facts adduced at the summary judgment stage, viewing any facts in dispute in the light most favorable to the plaintiff, the weight of the evidence must render a finding of conspiracy more likely than one of independent action. In our notation, it requires $P(C \mid PC \text{ \& } E) > P(I \mid PC \text{ \& } E)$.

This test looks very much like the one that the trier of fact would apply to render a decision if the evidence at the end of the trial consisted of that available at the summary judgment stage, namely, PC & E. In their comparative character and their determination of the totality of the record, the *Matsushita* summary judgment test and the decision rule of the trier are indeed of a piece. But what of the broad understanding of settled law requiring that '[on] summary judgment the inferences to be drawn from the underlying facts . . . must be viewed in the light most favorable to the party opposing the motion'?[100]

A narrow understanding of this requirement would restrict the favorable treatment

---

98   PHILLIP AREEDA, ANTITRUST ANALYSIS: PROBLEMS, TEXT, CASES 372–3 (2d ed. 1981).

99   '[I]n [*Monsanto*], we held that conduct *as consistent with permissible competition as with illegal conspiracy does not, standing alone, support an inference of antitrust conspiracy*'. *Matsushita*, 475 U.S. at 588 (citing Monsanto Co. v. Spray-Rite Service Corp., 465 U.S. 752 (1984)) (emphasis added).

100   United States v. Diebold, Inc., 369 U.S. 654, 655 (1962).

of the nonmoving party to instances in which the nonmoving party asserts a fact F, the moving party asserts not F, and the dispute is not resolved by the motion for summary judgment and the nonmoving party's response; for example, the plaintiff asserts that the elasticity of demand for the product is 1.2, the defendants say that it is 2.6, and each side submits an affidavit from an expert in support of its position. The application of such a narrow reading would be consistent with *Matsushita's* holding because it would require only that in cases of disputed facts a court should credit the facts asserted by the nonmoving party while allowing the court to evaluate which inferences from these facts are most reasonable in light of competing inferences.

What *Matsushita*, however, rejects for antitrust conspiracy cases is a broad reading of the directive to interpret all facts in the light most favorable to the nonmoving party at summary judgment. Assuming that the defendant is moving for summary judgment, such a reading would require the court to interpret the set of disputed facts pled by the nonmoving party as more consistent with conspiracy than with independent conduct, which would be the light most favorable to the plaintiff. But such a directive conflicts with the first principle established in *Matsushita's* holding, the requirement that courts engage in a comparative weighing of ambiguous evidence. The majority directly addressed this tension by observing that in a section 1 case, certain inferences from ambiguous evidence are, as a matter of substantive law, unreasonable and therefore cannot be drawn.[101]

In the next section, we show that the lower federal courts have interpreted and applied *Monsanto* and *Matsushita* in this way. Applying the 'tends to exclude' standard, every Circuit that has developed a test for section 1 cases under which a plaintiff alleges conspiracy and relies on circumstantial evidence makes the same demands of that plaintiff. Each holds that such a plaintiff cannot withstand a motion for summary judgment (and thus a jury cannot find for the plaintiff) unless the judge finds that the inference to be drawn from the plaintiff's evidence yields a probability that the defendants acted on the basis of unlawful agreement that is higher than the probability that they acted on the basis of independent decisions.

V   INTEGRATING PLUS FACTORS AND *MATSUSHITA* IN THE SUMMARY JUDGMENT TEST

Whether or not the *Matsushita* standard caused lower courts to engage in a different type of evaluation of summary judgment motions,[102] a review of post-1986 section 1 summary judgment cases reveals that the Circuit Courts integrated the 'plus factor' and 'tends to exclude' concepts into unified tests that plaintiffs defending against such motions must

---

[101]   *Matsushita*, 475 U.S. at 588 ('Respondents correctly note that "[on] summary judgment the inferences to be drawn from the underlying facts . . . must be viewed in the light most favorable to the party opposing the motion". But antitrust law limits the range of permissible inferences from ambiguous evidence in a § 1 case. Thus, in [*Monsanto*], we held that conduct as consistent with permissible competition as with illegal conspiracy does not, standing alone, support an inference of antitrust conspiracy') (internal citations omitted).

[102]   In particular, we cannot prove that but for the *Matsushita* standard the courts would have come out differently in the cases discussed below or understood their task in vastly different terms.

meet.[103] These tests require plaintiffs to put forward a certain *type* of evidence that rises to a specific *level* of probativeness such that conspiracy, and not independent action, is the more likely inference from the evidentiary record at summary judgment.

In this section, we review several of these tests set by Circuit Courts in response to *Matsushita*. Familiarity with these tests is essential to move to the next stage of our argument, where we shall show that the *Twombly* litigants were well aware of the stakes of importing these requirements into the motion to dismiss phase. They argued about the merits and drawbacks of doing so at the district court, court of appeals, and Supreme Court levels. In the last section we shall argue that precisely because of the comparative and evaluative requirements of the summary judgment tests described in this section, interpreting *Twombly*'s holding as explicitly incorporating the summary judgment standard for antitrust conspiracy cases is inconsistent with the ethos of the Federal Rules. Such an interpretation is normatively undesirable from the standpoint of safeguarding justiciable and economically rational standards in antitrust law.

Since *Matsushita*, Circuit Courts have put forward somewhat distinct formulations of the summary judgment test, yet the formal structure of the tests is remarkably consistent across jurisdictions. Each test contains the following elements. First, in a section 1 conspiracy case in which the plaintiff lacks direct evidence of an agreement, the plaintiff must show plus factors in addition to parallel conduct. Plus factors are discussed, circularly, as that class of evidence necessary to transform evidence of parallel conduct into a viable conspiracy case where the plaintiff lacks direct evidence of an agreement. Second, defendants can provide counter-explanations of such evidence to rebut the inference of conspiracy in favor of an inference of independent conduct. Third, the *Matsushita/Monsanto* 'tends to exclude' metric operates as the final standard by which the entirety of the evidence is evaluated. The totality of the plaintiff's plus factor and parallel conduct evidence must be sufficiently probative that, based on the record at summary judgment, the inference of conspiracy is stronger than the inference of independent conduct.

A possible formalization of these tests, utilizing the helpful concepts and notation of Bayesian probability, is as follows. Where the plaintiff lacks direct evidence of conspiracy, she must present circumstantial evidence – plus factors – that would revise the probability of conspiracy upward from the prior baseline that a fact-finder would infer from mere evidence of parallel conduct. Denote the baseline probability of conspiracy (C) given only evidence of mere parallel conduct (PC) as $P(C \mid PC)$. A plaintiff must assert at least one plus factor (PF) such that the probability of conspiracy given the parallel conduct and the plus factor is greater than the probability of such conspiracy given the parallel conduct alone

$$P(C|PC\&PF) > P(C|PC).$$

That is, the plus factor is any evidence that would make a rational trier of fact revise *upward* her estimated probability that the defendants engaged in concerted, conspiratorial action. A defendant can rebut the presumption that this evidence is sufficient to show conspiracy by proffering counter-explanations of the evidence to show that the plus factor is equally (or more) consistent with independent conduct.

---

[103]   See infra notes 106–26 and accompanying text.

To expand this Bayesian formalization, we need to recall that P(C | PC & PF) will be greater than P(C | PC) if and only if the plus factor is the sort of event or activity that is more likely to be present *with* parallel conduct when and where defendants have formed a conspiracy (C) than where defendants have engaged in independent conduct (I). Note that:

$$P(C|PC\&PF) = [P(PC\&PF|C)*P(C)] \div [P(PC\&PF|C)*P(C) + P(PC\&PF|I)*P(I)].$$

Here P(C) is the prior probability of conspiracy before anything is known about the defendants. It is the likelihood attached to conspiracy without information about the defendants' products or their behavior or the market(s) in which they operate. The prior probability P(C) can be based on a legal presumption or on economic logic about the likelihood of conspiracies to form and be stable, or empirical guesses about the frequency of conspiracies across the full panoply of markets. Correspondingly, P(I) is the prior probability of independent conduct, and since under our working definitions C and I are mutually exclusive and collectively exhaustive states, P(I) = 1 − P(C). To emphasize, because P(I) and P(C) are Bayesian priors, their values are not determined by anything specific to the defendant firms in the case or the particular market at issue.

Whether or not the plus factor leads us to revise the probability of conspiracy upward from its level given only parallel conduct depends on whether or not the plus factor *in combination with* parallel conduct is more likely to be associated with conspiratorial or independent action.[104] The second stage of the *Matsushita* assessment thus allows defendants to contest the relative values of P(PC & PF | C) and P(PC & PF | I). The court then applies the 'tends to exclude' standard as requiring that the totality of the plaintiff's proof rise to a substantive level at which the inference of conspiracy is stronger than the inference of independent conduct.[105] Where the plaintiff introduces n plus factors indexed by i, PF_i with i = 1, . . ., n, the court requires that:

$$P(I|PC\&PF_1\&PF_2\& \ldots \&PF_n) < P(C|PC\&PF_1\&PF_2\& \ldots \&PF_n).$$

This inquiry is phrased distinctively in different Circuits, but the essential elements are consistently present in the summary judgment tests articulated in most federal appeals courts. For example, in its seminal case applying the *Matsushita* standard in the Second Circuit, *Apex Oil Co. v. DiMauro*,[106] the appeals court addressed the sufficiency of the plus factor evidence adduced by the plaintiff oil refiner and retailer on a summary

---

[104]   We emphasize that the concern is with the conjunction of the plus factor and the existence of parallel conduct. Sometimes the language of courts or commentators suggests that what is relevant is whether a plus factor alone is more likely to be associated with conspiracy or independent conduct. That would imply that the crucial comparison is between P(PF | C) and P(PF | I), which is not the case.

[105]   Recall 'conduct as consistent with permissible competition as with illegal conspiracy does not, standing alone, support an inference of antitrust conspiracy'. *Matsushita Elec. Indus. Co. v. Zenith Radio Corp.*, 475 U.S. 574, 588 (1986) (citing Monsanto Co. v. Spray-Rite Service Corp., 465 U.S. 752, 762 (1984)).

[106]   Apex Oil Co. v. Di Mauro, 822 F.2d 246 (2d Cir. 1987).

judgment motion. The plaintiff's plus factor evidence consisted of various conversations and memoranda exchanged among the defendant competing oil companies. The Circuit Court first noted that '[s]ince mere parallel behavior can be consistent with independent conduct, courts have held that a plaintiff must show the existence of additional circumstances, often referred to as "plus" factors, which, when viewed in conjunction with the parallel acts, can serve to allow a fact-finder to infer a conspiracy'.[107] But the court went on to say that:

> plus factors may not necessarily lead to an inference of conspiracy . . . Such factors in a particular case could lead to an equally plausible inference of mere interdependent behavior, i.e., actions taken by market actors who are aware of and anticipate similar actions taken by competitors, but which fall short of a tacit agreement.[108]

The plus factor is not sufficient unless the court can be sure it '"tend[s] to exclude the possibility" of independent action'.[109] The Court concluded that, whether taken individually or in the aggregate, the plus factors Apex identified failed that test.[110] The Second Circuit continues to adhere to the test that it articulated in *Apex Oil*.[111]

The Fourth Circuit formulated a similar summary judgment test that incorporates the 'tends to exclude' standard to assess the plaintiff's proof in a section 1 conspiracy case.[112] In *Merck-Medco* the court affirmed the district court's grant of summary judgment for the defendants where the plaintiff, a managed care company (Medco), alleged that various pharmacies conspired to refuse to participate in a network plan to manage the prescription drug benefits program for Maryland State employees and retirees.[113] The court first noted that although the summary judgment standard is uniform across causes of action, 'the application of Rule 56 to antitrust cases is somewhat unique' because *Matsushita* made clear that conduct as consistent with permissible parallel action as with conspiracy cannot standing alone support the inference of conspiracy.[114] The court then

---

[107]   *Id.* at 253.

[108]   *Id.* at 254.

[109]   *Id.*

[110]   *Id.*

[111]   In its overturned *Twombly* decision, see the court's statement of its summary judgment test and its contrasting of that test with the test for a motion to dismiss: 'Thus, on a motion for summary judgment in a case involving alleged violations of Section 1, "courts have held that a plaintiff must show the existence of additional circumstances, often referred to as 'plus' factors, which, when viewed in conjunction with the parallel acts, can serve to allow a fact-finder to infer a conspiracy"'. Twombly v. Bell Atl. Corp., 425 F.3d 99, 114 (2d Cir. 2005) (quoting *Apex Oil*, 822 F.2d at 253).

[112]   See Merck-Medco Managed Care, LLC v. Rite Aid Corp., 201 F.3d 436, 1999 U.S. App. LEXIS 21487 (4th Cir. 1999).

[113]   The alleged reason was that since Medco also filled prescriptions by mail, it competed with the retail pharmacies, and also because as the Circuit Court explained, 'as a subsidiary of Merck, a very large drug manufacturer, [it] has a substantial advantage in discounting the price of prescription drugs'. *Merck-Medco*, 1999 U.S. App. LEXIS 21487, at *5.

[114]   *Id.* at *11. The court noted that when relying on circumstantial evidence, 'the range of permissible inferences that the court may draw from the evidence is limited . . . "conduct as consistent with permissible competition as with illegal conspiracy does not, standing alone, support an inference of antitrust conspiracy"'. *Id.* at *14–15 (quoting Matsushita Elec. Indus. Co. v. Zenith Radio

restated the *Matsushita* standard and described the showing required of plaintiffs on summary judgment as follows:

> conscious parallelism must be accompanied by 'plus factors'. While the Supreme Court has not recounted a list of plus factors, numerous plus factors, such as 'motive to conspire', 'opportunity to conspire', 'high level of interfirm communications', irrational acts or acts contrary to a defendant's economic interest, but rational if the alleged agreement existed, and departure from normal business practices, have been considered by other circuits. If a party establishes the existence of plus factors, a rebuttable presumption of conspiracy arises. Viewing all the evidence and taking the plus factors into consideration, the court must then determine if the evidence tends to exclude the possibility that the alleged coconspirators acted independently or based upon legitimate business purposes.[115]

The *Medco* plaintiffs presented plus factors of each type named above; the court discussed each in turn and then explored the defendant pharmacies' counter-explanations of their actions.[116] The court concluded, 'All of the evidence viewed together does not create a reasonable inference of conspiracy'.[117] The Fourth Circuit's summary judgment test demonstrates how lower courts have implemented *Matsushita* to require plaintiffs to present evidence that not only revises upward the probability of conspiracy but pushes the probability of conspiracy over the threshold value of one-half.[118]

In *Blomkest Fertilizer, Inc. v. Potash Corp. of Saskatchewan*,[119] the Eighth Circuit also articulated a three-step summary judgment test. The *Blomkest* plaintiffs comprised a class of direct purchasers of potash (a mineral used in fertilizer) who alleged horizontal price-fixing by six Canadian producers and two US producers selling the majority of the product exchanged in the United States. In addition to parallel pricing behavior, the plaintiffs proffered a host of plus factor evidence.[120] First, the court evaluated the plus factors put forward by the plaintiff class to see if they established a *prima facie* case for conspiracy; then it assessed the defendants' 'independent business justification for their actions'. Finally, the court weighed the competing inferences to find whether the plus factors succeeded in excluding the possibility of independent action.[121] The court described its test as follows:

> A plaintiff has the burden to present evidence of consciously paralleled pricing *supplemented with* one or more plus factors. However, even if a plaintiff carries its initial burden, a court must still find, based upon all the evidence before it, that the plaintiff's evidence tends to exclude the possibility of independent action.[122]

Corp., 475 U.S. 574, 588 (1986) (citing Monsanto Co. v. Spray-Rite Service Corp., 465 U.S. 752, 764 (1984))).

[115]   *Medco*, 1999 U.S. App. LEXIS 21487 at *26–7 (citations omitted).

[116]   *Id.* at *28–42.

[117]   *Id.* at *43.

[118]   Note in the above-quoted language in the text the Circuit Court's discussion of plus factors as familiar *types* of evidence and the *Matsushita* standard as applicable to the *quantum* of proof for the totality of evidence.

[119]   Blomkest Fertilizer, Inc. v. Potash Corp. of Sask., 203 F.3d 1028 (8th Cir. 2000).

[120]   *Id.* at 1033–8.

[121]   *Id.* at 1037.

[122]   *Id.* at 1033 (citations omitted).

The majority and the dissent in this narrowly decided case seemed to agree that some of the 'background plus factors' established the possibility of conspiracy, but the majority ultimately concluded that the plaintiff class had failed to 'carry its burden to rebut the producers' independent business justification for their actions' and therefore to exclude the possibility of lawful, parallel action.[123]

Other Circuit Courts also follow the same three-part structure in evaluating a section 1 summary judgment motion.[124] As a final example, the Ninth Circuit's test for summary judgment also contains the same three elements of a proffering of plus factors by the plaintiff, an opportunity for the defendants to rebut, and the requirement that the totality of the plaintiff's evidence reach a substantive threshold of probativeness. In *In re Citric Acid Litigation*, the court noted that:

> [a] section 1 violation cannot . . . be inferred from parallel pricing alone, nor from an industry's follow-the-leader pricing strategy . . . Parallel pricing is a relevant factor to be considered along with the evidence as a whole; if there are sufficient other 'plus' factors, an inference of conspiracy can be reasonable.[125]

The court described its approach to summary judgment assessment as follows:

> this circuit has outlined a two-part test to be applied whenever a plaintiff rests its case entirely on circumstantial evidence. First, the defendant can 'rebut an allegation of conspiracy by showing a plausible and justifiable reason for its conduct that is consistent with proper business practice'. The burden then shifts back to the plaintiff to provide specific evidence tending to show that the defendant was not engaging in permissible competitive behavior.[126]

We offer this selection of post-*Matsushita* summary judgment cases to demonstrate how the substantive evidentiary 'tends to exclude' standard articulated first in *Monsanto* became incorporated in the doctrine of plus factors to produce a canonical approach across the Circuits to summary judgment in antitrust conspiracy cases. The courts' tests have three key elements. First, plaintiffs relying on circumstantial evidence of conspiracy must adduce a specific class of proof to augment evidence of parallel conduct; they must come forward with plus factors that raise the probability of an inference of conspiracy above the likelihood implied by evidence of mere parallel behavior by defendants. Second, defendants can come forward with counter-explanations for these plus factors in an effort to show they are not necessarily more consistent with conspiracy than with independent action. Third, the court must undertake a comparative evaluation of that

---

[123]   *Id.* at 1037. The dissent's summary judgment analysis incorporated two possible under-standings of the *Monsanto/Mastsushita* standard by stating that 'it is useful to distinguish between "plus factors" that establish a background making conspiracy likely and "plus factors" that tend to exclude the possibility that the defendants acted without agreement'. *Id.* at 1044 (Gibson, J., dis-senting). By way of example the dissent noted that 'acts that would be irrational or contrary to the defendant's economic interest if no conspiracy existed, but which would be rational if the alleged agreement existed, do tend to exclude the possibility of innocence'. *Id.*

[124]   See, e.g., Intervest v. Bloomberg L.P., 340 F.3d 144 (3d Cir. 2003); Williamson Oil Co. v. Philip Morris USA, 346 F.3d 1287 (11th Cir. 2003).

[125]   In re Citric Acid Litig., 191 F.3d 1090, 1102 (9th Cir. 1999) (internal citations omitted).

[126]   *Id.* at 1094 (internal citations omitted).

proof to determine if it is more consistent with independent or conspiratorial action, and it must apply a particular substantive standard. Specifically, considering the accounts of both the plaintiff and defendant, a court must as a matter of law determine whether the proffered plus factors cum parallel conduct are more likely to be found where defendants are acting independently or more likely to be found where defendants are acting pursuant to a conspiracy.[127] The court must determine if the totality of the plaintiff's evidence of parallel behavior and evidence of plus factors is more consistent with conspiracy or with independent conduct, that is whether $P(C| PC \& PF)$ is greater than one-half.

In the following two sections we show that in *Twombly* both the lower court opinions and the briefs of the parties to the Supreme Court were framed in terms of whether or not it was appropriate to apply this summary judgment standard when ruling on a motion to dismiss.

VI   THE SECTION 1 DILEMMA IN THE CONTEXT OF A MOTION TO DISMISS: THE *TWOMBLY* CONFLICT IN THE LOWER COURTS

The divergence between the district court and the Second Circuit opinions in *Twombly* can be described as a disagreement over the applicability of the summary judgment standard in ruling on a motion to dismiss an antitrust conspiracy claim. The debate was framed in terms of accepting or rejecting a rule that would require the plaintiff to plead plus factors that would 'tend to exclude' the possibility of independent conduct.[128]

The district court held that the relevant standard for evaluating the sufficiency of the plaintiffs' claim 'required that plaintiffs allege plus factors in order to withstand motions to dismiss'.[129] The court concluded that the plaintiffs' complaint 'alleges nothing more than parallel conduct that appears to accord with the individual economic interests of the alleged conspirators', and therefore failed to meet this standard.[130] Although it is not clear that the district court necessarily intended that a plus factor pleading rule import whole cloth the summary judgment standard into the motion to dismiss context, the court drew its definitions of plus factors from cases that had applied the summary judgment standard.

The court began its discussion of the pleading standard by noting that because:

> the Supreme Court 'has never held that proof of parallel business behavior conclusively establishes agreement or, phrased differently, that such behavior itself constitutes a Sherman Act

---

[127]   Recalling the formalization above, this part of the test concerns whether $P(PC \& PF | C) > P(PC \& PF | I)$ or $P(PC \& PF | C) < P(PC \& PF | I)$.

[128]   Compare Twombly v. Bell Atl. Corp., 313 F. Supp. 2d 174, 180 (S.D.N.Y. 2003) (stating that '[t]he plus factors pleading requirement is . . . an expression of the longstanding rule that "a bare bones statement of conspiracy or of injury under the antitrust laws without any supporting facts permits dismissal" of a complaint') (quoting Heart Disease Research Found. v. Gen. Motors Corp., 463 F.2d 98, 100 (2d Cir. 1972)) with Twombly v. Bell Atl. Corp., 425 F.3d 99, 114 (2d Cir. 2005) (holding that 'plus factors are not required to be pleaded to permit an antitrust claim based on parallel conduct to survive dismissal') (emphasis omitted).

[129]   *Twombly*, 313 F. Supp. 2d at 179–80.

[130]   *Id.* at 189.

offense' . . . [c]ourts must therefore distinguish between conduct that represents the natural convergence of competitors' market behavior, and conduct that appears to have been taken pursuant to an agreement.[131]

In the summary judgment context, the court noted, the courts in the Second Circuit have required plaintiffs to show that parallel behavior is the result of an agreement 'by establishing at least one "plus factor" that tends to exclude independent self-interested conduct as an explanation for defendants' parallel behavior'.[132] Therefore, the district court understood that the plus factor requirement not only referred to a type of evidence but also entailed a substantive probativeness requirement – evidence of plus factors is probative only when, considered along with parallel conduct, it makes the inferred likelihood of conspiracy greater than the inferred likelihood of independent conduct.

The district court reasoned that a pleading rule requiring 'that plaintiffs allege plus factors in order to withstand motions to dismiss' was mandated by both substantive antitrust law and the Federal Rules of Civil Procedure.[133] Otherwise, the court argued, a complaint alleging nothing more than conscious parallelism could survive a motion to dismiss. That would effectively allow a plaintiff to proceed to discovery on the bare assertion of actions that are not themselves unlawful under section 1.[134] Hence, a section 1 complaint without plus factors satisfies neither section 1's requirement of actual conspiracy nor Rule 8's requirement to state an actual violation upon which relief can be granted.[135] Applying its standard to the plaintiffs' complaint, the district court ultimately concluded that '[t]he allegations of plaintiffs' complaint provide no reason to believe that defendants' parallel conduct was reflective of any agreement. The complaint therefore alleges nothing more than parallel conduct that appears to accord with the individual economic interests of the alleged conspirators'.[136]

The Second Circuit reversed the district court and reinstated the plaintiffs' complaint. The court of appeals characterized the district court's plus factor pleading requirement as effectively applying a summary judgment standard to the motion to dismiss,[137] and it rejected this equating of the two standards. The court held that from Rule 8, Rule 9, and recent Supreme Court decisions it followed that the 'notice' pleading standard ought to be interpreted liberally and that the heightened pleading standard of Rule 9 (requiring additional specificity) does not extend to antitrust actions. The court reasoned that at the complaint stage the plaintiff does not yet know if she will need to rely on indirect,

---

[131]   *Id.* at 179 (quoting Theatre Enterprises, Inc. v. Paramount Film Distrib. Corp., 346 U.S. 537, 541 (1954)).

[132]   *Twombly*, 313 F. Supp. 2d at 179.

[133]   *Id.* at 180.

[134]   *Id.* ('Viewed in this light, the plus factors are simply examples of allegations that are sufficiently suggestive of a conspiracy to warrant discovery').

[135]   The court noted that the 'requirement that plaintiffs allege specific facts suggesting a conspiracy is somewhat in tension with Fed. R. Civ. P. 8, which requires only a "short and plain statement of the claim", and allows plaintiffs to base their complaints on "statement[s] of ultimate facts"'. *Id.* But the court reasoned that in the context of section 1 substantive antitrust law, 'allegations of plus factors are necessary to give defendants' notice of plaintiff's theory of the conspiracy'. *Id.* at 181.

[136]   *Id.* at 189.

[137]   Twombly v. Bell Atl. Corp., 425 F.3d 99, 113–17 (2d Cir. 2005).

circumstantial evidence because discovery may yield direct evidence of conspiracy, in which case the plaintiff will not need to rely on showing parallel conduct in combination with plus factors.[138]

On this basis the Second Circuit held that the district court had erred in evaluating the sufficiency of the complaint using a standard indistinguishable from that appropriate to the summary judgment phase. To identify the standard to apply to a motion to dismiss, the court looked to *Conley v. Gibson*, which stated 'the accepted rule that a complaint should not be dismissed for failure to state a claim unless it appears beyond doubt that the plaintiff can prove no set of facts in support of his claim which would entitle him to relief'.[139] Citing *Apex Oil*, the Second Circuit in *Twombly* recounted that plus factors have been long required in the Circuit to survive a motion for summary judgment when the plaintiff relies on circumstantial, indirect evidence in addition to parallel behavior to make out a section 1 case of conspiracy.[140] But, the appeals court held, 'plus factors are not required to be pleaded to permit an antitrust claim based on parallel conduct to survive dismissal'.[141] Nevertheless, '[t]he factual predicate that is pleaded does need to include conspiracy among the realm of *plausible* possibilities'.[142]

Ironically, it was the Second Circuit's language of *plausibility*, not the district court's language of plus factor pleading, that the Supreme Court adopted to define the standard that should be used to evaluate the motion to dismiss.[143] Hence, it could be argued that

---

[138]   *Id.* at 114. The court was most likely influenced in this reasoning by the then recent Supreme Court case overturning the Second Circuit's pleading rule for employment discrimination cases that required Title VII plaintiffs to plead facts sufficient to state a *prima facie* case under McDonnell Douglas Corp. v. Green, 411 U.S. 792 (1973). See Swierkiewicz v. Sorema N.A., 534 U.S. 506 (2002).

[139]   Conley v. Gibson, 355 U.S. 41, 46 (1957).

[140]   *Twombly*, 425 F.3d at 113–14. 'Thus, on a motion for summary judgment in a case involving alleged violations of Section 1, "courts have held that a plaintiff must show the existence of additional circumstances, often referred to as 'plus' factors, which, when viewed in conjunction with the parallel acts, can serve to allow a fact-finder to infer a conspiracy"'. *Id.* at 114 (quoting Apex Oil Co. v. DiMauro, 822 F.2d 246, 253 (2d Cir. 1987)).

[141]   *Twombly*, 425 F.3d at 114 (emphasis omitted).

[142]   *Id.* at 111 (emphasis added). The Second Circuit offered the following definitional footnote to explicate the term 'plausible': 'One circuit court has employed this definition of "plausible" in another context: "superficially worthy of belief: CREDIBLE". *Mendoza Manimbao v. Ashcroft*, 329 F.3d 655, 664 (9th Cir. 2003) (quoting Webster's Third New International Dictionary 1736 (1976)). The Supreme Court in *Matsushita Electric Indus. Co., Ltd. v. Zenith Radio Corp.*, 475 U.S. 574, 106 S. Ct. 1348, 89 L. Ed. 2d 538 (1986), used the same term in the context of a motion for summary judgment. See *Matsushita*, 475 U.S. at 596–7, 106 S. Ct. 1348 ("[T]he absence of any plausible motive to engage in the conduct charged is highly relevant to whether a 'genuine issue for trial' exists within the meaning of Rule 56(e)".). As we note, however, language setting forth a summary judgment standard must be used with care in assessing a motion to dismiss'. *Id.* at 111 n.5 (alteration in original).

[143]   The Second Circuit opinion used the term again here: 'If a pleaded conspiracy is implausible on the basis of the facts as pleaded – if the allegations amount to no more than "unlikely speculations" – the complaint will be dismissed. But short of the extremes of "bare bones" and "implausibility", a complaint in an antitrust case need only contain the "short and plain statement of the claim showing that the pleader is entitled to relief" that Rule 8(a) requires'. *Twombly*, 425 F.3d at 111 (internal citations omitted). And, the court returned to its plausibility requirement

the Court's opinion was less a reversal of the Second Circuit's standard than it was a repudiation of its application of the standard to the complaint at issue.

The Second Circuit did not elaborate on what types of facts need to be shown or exactly how suggestive of conspiracy the complaint's facts must be to satisfy its standard. But the court did state that 'to rule that allegations of parallel anticompetitive conduct fail to support a plausible conspiracy claim, a court would have to conclude that there is no set of facts that would permit a plaintiff to demonstrate that the particular parallelism asserted was the product of collusion rather than coincidence'.[144] It appears, therefore, that the court intended that a plaintiff would be allowed to proceed on the basis of a complaint consisting of 'allegations of parallel anticompetitive conduct' so long as the particular parallel conduct considered in a specific context were to permit a *plausible* inference of conspiracy. Using this standard, the appeals court concluded that the plaintiffs' amended complaint did state sufficient facts to survive the defendants' motion to dismiss.[145]

VII THE DEBATE BETWEEN THE *TWOMBLY* PARTIES AT THE SUPREME COURT

In the previous section we showed that the district and Circuit Courts' disagreement in *Twombly* over the appropriate standard to apply in evaluating the motion to dismiss was framed in terms of the applicability of standards and requirements drawn from the summary judgment context. On appeal to the Supreme Court, the parties' briefs and those of their amici also framed the issue in terms of summary judgment concepts and terms.

The defendant-petitioners insisted that the appropriate standard to evaluate the motion to dismiss ought to be drawn from the summary judgment standard.[146] They argued that the Supreme Court's general pleading precedents established two requirements for a proper complaint: 'First, a complaint must allege facts, not merely conclusions, that show the plaintiff is entitled to relief under the governing substantive law. Second, it is the facts alleged, not unalleged facts that the plaintiff might later prove, that must support the claim to relief'.[147] Applied to a section 1 conspiracy complaint, those rules require a plaintiff to plead 'facts that themselves tend to exclude the likelihood that the conduct was unilateral'.[148] Any standard lower than the *Matsushita* 'tends to exclude' standard would permit, the petitioners said, the plaintiff to proceed on a complaint that states merely conclusory allegations.[149]

---

when it stated that the 'pleaded factual predicate must include conspiracy among the realm of "plausible" possibilities in order to survive a motion to dismiss'. *Id.* at 114.

[144] *Id.* at 114.

[145] *Id.* at 119.

[146] Brief for Petitioners, Bell Atl. Corp. v. Twombly, 550 U.S. 544 (2007) (No. 05–1126).

[147] *Id.* at 16 (citing Associated Gen. Contractors of Cal., Inc. v. Cal. State Council of Carpenters, 459 U.S. 519, 526 (1983) ('It is not . . . proper to assume that the [plaintiff] can prove facts that it has not alleged'); Wilson v. Schnettler, 365 U.S. 381, 383 (1961)).

[148] Brief for Petitioners, *supra* note 146, at 16 (citing Matsushita Elec. Indus. Co. v. Zenith Radio Corp., 475 U.S. 574, 588 (1986); Monsanto Co. v. Spray-Rite Serv. Corp., 465 U.S. 752, 764 (1984)).

[149] Brief for Petitioners, *supra* note 146, at 17.

The petitioners argued that because '[s]ubstantive antitrust law draws a sharp distinction between conspiracy prohibited by Section 1 and parallel but unilateral conduct, which Section 1 does not address', the Court must conclude that 'allegations of parallel conduct cannot by themselves satisfy the agreement element of Section 1'.[150] From this premise the petitioners concluded that the proper standard to determine whether a complaint presents conspiracy allegations, as opposed to alleging mere parallel conduct, is to implement at the motion to dismiss phase 'the basic principle articulated in *Matsushita* and *Monsanto* that "a plaintiff seeking damages for a violation of § 1 must present evidence 'that tends to exclude the possibility' that the alleged conspirators acted independently"'.[151] The petitioners noted that *Matsushita* was a summary judgment case, and they acknowledged that there are distinctions between the purposes of a motion to dismiss and a motion for summary judgment. They concluded, however, that applying the district court's standard drawn from *Matsushita* 'comports with the proper function of a motion to dismiss'.[152] With respect to the appeals court standard, the petitioners argued that even when

> collusion is one 'plausible possibilit[y]' underlying parallel conduct [it] does not mean that independent action is not also plausible, or even *more* plausible. The Second Circuit's mere-plausibility standard does not comport with the standard for antitrust conspiracy because it does not require facts that 'tend. . . to exclude' the possibility that defendants acted independently.[153]

The plaintiff-respondents' initial brief characterized the defendant-petitioners' position interchangeably as defending a plus factor pleading requirement[154] or transposing *Matsushita's* 'tends to exclude' summary judgment standard into the motion to dismiss context.[155] In various places the respondents characterized the petitioners' proposal as

---

[150]   *Id.* at 23–4.

[151]   *Id.* at 24 (quoting *Matsushita*, 475 U.S. at 588 (quoting *Monsanto*, 465 U.S. at 764)). The petitioners' brief cited a number of cases in support of this standard; all but one of them was decided in the posture of summary judgment or judgment as a matter of law. The petitioners cited Williamson Oil Co. v. Philip Morris USA, 346 F.3d 1287, 1301 (11th Cir. 2003) (summary judgment); In re Flat Glass Antitrust Litigation, 385 F.3d 350, 360–1 (3d Cir. 2004), cert. denied, 544 U.S. 948 (2005) (summary judgment); Viazis v. American Association of Orthodontists, 314 F.3d 758, 762, 764 (5th Cir. 2002) (judgment as a matter of law); Toys 'R' Us, Inc. v. FTC, 221 F.3d 928, 936 (7th Cir. 2000) (appeal from an FTC decision); Blomkest Fertilizer, Inc. v. Potash Corp. of Saskatchewan, 203 F.3d 1028, 1033 (8th Cir. 2000) (en banc) (summary judgment); In re Citric Acid Litigation, 191 F.3d 1090, 1100 (9th Cir. 1999) (summary judgment); and In re Brand Name Prescription Drugs Antitrust Litigation, 186 F.3d 781, 787–8 (7th Cir. 1999) (Posner, J.) (judgment as a matter of law). Brief for Petitioners, *supra* note 146, at 24–5.

[152]   Brief for Petitioners, *supra* note 146, at 25.

[153]   *Id.* at 13 (quoting *Matsushita*, 475 U.S. at 588) (alteration in original).

[154]   Brief for Respondents at 24, Bell Atl. Corp. v. Twombly, 550 U.S. 544 (2007) (No. 05–1126) ('Petitioners could not be clearer in arguing that the District Court's analysis was correct, in holding that there is a so-called "plus factors pleading requirement". Pet. App. 42a, 45a. To suggest that a "plus factors pleading requirement" would not be a "heightened pleading requirement" is a stark contradiction in terms').

[155]   *Id.* at 3 ('Petitioners' own proposal – to apply summary judgment standards of *Matsushita* at the Rule 12(b)(6) stage – is precisely analogous to proposals made to the Court, and decisively rejected, in *Swierkiewicz*'); see also *id.* at iv ('[Section] E: Petitioners' radical proposal, to apply *Matsushita* on a Rule 12(b)(6) motion, is utterly inconsistent with the Court's precedents').

one seeking 'to apply summary judgment standards of *Matsushita* at the Rule 12(b)(6) stage'.[156] The respondents argued that:

> the standard urged by Petitioners would stand conventional Rule 12(b)(6) standards on their head. Since the gist of *Matsushita* is that a plaintiff on summary judgment must offer evidence that 'tends to exclude the possibility' of independent conduct . . . – i.e., that the defendant receives the benefit of ambiguous inferences on such a motion – to apply *Matsushita* standards on a motion to dismiss would diametrically reverse the established rule that the plaintiff gets the benefit of such inferences on a motion to dismiss.[157]

Furthermore, the respondents observed that:

> the standard of 'excluding the possibility of independent action' in *Matsushita* is calibrated to the completely different context of summary judgment after discovery, when a plaintiff has fully collected his evidence, and when the magnitude of the risks from 'false positives' in a jury trial is vastly greater than the mere legal fees at stake on a motion to dismiss.[158]

The plaintiff-respondents also argued that in seeking to validate the district court's standard the petitioners were proposing a plus factor pleading rule, which would be contrary to the uniform notice pleading standard imposed by the federal rules.[159]

In their brief, the plaintiff-respondents advocated adoption of the Second Circuit's standard for evaluating a motion to dismiss. It would, they contended, have a court examine 'the particular parallelism asserted' to determine whether alleging the conspiracy is 'plausible'.[160] Throughout the brief, they emphasized the plausibility requirement, the term the Supreme Court would adopt to define a standard that evidently overruled the Second Circuit, and defended that requirement as a standard flexible and fair to defendants under notice pleading.[161]

The petitioners, in their reply brief, disclaimed any attempt to erect a 'heightened pleading standard'.[162] They reiterated their argument that because the plaintiffs' allegation relied on 'observations of public conduct and market circumstances'[163] to yield the inference of conspiracy, they must be required to state sufficient 'facts . . . to support the claim of agreement under the "tend to exclude" standard that governs such inferences'.[164] In short, the defendants' position was that the standard for Rule 12 should be equivalent to the standard *Matsushita* established for Rule 56.

Many of the amici briefs submitted on behalf of the petitioners argued in support of

---

[156] *Id.* at 3.

[157] *Id.* at 28 (quoting *Matsushita*, 475 U.S. at 588).

[158] Brief for Respondents, *supra* note 154, at 28.

[159] *Id.* at 24 ('Petitioners could not be clearer in arguing that the District Court's analysis was correct, in holding that there is a so-called "plus factors pleading requirement". Pet. App. 42a, 45a. To suggest that a "plus factors pleading requirement" would not be a "heightened pleading requirement" is a stark contradiction in terms').

[160] *Id.* at 4 (quoting Twombly v. Bell Atl. Corp., 425 F.3d 99, 114 (2d Cir. 2005)).

[161] In various places, the respondents used the term 'plausible' to describe the Second Circuit's standard. See Brief for Respondents, *supra* note 154, § G, at 35–8.

[162] Reply Brief for Petitioners at 5, Bell Atl. v. Twombly, 550 U.S. 544 (2007) (No. 05–1126).

[163] *Id.* at 11 (quoting Brief for Respondents, *supra* note 154, at 21).

[164] Reply Brief for Petitioners, *supra* note 162, at 12.

adopting for motions to dismiss antitrust conspiracy claims a standard drawn from the summary judgment context while the amici briefs submitted on behalf of the respondents opposed doing that.[165] Among the amici in support of the defendant-petitioners, only the Solicitor General's brief attempted to steer away from the petitioners' argument to conflate the summary judgment and motion to dismiss standards.[166]

Since the lower court opinions and the arguments of the parties to the Supreme Court were largely framed in terms of accepting or rejecting the plus factor doctrine or the 21-year-old *Matsushita* standard established for summary judgment motions, it is natural to look to this standard to give content to the seemingly fuzzy 'plausibility' standard articulated in the Supreme Court's *Twombly* decision. We shall argue, however, that interpreting the *Twombly* decision as importing the summary judgment standard into the motion to dismiss phase would be misguided, both as an interpretation of the majority's decision and as a policy for substantive antitrust and civil procedure law.

VIII   INTERPRETING *TWOMBLY*

Central to the debate in the lower courts and during briefing and oral arguments to the Supreme Court in *Twombly* was the appropriateness of importing terms and standards adopted for the summary judgment context into the motion to dismiss phase of litigation. The prevalence of this framework in the steps leading to the Supreme Court's decision sharply contrasts with the conspicuous *absence* of any summary judgment language in the Court's opinion setting forth its new standard.[167] Indeed, Justice Souter's majority opinion invoked *Matsushita*'s 'tends to exclude' language only twice: once to describe the summary judgment or trial proof standard[168] and once to describe the standard employed

---

[165]   See, e.g., Brief of Amici Curiae Legal Scholars in Support of Petitioners at 7, *Twombly*, 550 U.S. 544 (No. 05–1126).

[166]   See Brief for the United States as Amicus Curiae Supporting Petitioners at 22–3, *Twombly*, 550 U.S. 544 (No. 05–1126) ('That is not to say that a complaint asserting a claim under Section 1 of the Sherman Act must allege facts that would be sufficient to defeat summary judgment under the standard articulated in *Matsushita Electric*. 475 U.S. at 588. No special rules of pleading apply to antitrust cases, and accordingly there is no absolute requirement that a complaint alleging an antitrust conspiracy must be dismissed unless it alleges facts sufficient to establish the so-called "plus factors" that would ultimately be required to prove the existence of an illegal agreement by means of circumstantial evidence').

[167]   During oral argument, members of the Supreme Court mentioned the Second Circuit's view on whether or not a section 1 complaint required allegations of plus factors. See Oral Argument at 50, *Twombly*, 550 U.S. 544 (No. 05–1126). Yet the final opinion never took a position on this question, and it omitted any mention of this language from the opinion.

[168]   See *Twombly*, 550 U.S. at 554 ('we have previously hedged against false inferences from identical behavior at a number of points in the trial sequence. An antitrust conspiracy plaintiff with evidence showing nothing beyond parallel conduct is not entitled to a directed verdict, see *Theatre Enterprises* . . .; proof of a § 1 conspiracy must include evidence tending to exclude the possibility of independent action, see *Monsanto* . . .; and at the summary judgment stage a § 1 plaintiff's offer of conspiracy evidence must tend to rule out the possibility that the defendants were acting independently, see *Matsushita* . . .').

by the district court.[169] The majority opinion also mentioned the term 'plus factors' only twice. The first occasion was only in describing the Second Circuit's opinion.[170] In the second instance, the Court quoted the plaintiffs' brief where they expressed concern that 'transpos[ing] "plus factor" summary judgment analysis woodenly into a rigid Rule 12(b)(6) pleading standard . . . would be unwise'.[171]

Justice Souter's opinion steered a new, distinct course away from the choices presented in the lower court opinions and party briefs that had urged either straightforward, unequivocal adoption or rejection of a summary judgment standard for assessing a motion to dismiss. Instead, Justice Souter articulated the motion to dismiss standard in language unencumbered by summary judgment evidentiary baggage. Plaintiffs, he said, are required to plead sufficient 'facts that are suggestive enough to render a § 1 conspiracy plausible'.[172] Again, this plausibility language was present not in the district court opinion dismissing the complaint but in the Second Circuit opinion – the ruling overturned by Justice Souter's opinion.[173]

Justice Souter's majority opinion started by noting the perennial tension in section 1 law: the requirement that to qualify as an unlawful restraint of trade, there must have been an actual conspiracy animating parallel behavior and the difficulty of proving such a conspiracy with direct evidence.[174] The Court stated:

> The inadequacy of showing parallel conduct or interdependence, without more, mirrors the ambiguity of the behavior: consistent with conspiracy, but just as much in line with a wide swath of rational and competitive business strategy unilaterally prompted by common perceptions of the market. Accordingly, we have previously hedged against false inferences from identical behavior at a number of points in the trial sequence.[175]

The Court went on to restate the directed verdict, trial, and summary judgment standards from *Theatre Enterprises, Monsanto,* and *Matsushita* respectively, and noted that '[t]his case presents the antecedent question of what a plaintiff must plead in order to state a claim under § 1 of the Sherman Act'.[176]

---

[169]   See *id.* at 552 ('Thus, the District Court understood that allegations of parallel business conduct, taken alone, do not state a claim under § 1; plaintiffs must allege additional facts that "ten[d] to exclude independent self-interested conduct as an explanation for defendants' parallel behavior"') (quoting Twombly v. Bell Atl. Corp., 313 F. Supp. 2d 174, 179 (S.D.N.Y. 2003)) (alteration in original).

[170]   See *Twombly*, 550 U.S. at 553 ('The Court of Appeals for the Second Circuit reversed, holding that the District Court tested the complaint by the wrong standard. It held that "plus factors are not *required* to be pleaded to permit an antitrust claim based on parallel conduct to survive dismissal"') (quoting Twombly v. Bell Atl. Corp., 425 F.3d 99, 114 (2d Cir. 2005)).

[171]   *Twombly*, 550 U.S. at 569 (quoting Brief for Respondents, *supra* note 154, at 39) (alterations in original).

[172]   *Twombly*, 550 U.S. at 556.

[173]   See *Twombly*, 425 F.3d at 111 ('The factual predicate that is pleaded does need to include conspiracy among the realm of plausible possibilities . . . If a pleaded conspiracy is implausible on the basis of the facts as pleaded – if the allegations amount to no more than "unlikely specula-tions" – the complaint will be dismissed') (quoting DM Research, Inc. v. Coll. Am. Pathologists, 170 F.3d 53, 56 (1st Cir. 1999)).

[174]   *Twombly*, 550 U.S. at 553–4.

[175]   *Id.* at 554 (citations omitted).

[176]   *Id.* at 554–6.

The Court recited the general pleading and Rule 12(b)(6) standards and asserted that the test it was fashioning in this case is a function of 'applying these general standards to a § 1 claim'.[177] The upshot, Justice Souter concluded, is that a section 1 plaintiff must plead 'a complaint with enough factual matter (taken as true) to suggest that an agreement was made'.[178] The plaintiff must, therefore, present in the complaint 'facts that are suggestive enough to render a § 1 conspiracy *plausible*'.[179] Instead of clarifying the plausibility standard with familiar summary judgment language, the opinion employed the term plausible or plausibility several times in different formulations. For example, the Court stated, 'The need at the pleading stage for allegations plausibly suggesting (not merely consistent with) agreement reflects the threshold requirement of Rule 8(a)(2) that the "plain statement" possess enough heft to "sho[w] that the pleader is entitled to relief"'.[180]

A complaint alleging only parallel conduct, the Court held, does not plead a sufficient factual predicate to raise the conspiracy claim to the level of plausibility necessary to survive a motion to dismiss.[181] The opinion, however, did not specify exactly what *type* of facts the plaintiff ought to plead in conjunction with parallel conduct to render plausible the overall factual predicate of the complaint. It also did not peg the newly articulated plausibility standard to a particular *level* of probativeness.

Justice Souter explicitly eschewed a probability requirement in answering the question: what must a complaint accomplish for the plaintiff to be able to pass into the discovery phase? But his response's reference to a 'reasonable expectation' readily invites an interpretation in probabilistic terms.[182] To meet his test it must be the case that following discovery, one will be able to infer that there is a sufficiently high probability that the defendant engaged in a conspiracy. Perhaps, even more stringently, the judge must believe that if the plaintiff can proceed to discovery, there is a sufficiently high probability that the *Matsushita* standard will be met at the summary judgment stage. But Justice Souter's formulation in *Twombly* is not equivalent to that *Matsushita* standard. Moreover, he did not specify how firm that 'reasonable expectation' must be or, alternatively, how high the post-discovery probability of conspiracy must be.

The opinion does tell lower courts that for a plaintiff to survive a motion to dismiss, the party must present *something* more than mere parallel conduct: '[W]hen allegations of

---

[177]   *Id.* at 556.

[178]   *Id.*

[179]   *Id.* (emphasis added).

[180]   *Id.* at 557 (quoting Fed. R. Civ. P. 8(a)) (alteration in original).

[181]   *Twombly*, 550 U.S. at 556–7 ('In identifying facts that are suggestive enough to render a § 1 conspiracy plausible, we have the benefit of the prior rulings and considered views of leading commentators, already quoted, that lawful parallel conduct fails to bespeak unlawful agreement. It makes sense to say, therefore, that an allegation of parallel conduct and a bare assertion of conspiracy will not suffice. Without more, parallel conduct does not suggest conspiracy, and a conclusory allegation of agreement at some unidentified point does not supply facts adequate to show illegality').

[182]   See *id.* at 556 ('Asking for plausible grounds to infer an agreement does not impose a probability requirement at the pleading stage; it simply calls for enough fact to raise a reasonable expectation that discovery will reveal evidence of illegal agreement'). At the conclusion of the opinion the majority emphasized, 'we do not require heightened fact pleading of specifics, but only enough facts to state a claim to relief that is plausible on its face'. *Id.* at 570.

parallel conduct are set out in order to make a § 1 claim, they must be placed in a context that raises a suggestion of a preceding agreement, not merely parallel conduct that could just as well be independent action'.[183] The plausibility standard does require the facts pled to rise to a threshold level that sufficiently suggests conspiracy so that discovery would likely produce some evidence of the claim asserted. But as articulated by the Court in *Twombly*, it does not require these facts to show that the inference of conspiracy is more likely than the inference of independent conduct. The novel 'plausibility' language should be understood as intentionally leaving room for lower courts to develop through the cases they decide both what types of facts plaintiffs can plead to add something beyond parallel conduct and just how strong the totality of these facts must be to satisfy the plausibility standard. Such an approach is consistent with the common law tradition in antitrust wherein general principles are refined and elaborated in the crucible of deciding actual cases.[184]

Beyond these interpretive pointers drawn from the context and language of *Twombly* itself, other factors also lead us to reject construing its holding as conflating the summary judgment and motion to dismiss standards. For one, such a construction would contradict the holding of *Tellabs, Inc. v. Makor Issues & Rights, Ltd.*, a case that was decided later in the same term – indeed, within a month of *Twombly* – and concerned the motion to dismiss standard under the Private Securities Litigation Reform Act of 1995 (PSLRA).[185] This Act raised the pleading standards for private securities litigation as it required plaintiffs to plead with particularity both the facts of the alleged securities violation and the facts indicating the defendant's scienter intent.

The *Tellabs* Court held that the heightened pleading standard required by Congress in the PSLRA meant that 'an inference of scienter must be more than merely plausible or reasonable – it must be cogent and at least as compelling as any opposing inference of nonfraudulent intent'.[186] This assessment, the majority acknowledged, is 'inherently comparative . . . To determine whether the plaintiff has alleged facts that give rise to the requisite "strong inference" of scienter, a court must consider plausible nonculpable explanations for the defendant's conduct, as well as inferences favoring the plaintiff'.[187] Justices Alito and Scalia maintained that the PSLRA language necessitated a pleading standard akin to that employed when ruling on a motion for summary judgment or judgment as a matter of law. They argued that 'a "strong inference" of scienter, in the present context, means an inference that is more likely than not correct'.[188] Yet the majority

---

[183]   *Id.* at 557.

[184]   This is analogous to what the Court did later in the same term when it explicitly left to lower courts the task of giving more specific content to the Rule of Reason that Leegin Creative Leather Products v. PSKS, Inc., 551 U.S. 877 (2007), announced would now apply in cases of resale price maintenance.

[185]   Tellabs v. Makor Issues & Rights, Ltd., 551 U.S. 308 (2007).

[186]   *Id.* at 314. The Act requires the complaint to 'state with particularity facts giving rise to a strong inference that the defendant acted with the required state of mind'. 15 U.S.C. § 78u-4(b)(2) (2006).

[187]   *Tellabs,* 551 U.S. at 323–4.

[188]   *Id.* at 333–4. See *id.* at 335 (Alito, J., concurring in the judgment) ('I would also hold that a "strong inference that the defendant acted with the required state of mind" is an inference that is stronger than the inference that the defendant lacked the required state of mind'); *id.* at 329 (Scalia,

rejected this proposition and held that the statutory 'strong inference' of scienter pleading language does *not* require that the inference of conspiracy be the *most* probable inference in light of the competing interpretations of the facts offered by the two parties.[189] The *Tellabs* majority explicitly rejected equating the standard for ruling on a motion to dismiss with the standard for deciding on summary judgment or judgment as a matter of law.[190]

Interpreting *Twombly* to require the pleading of plus factors or satisfaction of *Matsushita*'s 'tends to exclude' standard would import the summary judgment standard into the motion to dismiss phase, where the claim is subject to only the general notice pleading requirements of Rule 8.[191] This is an improbable interpretation of *Twombly*'s holding precisely because in *Tellabs* the Court later rejected such a proposal when the claim was statutorily subject to the stricter pleading requirements of the PSLRA. Furthermore, in a case later in that same term, *Erickson v. Pardus*, the Court reiterated its commitment to notice pleading, and it cited *Twombly* quoting *Conley* for the proposition that notice pleading is still the ruling standard.[192]

The Court's recent decision in *Iqbal* provides further support for the position that *Twombly* maintained a distinction between the standard for deciding on a motion to dismiss and the one to apply to a motion for summary judgment. In *Iqbal* the Court stated explicitly that '[o]ur decision in *Twombly* expounded the pleading standard for "all civil actions"',[193] and in setting out the standard in *Iqbal*, Justice Kennedy quoted extensively from Justice Souter's opinion in *Twombly*.[194] Given the Court's strenuously maintained universality of the *Twombly* standard for ruling on a motion to dismiss a complaint, it would be implausible to identify that standard with the summary judgment standard in

---

J., concurring in the judgment) ('In my view, the test should be whether the inference of scienter (if any) is *more plausible* than the inference of innocence' (original emphasis)).

[189]   See *id.* at 324 (majority opinion).

[190]   See *id.* n.5 ('Justice Alito agrees with Justice Scalia, and would transpose to the pleading stage "the test that is used at the summary-judgment and judgment-as-a-matter-of-law stages". *Post* at 2516 (opinion concurring in judgment). But the test at each stage is measured against a different backdrop. It is improbable that Congress, without so stating, intended courts to test pleadings, unaided by discovery, to determine whether there is "no genuine issue as to any material fact". See Fed. Rule Civ. Proc. 56(c). And judgment as a matter of law is a post-trial device, turning on the question whether a party has produced evidence "legally sufficient" to warrant a jury determination in that party's favor. See Rule 50(a)(1)'). See Justice Alito's concurrence arguing that 'Justice Scalia's interpretation would align the pleading test under § 78u-4(b)(2) with the test that is used at the summary-judgment and judgment-as-a-matter-of-law stages, whereas the Court's test would introduce a test previously unknown in civil litigation. It seems more likely that Congress meant to adopt a known quantity and thus to adopt Justice Scalia's approach'. *Id.* at 335 (Alito, J., concurring in the judgment).

[191]   FED. R. CIV. P. 8(a).

[192]   See Erickson v. Pardus, 551 U.S. 89, 93 (2007) ('Federal Rule of Civil Procedure 8(a)(2) requires only "a short and plain statement of the claim showing that the pleader is entitled to relief". Specific facts are not necessary; the statement need only "give the defendant fair notice of what the . . . claim is and the grounds upon which it rests"') (quoting Bell Atlantic Corp. v. Twombly, 550 U.S. 544, 555 (2007) (quoting Conley v. Gibson, 355 U.S. 41, 47 (1957))).
Note the citation of *Twombly* itself in turn referencing *Conley*.

[193]   Ashcroft v. Iqbal, 129 S. Ct. 1937, 1953 (2009).

[194]   *Id.* at 1949–53.

one set of actions – namely, section 1 conspiracy claims – but to keep the standards distinct in all other civil actions.[195]

Our interpretation of *Twombly* is not only the most compelling reading of the Court's decision given the context in which it was decided; it is also the understanding most consistent with substantive antitrust and civil procedure considerations. Interpreting *Twombly*'s motion to dismiss standard, which is rooted in plausibility, as distinct from the standards for summary judgment and judgment as a matter of law is most consistent with the general principles of civil procedure that distinguish between pleading standards and evidentiary standards.[196] The *Matsushita* standard for summary judgment requires the plaintiff to adduce evidence sufficient to create an inference that conspiracy is more likely than independent conduct. Requiring plaintiffs to plead facts sufficient to yield the conclusion that the defendants *more* likely engaged in a conspiracy than in independent conduct would contravene settled civil procedure law that requires a complaint to provide only legally sufficient grounds for relief and fair notice to the defendant, as opposed to proof of the claim.[197] Conflating the summary judgment and motion to dismiss standards would be inconsistent with the Court's insistence in *Twombly* that it rejected the imposition of a heightened pleading standard for section 1 conspiracy complaints[198] and with the Court's oft-stated insistence that statutorily and Rule 9 specified exceptions to general notice pleading mark the exhaustive bounds of heightened pleading particularity requirements.[199]

Furthermore, as a matter of judicial practice, leaning on tests developed for summary judgment motions to evaluate motions to dismiss would invite a type of evidentiary

---

[195]   Justice Souter, the author of the *Twombly* opinion, dissented in *Iqbal*, and he was joined by Justices Stevens, Ginsburg, and Breyer. Justice Souter found that the majority had misapplied the pleading standard he had announced for the *Twombly* Court. *Id.* at 1955 (Souter, J., dissenting). In his dissent Justice Souter emphasized that in considering a motion to dismiss, 'a court must take the allegations as true, no matter how skeptical the court may be . . . [T]he relevant question is whether, assuming the factual allegations are true, the plaintiff has stated a ground for relief that is plausible'. *Id.* at 1959. In distinguishing the circumstances in *Iqbal* from those in *Twombly*, Justice Souter re-affirmed the view that in his assessment the *Twombly* plaintiffs had alleged only parallel conduct that was as consistent with legal behavior as with conspiracy, and hence their complaint had not presented a plausible basis for entitlement to relief. *Id.* at 1959–60.

[196]   See Swierkiewicz v. Sorema N.A., 534 U.S. 506, 512 (2002) (holding that a court cannot require a Title VII plaintiff to plead facts necessary to establish a *prima facie* discrimination case because, since the 'prima facie case operates as a flexible evidentiary standard, it should not be transposed into a rigid pleading standard for discrimination cases').

[197]   Justice Stevens feared the majority opinion did just this: 'Here, the failure the majority identifies is not a failure of notice – which 'notice pleading' rightly condemns – but rather a failure to satisfy the Court that the agreement alleged might plausibly have occurred. That being a question not of *notice* but of *proof*, it should not be answered without first hearing from the defendants (as apart from their lawyers)'. *Twombly*, 550 U.S. at 588 n.8 (Stevens, J., dissenting) (original emphasis).

[198]   See *id.* at 569 n.14 (majority opinion) ('In reaching this conclusion, we do not apply any "heightened" pleading standard, nor do we seek to broaden the scope of Federal Rule of Civil Procedure 9, which can only be accomplished "by the process of amending the Federal Rules, and not by judicial interpretation"') (quoting *Swierkiewicz*, 534 U.S. at 515).

[199]   See, e.g., *Swierkiewicz*, 534 U.S. at 513; Leatherman v. Tarrant County Narcotics Intelligence, 507 U.S. 163, 168 (1993).

inquiry inappropriate to the pleading stage of litigation. At issue in a motion to dismiss is the plausibility of successful discovery; at issue in summary judgment is the plausibility of the claim itself. Thus, *Twombly* and *Matsushita* speak to two different questions. The motion to dismiss standard must be fashioned with an eye to identifying legally sufficient complaints whose claimants have a reasonable possibility of being able to develop proof of conspiracy through the discovery process. The *Matsushita* summary judgment standard was fashioned with an eye to selecting for continued consideration those claims that are supported by sufficient evidence so that the plaintiffs making them have a reasonable probability of being able to prove their cases to a jury.

Courts trying antitrust conspiracy cases regularly repeat the Rule 56 mantra that in deciding motions for summary judgment, all inferences regarding disputed facts must be drawn in favor of the nonmoving party. Nevertheless, the *Matsushita* standard requires (to borrow the words of the *Tellabs* Court referring to the PSLRA context) an assessment of the plaintiff's evidence that is 'inherently comparative', because to 'determine whether the plaintiff has alleged facts that give rise to the requisite [inference] . . . a court must consider plausible nonculpable explanations for the defendant's conduct, as well as inferences favoring the plaintiff'.[200] This description applies equally well to summary judgment motions under the *Matsushita* standard because there the Court held that 'conduct as consistent with permissible competition as with illegal conspiracy does not, standing alone, support an inference of antitrust conspiracy', and that a plaintiff 'must show that the inference of conspiracy is reasonable in light of the competing inferences of independent action or collusive action that could not have harmed respondents'.[201]

Whether or not the upshot of this standard, as Justice White worried in his *Matsushita* dissent, requires a judge to 'invade the factfinder's province', he was prescient in predicting that the *Matsushita* standard would require a judge to 'decide for himself whether the weight of the evidence favors the plaintiff'.[202] We illustrated this practice at work in our overview of the post-*Matsushita* summary judgment tests that Circuit Courts apply in section 1 cases. Therefore, reliance on language or terms from the summary judgment context (such as plus factors or *Matsushita*'s 'tends to exclude' standard) to fill out the unfamiliar plausibility standard in *Twombly* ought to be rejected because this would invite a type of evaluative, comparative evidentiary inquiry that is inappropriate to the pleading stage.

Justice Stevens, dissenting in *Twombly*, remarked that the distinction between pleading facts and drawing inferences from those facts, on the one hand, and pleading legal conclusions, on the other, is a distinction more of rhetoric than of substance.[203] Hence, judges will necessarily undertake a mixed analysis of facts and law; they will read the basic factual allegations of parallel conduct and additional information about the economic, market, and behavioral context, and come to a judgment about whether these basic facts add up to a plausible story of conspiracy. This, however, does not mean that the judge is employing the summary judgment standard as to the quantum or strength of proof that

---

[200]   Tellabs Inc. v. Makor Issues & Rights, Ltd., 551 U.S. 308, 323–4 (2007).
[201]   Matsushita Elec. Indus. Co. v. Zenith Radio Corp., 475 U.S. 574, 588 (1986).
[202]   *Id.* at 599–600 (White, J., dissenting).
[203]   See *Twombly*, 550 U.S. at 589–90 (Stevens, J., dissenting).

must be presented in the pleadings. Judges ought to examine the facts pled to determine if they compose *a* plausible story of conspiracy that, as a result of discovery, could be supported with additional evidence. They ought not to examine those facts pled to determine whether they render conspiracy the *most likely* story, as applying *Matsushita*'s substantive 'tends to exclude' standard would require.

Could *Twombly*'s plausibility standard nonetheless be interpreted as importing the plus factor doctrine from the summary judgment context into the motion to dismiss context, thereby requiring a plaintiff to marshal the same types of facts in both stages? A plaintiff could certainly satisfy the plausibility standard in defending against a motion to dismiss by pleading one or several plus factors in addition to parallel conduct. But whether or not the *Twombly* plausibility standard implies or demands a 'plus factor pleading rule' depends on how such a rule would employ the term 'plus factor'.

Twombly held that a plaintiff must plead something more than just parallel conduct. Therefore, the complaint must allege *some* facts that would raise the posterior likelihood of conspiracy above the likelihood implied by mere parallel conduct. This additional evidence would be any fact (F) that together with parallel conduct is more consistent with conspiracy than is parallel conduct alone, so that $P(C \mid PC \& F) > P(C \mid PC)$.[204] If *this* is what a court would mean by a plus factor pleading rule, then such a rule is consistent with *Twombly*'s plausibility standard because the rule requires only that plaintiffs plead *some* additional evidence, in addition to parallel conduct, that when considered together 'nudge[s] their claims across the line from conceivable to plausible'.[205] As with plus factors in the summary judgment context, the additional facts in pleadings could relate to the structure of the market in question and the conduct of the firms in it, or they could relate to specific acts undertaken by the defendants in pursuit of the alleged conspiracy.

The difficulty, however, is that since *Matsushita* many lower courts have employed the term 'plus factors' to indicate a set of evidence that when combined with parallel conduct is sufficient to make an inference of conspiracy more likely than an inference of independent conduct.[206] If *this* is what a court would mean by a plus factor pleading rule, then such a rule would demand more of a plaintiff than *Twombly* does. It would require the

---

[204]   For example, Richard A. Posner in his seminal 1969 article argued that supracompetitive pricing does not automatically follow from the mere existence of oligopolistic market conditions. Instead, it requires some 'additional, voluntary behavior by sellers' that must include some form of signaling the intention to restrict output and increase prices above competitive levels and some positive acts of implementation and enforcement of supracompetitive price levels. Posner, *supra* note 16, at 1578. He therefore argued that instances of tacit collusion (successful supracompetitive pricing in oligopolistic markets) should be treated identically to instances of express collusion under section 1. For Posner, a number of types of proof would indicate the existence of tacit collusion, understood as encompassing interdependent reliance on the decisions of other firms in a concentrated market to restrict output and raise prices above competitive levels without an *express* agreement to such ends. For example, Posner noted the persistent existence of excess capacity, market-wide price discrimination, sustained abnormal profits, stable market shares, and price leadership as examples of facts that would raise the likelihood that firms were guilty of tacit collusion in oligopolistic markets. *Id.* at 1578–84. Judge Posner re-affirmed these views in RICHARD A. POSNER, ANTITRUST LAW 55–100 (2d ed., University of Chicago Press, 2001).

[205]   *Twombly*, 550 U.S. at 547.

[206]   We demonstrated this in section V.

plaintiff to plead a set of facts (plus factors 1, . . ., n) that would result in a likelihood of conspiracy that is higher than the likelihood of independent conduct, that is, such that:

$$P(C \mid PC \ \& \ PF_1 \ \& \ PF_2 \ \& \ . . . \ \& \ PF_n) > P(I \mid PC \ \& \ PF_1 \ \& \ PF_2 \ \& \ . . . \ \& \ PF_n).$$

This understanding of a plus factor pleading rule would be inconsistent with the *Twombly* decision because it demands a specific quantum of probative weight from the additional facts pled along with parallel conduct, namely, that in light of all the facts alleged, the probability of conspiracy must be greater than one-half.

It is arguable that *Twombly* requires more than that the plaintiff include in her complaint facts that increase the probability of conspiracy above that implied by parallel conduct alone. For example, the *Twombly* standard might demand that the facts pled in the complaint yield a probability of conspiracy that *substantially* exceeds the probability that follows from parallel conduct alone, so that $P(C \mid PC \ \& \ F) > P(C \mid PC) + K$, where K is some constant threshold by which the fact(s) F must increase the probability of conspiracy. The plaintiff cannot be required, however, to show more than that $P(C \mid PC \ \& \ F) > 0.5$, for if she satisfies this condition, then she has, in fact, met the *Matsushita* summary judgment test. Hence, the *Twombly* increased-probability test requires that $P(C \mid PC \ \& \ F) > \mathrm{Min} \ [P(C \mid PC) + K, 0.5]$; it does not generally demand of the plaintiff that she show that with all that she pleads – namely, PC & F – the probability of conspiracy exceeds the probability of independent conduct.

Therefore, although a plaintiff could satisfy the *Twombly* plausibility standard by pleading facts that have been recognized as plus factors in the summary judgment context, the *Twombly* plausibility standard should not be interpreted as requiring plaintiffs to plead plus factors as they have been understood in the summary judgment context. Plus factors in the latter context have come to connote those sets of facts that satisfy a particular evidentiary standard – that of *Matsushita*'s summary judgment standard of 'tends to exclude' – that is distinctly different from what should be required in making a determination on the basis of the pleadings alone.

As noted in the introduction, the question we address – what is required to plead an agreement? – and the logically prior question of what defines an agreement merge at this juncture. Specifically, if tacit collusion is recognized as a conspiracy proscribed by section 1, then a plaintiff ought to be able to proceed by pleading parallel conduct in the form of supracompetitive pricing and evidence of the character of the market or the good that economic theory strongly suggests makes the maintenance of an agreement more economically feasible. With tacit collusion so understood, pleading such facts could satisfy the $P(C \mid PC \ \& \ F) > \mathrm{Min} \ [P(C \mid PC) + K, 0.5]$ requirement because we would not expect the existence of parallel, supracompetitive pricing by all firms in such a market in the absence of conspiracy. Hence, that evidence relating to the market could yield a value of $P(C \mid PC \ \& \ F)$ sufficiently greater than $P(C \mid PC)$. Again, such market evidence taken alone could suffice *only* if the definition of an agreement were to include tacit collusion.[207]

In sharp contrast, if courts do not consider tacit collusion unlawful under section 1,

---

[207]   'If a firm raises price in the expectation that its competitors will do likewise, and they do, the firm's behavior can be conceptualized as the offer of a unilateral contract that the offerees accept

satisfying our proposed formalization of the *Twombly* standard could require certain types of facts suggestive either of actual instances of meeting and agreeing about prices, quantities, or other elements of firm policies or of compelling opportunities to do so. In *Twombly* itself the Supreme Court did seem to leave open the status of tacit collusion when it cited discussions of the phenomenon in a footnote expanding on the types of facts that might be sufficient 'to raise a reasonable expectation that discovery will reveal evidence of illegal agreement'.[208]

Finally, the *Twombly* majority expressed great concern about reports of growing litigation costs, specifically discovery costs, in antitrust cases.[209] But a plus factor pleading requirement would not necessarily promote the goal of minimizing the cost of false positives that are allowed to proceed to discovery. Instead, such a requirement might just promote a rigid and formalistic listing in complaints of officially recognized 'plus factors'. Because courts are not to evaluate the evidentiary sufficiency of facts alleged in a complaint, a plus factor pleading rule might lead courts simply to look at a checklist of these factors as opposed to evaluating the overall economic feasibility of the alleged conspiracy scheme. Furthermore, calling for an examination of plus factors at the pleading stage would likely elevate and might well distort their role throughout a case. It might well tend to ossify the approach to illegal section 1 behavior by leading finders of fact to focus on such factors one by one rather than taking a holistic approach to assessing the defendant's acts.

Table 8.1 summarizes the distinctions we have advanced between the motion to dismiss and summary judgment assessments.

IX   CONCLUSION: THE FUTURE OF THE PLAUSIBILITY STANDARD

We do not join the chorus of commentators who decry the 'plausibility' standard of the *Twombly* opinion as hopelessly ambiguous or disappointingly unclear. As we have sought to show by examining the extensive litigation history of the case and the jurisprudential

---

by raising their prices.' *In re High Fructose Corn Syrup Antitrust Litig.*, 295 F.3d 651, 654 (7th Cir. 2002).

[208]   *Twombly*, 550 U.S. at 556, n.4. 'Commentators have offered several examples of parallel conduct allegations that would state a § 1 claim under this standard. See, e.g., 6 Areeda & Hovenkamp para. 1425, at 167–185 (discussing "parallel behavior that would probably not result from chance, coincidence, independent responses to common stimuli, or mere interdependence unaided by an advance understanding among the parties"); Blechman, *Conscious Parallelism, Signalling and Facilitating Devices: The Problem of Tacit Collusion Under the Antitrust Laws*, 24 N.Y.L.S.L. Rev. 881, 899 (1979) (describing "conduct [that] indicates the sort of restricted freedom of action and sense of obligation that one generally associates with agreement"). The parties in this case agree that "complex and historically unprecedented changes in pricing structure made at the very same time by multiple competitors, and made for no other discernible reason" would support a plausible inference of conspiracy. Brief for Respondents 37; see also Reply Brief for Petitioners 12.'

[209]   See *Twombly*, 550 U.S. at 558–60 (citing various sources arguing that the costs and scope of discovery in federal antitrust is extensive and worrying that the 'threat of discovery expense will push cost-conscious defendants to settle even anemic cases before reaching those proceedings').

Table 8.1   Comparison of tests in antitrust for motions to dismiss and motions for summary judgment

Distinguishing factors	Motion to dismiss	Summary judgment
Guiding case articulating standard in antitrust context	Twombly	Matsushita
Federal Rule of Civil Procedure at issue	Rule 12(b)(6): motion to dismiss for failure to state a claim	Rule 56: motion for summary judgment
Motion designed to winnow cases deficient for which stage of litigation	Discovery: search for evidence to substantiate claim	Trial: assessment of evidence by fact-finder
Issue presented by motion at this stage of litigation	Legal sufficiency: does plaintiff have sufficient grounds for her claim in the law and in the facts she has pled to proceed to discovery?	Evidentiary sufficiency: has the plaintiff amassed sufficient evidence of defendants' conspiracy to show there is a genuine issue of material fact to proceed to trial?
Standard	Plaintiff must plead sufficient facts to suggest plausible story of conspiracy	Plaintiff must present evidence 'that tends to exclude the possibility' that the alleged conspirators acted independently (*Matsushita*, 475 U.S. at 588)
In section 1 cases lacking direct evidence of conspiracy, can parallel conduct alone satisfy standard?	No, something more is needed	No, something more is needed
Types of facts that satisfy something more	Any facts that raise the posterior probability of conspiracy above the baseline probability from parallel conduct alone or do so by a given amount	Plus factors such that the posterior probability of conspiracy given the plus factors and parallel conduct is greater than the probability of independent conduct given plus factors and parallel conduct
Formalization of 'something more' required in addition to parallel conduct	At least some fact F such that $P(C \mid PC \& F) > P(C \mid PC)$	A set of PF_i, $i = 1, \ldots, n$ such that: $P(C \mid PC \& PF_1 \& PF_2 \& \ldots \& PF_n) > P(I \mid PC \& PF_1 \& PF_2 \& \ldots \& PF_n)$
Absolute or relative level of probativeness?	Increase in level of probativeness $P(C \mid PC \& PF) > \mathrm{Min}[P(C \mid PC) + K, 0.5]$	Absolute level of probativeness $P(C \mid PC \& PF_1 \& PF_2 \& \ldots \& PF_n) > 0.5$

context of the question presented in *Twombly*, the Court was wise to choose a term hitherto unfamiliar for evaluating a motion to dismiss. That choice served to indicate the Court's rejection of the position that entrenched summary judgment practices should inform the Rule 12(b)(6) question.

In his *Twombly* dissent Justice Stevens argued that because Congress intended to encourage private enforcement of the antitrust laws (for example, by providing for treble damages and reimbursement of attorney fees) '[i]t is . . . more, not less, important in anti-trust cases to resist the urge to engage in armchair economics at the pleading stage'.[210] This well-sounded cautionary note serves as a reminder that motions on the pleadings should not be taken as an opportunity to pass on the probative prospects or evidentiary sufficiency of a plaintiff's nascent case. Given many legal academics' statements about *Twombly*, one might well believe that the majority gave the green light to lower courts to use Rule 12(b)(6) motions to screen out conspiracy antitrust cases that judges find have a low probability of success. This would be a troubling prospect indeed.

Twombly does not necessitate such an outcome. Lower courts have applied the *Matsushita* summary judgment standard to require a comparative evaluation of the plaintiff's evidence at the summary judgment phase and have granted the defendant's motion at that stage when the plaintiff could not show, on the record at that point, that conspiracy is a more likely inference than independent behavior. In the *Twombly* litiga-tion, the lower courts and the parties debated at great length the appropriateness of applying the summary judgment standard when ruling on the motion to dismiss. Yet in formulating its own standard applicable to deciding a Rule 12(b)(6) motion, the Court incorporates no reference to settled terms and standards from the summary judgment context. Instead of referencing a standard, such as plus factors or 'tends to exclude', with which lower courts are exceedingly familiar, the Court introduced a new standard with fresh language. The most compelling interpretation of the Court's decision is that it eschewed the summary judgment standard in the context of a motion to dismiss. Moreover, we have argued that as a matter of civil procedure and substantive antitrust law, we should reject an interpretation of the plausibility standard that incorporates summary judgment practices.

Some have found alarming the range of linguistic formulations of the motion to dismiss standard in the lower courts in the post-*Twombly* world.[211] This is not necessarily a distressing sign, unless the substance of the analysis being conducted with these diverse formulations indicates the courts are filling in the conceptual blanks by relying on tests or standards from the summary judgment context. We have sought to show why courts ought not to reach to the summary judgment standard to make the *Twombly* approach more precise. What is transpiring in the lower courts' application of *Twombly* fits with the common law tradition of antitrust. Over time, the courts will develop a repertoire of factual augmentation sufficient to satisfy the 'something more' beyond parallel conduct that will give content to the plausibility standard. This standard will acquire substance just as the entirety of section 1 has: from the broad proscription against 'contract, com-bination . . . conspiracy, in restraint of trade', courts have developed justiciable standards through their experience with a variety of factual contexts.

---

[210]   *Twombly*, 550 U.S. at 587 (Stevens, J., dissenting).
[211]   See, e.g., Redish and Epstein, *supra* note 11.

9 Monopsony, monopsony power, and antitrust policy

*Roger D. Blair and Jessica S. Haynes**

I INTRODUCTION

For the most part, antitrust enforcement has focused on monopoly problems – both real and imagined. Whether it was structural monopoly, collusive monopoly (overt or tacit), monopoly leveraging, market foreclosure, or trends in concentration, the focus has largely been on the selling side. Recently, however, some attention has shifted to the buying side and, therefore, to problems of monopsony. Monopsony is the flip-side of monopoly: instead of having a single seller, we have a single buyer in the market. As with pure monopoly, pure monopsony is rare, but its economic equivalent, a buying cartel, is not. Allegations of collusion among buyers have been raised against antique dealers, Major League Baseball owners, the NCAA, hospitals, and bidders for timber harvesting rights, among others. As an antitrust awareness of monopsony problems has grown, it is useful to examine the economics of monopsony. In section II of this chapter, we present and explain various models of monopsony: pure monopsony, collusive monopsony, dominant buyer, and oligopsony. We include a discussion of the social welfare losses associated with monopsony. In section III, we adapt the familiar Lerner Index to monopsony and discuss its significance. In section IV, we turn our attention to antitrust policy. Some final remarks are provided in section V.

II MODELS OF MONOPSONY

In this section, we present and explain structural and behavioral variants of monopsony. Profit-maximizing behavior will also be presented along with the consequences for social welfare.

A Pure Monopsony

When there is only one buyer of a sensibly defined input, that buyer is a pure monopsonist by definition. If the supply of the input is positively sloped, then the monopsonist can profit from its position as a single buyer. Start with a simple case of a firm that combines labor (L) and capital (K) to produce an output that it sells in an output market in which it may have some market power. With respect to the input markets, assume that it is the only employer of labor in the relevant market, but acquires capital in a competitive

* For past collaboration, we thank Jill Herndon, John Lopatka, and Christine Durrance.

capital market. Assuming that the supply of labor has a positive slope, the wage (w) will rise as the quantity of labor employed rises. Now, the firm's profit (π) function can be written as

$$\pi = PQ(L, K) - w(L)L - rK$$

where Q(L, K) is the production function and r is the price of capital. In order to maximize profit, the firm will expand its employment of labor and capital until

$$MRP_L - (w + Ldw/dL) = 0$$

and

$$MRP_K - r = 0$$

where MRP_L and MRP_K are the marginal revenue products of labor and capital, respectively.[1] Here, we are concerned with the first of these two conditions. Profit maximization leads the firm to limit its employment of labor to the quantity where the marginal revenue product is equal to the marginal factor cost, which is the increase in the total wage bill when employment is increased by a small amount. The total wage bill is w(L)L and, therefore, the change is found where

$$dw(L)L/dL = w + Ldw/dL$$

which is the marginal factor cost (MFC). Employing labor at the equality of MRP_L and MFC makes sense because the MRP_L measures the marginal benefit of adding one more unit of labor while the *MFC* measures the marginal cost of adding one more unit. This result and its consequences can be illustrated in Figure 9.1.

In the absence of monopsony, L_1 units of labor would be hired where demand (MRP_L) equals supply (S_L). The wage would then be w_1. Due to monopsony, however, employment is restricted to L_2 and the wage falls to w_2. The exercise of monopsony results in a deadweight social welfare loss that is analogous to the welfare loss associated with monopoly.

At the competitive solution, the employer enjoys some 'employer surplus' equal to area abw_1 while the workers garner 'supplier surplus' equal to area cbw_1.[2]

The monopsonist operates at L_2 and pays a wage of w_2. By doing so, the monopsonist converts some supplier surplus, $(w_1 - w_2)L_2$, into employer surplus. It is, of course, *privately* optimal to do so, but it is not socially optimal. At L_2, the social value of employing

---

[1]   These conditions for profit maximization are found by taking the first partial derivatives of π and setting them equal to zero. The marginal revenue product is the product of the marginal revenue and the marginal product of the input in question.

[2]   Employer surplus is analogous to consumer surplus and measures the difference between the employer's willingness to pay and what must be paid in the competitive market. Supplier surplus is analogous to producer surplus and measures the difference between the reservation wage and the competitive market wage.

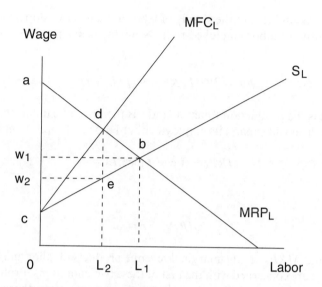

Figure 9.1   Monopsony in the labor market

one more unit is given by the height of the MRP_L curve. The social cost is given by the height of the supply curve. Since $MRP_L > w_2$ at L_2, some social value is lost. This is true for all units of labor between L_1 and L_2. The result is a deadweight social welfare loss equal to area dbe. This welfare loss is the economic foundation for objecting to monopsony.

B   The 'All-or-None' Variant

In the usual case, a buyer offers a price and the quantity that is found on the supply curve. To get more, the buyer must offer a higher price. In some circumstances, a monopsonist may make 'all-or-none' offers. In such cases, the monopsonist requires a specific quantity at a particular price. The supplier's option is to provide the requisite quantity at the price offered or supply nothing at all. This strategy will permit the monopsonist to extract all of the producer surplus. This result can be illustrated in Figure 9.2.

Put in the labor market context, demand is represented by MRP and the usual supply is denoted by S. The competitive solution is found where MRP equals S, i.e. at $w = w_1$ and $L = L_1$. The employer's surplus at the competitive solution is equal to area abw_1 while the supplier surplus is equal to area cbw_1. The sum of the employer surplus and the supplier surplus, which is area abc, is the maximum surplus that the market will generate.

Usually, a monopsonist would reduce its employment and thereby depress the wage below w_1 in order to maximize its profit. In an all-or-none setting, the monopsonist will demand L_1, but offer a wage of w_2. In this case, the employer offers to employ L_1 at w_2 or it will not hire anyone. By selecting the all-or-none wage optimally, the monopsonist can enjoy the total surplus of area abc and leave nothing for labor. Figure 9.2 depicts such a case.

At the competitive solution, the supplier surplus is area cbw_1. When the wage is reduced to w_2, labor would usually fall to L_2. This would generate a supplier surplus area of cew_2.

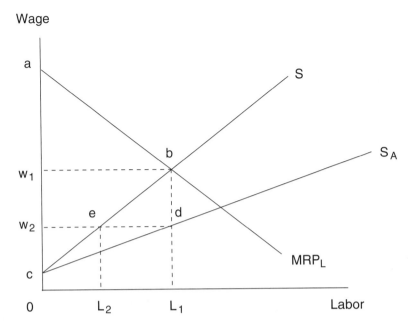

Figure 9.2   All-or-none supply

But the demand that L_1 units be supplied forces labor on to the all-or-none supply curve. At w_2 and L_1, area cew_2 is equal to area bde. Now, the employer surplus is equal to the area $abdw_2$ which is equal to area abc.

In this case, monopsony does not result in allocative inefficiency. The competitive quantity is employed, which means that the marginal social benefit of the last unit hired is equal to the marginal social cost. Consequently, the effect of monopsony is purely distributional; all of the surplus goes to the employer.

C   Collusive Monopsony

As we observed earlier, pure monopsony is rare, but collusive monopsony is not.[3] The organizational problems for a buyer cartel are analogous to those facing a seller cartel. The otherwise competitive buyers must agree to curtail purchases in order to depress price. The details of how much employment should be reduced and the allocation of buying quotas must be determined. Ideally, the cartel should behave as a multi-unit monopsonist would behave. This could involve differential quotas, which could be a destabilizing force if a profit-sharing mechanism cannot be devised that is mutually satisfactory.

As with any cartel, cheating poses a significant problem. Every cartel member will be operating where its marginal revenue product exceeds the depressed price. If everyone

---

[3]   A sample of these cases will be examined in section IV. For a more extensive discussion, see Roger D. Blair and Jeffrey L. Harrison, *Antitrust Policy and Monopsony*, 76 CORNELL L. REV. 297 (1991).

else adheres to the prescribed quota, one firm can increase its purchases substantially. This will cause a small increase in price, which is diffused across the entire market, while the cheater reaps the full benefit of cheating. The problem, of course, is that all cartel members have the same incentive to cheat, which would cause the cartel to collapse. In order to deter cheating by its members, the cartel must find a way to make cheating unprofitable. It must also monitor each member's behavior in an effort to detect cheating.

If the buying cartel is successful, it will behave precisely the way that a pure monopsonist would behave. Assuming that all-or-none offers are not feasible, the cartel will restrict its collective purchases to the point where the input's marginal revenue product equals the marginal factor cost. The effects will be those depicted in Figure 9.1: price will fall, buyer surplus will rise, and there will be a deadweight social welfare loss due to the allocative inefficiency.

D   Dominant Buyer

The dominant buyer is a close cousin of the pure monopsonist. In this model, a single large buyer is surrounded by a collection of small buyers, which are referred to collectively as the competitive fringe. Due to its size, the dominant firm recognizes that its purchases will influence the market price. As a result, this firm will act as a price setter rather than a price taker. Each fringe firm is small enough that it acts as a price taker because it believes that its purchases are too small to influence price in the market. In essence, the fringe of competitive buyers accepts the price that the dominant buyer pays as the market determined price. Behaving competitively, the fringe firms will buy the input up to the point where their collective demand equals the price set by the dominant buyer. Now, the dominant buyer's problem is to adjust its purchases to maximize profit subject to the competitive behavior of the fringe buyers. This is shown in Figure 9.3 where D_f represents the demand for the input in question by the competitive fringe, D_{df} represents the demand of the dominant firm, and S is the supply curve. The dominant firm recognizes that at any price that it sets, the fringe will purchase the quantity where D_f equals that price. The dominant buyer incorporates this behavior into its decision calculus by subtracting D_f from S to obtain the residual supply, which is denoted by S_r in Figure 9.3. The curve marginal to S_r, which is labeled MFC, represents the marginal factor cost for the dominant buyer. Given the presence of the competitive fringe, the dominant buyer acts like a monopsonist. The dominant buyer selects Q_{df} where MFC equals D_{df}, which determines price equal to P from the residual supply. At a price of P, the fringe firms will purchase Q_f where P equals D_f. At price of P, sellers will provide Q, which is equal to the sum of Q_{df} and Q_f. The marginal factor cost (MFC) exceeds the price of the input (P).

The profit-maximizing behavior of the dominant buyer leads to the same sort of allocative inefficiency that results from pure monopsony. Since MFC exceeds P, the value created by employing one more unit would exceed the social cost of doing so. As a consequence, dominant buyer behavior leads to a deadweight social welfare loss analogous to that of pure monopsony. The magnitude of the welfare loss will be smaller due to the presence of the competitive fringe. The ability of the dominant buyer to depress price below the competitive level is blunted by the fringe's willingness to expand purchases when price is reduced. But the fringe merely reduces and does not eliminate the social welfare loss.

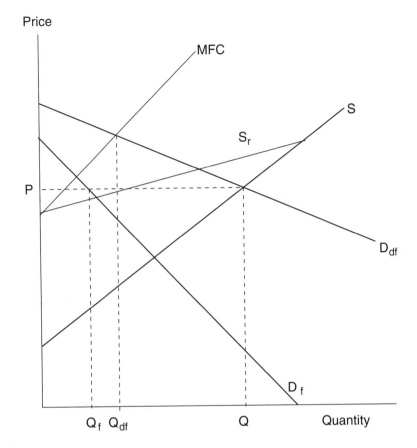

Price

MFC

S

S_r

P

D_{df}

D_f

Q_f Q_{df}

Q

Quantity

Figure 9.3 Dominant buyer

E Oligopsony

In markets where there are a small number of large buyers, the ability to depress the input price is more circumscribed than under monopsony. The exertion of oligopsony power relies on the mutual interdependence of firms' price and quantity decisions. Depending upon the choice of the decision variable[4] and the information structure of the game, the oligopsony equilibrium price will be between the monopsony and competitive input prices. In the case of Bertrand competition, the price will equal the competitive input price even with only two buyers.

In this subsection, we translate the standard Cournot, Bertrand, and Stackelberg[5]

---

[4] We examine both quantity and price as decision variables.

[5] See A. Augustin Cournot, Recherches sur les Principes Mathematiques de la Theorie des Richesses (Libraire des sciences politiques et sociales, M. Rivière & Cie, Paris, 1838) (English translation: Researches into the Mathematical Principles of the Theory of Wealth (Nathaniel T. Bacon trans., Macmillan Co., New York, 1929)); J. Bertrand, *Book review of Theorie*

oligopoly results into the oligopsony setting and discuss the implications for the exercise of oligopsony power.

1 Cournot

If firms independently and simultaneously choose the quantity of input to buy, a Cournot oligopsony provides the desired setting. For ease of explanation, we assume that supply is linear, $w = a + bX$, and the firms are identical. By assuming the firms are identical, we are assured that all firms have the same marginal revenue product. This is equivalent to assuming all firms have symmetric costs in the standard Cournot oligopoly game. We also assume that the oligopsonist only utilizes one input to produce its output. It is common and straightforward to think of this input as labor. Finally, to satisfy second-order conditions, the production function Q must be concave, i.e. must exhibit nonincreasing returns to scale.

Firm i's profit can be written as

$$\pi_i = PQ(x_i) - x_i\left(a + b\sum_{i=1}^{n}x_i\right), i = 1, \ldots, n$$

All n firms recognize their ability to affect the input price. Accordingly the firms choose the quantity of input to employ while recognizing that the price of the input increases in their own employment and the employment of others. Firms maximize profit as follows

$$\frac{\partial\pi_i}{\partial x_i} = PQ' - a - b\sum_{j\neq i}^{(n-1)}x_j - 2bx_i = 0$$

Since all the firms have the same marginal revenue product and face the same supply curve, $x_i = x_j$ for all i and j. This simplifies the above expression. The equilibrium in a Cournot oligopsony is, then, characterized by the following three equations:

$$x_i = \frac{PQ' - a}{b(n + 1)}$$

$$w = \frac{a}{n + 1} + \frac{n}{n + 1}PQ'$$

$$x = nx_i = \frac{n(PQ' - a)}{(n + 1)b}$$

In the first equation, we note that the quantity of input purchased by each firm is decreasing in the number of firms. In the second equation, we can see that the extent of oligopsony power is decreasing as the number of firms increases by looking at the input price. As $n \to \infty$, $w \to PQ'$ which is the competitive outcome.

---

mathematique de la richesse sociale and of Recherches sur les principes mathematiques de la theorie des richesses, 67 J. DES SAVANTS 499 (1883); H. VON STACKELBERG, MARKET STRUCTURE AND EQUILIBRIUM (Bazin, Urch and Hill trans., Springer, 2011 (1st ed. 1934)).

2   Bertrand

Oligopsony can also be analysed as a Bertrand game in which firms compete for the input by offering an input price w. When the decision variable is the input price, the competition between even two firms will drive the price up to the competitive level. This, of course, is the well-known Bertrand paradox. To show this result, we begin by analysing a Bertrand duopsony with homogeneous products. In this game, two firms offer input prices and the following quantity supplied results

$$x_1(w_1, w_2) = \begin{cases} 0 & if\, w_1 < w_2 \\ \frac{1}{2}X(w) & if\, w_1 = w_2 \\ X(w) & if\, w_1 > w_2 \end{cases}$$

The firms' profit functions are

$$\pi_i = P\, Q(x_i(w_i, w_j)) - w_i x_i(w_i, w_i), \quad i = 1, 2$$

If the input price offered by firm 1 is below the price offered by the other firm, then firm 1 will not be able to buy any of the input and will earn zero profit. Therefore firm 1 could do better by offering $w \geq w_2$. If both firms offer an equal price below PQ', then firm i will earn more profit by deviating and offering to pay a higher price. A small increase in w_i above w_j leads to a large increase in x_i. Since $PQ' > w_i$, it pays to offer such an increase. This process will continue until the firms bid the price up to the competitive level. In other words, Bertrand competition in oligopsony can be thought of as an ascending price auction with common values.

If we extend the analysis to n > 2 firms, all firms offering $w = PQ'$ will still be an equilibrium. There are also multiple equilibria where at least two firms offer the competitive price and all other firms offer a price arbitrarily below this price. The firms offering an arbitrarily low price of course are unable to buy any of the input and therefore earn zero profit.

3   Stackelberg

Oligopsony settings can also be analysed by changing the information structure of the game. In a Stackelberg duopsony model, the firms choose outputs (or prices) sequentially. Below we analyse a Stackelberg quantity game.

Firm 1 moves first and chooses a quantity that accounts for the profit-maximizing decisions of firm 2. The result of this is that firm 2 is worse off than in the Cournot game because it pays a higher price and consumes less of the input. The firms have the following profit functions

$$\pi_1 = PQ(x_1) - x_1(a + bx_1 + bx_2)$$

$$\pi_2 = PQ(x_2) - x_2(a + bx_1 + bx_2)$$

This game is then solved by backward induction, so firm 1 maximizes the following profit function

$$\pi_1 = PQ(x_1) - x_1\left(a + \frac{bx_1}{2} + \frac{PQ' - a}{2}\right)$$

The resulting optimal quantity for firm 1 is

$$x_1 = \frac{PQ' - a}{2b}$$

which is the quantity that would be chosen by a monopsonist. In turn, firm 2 chooses to buy quantity

$$x_2 = \frac{PQ' - a}{4b}$$

The resulting input price and total quantity supplied are

$$w = \frac{a + 3PQ'}{4}$$

$$X = \frac{3(PQ' - a)}{4b}$$

As noted above, the price in the Stackelberg quantity game exceeds the price in the Cournot setting. This price, however, will still be below the Bertrand/competitive price.

The duopsony game outlined above can be extended to a game with multiple first- and second-movers. As the number of second-movers increases, the total quantity supplied will increase. The quantity chosen by the individual second-movers, however, will decrease with the number of firms. Increased number of firms in turn leads to an increase in the input price. Again as $n \to \infty$, $w \to PQ'$.

To illustrate the results discussed above, we extend the Stackelberg game by allowing for two second-movers. These firms are $i = 1, 2$. Functions associated with the first-mover are denoted by the subscript f.

$$\pi_f = PQ(x_f) - x_f(a + bx_f + bx_1 + bx_2)$$

$$\pi_i = PQ(x_i) - x_i(a + bx_f + bx_i + bx_j), \quad i = 1, 2$$

Since firm f accounts for the profit-maximizing choice of firms 1 and 2, the profit function firm 1 maximizes is

$$\pi_f = PQ(x_f) - x_f\left(\frac{2PQ' + a + bx_f}{3}\right)$$

The following equations characterize the equilibrium of this game

$$x_f = \frac{PQ' - a}{2b}$$

$$x_1 = x_2 = \frac{PQ' - a}{6b}$$

$$X = x_f + x_1 + x_2 = \frac{5(PQ' - a)}{6b}$$

$$w = \frac{a + 5PQ'}{6}$$

The resulting quantities show that the individual firms further restrict the quantities they buy, while the first-mover does not change its quantity decision.

This result follows from the fact that the second-movers act as though the first-mover will not alter its purchases. Thus, they behave like Cournot quantity setters and split up the rest of the supply. As $n \to \infty$, the second-movers approach all of the remaining supply at the competitive price.

4   Chamberlin and tacit collusion

Edward Chamberlin introduced the notion of tacit collusion in a duopoly context.[6] Adapting his logic to duopsony is straightforward. Begin with a pure monopsony, which will purchase that quantity where MFC equals the marginal revenue product. This of course maximizes the incumbent's profit. When a second firm enters and competes on quantity, it will purchase the input in question to maximize its profits, which causes the input price to rise. This also begins the process of moving to the Cournot duopsony solution. In that event, the incumbent and the entrant will each buy the same amount and each will earn less than half of the monopsony profits. Chamberlin suggested that an alternative and more profitable solution is available. An enlightened incumbent will accommodate the entrant by reducing its purchases to one-half of its former level. If the entrant is smart it will hold its initial purchases constant. In that event, the two firms will keep the price at the monopsony level and each firm will earn half of the monopsony profit, which is more than half of any other profit. This unspoken agreement to accommodate one another's presence is known as tacit collusion.

It is clear that Chamberlin tried to address a multiperiod game with static tools. In a one-period game, Chamberlin's solution is not an equilibrium because either part can profit by deviating from one-half of the monopsony quantity. Modern game theory, however, provides room for Chamberlin in a repeated game context. The so-called Folk Theorem holds that any noncompetitive, noncollusive outcome – including the joint profit-maximizing solution – can prevail in a repeated game of indefinite duration.[7] Consequently, we may wind up at the monopsony solution even with duopoly.

---

[6]   EDWARD H. CHAMBERLIN, THE THEORY OF MONOPOLISTIC COMPETITION 46–7 (8th ed. 1962).
[7]   This result is outlined in JEAN TIROLE, THE THEORY OF INDUSTRIAL ORGANIZATION 268–9 (1988).

III   MONOPSONY POWER

In analysing any business practice that is governed by the rule of reason, market power is a central issue. In most instances, if there is no appreciable market power, then the conduct will not be deemed anticompetitive. When the antitrust concern is on the selling side of the market, we focus on monopoly power. But when the concern is on the buying side of the market, we are interested in *monopsony* power.[8] As a result, it is useful to have a measure of monopsony power. In this section, we provide such a measure, explain its meaning, and provide some numerical examples.

A   Concept of Monopsony Power

A monopsonist is not an '800-pound gorilla', although notoriously hard bargainers like Wal-Mart may seem to be. In truth, the power of a monopsonist lies in its ability to control the price of what it buys simply by adjusting the quantity.[9] Facing a positively-sloped supply curve, the profit-maximizing monopsonist pushes its purchase price below the competitive level by buying less than the competitive quantity. As we showed in section IIA, a profit-maximizing monopsonist will restrict its purchases below the quantity where its marginal revenue product is equal to the price. As a consequence, the monopsonist slides along the supply curve to a lower price. This, in a nutshell, is the way a monopsonist directly exercises monopsony power.[10]

B   Lerner Index of Monopsony Power

In the absence of monopsony power, a profit-maximizing firm will employ each input to the point where the input's marginal revenue product equals its price. As we have seen above, the monopsonist restricts its employment of a monopsonized input to the point where the marginal revenue product is equal to the marginal factor cost, which exceeds the price. An adaptation of the Lerner Index of monopoly will capture the competitive significance of monopsony.[11]

The profit-maximizing monopsonist will employ the monopsonized input, say labor, where

$$MRP = w + L\,dw/dL$$

which can be written as

---

[8]   This section depends heavily on Roger D. Blair and Jeffrey L. Harrison, *The Measurement of Monopsony Power*, 37 ANTITRUST BULLETIN 133 (1992).

[9]   This is the flip-side of monopoly power, which is the ability to control the selling prices by adjusting output.

[10]   There are examples of the indirect exercise of monopsony power. For instance, in United States v. Griffith, 334 U.S. 100 (1948), the defendant used its monopsony power in some local markets to extract concessions that enhanced its power in the output market in other locations.

[11]   Abba Lerner, *The Concept of Monopoly and the Measurement of Monopoly Power*, 1 REV. ECONOMIC STUDIES 157 (1934).

$$MRP - w = L dw/dL$$

Lerner suggested using the relative deviation from the competitive result as a measure of power. Following this suggestion, we divide both sides by w and use the definition of the elasticity of supply to find

$$\lambda = \frac{MRP - w}{w} = \frac{1}{\varepsilon}$$

where λ is the Lerner Index of monopsony power and ε is the elasticity of supply.[12]

The Lerner Index actually captures the extent of monopsonistic exploitation relative to the price paid.[13] The gap between MRP and w is exploitation in the sense that the marginal value of the labor service (as measured by MRP) exceeds the wage paid. Given the quantity purchased, competition would bid up the price to MRP. Thus, λ captures the deviation from the competitive price relative to the actual price at that quantity.[14]

The elasticity of supply measures the relative responsiveness of the quantity supplied to changes in price. As ε increases, suppliers are better able to adjust their outputs in response to price changes. As ε falls, they are less able to do so. Consequently, λ rises with reductions in ε and falls with increases in ε.[15] This can be seen quite easily in Table 9.1.

Table 9.1   Lerner Index for pure monopsony

ε	4	2	1	0.5	0.25
λ	0.25	0.5	1.0	2.0	4.0

It is clear that when the supply is extremely elastic (e.g., $\varepsilon = 4$), the Lerner Index is small ($\lambda = 0.25$), which indicates that the relative deviation from the competitive price is small. In contrast, an inelastic supply, say, $\varepsilon = 0.50$ leads to a large deviation ($\lambda = 2.0$). Thus, even a pure monopsonist's power to depress price below the competitive level will not be large if suppliers have other options.

C   Lerner Index for a Dominant Buyer

There is no doubt that pure monopsony is rare, but dominant buyers (Toys 'R' Us, Wal-Mart, the NCAA) are more common. Based on the dominant buyer model of section IID

---

[12]   The elasticity of supply measures the responsiveness of the quantity supplied to changes in price. It can be written as $\varepsilon = (dQ/dP)(Q/P)$ which is positive for a positively-sloped supply curve.

[13]   The 'monopsonistic exploitation' of labor can be traced to JOAN ROBINSON, THE ECONOMICS OF IMPERFECT COMPETITION (1933).

[14]   The monopsonistic exploitation of the input is not the same as the damages. Antitrust damages (Δ) would be equal to the difference between the price (P_{BF}) that would have been paid in the 'but for' world, i.e. the world without unlawful monopsony, and the actual price (P_A) paid times the quantity actually purchased (Q_A): $\Delta = (P_{BF} - P_A)Q_A$

[15]   Mathematically, we can check the sign of the first derivative: $d\lambda/d\varepsilon = -1/\varepsilon^2$ which is necessarily negative, thereby establishing the inverse relationship between λ and ε.

Table 9.2   Lerner Index for a dominant buyer with $\varepsilon = 1$ *and* $\eta = 1$ *(× 100)*

S (%)	10	20	30	40	50	60	70	80	90	100
λ	5	11	18	25	33	43	54	67	82	100

above, we can adapt the Lerner Index to the case of a dominant firm facing a fringe of competitive buyers.[16] Figure 9.3 reveals that the quantity supplied to the dominant buyer (Q_{DB}) equals the market supply (Q_M) minus the quantity demanded by the competitive fringe (Q_F)

$$Q_{DB} = Q_M - Q_F$$

It can be shown that the Lerner Index for the dominant buyer is:

$$\lambda = \frac{S}{\varepsilon + \eta(1 - S)}$$

where S is the share of total purchases accounted for by the dominant buyer and η is the elasticity of demand by the competitive fringe.[17] Thus, the Lerner Index for a dominant buyer depends upon the overall elasticity of supply (ε) and the elasticity of demand (η) for the fringe as well as the dominant buyer's share (S) of total purchases. It is easy to show that λ is positively related to S and inversely related to ε and η.[18]

Market share (S). The importance of market share seems intuitively obvious. If a buyer is relatively unimportant in the market, it cannot have much (if any) buying power. In Table 9.2, we show the value of λ for various values of S while assuming that $\varepsilon = 1$ and $\eta = 1$. As is plain to see, when S is small, λ is also small, but as S rises, so does λ. These results are consistent with our intuition and do not deserve much elaboration.

Elasticity of supply (ε). As we saw with the pure monopsonist, the elasticity of supply

---

[16]   This derivation provides the buying power analog to that on the selling side. For the latter, *see* Thomas R. Saving, *Concentration Ratios and the Degree of Monopoly,* 11 INT'L ECON. REV. 139 (1970) or William M. Landes and Richard A. Posner, *Market Power in Antitrust Cases,* 94 HARV. L. REV. 937 (1981).

[17]   For details of this derivation, see Blair and Harrison, *supra* note 8.

[18]   The effect of changes in S, ε, and η on λ can be signed by examining the signs of the partial derivatives of $\ddot{e}$:

$$\frac{\partial \lambda}{\partial S} = \frac{\varepsilon + \eta}{[\varepsilon + \eta(1 - S)]^2} > 0$$

$$\frac{\partial \lambda}{\partial \varepsilon} = \frac{-S}{[\varepsilon + \eta(1 - S)]^2} < 0$$

$$\frac{\partial \lambda}{\partial \eta} = \frac{-S(1 - S)}{[\varepsilon + \eta(1 - S)]^2} < 0$$

Table 9.3   Lerner Index for a dominant buyer with S = 0.75 and η = 1

ε	0	0.5	1	2	3	∞
λ	3	1	0.6	0.33	0.23	0

Table 9.4   Lerner Index for a dominant buyer with S = 0.75 and ε = 1

η	0	0.5	1	2	3	∞
λ	0.75	0.67	0.60	0.50	0.43	0

is an important determinant of the Lerner Index. As the value of ε rises, the value of λ falls. In Table 9.3, we illustrate the influence of ε for a case where $S = 0.75$ and $\eta = 1$. It is plain to see that low values of ε imply high values of λ and vice versa. For example, when $\varepsilon = 0.5$, $\lambda = 1$, but when $\varepsilon = 2$, λ is only 0.33.

Elasticity of fringe demand (η). When the elasticity of fringe demand increases, any price reduction will result in a large increase in the quantity demanded. This will tend to blunt any market power enjoyed by the dominant buyer. Thus, as η rises, λ falls. Table 9.4 illustrates this result for the specific case where $S = 0.75$ and $\varepsilon = 1$. As one can see, increases in η cause the value of λ to fall.

IV   MONOPSONY AND ANTITRUST POLICY

The economic theory of the preceding sections provides the economic foundation for a sound antitrust policy regarding monopsony and its variants. Here, we provide a brief overview of that policy.[19] As we will see, this policy is consistent with our attitudes toward monopoly and its variants.

A   Economic Rationale

In general, the economic rationale for a vigorous antitrust policy favoring competition resides in the allocative efficiency of competitive markets. When our scarce resources are efficiently allocated society gets the maximum output possible. The allocative inefficiency of monopoly explains the legal and economic objection to some forms of monopolizing behavior[20] and to cartels.[21] It is not the increase in price that accompanies monopoly that

---

[19]   For a more detailed examination, see ch. 4 in ROGER D. BLAIR AND JEFFREY L. HARRISON, MONOPSONY IN LAW AND ECONOMICS (2010).

[20]   Section 2 of the Sherman Act, 15 U.S.C § 2, prohibits monopolizing conduct and attempts to monopolize. For the Supreme Court's two-prong test for unlawful monopoly, see United States v. Grinnell Corp., 384 U.S. 563, 570–71 (1966). For an analysis, see Einer Elhauge, *Defining Better Monopolization Standards*, 56 STANFORD L. REV. 253 (2003).

[21]   Section 1 of the Sherman Act, 15 U.S.C § 1, forbids conspiracies in restraint of trade. A

offends economists; rather, it is the allocative inefficiency that the elevated prices cause that is the concern.[22]

Analogous objections hold for monopsony and its variants. Profit maximization by the monopsonist results in allocative inefficiency and consequent losses in social welfare. It is important to focus on these welfare losses because it is easy to get distracted by the lower prices extracted from suppliers by the monopsonist. After all, lower input prices usually lead to lower production costs, which in turn would lead to lower prices for consumers. This, it would seem, would be a good thing. But this reasoning is based on a misunderstanding of the effect of monopsony on the marginal and average cost curves of the monopsonist. In fact, the exercise of monopsony power causes the marginal cost curve to shift upward, which is what leads to the welfare losses.

1   Monopsony and marginal cost[23]

Continuing to use labor as an example, the marginal product of labor (MP_L) measures the increase in output that results from employing one more unit of labor. As a result, the increase in the quantity of labor necessary to expand output by one unit is given by the inverse of MP_L or $1/MP_L$. In the absence of monopsony power, the firm pays w to expand employment. Thus, the expenditure on labor necessary to increase output by one unit will be w/MP_L. This, of course, is marginal cost by definition:

$$MC = w/MP_L$$

But this changes with the introduction of monopsony power. The monopsonist recognizes that the supply of labor has a positive slope and, therefore, the increase in the wage bill accompanying a one unit increase in employment is the marginal factor cost (MFC):

$$MFC = w + Ldw/dL$$

Thus, the increase in cost necessary to expand output by one more unit for a monopsonist is

$$MC = MFC/MP_L = (w + Ldw/dL)/MP_L$$

Since Ldw/dL is positive, it follows that w is less than $w + Ldw/dL$ or $w/MP_L < (w + Ldw/dL)/MP_L$. In other words, monopsony causes the marginal cost curve to shift upward for all levels of output.

---

sweeping condemnation is provided in United States v. Socony-Vacuum Oil Co., 310 U.S. 150 (1940), which included depressing prices.

22   Higher prices hurt consumers and benefit sellers. Since buyers and sellers are both members of society, there is a transfer within society, which is a distributive matter. But the price rise also causes a reduction in total surplus, which is the economic objection to monopoly.

23   This presentation depends on Roger D. Blair and Richard E. Romano, *Collusive Monopsony in Theory and Practice: The NCAA*, 42 ANTITRUST BULLETIN 681 (1997).

2 Impact on consumers

Whether the monopsonist has market power in the output market or not, an upward shift in the monopsonist's marginal cost curve leads to a reduction in its (privately) optimal output. Accordingly, there is no improvement in consumer welfare resulting from monopsonistic reductions in wages. In fact, just the opposite will be the case. If the monopsonist has any degree of market power in the output market and thus faces a negatively-sloped demand curve, the monopsonist's reduced employment will lead to reduced output, which will cause the output price to rise and thereby will result in a loss in consumer surplus.

If the monopsonist has no market power in the output market, it will still reduce its output due to the upward shift in the marginal cost curve. Even though its effect on the market price will be small because its share of total output is small, it will be positive nonetheless. As a consequence, there will be a reduction – albeit a small one – in consumer surplus here as well.[24]

B Monopsonizing Behavior

Both a pure monopsonist and the dominant buyer profit from the exercise of monopsony power. As we have seen, this exercise imposes welfare losses on society. But the exercise of monopsony power does not offend the Sherman Act. As with monopoly, it is the use of exclusionary or predatory conduct to attain or maintain monopsony that offends section 2.[25] In the Supreme Court's recent decision in *Weyerhaeuser Co. v. Ross-Simmons Hardwood Lumber Co.*,[26] a small lumber mill had accused Weyerhaeuser of engaging in predatory bidding in an effort to monopsonize the market for hardwood sawlogs. If it had been proven that Weyerhaeuser had engaged in predatory bidding, then its conduct would have violated section 2.[27] Had Weyerhaeuser succeeded in monopsonizing the relevant market through such exclusionary practices, the resulting monopsony would have been unlawful.

C Collusive Monopsony

In *Socony-Vacuum*,[28] the Supreme Court ruled that price-fixing was a per se violation of section 1 of the Sherman Act:

---

[24] The benefit of being a monopsonist is found in the effect on *average* cost. At the monopsonist's optimal output, the average cost is lower than without monopsony power. As a result, profit is higher. This outcome holds whether the monopsonist has any market power in the output market. *Id.*

[25] Unilateral conduct is governed by section 2, which condemns those 'who shall monopolize'. 15 U.S.C. § 2. United States v. Grinnell Corp., 384 U.S. 563, 570–71 (1966), made it clear that monopolizing conduct is a necessary element of unlawful monopolization. This was recently reaffirmed in Verizon Communications v. Law Offices of Curtis V. Trinko, 540 U.S. 398, 407 (2004).

[26] 127 S. Ct. 1068 (2007).

[27] For an extensive analysis of the economic issues in this case, see Roger D. Blair and John E. Lopatka, *Predatory Buying and the Antitrust Laws*, Utah L. Rev. 415 (2008).

[28] United States v. Socony-Vacuum Oil Co., Inc., 310 U.S. 150 (1940).

Under the Sherman Act, a combination formed for the purpose and with the effect of raising, depressing, fixing, pegging, or stabilizing the price of a commodity in interstate commerce is illegal per se.[29]

This rule pertains to collusive monopsony as well. In *Mandeville Island Farms v. American Crystal Sugar Co.*,[30] several sugar refiners in northern California agreed among themselves to adopt a pricing formula that resulted in uniform prices being paid to sugar beet farmers. The sugar refiners had agreed not to compete on price in acquiring an important input. The result was lower prices than those that would have been paid in the 'but for' world. The Supreme Court analysed this case under *Socony-Vacuum*'s per se rule and found the agreement to be unlawful. The Court clearly recognized that this was an instance of colluding buyers:

> It is clear that the agreement is the sort of combination condemned by the Act, even though the price fixing was by purchasers and the persons specifically injured . . . are sellers, not customers or consumers.[31]

It is clear from this language that the Court knew that the collusion was among buyers and it extended *Socony-Vacuum* to cover collusive monopsony.

This extension clearly makes sense from an economic perspective. Collusive monopsony causes welfare losses that are not inevitable. While it is difficult to require an actual monopsonist to ignore its effect on the purchase price and behave in ways that will not maximize its profit, collusive monopsony is a very different thing. Competitive results emerge in the absence of a deliberate effort to avoid competition. Consequently, it is economically rational to demand that buyers compete rather than collude.

D   Oligopsony and Tacit Collusion

From the results presented in section IIE, we know that a market characterized by oligopsony will have a price and quantity below the competitive price and quantity (with the exception of the Bertrand game). This occurs because firms are aware of the impact of their decisions on the decisions of other firms. The awareness of other firms' actions and the resulting noncompetitive outcome is termed tacit collusion. In antitrust cases, this behavior is referred to as 'conscious parallelism'.[32]

The courts have established that the existence of parallel behavior alone does not infer agreement among competitors.[33] Tacit collusion is not a violation of section 1 of the Sherman Act because a section 1 violation requires proof of agreement.[34] This form of parallel behavior is instead the product of unilateral action by firms based on an inter-

---

[29]   *Id.* at 223.
[30]   334 U.S. 219 (1948).
[31]   *Id.* at 235.
[32]   *Restraints of Trade, infra* note 36, at 9.
[33]   This follows from the decision in Theatre Enterprises v. Paramount Film Distributing Corp., 346 U.S. 781 (1946).
[34]   See Roger D. Blair and Jill B. Herndon, *Inferring Collusion from Economic Evidence*, ANTITRUST 15, 17–21 (2001).

dependent market relationship. Firms may independently realize under certain market structures that common business practices, as well as corresponding price and quantity decisions, are mutually beneficial.

In cases where the market is characterized by oligopsony, proof of antitrust misbehavior requires evidence of an attempt to maintain this structure. The analysis must necessarily begin with an assessment of any direct evidence of collusion. Direct evidence would include videotapes of meetings, memos or contracts expressly referring to collusive action, or the admission of a conspirator. Often no direct evidence is available. The court recognized in *United States v. Washington* that '[b]y its nature conspiracy is conceived and carried out clandestinely, and direct evidence of the crime is rarely available'.[35]

Following a lack of direct evidence, the analysis then shifts to relevant circumstantial evidence. This evidence may include parallel business practices or other parallel behavior, as well as structures which could facilitate conspiracy. Posted price schedules and trade or industry organizations are common examples of such evidence. In analysing parallel business practices it is important to account for the oligopsony market structure. With homogeneous inputs, this structure will result in the same price being offered by all buyers. Differentiated inputs will similarly result in equilibrium price differentials. These are signals of tacit collusion rather than collusive action by firms.

To prove any antitrust violation the plaintiff must produce circumstantial evidence that it is not ambiguous. In *Monsanto Co. v. Spray-Rite Service Corp.*, the Supreme Court provided a useful standard for evaluating the relevance of evidence. The Court suggested 'that there must be evidence that tends to exclude the possibility of independent action by the [parties]'.[36] Therefore, while parallel behavior such as price and quantity decisions under oligopsony may be the result of conspiracy, its existence does not 'exclude the possibility of independent action'. Therefore, to infer conspiracy, the Court requires plaintiffs to demonstrate the existence of 'plus factors' which preclude unilateral action. The most important plus factors are those that show that the action of a plaintiff makes economic sense only under the assumption that other parties will act in concert.[37]

E   Monopsony and Merger Policy

Horizontal mergers, i.e. mergers between competitors, are governed by section 7 of the Clayton Act,[38] which forbids the acquisition of another firm's assets or stock where the effect of that acquisition in any line of commerce in any section of the country may be substantially to lessen competition or tend to create a monopoly. Whereas section 2 of the Sherman Act is a remedial measure, the design of section 7 is prophylactic. Congress wanted to prevent mergers to monopoly. Since the welfare losses associated with monopsony are analogous to those flowing from monopoly, it would seem appropriate to apply section 7 to mergers of buyers.

In order to evaluate the competitive significance of mergers of buyers, the relevant

---

[35]   United States v. Washington, 586 F.2d 1147, 1153 (1978).

[36]   *Restraints of Trade*, ch. 1 in ANTITRUST LAW DEVELOPMENTS, 5 (ABA Section of Antitrust Law, 5th ed. 2002).

[37]   *Id.* at 12.

[38]   15 U.S.C. § 18.

market, both product and geographic, must be defined. Based on this market definition, the merged firm's market power must be assessed to draw inferences regarding the
competitive effects of the merger. An excellent example of a merger to monopsony is
provided by *United States v. Rice Growers Association of California*.[39] This case involved
a merger of firms that bought paddy rice from farmers. These firms then milled the rice
before reselling it. Among other things, the Department of Justice objected to the merger
on the grounds that it might 'substantially lessen competition in the market . . . [for]
[t]he purchase or acquisition of paddy rice grown in California'.[40] The court found that
the merger violated section 7 of the Clayton Act because of the decrease in competition
among purchasers of paddy rice.

   In its analysis, the court considered the options available to the rice farmers. It found
that they had few. Switching to a different crop did not seem to be a feasible option.
From a product perspective, paddy rice was the product. The farmers could, of course,
ship rice elsewhere, but the court found that that was not a viable option. Thus, the line
of commerce was 'paddy rice' and the section of the country was 'California'. Based on
the limited options available to the farmers, the court inferred the reasonable likelihood
that the merger would tend to substantially lessen competition.

V   CONCLUDING REMARKS

Monopsony has always been with us, but it has received explicit attention from antitrust scholars only in recent years. The first articles focusing particularly on monopsony
appeared in 1991.[41] Since then, there has been an increased sensitivity to the competitive
significance of monopsony. This is reflected in the antitrust law and economics literature.[42]
In this chapter, we have provided the fundamentals of monopsony. More precisely, we
explained the basic theory of monopsony and its variants: collusion, dominant buyers,
and oligopsony. We also analysed the measurement of monopsony power. Finally, we
provided a brief overview of the antitrust policy applied to monopsony.

---

[39]   1986-2 Trade Case (CCH) para. 67, 288 (E.D. Cal., January 31, 1986).
[40]   *Id.* at 466, para. 61.
[41]   Roger D. Blair and Jeffrey L. Harrison, *Antitrust Policy and Monopsony*, 76 CORNELL L. REV.
297 (1991); and Jonathan Jacobson and Gary Dorman, *Joint Purchasing, Monopsony and Antitrust*,
36 ANTITRUST BULLETIN 1 (1991).
[42]   See BLAIR AND HARRISON, *supra* note 19, and the extensive references therein.

PART III

ANTITRUST ENFORCEMENT

10 Issues in antitrust enforcement
Abraham L. Wickelgren

I INTRODUCTION

While the literature on what antitrust law should and should not prohibit is vast, the literature on how best to enforce these laws is much smaller. That said, in recent years, there have been some important developments in the literature on optimal antitrust enforcement. While far from a comprehensive survey, this chapter discusses the literature on several issues in antitrust enforcement.

The next section in the chapter addresses the proper balance between public and private enforcement; that is, it examines the relative strengths of and weaknesses of public and private enforcement and attempts to shed some light on the circumstances in which one mode of enforcement is likely to be preferable to another. The following sections all discuss issues related to optimal enforcement by a public agency. Section III discusses the optimal welfare standard that a public antitrust enforcement agency (or a court) should use in evaluating potentially anticompetitive conduct. The two leading candidates are the total welfare standard (evaluating the effect on all players, including the benefits to the firms involved in the conduct), often advocated by economists, and the consumer welfare standard (only considering the effect of the conduct on consumers), which is most commonly used by regulators and courts. Section IV discusses the optimal timing of antitrust enforcement. An antitrust authority can either review and decide whether or not to prohibit conduct before it is undertaken (ex ante enforcement, commonly used in merger enforcement) or wait until after the conduct has occurred and evaluate it after observing (at least some of) its effects (ex post enforcement). This section examines the factors that affect the optimal combination of ex ante versus ex post enforcement. Section V considers enforcement in situations in which the firms have superior information to the enforcement agency and discusses strategies for inducing firms to reveal this information to the agency in order to improve agency decision-making. Section VI addresses some of the special issues that arise when multiple jurisdictions (countries) have authority over potentially anticompetitive conduct. Section VII concludes.

II PUBLIC VERSUS PRIVATE ENFORCEMENT

In much of the world, competition policy has been enforced primarily by the public sector. In the United States, by contrast, there are about 10 private antitrust suits for every public one.[1] This is not to say that private antitrust suits are prohibited outside the

---

[1] Ilya R. Segal and Michael D. Whinston, *Public versus Private Enforcement of Antitrust Law: A Survey*, EUROPEAN COMPETITION L. REV. 323 (2007).

United States. In the European Union, private parties can sue for damages resulting from an infringement of either Article 81 or 82 of the EU Treaty (the two main competition policy provisions in the European Union) in the courts of the Member States.[2] That said, private antitrust suits have been rare in Europe. The European Commission, however, has recently considered procedural changes that would encourage private suits.[3] This naturally raises the question of what are the conditions under which public enforcement, private enforcement, or a combination of both is optimal. This section will attempt to provide at least a limited answer to this question by discussing the (relatively sparse) literature on public versus private enforcement of antitrust laws.

Public and private enforcers differ on many dimensions. As Steven Shavell has pointed out generally, private parties' incentives to use the legal system differ from the socially optimal incentives.[4] In the antitrust context, private damages from antitrust violations may differ from the negative externality from the actual violation. For example, if the violation results in higher prices, consumer damages typically do not account for the lost consumer surplus from purchases not made (of course, this assumes consumers do not consider the possibility of collecting damages when making their purchasing decisions). If damages are trebled, as they are in the United States, then they would likely exceed the negative externality from the actual violation (though, because the probability of prevailing is less than one, expected damages could either exceed or be less than the magnitude of the externality). If competitors sue for damages from an antitrust violation, there is even less reason to think that the damages reflect the actual magnitude of the externality since the damages would not reflect any effect that the action has on consumer surplus.

Similarly, as Shavell argued more generally,[5] private antitrust plaintiffs do not have any reason to consider the deterrent effect of their decision to sue. This could lead to too few private suits if the expected damages a plaintiff could recover were likely smaller than the litigation costs but the prospect of suit would nonetheless deter an inefficient antitrust violation. Shavell also points out that private plaintiffs will not consider the social loss from the defendant's litigation costs in deciding whether or not to sue. This could lead to an excessive number of private suits if the net social cost of the action is quite small relative to the litigation costs but the prospect of suit still does not deter the violation.

In a recent paper, McAfee *et al.* argue that private antitrust plaintiffs may use the antitrust laws strategically to disadvantage their rivals.[6] On the other hand, they point out

---

[2]   Wouter P.J. Wils, *The Relationship Between Public Antitrust Enforcement and Private Actions for Damages*, 32 World Competition 3 (2009).

[3]   Segal and Whinston, *supra* note 1. The proposals that would facilitate private suits are in the EU Green Paper, *Damages Actions for Breach of the EC Antitrust Rules*, SEC (2005) 1732.

[4]   Steven Shavell, *The Social verus the Private Incentive to Bring Suit in a Costly Legal System*, 11 J. of Legal Studies 333 (1982).

[5]   *Id.*

[6]   R. Preston McAfee, Hugo Mialon, and Sue Mialon, *Private v. Public Antitrust Enforcement: A Strategic Analysis*, 92 J. Public Economics 1875 (2008). There are many papers that discuss how private antitrust suits are sometimes used to hurt rivals (or hostile acquirers) who have not actually committed an antitrust violation. See, for example, William J. Baumol and Janusz A. Ordover, *Use of Antitrust to Subvert Competition*, 28 J. Law and Economics 247 (1985); William Breit and Kenneth G. Elzinga, *Private Antitrust Enforcement: The New Learning*, 28 J. Law and Economics

that private enforcers may be more likely to detect violations of the antitrust laws. They integrate both these effects into a model that allows them to compare the ability of public and private antitrust suits to achieve optimal antitrust enforcement. In their model, there are two firms, 1 and 2, and a public enforcer, *GOV*. Firm 1 can choose to take an action, *A*, or not. This action is either procompetitive (with exogenous probability *p*) or anticompetitive (with exogenous probability $1 - p$). Either type of action transfers wealth from firm 2 to firm 1, but the procompetitive action also creates social surplus while the anticompetitive action reduces social surplus. Firm 2 knows whether firm 1's action is pro- or anticompetitive, while *GOV* only receives an imperfect (but better than random) signal of the type of the action. The court decision, if either firm 2 or *GOV* sues firm 1 (if it takes action *A*), is also imperfect (but better than random).

In this setting, they find that adding private enforcement to public enforcement increases welfare so long as the court is suffciently accurate. The reason is that since firm 2 has perfect information about whether or not firm 1's action is anticompetitive, if the court is suffciently accurate, it will sue if and only if firm 1 took the anticompetitive action.

If the court is less accurate, however, then firm 2 has an incentive to sue even if firm 1 took the procompetitive action in the hopes the court will mistakenly deem it anticompetitive and award firm 2 damages. In this case, it is better to rely on public enforcement even though the government misses some anticompetitive actions and sues firm 1 sometimes for procompetitive actions.

McAfee *et al.* also note two ways to eliminate the distortions associated with both public and private enforcement. First, they note that pure public enforcement can be made to achieve the first best if firm 2 is allowed to complain to the government enforcer provided it pays a fee. Since the court is more likely to rule for the government if the action is anticompetitive, firm 2's benefit from government suit is greater if *A* is anticompetitive than if it is procompetitive.[7] So, by setting the fee in between firm 2's expected benefit from a suit against a procompetitive action and its expected benefit from a suit against an anticompetitive action, firm 2 will only complain if it knows the action is anticompetitive. Second, they point out that by decoupling damages appropriately, they can reduce firm 2's payoff from suing if *A* is procompetitive just below the level at which it is profitable to sue. Since suit is more profitable if *A* is anticompetitive, however, firm 2 will still sue if *A* is anticompetitive. Using an appropriate damage multiple along with decoupling can then deter firm 1 from taking the action if and only if it is anticompetitive.

The McAfee *et al.* paper provides useful guidance on the question of whether it makes sense to allow significant private enforcement of the antitrust laws, as is currently being

---

443 (1985); William F. Shughart II, *Private Antitrust Enforcement: Compensation, Deterrence, or Extortion?*, 13 REGULATION 53 (1990); Joseph F. Brodley, *Antitrust Standing in Private Merger Cases: Reconciling Private Incentives and Public Enforcement Goals*, 94 MICHIGAN L. REV. 1 (1995); R. Preston McAfee and Nicholas Vakkur, *The Strategic Abuse of Antitrust Laws*, 1 J. STRATEGIC MANAGEMENT EDUCATION 1 (2004); and R. Preston McAfee, Hugo Mialon, and Sue Mialon, *Private Antitrust Litigation: Procompetitive or Anti-competitive?*, in THE POLITICAL ECONOMY OF ANTITRUST (V. Ghosal and J. Stennek eds., Elsevier, Amsterdam, 2007).

[7]   Action *A* hurts firm 2 whether it is pro- or anticompetitive, so a victory for *GOV* helps firm 2 in that it stops firm 1 from continuing *A*.

debated in Europe. In regimes where both public and private antitrust enforcement exist, as in the United States, however, it provides only limited suggestions about how the government should decide which cases to prosecute publicly and which cases should be left to private enforcement. That, however, is the major question that Schwartz and Wickelgren address in their paper on competitor suits.[8] In their model, there is an incumbent who can choose to take an action that increases the marginal cost of a potential entrant or decreases its own cost. After the incumbent decides to take this action, the entrant chooses whether or not to enter the industry. Then active firms compete in prices (with some product differentiation). Then the entrant has the option, if it has entered, to sue the incumbent if the incumbent took the action. The expected damages the entrant receives from suit are a multiple of its lost profit.

In the Schwartz and Wickelgren paper, there are two main effects from the entrant's ability to sue for damages based on lost profit. First, this provides an entry subsidy which can, if large enough, prevent the incumbent from using its action to deter entry. Second, because damages are based on lost profit, the incumbent can reduce its exposure to competitor suits by increasing its price and thereby reducing the entrant's lost profits from the incumbent's action. Thus, in situations in which entry is socially desirable,[9] while competitor suits can preserve some competition by enabling entry, they also soften post-entry competition by making the incumbent care about the entrant's profits. Since prices are generally strategic complements, this causes prices to be larger than they otherwise would be with entry. Of course, if the alternative is no entry at all, prices may still be lower with competitor suits, entry, and softer competition than they would be otherwise.

In their paper, Schwartz and Wickelgren show that if the incumbent's action primarily reduces its own costs and only increases the competitor's costs by a small amount, then competitor suits can work well, even if the damage multiple is very large. In this situation, the incumbent still makes the cost-reducing investment, and the entrant enters. The incumbent sets its price at the same level it would have if it had not taken the action that reduced its costs, thereby ensuring the entrant does not lose any profits as a result. Thus, while the cost-reducing investment does not lead to lower prices given entry, it does not lead to increased prices either since it cannot drive out the entrant. In contrast, the typical government suit in this case, if it were to occur, would enjoin the incumbent's action, thus preventing any cost reduction and leading to final prices that are identical to what they are with the cost-reducing action and the threat of a competitor suit. If there were neither competitor nor government suits in this case, then the cost-reducing investment could deter entry and lead to higher prices than without it.

On the other hand, if the incumbent's action only raises the entrant's marginal cost, competitor suits do not function well. This is an action that is clearly inefficient. The incumbent, however, can still profit from this action even if it is subject to competitor suits with a very large damage multiplier. The reason is that by charging a higher price, the incumbent can eliminate any lost profits to the entrant. Furthermore, Schwartz and

---

[8]   Warren F. Schwartz and Abraham L. Wickelgren, *Optimal Antitrust Enforcement: Competitor Suits, Entry, and Post-entry Competition*, 95 J. PUBLIC ECONOMICS 967 (2011).

[9]   See Gregory Mankiw and Michael D. Whinston, *Free Entry and Socially Ineffciency*, 17 RAND J. ECONOMICS 48 (1986) for a discussion of circumstances when entry might decrease total surplus.

Wickelgren show that if the increase in the entrant's cost is not too large, the incumbent's profit actually increases because the prospect of a competitor suit effectively enforces some degree of collusion (making both the incumbent's and the entrant's prices higher given entry). In this case, a government suit enjoining the action is clearly superior since it deters the inefficient action and preserves post-entry competition.[10]

The competition softening effect of private enforcement via competitor suits analysed by Schwartz and Wickelgren is related to a series of papers on the effect of treble damages suits against cartels by consumers. This literature began with Salant[11] and Baker.[12] Under the assumption that consumers and firms both know the firms' cost of production, the damage multiplier and the probability of a successful antitrust suit, they independently find that consumer suits cannot provide any deterrence against cartel price fixing unless the damage multiple is large enough to completely deter cartel formation. That is, if the damage multiple is t and the probability of detection is θ, they find that firms will form a cartel and sell the monopoly quantity and earn (net of damage payments) the monopoly profit in expectation as long as $t\theta < 1$. For $t\theta \geq 1$, firms do not form a cartel. The intuition is that both firms and consumers view antitrust damage suits as creating a discount on the price the firms charge. So that if a cartel charges a price of p while competitive firms would charge c, then, in expectation, consumers expect to pay p for each unit they buy but also to recover $t\theta(p - c)$ for each unit from the suit. It is the net price, $p - t\theta(p - t\theta)$, that determines consumer demand. The cartel then maximizes its net profit: $(p - t\theta(p - c) - c) *q(p - t\theta(p - c))$. This is, exactly, the monopoly pricing problem with $p - t\theta(p - c)$ serving as the price variable. As long as $t\theta < 1$, the cartel can increase p so that $p - t\theta(p - c)$ equals the monopoly price, and the outcome for firms and consumers is identical to what it would be without any antitrust enforcement at all.

Salant and Baker show that under conditions of perfect information, consumer antitrust enforcement cannot deter price increases by a cartel (or a monopoly firm) unless that enforcement is very effective. Under these conditions, government enforcement is clearly superior since consumers will no longer take expected damage payments into account when deciding on how much to purchase. This result, however, does depend on there being symmetric information between firms and consumers. Besanko and Spulber[13] reconsider this result in a setting in which consumers do not know the firms' costs, thus they cannot tell if high prices are a result of higher costs or cartel pricing. In this setting, consumer enforcement can induce a cartel to charge less than the monopoly price even if $t\theta < 1$. The reason is that consumers use a cartel's price to make an inference about its costs. Thus, the higher the price, the higher the consumer belief about the cartel's costs.

---

[10]   These findings are consistent with the general discussion of the relative advantages of public and private enforcement in Wils, *supra* note 2. There, he argues that public enforcement is superior for clarifying the law and deterring harmful behavior, while private enforcement is superior for compensating victims. In Schwartz and Wickelgren, *supra* note 8, compensation is valuable because it subsidizes entry.

[11]   Steven W. Salant, *Treble Damage Awards in Private Lawsuits for Price Fixing*, 96 J. POLITICAL ECONOMY 1326 (1987).

[12]   Jonathan B. Baker, *Private Information and the Deterrent Effect of Antitrust Damage Remedies*, 4 J. LAW, ECONOMICS, AND ORGANIZATION 385 (1988).

[13]   David Besanko and Daniel F. Spulber, *Are Treble Damages Neutral? Sequential Equilibrium and Private Antitrust Enforcement*, 80 AMERICAN ECONOMIC REV. 870 (1990).

If costs are higher, then for any given price, the consumer's expected damage award is smaller. Thus, the expected antitrust damages do not increase as quickly with price as they do under full information. This decreases the cartel's incentive to charge high prices to make up for the expected damage payment. That is, for a given level of cost, an increase in price increases the true expected damage payment more than consumers think it does, making price increases less profitable.

Thus, Besanko and Spulber show that if there is asymmetric information about costs, consumer antitrust enforcement can reduce the ability of a cartel (or a monopolist) to charge supracompetitive prices even if it is not strong enough to deter it altogether. That said, because consumers still do anticipate some increase in damages when prices go up, consumer antitrust enforcement is not as effective as it would be if consumers did not expect to receive any damages associated with higher prices. So, to the extent that the suits are otherwise equally effective, government enforcement in which the damages go to the treasury should still be more effective than consumer enforcement.

The literature on public versus private enforcement of antitrust shows that there are roles for both modes of enforcement. While private enforcement may sometimes lead to perverse incentives for higher prices or be used to harm rivals, it can stimulate entry and take advantage of information that market participants have that government enforcers may not. Thus, there is no clear case for eliminating either enforcement mechanism.

III   OPTIMAL WELFARE STANDARD

Another important issue in optimal antitrust enforcement is what is the appropriate welfare standard for the antitrust enforcement agencies and the courts to use when evaluating potentially anticompetitive conduct. In the United States and most of the rest of the world, consumer welfare is the dominant standard used; that is, firms can justify conduct that might otherwise be deemed anticompetitive if they can show that it makes consumers better off. This standard is in contrast to a total welfare standard, which is the standard typically advocated by economists. Under a total welfare standard, firms would only need to show that their conduct resulted in a positive change in the sum of the welfare of all affected parties. Typically, this means that the firms could justify the conduct if they could prove that even though consumers would be worse off, the firms' profits would increase by more than the loss to consumers.

As Farrell and Katz[14] point out in their article on welfare standards in antitrust, while there is good reason for thinking the ultimate objective of the antitrust laws should be to maximize total welfare, rather than just consumer welfare, this does not necessarily imply that antitrust agencies or courts should use a total welfare standard. The first part of this claim, that maximizing total welfare is a sensible objective for antitrust law, is relatively straightforward. The main objection to this goal would be a distributional one. Many aspects of government policy are focused on distributional concerns (progressive taxation and welfare programs are two of the largest). But antitrust law is not likely

---

[14]   Joseph Farrell and Michael Katz, *The Economics of Welfare Standards in Antitrust*, 2 COMPETITION POLICY INTERNATIONAL 3 (2006).

to be a sensible vehicle for addressing distributional concerns. First, while consumers might, on the average, be less wealthy than shareholders of defendant firms, there will be many situations where this is not the case. For example, in many antitrust cases the consumers are simply firms further down the vertical chain. There is no reason for thinking that the shareholders in these firms are any less wealthy than the shareholders in the upstream firms. Second, for many luxury goods, the consumers may be fairly wealthy on the average while the shareholders, who will often include many pension funds who hold the shares for the benefit of middle class workers, might not be as wealthy. Thus, using a consumer welfare standard generally would be an extremely noisy way to redistribute income.

The other alternative would be to use a consumer welfare standard only in those cases where it was clear the consumers were poorer than the shareholders. This creates two problems. First, it would greatly add to litigation expense and legal uncertainty to have to determine what standard should apply in a particular case based on the wealth characteristics of the shareholders of the firms and the likely consumers. Second, once we take wealth into account, then, as Kaplow and Shavell[15] have pointed out, we create the same work disincentives as the progressive tax system. Thus, there is no reason to prefer redistribution through legal rules than through taxation. And, since redistributive taxes are targeted much more effectively and do not create the additional distortion associated with inefficient legal rules, there is good reason to prefer the tax system for redistribution.

The case for a total surplus standard, however, rests not just on the fact that antitrust policy should maximize total surplus. The remaining question is whether total surplus is more likely to be maximized if antitrust agencies and courts use a total surplus standard rather than a consumer surplus standard. The answer to this question is far from obvious because, as Farrell and Katz note, there are many players involved in determining the effects of antitrust law. Since some of these players, the firms most notably, are definitely not maximizing total surplus, it may be desirable to skew the goals of other players in a different direction to make the final outcome closer to total surplus maximization. In particular, Lyons[16] and Fridolfsson[17] analyse the optimal welfare standard for mergers taking into account that firms choose their merging partners while the antitrust agencies and courts only evaluate those mergers in comparison to the status quo, not in comparison to other mergers the firms could have considered. Thus, they show that there are situations in which the use of a consumer surplus standard may induce firms to choose mergers that create more total surplus than they would choose under a total surplus standard. The intuition is simply that the most profitable merger that increases total surplus might not be the profitable merger that increases total surplus the most. If that latter merger increases consumer surplus while the former one does not, then total surplus is greater under a consumer surplus standard than under a total surplus standard.

---

[15] Louis Kaplow and Steven Shavell, *Why the Legal System is Less Efficient than the Income Tax in Redistributing Income*, 23 J. LEGAL STUDIES 667 (1994).

[16] Bruce R. Lyons, *Could Politicians be More Right than Economists? A Theory of Merger Standards* (mimeo, University of East Anglia, 2002).

[17] Sven Fridolfsson, *A Consumer Surplus Defense in Merger Control*, in THE POLITICAL ECONOMY OF ANTITRUST (V. Ghosal and J. Stennek eds., Elsevier, Amsterdam, 2007).

Armstrong and Vickers[18] analyse this problem quite generally. In their model, the agent has a choice of projects. Each project has two payoffs, u and v. The agent cares only about u. The principal cares about both u and v. In the antitrust context, we can think of the agent as the firm and the projects as mergers or other business strategies that might raise antitrust issues. The principal's problem is to commit to a function $r(u)$ so that she will approve the agent's project if and only if the external payoff $v \geq r(u)$. In the merger context, this says that the agencies or the courts will approve a merger that increases the firm's profit by u if and only if it increases consumer surplus (the v in this context) by at least $r(u)$. Thus, a consumer surplus standard would be one in which $r(u) = 0$ while a total surplus standard would be one in which $r(u) = -u$.

If we start from a given standard, call it $_r(u)$, and consider raising $r(u)$ for some u, there are two effects. The direct effect is that now projects (mergers) which produce total surplus of $u + {}_r(u)$ will no longer occur since the principal will now reject them. The indirect effect, what Armstrong and Vickers dub the strategic effect, is that the agent may now choose a different project. That is, under standard $_r(u)$, the agent chooses the project with the highest u provided that $v \geq {}_r(u)$. If the principal increases $r(u)$, the agent may now have to choose a project with a lower u but a larger v in order for the principal to approve the project.

If the principal wants to maximize total surplus, then analysing these effects yields two immediate conclusions. First, the principal should set $r(0) = 0$. The reason is that if $u = 0$ then there will be no strategic effect. The agent cannot be induced to choose a project with a u less than zero even if that is necessary for approval. If only the direct effect is operative, as is the case at $u = 0$, then the principal should approve all projects that maximize total surplus. Second, for $u > 0$, the principal should set $r(u) > -u$ (the standard should be stricter than a total surplus standard). The reason is that at $r(u) = -u$ the direct effect of increasing $r(u)$ has no negative effect on total surplus. It results in the principal rejecting projects with zero total surplus. The strategic effect, however, is beneficial since the agent may decide not to choose a project with zero total surplus which, under the new standard, would now be rejected and instead choose a different project with a lower u and a higher v and (in order for the principal to approve it) higher total surplus.

This analysis suggests that, to the extent firms have many options for merging partners or other projects with competitive implications, a total surplus standard will not maximize total surplus. That said, this does not necessarily mean a consumer surplus standard is optimal or necessarily superior. Armstrong and Vickers show that there is a particular set of distributions (u uniform over $[0, 1]$ and v uniform over $[-1, 1]$ and the number of projects is distributed according to a Poisson distribution with a mean of 4) for which a pure consumer surplus standard is optimal. As the expected number of projects increases, the optimal standard becomes more strict. So, if the expected number of projects is less than four, then the optimal standard is somewhere in between a total welfare standard and a consumer welfare standard. For a larger number of expected

18   Mark Armstrong and John Vickers, *A Model of Delegated Project Choice with Application to Merger Policy* (University of Oxford Department of Economics Discussion Paper, 2007).

projects, the optimal standard is substantially stricter than even a consumer welfare standard.[19]

Another potential justification for a consumer surplus standard was given by Besanko and Spulber.[20] In their model, firms have private information about a parameter that affects both profits and consumer surplus. Importantly, they assume that both profits and consumer surplus are increasing in this parameter. Thus, this model captures the case where firms have private information about the effciencies from the merger but not the case in which the firms have private information about the market power. Antitrust enforcers obtain no signal about the merger's effects, so they simply pick a probability p to reject the merger. Since rejection is costly, firms in this model only propose a merger if the effciencies are large enough so that the expected private payoff from proposing the merger is positive. Thus, the enforcer would like to pick a rejection probability, p^*, so that firms only propose mergers that increase total welfare. Importantly, however, in this model the enforcer cannot commit to a rejection probability. Thus, if the firms believe that the enforcer would reject the merger with exactly this optimal probability, they would only propose welfare-increasing mergers. In this case, however, the enforcer would want to approve all mergers with probability one.

To enable the enforcer to credibly threaten to reject any proposed merger with probability p^*, it must be that the enforcer's expected payoff from proposed mergers is zero. Since, under the policy of rejecting a merger with probability p^*, firms only propose total welfare-increasing mergers, the enforcer must have a payoff function that differs from total welfare. In particular, if the enforcer's payoff function weights consumer and producer surplus in just the right ratio, then its expected payoff from approving a merger in the set of total surplus-increasing mergers could be exactly zero. As with the Armstrong and Vickers paper, while this does not establish the superiority of a consumer surplus standard, it does suggest that deviations from a total surplus standard in the direction of the consumer surplus standard are likely optimal. That said, as Farrell and Katz have pointed out, a policy of taxing mergers and then approving them all would increase welfare by more in this model.[21] Furthermore, as pointed out above, their result relies heavily on the private information affecting firm profits and consumer surplus in the same direction, thus it is not applicable in situations where there is private information about the market power generated by the merger.

One can also make an ex ante justification for the consumer welfare standard. Posner has argued that monopoly profits are often dissipated by what firms spend to obtain

---

19   Armstrong and Vickers, *supra* note 18, also consider a model in which the agent has to engage in a costly search for projects. In this model, if search is suffciently costly, the principal may want to commit to allow projects that reduce total surplus in order to induce the agent to engage in search. They also analyse a model in which the agent passively waits for a project, but this seems less applicable to most competition applications.

20   David Besanko and Daniel F. Spulber, *Contested Mergers and Equilibrium Antitrust Policy*, 9 J. LAW, ECONOMICS, AND ORGANIZATION 1 (1993).

21   See Abraham L. Wickelgren, *A Simple Mechanism for Improving 'Up or Down' Regulation* (mimeo, 2009). He also finds that in a special case in his model, this policy of approving all mergers after the payment of a tax (he calls it a filing fee) can achieve the first best. See section V for more discussion of this model.

monopoly power.[22] Elhauge has recently argued that this justifies the use of a consumer welfare standard in monopolization cases.[23] He argues that the race to achieve market power will tend to lead to excessive investment in creating such market power (he uses the patent race as an example). Using a consumer welfare standard for monopolization cases can reduce the private returns to such market power, thereby reducing firms' incentives to acquire such market power. That said, to the extent that efforts to generate market power (such as innovations) also generate some consumer surplus, this would tend to provide firms with insufficient incentives to make such investments. Which effect is more important is ultimately an empirical question. That is, while the welfare standard in monopolization cases certainly affects the incentive to acquire monopoly power as well as affecting the actions firms with such power take, as a general matter it is not obvious what welfare standard optimizes a firm's ex ante incentive to acquire market power. That will certainly vary with the methods used for acquiring that market power and how much consumer surplus those methods create.

The question of what is the appropriate welfare standard for antitrust enforcement is obviously not just a question about what the proper goals of antitrust policy should be. While the case for protecting consumers at the expense of firms might be suspect as redistribution policy, it still might nonetheless be justified as a means for correcting for other distortions in the antitrust enforcement process. That said, while these distortions almost certainly suggest some standard other than a total welfare standard is optimal, a pure consumer welfare standard is only likely to be optimal in special circumstances. For the most part, some hybrid approach (where the optimal mix likely varies based on the area of enforcement) is probably optimal.

IV   OPTIMAL TIMING OF ENFORCEMENT

An important, but often overlooked, question in antitrust enforcement is when is the optimal time to evaluate an activity as potentially anticompetitive. The two main choices are prospectively (which I will often refer to as ex ante enforcement) and retrospectively (which I will often refer to as ex post enforcement). In the United States, mergers are most often reviewed prospectively; that is, firms propose a merger and the enforcement agency evaluates the merger to determine if the firms should be allowed to merge or, alternatively, if the agency should seek a preliminary injunction in an effort to block the merger before it is consummated. Most other antitrust cases are retrospective; that is, the government (or private parties) sue(s) a firm or firms for violating the antitrust laws after they have committed the alleged anticompetitive activity.

Ottaviani and Wickelgren[24] analyse the relative merits of ex ante and ex post enforcement to determine the optimal timing of antitrust enforcement in different

---

[22]   Richard A. Posner, *The Social Costs of Monopoly and Regulation*, 83 J. POLITICAL ECONOMY 807 (1975).

[23]   Einer Elhauge, *Tying, Bundled Discounts, and the Death of the Single Monopoly Profit Theory*, 123 HARVARD L. REV. 397 (2009).

[24]   M. Ottaviani and A.L. Wickelgren, *Approval Regulation and Learning, with Application to Timing of Merger Control* (mimeo, 2009).

situations.[25] In their model, both the enforcement agency and the firms are uncertain about the effects of the action (a merger being one natural application, but the model applies more broadly to actions such as exclusive dealing, tying, etc.) prior to doing the action. The basic tradeoff in the model is that the agency is better informed about the actual effects of the merger (I'll use the merger application for concreteness) after the fact, but reversing an inefficient merger is more costly than preventing it in advance. Not surprisingly, they find that ex ante enforcement is relatively more desirable if the cost of reversing a merger goes up, the duration of the merger is shorter, or as the magnitude of the uncertainty regarding the merger's effects declines.

They also find that there can be situations in which the regulator might benefit from committing not to review a merger ex post.[26] One leading situation in which this can occur is if there is substantial uncertainty about the effects of the merger on the ability of the firms to exercise market power but the merger also generates substantial efficiencies. In this case, it may be that in situations in which the merger generates very little market power, so it will not be reversed ex post, it will generate very little profit for the merged firms (this may be situations in which the efficiencies are largely passed on to consumers). If the profits necessary to make the firms propose the merger in the first place largely come from the states of the world in which the merger does generate substantial market power, then the firms may not propose the merger if threatened with ex post review. But, if the enforcement agency can commit only to ex ante review, it might approve the merger because in expectation it increases social welfare.

Another potential benefit to ex ante control that Ottaviani and Wickelgren identify is through what they call the manipulation effect; that is, the ex post optimal decision by the enforcement agency depends on the cost of reversal. Thus, the threat of ex post review will induce the firms to deliberately increase the cost of undoing the merger above the socially optimal level in order to at least partially deter the enforcement agency from reversing the merger ex post.

On the other hand, they identify a beneficial discipline effect from ex post review. This discipline effect occurs if the actual effect of the merger after the fact is only indirectly revealed to the merging parties. In this case, the enforcement agency will have to infer the merger's effects from the actions of the firm. In particular, imagine that the efficiencies generated by the merger are initially uncertain. If the merger generates substantial efficiencies, then ex post the firms would find lower prices optimal. If the merger is profitable even if the efficiencies are not that great, it may often be in the interest of the merging parties to charge lower prices than would otherwise be optimal in order to signal that the merger had substantial efficiencies in order to deter the agency from reversing it. While there can be a continuum of equilibria in this context, Ottaviani and Wickelgren show

---

[25]   See also Pedro Pita Barros, *Looking Behind the Curtain: Effects from Modernization of European Union Competition Policy*, 47 EUROPEAN ECONOMIC REV. 613 (2003). He examines a similar question in his paper on the European Union's decision to switch from requiring prior notice for horizontal agreements to a system of ex post control.

[26]   This possibility is also mentioned by Patrick Rey, *Towards a Theory of Competition Policy*, in ADVANCES IN ECONOMICS AND ECONOMETRICS: THEORY AND APPLICATIONS, EIGHTH WORLD CONGRESS 82–132, II (36) Econometric Society Monographs (Matthias Dewatripont, Lars P. Hansen, and Stephen J. Turnovsky eds., Cambridge University Press, 2003).

that there is a partially separating equilibrium in which the agency's reversal decision is unaffected by the private information, but in many states of the world the merging parties charge lower prices than they would have under full information. To the extent that the merging parties have some market power, their signaling through lower prices improves social welfare.

This analysis suggests that antitrust enforcement should contain a mix of ex ante and ex post enforcement. The more information the enforcers have, the more the mix should tilt toward ex ante enforcement. That said, incentive effects on both the regulator and the firms make this analysis somewhat more complicated. Ex post review can potentially undermine the regulator's ability to commit to an optimal policy. On the other hand, it can also provide either beneficial (inducing lower prices) or counterproductive (inducing excessive lock-in) incentives to the firms that potentially face ex post review.

V   ENFORCEMENT STRATEGIES UNDER ASYMMETRIC INFORMATION

In many, if not most, antitrust cases the defendant firms have superior information (relative to the enforcement agency) about either their actions or the likely effects those actions may have. In the context of fighting collusion, Besanko and Spulber[27] have analysed optimal enforcement strategies when the enforcement agency can only observe prices and quantities but not the firms' costs or whether or not they are colluding. Thus, if the enforcement agency observes a high price, it cannot tell for sure if costs are high or if the firms are colluding. The agency can, however, choose to audit the industry at a cost. Besanko and Spulber then determine the optimal audit policy that maximizes total welfare net of audit costs. Not surprisingly, they find that it is optimal only to audit firms if prices are high. More subtly, however, they also show that it is optimal to tolerate prices slightly above the competitive level for low cost firms. The reason is that the welfare loss from this is slight but it reduces the incentive of the low cost firms to pretend to be high cost firms by colluding on higher prices. This reduces the necessary frequency of audits when the agency observes high prices.

The Besanko and Spulber analysis assumes the firms in the industry can perfectly collude if they choose to do so. That is, as Rey[28] points out, they are effectively treated as a single entity. Rey informally discusses how recognizing that the firms are different entities with their own objective functions might be used to further deter collusion. In particular, he suggests that revelation mechanisms that work like guaranteed immunity for the firm that reveals collusion might be very effective at deterring collusion in some cases. In particular, he considers a policy in which the enforcement agency offers a firm the choice of reporting collusion and being exempt from a fine, or denying it and then being subject to a large fine if the agency, with some small probability, detects collusion on its own. Then, if collusion is a one-time event, it is a dominant strategy for the firm

---

[27]   David Besanko and Daniel Spulber, *Antitrust Enforcement under Asymmetric Information*, 99 Economic J. 408 (1989).
[28]   *Supra* note 26.

to report collusion, which would deter the collusion in the first place (provided the firms cannot collude at the revelation stage). Of course, as Rey acknowledges, because collusion is rarely a one-shot opportunity, one needs a dynamic framework to examine how revelation mechanisms might work when reporting collusion undermines the opportunity for further collusive profits.

Rey sketches just such a dynamic framework.[29] Firms have the choice to collude or compete in each period and then the enforcement agency asks each to report its choice. If a firm reports collusion, then it obtains a reduced fine in the event of a successful audit by the agency (which, of course, is made more likely by a report of collusion). Then, in order to deter firms from reporting collusion, there must be periods of competition (where the firms choose to compete instead of collude) after a successful audit. Otherwise, there would be no long term cost to reporting collusion. The larger the fine reduction (actual rewards would work even better), the longer the periods of competition must be after a successful audit in order to deter firms from voluntarily reporting collusion.[30]

Mechanisms designed to induce firms to reveal their private information can not only help deter collusion; they can also improve merger enforcement. Wickelgren[31] illustrates this in a simple model in which the merging parties have private information about the amount of market power and efficiencies that a merger will generate. Greater market power and efficiencies increase the profitability of the merger, while smaller market power and greater efficiencies increase the social desirability of the merger. The enforcement agency, through its investigation, will receive an imperfect signal of the market power and efficiency effects. It uses these signals to determine whether to allow the merger. Because these signals are imperfect, however, it will both approve some welfare-reducing mergers and reject some welfare-increasing mergers.

Wickelgren shows that the use of refundable filing fees can improve the agency's decisions by making the merging parties' decision about whether to file for a merger better aligned with social welfare. The basic intuition for this is that a refundable filing fee increases the firms' stake in agency approval, which is more likely if the merger increases social welfare. Without a refundable filing fee, the firms obviously want their merger to be approved, but this matters much more to them the more profitable the merger is. With a large refundable filing fee, the firms obtain a large payoff (or avoid a large loss) simply from approval itself. This reduces their incentive to file for welfare-reducing mergers. Since the agency knows that firms have a strong incentive only to file welfare-increasing mergers, it can greatly increase the probability of approval (approve for all but the worst values of the signal for social welfare). It is not possible to achieve the first best, since this would mean firms only file welfare-increasing mergers, which would mean that the agency approves all mergers regardless of its signals, thus inducing firms to file any profitable merger. But, if there is no bound on the size and refundability of the filing fee, one can

---

29   *Supra* note 26.
30   This assumes that the report to the agency can be kept secret. This is essential so that it is a successful audit rather than the report of collusion that triggers the periods of competition. If it is the latter, this would deter firms from reporting.
31   *Supra* note 21.

get arbitrarily close to the first best. With limits on the filing fee, the agency will improve its decision-making but will still make a nontrivial number of errors.

Given that antitrust enforcers necessarily operate under conditions of limited information, this section suggests that more effort should be made to design procedures that will induce firms to reveal information that can improve enforcement decisions. While designing the perfect system is clearly beyond the realm of what is possible, there are simple strategies that can produce at least some incentives for firms to reveal information that will enable enforcement agencies to make fewer errors and improve firms' incentives.

VI INTERNATIONAL ENFORCEMENT: THE EFFECT OF MULTIPLE ENFORCEMENT AGENCIES

In recent years, many of the most significant antitrust cases have been before the antitrust authorities in both the United States and the European Union (and sometimes other countries' antitrust authorities as well). In the case of mergers and joint ventures seeking approval, both jurisdictions must approve the action before the firms can go through with it (since, in most cases, it is not feasible to merge two firms in one jurisdiction and keep them separate in another). This means that each agency's decision only matters when the other agency approves the action.[32] This should make a significant difference in how each agency evaluates the action, though it is not clear that it actually does.

Notice that this problem is quite similar to a correlated values auction problem. Each agency, through its investigation, obtains a signal for the likely competitive effects of the merger, just as each bidder in an auction obtains a signal of the likely value of the good for sale. In both cases, the signals of the other players (agencies or bidders) affect each player's optimal action. Thus, just as there is a winner's curse in common value auctions if bidders do not consider the fact that they will only win if their signal is higher than all the others, there will be an 'over-enforcement' curse if each agency does not consider that its enforcement action only matters if the other agency's signal leads it to believe that the merger is procompetitive.

The international enforcement problem, however, is somewhat different from the typical auction problem in that the players are not ex ante identical. For example, it is commonly believed that antitrust agencies in the United States are much more likely to approve a merger than is the European Commission. One could represent this as being due to different preferences (private values as well as common values), but given that the articulated welfare standard on both sides of the Atlantic is the same, it is probably more accurate to characterize this as being due to different priors. Thus, if the US enforcement agencies are considering a merger of companies that do business in both the United States and Europe, they must know that the European Commission will require a stronger procompetitive signal than they would to approve the merger. As a result, the US decision to reject the merger will only matter if the European Commission gets a fairly strong

---

[32]   This is an extension of the seminal analysis of Raaj Kumar Sah and Joseph E. Stiglitz, *The Architecture of Economic Systems: Hierarchies and Polyarchies*, 76 AMERICAN ECONOMIC REV. 716 (1986).

procompetitive signal. This should induce the United States to reject the merger only if the signal is much more anticompetitive than it would normally require.

On the other hand, the European Commission should alter its approval standard much less as a result of the overlapping jurisdiction of the United States. Since the United States, based on the analysis in the previous paragraph, should reject the merger only if its signal is very strongly anticompetitive, approval in the United States is a weak, but not a strong, signal that the merger is likely to be procompetitive. Thus, while even the European Commission should be somewhat more lenient given possible enforcement in the United States, the effect should be much less drastic than it should be for US antitrust authorities.

Another way in which the international enforcement problem is different from the common value auction problem is that there is communication between the agencies. That is, while the bidders in an auction have no incentive to reveal their signals to their competitors, the competition authorities in different countries do talk to each other during merger investigations. That said, one must account for possible strategic behavior in this communication. Given that the two sides have different preferences over approval decisions given their different priors, truthful communication cannot be an equilibrium if the signals are soft information. In addition, full communication cannot be an equilibrium if the signals are hard information but made up of many different pieces of information, some of which can be hidden. To see this, notice that if full, truthful communication were an equilibrium, then the United States, say, would have an incentive to deviate by making its signal appear to be more procompetitive than it really is in order to make the European Union approve the merger for weaker signals.

While there will always be an equilibrium with no communication, if the priors are not too different, there may also be an equilibrium with coarse communication. That is, while the United States may not be able to credibly reveal its exact signal, it may be able to credibly reveal that its signal is in a certain range that is narrower than simply its approval or denial range.[33] The way such an equilibrium works is that if the signal for the United States, say, is in the range $(a, b]$, where higher values indicate the merger is more likely procompetitive, it can credibly signal this so long as if its signal is b, it does not want the Europeans to believe that its signal is in the next range $(b, c]$. This will be the case if (i) by reporting that its signal is in $(b, c]$, the Europeans believe that the United States signal is so strongly procompetitive that Europe is likely to approve the merger even when its own signal is so poor that the United States (knowing its signal is really b) would want Europe to reject it, and (ii) this is a greater concern than the risk that by reporting that its signal is $(a, b]$ Europe will reject a merger that the United States would want approved.[34]

Clearly, more work needs to be done to flesh out exactly how antitrust enforcers should respond to the presence of an additional regulator with different priors. This is particularly true in the area of improving communication between the different national enforcement agencies. Ideally, such work would lead in the direction of developing

---

[33] See Marco Ottaviani and Peter Norman Sorensen, *The Strategy of Professional Forecasting*, 81 J. FINANCIAL ECONOMICS 441 (2006) for a similar equilibrium in a slightly different context.

[34] I am currently working on formalizing this intuition and characterizing the possible communication more precisely.

mechanisms for more efficient use of the different signals created by the investigations of the multiple agencies looking at a particular transaction.

VII   CONCLUSION

While knowing what should be prohibited and what should be allowed under the antitrust laws is clearly of first order importance, using that knowledge effectively requires also knowing how best to enforce those laws. The survey in this chapter summarizes the recent literature in several areas of antitrust enforcement. Clearly, more work needs to be done. The papers discussed in this chapter all provide important contributions in how to think about antitrust enforcement and in identifying some of the key issues and trade-offs involved. But the existing literature is still short on specific results that enforcers or policy-makers can use to change the structure of enforcement. More applied research on these questions would be especially valuable.

11 Antitrust law in global markets
*Anu Bradford**

INTRODUCTION

Multilateral corporations' activities span across global markets. Yet antitrust laws regulating those activities remain national. Europeans can ban American companies from merging,[1] tell American companies how to design their products,[2] or determine what kind of discounts American companies are permitted to offer to their customers.[3] Chinese can impose conditions on off-shore mergers.[4] And Brazilians can insist on reviewing a transaction with minimal connections to the Brazilian market.[5]

As the global web of antitrust laws thickens, companies are forced to navigate an increasingly complex regulatory environment. The need to comply with multiple different domestic antitrust regimes exposes multinational corporations to additional transaction costs, delays, and uncertainty. Simultaneous application of many antitrust laws carries the risk of enforcement conflicts and is likely to lead to global overenforcement of antitrust laws. A lack of international antitrust regulation may also lead to antitrust protectionism if states underenforce their antitrust laws towards domestic corporations, while overenforcing those same laws towards foreign corporations.[6]

These concerns have sparked demands to move away from decentralized antitrust

*   Thanks to Hanna Chung for outstanding research assistance.

[1]   See, e.g., Commission Decision 2004/134 of 3 July 2001, Case No. COMP/M.2220 – General Electric/Honeywell, [2004] O.J. L48/1 (hereinafter '*GE/Honeywell* Commission Decision').

[2]   See, e.g., Case T-204/04, Microsoft Corp. v. Comm'n, [2007] E.C.R. II-03601, paras 231–3 (requiring Microsoft to design their products to have greater interoperability with competitors); Press Release, *Antitrust: Commission Confirms Sending a Statement of Objections to Microsoft on the Tying of Internet Explorer to Windows*, 17 January 2009, available at http://europa.eu/rapid/ pressReleasesAction.do?reference=MEMO/09/15.

[3]   See, e.g., Case T-457/08 R, Intel Corp. v. Comm'n, Order of the President of the Court of First Instance; Press Release, *Antitrust: Commission Imposes Fine of €1.06 Billion on Intel for Abuse of Dominant Position; Orders Intel to Cease Illegal Practices*, 13 May 2009, available at http:// europa.eu/rapid/pressReleasesAction.do?reference=IP/09/745&format=HTML&aged=0&langu age=EN&guiLanguage=en (finding that Intel offered rebates to computer manufacturers in return for purchasing Intel CPUs exclusively).

[4]   *Coca-Cola Purchase of Huiyuan Fails to Pass Antimonopoly Review*, XINHUA NEWS, 13 March 2009, available at http://news.xinhuanet.com/english/2009-03/19/content_11036911. htm.

[5]   See International Competition Policy Advisory Committee to the Attorney General and Assistant Attorney General for Antitrust, *Final Report* 103 (2000), available at www.usdoj.gov/atr/ icpac/finalreport.htm (hereinafter 'ICPAC Report').

[6]   FREDERIC M. SCHERER, COMPETITION POLICIES FOR AN INTEGRATED WORLD ECONOMY 15–16 (Brookings, 1994); Henrik Horn and James Levinsohn, *Merger Policies and Trade Liberalization*, 111 ECON. J. ROYAL ECON. SOC. 244 (2001).

enforcement in favor of an international antitrust regime.[7] However, no overarching international antitrust regime has been established. Instead, states seek to mitigate the negative externalities embedded in decentralized antitrust enforcement largely through bilateral cooperation and voluntary multilateral norms.

This chapter describes the key issues underlying international antitrust law.[8] Section I reviews the recent proliferation of antitrust laws around the world, explaining why states adopt antitrust laws and why such laws may differ across jurisdictions. Section II discusses the most important problems embedded in the current system of multijurisdictional antitrust enforcement, focusing on increased transaction costs and uncertainties, enforcement conflicts, antitrust protectionism, and global overenforcement of antitrust laws. Section III discusses efforts to mitigate these problems through international cooperation. After reviewing the current state of antitrust cooperation, it examines why, despite the well-accepted inefficiencies embedded in the current system, no global antitrust regime exists. The final section offers suggestions for the direction of future scholarship in the field.

I   PROLIFERATION OF ANTITRUST LAWS

Over the last two decades, the number of antitrust jurisdictions has increased dramatically. Today, over 100 countries have adopted domestic antitrust laws.[9] In 1989, 100 years after the first antitrust law was enacted in Canada, followed by the adoption of the Sherman Act in the United States one year later,[10] only 39 countries had antitrust laws.[11]

---

[7]   See, e.g., Andrew Guzman, *The Case for International Antitrust*, in COMPETITION LAWS IN CONFLICT: ANTITRUST JURISDICTION IN THE GLOBAL ECONOMY 99, 108–10, 117–20 (Richard A. Epstein and Michael S. Greve eds., AEI, 2004); Eleanor M. Fox, *Antitrust and Regulatory Federalism: Races Up, Down, and Sideways*, 75 N.Y.U. L. REV. 1781, 1805–6 (2000); PHILIP MARSDEN, COMPETITION POLICY FOR THE WTO chs. 4–5 (Cameron May, 2003) (describing proposals made by the EU and others for greater international cooperation and harmonization, but generally taking a critical stance toward them); WTO Competition Working Group, *Communication by the European Community and its Member States*, WT/WGTCP/W/62, 12–13 (5 March 1998), available at http://docsonline.wto.org/gen_search.asp?language=1; International Antitrust Working Group, Draft International Antitrust Code, 5 WORLD TRADE MATERIALS 126, 129–31 (September 1993); Ernst-Ulrich Petersmann, *Competition-Oriented Reforms of the WTO World Trade System: Proposals and Trade Options*, in TOWARDS WTO COMPETITION RULES 43, 48–9 (Roger Zäch and Carlos M. Correa eds, 1999); Robert D. Anderson and Peter Holmes, *Competition Policy and the Future of the Multilateral Trading System*, 5 J. INT'L ECON. L. 531, § IV (2002).

[8]   The concept of 'international antitrust law' can be misleading in the sense that there are no supranational antitrust rules or international enforcement mechanism; instead, international antitrust law refers to ways states seek to regulate cross-border business activity through their domestic antitrust laws.

[9]   See Keith Hylton and Fei Deng, *Antitrust Around the World: An Empirical Analysis of the Scope of Competition Laws and their Effects*, 74 ANTITRUST L.J. 271, 272 (2007); David S. Evans, *Trustbusting Goes Global*, in TRUSTBUSTERS: COMPETITION POLICY AUTHORITIES SPEAK OUT 7 (David S. Evans and Frédéric Jenny eds, Competition Policy International, 2009).

[10]   Michael Bliss, *Another Anti-Trust Tradition: Canadian Anti-Combines Policy, 1889–1910*, 47 BUS. HIST. REV. 177 (1973).

[11]   Evans, *supra* note 9, at 9, 11.

The 1991 collapse of the Soviet Union became a watershed moment for the adoption of antitrust laws. After the fall of the Berlin Wall, former communist countries began to embrace free markets, adopting domestic antitrust laws in the process.[12] The implementation of antitrust laws by Eastern European countries coincided with the awakening of the 'Asian tigers' to the ability of free markets and competition to stimulate economic growth. Following these developments, almost all developed countries (94%) and almost half of all emerging and developing countries in the world (47%) have now enacted domestic antitrust laws.[13]

A Why States Adopt Antitrust Laws

Motivations for adopting domestic antitrust rules vary. Some countries adopt antitrust laws because they believe that such laws increase their domestic welfare. Antitrust laws foster strong domestic competition, which also tends to increase the competitiveness of these same domestic firms in global markets.[14] Domestic antitrust regimes can also instill a sense of confidence in a country's regulatory environment, which helps the country attract more international investment.[15]

At times, countries adopt antitrust statutes in response to a change in the country's economic philosophy. Many developing countries in Latin America and Asia, for instance, discovered first-hand the harmfulness of import substitution, negative effects of price controls, and inefficiencies of state-owned enterprises. These experiences led them to pursue market-oriented policies, including enacting antitrust regimes to foster efficiency and stimulate competition.[16] Similarly, several former Soviet satellites wanted to distance themselves from the state-driven economic policies by voluntarily embracing laws that dismantled state monopolies and established economies with competitive pressures.[17] International institutions, including the World Bank, the IMF, and the OECD, have enthusiastically supported these endeavors. They have endorsed antitrust policies as drivers of economic development and offered technical assistance to support emerging economies' efforts to establish antitrust regimes.[18]

---

[12] *Id.* at 9–10.

[13] *Id.* at 11.

[14] Fox, *supra* note 7, at 1784; MICHAEL E. PORTER, THE COMPETITIVE ADVANTAGE OF NATIONS 636 (Simon & Schuster, 2d ed. 1998) (arguing that domestic competition improves corporations' ability to compete in the global market, rather than encumbering it).

[15] Fox, *supra* note 7, at 1784.

[16] See Clive S. Gray and Anthony A. Davis, *Competition Policy in Developing Countries Pursuing Structural Adjustment*, 38 ANTITRUST BULL. 425, 430–31 (1993); Evans, *supra* note 9, at 11–12.

[17] Fox, *supra* note 7, at 1784–5. See Evans, *supra* note 9, at 9, 12.

[18] Evans, *supra* note 9, at 11; Jean-François Pons, Deputy Director General of Competition for the European Commission, *Is it Time for an International Agreement on Antitrust?* 12, available at http://ec.europa.eu/competition/speeches/text/sp2002_027_en.pdf (envisioning that the International Competition Network (ICN) will cooperate with the WTO, UNCTAD, and the OECD who are already established in the field); Merit E. Janow, *Developing a Competition Policy: A Role for WTO*, 13 CONSUMER POL'Y REV. 17, 21 (2003) (noting that the OECD has supported technical assistance and capacity building in the past); William E. Kovacic, *Getting Started: Creating New Competition Policy Institutions in Transition Economies*, 23 BROOK. J. INT'L L. 403,

Other countries adopt antitrust laws more reluctantly, in response to international pressure or inducement to secure other benefits, including trade deals. International institutions' approach to lending support, for instance, has ranged from persuasion and assistance to imposing the requirement to adopt antitrust laws as a condition for loans and other funding. Indonesia and Zambia, for instance, adopted antitrust laws as part of structural adjustment programs that were financed by the IMF and the World Bank.[19] Several countries have adopted antitrust laws in response to their trading partners' demands to do so. For instance, Guatemala, Singapore, and Jordan enacted antitrust laws as a condition for securing a free trade agreement with the United States.[20] The EU employs the strategy of trade conditionality even more frequently and effectively. Aspiring Member States or states seeking trade agreements with the EU have to adopt antitrust laws as a condition for the trade agreement or in preparation for their membership.[21]

Some countries choose not to adopt antitrust laws. The reasons vary, but given that countries without antitrust laws are predominantly the least developed economies, an obvious reason is that antitrust enforcement is costly.[22] Adopting and enforcing antitrust laws requires institutional capacity, technical expertise, and economic resources that these countries lack. Even if an economic argument can be made that competitive markets support developing countries' quest for economic growth and higher levels of development,[23] antitrust laws may not be a regulatory priority given the limited

---

407 (1997–1998) (observing that the support of advisory bodies and multinational donors such as the World Bank, the OECD, and UNCTAD have played an active role in shaping developing countries' newly adopted laws).

[19]   Janow, *supra* note 18, at 18 and n.15 (reporting that the World Bank/IMF conditioned Indonesia's aid to the establishment of a domestic competition law); UNCTAD, *Report of the Third United Nations Conference to Review All Aspects of the Set of Multilaterally Agreed Equitable Principles and Rules for the Control of Restrictive Business Practices* para. 63, U.N. Doc. TD/RBP/CONF.4/15 (1996), available at http://daccessdds.un.org/doc/UNDOC/GEN/G96/511/11/PDF/G9651111.pdf (reporting that Zambia had enacted a statute establishing a Competition Commission as a part of its World Bank-financed 'structural adjustment programme'); Eleanor M. Fox, *Equality, Discrimination, and Competition Law: Lessons from and for South Africa and Indonesia*, 41 HARV. INT'L L.J. 579, 589 (2000).

[20]   Evans, *supra* note 9, at 5.

[21]   Evans, *supra* note 9, at 10, 12 (noting that countries such as Finland and Sweden enacted competition laws in order to join the European Union); see Mark R.A. Palim, *The Worldwide Growth of Competition Law: An Empirical Analysis*, 43 ANTITRUST BULL. 105, 120, 121 n.51 (1998) (noting that many current members of the European Community, such as the Czech Republic, Hungary, Slovak Republic, and Poland, adopted competition policies as a part of trade agreements before they were members).

[22]   See Fox, *supra* note 7, at 1794.

[23]   PORTER, *supra* note 14, at 636; Eleanor M. Fox, *Economic Development, Poverty and Antitrust: The Other Path*, 13 SW. J.L. AND TRADE AM. 211, 212–13 (2006–2007) (suggesting that, although developing nations stand to gain economic benefits from adopting antitrust laws, one should not expect the antitrust law of those nations to be identical to the law of developed nations, since developing nations have other pressing priorities, such as poverty); Peter A.G. van Bergeijk, *What Could Anti-Trust in the OECD Do for Development?*, para. 3 (Institute of Social Studies Working Paper No. 473, 2009), available at http://papers.ssrn.com/sol3/papers.cfm?abstract_id=1331830 (summarizing empirical studies documenting the costs that anticompetitive behavior imposes on developing nations).

government resources and the number of challenges these countries face.[24] Also, developed countries with small, open markets may conclude that antitrust laws would only yield marginal gains for them. Exposure to foreign competition may be sufficient to make domestic markets competitive.[25] This is a reason why Singapore and Hong Kong have taken such a long time to consider antitrust laws in earnest.[26]

B   The Global Reach of Local Antitrust Laws

Given that over 100 countries have antitrust laws, a critical question is to determine which laws apply to which international business activity. The jurisdictional reach of domestic antitrust laws is often determined according to an 'effects doctrine'. This doctrine entails that a state can apply its antitrust laws to any anticompetitive conduct that has an effect on its domestic market.[27] No state can exercise exclusive jurisdiction in antitrust matters.[28] Thus, if a multinational corporation operates in several markets, it is likely to be subject to multiple antitrust laws simultaneously.

The United States and the EU have frequently resorted to extra-territorial enforcement of their antitrust laws.[29] The early antitrust jurisprudence in the United States denied the principle of extra-territoriality. In the *American Banana* case, the US Supreme Court held that US antitrust laws only extend to acts that take place within the United States' borders.[30] Gradually, however, the Supreme Court moved away from the territoriality

---

[24]   Editorial, *The Real Lesson of the Cancun Failure*, FINANCIAL TIMES (London), 23 September 2003, at 16 ('It is absurd to push, as the EU has done, to impose rules in complex areas such as competition and investment on countries so poor that some cannot even afford WTO diplomatic representation').

[25]   Fox, *supra* note 7, at 1794.

[26]   As of date, Hong Kong has yet to enact an antitrust law. See Grace Li and Angus Young, *Competition Laws and Policies in China and Hong Kong: A Tale of Two Regulatory Journeys*, 7 J. INT'L TRADE L. AND POL'Y 186 (2008), available at http://papers.ssrn.com/sol3/papers.cfm?abstract_id=1421792 (manuscript at 15). Singapore did not enact its Competition Act until 2004. Thomas K. Cheng, *A Tale of Two Competition Law Regimes: The Telecom-Sector Competition Regulation in Hong Kong and Singapore*, 30 WORLD COMPET. 501, 502 (2007).

[27]   See Wolfgang Kerber, *The Theory of Regulatory Competition and Competition Law*, in ECONOMIC LAW AS AN ECONOMIC GOOD: ITS RULE FUNCTION IN THE COMPETITION OF SYSTEMS 38 (Karl Meessen ed., 2009), available at http://papers.ssrn.com/sol3/papers.cfm?abstract_id=1392163; Wolfgang Kerber and Oliver Budzinski, *Competition of Competition Laws: Mission Impossible?*, in COMPETITION LAWS IN CONFLICT, *supra* note 7, at 45; Fox, *supra* note 7, at 1789.

[28]   In this respect, antitrust differs from areas such as corporate law, where the internal affairs of the corporation are regulated exclusively by the laws of the state where the corporation was established. This creates a very different dynamic and incentives for regulatory competition.

[29]   The United States and the European Union apply their antitrust laws to the conduct of foreign corporations as long the conduct has had an 'effect' on their domestic market. See, e.g., United States v. Alcoa, 148 F.2d 416, 444 (2d Cir. 1945); Case T-102/96, Gencor Ltd v. Comm'n, [1999] E.C.R. II-00753, paras. 92, 96 (CFI); Federal Trade Antitrust Improvements Act of 1982 (FTAIA), 96 Stat. 1246, 15 U.S.C. § 6a (1982). See, e.g., Damien Geradin, Marc Reysen, and David Henry, *Extraterritoriality, Comity and Cooperation in EC Competition Law* 4–7 (July 2008), available at http://papers.ssrn.com/sol3/papers.cfm?abstract_id=1175003; Eleanor M. Fox, *National Law, Global Markets, and Hartford: Eyes Wide Shut*, 68 ANTITRUST L.J. 73, §§ IV–V (2000).

[30]   Am. Banana Co. v. United Fruit Co., 213 US 347, 356, 359 (1909); Andrew T. Guzman, *International Competition Law*, in RESEARCH HANDBOOK IN INTERNATIONAL ECONOMIC LAW 419 (Andrew T. Guzman and Alan O. Sykes eds., Edward Elgar, 2007).

principle and focused on the effects of foreign conduct on the domestic market.[31] The landmark case of extra-territoriality in the United States was the *Hartford Fire* case, where the Supreme Court affirmed that 'the Sherman Act applies to foreign conduct that was meant to produce and did in fact produce some substantial effect in the United States'. The Court held that considerations of international comity do not prevent US courts from attaching jurisdiction in cases where there is no true conflict between US and foreign law.[32] Most recently, the Supreme Court revisited the question of extra-territorial application of antitrust laws in the *Empagran* case. Invoking the principle of international comity, it limited the extra-territorial reach of the Sherman Act by holding that the Act did not extend to cases where a foreign plaintiff suffers an injury that is independent of any domestic harm.[33]

Notwithstanding its historically more cautious stand towards antitrust extra-territoriality, the EU today is prepared to extend its antitrust jurisdiction to foreign conduct.[34] The European Court of Justice re-affirmed the extra-territorial application of European antitrust laws in the *Wood Pulp* case.[35] The Commission has also exercised jurisdiction over mergers involving foreign companies whenever merging parties have exceeded the EU's revenue-based thresholds for notification.[36] However, many other

---

[31] See United States v. Aluminum Co. of Am., 148 F.2d 416, 443 (2d Cir. 1945) ('it is settled law – as "Limited" itself agrees – that any state may impose liabilities, even upon persons not within its allegiance, for conduct outside its borders that has consequences within its borders which the state reprehends; and these liabilities other states will ordinarily recognize'). Although this is a Second Circuit case, it has the binding effect of a Supreme Court case because the Court lacked quorum and had to refer the case. See *id.* at 416. The *Alcoa* case held that the Sherman Act extends to foreign conduct if such conduct 'were intended to affect imports and did affect them'. *Id.* at 444. But see Timberlane Lumber Co. v. Bank of Am. Nat'l Trust & Sav. Ass'n, 549 F.2d 597, 611–12 (9th Cir. 1976) (softening the *Alcoa* effects test with a requirement that courts must weigh the interests of foreign states); Hartford Fire Ins. Co. v. California, 509 U.S. 764, 797 (1993) (acknowledging that comity considerations may apply, but only where there is a 'true conflict').

[32] Implicitly, the Court also re-affirmed the simultaneous applicability of multiple antitrust laws, and the requirement that an individual must comply with all those laws absent true conflict. True conflict exists only when one jurisdiction requires (as opposed to permits) a conduct that is prohibited by another jurisdiction. In most cases, a company can therefore ensure its compliance with multiple antitrust laws by simply conforming to the strictest jurisdiction. This phenomenon of 'strictest regime wins' is discussed *infra*.

[33] F. Hoffman-La Roche Ltd. v. Empagran S.A., 542 U.S. 155 (2004); see also Ronald W. Davis, *Empagran and International Cartels: A Comity of Errors*, 19 ANTITRUST 58, 61 (2004); Victor P. Goldberg, *The Empagran Exception: Between Illinois Brick and a Hard Place* 11 (Center for Law and Economic Studies at the Columbia University School of Law Working Paper No. 345, 2009); Alvin K. Klevorick and Alan O. Sykes, *United States Courts and the Optimal Deterrence of International Cartels: A Welfarist Perspective on Empagran*, 3 J. COMPETIT. L. AND ECON. 309 (2007).

[34] Geradin *et al.*, *supra* note 29, at 4.

[35] Cases 89/85, 114/85, 116–117/85, 125–129/85, A. Ahlström Osakeyhtiö v. Comm'n (Wood Pulp), [1993] E.C.R. I-1307, para. 62; Case 48/69, Imperial Chem. Ind. v. Comm'n (Dyestuffs), [1972] E.C.R. 619, paras 125–42.

[36] Guzman, *supra* note 30, at 423. See, e.g., Commission Decision 97/26/EC, Case IV/M.619 (Gencor/Lonrho), [1997] O.J. L 11/30 para. 219; Commission Decision of 30 July 1997, Case IV/M.877 (Boeing/McDonnell Douglas), [1997] O.J. L 336/16 paras 8, 124; *GE/Honeywell*

jurisdictions beyond the United States and the EU have recognized the legitimacy of applying antitrust laws to the conduct of foreign firms as long as some anticompetitive effect is felt on the domestic market of that country.[37] China's recent decision to exert jurisdiction over Coca-Cola during its attempted acquisition of Chinese juice company Huiyuan offers an example of this.[38] India, departing from its previous practice of denying extra-territorial application of its antitrust laws, has also revised its antitrust laws to embrace the effects doctrine.[39]

C   Why Antitrust Laws Differ Across Jurisdictions

In principle, all states could enforce the same antitrust laws. The basic economic theory informing antitrust enforcement applies regardless of the particular market or the specific situation.[40] Most states' antitrust laws also purport to promote the same goal: consumer welfare. Yet, a closer look at the laws and their enforcement reveals remarkable differences across the jurisdictions.

Substantive laws may often appear similar, given that most antitrust jurisdictions have chosen to adopt either US- or EU-style antitrust laws.[41] However, many states, while sharing the fundamental policy goal of consumer welfare, seek to pursue a wider set of objectives through their antitrust laws. These may include the advancement of public interest or 'fair' competition, the protection of small- and medium-sized enterprises, employment, or more equitable distribution of ownership.[42] Even where the substantive

---

Commission Decision, para. 567. For all of these decisions, the legal basis of the decision came from EC Merger Regulation. Council Regulation 139/2004 of 20 January 2004, [2004] O.J. L24, art. 8(3).

[37]   See RESTATEMENT (THIRD) OF FOREIGN RELATIONS LAW OF THE UNITED STATES § 415 reporters' note 9 (1987).

[38]   See Sundeep Tucker and Jamil Anderlini, *China's Block on Coke Bid Raises Alarm Over M&A*, FINANCIAL TIMES, 19 March, 2009, at 16; Zhou Xin and Michael Wei, *China's Statement on Rejecting Coke's Huiyuan Bid*, REUTERS, 18 March 2009 (quoting a translation of the Chinese Ministry of Commerce's decision to reject Coca-Cola's bid for Huiyuan).

[39]   See Aditya Bhattacharjea, *India's New Competition Law: A Comparative Assessment*, 4 J. COMPET. L. AND ECON. 609, 624, 627 (2008) (noting that the 1969 Monopolies and Restrictive Trade Practices Act was interpreted not to have extra-territorial application, but that the new Competition Act of 2002 will apply to any practices that have 'an anticompetitive *effect* in India'); Rahul Singh, *Shifting Paradigms, Changing Contexts: Need for a New Competition Law in India*, 8 J. CORP. L. STUD. 143, 153 (2008); S. Chakravarthy, *Competition Act, 2002: The Approach*, in A FUNCTIONAL COMPETITION POLICY FOR INDIA para. 3.10 (Pradeep S. Mehta ed., 2006).

[40]   Evans, *supra* note 9, at 8.

[41]   See Fox, *supra* note 7, at 1799 (suggesting that the EU and the United States are locked in a competition to export their competition laws and become the dominant antitrust model for the world).

[42]   See Dina I. Waked, *Competition Law in the Developing World: The Why and How of Adoption and Its Implications for International Competition Law*, 1 GLOBAL ANTITRUST REV. 69, 82 (2008) (noting that South Africa, for example, has a broader range of competition law objectives, including 'the promotion of a more equitable spread of ownership' and 'the interests of workers'); Michael J. Trebilcock and Edward M. Iacobucci, *National Treatment and Extraterritoriality: Defining the Domains of Trade and Antitrust Policy*, in COMPETITION LAWS IN CONFLICT, *supra* note 7, at 167 (explaining that Canada may consider producer welfare in addition to consumer welfare); Eleanor M. Fox, *Toward World Antitrust and Market Access*, 91 AM. J. INT'L L. 1, 4–5 (1997) (suggesting

rules are similar, the actual enforcement (or, at times, nonenforcement) of those laws can lead to different outcomes in practice. Also, remedial options differ from one country to another: some countries choose to criminalize anticompetitive conduct; others prefer resorting to administrative fines and injunctive relief.[43]

Scholars have examined sources for divergence in states' antitrust laws. Some suggest that the size and openness of the economy determine the type of antitrust law that is optimal for a country.[44] Also, market structures and prevailing conditions for cooperation differ, at times calling for dissimilar antitrust laws. This may be a result of the country's history of state-owned businesses, or a reflection of the government's adherence to a different economic ideology.[45] Antitrust laws are also likely to reflect the level of economic development in the country.[46] Countries with abundant resources, well-established institutions, and technical expertise are more likely to be able to afford sophisticated antitrust regimes. Finally, the domestic political economy is dissimilar across the countries. The prospect of political rents leads the government to pursue different antitrust policies, depending on the relative influence of various interest groups in any given country.[47]

The need to explain the differences among countries' antitrust laws has give rise to a 'comparative antitrust law' scholarship. Comparative analysis of antitrust laws has thus far focused on US and EU antitrust enforcement.[48] Einer Elhauge and Damien Geradin's textbook, *Global Antitrust Law and Economics*, provides the most comprehensive comparative discussion of these two jurisdictions.[49] After discussing the similarities and the differences across the entire field of antitrust and merger control, they confirm that

---

that the EU has a 'fuller [antitrust] agenda' that involves social policies); Nathan Bush, *The PRC Antimonopoly Law: Unanswered Questions and Challenges Ahead*, 7 ANTITRUST SOURCE 1, 2 (2007), available at www.abanet.org/antitrust/at-source/07/10/Oct07-Bush10-18f.pdf (noting that the priorities of Chinese Anti-Monopoly Law are ambiguous because art. 1 lists so many: efficiency, consumer interests, fair market competition, the public interest, and the healthy development of the socialist market economy); Bhattacharjea, *supra* note 39, at 624, 627 (observing that public interest has been a consideration in past Indian competition cases, and noting that the clause in the new Competition Act 'keeping in view the economic development of the country' provides a potentially dangerous loophole).

[43]   Diane P. Wood, *Cooperation and Convergence in International Antitrust*, in COMPETITION LAWS IN CONFLICT, *supra* note 7, at 183. *Cf. infra* notes 56–62 and accompanying text.

[44]   Wood, *supra* note 43, at 181–2; Michal S. Gal, *Size Does Matter: The Effects of Market Size on Optimal Competition Policy*, 74 S. CAL. L. REV. 1437, 1441, 1450–67 (2001); see Fox, *supra* note 7, at 1794.

[45]   See Evans, *supra* note 9, at 8 (surmising that it is not unreasonable to treat firms with different historical and economic circumstances differently).

[46]   See discussion *infra*.

[47]   Anu Bradford, *International Antitrust Negotiations and the False Hope of the WTO*, 48 HARV. INT'L L.J. 383, 392 (2007).

[48]   See generally HANDBOOK OF RESEARCH IN TRANS-ATLANTIC ANTITRUST (Philip Marsden ed., Edward Elgar, 2006); Alberto Pera, *Changing Views of Competition, Economic Analysis and EC Antitrust Law*, 4 EUR. COMPETIT. J. 127, 150–59 (2008); ELEANOR M. FOX, THE COMPETITION LAW OF THE EUROPEAN UNION IN COMPARATIVE PERSPECTIVE: CASES AND MATERIALS (West, 2009); Alan J. Devlin, *Exploring the Source of Transatlantic Antitrust Divergence* 25 (bepress Legal Series Working Paper No. 1108, 2006), available at http://law.bepress.com/expresso/eps/1108/.

[49]   EINER R. ELHAUGE AND DAMIEN GERADIN, GLOBAL ANTITRUST LAW AND ECONOMICS (Thomson West, 2007).

increasing convergence is taking place between the two key antitrust jurisdictions.[50] Both the United States and the EU seek to maximize consumer welfare as the primary goal of antitrust enforcement.[51] The EU is also increasingly embracing the economic analysis of antitrust law, adopting analytical tools closer to those employed by the US courts and antitrust agencies.[52] The antitrust doctrine is also similar, in particular with respect to collusive behavior or horizontal mergers.[53]

Still, some important differences remain. The EU employs its antitrust laws to further the creation of a common European market. This way, it ensures that the anticompetitive practices of private enterprise do not re-erect trade barriers within the common market.[54] The EU also intervenes more frequently, believing less in the ability of the markets to

---

[50]   *Id.* at 1100.

[51]   Neelie Kroes, European Commissioner for Competition, Review of Insurance Block Exemption Regulation, Keynote Speech at the Insurance Block Exemption Regulation Conference, 2 June 2009, available at http://europa.eu/rapid/pressReleasesAction.do?reference=SPEECH/09/278&format=HTML&aged=0&language=EN&guiLanguage=en (declaring that improving consumer welfare is the most important goal of the Commission); Mario Monti, European Commissioner for Competition, A Reformed Competition Policy: Achievements and Challenges for the Future, Speech before the Center for European Reform, 28 October 2004, available at http://europa.eu/rapid/pressReleasesAction.do?reference=SPEECH/04/477&format=HTML&aged=1&language=EN&guiLanguage=en (declaring that 'consumer interest' has been confirmed as the main goal of competition policy). See Pera, *supra* note 48, at 127, 140–41 (observing that the more 'objective' economics-based analytical approach looking at consumer welfare has increasingly gained support, both in the United States and the EU); Devlin, *supra* note 48, at 11. However, the EU has goals other than maximizing consumer welfare; it also seeks to develop and maintain a single, integrated market. See Devlin, *supra* note 48, at 25.

[52]   See, e.g., Monti, *supra* note 51 (acknowledging that the trend in competition policy is to ground decisions in sound microeconomic reasoning, and making commitments toward that end); Makan Delrahim, Deputy Assistant Attorney General, Antitrust Division of the US Department of Justice, The Long and Winding Road: Convergence in the Application of Antitrust to Intellectual Property, Remarks at the George Mason Law Review Symposium, 6 October 2004, available at www.usdoj.gov/atr/public/speeches/205712.htm (speaking on 'reaching consensus on antitrust enforcement strategies that are grounded in sound economic theory' as a central goal of convergence and noting the progress that has been made between the United States and the EU); William J. Kolasky, Deputy Assistant Attorney General, Antitrust Division of the US Department of Justice, Global Competition: Prospects for Convergence and Cooperation, Remarks before the American Bar Association Fall Forum, 7 November 2002, available at www.usdoj.gov/atr/public/speeches/200446.htm (claiming that the EU and the United States have made 'substantial progress' toward convergence and noting favorably Commissioner Mario Monti's plan to hire a new chief economist as a step which will bring 'more rigorous economic analysis' to EU decision-making). See also Roger Van den Bergh, *The Difficult Reception of Economic Analysis in European Competition Law*, in POST-CHICAGO DEVELOPMENTS IN ANTITRUST LAW 34 (Antonio Cucinotta, Roberto Pardolesi, and Roger Van den Bergh eds, Edward Elgar, 2002); Pera, *supra* note 48, at 140–41; Devlin, *supra* note 48, at 38, 40.

[53]   For a standard book on European antitrust doctrine, see generally BELLAMY AND CHILD: EUROPEAN COMMUNITY LAW OF COMPETITION (Peter Roth and Vivien Rose eds, Oxford, 6th ed. 2007); RICHARD WHISH, COMPETITION LAW (Oxford, 6th ed. 2008).

[54]   See European Commission, *XXIXth Report on Competition Policy 1999*, 19 (2000) (explaining that the two principal objectives of EU competition law are the maintenance of competitive markets and the development of a single market). Also, social considerations such as promotion of employment or protection of small enterprises still play a role at the margins of the EU antitrust analysis. See Fox, *supra* note 42, at 4 n.17, 12.

self-correct.[55] As such, the EU is likely to err on the side of making 'false positive' decisions, whereas the United States is likely to err on the side of 'false negatives', fearing incorrect intervention. These transatlantic divergences are most notable in the regulation of unilateral conduct by dominant companies.[56] The EU is more likely to bring cases against dominant companies than to rely on the market.[57] Another key area of divergence is in the treatment of vertical restraints. Because the EU uses antitrust laws as a tool to facilitate a common market in Europe,[58] the EU is particularly hostile towards territorial restraints that threaten to partition the common market.[59] Finally, the *GE/Honeywell* case exposed critical transatlantic differences towards vertical and conglomerate mergers.[60]

While the substantive scope of antitrust in the EU appears to be wider than in the United States, it is not clear that corporations incur higher financial costs for complying with the EU's antitrust laws.[61] Assume that the narrower scope of US antitrust laws, together with the fear of 'false positive' decisions, causes the US antitrust agencies to underenforce their antitrust laws. Assume also that the more extensive scope of antitrust laws, together with the fear of 'false negative' decisions, causes the EU antitrust authori-

---

[55]   Gunnar Niels and Adriaan ten Kate, *Introduction: Antitrust in the U.S. and the EU – Converging or Diverging Paths?*, 49 ANTITRUST BULL. 1, 15 (2004). See Nuno Garoupa and Thomas S. Ulen, *The Market for Legal Innovation: Law and Economics in Europe and the United States*, 59 ALA. L. REV. 1555, 1579 (2008) (noting that those in the antitrust field in the United States have been far more receptive to free-market classical liberalism than those in the EU); Andreas Kirsch and William Weesner, *Can Antitrust Law Control E-Commerce? A Comparative Analysis in Light of U.S. and E.U. Antitrust Law*, 12 U.C. DAVIS J. INT'L L. AND POLY. 297, 308 (2006).

[56]   See ELHAUGE AND GERADIN, *supra* note 49, at 255; see also *id.* at 1100 (listing the main differences between the United States and the EU). The United States and the EU differ on whether excessive pricing by dominant companies should be considered anticompetitive; whether above-cost predatory pricing should be banned; whether a below-cost predatory pricing claim requires the showing of recoupment of predatory losses; when a dominant company has a duty to deal; and, finally, under which circumstances loyalty- and volume-based discounts should be allowed.

[57]   The European Commission's recent decisions against Microsoft and Intel are illustrative of this. See generally Commission Decision 2004/900 of 24 March 2004, Case No. COMP/C-3/37.792 – Microsoft, [2003] O.J. L1; Commission Decision of 13 May 2009, Case No. COMP/37.990 – Intel (not yet published).

[58]   *XXIXth Report on Competition Policy 1999*, *supra* note 54, at 19.

[59]   *Id.*

[60]   Eleanor M. Fox, *GE/Honeywell: The U.S. Merger that Europe Stopped – A Story of the Politics of Convergence*, in ANTITRUST STORIES 343–7 (Eleanor M. Fox and Daniel A. Crane eds., Foundation, 2007) (describing the fallout between the US Department of Justice and the EU Commission shortly after the GE/Honeywell merger had been shot down). However, developments since the *GE/Honeywell* case suggest that the differences raised in *GE/Honeywell* may not be as extreme as originally supposed. See *id.* at 353–5, 358–60 (arguing that EU rhetoric has largely converged to be compatible with the US school of thought, and suggesting that the *GE/Honeywell* decision might be an outlier in the long run); Case C-12/03 P, Comm'n v. Tetra Laval, [2005] E.C.R. I-1113 (involving another conglomerate merger, but resulting in annulment). For a recent attempt to clarify the European Union's stance on conglomerate mergers, see Commission Guidelines 2008/C 265/07, Assessment of Non-Horizontal Mergers under the Council Regulation on the Control of Concentrations between Undertakings, [2008] O.J. C265 6 (EC).

[61]   David S. Evans, *Why Different Jurisdictions Do Not (and Should Not) Adopt the Same Antitrust Rules* 8–9 (16 February 2009), available at http://papers.ssrn.com/sol3/papers.cfm?abstract_id=1342797.

ties to overenforce their antitrust laws. Despite these differences, critical procedural differences in the two antitrust jurisdictions may offset any assumed underenforcement in the United States and overenforcement in the EU. European antitrust law is enforced by the European Commission and national competition authorities of the EU Member States. Private plaintiffs have thus far had a limited, almost nonexistent,[62] right to sue corporations for their antitrust violations in European courts.[63] In contrast, private plaintiffs bring 95% of the federal antitrust cases in the United States.[64] The volume of antitrust litigation is therefore much higher in the United States.[65] Antitrust remedies differ as well: US agencies and courts employ more aggressive remedies, including imprisonment and treble damages, for antitrust violations.[66] These tools are not available for the European Commission and European courts.[67] Consequently, despite the differences in substantive antitrust laws, the US and the EU antitrust laws may deter anticompetitive behavior at similar levels, given the offsetting effects of the procedural and remedial choices made.

Another focus of comparative antitrust law scholarship has been developing countries. A debate has emerged as to assess whether developing countries should adopt different types of antitrust laws because of their developmental needs. Some argue that antitrust laws that are optimal for developing countries are different from those that are optimal for developed countries.[68] Because of their less efficient production, developing countries

---

[62] *Id.* at 8 n.23 (reporting that there have been 12 successful actions and 12 unsuccessful actions in the European Union).

[63] See Commission *White Paper on Damages Actions for Breach of the EC Antitrust Rules, COM(2008)165 final*, 2–3 (2 April 2008), available at http://ec.europa.eu/competition/antitrust/actionsdamages/files_white_paper/whitepaper_en.pdf (explaining that the 'right of victims to compensation' is guaranteed under Community law, but that in practice private victims rarely obtain reparation). However, the EU plans to expand the role of private litigation in enforcing its competition rules. See *id.* See also Mario Monti, European Commissioner for Competition Matters, Private Litigation as a Key Complement to Public Enforcement of Competition Rules and the First Conclusions on the Implementation of the New Merger Regulation, Speech before the International Bar Association 8th Annual Competition Conference, 17 September 2004, available at http://europa.eu/rapid/pressReleasesAction.do?reference=SPEECH/04/403&format=PDF&aged=1&language=EN&guiLanguage=en. A few scholars have weighed in on the role of private litigation in EU antitrust enforcement. See, e.g., Wouter P.J. Wils, *The Relationship Between Public Antitrust Enforcement and Private Actions for Damages*, 32 WORLD COMPET. (2009); Christopher Cook, *Private Enforcement of EU Competition Law in Member State Courts: Experience to Date and the Path Ahead*, 4 COMPET. POL'Y INT'L 3 (2008); Vincent Smith, *Will Europe Provide Effective Redress for Cartel Victims?*, 4 COMPET. POL'Y INT'L 65 (2008); Assimakis P. Komninos, *The Road to the Commission's White Paper for Damages Actions: Where We Came From*, 4 COMPET. POL'Y INT'L 81 (2008); Renato Nazzini and Ali Nikpay, *Private Actions in EC Competition Law*, 4 COMPET. POL'Y INT'L 107 (2008).

[64] Evans, *supra* note 61, at 8.

[65] *Id.*

[66] Evans, *supra* note 9, at 8.

[67] Most countries do not impose criminal penalties for antitrust violations. Notable exceptions include the United States and the United Kingdom. See *id.*

[68] See Waked, *supra* note 42, at 82; Paul E. Godek, *One U.S. Export Eastern Europe Does Not Need*, 15 REGULATION 20, 21 (1992); Paul E. Godek, *A Chicago-School Approach to Antitrust for Developing Economies*, 43 ANTITRUST BULL. 274, 262 (1998); Bernard Hoekman and Petros C. Mavroidis, *Economic Development: Competition Policy and the World Trade Organization* 8

may need to focus on productive efficiency rather than allocative efficiency in assessing competitive effects on their markets.[69] Also, economies of scale may also be more important for developing countries.[70] This, some would argue, justifies higher levels of concentration in their markets. Developing country markets may support only few firms, which need to be allowed to acquire market power in order to innovate and compete against large developed country firms.[71] Critics doubt the categorical presumption that economies of scale require more concentrated markets.[72] They also question whether lax antitrust rules and the protection of monopolists lead to enhanced competitiveness and innovations in these countries.[73] Higher levels of concentration increase the risk of collusion or abuse of market power, suggesting that developing countries need more, not less, antitrust enforcement.[74] Empirical studies have also shown a positive correlation between antitrust enforcement and high GDP, further indicating that antitrust enforcement helps rather than impedes the goals of development.[75]

Most recently, the antitrust community has turned its attention to developments in China. After 13 years of drafting, China adopted an Antimonopoly Law in August 2008. The new law entered into force a year later. The law states consumer welfare and efficiency as its goal. However, the new law also purports to advance 'fair market competition', 'public interest' and 'the healthy development of socialist market economy'.[76] It is unclear which priorities will come to dominate the enforcement. The legislative history revealed mixed motivations: some domestic groups favored the law as a tool to control the conduct of state-owned enterprises and to abolish trade barriers among different regions within China; others saw the new law as an opportunity to challenge foreign multinationals that are increasingly controlling the Chinese economy. China's first year of enforcement has reinforced concerns that the law will be used as a tool for protectionism. Most prominently, China prohibited Coca-Cola's proposed

---

(World Bank Policy Research Paper No. 2917, 2002), available at http://papers.ssrn.com/sol3/papers.cfm?abstract_id=636279; A.E. Rodriguez and Malcolm B. Coate, *Limits to Antitrust Policy for Reforming Economies*, 18 HOUS. J. INT'L L. 311, 320–22 (1996) (noting that several scholars have argued against applying the antitrust law of developed countries to developing countries, but also concluding that antitrust law has become an accepted part of developing countries' policies); Richard A. Posner, *100 Years of Antitrust*, WALL ST. J., 29 June 1990, at A12; ELHAUGE, *supra* note 49, at 1206–8; Gal, *supra* note 44, at 1441–2.

[69]   Ajit Singh and Rahule Dhumale, *Competition Policy, Development, and Developing Countries*, in WHAT GLOBAL ECONOMIC CRISIS? 133–4 (Philip Arestis, Michelle Baddeley, and John McCombie eds, Palgrave, 2001); ELHAUGE AND GERADIN, *supra* note 49, at 1207.

[70]   ELHAUGE AND GERADIN, *supra* note 49, at 1206 (discussing this yet questioning the basis of the argument).

[71]   Waked, *supra* note 42, at 86, 89. See ELHAUGE AND GERADIN, *supra* note 49, at 1206.

[72]   ELHAUGE AND GERADIN, *supra* note 49, at 1207.

[73]   *Id.*

[74]   *Id.* at 1206.

[75]   See WORLD BANK, WORLD DEVELOPMENT REPORT: BUILDING INSTITUTIONS FOR MARKETS 141 (2002). See generally Michael W. Nicholson, *An Antitrust Law Index for Empirical Analysis of International Competition Policy*, 4 J. COMPET. L. AND ECON. 1009 (2008).

[76]   See Anti-Monopoly Law of the People's Republic of China, Presidential Order No. 68 (National People's Congress, 2007, 2008), www.npc.gov.cn/englishnpc/Law/2009-02/20/content_1471587.htm (PRC), art. 1; Bush, *supra* note 42, at 2.

acquisition of a Chinese juice maker, Huiyuan, in March 2009.[77] A few months earlier, China imposed extensive conditions before approving the merger between two foreign brewers, American Anheuser-Busch and Belgian InBev.[78] These decisions, together with a similarly interventionist decision in the deal between Mitsubishi Rayon and Lucite International,[79] indicate that China's new law may indeed depart from antitrust laws of more established jurisdictions.

Assuming that all states have adopted antitrust laws that are optimal for their country (in maximizing either their domestic consumer welfare or their domestic total welfare), the differences across antitrust jurisdictions reflect legitimate policy choices. Those differences would therefore be difficult or costly to reverse without reducing the welfare of individual countries. Indeed, it is possible that no one-size-fits-all antitrust law exists.[80] Yet, the current system consisting of multiple, overlapping, and often inconsistent antitrust laws creates several externalities that fail to advance global welfare. These problems are discussed next.

II   PROBLEM OF DECENTRALIZED ANTITRUST REGIMES

A   Increase in Transaction Costs and Conflicts

1   Costs of compliance with multiple antitrust laws

Decentralized antitrust enforcement increases transaction costs, causes delays, and raises the likelihood of conflicting decisions.[81] Multijurisdictional merger review offers a pertinent example of this. Over 70 countries today have domestic merger control regimes, imposing overlapping notification obligations on merging parties. The sheer number of jurisdictions reviewing the transaction increases the costs of compliance. Further costs stem from inconsistent procedural requirements and conflicting substantive standards which different antitrust agencies use when assessing the competitive effects of transactions.

The costs associated with multijurisdictional merger review can be divided into three major categories. First, parties must expend management time and legal fees to ascertain whether a notification in a particular jurisdiction is required.[82] Opaque or

---

[77]   *China Rejects Coke Bid for Juice Maker*, NEW YORK TIMES, 18 March 2009, available at www.nytimes.com/aponline/2009/03/18/business/AP-AS-China-Coca-Cola-Huiyuan.html?dbk.

[78]   Li Jing, *MOFCOM Approves InBev, AB Merger*, CHINA DAILY, 19 November 2008, www.chinadaily.com.cn/bizchina/2008-11/19/content_7219360.htm.

[79]   See *Mitsubishi/Lucite Deal Approved with 'Conditions'*, CHINA LAW AND PRACTICE, May 2009, www.chinalawandpractice.com/Article/2194925/MitsubishiLucite-deal-approved-with-conditions.html.

[80]   See Wood, *supra* note 43, at 179–82. *Cf.* Daniel K. Tarullo, *Norms and Institutions in Global Competition Policy*, 94 AM. J. INT'L L. 478, 504 (2000).

[81]   Tarullo, *supra* note 80, at 482; Guzman, *supra* note 7, at 100–101; Guzman, *supra* note 30, at 428–9.

[82]   International Competition Network, *Report on the Costs and Burdens of Multijurisdictional Merger Review* 10–12 (November 2004), available at www.internationalcompetitionnetwork.org/media/library/conference_1st_naples_2002/costburd.pdf (hereinafter 'ICN Report').

difficult-to-interpret filing requirements in a given jurisdiction may magnify these costs.[83] Second, the process of notifying an upcoming merger to multiple authorities entails filing fees, legal fees, document production fees, and possible translation fees.[84] These fees are particularly high in jurisdictions that require parties to submit extensive information even for mergers that have a trivial effect on the market.[85] Finally, multiple notification requirements may lead to costly delays in implementing the merger.[86] These delays lead to a loss of efficiencies that motivated the transaction. At worst, they can be fatal to a particularly time-sensitive transaction.[87]

Many commentators have asserted that the proliferation of merger control regimes imposes significant costs on merging parties.[88] Antitrust agencies across jurisdictions have conceded that multiple filing requirements function as a 'tax' on international mergers, perhaps discouraging or delaying efficient transactions.[89] Until recently, however, there was little empirical evidence on the actual magnitude of the costs associated with multijurisdictional merger review. Diane Wood and Richard Whish, in their study entitled *Merger Cases in the Real World*, made an important early attempt to account for the costs of multijurisdictional merger filing.[90] Another noteworthy study examining the associated costs is the 2000 ICPAC report to the Attorney General and Assistant Attorney General for Antitrust, which examined the effects of globalization on US antitrust policy, including the costs of multijurisdictional merger review.[91]

In 2002, the International Bar Association and the American Bar Association commissioned a study from PricewaterhouseCoopers LLP to quantify the costs of multijurisdictional merger review ('Multijurisdictional Merger Survey' or 'Survey').[92] As the first serious attempt to measure the costs of multijurisdictional review, the Survey drew from a sample of 62 international M&A deals from 2000 to mid-2002, involving 382 notifications

---

[83]   *Id.* at 10–11; ICPAC REPORT, *supra* note 5, at 91.

[84]   ICN Report, *supra* note 82, at 7.

[85]   *Id.* at 14.

[86]   Guzman, *supra* note 30, at 429.

[87]   ICN Report, *supra* note 82, at 16.

[88]   See generally ICPAC Report, *supra* note 5; ICN Report, *supra* note 82.

[89]   See Konrad von Finckenstein, Commissioner of Competition, Canadian Competition Bureau, International Antitrust Cooperation: Bilateralism or Multilateralism?, Address to joint meeting of the American Bar Association Section of Antitrust Law and Canadian Bar Association National Competition Law Section, 31 May 2001, available at www.apeccp.org.tw/doc/Canada/Policy/1a.htm; Charles A. James, *Perspectives on the International Competition Network*, 16 ANTITRUST 36 (2001); Mario Monti, Competition Commissioner, European Commission, The EU Views on Global Competition Forum, Address before the American Bar Association, 29 March 2001, available at http://europa.eu/rapid/pressReleasesAction.do?reference=SPEECH/01/147&format=PDF&aged=1&language=EN&guiLanguage=en.

[90]   RICHARD WHISH AND DIANE WOOD, MERGER CASES IN THE REAL WORLD: A STUDY OF MERGER CONTROL PROCEDURES (OECD, 1994). The study reports several merger investigations and their outcomes in detail, describing the nature of the transaction, the steps taken during the proceeding, and the parties' reactions; it then proceeds to analyse the factors that affect cooperation and propose suggestions for strengthening cooperation across jurisdictions.

[91]   ICPAC Report, *supra* note 5.

[92]   PricewaterhouseCoopers LLC, *A Tax On Mergers? Surveying the Costs to Business of Multi-Jurisdictional Merger Review* (June 2003), available at www.pwc.co.uk/pdf/pwc_mergers.pdf (hereinafter 'PWC Report').

in 49 jurisdictions. [93] Though the Survey's small sample size and overrepresentation of European deals limits its applicability, the Survey provides an important empirical foundation for the discussion on the costs of decentralized antitrust enforcement. [94]

The Survey confirmed that the current system of multijurisdictional review imposes additional costs on firms in terms of time and money. It found that a typical international merger requires parties to file with six different antitrust agencies. On average, a multijurisdictional merger review took seven months to complete. A regression analysis showed that the duration of the review process for any given merger is a function of the number of jurisdictions reviewing the transaction. [95] As for monetary costs, the Survey found that an average merger generated €3.3 million (US $4.7 million) in *external* merger review costs. [96] If an antitrust authority issued a 'second request', these costs increased to €5.4 million (US $7.8 million). The results indicated that the number of required filings was the most important determinant of the total external costs in the absence of economies of scale. By contrast, the primary determinant of the extent of the total *internal* costs was the transaction's value, [97] since economies of scale do lower the internal costs associated with the review process.

The Survey also compared the costs associated with multijurisdictional merger review to the value of an average merger, finding that the average external transaction costs of reviewing a merger constitute 0.11% of the total costs of the average deal. Transaction costs of this magnitude are unlikely to deter transnational mergers. Still, these costs impose a 'relatively small, but regressive tax' on international mergers. [98] As long as the states maintain a decentralized merger review process, this regressive tax cannot be entirely eliminated. Thus, international efforts to foster cooperation among antitrust agencies have primarily focused on identifying[99] and eradicating[100] the 'unnecessary'

---

[93] See *id.* at 10–11, 44.

[94] ICN Report, *supra* note 82, at 5.

[95] PWC Report, *supra* note 92, at 34.

[96] *Id.* at 42. These represented approximately 85% of the overall costs of the merger review for the merging parties, comprising legal fees (65%), filing fees (19%), and other advisory fees (14%). *Id.* at 4.

[97] To measure the internal costs of the merger, the Survey looked at the time the management dedicated to the review process, measured in person-weeks. For Phase I reviews, average internal costs amounted to 28 person-weeks, whereas the costs increased to 120 person-weeks for Phase II reviews.

[98] See PWC Report, *supra* note 92, at 4. The 'regressive tax' is likely to have a disproportionately adverse impact on relatively small-value transactions.

[99] For instance, the ICN Mergers Working Group has identified four categories of unnecessary costs that it urges countries to reduce. These include costs associated with (1) imprecise or subjective notification thresholds; (2) notifications without an appreciable nexus with the reviewing jurisdiction; (3) unduly onerous filing requirements; and (4) unreasonable delays in the review process. ICN Report, *supra* note 82, at 9–18. See also OECD Business and Industry Advisory Committee and International Chamber of Commerce, Recommended Framework for Best Practices in International Merger Control Procedures §§ 2.1.2.2–2.1.2.5 (4 October 2001), available at www.biac.org/statements/comp/BIAC-ICCMergerPaper.pdf; Merger Streamlining Group, *Best Practices for the Review of International Mergers* 27 (November 2002), available at www.mcmillan-binch.com/mergerstreamlininggroup.html (hereinafter 'MSG Report'); ICPAC Report, *supra* note 5, at 91–92; American Bar Ass'n Section of Antitrust Law, *Report on Multijurisdictional Merger Review Issues* 8–11 (17 May 1999), available at www.abanet.org/ftp/pub/antitrust/icpac-mr.doc.

[100] The ICN Working Group proposes a set of Recommended Practices to reduce unnecessary

costs – costs that can be avoided while retaining the current system of multijurisdictional merger review.

2   Possibility of conflicting decisions

As discussed above, antitrust laws and enforcement practices differ across the jurisdictions. At worst, this can lead to inconsistent decisions among antitrust authorities. The most prominent enforcement conflict erupted when the European Commission enjoined the proposed merger between two American companies, General Electric and Honeywell, in June 2001,[101] despite the transaction's earlier approval in the United States.[102] Had it not failed, the transaction would have been the largest industrial merger in history.[103]

The reasons for the transatlantic divergence in the *GE/Honeywell* case have been extensively debated in the literature.[104] Most notably, the US and the EU authorities differed on two issues: the competitive effects of 'mixed bundling' and the existence of vertical foreclosure. 'Mixed bundling' refers to a practice of offering goods both separately and in a bundle. The European Commission was concerned about the merged entity's ability

---

costs. The ICN urges antitrust agencies to adopt clear notification thresholds and to offer pre-notification guidance to parties. These measures would mitigate uncertainties involved in ascertaining if a notification is required in a given jurisdiction. The ICN further suggests that states should only assert jurisdiction over mergers that have 'appreciable competitive effects within their territory' based on sales the merging parties generate or assets they possess within that jurisdiction. This would eliminate unnecessary filings to jurisdictions where the effects of a transaction are trivial. To alleviate the burden of notifications, the ICN proposes methods to limit the amount of information agencies require, at least at the initial stage. Finally, the Group proposes allowing for early notification of mergers and imposing strict time limits within which agencies must complete their reviews. ICN Report, *supra* note 82, at 18–22; ICPAC Report, *supra* note 5, ch. III; see generally MSG Report, *supra* note 99. See generally International Competition Network, Recommended Practices for Merger Notification Procedures (2002), available at www.internationalcompetition network.org/media/archive0611/mnprecpractices.pdf.

[101]   *GE/Honeywell* Commission Decision, *supra* note 1.

[102]   See Press Release, US Dep't of Justice, *Justice Department Requires Divestitures in Merger Between General Electric and Honeywell*, 2 May 2001, available at www.usdoj.gov/atr/public/press_releases/2001/8140.htm. For the cases that followed in the European Union, see *GE/ Honeywell* Commission Decision, *supra* note 1; Case T-209/01, Honeywell Int'l Inc. v. Comm'n, Case T-210/01, Gen. Elec. v. Comm'n, [2006] O.J. C48/26.

[103]   Fox, *supra* note 60, at 331, 332, 337 (reporting that the merger deal involved exchange of GE stock worth just under US$45 billion, which would have made the merger the largest ever).

[104]   See *id.* at 352, 355 (suggesting that the EU had not been accustomed to employing economic analysis of consumer welfare benefits in their relatively new merger law); Bradford, *supra* note 47, at 397, 406–7 (arguing against the theory that the EU was simply being protectionist); William J. Kolasky, Deputy Assistant Attorney General, Antitrust Division, US Department of Justice, Address before the George Mason University Symposium, 9 November 2001, available at www.usdoj.gov/atr/public/speeches/9536.htm (suggesting that the reasons for the divergence in the *GE/Honeywell* case might come from the number of economists on staff at the US Department of Justice as opposed to the Commission staff, the greater availability of judicial review in the United States, and the possibility that the EU has a fundamentally different stance toward the reliability of government intervention); Donna Patterson and Carl Shapiro, *Transatlantic Divergence in GE/Honeywell: Causes and Lessons,* ANTITRUST 18, 25 (Fall 2001) (concluding that the *GE/Honeywell* disagreement occurred because there are fundamental differences between the United States and the EU on whether mergers that lead to lower prices are procompetitive or anticompetitive).

to offer complementary products (GE engines and Honeywell avionics) as a bundle. According to the Commission, the merged entity's extensive product range and unparalleled access to capital would enable it to lower the price of the bundle until all the competitors were forced to exit the market.[105] The US antitrust authorities criticized the mixed bundling theory, suggesting that it may penalize firms for efficient conduct that will result in lower prices. The other analytical difference – the EU's concern for vertical foreclosure – stemmed from the fact that Honeywell, as a leading supplier of engine starters, could disrupt the supply of these essential inputs to GE's rivals, reinforcing GE's dominance in the engine market.[106] Again, the US authorities disagreed, asserting that the EU had underestimated the adaptive responses of other market participants.[107]

The *GE/Honeywell* transaction was not the first conflict between antitrust enforcers. In 1991, the European Commission prohibited the European-owned ATR from acquiring the Canadian-based de Havilland, even though the Canadian antitrust authorities had already approved the same transaction.[108] The Commission held that the merger would have given the new entity excessive market power in Europe.[109] Canadian antitrust authorities, on the other hand, supported the transaction, arguing that de Havilland was a 'failing firm' that would have gone out of business unless saved by an acquisition.[110] An enforcement conflict nearly occurred in another aircraft-industry merger involving Boeing and McDonnell Douglas, which the Commission threatened to enjoin despite the clearance decision in the United States.[111] The two jurisdictions were able to avoid conflict eventually, but only after extensive political pressure from the United States; the Commission ultimately backed down and agreed to clear a merger, subject to significant commitments.

The conflicts associated with decentralized antitrust regimes are not limited to mergers. Inconsistent remedies may result each time that corporations are targets of antitrust investigation in several jurisdictions simultaneously. For example, American, European, and Korean authorities imposed different remedies in their investigation of Microsoft's alleged abusive practices. The European Commission, for instance, concluded that

---

[105] The Commission relied on the theory of 'portfolio effects', referring to the advantage the merged entity would have had because of its broad product portfolio and superior access to capital through GE's subsidiary GE capital.

[106] Fox, *supra* note 60, at 339–40.

[107] Timothy Muris, Chairman of Fed. Trade Comm'n, Merger Enforcement in a World of Multiple Arbiters, Remarks before the Brookings Institution Roundtable on Trade and Investment Policy, 21 December 2001, available at www.ftc.gov/speeches/muris/brookings.pdf.

[108] Commission Decision of 2 October 1991, Aerospatiale-Alenia/de Havilland, Case No. IV/M.053, [1991] O.J. L334/42 (12 May 1991).

[109] See *id.* paras 32–3, 36–42; ROBERT HOWSE AND M.J. TREBILCOCK, THE REGULATION OF INTERNATIONAL TRADE 604 (3d ed. 2005).

[110] Ioannis Kokkoris, *Failing Firm Defence in the European Union: A Panacea for Mergers?*, 2006 EUR. COMPET. L. REV. 494, 497–8 (2006).

[111] See Commission Decision of 30 July 1997, *Boeing/McDonnell-Douglas,* Case No. IV/M.877, [1997] O.J. L336/16 (8 December, 1997); see generally Thomas L. Boeder, *The Boeing-McDonnell Douglas Merger*, in ANTITRUST GOES GLOBAL: WHAT FUTURE FOR TRANSATLANTIC COOPERATION? 139 (Simon J. Evenett, Alexander Lehmann, and Benn Steil eds., 2000); William E. Kovacic, *Transatlantic Turbulence: The Boeing-McDonnell Douglas Merger and International Competition Policy*, 68 ANTITRUST L.J. 805, 817–63 (2000–2001).

Microsoft had anticompetitively tied its Windows operating system to the Windows Media Player, and required Microsoft to offer an unbundled version of its products for European customers.[112] The Korean authorities' approach was similar to the Europeans': they also required Microsoft to unbundle its products.[113] In contrast, the US authorities did not require a comparable remedy in their settlement decree.[114]

Conflicting enforcement decisions have several economic and political consequences. William Kolasky, the former Deputy Assistant Attorney General for Antitrust, identified three key implications from the enforcement conflict in the *GE/Honeywell* case. First, when one jurisdiction blocks a merger that other jurisdictions find procompetitive, the former jurisdiction denies consumers around the world the benefits the merger might have delivered. Second, inconsistent substantive standards applied by the United States and the EU increase transaction costs associated with the multijurisdictional merger review process, possibly deterring efficiency-enhancing mergers. Third, the divergence akin to the one witnessed in the *GE/Honeywell* case undermines the political consensus supporting strong antitrust enforcement.[115]

Enforcement conflicts also increase tensions among antitrust regulators. The McDonnell Douglas controversy escalated into a political battle where the US administration considered a range of actions against the Europeans in response to the European Commission's threat to enjoin the merger, including the possibility of limiting transatlantic flights, imposing retaliatory tariffs on European aircrafts, and challenging the Commission's decision before the WTO.[116] The criticism was no less muted after the negative *GE/Honeywell* decision. The US Secretary of the Treasury, Paul O'Neil, described the decision as being 'off the wall', adding that the Commission was 'the closest thing you can find to an autocratic organization that can successfully impose their will on things that one would think are outside their scope of attention'.[117] Similarly, when the European

---

[112]   See Christian Ahlborn and David Evans, *The Microsoft Judgment and its Implications Towards Dominant Firms in Europe*, 75 ANTITRUST L.J. 887, § II.A (2009); Harry First, *Strong Spine, Weak Underbelly: The CFI Microsoft Decision* (NYU Law and Economics Research Paper No. 08-17, 2008), available at http://ssrn.com/abstract=1020850.

[113]   Korea Fair Trade Commission, *The Findings of the Microsoft Case* (7 December 2005), at 1, available at http://ftc.go.kr/data/hwp/micorsoft_case.pdf [*sic*]; Youngjin Jung, *Abuse of Market Dominance in Korea: Some Reflections on the KFTC's Microsoft Decision*, 36 LEGAL ISSUES OF ECON. INTEGRATION 57, 59 (2009).

[114]   Damien Geradin, *The Perils of Antitrust Proliferation: The Globalization of Antitrust and the Risks of Overregulation of Competitive Behavior*, 10 CHI. J. INT'L L. 189, 190 n.8 (2009); Harry First, *Netscape is Dead: Remedy Lessons from the Microsoft Litigation*, at 9–12 (New York University Law and Economics Working Paper No. 166, 2008), available at http://lsr.nellco.org/nyu_lewp/166/. A similar conflict between regimes occurred when the the European Union and the United States reviewed British Airways' and Virgin Airlines' loyalty discounts. The United States concluded that the conduct was permissible under its law, but the EU condemned the conduct as contrary to its law. See Virgin Atl. Airways Ltd. v. British Airways PLC, 257 F.3d 256 (2d Cir. 2001); Case T-219/99, British Airways PLC v. Comm'n, [2003] E.C.R. II-5917.

[115]   Kolasky, *supra* note 104.

[116]   Steven Pearlstein and Anne Swardson, *U.S. Gets Tough to Ensure Boeing, McDonnell Douglas Merger; Retaliation Plan in Works as Europe Threatens*, WASHINGTON POST, 17 July 1997, at C01.

[117]   Tom Brown, *Update 2: U.S. Treasury Chief Slaps at Europe Over GE Deal*, REUTERS, 27 June 2001.

Court of First Instance handed down its judgment in the *Microsoft* case, Tom Barnett, the Assistant Attorney General for Antitrust at the time, criticized the judgment vocally, accusing the Europeans of 'chilling innovation and discouraging competition'.[118]

The furor surrounding these high-profile merger controversies shadows the fact that the instances of actual conflict are extremely rare. Despite the common fear of inconsistent merger decisions, the *GE/Honeywell* and the *De Havilland/ATR* cases remain rare examples of mergers which resulted in different antitrust jurisdictions adopting contradictory decisions. This is remarkable given how frequently mergers are reviewed by multiple antitrust agencies applying different substantive standards and relying on dissimilar analytical processes.[119] One might also argue that corporations can avoid jurisdictional conflicts by conforming their conduct to the most stringent jurisdiction.[120] This, however, leads to another problem, where the most stringent antitrust jurisdiction has the ability to set the standards of competitive conduct in global markets, as will be discussed in section IIC.[121]

B Emergence of Antitrust Protectionism

Some commentators believe that states employ antitrust laws to further protectionist goals.[122] As traditional trade barriers have fallen following multiple rounds of trade

---

[118] See Thomas O. Bartnett, Assistant Attorney General, Antitrust Division, US Dep't of Justice, Statement on European Microsoft Decision (17 September 2007), available at www.usdoj.gov/atr/public/press_releases/2007/226070.htm..

[119] However, it is conceivable that the mere *possibility* of a negative decision by a certain authority leads to costs in terms of inefficiencies embedded in structuring the merger. The merging parties might, for instance, carve out certain assets of a transaction in order to avoid filing in a certain jurisdiction. Similarly, they may do this to pre-empt an in-depth investigation (a 'second request' equivalent in another jurisdiction) or to avoid having to agree to extensive commitments as a condition for clearance. It is difficult, if at all possible, to evaluate the costs of inefficiencies embedded in this type of precautionary action. Also, the issue is not limited to mergers. See Dave Heiner, *Working to Fulfill Our Legal Obligations in Europe for Windows 7* (11 June 2009), available at http://microsoftonthe-issues.com/cs/blogs/mscorp/archive/2009/06/11/working-to-fulfill-our-legal-obligations-in-europe-for-windows-7.aspx (discussing Microsoft's proposal to offer Windows 7 without Internet Explorer in the European Union); Brad Smith, *Microsoft Proposal to European Commission* (24 July 2009), available at www.microsoft.com/presspass/press/2009/jul09/07-24statement.mspx (proposing that Microsoft could release a version of Windows 7 with full browser capability, but giving the user the option of selecting which browser to install). Microsoft had proposed this design for Windows 7 to preempt a regulatory setback, not to provide consumers the features they demand. Similarly, companies may refrain from offering their products at the lowest competitive price, fearing investigations by jurisdictions with low evidentiary standards for predation.

[120] ELHAUGE AND GERADIN, *supra* note 49, at 1100.

[121] *Id.* See discussion *infra*.

[122] See, e.g., Nuno Garoupa and Thomas S. Ulen, *The Market for Legal Innovation: Law and Economics in Europe and in the United States*, 59 ALA. L. REV. 1555, 1632 (2008) (surmising that protectionism is a problem both in the United States and in the European Union, but that the size of the market may exacerbate the problem in the European context); Fox, *supra* note 60, at 336 (raising the more moderate hypothesis that agencies do not follow an explicitly acknowledged policy of protectionism, but may still have professional inclinations to cooperate with politicians' nationalistic agendas); Guzman, *supra* note 7, at 100–101; Kerber, *supra* note 27, at 44; Paul B. Stephan, *Against International Cooperation*, in COMPETITION LAWS IN CONFLICT, *supra* note 7, at 75.

negotiations, states are expected to look for alternative ways to protect their domestic markets.[123] Domestic firms seeking protection may increasingly turn to antitrust authorities, urging them to block the entry of foreign rivals on antitrust grounds, or to tolerate domestic firms' monopolistic practices in an effort to bolster their international competitiveness.[124] If successful, these protectionist pressures can convert antitrust laws into instruments of industrial policy, severely undermining the gains of trade liberalization.

Antitrust protectionism can take several forms: states may engage in systematic under- or overenforcement of antitrust laws depending on their terms of trade ('trade-flow bias'). States may also exempt domestic firms from antitrust scrutiny altogether ('statutory bias'). Similarly, antitrust agencies may engage in selective enforcement practices, disproportionately targeting foreign firms at the expense of domestic firms in their investigations ('enforcement bias'). Yet the key assumption behind all forms of alleged antitrust protectionism is the same: each antitrust jurisdiction internalizes the costs and the benefits incurred by its domestic producers and consumers, while externalizing the costs and the benefits sustained by producers and consumers in another jurisdiction.

1   Trade-flow bias in antitrust laws

Andrew Guzman has developed a theory on how trade flows across countries can impact the type of antitrust laws a country adopts ('trade-flow bias').[125] Consistent with rational choice theory, Guzman assumes that states 'externalize the costs and internalize the benefits of the exercise of market power across borders' to maximize their national welfare.[126] This behavior, according to Guzman, leads states to choose the appropriate level of antitrust regulation based on their trading status as a net-importer or a net-exporter. A net-importer country employs stricter-than-optimal antitrust standards (overregulation), since it does not internalize costs of overenforcement, which are primarily borne by foreign producers.[127] Conversely, a net-exporter country enacts laxer-than-optimal antitrust laws (underregulation), since the costs of the lax enforcement fall on foreign consumers. Both over- and underregulation are instances of suboptimal antitrust enforcement that reduces welfare globally.

Guzman does not draw on game theoretic insights when developing his theory. Implicitly, however, he seems to assume that the strategic setting underlying international antitrust cooperation resembles a prisoner's dilemma (PD). Guzman argues that

---

[123]   See Edward D. Mansfield and Marc L. Busch, *The Political Economy of Nontariff Barriers: A Cross-National Analysis*, in INTERNATIONAL POLITICAL ECONOMY: PERSPECTIVES ON GLOBAL POWER AND WEALTH 353 (Jeffrey A. Frieden and David A. Lake eds, Routledge, 4th ed. 2000); Henrik Horn and James Levinsohn, *Merger Policies and Trade Liberalization* 1 (Nat'l Bureau of Econ. Research Working Paper No. 6077, 1997), available at http://papers.ssrn.com/sol3/papers. cfm?abstract_id=226484.

[124]   See Kerber, *supra* note 27, at 45–6.

[125]   Guzman, *supra* note 7, at 101; Andrew T. Guzman, *Antitrust and International Regulatory Federalism*, 76 N.Y.U. L. REV. 1142, 1154–5 (2001).

[126]   *Id.*

[127]   'Optimal' antitrust laws would be globally efficient, as no state would engage in over- or underenforcement, but would choose the same antitrust laws as they would have absent trade flows. *Id.* at 108–9.

individual antitrust enforcers' uncoordinated action leads to a Pareto-suboptimal solution as each state seeks to increase its national welfare at the expense of other states. Individual states always maximize their own welfare by choosing a noncooperative strategy (over- or underregulation), even though choosing to enforce optimal antitrust laws (i.e., refraining from over- or underregulation) would maximize states' collective welfare.[128] Guzman also assumes that any agreement to overcome these suboptimal incentives would be difficult to sustain as the states would have the incentive to defect from their commitments.[129] These assumptions are consistent with a PD-type game.[130] In a PD situation, each state has the incentive to defect from the agreement, as it can increase its payoff by taking advantage of the other party's cooperation while refusing to cooperate itself. Thus, the primary impediment for cooperation is the constant fear of the other player's defection from the agreement.[131]

In a PD situation, a net-exporter can maximize its welfare by underregulating whereas a net-importer can maximize its welfare by overregulating.[132] State A, for instance, could obtain the highest individual payoff by choosing to overregulate (if a net-importer) or underregulate (if a net-exporter), if state B chose optimal antitrust laws. State B, however, will not choose optimal antitrust laws. It knows that if it chooses optimal antitrust laws and state A fails to reciprocate with the same strategy, it receives the lowest possible payoff.[133] Seeking to maximize their individual payoffs and fearing each other's defection,

---

[128]　*Id.* at 101 ('each state pursues its own interests without regard for the interests of other states'); *id.* at 108–9 ('The resulting policies are domestically optimal but are suboptimal from a global perspective'); *id.* at 110 ('Because cooperative policy is globally optimal, it must be the case that there are sufficient gains for a Pareto improving agreement to be reached').

[129]　Guzman, *supra* note 125, at 1158 ('The WTO has additional advantages that make it a desirable forum for the negotiation of a competition policy agreement. Most obvious among these advantages is the presence of a dispute settlement system. Dispute resolution is of great importance because if a deal is reached, some of the parties to the agreement will have consented to the system of international antitrust only because they were offered other benefits. In the absence of procedures to compel such compliance, these countries have little incentive to honor their commitments').

[130]　Similar claims are made by Wolfgang Kerber and Oliver Budzinski, who have explicitly likened countries' processes for choosing discriminatory competition policy to a prisoner's dilemma situation. See Kerber and Budzinski, *supra* note 27, at 44–5. Unlike Guzman, who finds that 'optimal *strategic* antitrust policy' can be rigid or lenient depending on a country's terms-of-trade, Kerber and Budzinski only describe lenient forms of strategic behavior (i.e., the lax antitrust enforcement that comes from a 'deliberate toleration of market power'). Such a characterization of country strategy ignores the possibility that strategic antitrust policy can also lead to excessive antitrust enforcement vis-à-vis foreign competitors. See also Oliver Budzinski, *Toward an International Governance of Transborder Mergers? Competing Networks and Institutions Between Centralism and Decentralism*, 36 N.Y.U. J. INT'L L. AND POL. 1, 6–8 (2004) (explaining ways in which a noncoordinated merger control regime presents a prisoner's dilemma situation).

[131]　Many international trade issues, for instance, can best be modeled as a PD. See JAMES D. MORROW, GAME THEORY FOR POLITICAL SCIENTISTS 262–3 (Princeton, 1994) (applying the prisoner's dilemma analysis to explain why enforcement of long-term relations, generally, is difficult because of incentives to defect from the cooperative enterprise, then suggesting that '[t]he regulation of international trade is one such problem').

[132]　In comparison, according to Kerber and Budzinski, the dominant strategy for each state would be to lower their antitrust standards. See Kerber and Budzinsk; *supra* note 27, at 41–3.

[133]　See *id.* at 44–5.

both states adopt suboptimal antitrust laws.[134] Consequently, both states are worse off than they would have been if they both adopted optimal antitrust laws.

Other authors have questioned that trade flows could lead to biased antitrust enforcement. Einer Elhauge and Damien Gerardin note that the effects doctrine compromises states' ability to engage in systematic underenforcement or overenforcement.[135] If a net-exporting country were to enact overly lax antitrust laws, its producers would still be subject to the antitrust laws of the importing jurisdiction, assuming their activities have an effect on that market.[136] The prospect of a concurrent jurisdiction by importing jurisdictions renders net-exporting countries' underenforcement irrelevant, steering them towards optimal regulation.[137] Elhauge and Geradin point out that the importing jurisdiction also has optimal incentives to regulate as long as it embraces the consumer welfare standard.[138]

Michael Trebilcock and Edward Iacobucci question whether trade deficits or surpluses would ever determine countries' preferred level of antitrust regulation, given that trade imbalances usually constitute only a small percentage of any nation's GDP.[139] John McGinnis notes that trade flows have a tendency to fluctuate, and doubts that countries amend their antitrust laws in response to their changing trade balances.[140] McGinnis further argues that trade-flow bias would be infeasible to apply in practice, considering that it is often difficult to categorize a multinational corporation as 'domestic' or 'foreign'. Hence, exercising bias against a 'foreign' corporation may have the unintended effect of harming the corporation's many domestic shareholders and employees.[141] Anu Bradford points out that biased policies may have similar unintended consequences on domestic industries that rely on intermediate goods, since such goods comprise approximately 50% of the total imports in developed countries.[142] Thus, if a country is a net-importer, predisposed to adopt overly strict antitrust laws, those strict antitrust laws would not only target the foreign producers attempting to penetrate the market but also domestic firms that depend on imported goods as inputs or raw materials.[143] This

---

[134]   Kenneth W. Abbott, *Modern International Relations Theory: A Prospectus for International Lawyers*, 14 YALE J. INT'L. L. 335, 358–9 (1989).

[135]   See ELHAUGE AND GERADIN, *supra* note 49, at 1012–14.

[136]   This assumes that the foreign antitrust agencies have adequate enforcement capacity, including access to evidence, which is not always the case.

[137]   See ELHAUGE AND GERADIN, *supra* note 49, at 1012–14.

[138]   Elhauge and Geradin assume that consumer welfare is the optimal standard for antitrust enforcement rather than total welfare. The US and EU antitrust laws both embrace a consumer welfare standard. According to Elhauge and Geradin, the case for a consumer welfare standard is even stronger internationally than domestically, because in the international situation it is less likely that increases in producer welfare will benefit consumers as employees, shareholders, or taxpayers. ELHAUGE AND GERADIN, *supra* note 49, at 1103.

[139]   Trebilcock and Iacobucci, *supra* note 42, at 168–9.

[140]   John O. McGinnis, *The Political Economy of International Antitrust Harmonization*, in COMPETITION LAWS IN CONFLICT, *supra* note 7, at 136.

[141]   *Id.* at 134.

[142]   Bradford, *supra* note 47, at 390–91. On trade in intermediate goods, see Jörn Kleinert, *Growing Trade in Intermediate Goods: Outsourcing, Global Sourcing, or Increasing Importance of MNE Networks?*, 11 REV. INT'L ECON. 464 (2003).

[143]   See *id.* at 464–5.

criticism, if accepted, suggests that trade flows have, at best, only a marginal effect on countries' level of antitrust regulation.

2 Export cartels as examples of antitrust protectionism

Antitrust protectionism can also manifest itself in the types of exemptions given to domestic companies. For example, scholars have frequently cited exemptions for export cartels in domestic antitrust laws as an example of biased antitrust enforcement that favors domestic firms.[144] An export cartel refers to an agreement between two or more firms to charge a specified export price or to divide export markets among them.[145] The difference between an export cartel and a normal cartel is that an export cartel restricts its collusive behavior to goods or services that are exported to foreign markets. Export cartels enhance the welfare of domestic firms, which can extract supracompetitive profits at the expense of foreign consumers. The export cartel's home state does not have the incentive to pursue the cartel's anticompetitive activity given that the entire anticompetitive harm falls outside of its jurisdiction.[146]

To illustrate how export cartels can serve states' protectionist interests, assume that state A is the exporting jurisdiction, and state B is the importing jurisdiction. Critics of export cartel exemptions fear that state A exempts export cartels because it fails to consider the cartels' anticompetitive effects on state B's consumers. Knowing this, state B likewise chooses to exempt export cartels from its antitrust laws, given that the anti-competitive harm falls on state A's consumers. As a result, both state A and state B fail to pursue export cartels, causing harm to both state A and state B consumers. This yields a suboptimal payoff for both states.

It is, however, unclear that the above description of the strategic situation is accurate.

---

[144] See Trebilcock and Iacobucci, *supra* note 42, at 152. See also Guzman, *supra* note 7, at 100 (referring to export cartels as the 'most obvious example' of states' biased application of their antitrust laws); Florian Becker, *The Case of Export Cartel Exemptions: Between Competition and Protectionism*, 3 J. COMPET. L. AND ECON. 97, 101–8 (2007).

[145] See discussion on the prevalence of export cartels in Margaret C. Levenstein and Valerie Y. Suslow, *The Changing International Status of Export Cartel Exemptions*, 20 AM. U. INT'L L. REV. 785, 793, 796 (2005).

[146] In contrast, some have defended the practice of exempting export cartels. The proponents of export cartel exemptions argue that they are predominantly formed to create export opportunities for small- and medium-sized companies who would not have the resources to engage in export activity alone. Export cartels are hence argued to generate new trading opportunities and enhance (instead of diminish) competition on markets where exporters would otherwise not compete at all. The United States, for example, defended the WPA and ETCA in the WTO in 2003 by arguing that these exemptions 'were conceived as mechanisms for domestic entities that lacked the resources to engage in effective export activity acting individually'. See WTO Fed. Rep., WT/WGTCP/M/21, at 15 (26 May 2003). See also Spencer Weber Waller, *The Failure of the Export Trading Company Program*, 17 N.C. J. INT'L L. AND COM. REG. 239, 250 (1992) ('[today] the ETC program has been used almost exclusively by small export intermediaries and by trade associations focusing on a small group of products, industries and markets'); *id.* at 251 ('the history of Webb-Pomerene Act suggests that few export associations will have sufficient global market power to exploit foreign markets'). See also Aditya Bhattacharjea, *Export Cartels: A Developing Country Perspective* 32 (Centre for Dev. Econ. Working Paper No. 120, 2004) (arguing that neither a per se prohibition nor a presumption of efficiencies constitutes an optimal policy response to export cartels exporting to developing countries).

One may argue that export cartel exemptions do not pose a serious international enforcement problem. Even when state A exempts the export cartel from its antitrust laws, state B can pursue the export cartel under its domestic antitrust laws as long as the cartel adversely affects competition in state B's domestic market.[147] One can even argue that the decision by state A not to prosecute the cartel represents optimal allocation of jurisdiction: state B is in a better position to evaluate the effects of the cartel on its own market. Of course, this argument assumes that state B has the resources to impose effective remedies on the cartel. Effective prosecution by state B may therefore require assistance from state A, in particular if the evidence is located in the jurisdiction of the latter.[148]

3   Antitrust protectionism embedded in biased enforcement

Antitrust laws rarely plainly favor local firms at the expense of their foreign counterparts. But even facially neutral antitrust laws can lead to discrimination if those unbiased laws are enforced selectively. Antitrust agencies are often vested with substantial discretion. Organized domestic interest groups could exploit that discretion by seeking protection from antitrust enforcement or by urging the domestic authorities to take on cases against their foreign competitors. This could lead to deliberate underenforcement of the anticompetitive conduct of domestic corporations, or to deliberate overenforcement of the anticompetitive conduct of foreign corporations.[149]

Biased enforcement differs from the trade-flow bias discussed above in that state A and state B would not generally underenforce or overenforce based on their status as a net-exporter or net-importer. Instead, both states would have optimal antitrust laws but would engage in selective enforcement of those laws case-by-case, depending on the nationality of the corporation that they are investigating. For instance, state A might approve an anticompetitive merger between two state A firms to build a national champion that can better compete internationally, while prohibiting a merger between two state B companies in order to protect their rival in state A who opposes the merger.

It seems plausible that antitrust enforcers deliberately overlook the anticompetitive conduct of domestic corporations in individual instances while disproportionately

---

[147]   This argument, however, assumes that the importing country is vested with adequate enforcement capacity and can hence be problematic if the prosecution of the export cartel requires evidence that is located in the exporting jurisdiction or if the importing jurisdiction cannot impose effective remedies.

[148]   Cf. *Intel Corp. v. Advanced Micro Devices, Inc.*, 542 U.S. 241, 256–7, 266 (2004) (noting that US law will permit agencies to lend discovery assistance to 'any interested person', even if that person is involved in a foreign proceeding).

[149]   Guzman, *supra* note 7, at 100. Guzman expects this type of 'favoritism toward locals' to take place at the administrative level, 'either because the regulators themselves view local firms more favorably or because political leaders bring pressure to bear on regulators and encourage them to pursue foreign firms rather than national champions'. See also McGinnis, *supra* note 140, at 128–9, 134 (explaining that regulators have an interest in maintaining an interventionist policy because it enables them to extract greater rents and acknowledging that regulators could discriminate between local and foreign firms); Kerber, *supra* note 27, at 41–4. See also an analysis of how domestic antitrust enforcement can become susceptible to bias in Fred S. McChesney, *Debate: Public Choice: Do Politics Corrupt Antitrust Enforcement? Economics versus Politics in Antitrust*, 23 HARV. J.L. AND PUB. POL'Y 133 (1999).

targeting foreign corporations.[150] Suspicions were reinforced when the EC Commission threatened to block the merger between the two US-based companies, Boeing and McDonnell Douglas, after the merger had been cleared in the United States.[151] Both the United States and the EU accused one another of engaging in industrial policy: the Europeans perceived the US clearance of the merger as an effort to create a US-based global monopolist in the large civil jet aircraft market, whereas the Americans accused the EU of opposing the merger to protect Boeing's main European rival, Airbus, from competition.[152] Distrust over antitrust protectionism escalated further in 2001, when the EU moved on to prohibit the *GE/Honeywell* merger.[153]

Despite the perception of protectionism, a deeper inquiry into the EU antitrust authorities' merger decisions does not reveal any systematic bias against US corporations. In fact, while 25% of the merger notifications the EU Commission received in 1995–2005 involved at least one US-based company, only 12% of the prohibited mergers involved a US corporation.[154] Similarly, only 17% of the mergers withdrawn after the notification involved a US corporation, 26% of the Commission's initiated phase II investigations ('second request') involved a US corporation, and 27% of the conditional clearances were granted in cases that involved a US company. These numbers suggest that any enforcement bias would be limited to a small number of individual cases, or that enforcement bias may not even exist. There are several reasons for this. For instance, the threat of judicial review may sufficiently deter antitrust agencies from engaging in blatant

---

[150] The claim that antitrust agencies engage in selective enforcement is consistent with well-developed public choice theories of agency capture. These theories explain how government agencies respond to the demands of organized interest groups. Tanya Heikkila, *The Contribution of Public Choice Analysis to Decision Making Theories*, in HANDBOOK OF DECISION MAKING 23–4 (Göktuğ Morçöl ed., CRC 2007) (discussing 'bureaucratic pathologies' where interest groups spend resources on lobbying rather than productive activity and bureaucrats allocate resources to strengthen their political base rather than to best fulfill their mission); JAMES M. BUCHANAN AND GORDON TULLOCK, THE CALCULUS OF CONSENT: LOGICAL FOUNDATIONS OF CONSTITUTIONAL DEMOCRACY 287 (Michigan, 1962) (using economic analysis to explain that interest groups become entrenched because the political process can give unequal advantages, and these unequal advantages then further strengthen interest groups and incentivize them to pursue further preferential treatment).

[151] See Commission Decision of 30 July 1997, Boeing/McDonnell-Douglas, Case No. IV/M.877, [1997] O.J. L336/16 (8 December 1997); Boeing Co., et al., Joint Statement Closing Investigation of the Proposed Merger, FTC File No. 971-0051 (1 July 1997), reported in 5 Trade Reg. Rep. (CCH) para. 24, 295.

[152] Kerber, *supra* note 27, at 42.

[153] See Fox, *supra* note 60, at 332 (citing Matt Murray, Phillip Shishkin, Bob Davis, and Anita Raghavan, *Oceans Apart: As Honeywell Deal Goes Awry for GE, Fallout May be Global – The U.S. Giant's Troubles in Europe Could Chill Mergers of Multinationals – Raining on Welch's Parade*, WALL ST. J., 15 June 2001, at A1 (quoting Sen. Ernest Hollings of the Senate Commerce Committee) ('EU disapproval gives credence to those who suspect that the EU is using its merger review process as a tool to protect and promote European industry at the expense of its US competitors'). Senator Hollings further accused the EU of 'an apparent double standard by swiftly approving mergers involving European companies and holding up those of US groups'.

[154] Commission Decision of 28 June 2000, MCIWorldCom/Sprint, Case No. COMP/M.1741, [2000] O.J. L300/1; *GE/Honeywell* Commission Decision, *supra* note 1. Note that the *MCIWorldCom/Sprint* merger was also challenged in the United States. In contrast, the *General Electric/Honeywell* merger was approved subject to limited undertakings in the United States.

parochialism. Agencies must also give reasons for their decisions, and will therefore find it difficult to depart manifestly from an established legal framework.[155]

Another question is whether some less established antitrust regimes with fewer institutional safeguards are more susceptible to antitrust protectionism. China's first enforcement decisions under its newly adopted Antimonopoly Law[156] offer some indication that antitrust review could be used as a vehicle for protectionism.[157] China's decision to prohibit Coca-Cola's proposed acquisition of the Chinese juice company Huiyuan,[158] for instance, raised suspicions on the motivations behind China's antitrust policy. While it is too soon to draw drastic conclusions based on China's limited enforcement record, the possibility of China becoming a major antitrust force that repeatedly applies its antitrust laws strategically to block the market entry of foreign companies has reinforced concerns of antitrust protectionism.

C   Global Overregulation

The final problem relating to decentralized antitrust enforcement is that the strictest antitrust jurisdiction always prevails when a real jurisdictional conflict arises. This leads to global overregulation. To illustrate this, assume that both state A and state B choose suboptimal antitrust laws: state A underregulates and state B overregulates. State A

---

[155]   McGinnis, *supra* note 140, at 134–5 (noting that institutional checks and craft interests help deter overly discriminatory policies).

[156]   See Sundeep Tucker, *InBev Ruling Sparks Fears for M&A in China*, FINANCIAL TIMES, 30 November 2008 (noting that the *InBev/Anheuser-Busch* deal was approved, but with a number of unanticipated restrictions that will prevent InBev from acquiring further interests in certain companies in the Chinese beer market); Gordon Fairclough and Carlos Tejada, *China's Coke Decision Threatens to Chill Investment*, WALL ST. J. (Eastern), 19 March 2009, at B9 (describing China's decision to block of the proposed Coca-Cola/Huiyuan merger after widespread nationalistic resentment of foreign ownership); Aaron Back and J.R. Wu, *China Flexes Global Merger Clout, Imposes Conditions on Lucite Deal*, WALL ST. J., 28 April 2009, at B6 (conditioning approval of the *Mitsubishi Rayon/Lucite* merger on a five-year ban that prevents it from acquiring any Chinese producer of methylmethacrylate or building factories in China making such products). *Cf.* Anti-Monopoly Law of the People's Republic of China, Presidential Order No. 68 (National People's Congress, 2007, 2008), www.npc.gov.cn/englishnpc/Law/2009-02/20/content_1471587.htm (PRC).

[157]   See Bruce M. Owen, Su Sun, and Wentong Zheng, *China's Competition Policy Reforms: The Antimonopoly Law and Beyond* 28 (Stanford John M. Olin Program in Law and Economics Working Paper No. 339, 2007), available at http://papers.ssrn.com/sol3/papers.cfm?abstract_id=978810 (explaining that administrative monopolies could create regional blockage leading to protectionism); Salil K. Mehra and Meng Yanbei, *Against Antitrust Functionalism: Reconsidering China's Antimonopoly Law*, 49 VA. J. INT'L L. 380, 421–3 (2009) (noting that China still needs to clarify how the Antimonopoly Law will balance social welfare concerns while avoiding improper protectionism). *Cf.* Adrian Emch, *Abuse of Dominance in China: A Paradigmatic Shift?*, 29 EUR. COMPET. L. REV. 615, 622 (2008) (explaining that the current scope of the Antimonopoly Law is unclear and that art. 7 may exempt 'industries vital to the national economy and national security').

[158]   Andrew Batson, *China's Statement Blocking Coca-Cola Huiyuan Deal*, WALL ST. J. (China Journal Blog), 18 March 2009, http://blogs.wsj.com/chinajournal/2009/03/18/china%E2%80%99s-statement-blocking-coca-cola-huiyuan-deal/. For the original Chinese statement, see Ministry of Commerce of the People's Republic of China, 商务部就可口可乐公司收购中国汇源公司案反垄断审查做出裁决 (18 March 2009), available at www.mofcom.gov.cn/aarticle/ae/ai/200903/20090306108388.html.

may choose to underregulate for protectionist or nonprotectionist reasons. It may be a net-exporter wishing to extract welfare gains at the expense of the importing jurisdiction or it may simply not believe in the benefits of strong antitrust intervention. In contrast, state B may choose to overregulate, similarly for a variety of protectionist and legitimate reasons. Assuming that state A (underregulator) and state B (overregulator) investigate the same transaction, state B prevails. This example exposes the key international antitrust paradox: the strictest regime wins.

Imagine that state A is the United States examining the *GE/Honeywell* transaction and state B is the EU examining the same transaction. Suppose first that the transaction would have an identical effect in both markets but that the antitrust authorities in the United States and in the EU differ in their assessments on whether the merger should proceed. The United States favors a permissive antitrust policy and chooses to approve the transaction. The EU favors an interventionist policy and chooses to prohibit the transaction. The inevitable outcome is that the EU antitrust policy prevails: the *GE/Honeywell* transaction is banned, not just in the EU, but around the world.

Now suppose that the *GE/Honeywell* transaction would have different effects in the US and the EU markets: the merger would increase consumer welfare in the United States and reduce consumer welfare in the EU. Assume further that the expected efficiencies of the merger in the United States would offset its alleged competitive harm within the EU. When evaluating the merger, the EU antitrust authorities would ignore the merger's possible efficiencies in the United States, in the same way the US authorities would disregard any alleged anticompetitive harm in the EU. Advancing domestic consumer welfare rather than global welfare is consistent with both US and EU antitrust laws. However, assuming that the merger's expected aggregate global efficiencies outweighed its expected aggregate global anticompetitive harm, the EU's decision to ban the merger would be globally suboptimal.

The *GE/Honeywell* case illustrates the more general phenomenon that the decentralized antitrust enforcement consisting of both under- and overenforcement is likely to lead to overregulation globally. It is debatable whether the United States or the EU was pursuing optimal antitrust policy in the *GE/Honeywell* controversy. But assuming that both the United States and the EU are equally likely to err toward under- and overregulation across the range of antitrust cases, the net effect is global overregulation.[159] If the EU antitrust decisions overall are more stringent than those of the United States, the United States effectively relinquishes the antitrust regulation of international business activity to the EU. This way, the EU becomes the de facto global antitrust regulator, simply by choosing more stringent enforcement policies.[160]

Damien Geradin illustrates the same problem by offering a hypothetical example of a firm A's decision to integrate a piece of software into its hardware. Firm B, which offers only the software in question, launches a complaint before antitrust authorities in jurisdictions X, Y, and Z, after having lost sales to firm A. Assume that antitrust authorities of jurisdictions X and Y note that there is consumer demand for the integrated product, and reach a decision that firm A's conduct is procompetitive. Assume further that this

---

[159]   ELHAUGE AND GERADIN, *supra* note 49, at 1100–1101.
[160]   See *id.* at 1101.

decision follows a sound economic analysis. The jurisdiction Z, however, decides to forgo any effects-based analysis and declares that firm A's conduct constitutes anticompetitive tying. It orders firm A to disintegrate the product and imposes a substantial fine. In the worst-case scenario, firm A would be forced to abandon the sale of its integrated product altogether. This might be the case if it is too expensive to design different products for different markets (for instance, integrated products for markets X and Y and separate products for the market Z).[161]

The problem of global overregulation could be mitigated if corporations could easily escape from the antitrust review of an overly zealous antitrust jurisdiction. This could be done, for instance, by carving out assets located in a particular jurisdiction when structuring a merger to avoid notification in that particular jurisdiction. Similarly, a corporation might cease to supply customers in a particular jurisdiction or it may change its product design or distribution practices in a particular market. For instance, the easiest way out for firm A in the previous example would have been to abandon business in jurisdiction Z. But this is generally an option only when the jurisdiction Z is insignificant enough to make abandonment commercially viable.[162] The merging parties in the *GE/Honeywell* transaction, for instance, could have evaded EU antitrust review only by withdrawing from the EU market altogether. But abandoning the world's largest market was never, obviously, a realistic option. As the most aggressive antitrust enforcers are generally the jurisdictions with the largest consumer markets (including the EU, Brazil, Korea, and maybe increasingly China),[163] escaping their jurisdiction is rarely feasible. Accordingly, global overregulation remains a significant problem.[164]

Antitrust differs from many other areas of law subject to jurisdictional competition in that the strictest regime governs firms' conduct in global markets. This defies the prevailing theories of regulatory competition. Regulatory competition is often believed to lead to either welfare-increasing legal rules and regulations ('race to the top') or welfare-reducing legal rules and regulations ('race to the bottom'). The jurisdictional competition of corporate charters in the United States is an example of the latter: corporations have the choice of law to incorporate in any state. This gives all states an incentive to adopt

---

[161]   Geradin, *supra* note 114, at 203–4.
[162]   *Id.* at 204.
[163]   *Id.* at 206.
[164]   Corporations may exacerbate this problem by forum shopping. Though they cannot engage in forum shopping for their own merger approvals (since a lone jurisdiction that blocks the merger can block the merger from happening anywhere), they can still shop for forums that will be most receptive to their complaints against *competitors'* mergers. For example, the European Commission has garnered enough of a reputation for aggressive investigation of anticompetitive practices that US companies will lodge complaints before the Commission rather than before a domestic agency. See, e.g., Bobbie Johnson, *Google Pledges to Support EU's Microsoft Case*, GUARDIAN, 25 February 2009, www.guardian.co.uk/technology/2009/feb/25/microsoft-internet; Miguel Helft, *Google Joins Europe Case Against Microsoft*, N.Y. TIMES, 24 February 2009 (noting that Google had attempted to lodge a complaint with the US Department of Justice in the past, and finding it unsurprising that Google would join Opera's complaint against Microsoft in the EU). *Cf.* European Commission, *Antitrust: Commission Confirms Sending a Statement of Objections to Microsoft on the Tying of Internet Explorer to Windows* (17 January 2009), available at http://europa.eu/rapid/pressReleasesAction.do?reference=MEMO/09/15&format=HTML&aged=0&language=EN&guiLanguage=en.

business-friendly corporate laws in order to attract corporations and thereby increase their tax base. At best, this incentive leads to more efficient and innovative rules. At worst, however, regulatory competition leads to a detrimental race to the bottom whereby jurisdictions compete to lower their regulatory standards, including environmental or labor standards, in order to attract businesses that are seeking to reduce their production costs.[165]

For regulatory competition to occur, firms must either be able to choose the laws that apply to them or be able to relocate to their chosen jurisdictions. Neither of these preconditions are present in antitrust law. The effects doctrine prevents corporations from choosing an applicable antitrust law through choice of law or relocation. The only possible race in antitrust enforcement is therefore the race to be the strictest jurisdiction among the states seeking to assert their norms globally, given that all other jurisdictions yield to the most aggressive regulator in case of a conflict.

The 'strictest regime wins' phenomenon could have some positive effects, however. For example, it could correct distortions stemming from suboptimally lenient antitrust enforcement. Some jurisdictions do not have the capacity to prosecute multinational companies who extract supracompetitive profits within their borders. Such countries rely on other aggressive jurisdictions with the resources to pursue anticompetitive cross-border conduct of multinational enterprises, hoping to free-ride on their investigations. For instance, suppose that an international cartel has anticompetitive effects in the United States, the EU, and several developing countries. The developing countries will look to the United States and the EU to prosecute and sanction the cartel. But if none of the anticompetitive effects are felt in jurisdictions that have enforcement capacity, a serious risk of underenforcement remains. The United States and the EU will not expend resources in pursuing a cartel that has trivial or no effects in their domestic jurisdictions. Some may therefore argue that global overregulation is desirable in that it compensates for the underenforcement of antitrust laws by weaker antitrust jurisdictions. However, many others advocate for more direct ways to mitigate the problem of underenforcement, such as offering technical assistance to help weak antitrust jurisdictions pursue their investigations.

III   TOWARDS AN INTERNATIONAL ANTITRUST REGIME?

The above problems of decentralized antitrust enforcement have led many states and numerous scholars to advance proposals to enhance international antitrust convergence. These proposals range from complete substantive harmonization of antitrust laws to various decentralized forms of cooperation. Some envision the establishment of a stand-alone international antitrust organization[166] that will enforce the harmonized

---

[165]   See Fox, *supra* note 7, at 1790–91; Oliver Budzinski, The Governance of Global Competition: Competence Allocation in International Competition Policy 80 (Edward Elgar, 2008) (explaining how countries can attract foreign business by either improving domestic competition conditions or offering lax standards).

[166]   See, e.g., Eleanor M. Fox, *Competition Law and the Millennium Round*, 2 J. Int'l Econ. L. 665, 675 (1999) (arguing for the creation of a 'World Competition Forum' for competition-specific

antitrust law.[167] Others propose incorporating substantive antitrust norms within the existing institutional framework, via organizations such as the WTO,[168] the Organisation for Economic Co-operation and Development (OECD)[169] and the United Nations Conference on Trade and Development (UNCTAD).[170] Some scholars remain skeptical of substantive harmonization but advocate limited WTO negotiations to prevent anticompetitive private practices from becoming trade barriers,[171] or propose rules allocating jurisdictional competence among states.[172] Still others remain skeptical of any

---

issues). But *cf.* Eleanor M. Fox, *Antitrust and Intellectual Property in a Global Context*, 13 Sw. J.L. AND TRADE AM. 211, 233 (2007) (suggesting, more flexibly, that the European Union's proposal for a worldwide competition policy could be implemented in the WTO *or* as a stand-alone project); Eleanor M. Fox, *International Antitrust, A Multi-Tiered Challenge: The Doha Dome*, 43 VA. J. INT'L L. 911, 925–6 (2003) (hereinafter '*Doha Dome*') (arguing that a stand-alone world antitrust institution would be theoretically preferable, but conceding that it would be very difficult to establish).

[167]   See Trebilcock and Iacobucci, *supra* note 42, at 169 (describing the International Antitrust Working Group's Draft International Antitrust Code and proposal for a mandatory World Antitrust Authority, but dismissing it as largely irrelevant to modern preoccupations regarding antitrust); Fox, *Doha Dome*, *supra* note 166, at n.36 (explaining that neither the EU nor the United States has the legitimate authority to enforce competition law on behalf of the world).

[168]   Fox, *Doha Dome*, *supra* note 166, at 929–30; Guzman, *supra* note 125, at 1158; Robert D. Anderson and Peter Holmes, *Competition Policy and the Future of the Multilateral Trading System*, 5 J. INT'L ECON. L. 531, 557–60 (2002) (explaining various proposals regarding implementing competition law under the WTO); Frédéric Jenny, *Globalization, Competition and Trade Policy: Convergence, Divergence and Cooperation*, in COMPETITION POLICY IN THE GLOBAL TRADING SYSTEM: PERSPECTIVES FROM THE EU, JAPAN AND THE USA 295 (Clifford A. Jones and Mitsuo Matsushita eds., Kluwer, 2002). See generally MARTYN TAYLOR, INTERNATIONAL COMPETITION LAW: A NEW DIMENSION FOR THE WTO? (Cambridge, 2006); MARSDEN, *supra* note 7.

[169]   See Tarullo, *supra* note 80, at 501 (proposing that the OECD be given substantial autonomy to evolve antitrust arrangements into more ambitious agreements).

[170]   Ioannis Lianos, *The Contribution of the United Nations to the Emergence of Global Antitrust Law*, 15 TUL. J. INT'L AND COMP. L. 415, 455–61 (2006–2007) (explaining that UNCTAD may play a role in garnering international support by facilitating antitrust negotiations with developing countries).

[171]   See, e.g., MARSDEN, *supra* note 7, at 284 (proposing the development of a 'trade and competition "guideline"' by which WTO Members would undertake to prohibit those arrangements that substantially impede access to their market and which are thereby likely to lessen competition substantially in the relevant market for the products at issue'); Trebilcock and Iacoburri, *supra* note 42, at 154–7 (proposing a 'national treatment principle' which would prohibit countries from enforcing domestic competition laws in a way that favors domestic producers over foreign producers); Fox, *supra* note 7, at 1806 (proposing a modest extension of WTO obligations for member states to prevent market closure, but not demanding a comprehensive antitrust agreement); Fox, *Doha Dome*, *supra* note 166, at 928–31 (suggesting two possible models for global antitrust governance, one based on agreeing on certain basic principles and establishing a protocol for dealing with clashes, and another that focuses more on technical assistance); Fox, *Competition Law and the Millennium Round*, *supra* note 166, at 670–72 (proposing that countries could begin by negotiating an agreement ensuring market access with any noncompetition considerations transparently disclosed). McGinnis is skeptical of negotiating substantive rules in the WTO but proposes including an 'antidiscrimination antitrust code' within its institutional framework. Such a code would ensure that the WTO's Dispute Settlement Mechanism has jurisdiction to condemn discriminatory antitrust laws that impede trading partners' market access. McGinnis, *supra* note 140, at 126–7, 136–7.

[172]   See BUDZINSKI, *supra* note 165, at 203–6 (describing a system of 'mandatory lead jurisdiction' where a supranational authority decides which market has suffered the most anticompetitive

binding international antitrust rules, preferring bilateral cooperation between antitrust agencies and endorsing voluntary multilateral convergence through the International Competition Network (ICN).[173]

The history of international antitrust cooperation reveals that none of the more ambitious proposals for an international antitrust regime have been realized in practice; despite the well-known inefficiencies of decentralized antitrust enforcement, no overarching international antitrust regime has been established. Instead, international cooperation today consists of bilateral cooperation agreements among key jurisdictions and pursuits of voluntary multilateral convergence. This section reviews the current stage of antitrust cooperation and discusses why efforts to write binding international antitrust rules have failed.

A   Current Status of International Antitrust Cooperation

States have attempted to launch international antitrust negotiations on several occasions.[174] In 1948, states negotiated international rules against anticompetitive business practices. These rules were incorporated into the Havana Charter, which contemplated establishment of an International Trade Organization (ITO).[175] The Charter failed to gain Congress' approval, and the world abandoned the ITO.[176] However, the need for multilateral coordination still remained, and the international community has periodically tried to revive antitrust negotiations in some other form.

In more recent history, the EU in particular has advocated including antitrust in

---

impact in order to assign which country gets exclusive jurisdiction over the case); Wood, *supra* note 43, at 186–7 (advocating an international clearinghouse for mergers, where companies could submit the filing form of their home jurisdiction to the international clearinghouse, which would then submit it forward to other jurisdictions for review and optional follow-up).

[173]   The United States, for example, has continued to stress that any antitrust cooperation should be voluntary, through mechanisms such as the ICN. See Antitrust Division, US Dep't of Justice, *Final Report of the Int'l Competition Advisory Comm. to the Att'y Gen. and Assistant Att'y Gen. for Antitrust* ch. 4 (2000), available at www.usdoj.gov/atr/icpac/finalreport.htm; Kolasky, *supra* note 52. See also Wood, *supra* note 43, at 185 (taking the stance that any attempt at harmonization would be premature); Anu Bradford, *International Antitrust Cooperation and the Preference for Non-Binding Regimes*, in COOPERATION, COMITY AND COMPETITION POLICY (Andrew Guzman ed., Oxford University Press, 2011) at 331, 333 (arguing that a binding agreement would only yield limited gains and that a nonbinding agreement would be able to capture much of the same gains with lower transaction cost); Paul B. Stephan, *Global Governance, Antitrust, and the Limits of International Cooperation*, 38 CORNELL INT'L L.J. 173, 215–17 (2005) (endorsing a system of regulatory competition for innovation and investment, suggesting that countries will have an incentive to adopt the best laws once they feel the pressure of a neighbor's technological progress).

[174]   See, e.g., MARSDEN, *supra* note 7, ch. 1; see also Nataliya Yacheistova, *The International Competition Regulation A Short Review of a Long Evolution*, 18 WORLD COMPET. LAW AND ECON. 99, 99–110 (1994).

[175]   See SUSAN A. AARONSON, TRADE AND THE AMERICAN DREAM: A SOCIAL HISTORY OF POSTWAR TRADE POLICY 43 (Kentucky, 1996); Final Act and Related Documents of the United Nations Conference on Trade and Employment ('Havana Charter'), April 1948, U.N. Doc. E/807, available at www.wto.org/english/docs_e/legal_e/havana_e.pdf.

[176]   See AARONSON, *supra* note 175, at 127–31. See also *id.* at 4–5, 50–8, 61 (discussing the various factors and competing priorities that led to the waning of support for the ITO in the United States).

the WTO's negotiation agenda. Following the EU's request, the WTO established a Working Group on the Interaction of Trade and Competition in 1996 to study the interface between trade and antitrust policy.[177] In the 2001 Doha Ministerial meeting, the WTO Member States agreed to launch WTO antitrust negotiations in the near future.[178] However, prospective antitrust negotiations came to halt in the 2003 Cancun Ministerial meeting, largely as a result of opposition from developing countries.[179] The efforts to revive antitrust negotiations by the WTO General Council in 2004 also failed, and antitrust was officially removed from the Doha agenda at that time.[180] With that decision, any further efforts to adopt antitrust rules within the WTO were abandoned, at least for the time being.

The failure to negotiate a binding international antitrust agreement has prompted states to pursue voluntary cooperation, both bilaterally and multilaterally.[181] Several states have negotiated bilateral agreements, which allow their antitrust authorities to cooperate, for instance, by exchanging market information, assisting each other in evidence gathering, coordinating investigations, and negotiating joint remedies.[182] The primary challenge for the case-by-case cooperation, however, is the agencies' inability to exchange confidential business information absent a waiver from the relevant corporations. For this reason, enforcement cooperation tends to be more successful in merger control investigations (where agencies can incentivize corporations to cooperate with the prospect of accelerated merger approval) than in cartel investigations (where cooperation could expose corporations to additional sanctions in another jurisdiction).[183]

Bilateral cooperation has been particularly successful between the United States and

---

[177]   BUDZINSKI, *supra* note 165, at 137. See World Trade Organization, Ministerial Declaration of 18 December 1996 ('Singapore Ministerial Declaration'), WT/MIN(96)/DEC.

[178]   See World Trade Organization, Ministerial Declaration of 20 November 2001 ('Doha Ministerial Declaration'), WT/MIN(01)/DEC/1.

[179]   See, e.g., *Day 5: Conference Ends Without Consensus*, available at www.wto.org/english/thewto_e/minist_e/min03_e/min03_14sept_e.htm. On 1 August 2004, the WTO General Council decided to officially drop antitrust policy from the Doha Round agenda of negotiations. See World Trade Organization, Decision Adopted by the General Council on 1 August 2004, WT/L/579, para. 1(g).

[180]   See *id.*

[181]   See generally Oliver Budzinski, *The International Competition Network: Prospects and Limits on the Road Towards International Competition Governance,* 8 COMP. AND CHANGE 223 (2004); Frederic Jenny, *International Cooperation on Competition: Myth, Reality and Perspective,* 48 ANTITRUST BULL. 973 (2003); Anu Piilola, *Assessing Theories of Global Governance: A Case Study of International Antitrust Regulation,* 39 STAN. J. INT'L L. 207 (2003). These cooperation arrangements have been extensively described elsewhere in the literature. See generally BRUNO ZANETTI, COOPERATION BETWEEN ANTITRUST AGENCIES AT THE INTERNATIONAL LEVEL (2002); BUDZINSKI, *supra* note 165.

[182]   Some states have concluded formal bilateral agreements, but these are more nonbinding than binding in character, since the decision to cooperate remains entirely at the discretion of domestic antitrust authorities.

[183]   Jenny, *supra* note 181, at 995. See also International Chamber of Commerce and Business and Industry Advisory Committee to the OECD, ICC/BIAC Comments on Report of the US International Competition Policy Advisory Committee (ICPAC) 8 (5 June 2000), available at www.biac.org/statements/comp/00-06-ICC-BIAC_comments_on_ICPAC_report.pdf.

the EU,[184] leading to significant convergence of their enforcement practices.[185] And while frequent cooperation does not eliminate the risk of conflicting decisions, as the controversial GE/Honeywell merger demonstrated,[186] enforcement conflicts between the United States and the EU are rare in practice.[187] Indeed, the *GE/Honeywell* decision remains the only merger case in which the US and EU authorities have reached a conflicting decision. In contrast, developed countries have rarely sought cooperation agreements with developing countries.[188] This might be because developed countries do not expect to gain much from such cooperation. Corporations based in developing countries are predominantly small and thus rarely able to acquire significant market power in developed country markets. Developed countries' domestic laws and superior enforcement resources also give them adequate power to regulate extra-territorially the conduct of developing country corporations, if necessary. Developed countries may also fear that they would be subject to frequent requests for enforcement assistance from developing countries, which do not have the resources to prosecute large corporations from developed countries.

Multilateral institutions have complemented bilateral efforts to foster nonbinding international antitrust cooperation. Both UNCTAD and the OECD have included antitrust matters on their agendas. UNCTAD has not played a major role in enhancing international antitrust convergence beyond its educational and capacity-building efforts, and its role in international antitrust governance today is marginal.[189] The OECD has

---

[184] See Agreement between the Government of the United States and the Commission of the European Communities regarding the Application of the Competition Law, US–EC, 23 September 1991, US State Dep't No. 91-216, 30 I.L.M. 1487, 1991 WL 495155; Agreement between the Government of the United States and the European Communities on the Application of Positive Comity Principles in the Enforcement of Their Competition Laws, art. III, US–EC, 4 June 1998, US State Dept. No. 98-106, 1998 WL 428268. See also Press Release, US–EU Merger Working Group, *Best Practices on Cooperation in Merger Investigations*, 30 October 2002, available at www. usdoj.gov/atr/public/international/docs/200405.pdf.

[185] The effectiveness of transatlantic antitrust cooperation was also recognized by Robert Pitofsky, the former Chairman of the Federal Trade Commission, who noted in 2000 that '[t]here has been a remarkable convergence in substance between the EC and the U.S. in merger review in the last ten years . . . In my view, it is hard to imagine how day-to-day cooperation and coordination between enforcement officials in Europe and the United States could be much improved'. See Robert Pitofsky, Chairman, Federal Trade Commission, EU and US Approaches to International Mergers: Views from the US Federal Trade Commission, Address at the EC Merger Control 10th Anniversary Conference, 14–15 September 2000, available at www.ftc.gov/speeches/pitofsky/pitintermergers.shtm.

[186] See *supra* note 60.

[187] For example, the EU prohibited a proposed merger between de Havilland and ATR, which was approved by the Canadian authorities. See Commission Decision of 2 October 1991, Aerospatiale-Alenia/de Havilland, Case No. Case No IV/M.053, [1991] O.J. L334/42 (12 May 1991).

[188] See Jenny, *supra* note 181, at 979, 993.

[189] See A. Douglas Melamed, Promoting Sound Antitrust Enforcement in the Global Economy, Address before the Fordham Corporate Law Institute, 19 October 2000, at § II–III, available at www.usdoj.gov/atr/public/speeches/6785.htm (noting that UNCTAD has given technical assistance, but noting that its mandate is not conducive to negotiating international convergence). In 1980, the United Nation's General Assembly adopted a nonbinding set of rules for the control of restrictive business practices ('RBP Code'). See UNCTAD, A Set of Mutually Agreed Equitable

been more influential. Its Governing Council and the Competition Committee have issued a series of nonbinding recommendations and best practice guidelines to facilitate cooperation and convergence among national antitrust regulators and their respective antitrust policies.[190] The OECD has not sought to harmonize national antitrust laws or create uniform enforcement institutions. Instead, it has emphasized the need to enhance voluntary convergence in principles underlying antitrust policy, domestic policy objectives, and enforcement practices.[191] The most active forum for nonbinding multilateral antitrust cooperation since 2001 has been the International Competition Network (ICN). As an informal network of antitrust agencies, the ICN seeks to enhance policy convergence, reduce transaction costs, and catalyse domestic reforms on a voluntary basis.[192]

Principles and Rules for the Control of Restrictive Business Practices, TD/RBP/CONF/10/REV.1 (1980). The RBP Code recommends member states to eliminate restrictive business practices by encouraging them to establish domestic antitrust regimes. In addition, the RBP Code urges businesses to refrain from engaging in anticompetitive practices. The RBP Code also established an Intergovernmental Group of Experts. The Group of Experts and the UNCTAD Secretariat have provided education and technical assistance to facilitate the adoption of antitrust laws in developing countries. See Lianos, *supra* note 170, at 427.

[190]   While the OECD also has the capacity to issue binding international norms, see, e.g., 1997 International Convention on Combating Bribery of Foreign Public Officials in International Business Transactions ('Anti-Bribery Convention'), 8 April 1998, OECD Doc. Daffe/IME/BR (97)20, 37 I.L.M. 1, cooperation within the antitrust domain has thus far been voluntary. Earlier OECD recommendations on antitrust cooperation focused on international consultation, notification, investigative assistance, and information exchange among agencies. The Recommendation Concerning Cooperation Between Member Countries on Anti-Competitive Practices Affecting International Trade was adopted in 1967 and amended in 1973, 1979, 1986, and 1995 ('OECD Recommendation'). See Revised Recommendation of the Council concerning Co-operation Between Member Countries on Anticompetitive Practices Affecting International Trade, 28 July 1995, OECD Doc. C(95)130/Final; OECD Revised Recommendation of the Council concerning Cooperation between Member Countries on Restrictive Business Practices Affecting International Trade, 21 May 1986, OECD Doc. C(86)44/Final; Recommendations of the Council of the Organisation for Economic Co-operation and Development concerning Co-operation between Member Countries on Restrictive Business Practices Affecting International Trade, 25 September 1979, OECD Doc. C(79)154/Final; Recommendation concerning a Consultation and Conciliation Procedure on Restrictive Business Practices Affecting International Trade, OECD Doc. C(73)99/Final (3 July 1973); Recommendation of the Council concerning Co-operation between Member Countries on Restrictive Business Practices Affecting International Trade, OECD Doc. C(67)54/Final (5 October 1967). More recent recommendations have dealt with, for instance, merger review and action against hard-core cartels. See 2005 Best Practices for the Formal Exchange of Information between Competition Authorities in Hard Core Cartel Investigations, available at www.oecd.org/dataoecd/1/33/35590548.pdf; 1998 Recommendation of the Council concerning Effective Action Against Hard Core Cartels, 25 March 1998, OECD Doc. C(98) 35/Final, available at www.oecd.org/dataoecd/39/4/2350130.pdf.

[191]   Jenny, *supra* note 181, at 987; Tarullo, *supra* note 80, at 494–6.

[192]   For example, the ICN identifies, develops, and publishes policy recommendations and best practices. ICN Report, *supra* note 82, at 18–23. See BUDZINSKI, *supra* note 165, at 228 (describing the ICN's functions and proposing to develop the ICN further to create an International Competition Panel that can exercise lead jurisdiction). The ICN, together with other international institutions, also offers technical assistance to developing countries with the view of strengthening antitrust advocacy, building institutional capacity, and supporting market reforms in those countries. For more information on the purpose and the functioning of the ICN, see www.internationalcompetitionnetwork.org. See also Jenny, *supra* note 181, at 976–7 (discussing in more

Following the collapse of the WTO antitrust negotiations in 2003, the ICN has become the most influential international regime facilitating multilateral antitrust cooperation today.

B Why Attempts to Negotiate International Antitrust Rules Have Failed

1 Disagreement on optimal rules

Section IIB explored the possibility that the risk of defection inherent in the prisoner's dilemma would impede states from pursuing international antitrust cooperation. However, some scholars have questioned this premise. They argue that the greatest impediment for international cooperation does not stem from the possibility of defection but from the difficulty of reaching the right set of rules in the first place. States prefer convergence to nonconvergence; they just cannot agree on optimal rules to converge on. Bradford, for instance, has argued against the widespread existence of PD-incentives,[193] asserting instead that the collective action problem underlying international antitrust cooperation resembles a 'coordination game' where the distributional consequences of various forms of coordination impede states' ability to settle on any given set of international rules.[194] This theory assumes that different antitrust rules are optimal for different states. The costs and the benefits of a harmonized antitrust regime would therefore be unevenly distributed among states, creating a distributional conflict. This distributional conflict impedes states' ability to agree on the focal point of coordination.[195]

The most prominent distributional conflict exists between the United States and the EU. Despite the increasing alignment of the US and EU antitrust laws over the last decade, some key differences persist, as discussed above in section IC.[196] These enduring differences explain why the United States and the EU have competed against each other to direct international convergence towards their respective antitrust laws.[197] Even if both entities recognize that increased international coordination would lead to greater

---

general terms the efforts between national competition authorities to enhance cooperation and advocate policy).

[193] Bradford, *supra* note 47, at 389–97.

[194] *Id.* at 397–400.

[195] See *id.* at 413–15; Wood, *supra* note 43, at 184 (concluding based on her government service that the differences between governments are too great at present to form a meaningful agreement); Guzman, *supra* note 125, at 1155 (noting that the interests of exporters in supporting weak antitrust laws would conflict directly with the interests of net-importers who would want strict antitrust laws); Stephan, *supra* note 122, at 74; Trebilcock and Iacobucci, *supra* note 42, at 169 (suggesting that, although countries may occasionally act opportunistically, most conflicts probably arise from good-faith differences of opinion). See also World Trade Organization, *Report of the Working Group on the Interaction Between Trade and Competition Policy to the General Council*, WT/WGTCP/6 (9 December 2002) (revealing a great diversity of viewpoints, even for smaller agenda items).

[196] See ELHAUGE AND GERADIN, *supra* note 49.

[197] See, e.g., Fox, *supra* note 7, at 1799 (explaining how the United States and the EU have actively exported their own antitrust laws to other countries in the recent decade in order to expand their regimes' influence).

efficiency, each would prefer to internationalize their respective domestic antitrust regimes.[198]

This type of strategic situation is known as a coordination game with distributional consequences (CGDC) or a 'battle of the sexes'.[199] In a CGDC, both states prefer a coordinated outcome to a noncoordinated outcome, even though both also favor coordinating at their respective preferred equilibrium. For instance, the United States and the EU might both prefer coordination to noncoordination given that their antitrust laws today are increasingly similar; neither the United States nor the EU would incur significant adjustment costs if they were to coordinate to each other's preferred equilibrium. Still, it is reasonable to assume that, given the choice, both players would favor their own respective regimes as the focal point of convergence. The challenge is to choose between the focal point the United States prefers (US antitrust law) and the focal point the EU prefers (EU antitrust law).

Similar distributional conflict exists between developed countries and developing countries.[200] Developed countries want any international antitrust regime to reduce multinational corporations' (MNCs') transaction costs of operating on global markets. They also seek to 'level the playing field' by enhancing MNCs' access to the developing-country markets.[201] In contrast, developing countries resist the idea of a level playing field, asserting that their small domestic corporations require protection to be able to compete against MNCs.[202] Developing countries struggling with capacity constraints also fear that an international antitrust agreement would impose unduly burdensome obligations on them. Both developed countries and developing countries would benefit from coordination, but they disagree on whether to coordinate around the focal point preferred by the former or the latter.

Even the proponents of an international antitrust agreement concede that the

---

[198]   This assumption rests on the presumption that the status quo of the domestic antitrust regime represents the domestic political equilibrium on this particular issue.

[199]   Simple coordination games that present no distributional consequences are relatively easy to solve as long as the parties can communicate. Neither player has a dominant strategy: there exist two Pareto-efficient outcomes that both players value equally and two Pareto-deficient outcomes that both players want to avoid. Since both parties are indifferent as to the choice between the two possible equilibria, the coordination is expected to be relatively smooth. In CGDC games, on the other hand, players hold different preferences as to the actual point of coordination. Players agree on mutually undesirable outcomes (noncoordination) but disagree as to which of the two Pareto-efficient equilibria to coordinate on (focal point of coordination). This makes coordination in a CGDC situation difficult.

[200]   Bradford, *supra* note 47, at 418–22.

[201]   *Cf.* Bernard M. Hoekman and Kamal Saggi, *International Cooperation on Domestic Policies: Lessons from the WTO Competition Policy Debate*, in ECONOMIC DEVELOPMENT AND MULTILATERAL TRADE COOPERATION 439, 446 (Simon J. Evenett and Bernard M. Hoekman eds., World Bank, 2006) (reporting that the European Union, the United States, and other OECD members wanted the WTO to address antitrust because they did not want national idiosyncrasies to impede market access).

[202]   Singh and Dhumale, *supra* note 69, at 127. Developing countries are also concerned with their inability to prosecute international cartels. See Margaret Levenstein and Valerie Y. Suslow, *Contemporary International Cartels and Developing Countries: Economic Effects and Implications for Competition Policy*, 71 ANTITRUST L.J. 801, 801–3 (2004).

unequal distributional consequences of any international agreement would present a challenge for cooperation.[203] This has led them to propose ways to overcome the distributional conflict. Eleanor Fox, for instance, invokes the spirit of cosmopolitanism as a solution to the existing disagreements among antitrust jurisdictions on optimal law and policy.[204] Fox calls on countries to bar government actions 'where the harm [the action] causes to world welfare perceptibly outweighs the benefit to the nation's citizens'.[205] However, critics have pointed out that this approach raises practical and moral concerns. On the practical level, data measuring 'world' and 'domestic' welfare would be hard to obtain and, once obtained, would remain controversial; it would also be difficult for countries in the WTO to agree when 'perceptible' net losses to world welfare have occurred. On an even more fundamental level, Fox's approach raises concern on whether 'world welfare' is the appropriate standard to use in the first place. As Marsden argues, the national government's obligations should lie with its national constituency.[206]

Andrew Guzman similarly recognizes that net-exporters and net-importers disagree on the optimal content of an international antitrust regime, the former seeking lax rules and the latter strict rules.[207] To overcome the distributional conflict between net-importers and net-exporters, Guzman proposes that states resort to transfer payments via the WTO.[208] This way, winners can compensate losers and thereby overcome their resistance to the agreement. Others have questioned the feasibility of transfer payments in the case of WTO antitrust negotiations. Bradford, for instance, argues that the costs and the benefits arising from an international antitrust agreement are likely to be diffuse, case-specific, and difficult to forecast. As long as states remain unable ex ante to identify the winners and losers under an agreement, they do not know who should compensate whom and by how much. As a result, transfer payments would be difficult to negotiate.[209] Moreover, Trebilcock and Iacobucci have noted that, even if such transfer payments were feasible, they might be normatively objectionable because some countries would have to adopt antitrust laws that would decrease their domestic welfare.[210]

Absent linkages, states are likely to be forced to negotiate compromises that lead to

---

[203]   See Guzman, *supra* note 125, at 1155–6 (noting that net-exporters and net-importers will have different objectives); Fox, *supra* note 42, at 12 (observing that many countries with more statist traditions may be concerned about different goals than the United States or the EU such as the distribution of wealth or tight control over the potential abuses of multinational corporations).

[204]   The cosmopolitan view, as Fox characterizes it, means taking 'concern for the interests of the entire community without regard to nationality, while recognizing the legitimate role for national and provincial governments to act in the interest of their citizens'. Fox, *supra* note 42, at 3 n.4.

[205]   *Id.* The WTO Secretariat has expressed similar sentiments, suggesting that 'the negative consequences for foreign interests must exceed the benefits to domestic agents' in order for the national competition policy to be deemed an inefficient allocation of resources from a global point of view. MARSDEN, *supra* note 7, at 197.

[206]   *Id.* at 251.

[207]   Guzman, *Antitrust and International Regulatory Federalism*, *supra* note 125, at 1155.

[208]   *Id.* at 1155–8.

[209]   Bradford, *supra* note 47, at 422–32.

[210]   Trebilcock and Iacobucci, *supra* note 42, at 171.

shallow international obligations.[211] The United States has resisted the WTO antitrust agreement precisely because of the fear that a binding international agreement would weaken antitrust laws throughout the world. Conflicting regulatory priorities would inevitably lead to a watered-down compromise, weakening antitrust laws worldwide.[212] At worst, the WTO antitrust agreement would merely codify the lowest common denominator among its broad and diverse membership.[213] Diane Wood similarly predicts that efforts to reach a compromise in the midst of vast disagreement would merely lead to international rules riddled with exceptions.[214] Proponents of the WTO antitrust agreement may respond that initially weak antitrust commitments could deepen with time as a result of voluntary convergence and gradual alignment of states' preferences.[215] However, the WTO does not generally lend itself well to the idea of 'gradualism'. Frequent revision of WTO obligations would call for new negotiations among over 150 states. These negotiations would inevitably be slow and costly, producing, at best, an uncertain outcome.[216]

2   Costs of international convergence

Limited net benefits stemming from the agreement   Another impediment for an international antitrust agreement is the perception that the net benefits of such an agreement would be limited. Several scholars have argued that the costs of a binding international

---

[211]   See, e.g., Bradford, *supra* note 173, at 7–9; Wood, *supra* note 43, at 186 (arguing that any consensus could only be achieved after diluting the law to the point that it lacks any real guiding content).

[212]   See Wood, *supra* note 43, at 186; Roscoe B. Starek, III, Commissioner, Federal Trade Commission, International Aspects of Antitrust Enforcement, Address at the Antitrust 1996 Conference, 29 September 1995, available at www.ftc.gov/speeches/starek/starekda.htm ('The sticking point is whether agreement can be reached on a sufficiently stringent set of antitrust policies. It is the fear of a "lowest-common-denominator" antitrust code that has made many American policymakers skeptical about pursuing a world code'); see also A. Douglas Melamed, Principal Deputy Assistant Att'y Gen., US Dep't of Justice, Antitrust Enforcement in the Global Economy, Address at the Fordham Corporate Law Institute, 25th Annual Conference on International Antitrust Law and Policy, 22 October 1998, available at www.usdoj.gov/atr/public/speeches/2043. htm ('any WTO rules would be lowest-common-denominator rules that would merely serve to justify weak national antitrust enforcement. Third, such lowest-common-denominator rules would serve little purpose'). Every new attempt to accommodate divergent preferences stripped the antitrust agreement of more meaningful content. The most recent proposal for a WTO antitrust agreement is the most unambitious yet: rather than proposing any substantive rules, it merely extends the fundamental yet vague WTO principles of 'transparency' or 'national treatment' to antitrust matters. See Bradford, *supra* note 173, at 8.

[213]   See Starek, *supra* note 212; Melamed, *supra* note 212.

[214]   Wood, *supra* note 43, at 185–6.

[215]   See, e.g., Fox, *Doha Dome*, *supra* note 166, at 926–32 (explaining that the world is not yet ready for a global consensus on principles and suggesting horizontal cooperation in the meantime); Guzman, *supra* note 30, at 437–40 (proposing several possibilities for small-scale cooperation). In general, this approach is advanced by the 'transformational approach'. Transformationalists endorse shallow framework agreements with broadest possible participation and claim that commitments that are initially shallow deepen with time. For a discussion and critique of transformationalism, see George W. Downs *et al.*, *The Transformational Model of International Regime Design: Triumph of Hope or Experience?*, 38 COLUM. J. TRANSNAT'L L. 465 (2000).

[216]   See Bradford, *supra* note 173, at 9; Stephan, *supra* note 122, at 80.

antitrust agreement may exceed its benefits.[217] There are three principal reasons for this. First, the benefits from such an agreement are hard to predict and possibly not as great as generally presumed. Second, the opportunity costs of forgoing the agreement are relatively low. Third, negotiating a binding international agreement would be costly, particularly when compared to the uncertain benefits stemming from coordination and the lack of high opportunity costs under the status quo.[218] These reasons are discussed below.

An international antitrust agreement may yield disappointing returns for several reasons. If the parties to the agreement dilute its substance to accommodate distributional tensions, the agreement will no longer generate any net benefits to offset the costs of negotiating the agreement.[219] Also, the externalities from multijurisdictional antitrust enforcement may not be as great as commonly presumed, making reform unnecessary. Scholars often point to multijurisdictional merger review as an example of an antitrust action that involves high transaction costs. However, as discussed above, these 'high' transaction costs seem relatively small when compared to the total costs of the deal.[220] Another example comes from a recent US International Trade Commission survey, which challenges the presumption that anticompetitive practices would constitute significant nontariff barriers that compromise the gains of trade liberalization.[221] Third, unlike in other areas involving regulatory competition, antitrust law does not carry the risk of a detrimental race to the bottom, as discussed above; this reduces the need to pursue international rules.[222]

Also the opportunity costs of forgoing global antitrust rules are relatively low.[223] Most states – the strong antitrust jurisdictions in particular – can apply their domestic antitrust laws extra-territorially as long as their respective domestic markets are affected by the alleged anticompetitive conduct. Extra-territorial enforcement by the importing jurisdiction limits externalities stemming from any underenforcement of antitrust laws by the exporting jurisdiction.[224] Further, the existing bilateral agreements and voluntary

---

[217]   Bradford, *supra* note 47, at 410–13.

[218]   McGinnis, *supra* note 140, at 126. McGinnis maintains that harmonization would be costly and likely to retard rather than advance the goals of antitrust enforcement. *Id.* at 129.

[219]   Bradford, *supra* note 173, at 9–11.

[220]   See discussion *supra*.

[221]   The USITC statistics analyse data collected by the USTR, the EU, and the WTO to evaluate the relative harmfulness of various nontariff barriers (NTBs) that may impede the free flow of goods and services. The study compiles data from 53 economies, dividing the information into 15 categories of NTBs, 'anticompetitive practices/competition policy' being one of them. As a category, 'anticompetitive practices/competition policy' was second to last in frequency among the NTBs. 'Anticompetitive practices/competition policy' was also second to last in terms of the number of economies in which the measure was reported. See Diane Manifold and William Donnelly, *A Compilation from Multiple Sources of Reported Measures which May Affect Trade*, in QUANTITATIVE METHODS FOR ASSESSING THE EFFECTS OF NON-TARIFF MEASURES AND TRADE FACILITATION 41–50 (Philippa Dee and Michael Ferrantino eds, World Scientific, 2005).

[222]   See discussion *supra* (discussing the 'strictest regime wins' problem, in which the law of the strictest jurisdiction has the power to set the de facto world standard).

[223]   Bradford, *supra* note 47, at 433–5 (comparing the relatively low opportunity costs to forgoing antitrust agreements to the relatively high opportunity costs of forgoing intellectual property agreements).

[224]   However, extra-territoriality does not solve the overenforcement problem raised by the 'strictest regime wins' phenomenon.

multilateral cooperation within the OECD and the ICN have enhanced convergence and reduced the frictions arising from decentralized enforcement. While voluntary guidelines and case-by-case cooperation may have their limits, they may lower the opportunity cost enough to make the expected benefits of a global antitrust regime no longer worthwhile.[225] Paul Stephan also argues that international rules are unnecessary because there are sufficient market incentives for states to refrain from over- and underenforcement of their antitrust rules. For instance, a state that chooses to protect domestic producers against welfare-enhancing competition does so at the expense of future investment and innovation, the welfare of its consumers, and the competitiveness of its industries.[226]

Finally, negotiating and implementing an international agreement would be costly. Contracting costs are particularly high in an institution like the WTO where numerous states with divergent preferences are seeking to agree on binding norms.[227] The need to secure domestic ratification of the agreement in (presumably) most WTO member states would add to the contracting costs. The negotiations would also be slow and cumbersome: the Uruguay Round of WTO negotiations required eight years to complete. The current Doha Round, launched in 2001, is still ongoing. Pursuing a WTO antitrust agreement would hence almost inevitably be a slow and costly process. Implementing and enforcing international rules would also be costly, in particular for developing countries with limited institutional capacity, technical expertise, and financial resources. The costs associated with international rules were a major reason why developing countries blocked the antitrust talks in the 2003 WTO ministerial meeting in Cancun.[228] Consequently, the prospect of international antitrust laws, while yielding certain undeniable efficiencies, may simply not have been a priority for states due to high costs, limited gains, and the absence of significant opportunity costs.

Agency costs and institutional limitations   The international antitrust regime could also entail higher agency costs, reducing the welfare effects of antitrust laws. Stephan has opposed delegating antitrust decision-making powers to the WTO precisely because of the prospect of higher agency costs.[229] All agencies vested with discretion have the capacity to act arbitrarily. Often, states can mitigate these agency problems by curtailing agencies' discretion ('bonding') ex ante and supervising their behavior ('monitoring') ex

---

[225]   Bradford, *supra* note 47, *Id.* at 439; Fox, *Doha Dome, supra* note 166, at 929–30.

[226]   Stephan, *supra* note 122, at 67.

[227]   States would negotiate each provision more cautiously when they know that they will be legally bound by the agreement.

[228]   See Editorial, *The Real Lesson of the Cancun Failure*, Financial Times (London), 23 September 2003, at 16 ('It is absurd to push, as the EU has done, to impose rules in complex areas such as competition and investment on countries so poor that some cannot even afford WTO diplomatic representation'). See also Taimoon Stewart, *The Fate of Competition Policy in Cancun: Politics or Substance?*, 31 Legal Issues of Econ. Integration 7 (2004). The developing countries would also have to sustain higher political costs because their import-competing industries and former state-owned enterprises would resist any reforms that would remove the government protection they enjoy. See William E. Kovacic, *Getting Started: Creating New Competition Policy Institutions in Transition Economies*, 23 Brook. J. Int'l L. 403, 404–5 (1997).

[229]   Stephan, *supra* note 173, at 198–201; Stephan, *supra* note 122, at 77–9.

post.[230] Bonding and monitoring an international agent that administers and enforces an agreement of substantive antitrust policy would, however, be particularly challenging, for two reasons. First, the principals (the WTO member states) do not share an understanding on optimal antitrust rules, making bonding difficult. This would leave an international agent with wide discretion. Second, monitoring the agent would be ineffective because of the difficulty of reforming international regimes even if states were dissatisfied with the agent.[231] Thus, according to Stephan, international antitrust agreement would entail a risk of replicating, if not magnifying, the government failures experienced at the domestic level.[232]

John McGinnis opposes international antitrust agreement on similar grounds. He argues that such an agreement would create higher agency costs, while depriving states of the distinct benefits that the decentralized enforcement regime provides.[233] For example, there are fewer ways of holding an international antitrust regime democratically accountable than there are for domestic agencies.[234] Being more opaque than domestic administrative processes, the monitoring costs of an international agent would be higher.[235] The dangers of agency capture would also be more severe: political rents available on a global scale are expected to be higher, inducing interest groups to expend more resources on costly lobbying.[236] Whereas interest groups have to capture numerous agencies under the decentralized antitrust regime, interest groups under the unified regime would only need to capture one agency to influence an outcome.[237]

Stephan also emphasizes the difficulties associated with creating institutions and reforming them. International institutions are inflexible in their decision-making and therefore often incapable of responding to changing circumstances. McGinnis agrees, emphasizing the high lock-in costs of international institutions in a rapidly changing world. These costs can deter beneficial change.[238] In contrast, decentralized antitrust enforcement creates opportunities for legal innovation, experiment, and mutual learning.[239] Wolfgang Kerber and Oliver Budzinski take this view. They argue that states can use each other's experiences to re-assess their own antitrust regimes, imitating successful regimes and correcting their own errors as necessary.[240] They maintain that no one country knows which rules are best ex ante, and see the freedom to experiment in multiple

---

[230]   See generally Michael C. Jensen and William H. Meckling, *Theory of the Firm: Managerial Behavior, Agency Costs, and Ownership Structure*, 3 J. FIN. ECON. 305 (1976) (proposing bonding and monitoring as an appropriate solution for agency problems).

[231]   See Stephan, *supra* note 122, at 66, 77–9.

[232]   See *id.*

[233]   McGinnis, *supra* note 140, at 129.

[234]   See *id.* at 126; Wood, *supra* note 43, at 185.

[235]   McGinnis, *supra* note 140, at 129.

[236]   *Id.*

[237]   But see Josef Drexl, *Comments on Harry First: Decentralized Antitrust Enforcement and the Evolution of an International Common Law of Antitrust*, in THE FUTURE OF TRANSNATIONAL ANTITRUST: FROM COMPARATIVE TO COMMON COMPETITION LAW 60 (Josef Drexl ed., Kluwer, 2003) (arguing that, in practice, the European Commission has been less subject to the political influence of private businesses than national governments).

[238]   McGinnis, *supra* note 140, at 126.

[239]   *Id.*

[240]   See Kerber and Budzinski, *supra* note 27, at 36–9 (describing the concept they call 'yardstick

jurisdictions as an opportunity to test competing theories. Indeed, several commentators have argued that the criticism directed at the EU in the aftermath of the *GE/Honeywell* decision prompted several changes in the European antitrust regime, shifting the EU's enforcement closer to that of the United States.[241]

The WTO also has serious institutional limitations that impede its ability to effectively embrace new areas of regulation, including antitrust.[242] Diane Wood, for instance, fears that incorporating antitrust within the WTO would lead to institutional and political overload of the organization.[243] At worst, this could weaken the WTO's ability to carry out its key mission: to liberalize world trade. Several commentators note that the WTO is predominantly a trade organization with limited expertise in antitrust.[244] They fear that the WTO could conflate antitrust issues with trade policy considerations in its decision-making.[245] The United States in particular has opposed a WTO antitrust agreement on these grounds.[246] It has repeatedly emphasized the need to avoid enmeshing antitrust with trade policy.[247] This stands in stark contrast to the EU, which is comfortable in entangling trade and antitrust policies. After all, the EU's antitrust laws were enacted predominantly to complement the goal of establishing a Common Market and ensuring that the efforts to remove trade barriers would not be frustrated by private barriers to trade.[248]

Consequently, opposition to a global antitrust regime revolves around several related

---

competition', in which countries mutually learn from one another by observing one another's successes and failures).

[241]   See, e.g., Mario Monti, Commissioner for Competition Policy, Feedback to the Green Paper: An Overview, Remarks Before the Conference on Reform of European Merger Control (4 June 2002), available at europa.eu/rapid/pressReleasesAction.do?reference=SPEECH/02/252&format=PDF&aged=1&language=EN&guiLanguage=en; McGinnis, *supra* note 140, at 131; Fox, *supra* note 60, at 353–4, 358–9.

[242]   See Stephan, *supra* note 122, at 80–81.

[243]   Wood, *supra* note 43, at 185. Stephan agrees, asserting that extending the scope of the WTO to new areas, including antitrust, would be precarious. At worst, it would reduce the WTO's capacity for effective intervention in traditional areas of trade liberalization. See Stephan, *supra* note 122, at 81.

[244]   See, e.g., D. Daniel Sokol, *Monopolists Without Borders: The Institutional Challenge of International Antitrust in a Global Gilded Age*, 4 BERKELEY BUS. L.J. 37, 91–2 (2007). In response to the criticism that the WTO does not have sufficient expertise in antitrust, Guzman proposes changes in the organizational structure of the institution: the WTO could be divided into specialized departments, each vested with the responsibility and corresponding expertise in a particular substantive area. See Andrew T. Guzman, *Global Governance and the WTO*, 45 HARV. INT'L L.J. 303, 306, 310 (2004). Under this proposal, a WTO department could develop specialized knowledge particular to the WTO, much as antitrust divisions in national jurisdictions do now.

[245]   See Tarullo, *supra* note 80, at 493–4 (predicting that broadening the WTO's agenda to include antitrust will strain its ability to address other trade-related parts of its mission). In contrast, scholars such as Fox are not worried about this potential conflation, and even welcome existing trade concepts as a potential platform on which to build basic consensus and protocol rules. See Fox, *Doha Dome*, *supra* note 166, at 926, 929–30.

[246]   See Melamed, *supra* note 189, at § II.

[247]   See, e.g., Melamed, *supra* note 212, at § III. See also Spencer Weber Waller, *The Decline of the Nation State and its Effect on Constitutional and International Economic Law: Contribution: National Laws and International Markets: Strategies of Cooperation and Enforcement of Competition Law*, 18 CARDOZO L. REV. 1111, 1123 (1996).

[248]   See Bradford, *supra* note 47, at 406–9; Bradford, *supra* note 173, at 6.

perceptions: that divergences across states loom too great, that such a regime would represent the lowest common denominator, that the global regime would not entail sufficient net benefits to make it a priority, or that it would magnify agency problems or even subject antitrust rules to trade policy. These reasons, taken together, help us understand why efforts to negotiate an international antitrust agreement have failed. Still, the idea of international antitrust governance continues to invite vibrant scholarly discussion. The last section of this chapter will sketch possible directions for that discussion going forward.

IV CONCLUSION

The above discussion has exposed the dual problem underlying international antitrust law. Section II discussed how decentralized antitrust enforcement can produce externalities and reduce global welfare. Section III discussed how seeking increased convergence across jurisdictions may not be optimal either. This has led international antitrust scholars to search for ways to reduce negative externalities embedded in the decentralized antitrust regime, while respecting each antitrust jurisdiction's freedom to design its own laws.

Debate on the optimal balance between convergence and divergence continues. Two trends have emerged to shape the direction of this debate. First, those engaged in the discussion are beginning to appreciate that the world of antitrust extends beyond the United States and the European Union. Second, scholars are beginning to realize the paucity of empirical scholarship on international antitrust law.

The United States and the European Union remain the two most significant antitrust jurisdictions in the world. Comparative inquiries into their antitrust laws and enforcement practices continue to be fruitful. However, the center of gravity for international business activity is increasingly shifting to emerging markets. Goldman Sachs has predicted that by 2035, the GDP of the 'BRIC' countries (referring to Brazil, Russia, India, and China) will exceed the GDP of the current G-7 countries.[249] The scholarship on international antitrust law should seek to anticipate the implications this development has for antitrust law. This also requires revisiting the distinction between developed countries and developing countries. Today, developing countries comprise a diverse group of states, with vastly different domestic markets, levels of openness, political economies, and institutional capacities. China and Kenya cannot be expected to balance similar concerns when designing their domestic antitrust regimes. The increasing heterogeneity among developing countries has given new impetus for the debate on how different market conditions and political economies shape antitrust laws, how universal the economic theories underlying antitrust enforcement are, and how adaptable these theories are for guiding countries that do not share the same economic or political history and that face different opportunities and challenges.

On the methodological side, while domestic antitrust law has for a long time benefited from sophisticated analytical tools, scholarship on international antitrust law has not

---

[249] Goldman Sachs, *BRICs and Beyond* 5 (November 2007), available at www2.goldmansachs.com/ideas/brics/BRICs-and-Beyond.html. The G-7 countries are Canada, France, Germany, Italy, Japan, the United Kingdom, and the United States.

taken full advantage of insights from economics or other disciplines. More recently, scholars have employed new tools, including game theory and empirical methods, to bring more analytical coherence into the field.[250] The ICN study measuring the costs of multijurisdictional merger enforcement was a welcome early step in the right direction.[251] Some areas of international antitrust law have already received more attention by empiricists. Margaret Levenstein and Valerie Suslow have studied the effect of international cartels on developing countries.[252] They have also made a significant contribution to our understanding of the prevalence and harmfulness of export cartels.[253] Building on work done by Nicholson,[254] Keith Hylton and Fei Deng have undertaken an ambitious project seeking to quantify antitrust laws around the world. Studying variations across antitrust jurisdictions, they developed a 'scope index' to measure the extent to which antitrust laws of a given country are likely to catch anticompetitive conduct.[255] Their findings are less credible because of their exclusive focus on antitrust laws in books – they do not incorporate actual enforcement realities when constructing the scope index. Still, they have contributed a founding work to empirical international antitrust law scholarship on which other scholars in the future are likely to build. Such future work will help us verify the importance of the problems underlying international antitrust law that are often assumed rather than empirically validated.

---

[250]   For a game theory-based analysis of antitrust cooperation strategies, see generally Bradford, *supra* note 47. In addition to empirical work mentioned in this section, see generally Daniel Sokol and Kyle Steigert, *An Empirical Evaluation of Long Term Advisors and Short Term Interventions in Technical Assistance and Capacity Building* (University of Missouri School of Law Legal Studies Research Paper No. 2008-03, 2008), available at http://papers.ssrn.com/sol3/papers.cfm?abstract_id=1095884; Çaglar Özden, *International Dimensions of Competition Policies: European Responses to American Mergers*, 56 REVENUE ECONOMIQUE 1413 (2005); Simon Evenett and Alexander Hijzen, *Conformity with International Recommendations on Merger Reviews: An Economic Perspective on 'Soft Law'* (University of Nottingham Research Paper No. 2006/04, 2006), available at http://papers.ssrn.com/sol3/papers.cfm?abstract_id=893034.

[251]   ICN Report, *supra* note 82.

[252]   Levenstein and Suslow, *supra* note 202, at 800–806.

[253]   Levenstein and Suslow, *supra* note 145, at 792–3.

[254]   See generally Michael W. Nicholson, *Quantifying Antitrust Regimes*, 3 ERASMUS L. AND ECON. REV. 41 (2007). For a more recent follow-up to the original study, see generally Nicholson, *supra* note 75.

[255]   See generally Hylton and Deng, *supra* note 9.

12 Antitrust and regulation
*Howard A. Shelanski**

INTRODUCTION

Antitrust enforcement has long helped to prevent anticompetitive conduct and protect consumer welfare in regulated industries. The federal courts were long reluctant to allow a firm's regulated status to immunize it from antitrust suits. Over the past decade, however, the Supreme Court has signaled a weakening of that reluctance. Notably, the Court's decisions in *Credit Suisse v. Billing*[1] and *Verizon v. Trinko*[2] have reduced the scope of antitrust enforcement against regulated firms in important circumstances. This chapter analyses the reasoning and potential consequences of the Court's recent decisions and discusses some possible future directions for antitrust policy in regulated markets.

Section I of this chapter describes the relationship between antitrust and regulation before 2004 and examines how the Supreme Court changed that relationship through its decisions in *Trinko* and *Credit Suisse*. Section II then offers a critique of the Court's rationale for limiting antitrust in regulated markets and discusses some important questions that the Court's decisions leave open. Section III discusses some suggestions for change that could improve on the current state of the law while still addressing the concerns that motivated the Supreme Court to adopt its restrictive stance toward antitrust enforcement in regulated industries. Section IV concludes.

I DOCTRINAL EVOLUTION OF REGULATORY IMMUNITY FROM ANTITRUST LAW

Before 2004, the federal courts did not view it as novel or surprising for antitrust agencies or private parties to intervene against conduct subject to regulation. In 1963, for example, the Supreme Court rejected the New York Stock Exchange's attempt to block a group of securities dealers from pursuing an antitrust suit against the exchange for having directed its members not to provide wire transfer services to the nonmember plaintiffs.[3] The Court ruled that the Securities Exchange Act of 1934 allowed some self-regulatory conduct by exchanges that might ordinarily run afoul of the antitrust laws, but held that the group boycott at issue was outside the permissible scope of such self-regulation and therefore

*   This chapter represents my personal views and not necessarily those of the FTC. I am grateful to Bobby Ahdieh, Bill Bratton, Julie Cohen, Kay Levine, Steve Salop, Catherine Sharkey, Phil Weiser, Kathy Zeiler, and workshop participants at Emory University, Georgetown University, and Northwestern University for helpful comments and suggestions.
1   127 S.Ct. 2383 (2007).
2   540 U.S. 398 (2004).
3   Silver v. New York Stock Exchange, 373 U.S. 341 (1963).

not exempt from antitrust suits.[4] The Court's decision narrowly construed exemptions from Sherman Act scrutiny in order to advance section 1's core objective of preventing anticompetitive collusion. Similarly, in 1973 the Court affirmed the government's application of section 2 of the Sherman Antitrust Act[5] ('section 2') to interconnection among rival electric utilities.[6] The Federal Power Commission had independent authority under the Federal Power Act to order and regulate such interconnection.[7] The Court nonetheless upheld the lower courts' decision to block a dominant utility from using its control over electrical generation to exclude a rival power distributor and monopolize the power market.[8] The Department of Justice (DOJ) had three times sued AT&T (in 1912, 1949, and 1974) for a variety of exclusionary practices against rivals in various telephone equipment and service markets.[9]

In several of the above cases the Supreme Court grappled expressly with whether the applicable regulation implied immunity from particular applications of antitrust law; in others the courts implicitly resolved the question of antitrust immunity by letting the antitrust case proceed without comment. The key point is that the federal courts generally presumed that the general antitrust statutes could operate in parallel with industry-specific regulatory statutes. This simultaneous operation was consistent with the respective statutory texts. Nothing in the Communications Act, the Securities Exchange Act, or the Federal Power Act expressly conferred immunity from antitrust law. Congress having been silent on the relationship between antitrust law and those statutes, the Supreme Court presumed against antitrust immunity. It established specific standards for the level of conflict – 'plain repugnancy' in the Court's words – between antitrust law and the regulatory statute that must be met before courts can imply immunity from antitrust.[10]

As will be discussed in detail below, *Credit Suisse* and *Trinko* weakened the presumption against implied immunity established by the earlier decisions and broadened the circumstances under which regulation could limit antitrust enforcement. *Credit Suisse* extended the idea of 'repugnancy' between regulation and antitrust law by finding antitrust claims 'repugnant' even if the only way they could conflict with regulation was through judicial error.[11] *Trinko* can be read to make it harder to bring antitrust claims that are not already established in precedent against firms whose competitive conduct is subject to regulatory oversight, even when Congress has included a savings clause that expressly preserves the simultaneous operation of antitrust and regulation.[12] The combined result is that through *Credit Suisse* and *Trinko* the Supreme Court has shifted the earlier cases' balance between antitrust and regulation in favor

---

[4]   *Id.* at 357.
[5]   15 U.S.C. § 2.
[6]   Otter Tail Power Co. v. United States, 410 U.S. 366 (1973).
[7]   *Id.* at 373.
[8]   *Id.*
[9]   See STUART BENJAMIN *et al.*, TELECOMMUNICATIONS LAW AND POLICY 713 (2d ed. 2006) (discussing the antitrust actions).
[10]   *Otter Tail*, 410 U.S. at 372.
[11]   551 U.S. at 284.
[12]   540 U.S. at 410–11.

of regulation. To understand the impact of the Supreme Court's recent decisions, this section begins with a discussion of the doctrinal relationship between antitrust and regulation before *Trinko* and then turns to a discussion of the *Credit Suisse* and *Trinko* decisions themselves.

A   Antitrust and Regulation Before 2004

1   Implied immunity without a savings clause

Regulatory statutes can do essentially three things with respect to the antitrust laws: expressly exempt conduct in a given industry from antitrust through a preemption or immunity clause;[13] expressly preserve antitrust enforcement through a savings clause;[14] or be silent on the question.[15] Most cases involving the limits of antitrust enforcement in regulated industries have arisen in contexts where the regulatory statute at issue said nothing about immunity. The rule that emerged from early cases, simple in its statement if not necessarily in application, was that the courts should disfavor implied immunity of the antitrust laws and require antitrust to cede to regulation only where, and to the minimum extent, necessary for the more specific regulatory statute to achieve its purpose.[16]

The Supreme Court characterized the standard for implied immunity as one of 'plain repugnancy' between antitrust enforcement and regulation.[17] In *Silver v. New York Stock Exchange*, for example, the Court held that courts should try to 'reconcile the operation of both' antitrust and regulation rather than precluding the effect of one or the other.[18] The Court then allowed the plaintiff's group-boycott claim under the Sherman Act because nothing in the Securities Act could be read to authorize such anticompetitive conduct.[19] In *Gordon v. New York Stock Exchange*, the Court took a broader view of what constitutes repugnancy in reviewing an antitrust claim against stockbrokers for conspiring to fix prices.[20] The securities laws authorized the Securities and Exchange Commission (SEC) to regulate brokers' rate-setting practices and to approve fixed rates.[21] The agency had in fact decided to prohibit the kind of rate fixing at issue.[22] The Court nonetheless found that despite the then-current compatibility between antitrust and regulation, the SEC's statutory authority to allow future rate setting would be nullified

---

[13]   See, e.g., 15 U.S.C. § 62 (the Webb-Pomerene Act, expressly exempting certain collective export associations from antitrust liability); 15 U.S.C. § 1011 (the McCarran-Ferguson Act, providing limited antitrust immunity to state-regulated insurance companies); 15 U.S.C. § 17 (exempting labor strikes).

[14]   See, e.g., 47 U.S.C. § 152 (express preservation of antitrust in the Telecommunications Act of 1996).

[15]   See, e.g., 15 U.S.C. §§ 77(b) *et seq.* (securities statute governing underwriters' behavior); 16 U.S.C. § 824 (Federal Power Act), 15 U.S.C. § 79 (Public Utility Holding Company Act).

[16]   See, e.g., Silver v. New York Stock Exchange, 373 U.S. 341, 357 (1963); Georgia v. Pennsylvania R. Co., 324 U.S. 439, 456–7 (1962); California v. Federal Power Comm'n, 369 U.S. 482, 485 (1945).

[17]   *Credit Suisse*, 551 U.S. at 267.

[18]   373 U.S. at 357.

[19]   *Id.* at 357–8.

[20]   422 U.S. 659 (1975).

[21]   *Id.* at 665–6.

[22]   *Id.* at 671–2.

by allowing the plaintiffs' antitrust suit to go forward.[23] The Court held antitrust law's potential interference with future exercise of regulatory powers under the securities laws sufficiently repugnant to warrant the implication of antitrust immunity.[24]

After *Silver* and *Gordon* the case law thus made clear that 'plain repugnancy' would be measured in terms of whether antitrust might disallow conduct that regulators could authorize under the regulatory statute. Actual conflict need not exist between antitrust and the actual implementation of the regulatory statute for courts to imply immunity; the potential for conflict would suffice. The Court clarified in *United States v. National Association of Securities Dealers* (*NASD*) that even absent active regulatory supervision of the specific conduct at issue in an antitrust claim a court could imply immunity if the challenged conduct could be allowed under the statute and if the agency generally exercised 'the kind of administrative oversight of private practices that Congress contemplated'.[25] Despite this broadened view of what could constitute repugnancy between antitrust and regulation, the Court's doctrine was grounded in the potential for antitrust actually to reduce or impede an agency's exercise of regulatory authority conferred by Congress.

The courts did not limit the repugnancy standard to securities regulation. In *United States v. Otter Tail Power,* the Supreme Court declined to find the Federal Power Act to provide immunity from the government's claim that the defendant had violated the antitrust laws by refusing to supply either interconnection to distribution facilities or power to competing municipal utilities.[26] The Supreme Court found that Otter Tail's conduct contradicted the objectives of the statute and that the Federal Power Commission (FPC) had authority to prevent the defendant's refusal to deal.[27] Because the FPC had no authority under the statute to authorize the refusals to deal at issue, however, the antitrust claims could only be duplicative of, but not repugnant to, any actual or potential exercise of the FPC's regulatory authority. The *Otter Tail* decision therefore shows that mere overlap between antitrust and regulation was not a valid basis for implied immunity.

In *Phonotele v. AT&T*, a case decided under the Communications Act of 1934 prior to the 1996 amendments that added an antitrust savings clause, the Ninth Circuit denied implied immunity from antitrust claims directly related to conduct the Federal Communications Commission (FCC) had regularly and actively overseen and regulated.[28] The plaintiff sued on grounds that AT&T had violated section 2 of the Sherman Act by denying customers the ability to connect a device that the plaintiff manufactured to the telephone network. AT&T claimed implied immunity on grounds that the Communications Act gave the FCC jurisdiction over such matters and that the FCC had in fact consistently held proceedings and issued orders on precisely the conduct of which the plaintiff complained. The Court of Appeals rejected a broad reading of *NASD* and *Gordon* and held that the antitrust suit reinforced, but was not repugnant to, the FCC's

---

[23]   *Id.* at 689.
[24]   *Id.*
[25]   425 U.S. 694, 728 (1975).
[26]   410 U.S. 366 (1973).
[27]   *Id.* at 373.
[28]   664 F.2d 716 (9th Cir. 1981).

regulation of the allegedly monopolistic conduct.[29] Key to the court's decision was the fact that from the FCC's perspective, the mere fact of overlap did not imply repugnancy because there was no conflict between the FCC's regulatory position against AT&T's conduct and the antitrust law's potential imposition of liability for those activities.[30] The Ninth Circuit thus distinguished overlap from repugnancy and dismissed the likelihood of potential conflict in the future. *Phonotele* shares essential features of the DOJ's 1974 antitrust suit that culminated in the break-up of AT&T in 1984.

2 Immunity and statutes with an antitrust savings clause

There is little case law prior to 2004 addressing the relationship between antitrust and regulatory statutes that contain an antitrust savings clause. The two notable cases are direct antecedents to *Trinko* and both arose under the Telecommunications Act of 1996, which expressly disclaims any modification, impairment, or supersession of antitrust law.[31] The first case is the Seventh Circuit's decision in *Goldwasser et al. v. Ameritech*.[32] Plaintiffs alleged that Ameritech had violated section 2 of the Sherman Act by refusing to comply with the local competition provisions of the Telecommunications Act of 1996. The court found that the plaintiffs had failed to support their antitrust claim with any allegation of conduct that was independent of the duties to deal with rivals specifically listed in the FCC's regulations implementing the 1996 Act.[33] Finding those regulations to go well beyond what antitrust alone would require in terms of a duty to deal and finding nothing at all in plaintiff's pleading to state that defendant's actions would violate section 2 in absence of the regulations, the Court of Appeals held that the plaintiffs failed to state a basis for antitrust liability and affirmed the trial court's dismissal of the claims.[34] The 1996 Act's antitrust savings clause did not come into play because the court found that the plaintiff had never stated an antitrust claim whose relationship to the regulatory scheme needed to be analysed.

Two years later the Second Circuit issued a decision coming to a different result in *Trinko*,[35] a case virtually identical to *Goldwasser*. The Second Circuit, however, reversed the district court's dismissal of the antitrust claim, finding that the plaintiff had independently asserted the kind of harm section 2 could recognize independent of any statutory duties under the 1996 Act.[36] As a technical matter, the Second Circuit's decision does not conflict with *Goldwasser*'s holding that the antitrust claim must have a basis independent from the defendant's purely regulatory obligations. The Second Circuit found such an independent section 2 claim in Trinko's complaint while the Seventh Circuit did not find one in Goldwasser's suit. The tension between the courts is mostly in how generously they read the respective pleadings before them. But, because the Second Circuit found the plaintiff Trinko to have pled a valid claim under antitrust law, its case at least implicitly

---

[29] *Id.* at 727–30.
[30] *Id.*
[31] 47 U.S.C. § 152.
[32] 222 F.3d 390 (7th Cir. 2000).
[33] *Id.* at 396.
[34] *Id.* at 402.
[35] 305 F.3d 89 (2d Cir. 2002).
[36] *Id.* at 108.

raised the question of the extent to which the 1996 Act's savings clause preserved antitrust jurisdiction; a question the court answered in allowing Trinko to pursue even his very vague section 2 allegation.

It is hard to know what to infer about the relationship between antitrust and regulation from the Second Circuit's treatment of Trinko's case. Even if one assumes the refusal-to-deal claim had an independent basis in antitrust law, it was a claim that directly implicated duties to deal governed by FCC rules. If a court found that Verizon was not liable under section 2 for refusing to deal, that result would have no bearing on Verizon's regulatory obligations. On the other hand, if a court did find section 2 liability, the result would either duplicate or expand the regulatory duty to deal. While duplication of the regulatory duty through antitrust enforcement need not conflict with the FCC's full exercise of its authority under the 1996 Act, expansion of regulatory obligations would interfere with the agency's administration of the statutory scheme. It would nullify a regulatory decision not to extend the duty to deal as far as the court saw fit to do under antitrust.

At first glance, allowing the antitrust claim to proceed despite the above-mentioned tension between antitrust and regulation appears consistent with the plain language of the 1996 Act's savings clause. On further analysis, however, such a reading of the savings clause is too strong. It is one thing for regulation not to supersede or modify antitrust law; it is another for a specific statutory program of regulation to yield to antitrust. It would be odd for Congress purposefully to establish a detailed regulatory scheme whose full exercise could be trumped by a more general, preexisting body of law without specifically stating such an intention. From a more theoretical perspective, it would be strange for Congress to pull a set of commercial interactions out of the free market and into the regulated sphere, only to subject exactly the same commercial interactions to antitrust law, which to a large extent uses the free market as a benchmark for defining anticompetitive conduct.[37] Because savings clauses in general should not be read to produce unnecessary conflicts of law, the 1996 Act's savings clause should be read to avoid applications of antitrust that conflict with and weaken the FCC's regulatory authority over the conduct at issue in *Trinko*.[38]

The Second Circuit's *Trinko* decision does not delve into the interpretation of the savings clause at issue and therefore provides at best only vague guidance about when antitrust immunity might arise under statutes containing such clauses. Insofar as the pre-2004 cases addressed the issue, however, they gave no hint that a regulatory statute with a savings clause could ever imply immunity from a properly pled antitrust claim. Both in those cases and in the implied immunity cases involving statutes without savings clauses, the prevailing doctrine was premised on preserving the domain of antitrust law, at least to the extent possible without conflicting with the underlying regulatory statute.

---

[37]   See Herbert Hovenkamp, *Antitrust and the Regulatory Enterprise*, COLUM. BUS. L. 335, 341 (2004) (discussing why regulation's removal of economic conduct from market forces implies a reduced role for antitrust).

[38]   *Id.* at 345 (citing Geier v. American Honda Motor Co., 529 U.S. 861 (2000)).

B   Antitrust and Regulation After 2004

1   *Credit Suisse v. Billing*

In *Credit Suisse* and *Trinko*, the Supreme Court shifted the earlier cases' balance between antitrust and regulation in favor of regulation. The effect of each case was to reduce the scope of antitrust enforcement in regulated industries.

Credit Suisse, the more recent of the two decisions, involved an attempted antitrust suit for collusion in the underwriting of initial public offerings of securities. The relevant regulatory statute gave the SEC authority to review joint underwriting activities and contained no specific antitrust savings clause.[39] It did, however, contain a general savings clause that 'the rights and remedies provided by this chapter shall be in addition to any and all other rights and remedies that may exist at law or in equity'.[40] In nonetheless finding the securities laws to imply immunity from the plaintiffs' antitrust claim, the Court went beyond *Gordon* and *NASD* in important ways.

The cases that came before *Credit Suisse* all drew a line between antitrust claims that could conflict with an agency's statutory authority to regulate a particular kind of conduct and those claims that could not conflict principally because they addressed activities the agency had no power either to approve or prohibit. The doctrinal progression from *Silver* to *Gordon* to *NASD* interpreted agency authority and 'plain repugnancy' with increasing breadth, but those cases did not imply immunity where the conduct underlying the antitrust claim was distinct from anything the securities laws would or could allow. In *Credit Suisse*, the Court applied those prior cases, but added a prudential consideration that would preclude some antitrust claims involving conduct the agency either has no specific statutory power to regulate or is certain to regulate in a manner that is consistent with the antitrust laws.

The plaintiffs in *Credit Suisse* had complained that defendants violated section 1 of the Sherman Act by going beyond the kinds of joint setting of securities prices that the securities laws allow. They alleged that the defendants had impermissibly engaged in tying and similar activities that are prohibited by both the antitrust laws and the securities statutes. Importantly, the Court took as given that the defendants' conduct was unlawful under the securities laws and would remain so.[41] The Court nonetheless extended the potential-conflict rationale for immunity established by *Gordon* to apply even where the antitrust claim, correctly construed, would not actually conflict with regulation. The Court reasoned that 'only a fine, complex, detailed line separates activity that the SEC permits or encourages (for which respondents must concede antitrust immunity) from activity that the SEC must (and inevitably will) forbid'.[42]

Credit Suisse goes beyond prior implied immunity cases by blocking some antitrust claims that are based on legitimate antitrust principles, are consistent with securities laws, and are not potentially repugnant to the regulatory scheme, but where the underlying conduct is similar enough to regulated conduct that a judge might confuse the two and

---

[39]   551 U.S. at 271, 276.
[40]   15 U.S.C. §§ 77p(a), 78bb(a).
[41]   *Credit Suisse*, 551 U.S. at 278–9.
[42]   *Id.*

create a conflict with regulatory authority. The Court's main concern was the potential for a flood of 'lawsuits through the nation in dozens of different courts with different non-expert judges and nonexpert juries'.[43] If plaintiffs could 'dress what is essentially a securities complaint in antitrust clothing', they could bypass the expert securities regulators in favor of generalist courts more prone to errors and more likely to impose unwarranted costs on defendants.[44]

The *Credit Suisse* analysis is important because it marks the first time in the line of implied antitrust immunity cases that the Court has found regulation to imply immunity from legitimate and nonrepugnant antitrust claims because of the potential effects of erroneous interpretations of fact by future courts. The Court moreover emphasizes the costs of erroneous conflicts with the securities laws without evident consideration of the costs of errors on the other side: regulatory approval of, or failure to enforce against, conduct that the agency mistakenly places on the legitimate side of the line. Ultimately, the Court opts for favoring regulation for two reasons: first, because antitrust risks deterring behavior the statute approves or encourages while the opposite effect of regulation on the goals of anti-trust is unlikely or expressly dominated by Congress' specific statutory objectives;[45] and second, because injured parties still have a remedy from the SEC even if barred from pursuing antitrust claims.[46] Both reasons are open to question. The case itself involves concerted conduct at the heart of what the antitrust laws prohibit; and the SEC had in fact failed to reach a resolution or remedy for precisely the kind of conduct plaintiffs were alleging.

While *Credit Suisse* is potentially alarming for antitrust enforcement, it remains to be seen how broadly the particular potential-conflict rationale of *Credit Suisse* will be applied to antitrust claims outside of the securities context. As Einer Elhauge has noted, the decision can be read in several places to limit itself to securities law, and moreover to allow implied exemption from antitrust liability only for conduct related to 'core' areas of the securities laws.[47] Without such a limiting interpretation, however, the logic and likely practical effect of *Credit Suisse* contract the scope of antitrust enforcement and expand the scope of implied immunity in industries regulated by statutes that fail expressly to save the operation of antitrust law.

What about the general savings clauses in the securities Acts mentioned above? The Court itself had previously interpreted those clauses to 'confirm that the remedies in each [securities] Act were to be supplemented by "any and all" additional remedies'.[48] That precedent formed the basis for Justice Thomas' dissent in *Credit Suisse* from the majority's implication of antitrust immunity.[49] The majority gave two reasons for putting aside the savings clauses, neither of them terribly convincing. One reason the Court gave was that the plaintiff had failed to present the effect of the savings clauses for consideration by the lower courts.[50] That is a peculiar rationale given that it was not the plaintiff but

---

43   *Id.* at 281.
44   *Id.* at 284.
45   *Id.* at 283–4.
46   *Id.* at 283.
47   E. Elhauge, U.S. ANTITRUST LAW AND ECONOMICS 37 (Foundation Press, 2008).
48   Herman and MacLean v. Huddleston, 459 U.S. 375, 383 (1983).
49   551 U.S. at 287–8.
50   551 U.S. at 275.

the defendant who, in asking for immunity, sought a ruling in tension with the savings clauses.

The Court's other reason for overriding the savings clauses was that two earlier securities cases, *NASD* and *Gordon*, had implied immunity to antitrust suits notwithstanding the same savings clauses.[51] But that reasoning ignores a crucial difference between *Credit Suisse* and those earlier cases: the necessity of choosing between giving full effect to the securities laws and full effect to the antitrust laws. In each of the earlier cases the antitrust suit, even correctly construed, could have directly conflicted with the SEC's exercise of regulatory authority under the securities laws. In such cases the securities law remedies would not be 'in addition' to antitrust law remedies, but exclusive of them. With such clear 'repugnancy' between the two sets of laws, the Court had to choose between them. The Court's decision to prioritize the more specific securities laws over the more general antitrust laws is in keeping with established cannons of statutory construction.[52] In *Credit Suisse*, however, the particular antitrust suit at issue could not have conflicted with the exercise of authority under the securities laws and the Court therefore did not face the situation of mutual exclusivity it had faced in *NASD* or *Gordon*. The Court's reliance on potential future errors by trial courts to block antitrust suits like that in *Credit Suisse* effectively gives short shrift to the savings clause, enlarges the zone of implied immunity beyond the area of genuine conflict, and discounts Congress' own judgment about the cost and benefits of applying antitrust and other laws in securities markets.

2   *Verizon v. Trinko*

The Court's emphasis in *Credit Suisse* on the costs and institutional shortcomings of antitrust enforcement was not new. Indeed, that case built on themes the Court had been developing for some time and had articulated three years earlier when it addressed the balance of antitrust and regulation under the Telecommunications Act of 1996 in *Verizon v. Trinko*.[53] Unlike the securities laws at issue in *Credit Suisse*, however, the regulatory statute in *Trinko* contains a specific antitrust savings clause.

In brief, the background of *Trinko* is this. The Telecommunications Act of 1996 tries to foster competition in the provision of local telephone services by requiring the incumbent monopolies to provide access to their networks to new entrants into the telecommunications market.[54] When such a new entrant wishes to provide service to customers in a given area, it typically asks the incumbent to connect the customer's line to the new entrant's routing and billing equipment. In this way the new entrant can provide service without building the 'last mile' line to each customer. AT&T, which had been out of the local telephone business since the company's divestiture in 1984, re-entered that market as a competitor after the 1996 Act. One of the retail customers AT&T signed up was the law office of Curtis V. Trinko. AT&T faced delays in providing service to the plaintiff

---

[51]   *Id.*
[52]   Morton v. Mancari, 417 U.S. 535 (1974) (a specific statute will not be controlled or nullified by a general one, regardless of respective dates of enactment).
[53]   540 U.S. 398 (2004).
[54]   47 U.S.C. §§ 151, 152.

because of a dispute with Verizon, the incumbent provider of local services in New York, over AT&T's access to Verizon's network facilities.[55]

The 1996 Act amended the Communications Act of 1934 to add an antitrust savings clause, which states that 'nothing in this Act . . . shall be construed to modify, impair, or supersede the applicability of any of the antitrust laws' in telecommunications markets.[56] The plaintiff, ostensibly because he could not obtain his choice of telephone service provider, sued Verizon under section 2 of the Sherman Antitrust Act as well as under the Communications Act.[57] He claimed that Verizon violated section 2 and the 1996 Act by discriminating against rivals like AT&T by refusing to supply them with the network connections they needed to provide service to customers like Trinko's law office.[58] The case reached the Supreme Court after the Second Circuit reversed the district court's dismissal of Trinko's suit.

The Supreme Court phrased the question presented in *Trinko* as 'whether a complaint alleging a breach of the incumbent's duty under the 1996 Act to share its network with competitors states a claim under § 2 of the Sherman Act'.[59] The Court answered that question in the negative, and reversed the Second Circuit. The concern with *Trinko* is not with the Court's ruling against the plaintiff in that particular case, but that the decision may be susceptible to broad interpretations by lower courts that would preclude antitrust claims, both private and public, even absent some of the factors that might have justified the result in *Trinko* itself.

Present in *Trinko* were three critical factors. First, the duties to deal that the 1996 Act imposed on incumbent telephone carriers were stronger than any such duties under section 2 of the Sherman Act, the antimonopoly provision on which the plaintiff had based his claim. Second, the FCC had issued a set of rules that directly regulated the conduct about which the plaintiff was complaining. And third, the FCC actively administered its duty-to-deal regulations under the 1996 Act. The Court's holding can be read to say that where such factors are present, a violation of the agency's rule does not constitute a separate violation of the antitrust laws. That ruling directly answers the question presented and establishes the principle that when regulatory statutes establish pervasive competition enforcement regimes they do not implicitly enlarge the scope of substantive liability under the antitrust laws.[60] As the Court put it, 'just as the 1996 Act

---

[55]   540 U.S. at 403–4.

[56]   47 U.S.C § 152.

[57]   540 U.S. at 405. The plaintiff had no standing to sue directly under the 1996 Act, which does not provide private rights of action in federal court. N. County Comm. Corp. v. Calif. Catalog & Technology, No. 08-55408 (9th Cir. February 10, 2010). Whether the plaintiff had standing to sue under the antitrust laws as an 'indirect purchaser' is also unclear; the *Trinko* majority does not address the issue although Justice Stevens in dissent, joined by Justices Thomas and Souter, would have decided the case solely on the basis that Trinko lacked standing. 540 U.S. at 416.

[58]   *Id.* at 404–5.

[59]   *Id.* at 401.

[60]   The specifics of the regulation will matter in deciding how a regulatory statute affects antitrust law; not every statute should be read to limit expansion of antitrust law. In the Court's words, '[j]ust as regulatory context may in other cases serve as a basis for implied immunity, it may also be a consideration in deciding whether to recognize an expansion of the contours of § 2.' *Id.* at 412 (internal citations omitted).

preserves claims that satisfy existing antitrust standards, it does not create new claims that go beyond existing antitrust standards'.[61]

Embedded in the Supreme Court's ruling so interpreted are underlying issues related to the comparative competency of sector-specific regulatory agencies and generalist courts or public antitrust authorities that are beyond the scope of this chapter. The Court speaks explicitly in both *Credit Suisse* and *Trinko* about the hazards of diverting claims from expert agencies to nonexpert courts. The risk is that the ability of plaintiffs to seek through antitrust what they could not obtain through the regulatory process could lead to a flood of costly litigation that, when multiplied by the likelihood that generalist courts will make errors at both the pleading and merits stages of litigation, could distort firms' competitive and innovative incentives in a way that will be costly to society.

Where a competent agency actively administers a rule whose standard for the competitive conduct at issue in litigation is more demanding on the defendant than antitrust law, the Court was right to find it relevant whether the marginal gains outweigh the potential costs of antitrust enforcement against the same conduct. The concern for antitrust enforcement is that *Trinko* could be read more broadly by lower courts to block antitrust claims even when regulation does not as directly or effectively address the alleged competitive harm as the Supreme Court found the FCC rules at issue in *Trinko* to do.

Trinko states that one key factor in deciding whether to recognize an antitrust claim against a regulated firm 'is the existence of a regulatory structure designed to deter and remedy anticompetitive harm' because '[w]here such a structure exists, the additional benefit to competition provided by antitrust enforcement will tend to be small'.[62] Had the Court made clear that to preclude antitrust claims a regulatory structure must, like the one at issue in *Trinko*, be directly relevant to the conduct at issue, be more demanding than antitrust law, and be actively administered, one might worry less about any collateral consequences for legitimate antitrust cases. The Court, however, goes on to pose as the contrasting scenario in which antitrust might be worthwhile the case where '[t]here is nothing built into the regulatory scheme which performs the antitrust function'.[63] Between 'nothing' and the actively enforced duties to deal under the 1996 Act there is a lot of room. The risk for antitrust enforcement is that, given the *Trinko* Court's emphasis on the 'sometimes considerable disadvantages' of antitrust, lower courts will preclude antitrust suits where the regulatory scheme is something greater than 'nothing' but something well short of the FCC's implementation of the 1996 Act's competitive access provisions.

After *Trinko*, therefore, the presence of regulatory authority over a competition-related matter may make it more difficult for a plaintiff to pursue an antitrust challenge to the same conduct if the antitrust claim in any way exceeded the clear boundaries of antitrust precedent. Perhaps the most illustrative way to explain *Trinko*'s effect is this: had the decision been in place 40 years ago, the government's ability to pursue the antitrust suit that led to the break-up of AT&T, and other cases in which the government publicly enforced the antitrust laws in regulated industries, would have been in question. To the extent regulatory authorities have become more successful or active in enforcing

---

[61]   *Id.* at 407.
[62]   *Id.* at 412.
[63]   *Id.* (quoting *Silver*).

competition-enhancing rules than they were in the past,[64] one might be inclined to worry less about the loss of such antitrust enforcement. But the *Trinko* opinion hinges on the existence of a regulatory structure, not clearly on its effectiveness, so the decision risks blocking antitrust cases where regulation looks good on paper but leaves an enforcement gap in practice.

The Supreme Court's line between the novel claims its rule would preclude and established antitrust claims that could proceed in light of the 1996 Act's savings clause does not alleviate the above concern. As a practical and legal matter, that line may be difficult to draw, especially in activities analysed under the fact-intensive rule of reason. The more factual dimensions there are to a liability determination, the more likely it is that every example of some kind of conduct will be distinguishable from every other example and, therefore, to some extent a novel expansion of doctrine that came before.

Moreover, in concluding that the duties to deal under the 1996 Act went beyond relief recognizable under the antitrust laws, the Court read antitrust precedent on unilateral refusals to deal very restrictively. Despite several cases in which the Supreme Court and lower courts had found grounds to hold dominant firms liable for denial of an essential input to competitors,[65] the Court in *Trinko* disclaimed ever having sanctioned an 'essential facilities' doctrine or any other general basis for refusal-to-deal liability.[66] The Court acknowledged that it had upheld liability for a unilateral refusal to deal in *Aspen Skiing v. Aspen Highlands*.[67] But it emphasized the unusual and specific facts of that case – notably, a prior course of dealing with the plaintiff and none but an anticompetitive explanation for changing course – and described *Aspen* as being 'at or near the outer boundary of Section 2 liability'.[68] The facts of *Trinko* not fitting those of *Aspen*, the Court found the plaintiff not to have stated a recognized antitrust claim; as a doctrinal matter the Court found that Trinko's claim simply fell outside the reasonable scope of established section 2 liability.[69]

On one hand, the Court rightly found US antitrust law to establish a strong presumption against duties to deal with competitors because such duties could interfere with desirable economic incentives and punish firms for the very kind of conduct – aggressive competition – that the antitrust laws seek to promote.[70] But there is also a good argument that the presumption had not previously been as strong as the Court found it to be in *Trinko*.

To reach its conclusion that the kind of dealing with a competitor addressed by the

---

[64]   The FCC had acknowledged its own ineffectiveness as a regulatory authority in the antitrust case leading up to the 1982 AT&T divestiture. *United States v. AT&T*, 552 F. Supp. 131, 168 (D.D.C. 1982).

[65]   Aspen Skiing v. Aspen Highlands, 472 U.S. 585 (1985); *Otter Tail*, 410 U.S. 366 (1973); MCI Comm. Corp. v. AT&T, 708 F.2d 1081, 1092 (7th Cir. 1983), cert denied 464 U.S. 891 (1983); Phonotele, Inc. v. American Tel. & Tel. Co., 664 F.2d 716 (9th Cir. 1981).

[66]   540 U.S. at 410–11.

[67]   472 US 585 (1985).

[68]   540 U.S. at 409.

[69]   For an analysis of why even this conclusion of the Court is subject to question, and in turn of why it is unclear how much of *Aspen* actually survives *Trinko*, see Eleanor M. Fox, *Is There Life in Aspen after Trinko? The Silent Revolution of Section 2 of the Sherman Act*, 73 ANTITRUST L. J. 153 (2005).

[70]   540 U.S. at 407–8.

1996 Act was novel to antitrust law, the Court arguably engaged in some sleight of hand by altering ex post the substantive scope of section 2 liability for refusals to deal to exclude Trinko's claim, essentially redrawing the boundary of liability after Trinko had filed suit to move his claim outside of existing antitrust precedent. At the time Trinko filed suit the presumption against liability for unilateral refusals to deal had never been found to be as strong as the Court later ruled it to be. *Aspen* itself did not adopt such a skeptical posture toward refusal-to-deal claims or confine liability for such conduct to its own facts, as the Court retrospectively did in *Trinko*. To the contrary, in *Aspen* the Court considered itself already to have 'squarely held' in *Lorain Journal*[71] that a monopolist's right to exclude competition through a refusal to deal is a qualified one.[72] Whereas *Trinko* expressly cabined refusal-to-deal liability to the facts of *Aspen*, the Court in *Aspen* itself adopted a more flexible approach in expressly stating that '[t]he qualification on the right of a monopolist to deal with whom he pleases is not so narrow that it encompasses no more than the circumstances of *Lorain Journal*'.[73] The *Trinko* Court interpreted *Aspen* to narrow *Lorain Journal*, whereas the *Aspen* Court itself interpreted *Lorain* to be a broader rule that could apply to the specific facts of the *Aspen* case.

It is also hard to reconcile the Court's description of refusal-to-deal liability with *Otter Tail*, in which the Court had no difficulty allowing antitrust claims that involved 'pure refusal to deal' to proceed in the regulated power sector. In *Trinko*, the Court suggests that *Otter Tail* fits the facts of *Aspen* because the defendant power company was refusing to supply some municipal utilities with the same goods and services it was already providing to others.[74] But if the Court is thereby implying that dealing with one firm could trigger antitrust liability for refusal to deal with other firms, then that rule is broader than *Aspen*'s. For in *Aspen* the key point was that the defendant had previously dealt with the very same party with whom it later refused to deal. By discounting that distinction between *Aspen* and *Otter Tail*, the Court would curtail a seller's discretion more than *Aspen* itself might do. Moreover, if the Court means what it says about *Otter Tail*, then it could be hard to distinguish Trinko's refusal-to-deal claim if Verizon was, similarly, allegedly refusing to supply AT&T the same kind of access it was supplying to other competitive entrants into the local telecommunications market. If *Otter Tail* and not *Aspen* is more accurately described as the outer boundary of section 2 liability, then the claim at issue in *Trinko*, though weak, does not look novel. The Court nevertheless posits its analysis to be a straightforward description of the existing state of antitrust law rather than as a normative ruling that changes the scope of antitrust liability.

Even if one thinks the Court is right in its reading of precedent, implementing the distinction between established and novel antitrust claims may not, as mentioned, be easy. The more factual dimensions there are to a liability determination, the more likely it is that every example of some kind of conduct will be distinguishable from every other example and, therefore, to some extent a novel expansion of doctrine that came before. Is a claim of liability for a defendant's refusal to continue dealing with the plaintiff (*Aspen*)

---

[71]   Lorain Journal Co. v. United States, 342 U.S. 143 (1951).
[72]   *Aspen*, 472 U.S. at 480.
[73]   *Id*. at 603.
[74]   540 U.S. at 410.

the same as a claim of liability for a defendant's refusal to supply the plaintiff the things the defendant has supplied to third parties (*Otter Tail*)? If so, could Trinko have made his claim nonnovel simply by alleging that Verizon was supplying other new entrants with the same network elements it was allegedly refusing to supply AT&T? How would such a claim differ from that at issue in *Otter Tail,* a case the Court in passing interpreted to be within the purview of liability established by *Aspen*? Distinguishing novel from existing grounds for liability might therefore be a far less clear-cut task than the Court implies.

Moreover, where the line between a novel and existing basis for liability is blurred, the Court makes clear that its major concern is with the likelihood of false positives, i.e., of enforcement against conduct that may constitute aggressive competition, the conduct the antitrust laws try to promote and protect, rather than with the likelihood of illicit anticompetitive strategies. The *Trinko* opinion emphasizes the costs of antitrust enforcement, first referring to antitrust enforcement's 'sometimes considerable disadvantages'[75] and later to how difficult antitrust cases are '[u]nder the best of circumstances'.[76] The Court's error-cost discussion implies that lower courts should choose false negatives over false positives: in other words, be generous in the definition of what constitutes expansion and parsimonious in the definition of existing law. The Court thereby places a thumb on the scale in favor of finding antitrust claims to be precluded in a market subject to competition-oriented regulation.

To be sure, Trinko's claim was a stretch and it likely would have failed once the court reviewed Verizon's conduct under a rule-of-reason inquiry. However, the Supreme Court's decision prevents district courts from engaging in that inquiry at all for claims that push the boundaries of antitrust in the context of a regulated industry, perhaps even cutting off inquiry into novel sets of facts to see if they are sufficiently equivalent to the facts on which existing antitrust law has recognized liability. While it is easy to shrug off the preclusive effect of such a rule in the context of a case like Trinko's, the Court's decision will also bind lower courts in cases with more complex facts and greater merit. The difficulties of attaching presumptions to the fact-intensive inquiries underlying antitrust law's rule of reason or a regulatory statute's implication of antitrust immunity are a good reason to be wary of short-circuiting the provisions of the antitrust statutes that assign the heavily fact-driven question of whether a particular course of conduct violates the law to the district courts.[77]

In sum, *Trinko* shows that the Court will interpret the substantive scope of antitrust liability narrowly in regulated settings even where Congress has expressly preserved the operation of antitrust law. This narrow interpretation of existing law diminishes the degree to which the anti-expansion approach may in fact preserve plaintiffs' recourse to pursuing antitrust claims against regulated firms and in turn gives narrow practical effect to the savings clause. In limiting access of plaintiffs to the process through which antitrust law evolves in regulated markets, the Court leaves only the regulatory process for challenging certain kinds of potentially anticompetitive conduct. Therefore, when an agency has authority over competition-related conduct, the Court leaves it to regulators rather

---

[75]   *Id.* at 412.
[76]   *Id.* at 414.
[77]   15 U.S.C. § 4, 26.

than to courts applying the antitrust laws to judge whether conduct that does not closely fit the factual profile of previously successful antitrust claims is on balance more harmful than beneficial to competition, or at least to the agency's competition-related goals.

II RATIONALE AND OPEN QUESTIONS

The principal reason the Court gives in *Credit Suisse* and *Trinko* for precluding antitrust claims is concern with the costs of false positives in enforcement. The Court is unusually explicit in its aversion to the potential costs of antitrust in *Trinko* notwithstanding that Congress, in including a savings clause in the 1996 Act, appears to have taken a different view. Cases that came after *Trinko* continued to raise barriers to antitrust plaintiffs in both regulated and unregulated settings. As discussed earlier, *Credit Suisse* confers immunity even from well-established antitrust claims like price-fixing if those claims involve conduct that is factually close to, though not within, activities covered by a regulatory statute. In *Twombly*, the Court increased the barrier to all antitrust claims through heightened pleading requirements.[78] Most recently, in *Pacific Bell v. Linkline*, the Court virtually eliminated 'price squeezes' as a cognizable claim under section 2,[79] a consequence flowing in large part from the Court's interpretation of refusal-to-deal liability in *Trinko*.[80]

On one hand, the Court's argument about the relevance of regulation to the value of antitrust enforcement is perfectly sound. When there is already a regulatory remedy, the marginal benefits of an antitrust remedy may be small (as the Court again noted in *Credit Suisse*). Regulation may also make it more difficult to assess anticompetitive harms for purposes of an antitrust case. For even if antitrust and regulation are consistent with each other, regulation's influence on the economic structure and conduct of an industry might make it harder for antitrust enforcers to link particular competitive effects to the

---

[78] Bell Atlantic v. Twombly, 127 S. Ct. 1955 (2007).
[79] Pacific Bell Tel. Co. v. Linkline Communications, Inc. (Slip Op., February 25, 2009). A price squeeze can arise when a monopolist in the market for a productive input is also a competitor in the market for the final product incorporating that input. The monopolist might then try to squeeze the profits of its wholesale customer (and downstream competitor) by first charging a high wholesale price for the necessary input and then charging consumers a low price for the final product in which the wholesale customer competes with the monopolist.
[80] The other requirement *Linkline* establishes for a price squeeze claim is that the defendant's retail prices for the final product be predatory as defined in Brooke Group v. Brown and Williamson, 509 U.S. 209 (1993), under which the plaintiff must prove that the defendant's retail prices were below cost and likely to give the defendant enough market power in the future to raise prices and 'recoup' the money it lost from its predatory conduct. *Linkline,* Slip. Op. at 10–12. A perplexing feature of the *Linkline* decision, which is beyond the scope of this chapter, is the absence of any real discussion by the Court of whether the interaction between monopoly power in the wholesale input market and low retail pricing in the final product market should give rise to a different definition of predatory pricing in price-squeeze cases than in straight predation cases. The Court quickly dismisses an amicus brief's argument for taking such an interaction into account. Slip Op. at 14 (citing Brief for American Antitrust Institute at 30). But it does not engage the underlying economics at any depth and simply asserts the independence for antitrust purposes of the defendant's behavior in the upstream and downstream markets. Slip. Op. at 15.

defendant's conduct and to design suitable remedies. It therefore makes perfect sense that precedent requires antitrust to take account of the nature and pervasiveness of state and federal regulation and of the particular legal and economic setting of any industry in which it is being applied.[81]

On the other hand, the 1996 Act's savings clause would appear to deny courts a basis for weighing the marginal costs and benefits of antitrust enforcement. The Court's statement that its bar to expansion of section 2 follows logically from the implied immunity cases falls apart on even cursory analysis. The rationale for implied immunity was antitrust law's potential interference with regulatory authority. In contrast, the rationale for *Trinko*'s bar to expansion of section 2 was the Court's opinion that antitrust enforcement's benefits were not worth its costs in the presence of regulation. The implied immunity cases therefore hinge on antitrust law's conflicts with regulation, while *Trinko* hinges on antitrust law's potential duplication of regulation. The former was clearly inconsistent with the statutes in the relevant cases; the latter was expressly provided for in the savings clause of the regulatory statute at issue in *Trinko*.

The centrality the Court assigns to the costs of antitrust enforcement is new in the implied immunity context. Antitrust cases under section 2 typically focus on the costs and benefits of the economic conduct at issue and on whether there is enough evidence to conclude that the particular conduct is harmful enough to warrant injunction or liability. As the DOJ explains the rule-of-reason approach to antitrust liability:

> the courts must undertake an extensive evidentiary study of (1) whether the practice in question in fact is likely to have a significant anticompetitive effect in a relevant market and (2) whether there are any procompetitive justifications relating to the restraint. Under the Rule of Reason, if any anticompetitive harm would be outweighed by the practice's procompetitive effects, the practice is not unlawful.[82]

The primary focus is thus on the underlying conduct, not on the collateral costs of enforcement.

Acknowledging regulation's effects need not amount to a general modification of antitrust to accommodate regulation; it might lead instead to a sensible determination that under the circumstances of a particular case antitrust liability is unwarranted. At a formal level, in such an analysis antitrust law remains *applicable*, as the savings clause requires, but for prudential reasons a court is finding antitrust law not to warrant actual application given a specific set of facts. As Herbert Hovenkamp has pointed out, the case-by-case determination of whether antitrust should apply or yield to active regulation of the conduct at issue is precisely the kind of antitrust inquiry that the savings clause should be interpreted to preserve.[83] Among other things, because economic regulation usually changes the terms on which market participants interact, the competitive effects and justifications relevant to the rule-of-reason inquiry are likely to change depending on whether or not regulation is taken into account. It therefore makes no sense to interpret

---

[81]   *Id.* at 411 (citing United States v. Citizens & Southern Nat. Bank, 422 U.S. 86, 91 (1975), and Concord v. Boston Edison Co., 915 F.2d 17, 22 (1st Cir. 1990)).

[82]   DOJ, ANTITRUST RESOURCE MANUAL, part 7, available at www.usdoj.gov/usao/eousa/foia_reading_room/usam/title7/ant00007.htm.

[83]   Hovenkamp, *supra* note 37, at 375–6.

an antitrust savings clause as if regulation did not exist or affect the impact of antitrust in the industry.[84]

The problem is that *Trinko* may lead courts too far in the opposite direction. The Court did not provide much guidance for lower courts in how and when to take account of regulation, of potential conflicts between the regulatory statute and antitrust, or of the marginal benefits of antitrust before they decide whether to allow a given antitrust claim against a regulated firm. Instead, the Court may in practice have established a conclusive presumption that competition-related regulation renders expansion of antitrust liability more costly in all cases.[85] As a matter of precedent, this presumption is a departure from the Court's own pronouncement in *Gordon* that 'the determination of whether implied repeal of the antitrust laws is necessary to make [a regulatory statute] work is a matter for the courts, and in particular for the courts in which the antitrust claims are raised'.[86] *Trinko* shifts the question from whether immunity is necessary to make a regulatory statute to that of whether immunity is more economically efficient; *Credit Suisse* is based on a very broad notion of what is necessary to make a regulatory statute work. As an empirical matter, the Court's assertions about the costs of allowing antitrust claims against regulated conduct to reach the courts may not be well grounded in fact.

A   Overemphasis on False Positives: Some Evidence

The Supreme Court's presumption that false positives are more costly than false negatives in the presence of regulation is questionable on several fronts. First, the cost/benefit assumption underlying the Court's bar to complex or novel claims against regulated firms may or may not be correct in a given case. Its accuracy depends on a number of factors and hinges more on empirics than systematic logic. For instance, the regulatory agency might not actively exercise its authority. So the benefits of adding antitrust enforcement will not necessarily be small or marginal just because Congress has given an agency the authority to regulate. But even if one assumes that the marginal payoff of antitrust is lower when a regulator actively pursues the same result, that payoff will not presumptively be so low that the net benefits from antitrust enforcement are negative.

Second, while the *Trinko* opinion emphasizes the costs of false positives in antitrust enforcement, precluding antitrust liability would ensure at least some number of false negatives in which anticompetitive conduct would go unpunished. To the extent the cases involving conduct that causes net harm to competition can be separated from others in which false positives are more likely, an overinclusive rule against liability will reduce consumer welfare. The Supreme Court takes the view that the risk and cost of such false negatives is minor compared to the risk of false positives. Even if it were true that any individual false positive result is on average more costly than any individual false negative, it is not necessarily true that the overall costs of false positives from antitrust enforcement are higher than the costs of false negatives. That balance depends on the comparative frequency of false positives. In its 2007 Report and Recommendations, the Antitrust Modernization

---

[84]   *Id.*
[85]   540 U.S. at 414–15.
[86]   422 U.S. at 686.

Commission discussed the importance of avoiding both overdeterrence and underdeterrence of anticompetitive conduct, but noted in its discussion of treble damages that '[n]o actual cases or evidence of systematic overdeterrence were presented to the Commission'.[87]

Third, substantive and procedural developments in antitrust law over the past 30 years have reduced the likelihood that cases will reach trial and the probability that plaintiffs will win once they get there. On the procedural side, the Supreme Court has over the years placed limits on who can sue under the antitrust laws[88] and has raised the pleading requirements for those who can.[89] More fundamentally, the Court has increased the substantive burdens on plaintiffs for a number of antitrust claims, in particular those alleging monopolization under section 2 of the Sherman Act. In ruling against plaintiffs in every antitrust case since 1992,[90] the Court has made it harder for plaintiffs to get to the merits, never mind win, on claims ranging from predatory pricing,[91] to vertical price restraints,[92] and, of course, to refusals to deal.[93] Those are only examples, and the Court has raised barriers to plaintiffs for numerous other kinds of antitrust claims as well.[94] The point here is not to debate the merits of any of those particular decisions, but to show that antitrust jurisprudence has evolved to reduce significantly the likelihood of false positives. The assumption that even more preclusive rules against liability are necessary to protect against investment deterrence and other costs of overenforcement requires more justification than the Court has offered in light of these developments.[95]

Finally, the case law provides additional empirical evidence that the prospect of false positives is not so great as to warrant the antitrust-precluding effect the Court gives to competition-oriented regulation. There have been relatively few successful claims of refusal-to-deal liability and the overall number of cases has not been so great as to suggest the administrative and deterrence costs of a rule-of-reason test will be higher than the benefits of such a rule. Glen Robinson has shown that from 1980 to 2000 there were a total of 71 district and circuit court opinions addressing essential-facilities claims.[96] Although essential-facilities claims are a subset of refusal-to-deal claims, they are a large subset and serve as a reasonable proxy for the volume of the latter. In only five of 28 circuit court opinions and six of 43 district court opinions did the courts find there to be even a triable issue of fact as to the existence of an essential facility.[97] My update of the data shows

---

[87] Antitrust Modernization Commission, *Report and Recommendations* 247 (2007).
[88] See, e.g., ARCO v. USA Petroleum Co., 495 U.S. 328 (1990); Illinois Brick v. Illinois, 431 U.S. 720 (1977); Brunswick v. Pueblo Bowl-O-Mat, Inc., 429 U.S. 477 (1977).
[89] Bell Atlantic v. Twombly, 127 S. Ct. 1955 (2007).
[90] The last antitrust plaintiff's victory in the Supreme Court was in Eastman Kodak v. Image Technical Services, 504 U.S. 451 (1992).
[91] Brooke Group v. Brown and Williamson, 509 U.S. 209 (1993).
[92] Leegin Creative Leather Products v. PSKS, 127 S. Ct. 2705 (2007).
[93] *Trinko*, 540 U.S. 398 (2004).
[94] See Stacey L. Dogan and Mark. A. Lemley, *Antitrust Law and Regulatory Gaming*, 87 TEX. L. REV. 685 (2009).
[95] As Dogan and Lemley point out, the landscape of antitrust law has changed significantly since Judge Frank Easterbrook's 1984 critique of antitrust law's propensity toward false positives. *Id.* at 700 (discussing Frank H. Easterbrook, *The Limits of Antitrust*, 63 TEXAS L. REV. 1 (1984)).
[96] Glen O. Robinson, *On Refusing to Deal with Rivals*, 87 CORNELL L. REV. 1177 (2002).
[97] *Id.* at 1206–7 n.129.

that from 2001 to 2008 there were 22 circuit court opinions addressing essential facilities claims, of which only three found a triable issue on the merits.[98] Those three include the Second Circuit's *Trinko* decision that the Supreme Court later reversed. During that same recent period there were 40 district court cases (distinct from the circuit court cases just mentioned) that dealt to differing degrees with the essential facilities doctrine, only eight of which declined to dispose of the claim on dismissal or summary judgment.

The case precedent therefore shows that even under the essential-facilities approach the court disdained in *Trinko*, the courts have been able to weed out the majority of cases and that potential liability will not necessarily be a broad deterrent to innovation. To be sure, even the majority of cases that ended with dismissal or summary judgment entailed costs for defendants and the courts, although those costs are presumably much less than those that would have resulted from mistaken findings of liability. But the overall number of essential-facilities cases, which I take as a proxy for the broader universe of refusal-to-deal cases, has been modest. As precedent develops, courts and plaintiffs gain increased guidance for the disposition of future cases. To the extent specific factual circumstances (like those of *Aspen*) can be identified in which refusal-to-deal liability may be warranted, those facts can become elements that constrain the rule-of-reason inquiry and limit the incidence of false positives in enforcement. In sum, the evidence from past experience does not on its face suggest such indiscriminate disposition by the courts or such a large number of cases that the deterrent and other costs of antitrust enforcement justify a presumptive preference for agency regulation over judicial disposition.

The basis on which the Court elevates one form of government intervention over the other is therefore opaque. One possible answer is that antitrust suits are more discretionary than regulation, and that while antitrust can adjust in the face of regulation, the reverse may not be true depending on the agency's obligations under the regulatory statute. This logic would provide a rationale for presuming against novel antitrust theories that might interfere with specific statutory provisions. It does not, however, provide a basis for more broadly limiting strong antitrust enforcement on matters within a regulatory agency's jurisdiction where Congress has specifically provided otherwise. The Court rightfully does not second-guess Congress' judgment about the benefits of regulation under the 1996 Act. Congress' inclusion of the antitrust savings clause suggests that Congress also determined the costs of antitrust enforcement to be worthwhile in telecommunications markets.[99] The Court should have deferred here as it has in the past where 'Congress itself expressed a willingness to bear the costs'.[100]

---

[98]   To do this update, I followed Robinson's method of searching all federal court cases in the LexisNexis database that expressly addressed 'essential facilities'. To avoid double counting, any district court case that was appealed was counted as an appellate case, and the district court category contained only cases for which there was no subsequent opinion on appeal. See *supra* note 96 for the reference to Robinson's method. Search records on file with author.

[99]   If anything, the fact that Congress has both preserved antitrust and seen fit to address competitive conduct through a specific regulatory statute suggests greater concern with the conduct at issue and hence greater willingness to bear any costs of antitrust enforcement than otherwise. See, e.g., Elhauge, *supra* note 47, at 37.

[100]   United States v. Winstar, 518 U.S. 839, 883 (1996) (deferring to costly regulation where 'Congress itself expressed a willingness to bear the costs').

B   Public versus Private Antitrust Actions

Both *Trinko* and *Credit Suisse* involved private antitrust suits rather than public enforcement actions by the Federal Trade Commission (FTC) or DOJ. The Supreme Court's decisions, however, affect public and private actions equally. The Court nowhere confines its holdings to private cases and US antitrust doctrine draws no distinction between public and private enforcement. This is unfortunate because the Court's animating concerns about costs are most salient in private suits, while the benefits of antitrust law as a complement and substitute for regulation are likely to be greatest through public enforcement. These differences arise because of differences in the incentives and capabilities of public and private antitrust plaintiffs.

Phrased broadly, the Court's concern is that antitrust is always costly and in the presence of regulation is likely to have little additional benefit for competition. Private plaintiffs have much less incentive to ensure that the net benefits of an antitrust case, even if modest, are positive. The payoff for a successful private plaintiff will be damages, an injunction that helps its competitive position, or both. Whether the case harms or helps consumers, the regulatory agency, or the defendant's other competitors does not factor into private incentives to seek antitrust relief. A public agency, on the other hand, does not collect revenue or otherwise directly benefit from a successful civil enforcement action. The government has no incentive to use antitrust law against a regulated firm unless doing so can yield net benefits on top of those the market already gets through regulation. The federal antitrust agencies therefore have more incentive than private plaintiffs do to assess the potential costs of an antitrust case, to identify the potential benefits that regulation will not provide, and to balance the two in the public interest.

The public antitrust authorities also have greater ability than private plaintiffs to assess the costs and benefits of antitrust enforcement and to avoid interfering with regulatory objectives. The FTC and DOJ can both investigate private conduct through a variety of tools, for example voluntary access letters, that don't require the costly discovery process of a trial and that can be focused narrowly on relevant conduct and information.[101] As needed, the agencies can move to more formal procedures like civil investigative demands (CIDs) to obtain the information needed to determine whether a suit is warranted.[102] These procedures are not costless, but they can be narrowly tailored and they occur in advance of litigation, unlike private discovery which occurs after litigation has been initiated and where plaintiffs have incentives to be much less discriminating in the information they demand from defendants.[103] Public antitrust agencies have greater ability and incentive to coordinate with relevant government regulatory agencies to avoid conflicts and unnecessary administrative costs.

---

[101]   FTC Practice and Procedure Manual 86. (American Bar Association, 2007).

[102]   *Id.*

[103]   See Steven F. Cherry and Gordon Pearson, *Why* Twombly *Does (and Should) Apply to all Private Antitrust Actions, Including Alleged Hard-Core Cartels,* The Antitrust Source 1, n.31 (December 2007) (distinguishing public enforcement from the 'extraordinary costs' of private civil litigation); J.-Peter Jost, *Disclosure of Information and Incentives for Care,* 15 Int'l Rev. L. and Econ. 65 (1995) ('if government officials act in the public interest, public administration is best suited to compel the disclosure of private information' through discovery).

As a result, public antitrust enforcement is much more likely than private litigation to avoid claims that will be prone to judicial errors, that will interfere with regulation, or that will fail to yield net benefits over regulation. Although the rationales of *Trinko* and *Credit Suisse* apply more to private suits than public enforcement, their precedent will have a preclusive effect on both.

C Open Questions

1 What kind of regulation triggers *Trinko*'s antitrust preclusion?

How powerful the impact of *Trinko* will be depends partly on how directly regulation must address the conduct at issue in order to bar an antitrust claim against that same conduct. On this point *Trinko* is ambiguous. At a minimum, the Court's ruling would bar novel claims when (1) they are beyond the scope of established duties under section 2 of the Sherman Act, *and* (2) the operative regulatory statute specifically addresses the very conduct underlying the claims. So interpreted, the case would not block novel antitrust claims against telecommunications carriers for conduct not expressly addressed in the 1996 Act. In Trinko's case, Verizon's alleged refusal to deal with AT&T was directly and specifically within the FCC's authority to regulate. In the 1996 Act Congress mandates the FCC to determine which network facilities incumbent telecommunications carriers must make available and which are not economically necessary for competition.[104] Trinko neither addressed any aspect of network unbundling ungoverned by the FCC nor explained why breach of the FCC's rules was independently grounds for antitrust liability.

Lower courts might read the case narrowly and require a close link between the antitrust claim and regulated conduct – perhaps as close a link as existed between the unilateral duty to deal Trinko sought to enforce and the duties to deal the 1996 Act imposes – before dismissing the antitrust claim. But in *Trinko* the Court provides both language and a rationale for a broader presumption against antitrust. The Court's emphasis on the costs of antitrust and the marginality of its benefits in a regulated industry could apply to any antitrust claim, not only one that is novel or that marks an expansion of settled doctrine. Moreover, the language of the decision gives broad effect to regulation that addresses economic competition. Thus, *Trinko* could reasonably be read to bar a court's consideration of an aggressive predation, tying, or other monopoly maintenance claim in the telecommunications industry even though the 1996 Act's competition provisions do not as specifically address those issues as they do refusals to deal. In such cases there seems much less reason than with Trinko's particular claim to presume a reduction in the marginal benefits of antitrust. But in light of *Credit Suisse*'s broad concern about likely errors in distinguishing different kinds of economic conduct, the current state of the law makes it likely that such related economic conduct will be beyond the reach of antitrust suits in regulated industries, even if prohibition of that conduct would not be inconsistent with the statutory scheme. *Trinko* is therefore ambiguous about the kind of connection between regulation and the conduct at the root of an antitrust claim that is required before courts should imply immunity from antitrust. The decision appears to provide

---

[104]   47 U.S.C. § 251(c).

some room for interpretation by lower courts that could lead the scope of immunity, while broader than before *Trinko*, to vary across the federal judicial circuits.

2   How actively must an agency regulate?

Trinko also leaves open the important question of what level of regulation is necessary to trigger the bar to novel antitrust claims. How pervasively or actively must the agency regulate for *Trinko* to apply? The decision itself is ambiguous. At one point the Court cites precedent that expressly refers to 'pervasive' regulation.[105] But at other points the Court refers merely to the existence of regulation or regulatory authority.[106] A fair reading of the decision shows the Court to aim its presumption against antitrust only when particular kinds of regulation apply. In the Court's words, 'One factor of particular importance is the existence of a regulatory structure designed to deter and remedy anticompetitive harm'.[107] Similarly, the opinion states that there must be something 'built into the regulatory scheme which performs the antitrust function'.[108] Unanswered, however, is whether the competition-focused regulation has to be actively enforced or whether its mere existence on the books is sufficient to forestall aggressive antitrust. This is a key question after *Trinko*. If a presumption against antitrust can apply absent active enforcement of a regulatory statute that ostensibly 'performs the antitrust function', then a little regulation could be a dangerous thing for competition enforcement in regulated industries.

III   ALTERNATIVE SOLUTIONS TO BALANCING ANTITRUST AND REGULATION

The more broadly *Trinko* precludes antitrust claims, the greater the gap in competition regulation is likely to be as industry structure evolves and the less inclined agencies will be to repeal costly rules. The situation is exacerbated in industries, like electric power, whose statute contains no antitrust savings clause and in which immunity could sweep especially broadly under *Credit Suisse.* There are a variety of ways that the unintended and harmful consequences of *Trinko* and *Credit Suisse* could be mitigated. The challenge is in overcoming the overbroad removal of antitrust from the regulatory balance while still preserving the beneficial aspects of those cases.

One possibility is that some lower federal courts will interpret *Trinko* and *Credit Suisse* narrowly. As mentioned in section I of this chapter, *Trinko* leaves open the questions of how closely regulation must address the conduct underlying an antitrust claim and how actively the regulatory supervision must be to trigger preclusion of an antitrust claim. The higher the standard lower courts apply, the fewer the antitrust claims that will be blocked. Similarly, lower courts could take a very narrow view of what constitutes 'expansion' of existing antitrust law or of what claims are likely to confuse district courts, and reduce the scope of implied immunity in that way. Such decisions would lead to less immunity from

---

[105]   *Trinko*, 540 U.S. at 411 (quoting United States v. Citizens & Southern Nat. Bank, 422 U.S. 86 (1975)).

[106]   *Id.* at 412.

[107]   *Id.*

[108]   *Id.* (quoting Silver v. New York Stock Exchange, 373 U.S. 341, 358 (1963)).

antitrust for regulated firms in those jurisdictions. If enough diversity developed among the federal courts, the Supreme Court might at some point revisit and refine their balance between antitrust and regulation.

Another possibility would be for Congress (or the Supreme Court in a future case) to establish clearer standards for antitrust immunity and to assign the case-by-case immunity determination to district courts. This is the position the Solicitor General's office took in *Credit Suisse*, essentially asking the court to clarify its standard of incompatibility between antitrust and regulation and to let district courts decide which cases met that standard.[109] As discussed, the Court believed the line-drawing problem to be too difficult for courts and decided to err in favor of precluding valid claims rather than allowing claims that should have been barred by the regulation. From a judicial economy and consistency perspective, the Solicitor General's solution is costlier than the Court's immunity approach, but it also preserves the benefits of antitrust, avoids costs of underenforcement, and would have benefits as markets change and courts could respond accordingly to claims of anticompetitive behavior. The Supreme Court's recent ruling in *Twombly*,[110] holding that plaintiffs must plead antitrust claims with heightened specificity or face dismissal, will likely mitigate the kinds of line-drawing hazards for regulated industries that the Court indentifies in *Credit Suisse* and will reduce the likelihood of false positives of concern to the Court in *Trinko*.[111]

Alternatively, Congress could compensate for the gap that *Trinko* and *Credit Suisse* create by exempting the FTC and DOJ from those rulings, thereby at least preserving more flexible public antitrust enforcement in regulated industries. Congress could also reduce the potential consequences of the Court's rulings by expressly giving regulatory agencies antitrust-like authority to make case-by-case determinations about allegedly anticompetitive conduct even in the absence of a formal rule-making proceeding. Such an approach is not without cost, as agencies will likely have to undertake an increased amount of adjudication. Increasing the ability of regulatory agencies to intervene ex post to resolve competition concerns on a case-by-case basis, rather than ex ante through a broadly applicable rule, could nonetheless help to bridge the antitrust gap that arises as regulated industries shift to more competitive structures and conventional regulation becomes less beneficial and more costly.

The Supreme Court's trend in adopting blunt forms of claim preclusion in regulated industries throws out good cases along with the bad, and private cases along with those brought by public enforcement agencies, and makes no provision for the comparative advantages of antitrust and regulation in different settings. Whether through the above or some other approaches, the gap in competition enforcement and reduction in regulatory flexibility the Court has created warrants policy attention. Courts, Congress, and the

---

[109] *Credit Suisse*, 551 U.S. at 284–5.

[110] Bell Atlantic v. Twombly, 127 S. Ct. 1955 (2007).

[111] While more stringent pleading standards might help, they will also potentially defeat meritorious cases in which the facts necessary for heightened pleading are beyond the plaintiff's reach. Such an approach risks converting motions to dismiss into summary judgment proceedings before the plaintiff has even had a chance for discovery. See Richard Epstein, *Bell Atlantic v. Twombly: How Motions to Dismiss Become (Disguised) Summary Judgments*, available at http://papers.ssrn.com/sol3/papers.cfm?abstract_id=1126359# (2008).

antitrust agencies should work to restore the balance between antitrust and regulation, while mitigating the kinds of enforcement costs that have motivated the Supreme Court to reconfigure that relationship so strongly in favor of regulation.

IV   CONCLUSION

As the law stands today, antitrust will likely play a diminished role in regulated industries compared to the important role it played before 2004. The Supreme Court's decisions in *Trinko* and *Credit Suisse* read the implicit immunizing effect of regulation broadly and read express savings clauses narrowly. This is a change from the past, in which the Court disfavored immunity and antitrust often worked as a constructive complement and addition to regulation in the absence of any express statutory savings provision. This change by the Court is particularly striking given that Congress has gone in precisely the opposite direction, adding an antitrust savings clause to the Communications Act through the 1996 amendments and expressly disclaiming immunity in the Securities Act.

The Court's rationale for its recent decisions hinges on its own view of the costs of antitrust, particularly the costs of false positives in enforcement. Concern for false positives in antitrust cases is warranted, but it can be taken too far. Neither the evidence from previous antitrust actions in regulated industries nor the antitrust case law more generally provides a basis for such disproportionate avoidance of false positives compared to false negatives or for the Court's implicit presumption that regulation will be more efficient than antitrust enforcement. As this chapter has argued, the latter presumption may not be empirically grounded. In several important sectors like telecommunications and energy, the traditional monopoly structure is giving way to competition in the face of technological change and shifting consumer demand. Antitrust law can play a supporting role that allows regulators to retreat from increasingly inefficient and costly forms of competitive oversight in favor of more targeted antitrust enforcement. *Trinko* and *Credit Suisse* weaken that important relationship between antitrust and regulation. Until the balance is restored, regulators could face difficult choices between overregulation and underregulation, with consequences potentially far more costly than those that would have arisen from errors in antitrust enforcement in the regulated markets at issue.

13 The intersection of patent and antitrust law
Christopher Jon Sprigman*

INTRODUCTION

Antitrust law's treatment of potentially anticompetitive business conduct involving patents has oscillated between aggressive intervention and acceptance bordering on complacency. Pre-Chicago antitrust viewed patents as monopolies, and the exercise of patent rights as likely to raise antitrust concerns. This view led antitrust courts to construe the scope of patents narrowly, and to intervene to police licensing terms, price restraints, and other business conduct of patentees that might harm competition.[1] It also led the federal antitrust agencies toward close policing of patent licenses.[2]

Following its Chicago reformulation, antitrust has slowly moved away from its former hostility. Some of this movement reflects a reappraisal of the respective roles that antitrust and intellectual property (IP) play in consumer and social welfare. By the advent of the agencies' 1995 Antitrust Guidelines for the Licensing of Intellectual Property,[3] the prevailing view had shifted markedly away from the presumed antagonism that characterized the patent–antitrust interface pre-Chicago. The IP Guidelines denied, at least implicitly, any foundational incompatibility, stating instead that '[t]he intellectual property laws and the antitrust laws share the common purpose of promoting innovation and enhancing consumer welfare'.[4] Based in part on this shift in background presumptions, the IP Guidelines asserted that IP licensing was broadly procompetitive, and that the rule of reason would be applied in the antitrust analysis of licensing restraints.

---

*   The author wishes to thank Einer Elhauge for comments on a previous draft.

[1]   See, e.g., Sears, Roebuck & Co. v. Stiffel Co., 376 U.S. 225, 230 (1964) ('Once the patent issues, it is strictly construed, it cannot be used to secure any monopoly beyond that contained in the patent, the patentee's control over the product when it leaves his hands is sharply limited, and the patent monopoly may not be used in disregard of the antitrust laws') (internal citations omitted); United States v. Masonite Corp., 316 U.S. 265 (1942) (invalidating price restraints imposed by a patent owner on its licensees); United States v. Line Material, 333 U.S. 287 (1948) (same); Morton Salt Co. v. G.S. Suppiger Co., 314 U.S. 488 (1942) (condemning use of patent in tying arrangement).

[2]   See Bruce B. Wilson, *Patent and Know-How License Agreements: Field of Use, Territorial, Price and Quantity Restrictions*, in ANTITRUST PRIMER: PATENTS, FRANCHISING, TREBLE DAMAGE SUITS 11, 12–14 (1970) (setting out antitrust agencies' 'Nine No-Nos' of intellectual property licensing).

[3]   US Dep't of Justice and Federal Trade Comm'n, Antitrust Guidelines for the Licensing of Intellectual Property (1995) (hereinafter 'IP Guidelines'), reprinted in 4 Trade Reg. Rep. (CCH) para. 13,132, available at www.usdoj.gov/atr/public/guidelines/ipguide.htm.

[4]   IP Guidelines § 1.0. See also Atari Games Corp. v. Nintendo of America, Inc., 897 F.2d 1572, 1576 (Fed. Cir. 1990) ('the aims and objectives of patent and antitrust laws may seem, at first glance, wholly at odds. However, the two bodies of law are complementary, as both are aimed at encouraging innovation, industry, and competition').

Influenced, undoubtedly, by these deep ideological shifts, the Supreme Court and the federal Circuit Courts are now well forward toward dismantling the structural elements of the earlier hostility.

For example, in its 2006 decision in *Illinois Tool Works, Inc. v. Independent Ink, Inc.*,[5] the Supreme Court ruled that in a tying case the existence of a patent on the alleged tying product was insufficient, absent some other evidence that the defendant had power over price, to establish the market power predicate for tying liability. In so ruling the Court overturned its prior rule, in place since the 1947 decision in *International Salt Co. v. United States*,[6] presuming that a defendant enjoyed market power in a patented tying product.

Similarly, the Federal Circuit in *CSU v. Xerox*[7] ruled that patent owners have a presumptive right to refuse to sell or license products incorporating the patented technology without fear of antitrust liability for unlawful refusal to deal. In so doing, the Xerox court created a special category within the antitrust law wherein refusals to deal in intellectual property are treated more leniently than refusals involving other forms of property.

The continuing course of antitrust's gradual liberalization respecting IP rights raises important questions. Has liberalization gone far enough? Has it gone too far? Unfortunately, we ask these questions against the backdrop of our continuing ignorance regarding the conditions conducive to innovation. Is innovation best encouraged by the spur of competition? Or by the shelter from competition that IP rights sometimes provide? This chapter will examine the most important recent and recurring issues at the intersection of antitrust and patent law, with the goal of assessing whether the development of the law is consistent with underlying economic principles.

I   ANTITRUST, INTELLECTUAL PROPERTY, AND POTENTIALLY CONFLICTING CONSUMER WELFARE STRATEGIES

The antitrust laws aim to safeguard consumer welfare by preserving market competition – or, more precisely, by ensuring that markets remain contestable even where, through superior 'skill, foresight and industry'[8] (and not via anticompetitive conduct), firms exercise significant market power or even monopoly power. In its focus on maintaining rivalry (or at least the prospect of rivalry) in the provision of products and services, antitrust functions as an integral part of a free-market economy, which is based on the expectation that robust competition will benefit consumers and social welfare via lower prices, better-quality products and services, and increased innovation.

Intellectual property law also has a consumer welfare focus, but one that is distinct from antitrust's. IP proceeds (or, more precisely, patent, copyright, and trade secret law proceed) from the expectation that for certain goods, namely, scientific and technical inventions, artistic and literary works, and certain forms of competitively-sensitive

---

[5]   547 U.S. 28 (2006).
[6]   332 U.S. 392 (1947).
[7]   203 F.3d 1322 (Fed. Cir. 2000).
[8]   United States v. Grinnell Corp., 384 U.S. 563, 570–71 (1966).

business information, competition from copyists will remove incentives to invest in the continuing creation of these goods. IP's strategy is to preempt this potential market failure by limiting competition from copyists.

Toward this end, patent creates limited-term exclusive rights to make, use, or sell certain useful, novel, and nonobvious scientific and technical inventions.[9] Copyright establishes a set of more durable but narrower exclusive rights to reproduce, adapt, distribute, or publicly perform or display original artistic and literary works.[10] Trade secret law, which is governed by state rather than federal statutes and judicial decisions, affords potentially perpetual protection against unauthorized disclosure for certain forms of confidential business information (such as formulas, processes, designs, or compilations of information) which are not generally known or reasonably ascertainable, and by which a business can obtain an economic advantage over competitors or customers.[11] (The recipe for Coca-Cola is an example of a famous and long-standing trade secret.)

Thus, patent, copyright, and trade secret are all legal tools aimed at a similar goal: the preservation of adequate incentives to invest in the creation of new inventions and creative works via suppression of the competition that copyists would otherwise provide.[12]

Unlike patent, copyright, and trade secret, trademark is not an inducement scheme. Trademark is, however, also premised on a concern related to competition. Trademark aims to facilitate competition by protecting commercial marks, i.e., distinctive signs or indicators (a famous example would be the Nike 'swoop') that businesses use to identify themselves as the source of their products or services,[13] against unauthorized use by

---

[9]   35 U.S.C. §§ 101, 102, 103, 154(a) (2004).

[10]   17 U.S.C. §§ 102, 106 (2004).

[11]   See Uniform Trade Secrets Act (1985), § 1(4) (defining 'trade secret').

[12]   The incentives theory may be sound as a general matter, but that does not mean that it applies equally to every form of creativity. Recent scholarship has demonstrated that in areas as diverse as academic research, creative cuisine, stand-up comedy, and production of open source software, maintenance of incentives to create either does not depend on or appears frequently to ignore the formal intellectual property law. See, e.g., Yochai Benkler, *Coase's Penguin, or, Linux and the Nature of the Firm,* 112 YALE L.J. 369 (2002) (detailing collaborative production in open source software); Katherine J. Strandburg, *Sharing Research Tools and Materials: Homo Scientificus and User Innovator Community Norms* (unpublished manuscript, 23 May 2008), available at http://ssrn.com/abstract=1136606) (examining social norms governing the sharing of academic science research); Emmanulle Fauchart and Eric Von Hippel, *Norms-Based Intellectual Property Systems: The Case of French Chefs* (Mass. Inst. of Tech. Sloan Sch. of Mgmt MIT Sloan Working Paper 4576-06, 2006), available at http://ssrn.com/abstract=881781 (describing the informal norms system discouraging appropriation without attribution among French haute cuisine chefs); Christopher J. Buccafusco, *On the Legal Consequences of Sauces: Should Thomas Keller's Recipes be Per Se Copyrightable?,* 2524 CARDOZO ARTS AND ENT. L.J. 1121 (2007) (examining anti-appropriation norms among elite chefs); Dotan Oliar and Christopher Sprigman, *There's No Free Laugh (Anymore): The Emergence of Intellectual Property Norms and the Transformation of Stand-Up Comedy,* 94 VIRGINIA L. REV. 1787 (2008) (examining anti-appropriation norms and enforcement mechanisms among stand-up comedians). Nor is the phenomenon of non-IP incentives confined to the economic margins. For an example of a major industry in which widespread copying and derivative reworking does not appear to suppress innovation incentives, see Kal Raustiala and Christopher Sprigman, *The Piracy Paradox: Innovation and Intellectual Property in Fashion Design,* 92 VA. L. REV. 1687 (2006) (examining the impact of piracy on the fashion industry).

[13]   15 U.S.C. § 1127 (defining 'trademark' and 'service mark').

others in a manner that would confuse consumers regarding the source of the product, or 'dilute' the mark by diminishing its ability to indicate source.[14] By protecting these marks, trademark law protects the associations that consumers make between the marks and product attributes, such as reputation, quality, and value, that form the basis for competition on the merits.

In different ways, then, all of the branches of IP law described above are, like the antitrust law, concerned with competition, innovation, and consumer welfare. But the concerns are congruent only at the most general level.

Antitrust's prime directive is the preservation of competition in both the short and long run. Viewed through antitrust's lens, competition is benign. It disciplines price and quality, drives incentives to innovate, and undergirds consumer welfare. Accordingly, antitrust is aimed at maintaining competition to ensure both static efficiency (i.e., lower prices and higher product quality driven by competition in the short term) and dynamic efficiency (i.e., higher rates of competition-driven innovation over time).

IP law, by contrast, proceeds from a darker view of competition: the law is founded on the view that for certain goods, in particular, for nonrivalrous, nonexcludible goods like artistic and literary expression (copyright) and scientific and technical inventions (patent and trade secret), unrestrained competition will often suppress incentives to innovate, thereby reducing long-term consumer welfare by an amount far greater than any immediate gain that more vigorous competition might provide. The protections granted by patent, copyright, and trade secret may impair static efficiency; these forms of IP limit competition from copyists that (at least in a notional world where all other variables are held constant[15]) would otherwise exist.

Given their fundamentally incompatible baseline assumptions regarding the consequences of competition for innovation, it makes little sense to insist, as some have done, that there is no essential conflict between IP and the antitrust laws.

The conflict is most pronounced in the case of patent, which grants the most powerful set of property rights of any form of IP.[16] A patent gives the inventor of any 'new and useful process, machine, manufacture, or composition of matter', any 'distinct and new variety of plant', or any 'new, original and ornamental design for an article of manufacture' the exclusive right to make, use, or sell the invention and its close equivalents (or to authorize others to do so) throughout the United States.[17] The term of US patents is typically 20 years from the date the patent application is filed.[18]

A strong patent (e.g., one claiming a particular molecule with important therapeutic effect) may create very substantial market power or, in the case of a true 'blocking patent',

---

[14]   See 15 U.S.C. 1125(a) (confusion), 1125(c) (dilution).

[15]   In some instances, of course, the absence of patent protection would delay or perhaps even foreclose the innovation, and so leave the public with no benefit (at least for the time required for the invention to be produced under competitive conditions) from either inventors or copyists.

[16]   Article I, Section 8, Clause 8 of the US Constitution grants Congress the power to create both patents and copyrights. That clause provides that 'The Congress shall have Power . . . [t]o promote the Progress of Science and useful Arts, by securing for limited Times to Authors and Inventors the exclusive right to their respective Writings and Discoveries'. US Const., Art. I, § 8, cl. 8.

[17]   See 35 U.S.C. §§ 101, 154, 161, 171.

[18]   *Id.* at § 154(a)(2).

even a monopoly. It is nonetheless true that most patents create no market power (e.g., a patent on an outmoded or commercially non-viable technology, or one for which it is easy to design a functional substitute without impinging on the patent, will not create any significant market power).[19]

Compared with patent, copyright is in general less likely to harm competition. Importantly, the copyright law grants narrower legal rights. Copyright protects creative expression but not the ideas underlying the protected expression, and therefore the public are left free to use the ideas conveyed by any particular creative work to make new creative expression of their own.[20] Because of the relative narrowness of the legal right, copyrights create significant market power far less frequently than patents do. Of course, less frequently does not mean never, and in some cases (e.g., copyrights protecting the source and object code describing software interfaces[21]) copyright might occasionally grant very significant market power.

Much the same is true of trade secret. Unlike patent, trade secret does not grant broad property rights against all use. Rather, trade secret prohibits unauthorized disclosure of confidential and competitively-sensitive business information, but does not prohibit mimicry, independent discovery, or reverse engineering of the protected information.[22] As a result, trade secrets are less likely to grant the kind of broad market power that patents sometimes create.

Finally, trademarks often convey some market power, but the property rights associated with trademark are in most instances even less preclusive than those granted by

---

[19]   See Illinois Tool Works, Inc. v. Independent Ink, Inc., 126 S. Ct. 1281 (2006) (reversing previous rule holding that in tying cases possession of patent on tying product creates presumption of market power). There is also another way in which IP can impair both static and dynamic efficiency. In the case of patent, Carl Shapiro has argued that in industries such as semiconductors, biotechnology, and computer software, the patent law has created numerous and overlapping property claims (which Shapiro labels 'patent thickets') that hinder innovation and slow the commercialization of new technologies, first by requiring innovators to seek licenses from a large number of rights-holders, and second (and relatedly) by creating opportunities for holdup. Carl Shapiro, *Navigating the Patent Thicket: Cross-Licenses, Patent Pools, and Standard Setting*, in 1 INNOVATION POLICY AND THE ECONOMY 119, 120 (Adam Jaffe *et al.* eds, 2001). Michael Heller and Rebecca Eisenberg identify some of the same difficulties attending a patent 'anticommons' in biomedical research, in which the wide distribution of property rights among many patent holders creates significant transaction costs on progressive innovation. Michael A. Heller and Rebecca Eisenberg, *Can Patents Deter Innovation? The Anticommons in Biomedical Research*, 280 SCIENCE 5364 (May 1998).

[20]   17 U.S.C. § 102(b) (setting out distinction between copyrightable expression and uncopyrightable ideas, principles, processes, methods of operation, etc.). See generally R. Polk Wagner, *Information Wants to be Free: Intellectual Property and the Mythologies of Control*, 103 COLUM. L. REV. 995 (2003).

[21]   The copyrightability of software interfaces has been thrown into doubt following the decisions of the Second and Ninth Circuits in Computer Associates v. Altai, 982 F.2d 693 (2d Cir. 1992) and Sega Enterprises, Ltd. v. Accolade, Inc., 977 F.2d 1510 (9th Cir. 1992). For a helpful account of the rise and subsequent decline of software copyright, see Pamela Samuelson, *The Strange Odyssey of Software Interfaces and Intellectual Property Law* (UC Berkeley Public Law Research Paper No. 1323818, 12 December 2008), available at http://ssrn.com/abstract=1323818.

[22]   See Katarzyna A. Czapracka, *Antitrust and Trade Secrets: The U.S. and the EU Approach*, 24 SANTA CLARA COMPUTER AND HIGH TECH L.J. 207, 212 (2008).

copyright or trade secret: use of a protected mark is proscribed only if the effect is to confuse consumers regarding the source of products, or to damage the source-indicating value of the mark. Virtually all trademarks lack the 'blocking' nature of a strong patent and, as in the case of copyright, the law has developed some internal limitations that mitigate potential antitrust concerns, e.g., the doctrine of nominative fair use, which allows wide use of protected marks in comparative advertising.[23]

For the reasons noted briefly above, antitrust issues involving copyrights, trade secrets, and trademarks arise far less frequently than those involving patent, and to the extent that antitrust issues arise in IP cases not involving patents, the Supreme Court has suggested that antitrust law regulates the use of all forms of IP similarly.[24] Accordingly, this chapter focuses on the intersection of antitrust and patent; cases involving copyright, trademark, and trade secret are not separately treated here.

II 'UNILATERAL' REFUSALS TO LICENSE PATENTS

The issue of antitrust liability for unilateral refusal to license patents reflects most directly the current conception of the patent right as a powerful and socially beneficial 'right to exclude' that commands deference from the antitrust law. Most courts considering the issue have held that a simple unilateral refusal to license a patent cannot be the basis for antitrust liability.

An early and extreme example of this view is the Supreme Court's 1908 opinion in *Continental Paper Bag Co. v. Eastern Paper Bag Co.*,[25] where the Court held that a firm holding patents on an improved machine was under no obligation either to build the patented machines or to license others to do so:

> As to the suggestion that competitors were excluded from the use of the new patent, we answer that such exclusion may be said to have been of the very essence of the right conferred by the patent, as it is the privilege of any owner of property to use or not use it, without question of motive.[26]

The meaning of this passage from *Continental Paper Bag* is not entirely clear: does a property owner's privilege to 'use or not use' equate to an absolute privilege to deal or not, as he likes, without antitrust consequence? That is one possible reading, but it would be, to modern eyes, an overstatement: there is a narrow but well-established area of anti-

---

[23] See 15 U.S.C. § 1115(b)(4) (Lanham Act fair use provision); KP Permanent Make-Up, Inc. v. Lasting Impression I, Inc., 543 U.S. 111 (2004) (holding that fair use defense applies even where evidence shows consumer confusion).

[24] See United States v. Paramount Pictures, 334 U.S. 131, 144 (1948) (antitrust violation found in motion picture studio's requirement that theatres maintain minimum admission prices, and violation not excused by studio's ownership of copyright in subject films: 'a copyright may no more be used than a patent to deter competition between rivals in the exploitation of their licenses'). The Department of Justice and the Federal Trade Commission have stated explicitly that they will apply equivalent antitrust principles to patents, copyrights, and trade secrets. See IP Guidelines, *supra* note 3, § 1.

[25] 210 U.S. 405 (1908).

[26] *Id.* at 429.

trust liability for refusals to deal which harm competition, so it cannot be true that it 'is the privilege of any owner of property to use or not use it, without question of motive'.

The salient question is whether a narrower immunity from antitrust liability can be defended for refusal to license a *patent*. Some commentators have suggested that because the refusal does nothing more than implement the right to exclude others from the subject matter within the scope of the patent grant, antitrust liability is incompatible with the patent grant.[27] This view animated the Federal Circuit's holding in *In re Indep. Serv. Orgs. Antitrust Litig. v. Xerox Corp.*,[28] a case considering Xerox's potential antitrust liability for its refusal to distribute parts for its copiers to independent copier repair organizations. In that case, the Federal Circuit held that, at least where foreclosure of rivals 'is not illegally extended beyond the statutory patent grant', refusal to deal in IP does not violate the antitrust laws except in three narrow circumstances:

> In the absence of any indication of illegal tying, fraud . . ., or sham litigation, the patent holder may enforce the statutory right to exclude others from making, using, or selling the claimed invention free from liability under [section 2].

The Federal Circuit's opinion in *Xerox* represents a tightening of the standards for refusal to deal in patents beyond the already narrow grounds for liability for refusal to deal in other forms of property. Earlier cases had suggested that patent-based refusals to deal would be judged according to the same standards applied generally. For example, the Ninth Circuit, in a case involving similar allegations against rival copier maker Kodak, reached a conclusion less constraining than the Federal Circuit's, holding in *Image Technical Servs., Inc. v. Eastman Kodak Co.*[29] that although a firm's desire to exclude others from the use of its IP is a presumptively valid business justification for a refusal to deal, that presumption was rebuttable if an antitrust plaintiff demonstrated that the assertion of IP rights was pretextual.[30] The First Circuit reached a conclusion similar to the Ninth's, albeit in a case involving a unilateral refusal to license a copyrighted work, in *Data General Corp. v. Grumman Systems Support Corp.*[31]

Much of the debate over the antitrust consequences of unilateral refusal to license patents has conceptualized these cases as posing a theological question about the nature of the patent right: i.e., whether the patent 'right to exclude' conveys an unqualified right not to deal that cannot be limited by the antitrust law. The answer to that question is rather obviously no. Patent conveys the same right to exclude as do other forms of property law – the law of trespass, for example. And refusals to deal in non-IP forms of

---

[27]   See, e.g., Jonathan Gleklen, *Antitrust Liability for Unilateral Refusals to License Intellectual Property: Xerox and its Critics* (2001), available at www.ftc.gov/opp/intellect/020501gleklen.pdf.

[28]   203 F.3d 1322 (Fed. Cir. 2000).

[29]   125 F.3d 1195 (9th Cir. 1997).

[30]   The Ninth Circuit's focus on demonstrating pretext via evidence of a subjective intent to monopolize has been subject to severe criticism, but the commentators are mostly attacking a strawman. The Ninth Circuit's holding reflected the fact that Kodak offered its patent as justification for its refusal to license only years into the litigation, thus fairly raising the question whether the asserted justification was merely pretext to cover an intent to monopolize. In any event, because such evidence will ordinarily not be available, the scope of potential antitrust liability for unilateral refusal to license IP is quite narrow even under the *Kodak* standard.

[31]   36 F.3d 1147 (1st Cir. 1994).

property are subject to antitrust scrutiny, and, under narrow circumstances, have been held unlawful.[32]

There is no sense in which patent's right to exclude is any more categorical than the right to exclude that attends possession of real or personal property. Indeed, the structure of patent law's remedies provisions make that point clear. The patent law features substantive rights that are structured as strong property rules but also remedies provisions that are oriented more directly at compensation, rather than deterrence. In particular, US patent law limits monetary damages to a reasonable royalty.[33] The award may be trebled for willful infringement,[34] but courts do this sparingly.[35] Similarly, awards of attorneys' fees are limited to 'exceptional cases' and are, relative to the rate at which they are awarded in copyright infringement lawsuits, rarely ordered.[36]

US patent law also provides for preliminary and permanent injunctions,[37] but since the Supreme Court's opinion in *eBay Inc. v. MercExchange, L.L.C.*,[38] it has been clear that injunctions are not available as a matter of course, but rather the need for relief beyond monetary compensation must be established by the plaintiff according to traditional rules of equity.[39]

In short, patent's remedies regime does not align with the theological argument that the patent law provides an 'unqualified' or 'categorical' property right. Indeed, patent law provides remedies that, at least in cases where damages are limited to those required to compensate and equitable relief is held inappropriate, are effectively equivalent to a liability rule, i.e., an arrangement where a would-be user of the patented technology is free to take, and held liable only to pay compensation.

Whether the current remedies regime in US patent law is good innovation policy is not a relevant question here, and, in any event, if Congress is dissatisfied with the Court's understanding of the meaning of patent's 'right to exclude' it can displace it by amending the patent statute to make deterrent or punitive damages more widely available, or to provide for automatic or at least presumptively available injunctions following a

---

[32]   See Verizon Communications v. Law Offices of Curtis V. Trinko, L.L.P., 540 U.S. 398 (2004) (summarizing standards governing antitrust liability for refusal to deal).

[33]   See 35 U.S.C. § 284 ('Upon finding for the claimant the court shall award the claimant damages adequate to compensate for the infringement, but in no event less than a reasonable royalty for the use made of the invention by the infringer, together with interest and costs as fixed by the court').

[34]   *Id.*

[35]   The Patent Act provides that courts have discretion to impose damages up to three times the amount of the infringement, see 35 U.S.C. § 284, but the courts have long held that an award of enhanced damages requires a showing that the defendant's infringement was willful. Jurgens v. CBK, Ltd., 80 F.3d 1566, 1570 (Fed. Cir. 1996) (holding that bad faith infringement, which is a type of willful infringement, is required for enhanced damages). Recently, the Federal Circuit (the federal appellate court that has the principal role in judicial interpretation of the Patent Act) made clear that a finding of willfulness required evidence that the defendant's infringing conduct was objectively reckless. In re Seagate Technology, L.L.C., 497 F.3d 1360 (Fed. Cir. 2007).

[36]   With respect to attorneys' fees, the Patent Act makes clear that they may be awarded only in 'exceptional cases'. 35 U.S.C. § 285.

[37]   See 35 U.S.C. § 283.

[38]   547 U.S. 388 (2006).

[39]   See *id.* at 390.

judgment of infringement. In any event, patent law's remedies regime makes clear that the 'right to exclude' granted by patent is not exceptional; the patent right, like property rights generally, is not inviolable and must be balanced with other interests. One such interest is the market competition that antitrust law is charged with protecting.

For the same reasons, courts that distinguish (as the Federal Circuit did in *Xerox*) between foreclosure 'within' versus 'beyond' the scope of the patent, and which suggest that the former is largely immunized from antitrust scrutiny, are relying on an empty distinction – or, more precisely, one that does not do the work they believe it should do. If the property rights granted by patent are not categorically immune from antitrust scrutiny, then even foreclosure 'within' the scope of the patent, such as via a flat refusal to license, should be actionable if it meets one of the general standards for refusal to deal liability (such as if, for example, the refusal to license can be explained only as a strategy whereby the patent holder sacrifices current profits in exchange for exclusion and the promise of eventual recoupment). Foreclosure 'inside' the scope of the patent would be analogous, in other words, to anticompetitive conduct 'inside' any other sort of property right (such as, for example, an incumbent power company's refusal to allow rival electricity generators' power to be 'wheeled' over its electricity lines to former municipal customers who choose to purchase power from the rivals).[40]

There is nonetheless a sound reason to vary the antitrust treatment of patent conduct 'inside' versus 'outside' the scope of the claims of a particular patent. Conduct that achieves foreclosure 'outside' the patent grant (e.g., a patentee's demand that prospective licensees refrain from competing with it in the development of technologies not covered by the claims of the patentee's patent) may increase the degree of antitrust scrutiny that is due relative to conduct that is 'within' the scope of the patent. There is no presumption, rebuttable or otherwise, of legitimacy attaching to business conduct that forecloses outside the scope of the property right granted by the patent. But the increase in antitrust scrutiny is not from a baseline of zero; it is, rather, a widening of the narrow but nonetheless real grounds for liability that attach to refusals to deal in any sort of property.

If this is true, and if the ordinary principles of refusal to deal liability apply to refusals to deal based in patent rights, then why all the debate over the antitrust consequences of refusals to license patents? To some degree, the insistence by some that refusals to license patents are immune from antitrust proceeds from an ideology, widespread for some time now among the public at large, that idealizes patents, and other forms of IP-like copyrights, as indispensible engines of innovation. For those who work from this presumption, antitrust scrutiny of refusal to license patents interferes with the patentee's ability freely to exploit his patent rights – and this freedom is key to innovation.

That is certainly a coherent view, but to many of those who work close to the ground in the world of IP, however, the picture appears much more equivocal. As has been earlier stated, the patent law itself is not structured in a way that suggests that the exercise of patent rights must be free of, or even especially resistant to, antitrust limitations. But the critique of the 'IP supremacist' position goes deeper. Strong and enforceable IP rights may be, in some cases, a necessary precondition of innovation. The paradigm example is the pharmaceutical industry, where the exclusive rights granted by patents

---

40   See *Otter Tail Power Co. v. United States*, 410 U.S. 366 (1973).

are an important element in incentivizing firms to devote huge amounts of their capital to the development and testing of new drugs. But in other innovative industries, the case for patent is much weaker. In the enormous and highly innovative software market, for example, patents play only a minor role. The concern, in industries like software where patents are not a sine qua non, is that the patent right will function not chiefly as a driver of innovation, but as protection for incumbent firms. Patents can be used to deter entry, raise rivals' costs, and slow or even freeze innovation, at least for a time.

The general point is that while the patent system serves a socially useful function overall, patents are neither as necessary to many forms of innovation as the IP suprema-cist position suggests, nor are they in any instance wholly benign. There are particular uses of patents that can harm social welfare. Antitrust cannot police all of these, but it should be available to preempt uses that can be shown to cause harm through suppression of competition that significantly outweighs any procompetitive benefits. In its most basic justification, antitrust's narrow intervention into the patent system is entirely consistent with the case for its limited superintendence of property rights generally.

Relatedly, it is worth noting that some measure of the unease attending antitrust limits on the exercise of the patent right stems not from any particular affinity for patent, but from a general dissatisfaction with the antitrust standards determining liability for refus-als to deal. Those whose insistence on antitrust immunity for refusal to license patents stems from their general taste for refusal to deal liability are, in effect, attempting to roll back the general doctrine, or at least prevent its expansion. A full discussion of the various standards that have been proposed is beyond the scope of this chapter.[41] It is true that courts and commentators have articulated differing standards for refusal to deal liability, and work remains to define a standard that will deter anticompetitive conduct across a range of monopolization cases, while preventing deterrence of too much procom-petitive conduct. It is nonetheless common cause that the standards under which antitrust liability may be imposed for refusals to deal in any sort of property are and should be narrow. It is also widely acknowledged that various forms of monopolization, including refusals to deal, threaten significant social harm.

A workable antitrust standard need not sort anticompetitive from procompetitive conduct perfectly. It must do so reliably enough that, over the run of cases, more social welfare is realized from anticompetitive conduct terminated or deterred than from pro-competitive conduct preempted or chilled. That point is a general one: there are many instances, inside and outside of antitrust, in which the law steps in to preempt social harm even where it lacks a precise understanding of when and how it should do so. For this reason, and given the narrowness of the refusal to deal standards that have been proposed, the prospect of continuing uncertainty over the proper standard of liability, although it does counsel caution, does not present a strong case to immunize refusals to deal, either in the patent context or generally.

In any event, so much of the discussion around the 'unilateral exclusion' opinions has been taken up with parsing the meaning of patent's 'right to exclude' that a far more inter-esting question has passed largely unnoticed. Both the *Kodak* and *Xerox* cases involved

---

[41]   For a comprehensive recent analysis of the proper standard for monopolization liability, see Einer Elhauge, *Defining Better Monopolization Standards*, 56 STANFORD L. REV. 253 (2003).

copier firms cutting off independent copier repair firms, aka independent service organizations (ISOs), from access to a range of copier parts. The question is a practical one and can be phrased very simply: why would firms like Xerox and Kodak want to cut off ISOs' access to replacement parts in the first place? Is there a reason to do so unrelated to the firms' desire to limit competition?

There are at least two explanations for the cut-off that suggest a pernicious motivation. First, Einer Elhauge has pointed out that the cut-off, which results in a tie between parts and service, could increase the copier firm's rent extraction in the short run; namely, it might increase tying market power in parts by raising prices for service, which is likely to function as a partial substitute for parts (if copiers serviced regularly break down less often). Or, it could increase, in at least two ways, the copier firm's ability to price discriminate. First, if the amount of service consumed by a customer meters that customer's valuation of copier parts, then the copier firm is able to extract surplus from high-valuing customers via higher prices for service. Second, the tie could facilitate price discrimination between self-servicing and service-purchasing customers: if service-purchasing customers are less sophisticated and therefore willing to pay more, the copier firm can extract surplus from this group via higher prices for service.[42]

The tie actuated by the refusal to deal also creates long-run opportunities for rent extraction. To see this, it is necessary to step back and consider the market structure pre- and post-tie. Kodak and Xerox are operating at least three related but not coterminous businesses. First, they sell copiers. Second, they sell replacement parts: before the cut-off, to both ISOs and end-users; after the cut-off, only to end-users. Third, they sell copier service. Before the cut-off, they competed with both customer self-service and ISOs; after the cut-off they competed with only the former.

The large copier firms sell copiers in a product market distinct from the markets for parts and service, both of which are in fact referred to as 'aftermarkets', thus distinguishing them from the copier market. Sales of parts and service are often made together, but the copier firms also sell parts as stand-alone aftermarket products, and repair services as a stand-alone aftermarket service. Accordingly, while sales of parts and service are often intertwined, substantial demand exists for each aftermarket element standing on its own. This substantial disaggregated demand suggests that for many consumers, suppliers of copier parts and suppliers of copier service compete in separate markets.

It bears mention that in both the *Kodak* and *Xerox* cases, only a small fraction of the copier parts at issue were indeed subject to patent claims. Most of the parts were subject to no IP rights at all. This raises a question whether the copier firm defendants in the case properly should enjoy any immunity from refusal to deal liability when they are using patent rights as a justification to restrict access to parts that are not covered by claims in those patents. In such an instance, assuming that the other requirements for refusal to deal liability are met, if a plaintiff could show that the refusal to deal was broader than the underlying patent claims, and that the extra scope of the refusal made a difference in terms of additional harm to competition, then the refusal should be actionable. This path was not explored in either the *Kodak* or the *Xerox* case.

---

[42]   See Einer Elhauge, *Tying, Bundled Discounts, and the Death of the Single Monopoly Profit Theory*, 123 Harvard L. Rev. 397, 445–6 (2009).

In any event, the question remains: why would a vertically-integrated copier firm seek to cut off the access of rival service firms to the supply of copier parts? Prior to the cut-off, the copier firm may extract whatever rents its IP will yield via supracompetitive prices charged to ISOs and customers for parts covered either by patent, copyright (in the case of software), or trade secret (inhering, for example, in a secret process for manufacturing a particular part). After the cut-off, the copier firm ceases to extract IP-created rents via sales of parts to ISOs, and does so by charging a supracompetitive price for parts sold to self-servicing customers, and for service performed by its own technicians for customers who do not self-service. Is there an opportunity for the copier firm that explains the cut-off and resulting forced tie?

There are two potential opportunities. As mentioned earlier, the cut-off may afford the copier firm additional rents via enhanced ability to price discriminate. Additionally, the cut-off may allow the copier firm to increase the *length of time* during which it will be able to extract rents.

How might this be so? Prior to the cut-off, the ISOs are able to work with the copier firm's parts. Through their experience with the various parts, the ISOs may learn how to invent around the copier firm's patents and create functionally useful replacements that do not trespass upon the copier firm's IP. Similarly with parts covered by trade secret; via repeated use and interaction, the ISOs may unravel the secrets of a part's function or manufacture, thereby vitiating entirely the narrow trade secret protection. And once an ISO is able to provide a workable replacement (or, perhaps more often, a workable *repair*) for the copier firm's proprietary part, either through a patent work-around or by piercing a trade secret, competition from the ISOs will dispel some of the rents that the copier firm currently enjoys.

After the cut-off, of course, the ISOs are deprived of much of their former opportunity to work with and learn from the copier firm's proprietary parts. So the motivation for the cut-off may be explained not only by the ability to extract rents in the short run, but additionally by the *length of time* during which rents may be extracted.

Should a firm's refusal to deal aimed at extending the period during which it is able to extract rents from its patent be shielded from antitrust liability? That is a much more difficult question than the one typically posited in cases like *Kodak* and *Xerox*. Patents do convey rights to exclude, but they do so only if the patent applicant provides a description of the subject matter for which the patent is sought in the detail required to enable a person ordinarily skilled in whatever scientific or technological field the patent covers to replicate the claimed invention. These descriptions are mandatory – a patent grant will not issue unless the application 'enables' replication of the invention[43] – and the patent system makes these descriptions public.

Patent law's enablement requirement shows that the system pursues two commitments that are both foundational and in tension. First, patent seeks to induce investment in the creation of new inventions via the provision of limited-term exclusive rights. Second, patent works to spread knowledge of the inventions as widely as possible – inventions that, but for the lure of the patent system's grant of exclusive rights, might have remained trade secrets and thus at least for a time unknown to the public.

---

[43]   See 35 U.S.C. § 112.

So patent protects inventions, but it also undermines them by facilitating work-around approaches. In light of these competing goals of the patent law, it makes little sense to say that the patent grant immunizes patentees from antitrust liability when they take steps to prevent the kind of work-around activity that is fostered by the patent system itself.

III   TYING

As in the instance of recent decisions regarding refusals to license patents, recent cases analysing tying arrangements where the tying product is protected by a patent have suggested only the narrowest potential for antitrust liability. Is the current antitrust retreat from regulation of tying arrangements defensible?

A tying arrangement is an agreement by a party to sell one (tying) product premised on the requirement that the buyer also purchases a different (or tied) product. In the patent context, consider the example of a firm holding a patent on a machine for depositing salt in canned goods. The patentee grants licenses to other firms to use its patented canning machines on the condition that the licensees purchase all of their salt requirements from the patentee. These were the facts in *Morton Salt Co. v. G.S. Suppiger Co.*,[44] where the Supreme Court held that such a tie was a misuse of the patent monopoly and refused to countenance a patent infringement lawsuit aimed at enforcing the tie. The holding in *Morton Salt* did not rely on any analysis of market conditions; it presumed, rather, that the tie of the patented product to the sale of unpatented goods suppressed competition that would otherwise occur in the sale of the tied product.

That presumption of market harm migrated into the antitrust law in *International Salt Co. v. United States*,[45] a case involving facts closely similar to those in *Morton Salt*. The Court, relying on the government's argument that tying arrangements 'ten[d] . . . to accomplishment of monopoly', invalidated the tie. And in a case issued in the same term, the Court characterized its opinion in *International Salt* as holding that the licensing of 'a patented device on the condition that unpatented materials be employed in conjunction with the patented device' is a restraint that is 'illegal per se'.[46]

Starting, then, with the Supreme Court's 1947 decision in *International Salt*, and continuing through a string of Supreme Court and lower court opinions to the 1984 decision in *Jefferson Parish*, courts have held that the presence of patent rights protecting the tying product raises a presumption that the defendant enjoyed substantial market power in that product. This point was made unambiguously in *Jefferson Parish*, where the Court stated that 'if the Government has granted the seller a patent or similar monopoly over

---

[44]   314 U.S. 488 (1942).

[45]   332 U.S. 392 (1947).

[46]   United States v. Columbia Steel Co., 334 U.S. 495, 522–3 n.22 (1948). The Court's treatment of a forced tie relying on a patented tying product was consistent with its early treatment of tying agreements as a suspect category. In its early encounters with forced ties, the Court consistently assumed that '[t]ying arrangements serve hardly any purpose beyond the suppression of competition'. Standard Oil Co. of Cal. v. United States, 337 U.S. 293, 305–6 (1949).

a product, it is fair to presume that the inability to buy the product elsewhere gives the seller market power'.[47]

The Supreme Court overturned this presumption in its 2006 opinion in *Illinois Tool Works, Inc. v. Independent Ink, Inc.*[48] Illinois Tool Works manufactures and distributes, through its wholly-owned subsidiary Trident, patented ink jet printheads to original equipment manufacturers (OEMs). Trident owns patents both on the printhead and on an ink container used in combination with the printhead. The OEMs manufacture printers incorporating Trident's printhead technology that print barcodes on corrugated materials and paper. In addition, Trident manufactures and sells unpatented ink for use with its patented printheads.

Independent Ink manufactures and supplies ink in direct competition with Trident. Independent's ink has the same chemical composition as that sold by Trident, and is readily usable in Trident's printheads.

Trident licenses its patented printhead technology to the OEMs. The standard form licensing agreement requires 'OEMs to purchase their ink for Trident-based systems exclusively from Trident' in order to use Trident's patented printhead technology.

The license agreement, by its very terms, is an explicit tying arrangement, and the existence of a forced tie between the patented printhead technology (the tying product) and the unpatented ink (the tied product) was never in dispute. Rather, the case turned entirely on whether the patented technology conferred market power on Trident.

Independent Ink relied upon the rebuttable presumption of market power that cases like *International Salt* and *Jefferson Parish* held would be conferred on Trident by its patent. Indeed, Independent Ink never presented to the district court any free-standing analysis demonstrating that Trident's patent gave it market power; Independent Ink offered virtually no evidence relating to any of the fundaments of market power analysis, including the relevant geographic market, relevant product market, and substitutability of Trident's patented technology with other technologies or products.

The Court agreed with Illinois Tool Works/Trident, and rejected any presumption of market power, rebuttable or otherwise, arising from the mere presence of a patent controlling access to a tying product:

> Congress, the antitrust enforcement agencies, and most economists have all reached the conclusion that a patent does not necessarily confer market power upon the patentee. Today, we reach the same conclusion, and therefore hold that, in all cases involving a tying arrangement, the plaintiff must prove that the defendant has market power in the tying product.[49]

The Court based its decision, in important part, in deference to the agencies' Antitrust Guidelines for the Licensing of Intellectual Property ('IP Guidelines'), which state that with respect to the first prong of the test for an unlawful tie the agencies 'will not presume that a patent, copyright, or trade secret necessarily confers market power upon

[47] Jefferson Parish Hospital Dist., No. 2 v. Hyde, 466 U.S. 2, 16 (1984).
[48] 126 S.Ct. 1281 (2006) (hereinafter '*ITW*').
[49] 126 S.Ct. at 1293.

its owner'.[50] At the time the IP Guidelines were promulgated, this statement by the agencies represented a departure from the law. But the statement also reflected a clear evolution in economic thinking about tying arrangements that allowed the agencies to better understand the circumstances in which ties could be procompetitive and serve consumer welfare.

The Court's narrow holding in *Illinois Tool Works* (*ITW*) seems on the surface correct: considering that most patents are commercially worthless and only very few accord the rights-holder any real power over a relevant market, it seems sensible to oblige plaintiffs to provide evidence of market power, rather than simply presuming its existence. But this argument is met by an important practical objection. For a tie on separate products successfully to be enforced via restrictions in a licensing agreement for a patent or patents covering the tying product, the underlying patents must afford the licensor a significant degree of market power, else potential licensees who objected to the tie would simply look elsewhere.[51] For this reason, if a tie that relies on a patented tying product actually produces litigation, rather than simply being ignored by potential licensees, then a rebuttable presumption that the patent at issue grants market power makes sense.

There is a broader and more important objection to the result in *ITW*, i.e., that a forced tie involving complementary products (e.g., printers and ink) should attract a presumption of market power *without regard to whether a patent covers the tying product*.

There are two very powerful arguments for this result. The first is a corollary to the argument above for a rebuttable presumption: regardless of whether the tying product is patented or not, if the tying and tied products are in fact separate products, then the ability of the licensor to force a tie against an objecting licensee (the effect of which is to transfer to the licensor significant surplus from high-valuing licensees) is evidence of market power, for absent that power, potential licensees who objected to the tying arrangement would simply look elsewhere. For these reasons, a rebuttable presumption of market power would be sensible whenever the licensor is able to force a tie on two otherwise separate products in the face of objections from a licensee.[52]

Ties like the one in *ITW* are often defended as implementing price discrimination schemes, and price discrimination is possible even in markets that are quite competitive, though not *perfectly* competitive. But if a tie succeeds in transferring substantial surplus away from consumers and to a producer – and is thus worth launching expensive federal litigation over – then it is evidence of the existence of significant market power that exceeds the threshold relevant to the antitrust law. Evidence in *ITW* suggested that

---

[50]   Under the IP Guidelines the antitrust agencies will apply the rule of reason to tying provisions in IP licenses, evaluating both the anticompetitive effects and the procompetitive efficiencies attributable to a tie. The agencies are likely to challenge a tying arrangement if '(1) the seller has market power in the tying product, (2) the arrangement has an adverse effect on competition in the relevant market for the tied product, and (3) efficiency justifications for the arrangement do not outweigh the anticompetitive effects'.

[51]   This argument appears in Frederick Scherer's amicus brief in *ITW*. F.M. Scherer, Amicus Curiae in Support of Respondent, Illinois Tool Works Inc. v. Independent Ink, Inc., 126 S. Ct. 1281 (2006) (No. 04-1329), available at www.som.yale.edu/Faculty/bn1.

[52]   See Barry Nalebuff, *Unfit to be Tied: An Analysis of Trident v. Independent Ink*, in THE ANTITRUST REVOLUTION: ECONOMICS, COMPETITION, AND POLICY (John Kwoka and Lawrence White eds., Oxford University Press, 5th ed. 2008).

Trident charged between 2.5 and 4 times as much as Independent Ink for printer ink that was identical chemically and in all other relevant respects. That is the kind of evidence that should lead to a rebuttable presumption of market power regardless of whether the tying product is patented or not.

The second argument suggests that in the case of requirements ties involving complementary products, a presumption of market power is justified by the potential harm to overall social welfare that represents the most conservative case for antitrust intervention. Forced ties on complementary products are most often pursued because they allow licensees to price discriminate via metering of demand.[53] So, for example, by enforcing its tying agreement, Illinois Tool Works was able to capture additional rents from high-volume users via additional sales of ink.

Whether this conduct is objectionable categorically raises a deep and unresolved question about antitrust's theory of harm. Does antitrust object only to business conduct that harms overall welfare? Or is antitrust focused on *consumer* welfare, such that strategies, exemplified by ITW's tying arrangement, that shift rents from consumers to producers should be subject to antitrust intervention?

Addressing this question is outside the scope of this chapter, but even for those who adhere to the social welfare criterion, under which price discrimination that transfers rents from consumers to producers would not be categorically impermissible, there remains an important inquiry. While perfect (i.e., costless) price discrimination would be unobjectionable under the social welfare criterion, price discrimination is never perfect – all such schemes impose costs. Firms do not have perfect information about customers' valuation, and so must glean what information they can via purchase behavior or group characteristics. Firms must spend significant resources to obtain this information, and then of course high-valuation customers may also devote significant resources to evading any metering scheme such information permits, by, for example, creating less-efficient substitutes for the product that imposes the metering tariff. And, importantly, forced ties are an imprecise tool for implementing price discrimination schemes, for a particular consumer's tied product usage does not reliably sort customers according to how highly they value the tying product.[54] Some buyers may use relatively little of the tied product, but employ the tying product for a particularly high-value use. For other customers, the story may be reversed; they use a lot of the tied product, but put the tying product to a relatively low-value use, and therefore value it less than the metering scheme suggests. Because forced ties are subject to these errors, they are likely to be costly forms of price discrimination.

---

[53]   Tying agreements are sometimes defended as cost-reduction strategies, i.e., tying is employed when it is more efficient to supply two products together rather than separately. But this is a poor explanation for forced ties, for if tying leads to substantial cost savings, then we would expect producers to offer the complementary products together, and for consumers to seek to purchase the products as a bundle. Thus, we would not see forcing; we would, rather, observe voluntary 'ties'. Moreover, under the legal framework used to analyse tying arrangements, we would not view the products as 'separate', and there would be no prospect of liability even if we saw producers only offering the products as a package.

[54]   See Einer Elhauge, *Tying, Bundled Discounts, and the Death of the Single Monopoly Profit Theory*, 123 HARVARD L. REV. 397, 431 (2009).

For these reasons, metering schemes implemented via price discrimination will reliably lead to reductions in consumer welfare, but yield no commensurately reliable increase in total welfare. Indeed, under certain conditions price discrimination may reduce both consumer welfare and total welfare.[55] The facilitation of price discrimination is thus a weak general justification for forced ties. Price discrimination may serve as a legitimate justification for a forced tie in a particular case (at least under the narrow total welfare criterion), but to understand whether a particular tie results in welfare gains courts must, at the very least, have some understanding of the costs of price discrimination, and of consumers' ability to circumvent the scheme, in the particular context in which a scheme is implemented.

IV   ANTITRUST CONCERNS ARISING FROM PATENT LICENSES

Unilateral refusals to license and patent-actuated tying agreements are the most important recently-litigated issues at the antitrust/patent interface. Yet there are many other issues involving the interaction between patents and antitrust where there has been continuity in the legal analysis but yet cases continue to recur, or where the issue has not yet reached the Supreme Court and so no definitive analysis has emerged. In the first category is a clutch of antitrust issues that attend patent licensing.

In general, patent licensing is viewed as procompetitive – indeed, licensing is the primary mechanism through which the patent law transfers control over technologies from innovators to those best positioned to commercialize them. Additionally, because some of the gains from licensing flow to the innovator, wide freedom to license magnifies the ex ante incentive to innovate that patent law seeks to create and maintain.[56]

Although antitrust law generally views patent licenses as benign, there are instances in which licensing can raise antitrust concerns. A restraint in a patent license is obviously objectionable, for example, if it facilitates price-fixing or market division. But even in cases where there is no such prospect, patent licenses can create competitive harm, especially in instances where the licensing parties are horizontal competitors, or would have been actual or likely potential competitors in some relevant market in the absence of the license.

An example would be two firms, A and B, which compete in a relevant product market with similar products manufactured using different processes. Both firms hold patents

---

[55]   See *id.* at 397, 430–34, 439–42, 479–81 (2009); E. Elhauge, *The Failed Resurrection of the Single Monopoly Profit Theory*, 6(1) COMPETITION POLICY INTERNATIONAL 155, 166–7 (Spring 2010).

[56]   U.S. Department of Justice and Federal Trade Commission, IP Guidelines, *supra* note 3 (noting that intellectual property licensing 'can lead to more efficient exploitation of the intellectual property, benefiting consumers through the reduction of costs and the introduction of new products . . . By potentially increasing the expected returns from intellectual property, licensing can also increase the incentive for its creation and thus promote greater investment in research and development'). See, however, Christopher Buccafusco and Christopher Jon Sprigman, *The Creativity Effect*, 78 U. CHI. L. REV. 31 (2011) (demonstrating significant endowment effects attending transactions in created goods – effects that may reduce the social value of IP licensing).

covering their manufacturing processes. The firms reach an agreement whereby firm A licenses its process patent to firm B. A provision in this license requires firm B to use firm A's process exclusively, and to refrain from licensing firm B's own process patent to competitors.

The antitrust agencies will typically evaluate provisions like these under the rule of reason, with a focus on whether the provision raises the risk that competitors will coordinate pricing, restrict output, or acquire or maintain market power – a possibility, in this example, if the license provision restricting firm B's licensing of its patent would give firm A significant power in the market for licensing process technology needed to produce the product at issue.

Even in the case of patent license provisions that raise the risk of harm to competition, the agencies will also assess whether on balance the provision at issue promotes competition by allowing the parties to achieve efficiencies such as economies of scale and integration of complementary factors of production such as research and development programs and production processes. In the example above, the agencies would consider whether the restraint would increase the incentives and the capacity of both the licensor and the licensee to develop and market the licensed technology.

There are a number of common provisions in patent licenses that can raise the risk of harm to competition. The example above illustrates an explicit exclusive dealing arrangement, and patent licenses often are exclusive. Exclusivity need not be explicit, however, to raise antitrust concern. Certain types of licensing provisions may effectively make a nominally nonexclusive license in fact exclusive. An example can be found in an early antitrust lawsuit brought by the Antitrust Division against Microsoft, which charged that Microsoft maintained a monopoly in its Windows operating system by requiring that computer manufacturers pay royalties to Microsoft on each computer shipped, regardless of whether that computer used a Microsoft operating system. Microsoft settled the Division's complaint and agreed to cease using per-unit royalties in its licensing agreements and cease enforcing those provisions in existing agreements.[57] Because the manufacturers were obliged to pay a fee to Microsoft for every unit shipped, they were unlikely to pay twice to install an operating system from one of Microsoft's competitors.

'Grantback' clauses are another common feature of patent licenses that may raise antitrust concern. The precise effect of such clauses differs license to license, but they generally require that licensees either (a) grant royalty-free nonexclusive licenses to any improvements the licensee makes to the licensor's technology, or (b) grant exclusive licenses or even assignment of all rights in any improvement. These clauses, especially the more limited versions creating nonexclusive licenses, may serve the interests of competition by ensuring wide access to improvements. But grantback clauses may also harm competition by stifling licensees' incentives to innovate and, in some cases, to compete with the licensor.

Recognizing this possibility, the IP Guidelines state that '[g]rantbacks may adversely affect competition . . . if they substantially reduce the licensee's incentives to engage in

---

[57]   United States v. Microsoft, Inc. 159 F.R.D. 318 (D.D.C.), rev'd on other grounds, 56 F.3d 1448 (D.C. Cir. 1995).

research and development and thereby limit rivalry in information markets'.[58] Because they may be either pro- or anticompetitive, the Supreme Court and the federal antitrust agencies have made clear that grantback provisions must be analysed under the rule of reason,[59] and courts applying the rule of reason have focused on a set of factors that tend to differentiate between benign and possibly malignant grantbacks:

(1)   whether the grantback is exclusive or nonexclusive;
(2)   if exclusive, whether the licensee retains the right to use its improvements;
(3)   whether the grantback forbids, permits, or requires the licensor to sublicense patents it acquires via the provision;
(4)   whether the grantback is limited to the subject matter of the licensed patents, or whether it covers inventions outside the scope of the licensed patents;
(5)   whether the grantback expires with the license or outlives it;
(6)   whether the grantback produces royalties for the licensee, or is royalty-free;
(7)   whether the parties to the license, either separately or jointly, exercise significant market power;
(8)   whether the parties to the license are competitors in relevant product or technology markets.

None of these factors are determinative standing alone, including the first. Exclusive grantbacks have been upheld if other factors suggest that they will not, on balance, harm competition. Nonexclusive grantbacks have been held unlawful where they are found, along with other restrictions present in the license, to harm competition.

Patent licensing arrangements much more frequently involve patent owners and licensees who are not horizontal competitors but are instead in a vertical relationship. For example, the patent owner may be a firm that does not market a product that competes with any product marketed by the licensee, but which nonetheless maintains research and development activities relevant to the licensee's business.

The restraints most commonly found in vertical licensing arrangements are 'field of use' and geographic limitations on the licensee's use of the patented invention. An example would be a license permitting access to a patented algorithm that uses historical data to predict changes in long-term interest rates. Field of use restrictions might limit a particular licensee to use of the algorithm in the underwriting of home mortgages. Other licensees might be limited to use of the algorithm in the marketing of life insurance policies. The license might also include geographic restrictions, limiting, for example, one licensee to use of the algorithm to predict interest rates in the United States, and another to predict rates in the United Kingdom.

Generally patent licenses between parties in a vertical relationship, and the field of use and geographic restrictions that they often contain, do not raise antitrust concerns, absent the possibility that they are present in the license as a means of enforcing a related cartel

---

58   IP Guidelines, *supra* note 3, § 5.6.
59   *Id.* See also Transparent-Wrap Machine Corp. v. Stokes & Smith Co., 329 U.S. 637 (1947) (applying rule of reason to grantback provision); United States v. National Lead Co., 332 U.S. 319 (1947) (approving grantback provision granting nonexclusive license at uniform, reasonable royalty).

arrangement (for example, by enforcing an agreed-upon customer or market allocation). Other provisions in licenses between parties in a vertical relationship may nonetheless be troubling. For example, an exclusive dealing provision, such as that posited above in the context of a license between horizontal competitors, may harm competition in the vertical context if (a) it prevents the licensee from licensing, selling, distributing, or using technologies that compete with the licensor's patented technology, and (b) the restraint would contribute to the licensor's ability to gain or maintain substantial market power.

V   CROSS-LICENSING AND PATENT POOLING

Patent cross-licensing and pooling arrangements are agreements of two or more owners of different patents to license one another or third parties. In a typical cross-license, two patent owners each grant reciprocal rights that permit each party to use the patents owned by the other.

This practice is especially common in concentrated industries where a small number of large firms hold substantial patent portfolios. An example is the semiconductor industry, where firms seek to acquire a large portfolio of patents not primarily for the purpose of offensive litigation, but rather as part of a 'balance of terror' strategy vis-à-vis other large competitors. The firms that have achieved this balance often enter into cross-licenses, thereby gaining certainty and wide freedom to pursue new semiconductor designs without fear of infringing the patents of their cross-licensed competitor.[60]

Cross-licensing may be procompetitive if used to integrate complementary technologies, reduce transaction costs, clear blocking positions, and avoid the cost and uncertainty of litigation.[61] But cross-licensing can also be a tool to suppress competition, when used either to enforce a price-fixing or market allocation agreement, or to suppress incentives to innovate. In *United States v. Automobile Manufacturers Ass'n*,[62] the DOJ alleged that a royalty-free cross-license applying to patents on certain emissions control technologies was unlawful where it worked to inhibit innovation in this area. The consent decree in this case prohibited the royalty-free cross-licenses and prohibited information exchanges that the government concluded would deter investment in new emissions control technologies.

Patent pools are created via agreement between multiple patent owners to license or transfer their patents to a separate entity or jointly-controlled venture for the purpose of licensing the pooled patents as a package to third parties. Patent pooling often is undertaken when the patent rights necessary to deploy a particular device or technology are dispersed among a large enough number of firms that cross-licensing is impractical. Patent pools can benefit competition by reducing transaction costs and facilitating access to the

---

[60]   Cross-licenses may be royalty-free or they may involve fixed or running royalties running either to one or both parties (depending on the relative strength of each party's portfolio). Cross-licenses may include field-of-use or territorial restrictions, may cover all or only some of the patents owned by each party, and may be limited to patents already issued or applied for as of the date of the license, or alternatively may extend beyond the current portfolios to patents to be obtained by each party in the future.

[61]   See IP Guidelines, *supra* note 3, § 5.5.

[62]   307 F. Supp. 617 (C.D. Cal. 1969).

patented technologies necessary to offer new or improved products. But patent pools may also harm competition. Pools operate as a form of cartel, because the participants typically agree on the price to be charged for the pooled patents. In addition, patent pooling creates the risk that patents that would otherwise compete in a licensing market, i.e., patents covering separate but reasonably interchangeable technologies, will be mingled in the pool with a resulting loss of competition that would have occurred absent the pool.

Patent pools have been used for many decades, and antitrust scrutiny of patent pooling dates back at least to the Supreme Court's 1931 opinion in *Standard Oil Co. v. United States*.[63] There, the Supreme Court addressed an agreement among several oil companies to pool patents controlling various processes for 'cracking' heavy crude oil to extract gasoline. Provisions of the pooling agreements fixed the price for a license to the pooled patents and created a formula for distributing the royalty payments among the pool participants. Despite the agreement on price, the Court validated the pool, finding that the participants' share of the relevant market was too low for the pool to have any harmful effect on competition.

The Court noted that the pooling arrangement was intended to and actually did clear what would otherwise have been blocking patent positions. Each of the defendant patent owners had developed a cracking process that arguably infringed the process patents of the other defendants. The Court observed that '[a]n interchange of patent rights and a division of royalties according to the value attributed by the parties to their respective patent claims is frequently necessary if technical advancement is not to be blocked by threatened litigation'. The Court also noted that the pool did not fix prices for end-users or limit the participants' use of nonlicensed cracking technologies. The Court clearly understood, however, that given different circumstances the arrangement would create a substantial risk, warning that '[i]f combining patent owners effectively dominate an industry, the power to fix and maintain royalties is tantamount to the power to fix prices. Where domination exists, a pooling of competing process patents . . . is beyond the privileges conferred by patents and constitutes a violation of the Sherman Act'.

The analysis in *Standard Oil* remains, at bottom, the way in which the competitive risks of patent pools are assessed today. The legacy of that opinion can be seen in the DOJ's 1990s-era business review letters for the MPEG-2 and DVD patent pools,[64] which aim to 'provide a template for patent pooling arrangements that should not run afoul of the antitrust laws'.

In approving these pools, the Antitrust Division noted several important features, set out in the rules governing both pools, which tended to increase their procompetitive potential and reduce the risk of competitive harm. First, only technically 'essential' patents would be eligible for pooling. Essential patents are, by definition, not competing in any relevant licensing market, because each patent is a 'must have' for firms wishing to deploy products meeting the established technical specification. Second, the pooled patents would be clearly identified and would remain available to be licensed individually

---

[63]   283 U.S. 163 (1931).

[64]   See DOJ Business Review Letter to Hitachi, Ltd., 1999 DOJBRL LEXIS 7 (10 June 1999); DOJ Business Review Letter to Koninklikje Philips Elec., N.V., 1998 DOBRL LEXIS 15 (16 December 1998).

as well as in a package. The continued availability of individual licenses meant that firms offering end-user products would be able to compete with more diverse products offering more or fewer features. Third, the licensees' royalty obligations would be based on actual use of the licensed patents, which meant that licensees did not face substantial disincentives to explore competing non-licensed technologies. Fourth and relatedly, the pools provided for explicit freedom of the licensees to develop and use alternative technologies. Fifth, and finally, the pool agreements both included grantback requirements, but these were limited in the sense that licensees were obliged only to grant back nonexclusive, nondiscriminatory licenses to use patents that are essential to comply with the technology.

The Antitrust Division's approval of the MPEG-2 and DVD pools may be contrasted with the FTC's attack on a patent pool formed by Summit Technology, Inc. and VISX, Inc., two manufacturers of equipment used in laser vision correction surgery. The FTC alleged that Summit and VISX, 'the only two firms legally able to market equipment for PRK [photorefractive keratectomy], placed their competing patents in a patent pool and shared the proceeds each and every time a Summit or VISX laser was used, a violation of antitrust laws'. In March 1999, the FTC issued consent orders, whereby the participants agreed to dissolve the pool. The consent orders were 'intended to make Summit and VISX vigorous competitors both in selling their lasers and in licensing their intellectual property to rivals'.[65]

The outcome in the Summit/VISX pooling case is not, in retrospect, surprising. In pooling competing patents, the parties aimed to eliminate competition (in both products and technology licenses) that would otherwise have existed between them. They aimed, in short, to become joint monopolists, and the pooling agreement was therefore akin to the agreement to share monopoly profits that often attends the formation of a cartel.

VI   MERGERS AND ACQUISITIONS

As the salience of IP to the fortunes of firms increases, mergers and acquisitions are often driven by the efficiencies (or on occasion the competition-suppressing potential) of combining patent portfolios. As with patent pooling, M&A activity involving firms holding patents may be anticompetitive if it is part of an agreement to restrain trade,[66] or if it results in the ownership by the acquiring firm of patents that would otherwise compete in a licensing market, and, in the absence of the merger, facilitate the competitive offering of products employing the licensed technology.[67] M&A may also be procompetitive, however, when it helps to resolve a patent block. If the acquired firm could not practice its own patents without infringing the patents of the acquiring firm, then competition is not threatened by the acquisition – at least not competition for licenses to the blocked patent or respecting products that the acquired firm is prevented by the block from offering. The blocking patents justification obviously requires that the acquiring firm's claims about

---

[65]   In re Summit Tech., Inc., No. 9286, 63 Fed. Reg. 46,452, 46,453 (FTC August 21, 1998).

[66]   See United States v. Singer Manufacturing Co., 374 U.S. 174 (1963) (transfer of patent unlawful where done to facilitate scheme to drive out competitors).

[67]   See Kobe, Inc. v. Dempsey Pump Co., 198 F.2d 416 (10th Cir. 1952) (acquisition of 'every important patent' in particular field with intent to exclude competitors held unlawful).

the validity and scope of its patents are correct; the government and/or judicial analysis of the merger may need to evaluate these complex questions, a task that is necessary but for which both the antitrust agencies and generalist courts are ill-suited.

If a merger or acquisition involving patents is likely to reduce licensing competition that is otherwise viable, then possible merger remedies include divestiture of patent holdings to a firm that will be well placed to maintain licensing competition and/or compulsory licensing of the merged patents. For example, a 1997 FTC challenge to the proposed merger of Ciba-Geigy Ltd. and Sandoz Ltd., both of which owned several pioneering patents on important gene therapy technologies, was ultimately resolved by requiring the merged entity to license several essential patents on a nondiscriminatory and royalty-free basis.[68]

VII   SETTLEMENT OF PHARMACEUTICAL PATENT LITIGATION

As with settlement of litigation generally, settlement of patent litigation is almost always thought to be desirable relative to the prospect of protracted and expensive proceedings that consume both private and government resources. Over the past decade, however, the instance of 'reverse payments' in settlements involving pharmaceutical patent infringement litigation has emerged as a recurring antitrust issue. Reverse payments sometimes occur in the settlement of litigation between owners of patents on branded drugs and their would-be generic drug competitors.

The antitrust concern is actuated by a complex statutory scheme, the Drug Price Competition and Patent Term Restoration Act of 1984, referred to more commonly as the Hatch-Waxman Act, which regulates the market entry of generics. Firms that manufacture generic equivalents of patented drugs often seek entry onto the market before the expiration of the relevant patents. In these cases, entry often sparks litigation between the branded and generic firms over patent infringement and patent validity.

The Hatch-Waxman Act put in place a scheme whereby a generic manufacturer can file an Abbreviated New Drug Application (ANDA) with the Food and Drug Administration seeking the FDA's approval to market a generic version of a patented drug prior to the patent's expiration. Pursuant to the statutory process, the generic firm will certify that its version will not infringe the patent at issue and/or that the patent is invalid. In response, the patent holder can bring an immediate infringement lawsuit – jurisdiction will lie even though the generic is not yet selling any product.

Once the lawsuit is timely filed, the FDA automatically delays approval of the generic's ANDA for 30 months. If the branded firm's patent is declared invalid or not infringed by the generic firm's proposed formulation, the automatic delay in FDA approval terminates, and with the FDA's approval of its ANDA the generic firm can enter the market.[69]

---

[68]   See In the Matter of Ciba-Geigy Ltd, No. C-3725 (FTC Decision and Order), available at www.ftc.gov/os/1997/04/c3725.do.htm.

[69]   Alternatively, if the court upholds the patent's validity and finds that the generic infringes, then FDA approval of the generic firm's ANDA will be postponed until the branded firm's patent expires.

As an inducement to generic firms to navigate the Hatch-Waxman process, the first generic entrant for any particular drug under this scheme is awarded a 180-day period of exclusivity in which to market its generic version; no other firms making generic equivalents of the same drug can enter the market during this time. This six-month exclusivity period can be very lucrative for the first generic entrant; entry under these conditions often allows the generic to price just under the price of the branded drug, shifting significant demand to it and at a very high margin.

The prospect of this significant payoff, combined with the desire of branded firms to avoid generic entry that will shift share and depress prices, raises the risk that branded firms will engage in strategic settlement behavior aimed at delaying the entry of the first-mover, with the effect of preventing the commencement of the 180-day period, thereby freezing out additional entrants. Antitrust concerns have been raised most sharply in instances where branded firms have paid generic firms to settle litigation commenced under the Hatch-Waxman process, conditioned on the generic firm's agreement to delay market entry.

It seems odd for the plaintiff in a patent infringement lawsuit to be paying money to the defendant in a settlement, and also facially anticompetitive for the agreement to delay entry. But matters are more complicated than that. From the perspective of the litigating parties, there is significant uncertainty about how to value settlement, and it is difficult for nonparties to discern whether settlements (even settlements involving reverse payments) reflect the parties' calculation of the risk of proceeding to a final judgment or are aimed at preventing competition that would have eventuated had a final judgment been rendered. If the litigation proceeds to final judgment and the patent is found valid and infringed, the generic would be barred from entering the market until the patent expires. On the other hand, if the patent is invalidated and/or found not to have been infringed, then the generic could enter the market immediately (as the exclusive entrant for the 180-day statutory period). Why might the parties' settlement include reverse payments flowing from the owner of the branded patent to the generic potential entrant?

Typically, settlement will terminate the generic firm's challenge to the validity of the patent and the patent owner will retain some or all of the remaining patent term as the exclusive producer of the patented drug. There is another benefit to the branded firm: as long as the generic firm does not enter the market with an equivalent drug, its statutory 180-day exclusivity period is not triggered. As a result, any generic firm filing a subsequent ANDA is indefinitely barred from entry.

Do agreements like this harm competition that would otherwise have occurred? In the absence of a final verdict in the underlying patent suit, it is in most instances very difficult to say. If the generic had been held in the litigation to have infringed a valid patent, then the patent owner would have been entitled to market exclusivity during the remaining term of its patent. In that case, a settlement agreement that includes a reverse payment does not result in any less competition relative to the result in the litigation. However, had the generic firm been successful in the lawsuit, either on validity or noninfringement grounds, the branded and generic firms would have been competitors in the marketplace. From this perspective, a settlement with a reverse payment looks like an illegal agreement between horizontal competitors to maintain a monopoly and divide its rents.

It is important to realize that both the branded and first-filer generic firms have powerful incentives to share a monopoly. The branded firm, obviously, wishes to maintain its high prices for the remainder of the patent term. From the generic's perspective, dividing the rents from a durable monopoly may be preferable to entry, not least because after the expiration of its six-month exclusivity period, follow-on generic entrants are likely to reduce prices markedly (the FTC estimates that prices fall as much as 90% following entry by subsequent-filing generic competitors).[70]

This is a pressing concern, not least because a 2002 FTC study reveals that in patent lawsuits between branded and generic firms, the generic firms prevail in *almost two-thirds of the cases.*[71] This suggests that, in many instances, the underlying lawsuit, if litigated to a final judgment, would lead to market competition from the first-to-file generic and then from follow-on generic entrants.

The antitrust law's treatment of these reverse payment settlements has been inconsistent. The Federal Trade Commission has brought enforcement actions in several cases, and in two cases the branded firms settled by agreeing not to enter into settlements that prevented the running of the 180-day period.[72] In cases that have proceeded to litigation, the federal Circuit Courts have split on the propriety of such payments. Two Circuits have applied a rule of reason approach and rejected liability unless the plaintiff shows patent invalidity or noninfringement.[73] Most notably, the Eleventh Circuit, in *Valley Drug Co. v. Geneva Pharm., Inc.,*[74] held that the exclusionary power of the pharmaceutical firm's patent must be considered in the antitrust analysis and that the challenged settlement agreements must be judged under the rule of reason. The Sixth Circuit in *In re Cardizem CD Antitrust Litigation*[75] adhered to a rule of per se invalidity, holding that the interim patent settlement agreement before it was a per se illegal horizontal market allocation.

The Supreme Court has not yet weighed in on this issue, having denied certiorari in both the *Cardizem* and *Valley Drug* cases. If the Court does eventually take a case involving reverse settlements, it should make clear that a presumption of illegality attends them. Such a stance would faithfully reflect Congress' determination, implicit in the structure of the Hatch-Waxman Act, to encourage litigation between branded firms and generic entrants. In enacting the Hatch-Waxman Act, Congress expected that many of these

---

[70]   See Jon Liebowitz, Chairman, FTC, *'Pay for Delay' Settlements in the Pharmaceutical Industry: How Congress Can Stop Anticompetitive Conduct, Protect Consumers' Wallets, and Help Pay for Health Care Reform (the $35 Billion Solution)* 3 (presented at Center for American Progress, 23 June 2009), available at www.ftc.gov/opa/2009/06/capspeech.shtm.

[71]   *Id.,* at 3.

[72]   In re Abbott Labs, Nos. C-3945, C-3946 (complaint), FTC LEXIS 65 (2000); In re Hoechst Marion Roussel, Inc., No-C9293 (complaint), FTC LEXIS 16 (2000).

[73]   See In re Tamoxifen Citrate Antitrust Litig., No. 03-7641, 2006 WL 2401244, at *1 (2d Cir. August 10, 2006); Schering-Plough Corp. v. FTC, 402 F.3d 1056, 1076 (11th Cir. 2005); see also Valley Drug Co. v. Geneva Pharm., Inc., 344 F.3d 1294, 1304, 1312–13 (11th Cir. 2003) (rejecting per se condemnation of interim settlement as 'premature', and remanding for further proceedings). The law in the Eleventh Circuit after the appellate panel's opinion in *Valley Drug* has trended toward increased receptivity to antitrust enforcement. One panel considering a settlement rejected a motion to dismiss. Andrx Pharm., Inc. v. Elan Corp., 421 F.3d 1227, 1235–6 (11th Cir. 2005). On remand from the Court of Appeals decision in *Valley Drug*, a district court found per se antitrust liability. In re Terazosin Hydrochloride Antitrust Litig., 352 F.Supp.2d 1279, 1286 (S.D. Fla. 2005) (condemning settlement as per se violation of Sherman Act).

[74]   344 F.3d 1294 (11th Cir. 2003).

[75]   481 F.3d 355 (6th Cir. 2004).

lawsuits would lead to entry, and presumably favored that result. Reverse settlements are a frustration of the statutory scheme, and antitrust law should accommodate the particular balance between competition and innovation that Congress set in this field.[76]

VIII   ENFORCEMENT OF PATENT OBTAINED VIA FRAUD ON THE PATENT AND TRADEMARK OFFICE

In *Walker Process Equipment, Inc. v. Food Machinery & Chem. Corp.*,[77] the Supreme Court held that enforcement of a patent obtained by fraud on the US Patent and Trademark Office may be the basis of an antitrust action under section 2 of the Sherman Act. Permitting such actions, the Court observed, would promote the policies it had earlier articulated in *Precision Instrument Mfg. Co. v. Automotive Maintenance Mach. Co.*:

> A patent by its very nature is affected with a public interest . . . [It] is an exception to the general rule against monopolies and to the right to access to a free and open market. The far-reaching social and economic consequences of a patent, therefore, give the public a paramount interest in seeing that patent monopolies spring from backgrounds free from fraud or other inequitable conduct and that such monopolies are kept within their legitimate scope.[78]

Antitrust claims based on the allegations of the patentee's fraudulent conduct before the USPTO are commonly referred to as '*Walker Process* claims'. The Federal Circuit has stressed that to succeed, the fraud alleged must meet the common law requirements – in particular, it must be knowing and willful. In addition to the requirement that the defendant be shown to possess either market power or a dangerous probability of attaining it, the antitrust claimant must show by clear and convincing evidence (1) that the patent owner acquired the patent by means of either a fraudulent misrepresentation or a fraudulent omission; (2) that there was intent to deceive, as contrasted to mere inequitable conduct; and (3) that the patentee was aware of the fraud when bringing suit to enforce its patent.[79]

There are two types of antitrust claims related to the *Walker Process* claim. A *Handgards* antitrust claim is based upon competitive harm caused by assertion of a patent known to be invalid.[80] A *Loctite* antitrust claim is based upon competitive harm caused by assertion of a patent known not to be infringed.[81]

More recently, the Federal Circuit in *Unitherm Food Sys., Inc. v. Swift-Eckrich, Inc.*[82] held that *threatened* enforcement of a patent procured by *Walker Process* fraud can underpin antitrust liability, even prior to the filing of an actual infringement suit. Unitherm brought a declaratory judgment action against patentee ConAgra, seeking a declaration that ConAgra's patent was invalid and unenforceable. Unitherm included in

---

[76]   See C. Scott Hemphill, *Paying for Delay: Pharmaceutical Patent Settlement as a Regulatory Design Problem*, 81 N.Y.U. L. Rev. 1553 (2006).

[77]   382 U.S. 172 (1965).

[78]   324 U.S. 806 (1945).

[79]   Nobelpharma AB v. Implant Innovations, Inc., 141 F.3d 1059, 1070 (Fed. Cir. 1998).

[80]   Handgards, Inc. v. Ethicon, Inc., 743 F.2d 1282 (9th Cir. 1984).

[81]   Loctite Corp. v. Ultraseal Ltd., 781 F.2d 861 (Fed. Cir. 1985).

[82]   375 F.3d 1341 (Fed. Cir. 2004).

its declaratory judgment complaint a *Walker Process* antitrust claim. The Federal Circuit approved the claim, holding that the same standards that determine jurisdiction in a declaratory judgment action alleging patent invalidity 'also define the minimum level of "enforcement" necessary to expose the patentee to a *Walker Process* claim for attempted monopolization'. The initial inquiry, under the general jurisdiction standard that applies to complaints seeking declaratory judgment, is whether sufficiently threatening actions have been taken by the patentee to create a reasonable apprehension of suit.

IX   SHAM PATENT INFRINGEMENT LITIGATION

The Federal Circuit in *Nobelpharma AB v. Implant Innovations, Inc.*[83] recognized the 'sham' enforcement of a patent as a type of anticompetitive act independent from the enforcement of a patent obtained by *Walker Process* fraud. Antitrust liability for 'sham' patent litigation fits within the 'sham litigation' exception to Noerr-Pennington antitrust immunity; while patentees' enforcement efforts cannot generally serve as a basis for antitrust liability, there are limited circumstances in which enforcement causes competitive harm for which the antitrust law will provide a remedy.

To prevail on a sham litigation claim, the antitrust claimant must show that the patentee's 'infringement suit was "a mere sham to cover what is actually nothing more than an attempt to interfere directly with the business relationships of a competitor"'. More specifically, the antitrust claimant must establish that (1) the lawsuit was 'objectively baseless in the sense that no reasonable litigant could realistically expect success on the merits'; and (2) that the baseless lawsuit concealed 'an attempt to interfere directly with the business relationships of a competitor through the use of the governmental process – as opposed to the outcome of that process – as an anticompetitive weapon'. [84]

CONCLUSION

Antitrust's intersection with the intellectual property law tends increasingly toward deference. In some cases, that deference seems overdone. The Federal Circuit overstepped in declaring unilateral refusals to license a patent categorically immune from antitrust scrutiny. Similarly, the Supreme Court's removal of the presumption of market power from cases involving forced patent ties, while narrowly correct, misses a much broader point about the ways in which these ties can harm competition.

These instances, and others described here, suggest that the antitrust/patent intersection is due for revision. That task, if it is ever to come to pass, awaits the work necessary to revive antitrust from its current somnolence.

---

[83]   141 F.3d 1059, 1070 (Fed. Cir. 1998).
[84]   Professional Real Estate Investors, Inc. v. Columbia Pictures Indus., Inc., 508 U.S. 49 (1993).

14 Antitrust damages
Daniel L. Rubinfeld*

I INTRODUCTION

Antitrust private actions have been an important component of civil enforcement in the United States since the passage of the Clayton Act.[1] Private actions have been seen, in combination with public enforcement, as a means of achieving an appropriate level of deterrence. However, they have also been viewed as a mechanism for compensating those who were injured by illegal anticompetitive activities.[2] In recent years, private antitrust enforcement has been growing outside the United States. Such actions are now available in parts of Asia (e.g., Japan) and in England. Private actions will almost certainly grow throughout the European Union as well.[3]

To obtain a financial recovery in a private action, the plaintiff must prove three distinct elements: (1) an antitrust violation; (2) antitrust injury;[4] and (3) damages – a measure of the extent of the injury. In this chapter, I focus entirely on the important third element – antitrust damages. While much of the analysis is conceptual in nature, the analytical details do depend on the institutional context in which damages are applied. Therefore, unless otherwise noted it will be presumed that we are operating within the US private civil litigation system.[5]

In order to pursue an antitrust case, the plaintiff must have been injured, i.e., have standing to sue. Under federal law, only direct purchasers have such standing.[6] Direct purchaser suits can be brought through the class action mechanism or individually.[7]

---

* I wish to thank Justin McCrary and Abe Wickelgren for their helpful comments, and Ashok Ayyar for his capable research assistance.

[1] Section 4 of the Clayton Act provides for private actions with treble damages as a remedy. 15 U.S.C. § 15 (2009).

[2] For an insightful discussion of the objectives associated with the payment of antitrust damages, see Herbert Hovenkamp, *Damages*, in FEDERAL ANTITRUST POLICY: THE LAW OF COMPETITION AND ITS PRACTICE (3d ed. 2005).

[3] See, e.g., European Commission, *Green Paper on Damages Actions for the Breach of EC Antitrust Rules* (2005); European Commission, *White Paper on Damages Actions for Breach of the EC Antitrust Rules* (2008).

[4] In Brunswick Corp. v. Pueblo Bowl-O-Mat, Inc., 429 U.S. 477, 489 (1977), the Court ruled that damages can be recovered only for injuries that flow from the wrongful anticompetitive conduct.

[5] I note that the US Supreme Court has set a higher standard for proof of violation and causation than for proof of damages. See Story Parchment Co. v. Paterson Parchment Paper Co., 282 U.S. 555, 562 (1931).

[6] See Illinois Brick Co. v. Illinois, 431 U.S. 720, 746 (1977); see also Hanover Shoe, Inc. v. United Shoe Mach. Corp., 392 U.S. 481, rehearing denied, 393 U.S 901 (1968).

[7] The first case supporting overcharges was Chattanooga Foundry & Pipe Works v. Atlanta, 203 U.S. 396 (1906).

When suits are brought as class actions, plaintiffs' damage claims are based on alleged overcharges,[8] which are trebled if liability is proven. Individual suits may claim either overcharges or lost profits. Indirect purchasers can sue, but only in states that have passed *Illinois Brick* 'repealer' statutes. By 2008, 35 states had done so.[9]

Almost all damage awards are paid in dollars. However, the vast majority of antitrust cases that continue beyond summary judgment motions settle. Furthermore, a substantial number of those settlements involve coupon payments as well as cash.

Not surprisingly, the complexity of the US system of private antitrust enforcement raises many important but difficult damages-related issues. This chapter treats a number of those issues, some of which are explicitly normative and others of which are not. I begin in section II with an analysis of antitrust overcharges. I describe the primary approaches to the analysis of overcharges and offer commentary on those methods. In section III, I move to an analysis of lost profits as an alternative to overcharges. This leads naturally to a discussion of the deterrence as well as compensation goals of antitrust. Section IV focuses on indirect purchasers; I emphasize the importance of pass-through analysis in evaluating indirect purchaser damages. Finally, in section V, I describe and evaluate the use of coupons in lieu of cash in the settlement of antitrust claims.

II OVERCHARGES

Overcharges are measures of overpayments by individuals or businesses that have been injured as the result of an antitrust violation. Overcharges can result from price-fixing and other restraints of trade or from illegal monopolizing behavior. To simplify the methodological issues to be discussed I will take as our prototypical case a price-fixing arrangement which leads to prices that are higher than they would be in a but-for world of no price-fixing. The analysis of overcharges associated with exclusionary practices such as tying and exclusive dealing contracts can be more involved, since they often involve nonprice restraints and they may also involve lost profit claims rather than claims for overcharges. Furthermore, most price-fixing cases arise under a per se rule, whereas most exclusionary practices are evaluated under a rule of reason standard. In rule of reason cases, proof of causality and the damages that are the result of the illegal behavior can be a significant hurdle for plaintiffs, especially when some or all of the harm has yet to occur.[10]

I note in passing that overcharges may over- or undercompensate the direct purchasers of the product or products at issue in a case. Overcompensation would arise, for example, if the direct purchaser is able to pass on its higher costs to downstream customers. Undercompensation would arise if the purchaser would have increased the quantity purchased absent the wrongful behavior.

A number of approaches have been used by experts to evaluate overcharges in

---

8 See Paper Sys. Inc. v. Mitsubishi Corp., 193 F.R.D. 601, 614 (D. Wis. 2000).

9 See Antitrust Modernization Commission, *Report and Recommendations* 18, 269 (2007), available at http://govinfo.library.unt.edu/amc/.

10 See Brunswick Corp. v. Pueblo Bowl-O-Mat, Inc., 429 U.S. 477, 487 (1977).

antitrust litigation. The two most common involve the use of *yardsticks* and *benchmarks*.[11] In a typical yardstick approach, one compares prices, margins, or rates of return during the period in which the antitrust violation is believed to have had an effect (the 'impact period') to prices, margins, or rates of return in other markets that are deemed to be reasonably comparable to the market at issue. In contrast, the benchmark approach evaluates prices only in the market at issue, comparing prices in the impact period to available prices before and/or after the alleged period of impact (the 'nonimpact period'). I comment first on the yardstick approach, after which I consider benchmarks.[12]

A   Yardsticks

Under the yardstick approach, damages are measured by obtaining a 'but-for price' from a market (the 'comparable market') that closely approximates the market in which the violation occurred.[13] The 'but-for price' is a measure of what the price of the product would be if the wrongful behavior had not occurred. A yardstick can come from a different but related product market in the same or similar geographic market, or from a different but related geographic market in which the same product or products are sold.

Ideally, the comparable market product should reflect the same degree of competition, the same costs, and the same demand conditions that would have prevailed in the market at issue had there been no wrongful behavior. Of course, it is quite possible for there to be no suitable yardstick in some cases. If an appropriate yardstick is available, it is important to take into account any differences in costs and the extent of competition between the yardstick market and the market at issue in the but-for world.

Regression analysis offers one tool that can be useful in a yardstick analysis. To illustrate, suppose that there are available price data for the market at issue in a case and for the yardstick market. Suppose also that the yardstick market and the market at issue are both differentiated product markets subject to Bertrand competition. However, the yardstick market has fewer firms and a lesser degree of competition among those firms. Then, a regression analysis relating price in the yardstick market to one or more measures of the degree of competition could allow one to predict what prices in the yardstick market would be when the degree of competition was the same as in the market at issue. This 'adjusted yardstick' price series could be used as the but-for price in the damages analysis in the case.[14]

---

[11]   Alternative approaches involve a comparison of rates of return and/or profit margins across industries. For a broad overview of the various approaches, see Daniel L. Rubinfeld, *Econometrics in the Courtroom*, 85 COLUM. L. REV. 1048 (1985); see also Franklin Fisher, *Multiple Regression in Legal Proceedings*, 80 COLUM. L. REV. 702 (1980).

[12]   For a broad discussion of these alternative measures, see Hovenkamp, *supra* note 2.

[13]   The yardstick approach was first cited by the Supreme Court in Bigelow v. RKO Radio Pictures, Inc., 327 U.S. 251, rehearing denied, 327 U.S. 817 (1946).

[14]   A similar approach could be used if one were analysing profit margins or rates of return. However, an appropriate margin analysis must account not only for pricing differences, but also for differences in costs between the two markets.

B   Benchmarks[15]

In essence, the benchmark approach involves using the periods before and/or after the alleged wrongful behavior as a benchmark. As with the yardstick approach, it is essential that the nonimpact period be as similar as possible to the impact period. This requires that one take into account any cost, demand, or competitive differences between the nonimpact behavior and the impact period, but -for the wrongful behavior. However, the benchmark approach does have one potentially important advantage in comparison to the yardstick approach. If sufficient data are available, regression analysis can be used to distinguish the effects of the alleged wrongful behavior on price from those effects that are not causally related to that behavior.

To be specific, when the time period or periods in which the alleged antitrust behavior impacted prices is sufficiently long and the necessary data are available, a standard approach to the evaluation of damages is to estimate a regression model for prices using only data for the nonimpact period in which the market was unimpeded and to utilize that regression model to predict but-for prices in the impact period.[16] This 'forecasting' (or 'before–after') approach relies heavily on the assumption that the regression specification adequately characterizes the nature of competition in both the impact and control periods. An alternative approach, often utilized when there are not sufficient data to estimate with confidence a regression model in the nonimpact period, estimates a regression model for the entire period for which data are available, and evaluates damages by looking at the statistical significance and magnitude of the coefficient on a dummy variable that distinguishes the impact period from the nonimpact period.

With either the forecasting or the dummy variable approach, it is essential to account for the effects of noncollusive variables on price. If these variables are not taken into account, it is quite possible that damages will be biased and highly inaccurate. To illustrate the possibility of upward bias, suppose that one is using the forecasting approach but fails to account for the fact that input costs have increased due to independent supply shocks. Failure to account for these noncollusive costs is likely to lead the expert to understate but-for prices – in essence omitting the likely upward pressure on but-for prices resulting from the higher input costs. Alternatively, suppose one is using the dummy variable approach. The failure to include an appropriate measure of input costs will similarly cause one to underestimate but-for prices.

With either approach, it is also essential to evaluate whether any explanatory variables ('covariates') included in the model to account for demand or cost changes are variables that are not causally affected by the alleged anticompetitive behavior. Failure to do so could lead one to mis-estimate the but-for price series and damages. This might arise, for example, if the anticompetitive behavior were to affect a key input price. Then, part of the influence of the wrongful behavior will have been accounted for by the input price variable itself, and this component will not be appropriately accounted for in the damages

---

[15]   This subsection borrows heavily from Justin McCrary and Daniel L. Rubinfeld, Measuring Benchmark Antitrust Damages (unpublished draft, 2009) (on file with authors).

[16]   There must be sufficiently variability to allow one to appropriately account for noncollusive variables that might have affected price in the impact period.

analysis.[17] Alternatively, a cartel might be able to take advantage of shifts in demand and cost that occur outside the cartel. This might happen if demand or cost conditions are heavily affected by expectations, since the cartel can heavily influence those expectations. As an example, Rubinfeld and Steiner explain how the uranium cartel was able to take advantage of an oil embargo to alter expectations about the likely price of uranium.[18]

When using the dummy variable approach, a secondary issue arises. Should one evaluate damages by assuming a constant price differential through the impact period (as suggested by the coefficient on the dummy variable) or should one allow for nonconstant price differentials?

To evaluate these questions in greater detail, I utilize the most basic pricing model.[19]

Let P_t = a measure of the outcome of an alleged price-fixing arrangement (typically price)

X_t = a list (i.e., a vector) of exogenous covariates not causally affected by the price-fixing (e.g., demand and cost variables)

D_t = a dummy variable indicating the period of the alleged price fix, i.e., the impact period

I assume for simplicity that the covariates are not causally related to the conspiracy and that the damage period and the conspiracy period are identical.[20] I focus first on what is to be done in the scenario where either approach might be appropriate. I therefore assume that there is no causal effect of the price-fixing on the covariates in the impact period. Were this not the case, other econometric methods (e.g., instrumental variables) would be needed to estimate the model, but the discussion that follows would otherwise apply. Note that assuming no *causal* relationship between the covariates and the price-fixing does not rule out the possibility that the covariates are *correlated* with the price-fixing.

The model that characterizes the determination of the outcome of the alleged conspiracy is given by:

$$(1) \qquad P_t = \alpha + X_t\beta + \theta D_t + \gamma D_t X_t + \varepsilon_t$$

This model takes into account the possibility that the alleged price-fixing will affect price directly, as given by θD_t (e.g., through an increase in price at each point in time in the impact period). It also takes into account the possibility that the effect of the conspiracy on price will also be felt indirectly through one or more of the demand and cost variables,

---

[17]   See Halbert White, Robert Marshall, and Pauline Kennedy, *The Measurement of Economic Damages in Antitrust Civil Litigation*, 6 ABA ANTITRUST SECTION, ECONOMIC COMMITTEE NEWSLETTER (2006).

[18]   Daniel L. Rubinfeld and Peter O. Steiner, *Quantitative Methods in Antitrust Litigation*, 46 L. AND CONTEMP. PROBS. 69 (1983).

[19]   A similar approach would apply if other wrongful activity was at issue.

[20]   For the forecasting approach, the forecast is based on covariates and is tainted if the covariates are caused by the conspiracy. For the dummy variable approach, the covariates are endogenous, which requires a more complex econometric model. The forecasting approach will also require a more complex model that correctly specifies the values of the taint-free covariates in the impact period.

as given by the term $\gamma D_t X_t$. To be specific, this term represents the fact that collusion could affect the correlation between the covariates and price.

To apply the dummy variable approach, we estimate equation (1) for the entire time period. The parameter θ measures the 'average' direct effect of the conspiracy on price per unit of time. However, if we now allow the covariates to be correlated with the timing of the conspiracy, the overall (direct and indirect) effect of the conspiracy on price in each time period is given by $(\theta + \gamma X_t)$. If Q_t represents output, and all covariates are deemed to be associated with the alleged price-fixing, then aggregate overcharges, OC_1, are determined by the following formula:

$$(2) \qquad OC_1 = \theta \Sigma D_t Q_t + \gamma \Sigma D_t Q_t X_t$$

where the summation signified by the Greek letter 'Σ' applies to all time periods, and θ and γ are regression estimates of the parameters.

For some purposes, it may be desirable to impose the restriction that $\gamma = 0$. This presumes that none of the covariates are correlated with the price-fixing period. In this case, we would obtain a different estimate of overcharge damages, given by

$$(3) \qquad OC_2 = \theta_s \Sigma D_t Q_t$$

where the subscript 'S' indicates that the θ parameter is obtained from the 'short' regression that omits the interaction between covariates and the impact period dummy variable. Our main focus is on OC_1, but I will offer brief comments about OC_2 as well.

The forecasting approach estimates the following model:

$$(4) \qquad P_t = \alpha + X_t \beta + e_t$$

for the pre-conspiratorial period. Overcharges are then based on the difference between the predicted outcome (e.g., price) in the impact period and the actual outcome. Applying this approach to the case in which price is the outcome and Q represents quantity of sales, and P_t^f is the predicted price in the damage period, aggregate overcharge damages are given by:

$$(5) \qquad OC_3 = \Sigma D_t (P_t - P_t^f) Q_t$$

As a general rule, the forecasting approach and the dummy variable approach will generate different damage estimates. How does one choose between the two? One way to think about this is to note that in equation (1) $\alpha + X_t \beta + \theta D_t + \gamma D_t X_t$ represents a regression prediction of prices, and we can think of ε_t as a price residual that reflects the cumulative effect of all omitted variables on price. The price residual will have zero correlation with the regression prediction of price, a result that follows directly from the fact that the regression model is estimated by least squares – it minimizes the residual sum of squares and by construction assures that the residual is uncorrelated with all of the covariates in the model. Since the prediction is a weighted average of the covariates, it is also uncorrelated with the residual.

McCrary and Rubinfeld have shown a number of results that allow for a comparison of the forecasting and dummy variable approaches.[21] When the quantity of sales of the product is assumed to be constant over the price-fixing period, the forecasting and dummy variable approaches yield numerically identical overcharge estimates. When one takes into account the fact that the quantity varies over the price-fixing period, the forecasting and dummy variable approaches will differ, depending on whether or not the quantity is correlated with the residual during the conspiracy period.

How does one choose between the two approaches when the damage estimates vary? McCrary and Rubinfeld have shown that, assuming quantity is not correlated with omitted factors, the dummy variable and forecasting approaches generate econometrically consistent estimates (the estimates will tend to be the same as the data sample gets larger).[22] This provides important support for each of the two approaches. However, McCrary and Rubinfeld have also shown (assuming that the econometric specification of the model is the appropriate one) that the forecasting approach produces a noisier estimate of damages (having greater variability) than does the dummy variable approach.

While the dummy variable approach is more appealing on purely econometric grounds, a case can be made for the forecasting approach. Assuming that the underlying competitive structure that determines price in the but-for nonimpact period has not changed substantially, a pricing model can be selected for the nonimpact period using robust search methods.[23] By construction, the specification of that model will have been uncorrupted by the alleged anticompetitive behavior in the impact period.

If data during the impact period are used to choose the regression model, then there is a risk that the model will produce a biased damages estimate, perhaps inappropriately. In principle, it is always possible to use an in-sample model selection procedure to produce a damages estimate of zero, just by adding a sufficient number of irrelevant variables to the regression specification so that the model fully explains prices in the impact period. A forecasting approach that is based on an appropriate model selection methodology serves as a good disciplining device.[24]

The disadvantage of the forecasting approach is that it may be too disciplining. In particular, it prevents the expert from selecting a model using his or her knowledge of the economics of the problem. Particularly in dynamic markets, the relationship between covariates and prices may be so rapidly evolving that the pre-conspiracy period will not be a particularly good guide to model selection for the conspiracy period. In such a setting, prior knowledge may be of great value and the expert may want to use such knowledge. Suppose, for example, that the market at issue is a highly innovative one in which new technologies are developed on average every two years, but that the rate of innovation is growing over time. Suppose also that the conspiracy period is four years

---

[21]   McCrary and Rubinfeld, *supra* note 15.
[22]   *Id.*
[23]   See, e.g., Halbert White, *Time Series Estimation of the Effect of Natural Experiments*, 135 J. ECONOMETRICS 527 (2006).
[24]   The second advantage of the forecasting approach is more technical. If model selection is based purely on the nonimpact, and one believes that observations before the price-fixing are (approximately) independent of observations during the price-fixing period, then the model selection process does not affect the standard errors associated with the damages estimates.

long. Then, the forecasting approach is likely to underestimate the extent of innovation that would likely have occurred in the but-for world during the impact period.

III   LOST PROFITS

A   Optimal Deterrence

As mentioned previously, overcharge damages (and lost profits damages) will not necessarily achieve optimal deterrence. This point is easily seen if we treat the hypothetical case in which an otherwise competitive market has been monopolized through illegal anticompetitive behavior. The higher monopolized price will result in a reduction in the quantity of the good that is purchased. For those actual purchasers, the monopolizing behavior will have led to higher prices; this involves a transfer of income from consumers to the monopolizing producer or producers. However, for those sales that did not occur (the difference between actual sales and the higher but-for sales that would have occurred had the price been competitive, consumers and producers have been injured.

If optimal deterrence is to be achieved, the deadweight loss of both consumer surplus and producer surplus must be taken into account. Some consumers have been injured because they would have purchased the product had the price been lower. Unfortunately, from an efficiency perspective, these individuals do not have standing to sue.[25] Moreover, some producers (not necessarily those involved in the monopolizing conduct) will have been injured to the extent that the additional production in the but-for world would have been undertaken at a cost that is less than the but-for price.[26]

While deadweight loss ought to be accounted for in theory, it has not been in antitrust doctrine. This omission may be pragmatic. First, consumers who would have purchased the product in the but-for world but did not make purchases in the actual world do not have standing to sue.[27] Were standing to be extended to any person claiming that they would have purchased in the but-for world, the courts would face a difficult information problem, in that presumably many individuals who would not have purchased in the but-for world would falsely claim that they would have, in order to avail themselves of damages. Second, courts frequently use an overcharge damage methodology, which inherently rules out deadweight loss considerations. This may also be a pragmatic choice. Deadweight loss can be difficult to measure in practice, since it depends on the shape of the demand curve for the product as well as the nature of the incremental cost of producing the product.

---

[25]   This restriction applies both to those customers who would have purchased the product at lower price had prices not been artificially high and to those suppliers that would have purchased more had there not been monopsonistic buying behavior. See Associated Gen. Contractors of Cal., Inc. v. Carpenters, 459 U.S. 519 (1983).

[26]   For a nice overview of this and related deterrence issues, see Christopher R. Leslie, *Antitrust Damages and Deadweight Loss*, 51 ANTITRUST BULL. 521 (2006). Leslie argues that there should be a remedy for deadweight loss.

[27]   Those consumers who do have standing recover only for purchases made, not those that would have been made in the but-for world.

These practical motivations notwithstanding, failure to account for deadweight loss will, in itself, lead to underdeterrence. However, most antitrust violations allow for treble damages recoveries (some criminal violations allow for criminal penalties as well). It is theoretically possible that the trebling of damages could increase deterrence sufficiently so as to counter the underdeterrence associated with deadweight loss. Such a balance would seem to be fortuitous at best. Indeed, there has been substantial debate as to whether trebling damages leads to appropriate deterrence, with little resolution. Some have pointed to the social costs (including substantial litigation costs) that are created by the treble damages regime, while others have pointed to the likely underenforcement of cartel activity.[28]

In any case, the analysis of optimal deterrence is complicated further by the fact that direct purchasers will, in many cases, pass on some or all of the overcharges to downstream customers.[29] The ability of direct purchasers to pass on some or all of the higher costs associated with illegal monopolizing behavior can affect not only who is injured but also the extent of injury and the resulting ideal level of deterrence. I turn to the complexities associated with pass-through in section IV. First, however, I discuss the measurement of lost profits.

B   Measuring Lost Profits

Lost profits claims are typically made by businesses claiming that their sales (either actual or potential) have been adversely affected by the behavior of a defendant or defendants. In some cases the plaintiffs might be competitors that allegedly lost profits as the result of exclusionary behavior, while in other cases the plaintiffs might be downstream purchasers that were adversely affected by collusion. In either case, the basic principle associated with lost profits is relatively straightforward: the plaintiff should receive compensation that would put it in the same position as it would have been had the bad acts not occurred. In practice, however, the measurement of lost profits can be quite difficult.

To keep the discussion focused, assume that the plaintiff is a downstream customer. If the plaintiff has been in business throughout the period of alleged harm, then either the benchmark or yardstick overcharge method can be applied. Of course, there will be additional steps involved, since one must take into account that overcharges are not lost profits. To do so, it is essential to predict but-for prices. However, it is also essential to estimate a demand model that will allow one to estimate but-for quantities as well.

---

[28]   See, e.g., Jeffrey Perloff and Daniel L. Rubinfeld, *Settlements in Private Antitrust Litigation*, in PRIVATE ANTITRUST LITIGATION 149 (Lawrence J. White ed., MIT Press, 2006); John M. Connor, *Forensic Economics: An Introduction with Special Emphasis on Price Fixing*, 4 J. COMPETITION L. AND ECON. 31 (2008).

[29]   It is also further complicated by the possibility that some consumers will have purchased the product in the expectation of obtaining damages (especially if this is an intermediate goods market). For an analysis of this point, see David Besanko and Daniel F. Spulber, *Delegated Law Enforcement and Noncooperative Behavior*, 5(1) J. LAW ECON. AND ORG. 25 (Spring 1989). See also Steven Salant, *Treble Damage Awards in Private Lawsuits for Price Fixing*, 95(6) J. POLIT. ECON. 1326 (1987) and Jonathan Baker, *Private Information and the Deterrent Effect of Antitrust Damage Remedies*, 4(3) J. LAW, ECON. AND ORG. 385 (1988).

Once prices and quantities are estimated for the but-for world, the final step involves an analysis of but-for costs, so that but-for revenues can be translated into but-for profits.

In addition to the benchmark and yardstick approaches to measuring lost profits, there is also a 'market share method'. In its most general form, this methodology involves comparing the profits enjoyed by the plaintiff in the actual and but-for worlds. If there is a loss of market share that can reasonably be attributed to the defendant's wrongful behavior, then the difference between the actual and but-for market shares can be translated into a measure of lost profits damages.

One virtue of the market share approach is that it provides a means of controlling for (and thus not taking into account) economic shocks not associated with the anticompetitive behavior that affect the industry and the plaintiff. There are, however, a number of significant disadvantages. First, as a practical matter it can be very difficult to control for noncollusive factors that led the plaintiff's market share to decline from those factors that were associated with the anticompetitive behavior. Second, market shares often fluctuate in a manner that can only be attributed to noise (a confluence of many economic forces). If plaintiffs only sue when their market shares decline, the selection effect will tend to yield damages associated with declining market shares that are not causal in nature. Third, if the lost market share approach is applied to a relatively new entrant into an industry (an entrant whose market share was naturally increasing), the approach can generate highly unreliable projections of lost share. The reason is that projections reasonably far into the future based on a short period of actual production and a small actual market share are likely to yield estimates of lost market share that are highly unreliable.[30]

Consider one particularly striking example. In *Conwood*, the plaintiffs put forward a market share projection based solely on market share growth.[31] However, the plaintiffs failed to distinguish the alleged wrongful behavior from legitimate noncollusive behavior (including the entry of several firms into the industry). Furthermore, the plaintiffs' market share estimates were highly unstable; the removal of a single data point from the plaintiffs' expert's market share regression analysis reduced alleged damages from over US$1 billion to zero.[32]

The likely unreliability of market share projections for firms that have not entered the industry presents a policy dilemma. Anticompetitive behavior can harm firms that have yet to enter the industry: what then is an appropriate damage remedy? I find a proposal by Herb Hovenkamp to be particularly intriguing.[33] Hovenkamp suggests that precluded entrants receive all sunk (unrecoverable) costs associated with the attempt at entry plus the fair market value of any contractual obligations which they have received

---

[30]   If the plaintiff's entry into the industry had been blocked due to the alleged anticompetitive behavior, then a market share approach based on business projections may be the plaintiff's only alternative. However, projections based on business plans must be evaluated with caution since such plans are often optimistic about future growth.

[31]   Conwood, Co. v. U.S. Tobacco Co., 290 F.3d 768, 784 (6th Cir. 2002), cert. denied, 537 U.S. 1148 (2003).

[32]   Motion for Leave to File Brief and Brief of Washington Legal Foundation, Stephen E. Fienberg, Franklin M. Fisher, Daniel L. McFadden, and Daniel L. Rubinfeld as Amici Curiae in Support of Petitioners, *Conwood*, 537 U.S. 1148 (No. 02-603).

[33]   Hovenkamp, *supra* note 2, at 689.

but have not been able to perform. While this approach may underestimate damages in some cases, it is likely to be substantially more reliable than would market share calculations.

IV   INDIRECT PURCHASERS: PASS-THROUGH

A   Complexities of Indirect Purchaser Cases

The analysis of anticompetitive injury and damages can be especially difficult when the plaintiffs are indirect purchasers. In such cases there is likely to be a relatively long supply chain. The prototypical case might involve an allegation of wrongful behavior by a manufacturer, which sells directly to wholesalers, which in turn sell to retailers, which in turn sell to the ultimate consumers. A higher price at the manufacturing level will likely lead to higher prices at the wholesale and retail levels, and ultimately higher prices to consumers. However, the extent to which a particular indirect purchaser is damaged will require analysis of the pass-through of the higher costs at each level in the supply chain.

Adding to the complexity of the indirect purchaser analysis is the fact that there may be multiple supply chains. To illustrate, the manufacturer might sell directly to some retailers and indirectly to others. Alternatively, some manufacturers might be vertically integrated (e.g., manufacturing and wholesaling) whereas others may not. Furthermore, the ultimate injury to final customers will in some cases depend on whether those customers had the opportunity to obtain insurance coverage. Consider, for example, the hypothetical injury caused by monopolizing conduct of a pharmaceutical company. Most individuals with health-care pharmaceutical coverage make a co-pay for covered drugs. In these situations, they will only be injured to the extent that the higher costs lead to higher insurance premiums.

The complications run even deeper. An analysis of pass-through along the supply chain will depend at each step on the extent to which the relevant market or markets are or are not competitive, and if not competitive, the nature of the strategic interaction among the firms.[34] Each of these complicating factors increases the likelihood that the injuries suffered and the damages to be recovered by downstream customers will vary from individual to individual. This suggests that certification of a class of indirect purchasers may not be sensible in many indirect purchaser situations. It also suggests that it will likely be quite difficult to fully specify and estimate a structural model of demand and cost associated with the complete supply chain. Whether a class is certified or not certified, the use of nonstructural empirical models may provide the most suitable means of analysis. I discuss these 'reduced form methods' in the following subsection.

---

[34]   For a recent analysis of these complexities, see Martijn A. Han, Maarten Pieter Schinkel, and Jan Tuinstra, *The Overcharge as a Measure for Antitrust Damages* (Amsterdam Center for Law and Economics Working Paper No. 2008-08, 2009). See also George Kosicki and Miles B. Cahill, *Economics of Cost Pass Through and Damages in Indirect Purchaser Cases*, 51 ANTITRUST BULL. 599 (2006).

B   Using Reduced Form Methods to Measure Pass-Through

The pass-through rate is a building block for assessing the net effect of the transaction on prices paid by buyers.[35] For example, if a proposed merger appears likely to increase prices by 5% because of the loss of rivalry between the firms (that is based on considerations other than the possibility of cost savings accruing to the merging parties), and the merger will permit the parties to reduce marginal costs by 10%, price would still be expected to increase unless the pass-through rate for cost reductions is 50% or greater.[36]

The most common statistical method employed to identify the rate at which a firm has historically passed through firm-specific cost changes to prices involves the estimation of *reduced form* price equations.[37] This technique explains the variation in a particular price by variables related to cost, demand, and market structure, and a series of dummy variables that allow the intercept to differ among relevant groups of observations. The model is called 'reduced form' because the price equation is thought of as derived from other, prior economic relationships, in this case the interaction of a demand function with a supply relation. The parameters of a reduced form equation are typically themselves functions of a number of the structural parameters (the parameters of the underlying economic relationships).

Inferences about the firm-specific pass-through rate can be made from estimating a reduced form price equation relating a firm's price (p) to its own costs (c) and its rival's costs (c_R) and a series of fixed effects dummy variables (D), as in the following equation (from which firm and time subscripts have been omitted):

$$(6) \quad p = \alpha + \beta_1 c + \beta_2 c_R + \gamma D + \varepsilon$$

The fixed effect variables are a collection of dummy variables that control for time-invariant firm-specific attributes, cross-section invariant time effects, and product-specific effects. In this model, the competitor's cost variable is thought of as a proxy for industry-wide costs. With industry-wide costs included, the cost variable would pick up only the effect of firm-specific cost variation on prices.[38]

---

[35]   The material in this subsection builds on the work of Baker and Rubinfeld; see Jonathan B. Baker and Daniel L. Rubinfeld, *Empirical Methods in Antitrust Litigation: Review and Critique*, 1 AM. L. AND ECON. REV. 386 (1999).

[36]   The magnitude of the firm-specific pass-through rate depends upon the curvature (second derivative) of the demand curve faced by the firm. Intuitively, the rate is less than (greater than) one-half if the firm's residual demand function grows more (less) elastic when price rises relative to the change in elasticity associated with linear demand. Because the curvature of demand is not constrained in economic theory, the magnitude of the firm-specific pass-through rate must be determined empirically.

[37]   Perhaps the best example came out of the FTC's *Staples* litigation. See generally Orley Ashenfelter, David Ashmore, Jonathan B. Baker, and Signe-Mary McKernan, *Identifying the Firm-Specific Cost Pass-Through Rate* (Federal Trade Commission Working Paper No. 217, January 1998); see also ABA ANTITRUST SECTION, ECONOMETRICS: LEGAL, PRACTICAL, AND TECHNICAL ISSUES (John Harkrider and Daniel L. Rubinfeld eds, 2005).

[38]   In *Staples*, for example, Professor Ashenfelter concluded that Staples had historically passed-through only 15% of firm-specific cost reductions to consumers, and the court accepted this

It is important to understand with respect to mergers that the firm-specific pass-through rate may not be the appropriate rate to apply to the efficiencies that would be achieved, given that the merger might change the extent to which the firms competed. In *Staples,* this did not turn out to be a problem, since the inclusion of variables related to market structure in the regression model did not substantively change the regression results.

C   Welfare Implications of *Illinois Brick*

The mix of *Illinois Brick* in federal cases and *Illinois Brick* repealers in many states creates a complex of normative issues for those interested in designing a combined federal–state system that creates incentives for optimal deterrence. Fortunately, that is not my purpose here. Rather, I simply note that it seems likely that the current system leads both to excess deterrence and to excessive litigation costs.

The excess deterrence conclusion follows from the assumption (largely unsupported) that the federal treble damages rule was designed to generate optimal deterrence. To the extent that this is the case, the addition of indirect purchaser cases is likely to overdeter. I note, however, that the evidence concerning the optimality of treble damages is weak at best. A more reasonable characterization may be that the federal system has overdeterred certain types of alleged exclusionary practices such as bundled rebates, but has underdeterred classic price-fixing.[39]

The most recent evidence concerning the duplication of damages that results when both direct and indirect purchasers sue was presented to the US Antitrust Modernization Commission (AMC). After hearing substantial testimony, the AMC recommended that direct purchasers continue to have standing, but that defendants be allowed to put forward a passing-on defense. The AMC also recommended that indirect purchasers be given standing to sue under federal law.[40] This proposed remedy would clearly remove the duplication of damages present under the current system. Whether the remedy would improve deterrence and efficiency more generally remains an open question.[41]

---

figure rather than the two-thirds rate suggested by defendants in reaching its decision to enjoin the merger. See Federal Trade Commission v. Staples, 970 F.Supp. 1066, 1090 (D.D.C. 1997).

[39]   For a critique of the bundled rebate decision in *LePage's v. 3M,* see Daniel L. Rubinfeld, *3M's Bundled Rebates: An Economic Perspective,* 72 U. CHI. L. REV. 243 (2005). For empirical evidence that detection of cartels is difficult, see Peter G. Bryant and E. Woodrow Eckard, *Price Fixing: the Probability of Getting Caught,* 73 REV. ECON. AND STAT. 531 (1991); see also John M. Connor, *Price Fixing Overcharges: Legal and Economic Evidence* (American Antitrust Institute Working Paper No. 04-05, 2004).

[40]   AMC Report, *supra* note 9.

[41]   Han *et al., supra* note 34, show that when there is a complex supply chain the direct purchaser overcharge provides a poor measure of antitrust harm. They suggest that the overcharge may underestimate the actual antitrust harm, with the extent of the underdeterrence depending on demand, competitive interactions, and the level of the supply chain in which the antitrust injury has occurred. In another interesting paper, Martin Hellwig shows that the deadweight loss resulting from a cartel is equivalent to the amount of the overcharge that a direct purchaser monopolist could pass on to its downstream customers and that the overcharge is a good measure of the harm suffered by the direct purchaser; the overcharge would, of course, lead to underdeterrence. See Martin Hellwig, *Private Damage Claims and the Passing-on Defense in Horizontal Price-Fixing Cases: An*

The European Commission has been leaning towards a different approach. In its 2008 White Paper, the Commission emphasized the goal of competition in the design of a system of private enforcement and therefore supported the use of overcharges and lost profits analysis for both direct and indirect purchasers.[42]

V   COUPON REMEDIES

Damage awards are typically awarded by payment in dollars. However, consumers injured by price overcharges are often awarded coupons that can be used for a limited period of time to purchase the good at a price below that which prevails after the overcharge has been eliminated. In this section, I highlight some of the concerns raised by the use of coupon remedies and I point to the possible benefit of a remedy that mixes the use of coupons and cash.

Coupons have appropriately been criticized because they facilitate settlements in class action cases between the lawyers representing the consumer class and the defendant that are not in the interests of the consumers. The plaintiffs' attorneys have an incentive to convince the judge that the coupons are worth close to their face value, even though the actual redemption rate is likely to be small.[43] If the attorneys are successful, they will be well rewarded, while the effective cost to the defendant will be relatively low and the actual compensation to consumers will be of relatively little value. There has been some effort to remedy this problem; the Class Action Fairness Act requires that coupon remedies be valued based on their redemption rate. However, the problem remains in nonclass cases and it is likely to continue in class cases so long as the prediction as to the likely redemption rate is overly optimistic.[44]

Coupon remedies can also distort consumption decisions and therefore create deadweight loss. In a recent article, Polinsky and Rubinfeld explain why.[45] Suppose that consumer demand varies over time. Now, consider a consumer whose demand when the coupons are awarded is substantially lower than his or her demand during the period in which the antitrust injury has occurred. This consumer will have a surplus of coupons

---

Economist's Perspective, in PRIVATE ENFORCEMENT OF EC COMPETITION LAW 121 (J. Basedow ed., Kluwer Law International, 2007).

    [42]   European Commision White Paper, *supra* note 3.

    [43]   According to Frederick Gramlich, the average coupon redemption rate for consumer plaintiffs is 13.1%. See Frederick Gramlich, *Scrip Damages in Antitrust Cases*, 31 ANTITRUST BULL. 261 (1986).

    [44]   Class Action Fairness Act of 2005, Pub. L. No. 109-2, 119 Stat. 4 (codified as amended in scattered sections of 28 U.S.C.) only allows the value of the coupons redeemed in calculating attorneys' fees. To be specific, 28 U.S.C. 1712, states: '(a) Contingent fees in coupon settlements – If a proposed settlement in a class action provides for a recovery of coupons to a class member, the portion of any attorney's fee award to class counsel that is attributable to the award of the coupons shall be based on the value to class members of the coupons that are redeemed'.

    [45]   The material in this section is based largely on the analysis in A. Mitchell Polinsky and Daniel L. Rubinfeld, *The Deadweight Loss of Coupon Remedies for Price Overcharges*, 56 J. INDUS. ECON. 402 (2008). For a broad overview, see Roger D. Blair and Christine A. Piette, *Coupon Settlements: Compensation and Deterrence*, 51 ANTITRUST BULL. 661 (2006).

and consequently will be encouraged to buy an excessive amount of the good at issue. In effect, the coupon remedy has lowered the price of the good below the price in the remedy period, which (assuming an effective remedy) is the but-for competitive price.[46] Of course, if the consumer's demand does not decline there will be no distortion; the consumer will purchase more of the good at the competitive price than he or she did during the period in which there was antitrust injury, and consequently will run out of coupons.

How large is the deadweight loss likely to be? Polinsky and Rubinfeld show that the deadweight loss from excessive consumption can be comparable to the magnitude of the deadweight loss that results from the price overcharge itself. The magnitude of the deadweight loss depends crucially on the variability of demand. It follows that as the variability of demand goes to zero, so does the deadweight loss.

It might seem sensible to extend the remedy period; the hope would be that the longer a consumer has to use coupons, the more likely the coupons will be used for purchases that would have been made anyway. However, Polinsky and Rubinfeld show that extending the remedy period does not eliminate the distortion, because with a reasonably high discount rate consumers have an incentive to use coupons early to make purchases they would otherwise have not made. Moreover, the value of these distorting purchases will, in general, exceed the present value of the later inframarginal purchases.

Polinsky and Rubinfeld offer an example of how such a system might work.[47] Assume that drivers in urban areas have higher expected damages resulting from a faulty tire than do drivers in suburban areas. Assume also that it would be prohibitively expensive to determine the driving habits of the class of all drivers with faulty tires. Consider, then, a remedy of coupons good for the purchaser of four new tires during the next year with a US$1000 face value, or US$500 in cash. The coupons will be more valuable to individuals who drive mainly in urban areas, whereas the cash will be beneficial to those that drive in suburban areas. With this remedy, the costs to the defendant tire manufacturer will be a function of the driving habits of tire buyers and therefore the harm suffered by those drivers. The traditional cash remedy, however, would not enable the court to determine the harm suffered, which is likely to lead to an incorrect estimate of the damages suffered by putative class members.

While the case against coupon remedies is a strong one, there is one argument to be made in their favor. Polinsky and Rubinfeld show that giving plaintiffs the appropriately designed choice between coupons and cash can offer a damage remedy that is superior to cash alone.[48] The authors show that the optimal coupon–cash remedy offers a cash amount that is less than the value of the coupons to consumers who suffer relatively

---

[46]   This model assumes that the equilibrium price is exogenous. For an analysis of the case in which price is endogenous, see Severin Borenstein, *Settling for Coupons: Discount Contracts as Compensation and Punishment in Antitrust Lawsuits*, 39(2) J. LAW AND ECON. 379 (October 1996).

[47]   The example is motivated by Notice of Pendency of Class Action, Proposed Settlement of Class Action, and Settlement Hearing, Tuchman v. Volvo Cars of N. Am., No. BER-L-1808-97 (N.J. Super. Ct. App. Div. 1999), available at www.gardencitygroup.com/cases/fullcase/1003. The settlement offered a choice of four new replacement tires, a US$1,000 credit toward the purchase or lease of a new Volvo, or US$500 in cash.

[48]   A. Mitchell Polinsky and Daniel L. Rubinfeld, *A Damage-Revelation Rationale for Coupon Remedies*, 23 J.L. ECON. AND ORG. 653 (2007).

high harm. This induces these plaintiffs to choose coupons, whereas consumers who suffer relatively little harm choose cash. Sorting consumers in this way leads to improved deterrence because the costs borne by defendants (the cash payments and the cost of providing coupons) more closely approximate the harms that defendants have caused.

Index